Global Islamic Politics

D1136238

Global Informed Logistics

Global Islamic Politics

Mir Zohair Husain
University of South Alabama

■HarperCollins*CollegePublishers*

Editor in Chief: Marcus Boggs
Project Editor: Andrew Roney
Design Supervisor: Nancy Sabato
Cover Design: Molly Heron
Electronic Production Manager: Valerie A. Sawyer
Desktop Administrator: Sarah Johnson
Manufacturing Manager: Helene G. Landers
Electronic Page Makeup: RR Donnelley Barbados
Printer and Binder: RR Donnelley & Sons Company
Cover Printer: RR Donnelley & Sons Company

Global Islamic Politics

Library of Congress Cataloging-in-Publication Data

Husain, Mir Zohair
    Global Islamic politics / Mir Zohair Husain.
        p.   cm.
    Includes bibliographical references and index.
    ISBN 0-06-501484-7
    1. Islam—20th century.   I. Title.
BP60 .H87   1994
322 ' . 1 ' 0917671—dc20   94-20363
                                        CIP

94 95 96 97   9 8 7 6 5 4 3 2 1

To my beloved parents and my wife

Contents

Preface

The global Islamic revival has consistently and dramatically caught the attention of the West in recent decades. With the end of the cold war, dismemberment of the Soviet Union, and demise of communism in the former Soviet bloc, political Islam—also known as Islamic fundamentalism, Islamic revivalism, or the Islamic revival—is now recognized as an influential force in international relations; it is in the forefront of Western consciousness. Initiating both reform and revolution throughout the Muslim world, political Islam fueled Iran's 1979 Islamic Revolution and the concurrent Islamization campaign in Pakistan and Sudan. It contributed to turmoil in Lebanon, chased the well-equipped Soviets from Afghanistan, was responsible for the assassination of Egypt's President Anwar al-Sadat, and has been an essential factor in the continuing Arab-Israeli dispute. Political Islam is also an important element in the Israeli-occupied West Bank and Gaza Strip, Jordan, Tunisia, Morocco, and Egypt. More recently, Islamic political parties working within the Algerian political system enjoyed marked success. Such success contributed, however, to a reactionary and decidedly antirevivalist military coup.

There is no question that a closer examination of Islamic revivalism is warranted. The size and potential power of the Muslim world, although currently a "house divided," makes the subject important for any student of international relations. Muslims number 1 billion people, one-fifth of humanity. They constitute a majority in nearly fifty countries, a substantial minority in another seven countries, and a sizable minority in at least nine others. While present throughout the world, exhibiting numerous cultures and speaking as many different languages, Muslims are most heavily concentrated in Asia, where they constitute 68.3 percent of the population. Africa comprises the second greatest concentration of Muslims, where they constitute 27.4 percent of the population.* Muslim countries are active participants in a number of international organizations, the most prominent being the Organization of Arab Petroleum Exporting Countries (OAPEC), the Organization of Petroleum Exporting Countries (OPEC), the Arab League,

---

*John R. Weeks, "The Demography of Islamic Nations," *Population Bulletin*, Vol. 43, No. 4, December 1988, pp. 5, 8–9. According to Dr. Zein al-Abidin, editor of *Muslim Minority Journal*, there are 1.2 billion Muslims in the world. Of this number, 336.42 million live as minorities. Muslims are considered a minority in a country when they live under non-Muslim jurisdiction and in a society where Islam is not the prevailing religion or culture (Zein al-Abidin, *The Minaret*, Vol. 13, No. 4, July/August 1991, p. 20).

the Organization of African Unity (OAU), the Association of Southeast Asian Nations (ASEAN), the Group of 77, the Organization of the Islamic Conference (OIC), the Non-Aligned Movement (NAM), and the United Nations.

A closer examination of global Islamic politics is further merited by the proximity of the Muslim world to seven strategically important sea routes, namely the Mediterranean Sea, the Bosphorus, the Black Sea, the Suez Canal, the Red Sea, the Persian Gulf, and the Straits of Malacca. In addition, Muslim countries possess innumerable raw materials, produce nearly half the oil consumed in the West, and control two-thirds of the world's known oil reserves. Owning an exhaustible and vital international commodity—for which there are countless uses and no immediate substitutes—has greatly empowered the ten predominantly Muslim nations in the twelve-member Organization of Petroleum Exporting Countries (OPEC). Moreover, the Muslim world also possesses a substantial pool of inexpensive labor and is a lucrative market for goods and services. Consequently, significant political changes in the Muslim world interest and concern the interdependent international community. In recent years, the West has discouraged any political change that might threaten a "satisfactory" status quo in an area of such vital importance. Islamic revivalism represents just such a change.

In the West today Islamic revivalism is as thoroughly reviled an ideology as Soviet communism had been. In fact, the struggle against political Islam has heightened with the collapse of the Soviet Union. However, Western fear of political Islam is rooted less in reality than in misunderstanding. The Western mass media, focusing on the most sensational aspects of Islamic revivalism, have contributed to its distortion by characterizing it as a monolithic and inherently anti-Western force; it is neither. The primary intention of this book is, therefore, to accurately and comprehensively portray global Islamic politics, its causes, consequences, and implications.

Voltaire wrote: "Define your terms, you will permit me again to say, or we shall never understand one another." The single greatest barrier to an intelligent inquiry into political Islam is the ambiguity of related terminology. Terms like *Islamic revival, Islamic fundamentalist, Islamic neo-fundamentalism, Islamic traditionalist, Islamic neo-traditionalist, Islamic conservative, Islamic modernist,* and *Islamic state* are often vaguely and inconsistently approached. When a definition is attempted in Islamic revivalist literature, it is seldom satisfactory or comprehensive.

To help clarify political Islam, this book provides in-depth definitions of relevant terms. More than that, however, *Global Islamic Politics* is an attempt to present multilevel, multidisciplinary, and typological perspectives of the causes and manifestations of Islamic revivalism. Another objective of this book is to examine the historical precedents to modern Islamic revivalism, and to present essential general information on the Muslim world through concise profiles of Islamic revivalist individuals and institutions. Also included are a glossary of important Islamic terms and a bibliography to assist those interested in further reading or research in the field. Finally, this work offers suggestions for ameliorating the relations between Islam and the West, in the hopes these recommendations may contribute to peace and understanding.

ACKNOWLEDGMENTS

I wish to express my gratitude to my former professor and guru Donald E. Smith for making invaluable comments and suggestions on the first draft of the manuscript.

I would like to acknowledge the generous help of student and friend David M. Rosenbaum for meticulously editing the manuscript, greatly helping me with the research on some sections (especially Chapter 11: "Islamic Revival in Central Asia"), and always being there with constructive criticism.

I would also like to express my deep appreciation to Cornelia Guest for her painstaking and expert copyediting, insightful comments and criticisms, and invaluable suggestions.

Finally, I owe a profound debt of gratitude to my parents and my wife for their love, moral support, and patience—factors that gave me the inner strength to carry this lengthy book project to its conclusion. With their constant encouragement and prayers they contributed more than they may realize.

Mir Zohair Husain

Chapter
1

Introduction to Islam and Islamic Revivals

Obvious manifestations of the global revival of political Islam abound in the modern world. Sometimes reactionary, sometimes revolutionary, sometimes reformist, and always relevant, political Islam or Islamic revivalism has become an influential force in international relations, a force that the West can ill afford to ignore, to discount, or to misunderstand in an increasingly interdependent world. However, by sensationalizing the most radical, militant, and reactionary aspects of political Islam, usually represented by Fundamentalist revivalists, the Western mass media have demonized all forms of Islamic revivalism, even forms essentially tolerant of the West. In essence, the West decried the 1979 Islamic Revolution in Iran and, thereafter, has consistently fashioned policy hostile to Islamic organizations whether they seek violent revolution or peaceful reform. In Algeria, for example, the Islamic Salvation Front (FIS) participated in good faith and with neither violent nor subversive intentions in the general election of December 1991. However, when the FIS was about to win the elections, the secularists in the Algerian army struck back. In mid-January 1992, they overthrew the government, disrupted the democratic process, and began jailing FIS leaders and activists. Then in March 1992, the new military government banned the peaceful and reform-oriented FIS. Ironically, the West, which aggressively promoted human rights and democracy in the communist world, remained silent and imposed no punitive sanctions. It appeared that the West had convinced itself that political Islam, no matter the facts or the circumstances, is inherently anti-Western fundamentalism and narrow-minded fanaticism that must be contained, neutralized, and, if possible, eradicated.

Islamic fundamentalism is no more the sole expression of Islamic revivalism than Christian fundamentalism is the sole expression of the Christian faith. However, the mass media have focused on zealous and extremist Muslim Fundamentalists, overlooking the more moderate and pragmatic revivalists, who do not engage in violent acts. While television's attention to radical and revolutionary brands of Islamic revivalism is understandable in light of its news formats and interests, this limited presentation has contributed to the misconception that Islamic fundamentalism is synonymous with Islamic revivalism. Although a cursory glance at the major political events rocking Muslim countries may reinforce that conviction, a closer and more thoughtful examination of political Islam debunks these false presumptions.

While all Fundamentalists are necessarily revivalists, not all revivalists are Fundamentalists. Indeed, Fundamentalists represent only one end of a spectrum, insofar as divisions within Islam, among Islamic nations, and between interpretations have engendered countless schisms and rivalries among revivalists. The purpose of this book is to describe political Islam in all its avatars and manifestations and to provide the student of global Islamic politics with a more comprehensive and balanced perspective of the subject. Understanding political Islam first requires an introduction to Islam and to its geographical and historical setting.

Many Westerners erroneously equate Islam, Muslims, and the Muslim world with Arabs and the Arab world. Certainly there is a relationship. After all, Prophet Muhammad, who began to propagate Islam in Mecca and Madina (located in present-day Saudi Arabia), was an Arab. The close companions of Prophet Muhammad were Arabs. They were responsible for writing down the Quranic verses (revealed in Arabic), *Hadith* (Prophet Muhammad's sayings), and *Sunnah* (the sayings and deeds of Prophet Muhammad), and then disseminating them to the rest of the world. Many of the holiest Islamic sites are located in the Arab world, especially in the holy cities of Mecca, Madina, and Jerusalem. In fact, it is to Mecca that Muslims turn to say their prayers in Arabic, and it is where they go to perform their *haj* (pilgrimage). Furthermore, the first Muslim armies that spread Islam throughout the Middle East, Asia, Africa, and Europe were Arab. And the multinational Islamic empire that those armies forged was, likewise, an Arab empire.

However, not all Arabs are Muslims, nor do all Muslims belong to the Arab world. Indeed, the majority of the 1 billion Muslims are not Arabs. Adherents of Islam include Persians, Turks, Indonesians, Indians, Pakistanis, Bangladeshis, Malaysians, Chinese, Africans, Russians, Europeans, Americans, and numerous other nationalities and ethnic groups. Meanwhile, although most Arabs are Muslims, millions of Christian and Jewish Arabs live among them in the Arab world. In fact, both the Christians and the Jews have made significant contributions to Arabic culture and civilization while, today, a number of Palestinian leaders eloquently espousing the Palestinian cause are Christians. Any individual who speaks Arabic and adopts the Arab culture is an Arab. While there are 200 million Arabs, 5 percent to 7 percent are non-Muslims; the remaining 186 million Arabs constitute only 20 percent or one-fifth of all Muslims. Indeed, more Muslims live in India and Pakistan (250 million) than live in the entire Arab world.

Thus, the setting of Islamic revivalism is not purely in the Arab world or in the Middle East, which is an even more nebulous term. Rather, the global revival of political Islam affects Muslims speaking numerous languages in myriad cultures throughout the world. In fact, were it not for Islam, the countries of the Muslim world would have little in common.

Some Muslim countries are ancient in origin, like Iran, Iraq, Egypt, and Yemen, while others are recent creations of the colonial powers, like Nigeria and Pakistan, or are federations of formerly separate peoples, like Malaysia. By the same token, Muslim countries have different political histories. The impact of various imperialists and colonialists has contributed to differentiation of political and economic development among the nation-states of the Muslim world. Many were colonized for decades before finally gaining independence, while a few, like Afghanistan, endured only a decade-long colonialist era (1979–1989).

Muslim countries like Bangladesh, Egypt, Pakistan, Indonesia, Nigeria, Jordan, and Malaysia are dangerously overpopulated, while others, like Libya, Saudi Arabia, the United Arab Emirates, Qatar, and Kuwait, are sparcely populated. Others, like Lebanon and Bahrain, are largely urbanized societies, while Sudan, Pakistan, Bangladesh, Jordan, Egypt, Morocco, Tunisia, Algeria, Malaysia, and Indonesia are predominantly agrarian societies.

Some Muslim nations are enormous in territorial size, like Saudi Arabia, Iran, Egypt, and Sudan, while others like Djibouti, Brunei, Kuwait, Bahrain, Qatar, Oman, and the Maldive Islands are mere specks on the world map. Muslim nations like Egypt have a population that is relatively homogeneous, while others, including Iran, Iraq, Pakistan, Malaysia, and the Sudan, have heterogeneous populations.

Arabs are often characterized by the Western media as oil-rich shaikhs. The truth is that petrodollars belong to the Arabs no more than the enormous wealth of Wall Street belongs to New Yorkers and Hollywood's assets belong to Los Angelenos. The vast majority of the 8.5 million Somalis, 25 million Sudanese, 55 million Egyptians, 4 million Jordanians, 12 million Syrians, 26 million Moroccans, 10 million Yemenis, 18.5 million Iraqis, 8 million Tunisians, 3 million Lebanese, and 1.5 million Omanis are among the most impoverished people in the world.[1] In fact, the majority of Muslim nations are poor in petroleum resources and must import oil from the few oil-rich states like Saudi Arabia, Kuwait, Libya, the United Arab Emirates (U.A.E.), Iran, Nigeria, and Indonesia.

Although the peoples of the Muslim countries are predominantly Muslims, there are divisions within the "House of Islam" that are partly reflected by national boundaries. Iran, for example, has an overwhelmingly Shi'ah population, while across the Persian Gulf, Saudi and Qatari citizens follow the Hanbali sect of Sunni Islam. The adherents of the Shi'ah and Hanbali sects are poles apart and view each other with antipathy.

Politically, many Muslim countries are governed by monarchs, others by military juntas, and still others by authoritarian one-party regimes; only a few can be considered democratic. Likewise, some Muslim countries are based on the socialist economic model, while others are capitalist.

---

[1]Mansour Farhang, *U.S. Imperialism: The Spanish-American War to the Iranian Revolution*, Boston: South End Press, 1981, p. 130.

In short, the Muslim world is not a monolithic bloc. There are over fifty predominantly Muslim countries, each with its own national interests. By extrapolation then, political Islam is neither monolithic nor homogeneous, but pluralistic and heterogeneous.

Islam is the common thread that binds Muslims of diverse nationalities and ethnic groups throughout the Muslim world. Therefore, an understanding of the elemental principles and precepts of Islam is a prerequisite to an understanding of global Islamic politics (see Box 1.1).

THE MEANING OF ISLAMIC REVIVALS

An Islamic revival can be defined as the reawakening of interest in Islamic symbols, ideas, and ideals subsequent to a period of relative dormancy. It is the reemergence of Islam as a sociopolitical force in the world. According to Ali E. Hillal Dessouki, Islamic resurgence refers to

> [A]n increasing political activism in the name of Islam by governments and opposition groups alike. . . . Islamic groups have assumed a more assertive posture and projected themselves in many Arab and Islamic countries as contenders for public allegiance and political loyalty. . . . Thus, Islamic resurgence refers to the increasing prominence and politicization of Islamic ideologies and symbols in Muslim societies and in the public life of Muslim individuals.[2]

According to Chandra Muzaffar, Islamic resurgence

> conveys the impression that Islam is becoming important again. . . . Secondly . . . there are elements in the present rise of Islam which are linked to . . . the cherished path trodden by the Prophet Muhammad and his companions. . . . Thirdly, 'resurgence' as a term embodies the notion of challenge to the dominant social systems.[3]

Manifestations of the Islamic revival include *(a)* a groundswell or resurgence—involving a broad spectrum of the Muslim society—of public sentiment for and interest in an Islamic system, which has been referred to both as an Islamic resurgence and as "Populist Islam"; *(b)* grass roots or populist Islamic movements (also referred to as "Populist Islam"), involving selected segments of Muslim society—for example, members of the working class or those of the student community—who want to establish an Islamic system; and *(c)* government-sponsored Islamic programs that reassert religion as a primary ideological force (referred to variously as "Governmental Islam" or "Official Islam"). In the latter programs the leadership in power may be resorting to Islam for any number of reasons, including sincere religious beliefs, appeasement of an influential domestic religious pressure group, enhancement of governmental legitimacy, assistance in the integration of a fragmented society, and acquisition of funds from rich Muslim countries.

---

[2]Ali E. Hillal Dessouki, "The Islamic Resurgence: Sources, Dnyamics, and Implications," in Ali E. H. Dessouki, ed., *Islamic Resurgence in the Arab World,* New York: Praeger Publishers, 1982, p. 4.

[3]Chandra Muzaffar, "Islamic Resurgence: A Global View," in Taufik Abdullah and Sharon Siddique, eds., *Islam and Society in Southeast Asia,* Singapore: Institute of Southeast Asian Studies, 1987, p. 5.

Box 1.1   A BRIEF INTRODUCTION TO ISLAM

ISLAM is an Arabic word derived from the root *salama,* which means peace. The meaning of the word is subject to interpretation and has been translated variously as "peace," "submission," "resignation," and "obedience to the will of Allah."

ALLAH is the Islamic term for the one and only omnipotent, omnipresent, just, and merciful God. Belief in Allah, who has neither feminine nor plural attributes, is the first tenet of the Islamic faith.

MUSLIMS believe that Islam is God's final and perfect religion. Muslims also believe that only by totally surrendering to God's will and by obeying His laws can one achieve true happiness in this world and in the hereafter.

MUHAMMAD was born into the Hashemite clan of Mecca's Qureish tribe in A.D. 570. Even before his first revelation, Muhammad was a spiritual and sensitive human being disturbed by the ignorance and corrupt customs prevalent in Arabia. At the time, the practice of female infanticide was common; slavery, alcoholism, and gambling were widespread; wealthy men kept harems; widows and orphans suffered poverty and terrible indignities; and tribal wars were frequent.

While Muhammad sought in his heart for spiritual answers to these social ills, he earned his living as a merchant-trader. By his mid-twenties he had acquired so great a reputation in Mecca for honesty, integrity, and trustworthiness that men often came to him to settle their disputes and to leave their valuables for safekeeping while they were out of town. Hearing of Muhammad's impeccable character, Khadijah bint Khuwaylid, a wealthy and influential woman of one of Mecca's successful trading houses, employed him. Muhammad's personality and performance so impressed Khadijah that she asked him to marry her, to which he agreed. They had three daughters and two sons. The sons died in infancy, but Muhammad's younger daughter Fatimah lived to marry Muhammad's cousin, Ali ibn Abi Talib, and carry on the family of the Prophet.

In his thirties, Muhammad meditated regularly in the Meccan cave of Hira. When he reached forty in A.D. 610, according to Muslims, Muhammad was visited in the cave by the archangel Gabriel, who told him that he should announce his prophethood and preach the message of Islam. Khadijah and a handful of relatives converted immediately to Islam.

So brutal was the persecution suffered by the first Muslims at the hands of the corrupt leaders of Mecca that in A.D. 622 Muhammad led his followers to the nearby city of Madina where a small band of converts had invited him. This migration, called the *hijra,* marks the beginning of the Islamic calendar.

In Madina, Muhammad established and governed the first Islamic state. The Meccans, however, gave the Prophet no peace, and a series of wars between the Meccans and the Muslims ensued for a period of nine years, a period that ended only when Muhammad conquered Mecca and accepted the conversion to Islam of his former enemies. In A.D. 632, at the age of sixty-three, Muhammad died, leaving behind a young and dynamic faith and the foundations for a great empire.

QURAN: While accepting both the Torah and the Gospels as revered and holy scriptures, Muslims believe that the Quran represents the last edition of God's holy books. Quran is Arabic for "recitation," and the book is believed by Muslims to be the literal "Word of God" revealed in Arabic to Prophet Muhammad over a period of 22 years by the archangel Gabriel. Muhammad recited these revelations to his companions, who faithfully recorded them.

IMAN literally means "faith" or "spiritual convictions." In Islam it refers to the five articles of the Islamic creed; *(a)* belief in God; *(b)* belief in angels; *(c)* belief in the Prophets of God with Adam as the first Prophet and Muhammad as the last; *(d)* belief in the holy books revealed by God; the Torah, the Bible, and the Quran; and *(e)* belief in the Day of Judgment.

HADITH are a collection of eyewitness accounts, narratives, and reports of the sayings of Prophet Muhammad. Each account is passed through a chain of presumably reliable oral transmitters. The *Hadith* is second in importance only to the Quran as a source of Islamic theology and law.

SUNNAH literally means "a path," "a road," or "a way." It is a record of the sayings and deeds of the Prophet Muhammad. Unlike the *Hadith,* which includes only the Prophet's sayings, the *Sunnah* presents what Prophet Muhammad said *and* did. As a major source of Islamic faith and practice, the *Sunnah* complements the Quran.

SHARIAH: Literally, "the way," "the path," or "the road" of Islam showed by Prophet Muhammad. Also, the comprehensive, eternal, immutable, and sacred body of canon law governing the individual and community life of Muslims.

FARAIDH literally means "compulsory duties" or "obligations." Muslims believe that neglect of the five *faraidh* (also known as the five pillars of Islam) will be punished in the next world while their fulfilment will be rewarded. The five *faraidh* enjoined on all Muslims are the *shahadah, salat, sawm, zakat,* and *haj.*

> **Shahadah** is Arabic for "witnessing," "professing," or "declaring." It is the first pillar of Islam and refers to the declaration of faith in God and in Muhammad as God's last Prophet. It reads: "There is no God but God and Muhammad is His Prophet."

Salat is the second pillar of Islam and refers to the ritual of daily prayers in Islam. Adult Muslims are enjoined by their faith to perform five prayers daily. Each prayer is offered in a fixed pattern of recitation of Quranic verses coupled with prostrations.

Sawm is the third pillar of Islam and represents the obligation of all able adult Muslims to fast from dawn to dusk during the ninth Islamic calendar month of Ramadan. The word Ramadan is derived from the Arabic root *ramz*, which means "to burn." Ideally, *sawm* during Ramadan should burn away one's sins.

Zakat is the fourth pillar of Islam. It enjoins Muslims to donate 2.5 percent of their wealth in alms to the needy or to a charitable institution.

Haj, which is the fifth pillar of Islam, represents the obligation of all adult Muslims of sound mind and body to make a religious journey to Mecca and Madina at least once in their lifetime. The pilgrimage is supposed to take place between the seventh and tenth days of the Islamic month of *Dhul-Hijj,* which is the twelfth and last month in the Islamic calendar. The pilgrim who completes the *haj* during the annual *haj* season is called a *haji.* A Muslim undertaking a pilgrimage to Mecca and Madina at any time other than the annual *haj* season will be performing an *umrah.*

SUNNIS AND SHI'AHS: The Muslim world is divided into several sects, of which there are two principal groups: the Sunnis and the Shi'ahs. The Sunni sect is the larger of the two and comprises 85 percent of the *umma* (the community of Muslims). The word *Sunni* is Arabic in derivation and literally means "those who follow the sayings and deeds of Prophet Muhammad."

The minority Shi'ah sect comprises 15 percent of the world's *umma.* The term *Shi'ah,* which is an abbreviation for *shi'at-i-Ali* (Ali's faction), means "partisan" and describes any Muslim who believes that Prophet Muhammad nominated Ali to be the first caliph or *imam* of the *umma.* To the Islamic credo alluded to by the *shahadah* ("There is no God but God and Muhammad is His Messenger"), Shi'ahs often add the phrase, "Ali is the beloved of God." Although Ali did become Islam's fourth caliph, he was preceded by Abu Bakr, Umar, and Uthman. Therefore, while Sunnis revere the first four "rightly guided" or "pious" caliphs, Shi'ahs usually reject the legitimacy of Ali's three predecessors and all his successors. This difference in belief is an obstacle to Shi'ah and Sunni reconciliation and reunification.

In addition, Sunnis insist that Prophet Muhammad was illiterate and a mere human being through whom God revealed his message (as recorded in the Quran), while Shi'ahs contend that the Prophet was literate, infallible, and possessed semidivine attributes because of the *Nur-iElahi* (Divine Light) shared by all of God's prophets. Moreover, Shi'ahs assert, elements of the *Nur-i-Elahi* were bestowed upon Muhammad's daughter, Fatimah, her husband, Imam Ali, and their descendants through their male progeny. While Sunnis respect Ali and his descendants, they do not revere them to the extent that Shi'ahs do. Indeed, the Sunnis reject the Shi'ah contention that Muhammad or any of his descendants possessed qualities of divinity, and they repudiate the Shi'ah institution of the *Imamat* (the divine right of Ali and his male descendants to lead the *umma*). These differences in doctrine have also contributed to Shi'ah-Sunni conflict.

Closely connected to the institution of the Imamate is the doctrine of the *Ithna Ashari* (Twelver) Shi'ah sect regarding the disappearance of the twelfth apostolic *Imam* in A.D. 873 and his expected reappearance as the *Mahdi* (the divinely guided one or messianic savior). According to this doctrine, this reappearance will usher in a golden age of Islamic justice, equality, and unity of the *umma*. So powerful is the idea of the *Mahdi* that many Sunnis have accepted it as well.

Another major difference between Shi'ahs and Sunnis is in the realm of *fiqh* (Islamic jurisprudence). While Sunnis recognize four schools or rites of *fiqh* (the Hanafi, Hanbali, Maliki, and Shafi'i sects), the Shi'ah have only one major *madhab* (sect), *Fiqh-i-Jafariyyah,* which was compiled and codified by the sixth Shi'ah Imam, Ja'faral-Sadiq (d. A.D. 765). Shi'ahs promote the exercize of *ijtihad* (independent reasoning and judgment) by experienced *mujtahids* (learned theologians, or *ulama*, entitled to exercise *ijtihad*) and reject the Sunni concept of *qiyas* (deduction by analogy) as the fourth source of Islamic law after the Quran, the *Sunnah*, and *ijma* (consensus). Furthermore, differences exist between Shi'ahs and Sunnis in the laws of marriage, divorce, and inheritance. Twelver Shi'ahs, for example, permit temporary marriage, or *mut'ah*. For Sunnis, any marriage contract that sets a limit to the duration of marriage is sinful. However, Shi'ahs place greater restrictions than do Sunnis on the husband's right to divorce his wife. In addition, in matters of inheritance, female heiresses often are treated far more generously in the Shi'ah *Fiqh-i-Jafariyyah* than under the Hanafi, Hanbali, Maliki, or Shafi'i schools of Sunni *fiqh*.

Further differentiating Shi'ahs from Sunnis is the exclusively Shi'ah practice of *taqiyyah* (concealment), which permits an individual to conceal his true religious, ideological, or political beliefs to avoid persecution or death at the hands of enemies. This practice evolved in response to 1,400 years of persecution of Shi'ahs throughout the Muslim world.

The two major sects of Islam likewise differ with respect to religious tradition. The Shi'ahs engage in more rituals than do the Sunnis. Indeed, Sunni fundamentalists often denounce Shi'ahs for their adulation of saints, especially the most prominent members of the *Ahl al-Bayt* (Prophet Muhammad's extended family), and their pilgrimages to the mausoleums of saints in Iraq, Iran, and Syria. Portraits of Prophet Muhammad, Imam Ali,

Imam Hussein, and the battle of Karbala are publicly displayed and sold in Iran. Such pictures would never be found in predominantly Sunni societies.

The practice of daily liturgical prayers also differs between Sunnis and Shi'ahs. Shi'ahs are permitted to recite their five daily prayers three times a day (between dawn and sunrise, between midday and sunset, and betweem sunset and midnight) instead of the five times practiced by Sunnis (before sunrise, around midday, in the late afternoon, at dusk, and before midnight). The two sects' calls to prayer also differ, as do their manners of praying: Shi'ahs stand with their arms hanging straight down, while Sunnis fold their arms in front of themselves.

Shi'ahs and Sunnis differ greatly in their commemoration of Muharram, the first month in the Islamic calendar and the month in A.D. 680 in which Prophet Muhammad's grandson Hussein ibn Ali and his male followers were martyred on the battlefield of Karbala by Ummayad caliph Yazid's army. While Sunnis revere Hussein and lament his martyrdom, the *Ithna Ashari* (Twelver) Shi'ahs engage in elaborate mourning processions, *ma'atam* (breast-beating), and self-flagellation to commemorate the tragic death of Hussein and to atone for their failure to rescue Hussein and his clan from martyrdom. Shi'ahs believe that this dramatic display of mourning will have an unforgettable instructional impact on Muslims and non-Muslims. Shi'ahs also maintain that Imam Hussein will act as intercessor on the Day of Judgment and help them enter Heaven. Sunnis, however, feel that Shi'ahs have created an inappropriate cult around the personalities of Hussein and his father, Ali, strongly criticize the manifest masochism of some Shi'ahs during Muharram.

Although Shi'ahs and Sunnis have their differences, as do adherents of the four Sunni sects, Muslims of all sects agree that they have much in common. Not only do they share most fundamental religious beliefs, but the devout members of all Islamic sects express their conviction that Islam provides answers and guidance in all endeavors, even political. Thus, Muslims of all sects are sharing in the Islamic revival that is sweeping through the Muslim world.

FIQH is the science of Islamic jurisprudence. Although *fiqh* is not as comprehensive, divine, eternal, and immutable as the *Shariah,* it does cover most aspects of religiopolitical and socioeconomic life. While the Shi'ah sect is based on *Fiqh-i-Jafariyyah,* the Sunni sect is further subdivided into four *madhabs* that are based on the Hanafi, Hanbali, Maliki, and Shafi'i schools of Islamic jurisprudence.

The Islamic revival of the past two decades encompasses at least five prominent features: First, the spread of Islam from homes, *masjids* (mosques), and *madrassahs* (Islamic schools) into the mainstream of not only the sociocultural life of Muslim societies, but the legal, economic, and political spheres of the modern-day Muslim nation-states as well. The majority of Islamic revivalists (except for the Muslim Pragmatists) stress the observance of the five *faraidh,* or the five pillars of Islam: *shahadah* (belief in one god), *salat* (prayer rituals), *sawm* (Ramadan fasting), *zakat* (giving alms to the poor), and *haj* (making a religious pilgrimage to Mecca and Madina). They also emphasize modesty in dress for all, the *hijab* (veil) for women, and segregation of the sexes wherever possible. The Muslim Fundamentalists, Traditionalists, and Modernists within these movements exert considerable pressure on their respective governments to ban alcohol, gambling, nightclubs, prostitution, pornography, and a number of other corrupting influences. They further demand the formulation of an Islamic constitution and the implementation of the *Shariah,* the comprehensive and divine Islamic law that includes severe penalties for a broad spectrum of crimes. During Islamic revivals the governments of Muslim countries often display their Islamic credentials by stepping up mosque construction and increasing their funding of mosques and *madrassahs.* There is also an increased attendance of Muslims of all walks of life at *Jum'ah* (Friday) prayer services and during the annual *haj* to Mecca in the Islamic calendar month of *Dhul-Hijj.*

Second, all Islamic revivals engender widespread discussion and debate of Islamic issues in the mass media, leading to a proliferation of books and articles on Islamic theology, history, jurisprudence, culture, and civilization. More important, such Islamic revivals produce efforts at the reformulation and revision of Islamic theory and practice in light of contemporary times. This has been achieved particularly by Muslim Modernists through *ijma* (consensus) and *ijtihad* (independent reasoning and judgment). *Ijma* requires dissemination of pertinent information by the *ulama* (learned theologians) and Islamic experts of various schools of thought, so that an enlightened consensus can result from informed public opinion. *Ijtihad* demands that *mujtahids* (*ulama* who practice *ijtihad*) provide relevant solutions to contemporary problems.

Third, coming at a time of great economic disparity between the affluent elite and the impoverished majority, as well a time of sociopolitical injustice in most Muslim societies, Islam's emphasis on socioeconomic equality and justice has significant populist appeal. In fact, this appeal is one of the most important features in the Islamic revival.

Fourth, Islamic revivals often reassert the relevance of the religious (Islamic) approach to solving contemporary problems, while at the same time presenting a critique of the dominant materialist values imported from the West or the socialist-communist world. For instance, secularization is especially denounced by Muslim Fundamentalists and Traditionalists as "un-Islamic" because it implies that almighty Allah and His guidance are relegated to the personal domain of an individual's life, and that the larger political, economic, and sociocultural areas should be independent of His influence. Many contemporary Islamic revivalists are eager to accept modern scientific methods and technology from anywhere in the world. However, they are adamantly opposed to and totally reject whatever they perceive as "un-Islamic" and harmful to the *umma* (the Muslim "nation").

Last but not least, Islamic revivalist movements have strong anti-imperialist and anticolonialist undercurrents. The Islamic revivalists call for an end to international dependence on Western and/or communist powers. Instead, they champion the development of a united Islamic bloc of fraternal Muslim nations, which in turn could become an influential force in international relations for the good of the *umma.*

Although Islamic revivalism is defined here in the most general terms, it must be understood that it is no monolithic force under a single leadership. Indeed, there is a different expression of Islamic revivalism for each self-proclaimed Islamic revivalist. Generally, however, differing and sometimes contradictory views of Islamic revivalism prevail in the Muslim world.

The term Islamic *revivalist* refers generically to anyone who has contributed significantly to the revival of Islam. In propagating their perception of the "true" Islam, Islamic revivalists frequently, but not necessarily, promote the creation of an "Islamic state" by teaching, preaching, and/or writing, and on rare occasions by resorting to the force of arms. The individuals, groups, and movements that have fueled Islamic revivals fall into four ideal-typical categories: the Muslim Fundamentalists, the Muslim Traditionalists, the Muslim Modernists, and the Muslim Pragmatists. Like any classification scheme, this typology imperfectly represents reality. Many revivalist leaders may combine elements of two (or more) of these major categories, depending on specific issues and circumstances. But for the sake of clarity and simplicity, individual revivalists are categorized according to the principal thrust of the beliefs. (See the table following p. 151.)

The Fundamentalist revivalists tend to be puritanical and revolutionary in their religiopolitical orientation. They support *ijtihad,* independent reasoning, in matters of Islamic law and theology, while rejecting Western ideas and ideals. However, Fundamentalists are not inherently opposed to the nations of the West, only to their undue influence; nor do Fundamentalists always struggle through revolution. Many are willing, if given the opportunity, to participate in democratic elections and to abide by those elections. In general, however, Fundamentalists passionately desire to establish an "Islamic state" based on the comprehensive and rigorous application of the *Shariah.*

The Traditionalist revivalists are often Islamic scholars who want to conserve and preserve the Islamic laws, customs, and traditions practiced in the classical and medieval periods of Islam. In contrast to both Sunni and Shi'ah Fundamentalists, Sunni Traditionalists reject *ijtihad* and believe instead in *taqlid,* the rigid and unquestioning adherence to certain legal rulings compiled during Islam's medieval period. Some Shi'ah Traditionalists likewise split with the Sunni Traditionalists on the question of *ijtihad.* Among the Shi'ah Traditionalists there is a minority who after much learning and scholarship have gained the stature of *majtahids* (*ulama* entitled to exercise *ijtihad*), and these few *mujtahids* do exercise *ijtihad.* However, most Shi'ah Traditionalists (the majority of whom are not *mujtahids*) closely and rigidly adhere to the *Fiqh-i-Jafariyyah,* just as Sunni Traditionalists rigidly adhere to one of their four schools of jurisprudence—namely, the Hanafi, Maliki, Shafi'i, or Hanbali *fiqh.* While both Sunni and Shi'ah Traditionalists are often apolitical, passive, and status-quo oriented, these scholarly custodians of Islam do get involved in politics when they perceive Islam and/or the *umma* to be in imminent danger.

The Muslim Modernists, also called adaptationists, apologists, syncretists, and even revisionists, are religiously devout but unafraid of Western sciences and learning. In contradistinction to the conservative Traditionalists and the puritanical Fundamentalists, the Modernists advocate the reconciliation of traditional religious doctrine with secular scientific rationalism. Predictably, the Modernists are vehement critics of *taqlid* and vigorous proponents of *ijtihad.* They advocate the incorporation of many "modern-day" ideas and revisions of Islamic law. The radical Fundamentalists, in contrast, reject anything "modern" as un-Islamic.

The final category, the Muslim Pragmatists, are generally Muslims by name and birth who cherish Islamic ideals and values, identify with the Muslim community and culture, and are perceived as Muslims by non-Muslims. However, devout Muslims sometimes consider Muslim Pragmatists as non-Muslims or nonpracticing Muslims. Many Pragmatists do not fulfill the five *faraidh* expected of all Muslims; rather, they follow Islam's various basic ethical, moral, and spiritual principles, including belief in equality, justice, liberty, freedom, honesty, integrity, brotherhood, tolerance, and peace. Many of these nominal Muslims have been exposed to secular Western education and may have a better understanding of Western than Islamic thought. Accordingly, these Pragmatists view the classical and medieval Islamic doctrines and practices as anachronistic and impractical in the modern era. Pragmatists look instead to a broad spectrum of philosophies for political and socioeconomic models, including ideas from both capitalist and socialist countries. Pragmatists use Islamic rhetoric and symbolism to promote their economic, social, and political policies and programs of modernization and Westernization to an often hostile population; to draw support away from the Fundamentalists, Traditionalists, and Modernists; to enhance their own legitimacy; to integrate and unite their fragmented citizenry; and to inspire and galvanize the Muslim masses. The Muslim Pragmatists have governed most Muslim countries since they gained their independence from Western colonial rule.

Thus, their is a broad spectrum of belief and orientation in the revivalist movement sweeping the Muslim world. In fact, the greatest domestic enemies of the Muslim Fundamentalists are the Muslim Pragmatists, as both are vying for the support of the Muslim masses.

ISLAMIC REVIVALS PAST AND PRESENT

Historically, Islamic revivalism appeared in cycles followed by periods of relative dormancy. The present revival, like those of the past, advocates simplicity, purity, and piety in a time of trouble and confusion. However, two major differences separate the contemporary Islamic revival from past revivals. First, the current Islamic revival is not merely a localized or even regional phenomenon, but is global in scope. Second, this Islamic revival is not monolithic, but polycentric, heterogenous and multifaceted.

The Global Nature of the Current Islamic Revival

The universal application of the current Islamic revival can best be understood through such theoretical concepts in international relations as "transnational relations," "linkage politics," and "global interdependence." These three phenomena have occurred in conjunction with the peaceful and constructive revolutions in mass communications and mass transportation that have led to the shrinking of time and space. Joseph S. Nye and Robert O. Keohane have defined transnational relations as "the movements of tangible or intangible items across state boundaries when at least one actor is not an agent of a government or an intergovernmental organization."[4] For instance, due to the low cost and relative ease of modern mass transportation, as well as on account of the Islamic revival in the Muslim world, the number of pilgrims annually performing the *haj* has increased dramatically in the last fifteen years. In 1930, just over 230,000 Muslims performed the *haj,* and in 1940, the number was over 280,000. By 1950, the number of *hajis* (those who have performed the *haj*) had reached 895,000. Throughout the 1950s and 1960s approximately 1 million pilgrims performed the *haj* annually. But the decade of the 1970s witnessed the dramatic doubling of pilgrims to almost 2 million each year. In 1983, this number reached 2.25 million.[5] Since then, 2-to-2.5 million Muslims have performed the *haj* annually.

Some of the many participants in transnational relations are the nongovernmental, religiopolitical organizations that operate across the international boundaries of a number of countries. The *Ikhwan al-Muslimun* (Muslim Brotherhood) is one such organization (see Box 1.2). The group was founded in Egypt in 1928 and in due course established branches in several Arab countries including Syria, Jordan, and Sudan. Not only does the Egyptian *Ikhwan al-Muslimun* maintain close contacts with its branch organizations, but it is reported to have received financial assistance from the regimes of Saudi Arabia and Libya during the 1970s. Another such organization is the *Jamaat-i-Islami* (Islamic Association) of Pakistan (see Box 1.3). Not only does it keep in regular touch with a number of friendly Muslim governments (such as Saudi Arabia) and global Islamic institutions (such as *Al-Azhar* in Cairo), but it also publishes numerous books and monographs that are translated from Urdu into many languages and distributed internationally. (Libya's Muammar al-Gaddafi is also known to have funded the Moro Muslims of the Southern Philippines who are waging their *jihad* (holy struggle) for greater autonomy.) The external support given to the *Ikhwan al-Muslimun* (particularly during the era of Gamal Abdel Nasser in Egypt), the *Jamaat-i-Islami* (during the era of Zulfikar Ali Bhutto in Pakistan), and the Moro rebels (during the 1970s) was strongly resented by the governments in whose territories these Islamic move-

---

[4]Quoted in Walter S. Jones, *The Logic of International Relations,* 7th ed., New York: HarperCollins Publishers Inc., 1991, p. 626; Joseph S. Nye and Robert O. Keohane, "Transnational Relations and World Politics: An Introduction," *International Organization,* Vol. 25, 1971, pp. 329–349.

[5]Ziauddin Sardar, "The Greatest Gathering of Mankind," *Inquiry,* Vol. 1, No. 4, September 1984, p. 27; David Lamb, "Muslim Faithful Worldwide Preparing for Annual Pilgrimmage to Mecca," *Los Angeles Times,* August 19, 1984, Part I, p. 28.

Box 1.2   EGYPT'S IKHWAN AL-MUSLIMUN

The *Ikhwan al-Muslimun* (Muslim Brotherhood), also called more simply the *Ikhwan,* originated in the 1930s in Egypt under the direction of Hassan al-Banna, an Egyptian elementary-school teacher and Muslim Fundamentalist. A party dedicated to Islamic revivalism and social, economic, and political equity, the *Ikhwan* experienced rapid growth throughout its first decade; by the 1940s, its membership had swelled into a mass movement. The *Ikhwan* filled a religious and political void for many Egyptians. The mystical Sufi orders, which had flowered in the 1920s, and the Traditionalist *ulama* were passive, apolitical, and out of touch with the social, economic, and political realities of the time. Consequently, the *Ikhwan*'s activist message of radical reform appealed to the unemployed and underemployed Egyptians of the depression. In addition, the *Ikhwan* blamed Egypt's problems on Western colonial powers and Egypt's secular dictators under their influence—an ever-popular opinion.

The *Ikhwan* also owed its growth to the rapid industrialization and urbanization of Egyptian society and the consequent migration of countless villagers into the cities in search of jobs and a better standard of living. The resulting rootlessness, alienation, and culture shock experienced by these migrants led them to turn to the well-organized *Ikhwan* as a source of identity and direction in their lives.

By the mid-1940s, active and tightly knit "cells" of the *Ikhwan* had infiltrated educational institutions, factories, and trade unions. Indeed, the *Ikhwan* operated several businesses, including a publishing house where it printed its propaganda for nationwide distribution. The *Ikhwan* also owned and operated a textile company, an engineering company, an insurance company, and paramilitary training camps.

The *Ikhwan* expanded its base of support when the Egyptian monarchy suffered humiliating defeat after the botched invasion of the newly created state of Israel. The *Ikhwan,* in contrast, had sent its own volunteers to fight alongside the Arab armies against Israel, thus proving its pan-Islamic credentials. The *Ikhwan* viewed the expropriation of Palestine by the Zionists as a crime against the Palestinian people and Zionism as an extension of Western imperialism. By the end of the 1940s, with the Egyptian monarchy seriously discredited by its own ineptitude, the *Ikhwan* enjoyed its greatest influence and popularity and was widely seen as the only institution in the Muslim world seriously committed to the recovery of Palestine and to the restoration of Muslim honor.

In 1952, the *Ikhwan* supported the Free Officers Movement that toppled the government of Egypt's King Farouk. In fact, not only did the *Ikhwan* assist the insurrection, it cooperated with the Free Officers Movement to maintain law and order in Egypt. However, although the *Ikhwan* and the Free Officers had a common dislike of the Egyptian monarchy, their compatibility ended there. The Free Officers, led by Colonel Gamal Abdel Nasser and his clique of army officers, were secular nationalists and socialists dedicated to the un-Islamic notions of Egyptian nationalism, pan-Arabism, and Arab socialism. Once empowered, Nasser excluded *Ikhwan* leaders from his government and rejected the *Ikhwan*'s goals of an Islamic state at home and the promotion of pan-Islamism abroad. The *Ikhwan* was incensed; the new military regime refused even to educate Egyptian youth in Islamic values, to close gambling casinos, or to prohibit sales of alcohol.

Fearful of the power of the *Ikhwan,* Nasser accused the organization in 1954 of plotting to assassinate him and ordered the arrest of all *Ikhwan* activists. Nasser's information of the *Ikhwan*'s leadership and cells helped his government swiftly arrest, convict, and give extended prison sentences to numerous *Ikhwan* activists. Many of these activists were tortured, and a few were even executed. For the next decade the influence of the *Ikhwan* declined for lack of leadership. However, in the later 1960s the *Ikhwan* was revitalized, partially in reaction to the silence of the Traditionalist *ulama* to Nasser's socialism and dictatorship and to undue Soviet influence in Egypt. In addition, the organization gained ideological vitality when an imprisoned leader of the *Ikhwan,* Sayyid Qutb, wrote a book in which he revised Hassan al-Banna's dream of establishing an Islamic state in Egypt after the nation was thoroughly Islamized. Sayyid Qutb recommended that a revolutionary vanguard should first establish an Islamic state and then, from above, impose Islamization on Egyptian society and export Islamic revolutions throughout the Muslim world. The popularity of Qutb's ideas alarmed Nasser. In response, the Nasser regime again persecuted the *Ikhwan,* driving it underground.

After the terrible defeat suffered by the Arab armies during the 1967 Arab-Israeli War, President Nasser turned to Islamic themes and ritual observances to relieve Egypt's trauma. In 1970 Nasser died and was succeeded by his vice-president, Muhammad Anwar al-Sadat, who, to counter the Nasserite threat to his power, unleashed the *Ikhwan.* He freed members of the *Ikhwan* from jail, encouraged their exiled leaders to return to Egypt, permitted the *Ikhwan* to recruit new members, and allowed the *Ikhwan* to obtain financing from abroad. However, as the *Ikhwan* grew in strength, Sadat increasingly became the target of their criticism. For example, the *Ikhwan* criticized Sadat's close ties to the United States; complained about Western multinational corporations welcomed to Egypt by Sadat; and voiced alarm at the growth of nightclubs, prostitution, gambling, and liquor sales. In 1977, to protest Sadat's reduction of bread subsidies, the *Ikhwan* took to the streets and destroyed casinos, nightclubs, and bars.

The *Ikhwan* was further incensed when Sadat traveled to Jerusalem in 1977 and signed a peace treaty with Israel in 1979. The *Ikhwan* declared that Sadat had sold out Islamic Palestinian land. In 1980, Sadat again enraged the

Ikhwan by granting asylum to the deposed shah of Iran and, at the shah's death, providing him with an elaborate funeral at state expense. Then, in 1981, to stem Muslim-Coptic violence and to suppress growing dissatisfaction with his regime, Sadat persecuted and imprisoned Islamic leaders throughout Egypt. On October 6, 1981, Sadat was assassinated by an *Ikhwan* splinter group called Islamic *Jihad* (holy struggle).

Since Sadat's death, Egypt's President Hosni Mubarak has pursued the *Ikhwan* and other Islamists aggressively. However, Egyptians continue to turn to the *Ikhwan* and its radical spin-offs as disillusionment with and alienation from the Egyptian government persists. The *Ikhwan* has been impeded, however, by its ideological inconsistency and incoherent organizational structure. Thus, it is impossible to talk about the methods or aspirations of the *Ikhwan* as a generality. This lack of organizational discipline has obstructed the *Ikhwan*'s effectiveness as a political party and has enabled splinter groups like Islamic *Jihad* to steal much of the *Ikhwan*'s thunder in recent years.

Sources: Bruce Maynard Borthwick, *Comparative Politics of the Middle East: An Introduction,* Englewood Cliffs, NJ: Prentice-Hall, Inc., 1980; Ibrahim Ibrahim, "Islamic Revival in Egypt and Greater Syria," in Cyriac K. Pullapilly, ed., *Islam in the Contemporary World,* Notre Dame, IN: Cross Roads Books, 1980; John Waterbury, "Egypt: Islam and Social Change," in Philip H. Stoddard, David C. Cuthell, and Margaret W. Sullivan, eds., *Change and the Muslim World,* New York: Syracuse University Press, 1981; Gabriel R. Warburg, "Islam and Politics in Egypt: 1952–1980," *Middle Eastern Studies,* Vol. 18, No. 2, April 1982; Abd al-Moneir Said Aly and Manfred W. Wenner, "Modern Islamic Reform Movements: The Muslim Brotherhood in Contemporary Egypt," *The Middle East Journal,* Vol. 36, No. 3, Summer 1982; Ali E. Hillal Dessouki, "The Resurgence of Islamic Organization in Egypt: An Interpretation," in Alexander S. Cudsi and Ali E. Hillal Dessouki, eds., *Islam and Power in the Contemporary Muslim World,* Baltimore: The Johns Hopkins University Press, 1981; Raphael Israeli, "Islam in Egypt Under Nasir and Sadat: Some Comparative Notes," in Metin Heper and Raphael Israeli, eds., *Islam and Politics in the Modern Middle East,* New York: St. Martin's Press, 1984; Nazih N. M. Ayubi, "The Political Revival of Islam: The Case of Egypt," *International Journal of Middle East Studies,* Vol. 12, No. 4, December 1980; Saad Eddin Ibrahim, "An Islamic Alternative in Egypt: The Muslim Brotherhood and Sadat," *Arab Studies Quarterly,* Vol. 4, Nos. 1 and 2, Spring 1982.

ments operated and, in fact, still operate. Another transnational entity is the Organization of the Islamic Conference (OIC), whose multifarious organs help promote its objectives in the Muslim world (see Box 1.4).

In Iran, Ayatollah Khomeini engaged in transnational relations when he brought about the first "cassette revolution." According to Anthony Sampson, the exiled cleric found a way to take advantage of the proliferation of audiocassette players throughout Iran. After first recording his revolutionary religiopolitical ideas and antigovernment speeches on audiocassette tapes, his former students and supporters would then smuggle these tapes into Iran from Najaf, Iraq, where Khomeini lived. Because they were small, cheap, widely accessible, easily conceal-

Box 1.3 SOUTH ASIA'S JAMAAT-I-ISLAMI

The *Jamaat-i-Islami* (JI) was founded in 1941 in India by a devout Muslim journalist and Islamic scholar, Sayyid Abul A'la Maududi. As its founder and leader, Maududi wielded absolute power over the JI until 1972, when he retired and was replaced by Mian Tufail Muhammad.

The tightly organized, highly disciplined, and revolutionary JI was originally designed to oppose British colonial rule of India, to protect Muslims in India from the Hindu majority, to instill in Muslims Islamic fervor, to influence those in power to oversee the wants and needs of the Muslim community, to foster the Islamic revival, and eventually to transform India into the *dar al-Islam* (Abode of Islam) again. Following the partition of India and the creation of Pakistan, the JI dedicated itself to fashioning Pakistan into an Islamic state.

The JI's practice of selective recruitment has impeded its growth, however. The JI is no mass movement like Egypt's *Ikhwan al-Muslimun*, although the JI is better organized. The JI's members must pledge themselves not to Pakistan, its constitution, or its flag, but to the principles and ideals of the JI. If an individual, whether through lack of credentials or of time, cannot join the JI as a full member, that person may be invited to join the outer circle of sympathizers and from there potentially gain entry to the JI at a later time.

Among the JI's affiliates are a women's wing and a student association, which has won numerous student-union elections at universities throughout Pakistan since the 1950s. Other affiliates include the Labor Welfare Committee and the Peasant Organization.

By the rules of the JI's constitution, the leader of the organization is the *amir*, who is elected by an absolute majority of votes cast by the organization's entire membership every three years. The second highest position in the JI is the secretary general, who is responsible for directing the organization's various social, political, and educational departments.

Fifty members comprise the consultative assembly, the JI's second-highest policy-making body. Members of the assembly are elected by the JI's entire membership every three years. The assembly is responsible for reviewing the work of the *amir*, interpreting and amending the JI's constitution, and passing the budget.

The JI also serves as an educational and social-welfare organization in Pakistan. It operates schools and orphanages, where children are indoctrinated in the JI's Islamic ideology. The JI provides financial support for widows and runs health clinics. Furthermore, JI leaders travel throughout the world to attend Muslim Association conferences and to maintain contact with Islamic leaders, scholars, and organizations. The JI maintains it is non-aligned and, if empowered, promises to make Pakistan a leading member of the Islamic bloc. Indeed, during the Soviet invasion of Afghanistan, the JI contributed money to Afghan *mujahideen* groups (Muslims fighting a *jihad*).

Although the JI is influential politically, its success in elections has been limited. The organization's strict insistence on ideological purity, narrow interpretation of Islamic theory and practice, and zealous propagation of fundamentalist Islam have frightened away the support of both the Modernists and secularists who comprise the economic, social, and political elite. Moreover, the JI's promise to bring equity to the lord-serf relationship in Pakistan's countryside has earned them the vehement opposition of the *pirs* (spiritual guides), *zamindars* (large landlords), and *sardars* (tribal chieftains). Likewise, the *Jamaat-i-Islami*'s plan to segregate women from men in Pakistani society has alienated many women. The JI has also been engaged in heated doctrinal disputes with the two other prominent Islamic political parties of Pakistan: the *Jamiat-i-Ulama-i-Islam* (Association of the *Ulama* of Islam) and *Jamiat-i-Ulama-i-Pakistan* (Association of the *Ulama* of Pakistan).

The JI has other electoral liabilities; Its leaders thus far have lacked charisma, political shrewdness, and the ability to electrify the masses with their speeches; its original opposition to the Pakistan Movement and its leadership, put the JI's own loyalty to Pakistan in doubt; its religious appeal has been diminished by the Muslim Pragmatists' use of the same Islamic symbols and imagery; and the JI's selective recruitment has limited appeal. Most important, however, the JI has forged no realistic developmental strategy for Pakistan in a modern and increasingly interdependent world. For example, the JI offered no response to the serious inflation, unemployment, underemployment, and polarization of wealth during the 1960s except vague references to "Islam in Danger." By relying on sloganeering rather than formulating a plan of action, the JI proved ineffective in addressing the pressing needs of the population. Yet although the JI has failed to capture power, it remains an effective interest group commanding considerable influence. Indeed, the JI has collaborated, if briefly, with Zia's military government (1978–1983) and, later, with the current government of Nawaz Sharif. But the unpopularity of both governments has tarnished the image of the JI and it has had diminished success at the ballot box.

Sources: Khurshid Ahmad and Zafar Ishaq Ansari, "Mawlana Sayyid Abul A'la Mawdudi: An Introduction to his Vision of Islam and Islamic Revival," in Khurshid Ahmad and Zafar Ishaq Ansari, eds., *Islamic Perspectives: Studies in Honor of Maulana Sayyid Abul A'la Mawdudi,* Leicester, England: The Islamic Foundation, 1979; Abul A'la Maududi, *Islamic Law and Constitution,* 6th ed., trans. and ed. Khurshid Ahmad, Lahore, Pakistan: Islamic Publications Ltd., 1977; Asaf Hussain, *Islamic Movements in Egypt, Pakistan and Iran: An Annotated Bibliography,* London: Mansell Publishing Ltd., 1983; Khalid Bin Sayeed, "The Jama'at-i-Islami Movement in Pakistan," *Pacific Affairs,* Vol. 30, No. 1, March 1957; Sarvat Saulat, *Maulana Maududi,* Karachi, Pakistan: International Islamic Publishers, 1979; Sayyid Abul A'la Maududi, *Nationalism and India,* 2nd ed., Pathankot, India: Maktab-e-Jamaat-e-Islami, 1947; Aziz Ahmad, "Maududi and Orthodox Fundamentalists in Pakistan," *Middle East Journal,* Vol. 21, 1967; Nafis Ahmad, "Reactionary Politics of Jamaat-i-Islami," *Mainstream,* June 21, 1969;

Syed Abul A'la Maududi, *The Process of Islamic Revolution,* Lahore, Pakistan: Islamic Publications Ltd., 1970; Kalim Bahadur, *The Jama'at-i-Islami of Pakistan: Political Thought and Political Action,* New Delhi: Chetna Publications, 1977; Charles J. Adams, "The Ideology of Mawlana Mawdudi," in Donald Eugene Smith, ed., *South Asian Politics and Religion,* Princeton: Princeton University Press, 1966.

able, simply reproducible, and effortlessly transportable, these audiocassette tapes were widely disseminated, thus influencing numerous Iranians throughout the length and breadth of Muhammad Reza Shah Pahlavi's domain. In this way Khomeini totally bypassed the tightly controlled government mass media and reached Iranians directly, making it possible for them to listen to the tapes over and over again in the privacy of their homes and in the sanctuary of mosques—in other words, away from the prying eyes and ears of the Shah's feared secret police.[6]

Linkage politics also helps explain the global nature of the current Islamic revival. The term comes from James Rosenau's "linkage approach," which stresses that domestic and international environments cannot be artificially separated as some scholars tended to do until the late 1960s; the two environments are inextricably interrelated and "linked." This approach also studies the linkage between the domestic and foreign policies of a country, and among the social, economic, political, and cultural facets of a society. Linkage views the current domestic and foreign policies of a country as dynamic, rather than as a set of static and isolated events.[7]

Joseph Frankel defines linkage as "any recurrent sequence of behavior that originates in one system and is reacted to in another."[8] He discusses three major types of linkages: the "penetrative," the "reactive," and the "emulative."

The "penetrative linkage," according to Frankel, is one in which the government of one country participates in the decision-making process of another country's government. The foreign government thereby shares its authority to allocate values within the "penetrated" country. This category embraces economic, social, cultural, political, and military imperialism, colonialism, and neo-colonialism/dependency.[9] An example of penetrative linkage is Saudi Arabia's peaceful and constructive "penetration" and domination of the sparcely populated and politically fragile kingdoms of the Persian Gulf.

---

[6]From the account of Anthony Sampson, *New York Times,* May 6, 1979, p. 27.

[7]Patrick M. Morgan, *Theories and Approaches to International Politics: What Are We To Think,* 3rd ed., New Brunswick, NJ: Transaction Books, Inc., 1981, p. 176; see James N. Rosenau, ed., *Linkage Politics,* New York: Free Press, 1969.

[8]Quoted in Rosenau, *Linkage Politics,* p. 44.

[9]Joseph Frankel, *Contemporary International Theory and the Behavior of States,* London: Oxford University Press, 1973, p. 42.

Box 1.4 ORGANIZATION OF THE ISLAMIC CONFERENCE (OIC)

The Organization of the Islamic Conference (OIC) was established in 1969 to promote Islamic solidarity and to foster political, economic, social and cultural cooperation among member Muslim states. This organization comprises the following 54 Muslim countries (the percentage of Muslims, in parentheses, follows each country name):

(1) Afghanistan (99%); (2) Albania (70%); (3) Algeria (99%); (4) Azerbaijan (83%); (5) Bahrain (99%); (6) Bangladesh (83%); (7) Benin (60%); (8) Brunei (60%); (9) Burkina Faso (25%); (10) Cameroon (22%); (11) Chad (51%); (12) Comoro Islands (86%); (13) Djibouti (94%); (14) Egypt (94%); (15) Eritrea (75%); (16) Gambia (90%); (17) Guinea (85%); (18) Guinea-Bissau (30%); (19) Indonesia (88%); (20) Iran (98%); (21) Iraq (97%); (22) Jordan (95%); (23) Kazakhstan (50%); (24) Kirgizstan (65%); (25) Kuwait (85%); (26) Lebanon (75%); (27) Libya (97%); (28) Malaysia (53%); (29) Maldives (100%); (30) Mali (90%); (31) Mauritania (100%); (32) Morocco (98.7%); (33) Niger (80%); (34) Nigeria (50%); (35) Oman (99%); (36) Pakistan (97%); (37) Palestine/Israeli-occupied West Bank & Gaza (85%); (38) Qatar (95%); (39) Saudi Arabia (99%); (40) Senegal (92%); (41) Sierra Leone (30%); (42) Somalia (99%); (43) Sudan (70%); (44) Syria (87%); (45) Tajikistan (88%); (46) Tunisia (98%); (47) Turkey (98%); (48) Turkmenistan (84%); (49) Uganda (16%); (50) United Arab Emirates (96%); (51) Upper Volta (56%); (52) Uzbekistan (80%); (53) Yemen (99%); (54) Zanzibar (87%; former Sultanate of Zanzibar joined Tanganyika to form the United Republic of Tanzania in April 1964, which joined the OIC in 1993)

The major objectives of the OIC are *(a)* to promote Islamic solidarity among member states; *(b)* to consolidate cooperation among member states in the economic, social, cultural, scientific, and other vital fields of activity; *(c)* to carry out consultations among member states in international organizations; *(d)* to eliminate racial segregation and discrimination; *(e)* to eradicate colonialism in all its forms; *(f)* to support international peace and security founded on justice; *(g)* to coordinate efforts for safeguarding the holy places; *(h)* to help the Palestinian people regain their rights and liberate their land; *(i)* to support all Muslim peoples in maintaining their dignity, independence, and national rights; and *(j)* to create a suitable atmosphere for the promotion of cooperation and understanding betwen member states and other countries.

Source: For percentage of Muslims in countries belonging to the OIC: John W. Wright, ed., *The Universal Almanac,* Kansas City, MO: Universal Press Syndicate, 1993.

Frankel's second category of linkage, the "reactive," "is caused by boundary-crossing reactions without direct foreign participation made within the unit."[10] One country does not penetrate and control or unduly influence the decisions or

[10]bid., p. 42.

actions of another in its favor, but instead evokes a strong reaction from the other country. For example, the defeat of the Arabs in their June 1967 war with Israel was so humiliating that Egyptian Muslims in particular came to believe that *Allah* had punished them for having strayed from the "straight path." Egyptian Muslims "reacted" to this overwhelming defeat by turning to Islam for comfort and reassurance.

Another vivid illustration of "reactive linkage" is the takeover of the Grand Mosque in Mecca by a band of armed Muslim Fundamentalists on November 20, 1979 (see Box 1.5). The rumor that the United States and Israel were behind that incident enraged devout Muslims the world over. Anti-American demonstrations occurred in Thailand, the Philippines, Kuwait, Bangladesh, Turkey, and India. In Pakistan and Libya the "reaction" to the rumor assumed a more violent character as mobs assaulted, sacked, and burned the U.S. embassies in Islamabad and Tripoli.[11]

In fact, due to the revolution in mass communications (which includes print media, radio, and television), news of any major adversity, defeat, or victory experienced by Muslims anywhere in the world is transmitted through the mass media and grieved or celebrated respectively by Muslims worldwide the very same day. Graphic images of Israel's invasion of Lebanon in the summer of 1982; the massacre of Palestinians by the Phalangists in the Sabra and Shatila refugee camps in September 1982; the slaughter of Muslims by Hindus in Assam in February 1983, in Bombay in May 1984, and in Kashmir for much of 1994; the genocide of Bosnian Muslims by Serbs and Croats in the former Yugoslavia since February 1992; and the civil war and starvation of Somalis for much of 1992–1993 were moments of terrible grief for the *umma* worldwide. Conversely, moments of exhilaration and ecstasy were provided by transmissions of Yasir Arafat's address to the United Nations in November 1974; the periodic summit meetings of Muslim leaders; Ayatollah Khomeini's triumphant return to Iran in February 1979; the takeover of the government in Afghanistan by the Afghan *mujahideen* in April 1992; and the congregation of Muslims from all over the world in Mecca to perform the *haj*. It is clear from these examples that the revolution in mass communications and the "reactive linkage" have greatly enhanced and reinforced Islamic brotherhood and solidarity.

The third type of linkage discussed by Frankel is "emulative." With emulative linkage a response, which can be attitudinal and/or behavioral, is very similar to the action that triggers it.[12] An example of this "diffusion" or "demonstration effect" is the emulation of a successful Islamic revival in one country (such as that in Iran) by grass roots Islamic revivalist movements in other Muslim countries.

The three types of linkages have often manifested themselves simultaneously in the Muslim world, particularly in relation to the spread of Islamic revivalism. The current revival of political Islam is sustained and perpetuated by continuous chain reactions, which affect the world systematically through three linkages. Unlike previous revivals, however, this latest and most widespread of Islamic revivals

---

[11]*U.S. News & World Report*, December 3, 1979, pp. 11–12; *Time*, December 10, 1979, p. 47.

[12]Frankel, *Contemporary International Theory and the Behavior of States*, pp. 42–43.

Box 1.5 SEIZURE OF THE GRAND MOSQUE

The Grand Mosque in Mecca, Saudi Arabia, is considered to be the holiest mosque in Islam. At the center of the Grand Mosque is the *Ka'aba,* which is a cube-shaped shrine also known as *Al-Bayt al-Haram* (the holy house). The original *Ka'aba* was built by Prophet Abraham and his son Ishmael for worship of one God. It was later rebuilt by Prophet Muhammad in A.D. 605 for the worship of Allah. It houses the venerated "Black Stone," called *Hajr al-Aswad,* which was given to Abraham by God. The *Ka'aba* is covered with a black brocaded cloth into which is woven the Muslim credo: "There is no God but Allah and Muhammad is His Prophet." Muslims all over the world turn towards the *Ka'aba* when they pray. Muslims have also been enjoined by their faith to visit the *Ka'aba* once in their lifetime when they perform the *haj.*

Encouraged by the remarkable success of the Iranian Revolution and by the seizure of the U.S. Embassy in Tehran on November 4, 1979, 350 Muslim Fundamentalist zealots seized the Grand Mosque soon after the early morning prayers on November 20, 1979, the first day of Islam's 15th century. As many as 50,000 pilgrims were trapped within its holy confines. The leader of the hostage-takers, Juhayman ibn Saif al-Utaybi, was a charismatic 20-year-old cashiered corporal from the Saudi National Guard who had received some U.S. military training. Juhayman had persuaded his followers that his brother-in-law, Muhammad Abdullah al-Qahtani, a failed theology student, was the *Mahdi.* In the weeks before the operation, the hostage-takers had secretly squirreled away small arms and food inside the Grand Mosque. On the day of the operation, the zealots brought heavy weapons, walkie-talkies, and food in coffins. The guards and pilgrims were not alarmed to see people carrying coffins because it was common for Meccans to bring in their relatives and friends, who had died during the night, to the Grand Mosque for a final blessing before taking them for burial. After reciting a passage from the Quran, Juhayman began to denounce the Saudi Arabian government under the House of Saud for impiety, injustice, corruption, nepotism, and decadence. Juhayman also decried the presence of Westerners and alcohol in Saudi Arabia, demanded only Islamic programming on radio and television, voiced opposition to the higher education and employment of women, and generally advocated an Islamic purification of the Saudi kingdom.

Fearful of a replay of events in Iran, the Saudi government acceded to none of the demands of the hostage-takers in the Grand Mosque. Within two weeks, the Saudi government's security forces, with significant help from Western advisors (particularly of a few members of the elite French antiterrorist unit), overpowered the Wahhabi zealots who had seized the Grand Mosque. The event was significant not only as an aftershock of militant political Islam in Iran but as a cause of further Fundamentalist militancy throughout the Muslim world. The seizure of the Grand Mosque in the holi-est city of Islam, the point of adoration, shook the foundations of Saudi Ara-bia's House of Sa'ud, sent shock waves through the secular and Pragmatist governing elites of neighboring Muslim countries, and captivated audiences worldwide, bringing to their attention the powerful revival of militant politi-cized Islam. If Saudi Arabia, the geographic birthplace of Islam and Wahhabi Fundamentalism, the site of two of Islam's holiest cities, one of the most re-ligious Muslim nations in the world, and a principal exponent of a moderate brand of Islamic fundamentalism was vulnerable to accusations of religious laxity, then what indictment would be made against those Muslim countries where the secularization process had progressed much further?

Sources: Jim Paul, "Insurrection at Mecca," *MERIP Reports*, No. 91, October 1980,0 pp. 3–4; David B. Tinnin, "The Saudis Awaken to Their Vulnerability," *Fortune*, March 10, 1980, pp. 48–56.

has not quickly snuffed itself out. Indeed, it has grown stronger and shows no sign of letting up. In addition, the modern revival of Islam is, again unlike prior cycles of revivalism, a global phenomenon, with worldwide repercussions. Its endurance may continue indefinitely, insofar as the circumstances fueling revivalist move-ments show little sign of abating.

Iran's Islamic Revolution (1978–1979) still exerts a powerful influence on people and events in the Muslim world. The reverberations of this Islamic revolu-tion have been sustained, despite the indefatigable enmity of the West, partly through penetrative and reactive linkages but particularly through emulative link-ages. Again and again, Fundamentalist organizations take their inspiration and sometimes even their money and leadership from Tehran. Organizations like *Hamas* (Zeal) in the Israeli-occupied Gaza Strip and West Bank; Islamic *Jihad,* Is-lamic *Amal* (Hope), and *Hezbollah* (Party of God) in Lebanon; and Iraq's *Dawa* (The Call) are supported directly or indirectly by the Islamic Republic of Iran.

The emulative linkages of the Iranian revolution, however, are generally more subtle, insofar as Iran is a predominantly Shi'ah nation while most Muslim coun-tries have a Sunni majority. Nevertheless, organizations like Algeria's Islamic Sal-vation Front (FIS), Tunisia's *Ennahdah* party, the Islamic Renaissance Party (IRP) of the Central Asian Republics and Azerbaijan, and the *Ikhwan al-Mus-limun, al-Takfir w'al-Hidjra,* Islamic *Jihad,* and *al-Jama'a al-Islamiyya* in Egypt, despite their ideological differences and notwithstanding severe governmental re-pression, have not only endured, but look with hope to the survival and consolida-tion of Iran's Islamic government. Meanwhile, governments in Afghanistan and the Sudan, which have recently begun the process of building Islamic states, also look to the Iranian example for inspiration. In turn, organizations like *Hamas, Hezbollah,* and the Islamic *Amal* as well as governments like those of Afghanistan and Sudan perpetuate the emulative linkage for which Iran was the catalyst. Now the latter two fundamentalist states are becoming an influential inspiration to other Muslim countries. Consequently, the political revival of Islam is becoming self-perpetuating.

The former Soviet Union's predominantly Muslim republics (Azerbaijan, Kazakhistan, Turkmenistan, Uzbekistan, Kirgizistan, and Tajikistan) are experiencing an Islamic revival after emerging from the 74-year-old Soviet communist shadow. Iran, Pakistan, Saudi Arabia, and Turkey are actively competing for influence in the region by sending money, building and renovating mosques and *madrassahs*, and sending clerics and Islamic literature. Iran and Afghanistan have already exerted considerable sway in neighboring Tajikistan. There, Afghans are smuggling arms to the Fundamentalist IRP, which enjoys a powerful base of support in the mountain regions. Moreover, the Tajiks, unlike the other Central Asian Muslims and Azerbaijanis, have strong cultural and linguistic ties to neighboring Iran. Thus, as the political situation in the republic degenerates into civil war, the Islamic fundamentalists are gaining new converts to their cause every day. The example provided by Tajikistan may, in turn, inspire fundamentalist revivalists throughout the other Muslim former Soviet republics. Already, neighboring Uzbekistan is feeling the linkages.

The revolution in mass communications and mass transportation, combined with the immensely significant phenomena of "transnational relations" and "linkage politics," have helped make this an era of "global interdependence." According to Oran Young, global interdependence can be defined along a continuum, measured by "the extent to which events occurring in any given part of the world system affect (either physically or perceptually) events taking place in each of the other parts or component units of the system."[13] According to Kenneth Waltz, "interdependence is a condition in which anything that happens anywhere in the world may affect somebody or everybody elsewhere."[14] Witness, for example, the far-reaching consequences of the OPEC oil-price increases, which affected the economic, political, and social structures of many countries and dictated adjustments that in turn begat their own unique results. A pebble dropped in the pool of human endeavor makes ripples far away from the point of impact, and the pool is never the same again.

The Polycentric and Multifaceted Islamic Revival

The contemporary Islamic revival is polycentric, heterogeneous, and multifaceted because of a number of factors. First, all four types of Islamic Revivalists (Fundamentalists, Traditionalists, Modernists, and Pragmatists) are very active simultaneously, and each group believes that it is working for the greater good of the *umma*. A contemporary example of struggles among well-meaning partisans of each of these groups is illustrated in the short history of the Iranian Revolution.

---

[13]Oran Young, "Interdependence in World Politics," *International Journal*, Vol. 24, Autumn 1969, p. 726.

[14]Kenneth Waltz, *Theory of International Politics*, Reading, MA: Addison-Wesley Publishing Co., 1979, p. 139.

All four groups were very clearly delineated: Fundamentalists typified by Ayatollah Ruhollah Khomeini, Ayatollah Hussein-Ali Montazeri, Ali Khamanei, and Ali Akbar Hashemi Rafsanjani; Traditionalists exemplified by Ayatollah Shariatmadari; Modernists represented by Mehdi Bazargan and Abolhassan Banisadr; and Pragmatists, initially represented by Shahpour Bakhtiar, Karim Sanjabi, and Masoud Rajavi.

Second, in this age of nation-states, the twin ideals of nationalism and national interest are motivating the present leaders of most Muslim countries far more than the utopian ideal of an integrated and unified Islamic empire, or even the more attainable vision of a unified Islamic bloc. This was vividly illustrated in Khomeini's failure to create a pan-Islamic bloc. Despite some conviction at the grass roots level, the forces of nationalism overwhelmed any incipient movement in the pan-Islamic direction.

Third, because the leaders of nearly all Muslim states have different worldviews, they find it difficult to unite for any sustained period on more than a few issues. Some leaders are revolutionary Fundamentalists with an anti-American bias, as Khomeini was and Gaddafi remains. Others are pro-Western and status-quo oriented, such as King Fahd of Saudi Arabia, King Hassan of Morocco, and King Hussein of Jordan. Others are Muslim Pragmatists who develop their alliances with the goal of promoting personal and national objectives: Pakistan's Prime Minister Zulfikar Ali Bhutto, Egypt's President Muhammad Anwar al-Sadat, and Iraq's President Saddam Hussein.

Martin Kramer probably best summed up the diversity of the Muslim world:

> There is [as yet] no prestigious center for the propagation of the true faith, no compelling leader to whom the faithful look for authoritative pronouncements, no model Islamic order to which all turn in emulation. An Islamic order is in truth many orders, many nostalgias, many visions of the future. There are those across Asia and Africa who do call for Islam, who proclaim in harmony that 'the Quran is our constitution,' but beyond the single slogan are countless ideals.15

The "multipolarization" of the global system that began in the early 1970s has continued to grow. Likewise at the level of the Muslim world a number of different power centers have also evolved, namely, Saudi Arabia, Iran, Egypt, Turkey, Indonesia, Libya, Syria, and Pakistan. Thus, the Muslim world is not experiencing the homogeneous and monolithic Islamic revival necessary to help make it an international power bloc.

Nevertheless, Islamic revivalism is a potent and significant international movement. Representing a potentially powerful political ideology that all Muslims can embrace and support, Islamic revivalism is growing exponentially as a popular idiom of protest against unjust and repressive "un-Islamic" regimes. A number of major questions remain, however: What shape will political Islam take? Which of the four revivalist types will enjoy the greatest support in the Muslim world? And

---

15Martin Kramer, "Political Islam," *The Washington Papers*, Vol. 8, No. 73, Beverly Hills: Sage Publications, 1980, p. 39.

above all, what specific Islamic doctrines apply to political action? How is Islam, unlike Christianity, a vehicle for political action?

SUMMARY

Islam is an influential force in international relations today due to the revival of political Islam (Islamic revivalism) in many countries around the world. Manifestations of the modern Islamic revival include a groundswell of public support for an Islamic system (Islamic resurgence); the ceaseless efforts of Islamic movements, parties, and/or interest groups to establish an Islamic system; and government-sponsored Islamic policies and programs that reassert Islam, sometimes sincerely but most often to appease an influential domestic lobby, to enhance governmental legitimacy, to assist in the integration of a fragmented society, and/or to acquire funds from rich Muslim countries. These manifestations include at least five prominent features:

> the spread of Islamic principles, *faraidh* (duties), and practices from homes, *masjids,* and *madrassah*s into the mainstream of not only the sociocultural life of Muslim societies, but also the political, legal, and even economic spheres of Muslim countries

> a widespread discussion and intense debate of Islamic issues, problems, and events in the mass media that attempt to revise Islamic theory and practice in light of contemporary times

> Islamic revivals that stress the centrality of socioeconomic and political justice in Islam

> Islamic revivals that often reassert the relevance of Islamic solutions to contemporary problems

> Islamic revivals that have strong anti-imperialist and anticolonialist undercurrents, stressing autarky and pan-Islamism instead.

Historically, Islamic revivalism came in cycles followed by periods of relative dormancy. The present Islamic revival, like those of the past, advocates simplicity, purity, and piety in a time of trouble and confusion. However, two major differences separate the contemporary Islamic revival from those of the past. First, the current Islamic revival is not merely a localized or even regional phenomenon; it is instead global in scope. Second, this global Islamic revival is neither monolithic nor homogeneous, but polycentric, pluralistic, heterogenous, and multifaceted. The individuals, groups, and movements that have contributed to Islamic revivals in our interdependent world fall into four ideal/typical categories: the Muslim Fundamentalists, the Muslim Traditionalists, the Muslim Modernists, and the Muslim Pragmatists. The current Islamic revival is a product of the action, reaction, and interaction of all four types of Islamic revivalists.

Chapter
2

Islam

A Vehicle for Political Action

In the West, the domain of religion, represented by the church, and the domain of politics, represented by the state, are separate and coexist with their own distinct laws and chains of authority. This concept of separating church and state in the West follows the Christian maxim, "Render unto Caesar the things that are Caesar's, and unto God the things that are God's."[16] The same idea was also discussed in the writings of Benedict de Spinoza, John Locke, and the philosophers of the European Enlightenment. The idea was implemented in the West only three hundred years ago after much sectarianism and bloodshed.[17]

In Islam, however, religion and politics are inseparable. The domain of Caesar (civil/temporal authority) and the domain of Allah (the religion of Islam) are mutually inclusive. According to the famous Muslim philosopher Al-Ghazali (1058–1111): "religion and temporal power are twins." They are two sides of the same coin.

In essence Islam is both this-worldly and other-worldly. While the faithful are enjoined to be actively involved in this world and to enjoy the good things that life has to offer, they are just as strongly commanded to lead virtuous, righteous, pious, and God-fearing lives so that they can end up in Heaven in the next world. Islam is more than a set of obligatory rituals, like praying and alms-giving. It is an integrated and holistic belief system governing all aspects of a Muslim's life, making no distinction between religious and political responsibilities. The Quran is the devout Muslim's ultimate authority in all matters, offering "Divine Guidance for all fields of human life, may they be private or public, political or economic, social

---

[16]Luke 20:25.

[17]Bernard Lewis, "The Roots of Muslim Rage," *The Atlantic*, Vol. 266, No. 3, September 1990, p. 47.

or cultural, moral or legal and judicial. Islam is an all-embracing social ideology."[18] Islam thus provides models for both individual and political action. Hence, when secular ideologies fail in the Muslim world, Muslims often turn to the Islamic alternative. An Islamic revival is the end result.

Islam is both a "historical" and an "organic" religion.[19] These concepts help explain why and how Islam becomes a vehicle for political change in the Muslim world.

ISLAM: A "HISTORICAL" RELIGION

Unlike "ahistorical" religions like Hinduism and Buddhism,[20] Islam perceives history as divinely ordained. Muslims see the hand of God purposefully guiding history, presumably toward a "Kingdom of God" on Earth. As Wilfred Cantwell Smith wrote, "In essence, Islamic history, therefore, is the fulfillment, under divine guidance, of the purpose of human history."[21] The greater a religion's emphasis on history as divinely ordained, the greater the likelihood that religion will assume a significant role in the region's political life.[22] This is true in Islam. Within a "historical" religion, human history is, in general, a process of progressive revelation and promised fulfilment. Religion explains the beginning and end of human history and the direction it must take. But, because "particular historical events are [considered] crucial acts of revelation,"[23] such events set specific precedents for establishing a socioeconomic and political order that conforms to a divine design. In effect, what Muhammad did is as important to devout Muslims as what Muhammad said; and it is lost on no believer that Muhammad, escaping persecution in Mecca, established the first Islamic state in the neighboring city of Madina.

Prophet Muhammad frowned upon celibacy and the renunciation of one's responsibilities to one's work, family, colleagues, and friends in this world for otherworldly pursuits, such as praying and meditating. Indeed, Muhammad's life exem-

---

[18]Sayyid Abul A'la Maududi, *Islamic Law and Constitution*, 6th ed., trans. and ed. Khurshid Ahmad, Lahore, Pakistan: Islamic Publications Ltd., 1977, p. 1.

[19]See Donald Eugene Smith, *Religion and Political Development*, Boston: Little, Brown & Co., 1970, pp. 24–40, 248–249; Donald Eugene Smith, ed., *Religion and Political Modernization*, New Haven: Yale University Press, 1974, Chp. 1.

[20]According to Donald Eugene Smith, "ahistorical religions" like Hinduism and Buddhism consider history irrelevant to the spiritual quest, although the guidance of religious leaders both past and present may be useful. Moreover, in these religions "history has no divine purpose, no beginning, no end, and may be cyclical in nature. Individual salvation or self-realization is the goal of the spiritual quest, and historical events bear no significant relationship to the process" [D. E. Smith, *Religion and Political Development*, p. 249; also see Donald Eugene Smith, ed., *Religion and Political Modernization*, Chp. 1].

[21]Wilfred Cantwell Smith, *Islam in Modern History*, New York: Mentor Books, 1957, pp. 14, 24, 47, 11–47.

[22]D. E. Smith, *Religion and Political Development*, pp. 24–40, 248–249.

[23]Ibid., pp. 248–249.

plifies the importance of adopting an active and assertive worldly orientation. Islam demands the building of a political, social, and economic order, which, because the religion is "historical," is based on divine principles laid down not only in Islamic theology, jurisprudence, and the *Shariah,* but in specific historical precedents set by Muhammad and his first four "rightly guided caliphs."

In Islam today, Muhammad remains, to the devout believer, the most significant model. The Prophet was a charismatic religious leader, a statesman with vision, a just judge, a competent administrator, a courageous military general, a loving husband and father, and a trustworthy friend. Hence, throughout the Muslim world, Muhammad has "had a greater immediate impact on the course of history than any other religious leader," while "Islam has been the [religion] most fully involved in the events of social and political life."[24] Islam, both at its inception and at its peak of glory, becomes the blueprint by which today's Islamic revivalist, disillusioned by secular ideologies, seeks to build a true Islamic state.

Although Muhammad is the most significant role model to Islam, other historical personalities and events provide models to emulate or interpret. For example, victory in battle has always been considered a sign of God's favor, and defeat either punishment for deviation from Islam's "Straight Path" or a test of faith. Muhammad's victory in the Battle of Badr (A.D. 624) against the numerically superior Meccan forces signified that "Allah willed that He should cause the truth to triumph by His words, and cut the root of the disbelievers." (8:7–9)[25] Moreover, Muhammad's victory was purely God's doing; "Ye slew them not, but Allah slew them. . . ." (8:17)

Likewise, defeat in battle was also God's doing. Following the Battle of Badr, the Prophet's army was overwhelmed by the Meccans in the Battle of Uhud. The Quran provides two explanations for this defeat. The first suggests that God was testing the Muslims to distinguish the true believers from the hypocrites; "If you have suffered from a wound, so did the [disbelieving] people. We alternate these vicissitudes among mankind so that Allah may know the true believers and choose martyrs from among you. . . ." (3:140) The second explanation implies that a portion of Muhammad's army had incurred God's displeasure by disobeying the Prophet's orders and abandoning a strategic pass when the Meccans fled. These Muslims who were gathering booty left behind by the retreating Meccans, were unprepared for the returning Meccan forces and were overcome.[26] The Quran explains: "Allah fulfilled His pledge to you when, by His leave, you went on killing

---

[24]Newell S. Booth, "The Historical and Non-Historical in Islam," *The Muslim World,* Vol. 60, No. 2, April 1970, p. 109.

[25]Interpretations of most Quranic verses in this work are derived from three sources: *The Meaning of the Quran,* 5th ed., checked and revised by Mahmud Y. Zayid, Beirut, Lebanon: Dar al-Choura, 1980; Mohammed Marmaduke Pickthall, *The Meaning of the Glorious Koran,* New York: Mentor Books, 1953; and N. J. Dawood, *The Koran,* 4th ed., Baltimore: Penguin Books, 1974. Often the Quranic interpretations appearing here are a synthesis of all three aforementioned sources. All sources from the Quran are presented at the end of the Quranic verse in parentheses. First the *sura* (chapter) number is given, followed by a colon and then the number of the specific Quranic verse(s).

[26]W. Montgomery Watt, *Muhammad in Medina,* Oxford: Clarendon Press, 1968, pp. 26–27.

them. But afterwards your courage failed you, and you disobeyed [the Apostle] after he had brought you within view of what you wished for."(3:152)

Therefore, according to devout Muslims, the outcome of the battles of Badr and Uhud, and by implication of all battles throughout Islamic history, depended on the favor of Allah. Moreover, Islam's conspicuous success and expansion in its first three centuries confirmed "divine support and power."[27] Such historical glory, in turn, provided the devout Muslim both failures to be avoided and successes to be emulated. And since Muslims believed historical success resulted from the establishment of a spiritually unified Islamic state, the conviction was reinforced that "true faith was indeed inseparable from social and political action in this world."[28]

Today's Muslims likewise interpret recent successes and failures in the Muslim world from a religious context. The establishment of the new nation-state of Pakistan, the economic empowerment of OAPEC, the success of Khomeini in defiance of the United States, and the Afghan *mujahideen's* expulsion of the Soviets from Afghanistan are each events perceived by Muslims as God's vindication of the righteous. Meanwhile, the dismemberment of Pakistan and the defeat of the Arabs by Israel in the 1967 war are interpreted by many Muslims as divine punishment for the Muslim world becoming too secular and Western, thus straying from the "Straight Path."

As a "historical" religion, orthodox Islam, at least in theory, bridges the gulf between the sacred and the profane, the religious and the political.[29] In essence, "Islam has been inseparable from the political vicissitudes of the Islamic peoples to such an extent that the history of Islam turns out to be political history. . . ."[30] Moreover, for the Islamic revivalist, history serves as both model and warning for the future.

ISLAM: AN "ORGANIC" RELIGION

While "church" religions emphasize the role of a well-established and well-structured clerical organization that, in theory and in structure, has a separate identity from both government and society, an "organic" religion maintains no such church hierarchy or priestly class. In fact, within an "organic" religion, "sacral law and sacral social structure are of the essence. . . . Religion is largely equated with society, and distinct ecclesiastical organizations . . . are secondary."[31]

By the above definition, Islam is an "organic" religion possessing a comprehensive code of ethics, morals, instructions, and recommendations for individual

---

[27]Booth, "The Historical and Non-Historical in Islam," pp. 109–110.

[28]Ibid.,pp.109–110.

[29]Binnaz Toprak, *Islam and Political Development in Turkey,* Leiden, The Netherlands: E. J. Brill, 1981, pp. 22–23.

[30]Booth, "The Historical and Non-Historical in Islam," p. 109.

[31]D. E. Smith, *Religion and Political Development,* p. 249.

action and social interaction. It is also a legalistic religion whose rules and regulations later formed the basis of a divine law governing every aspect of the devout Muslim's life. Islam provides political ideology that has mobilized, integrated, and governed all sects and all classes of believers.

In an "organic" religion the distinction between religious and social systems is obscured; the two systems virtually merge.[32] In Islam, this merger is both prescribed and effected by the *Shariah,* which Fundamentalists and Traditionalists throughout the Muslim world endow with the force of law.

Drawn from the Quran and the *Sunnah* (Prophet Muhammad's words and deeds), the *Shariah* has something to say about ever aspect of life: manners and hygiene, marriage and divorce, crime and punishment, economics and politics, war and peace, and so forth. By strictly regulating a devout Muslim's life, the *Shariah* binds the temporal to the eternal.

Acceptance of the divine origin of the *Shariah* implies a concurrent acceptance of the divine basis of society. Thus, religious law becomes civil law and becomes the principal means of social and political action. No social or political theory exists separately from what is prescribed in the *Shariah.* Society is the *umma;* the state is the political expression of God and the political organization of His *umma.* The *umma* in Islam, therefore, enjoys a dual character—it is both a religious community and a political society. Theoretical distinctions in Christianity between the realms of God and of king are absent in Islam. The *Shariah* incorporates the temporal within the all-encompassing spiritual realm. The divinity of the *Shariah* presupposes that both the private and public lives of an entire community are subject to divine guidance. Islam is not only a belief system in the religious sense, but a political doctrine that sets the limits of authority and obligation within the Muslim community. The Islamic community, based on God's Revelation, is the Muslim's ideal political model, whose laws and institutions are comprehensive and infallible.[33]

Thus, in Islam, political institutions are designed to defend and promote Islam, not the state. Moreover, such institutions are intended to establish and uphold an Islamic system based on the *Shariah.*[34] Furthermore, the primary loyalty of Muslim citizens is to the *umma,* rather than the state, and to the *Shariah,* rather than the ruler because, "at the heart of Islamic political doctrine lies neither state, nor the individual, nor yet a social class, but the *umma,* the Islamic community tied by bonds of faith alone."[35] When a ruler in a predominantly Muslim country is unjust or perceived as "un-Islamic" and imposes laws incompatible with the *Shariah,* the devout Muslim is enjoined by the Quran to take political action. This has been the primary impetus driving periodic and cyclical Islamic revivals today and throughout history.

---

[32]Toprak, *Islam,* p. 23.

[33]Ibid., p. 24.

[34]Ibid., pp. 24–25.

[35]Henry Siegman, "The State and the Individual in Sunni Islam," *The Muslim World,* Vol. 54, No. 1, January 1964, p. 14.

As both a "historical" and "organic" religion, Islam clashes with conspicuous elements of Western-style modernization, including secularization and Westernization. The secularization process in Muslim societies where the majority of Muslims are still steeped in the Islamic tradition (e.g., Pakistan, Afghanistan, Lebanon, Iran, Sudan, Algeria, and Tunisia) is punctuated with periodic regressions. This is because modernization, adopted wholesale from the West and implemented hastily, has not been thoughtfully adapted to the Muslim world. Unreconciled with Islamic principles that emphatically discourage secularization and the complete separation of the religious realm from the political, social, and economic realms, the process of modernization only perpetuates and intensifies Islamic revivals.

THE CENTRALITY OF SOCIOECONOMIC EQUITY AND JUSTICE IN ISLAM

The modernization process occurring throughout the Muslim world has not only caused secularization, which devout Muslims oppose and which most Islamic revivalists seek to reverse, but has also led to a concentration of wealth into fewer and fewer hands, a situation inconsistent with the teachings of Islam. Such economic polarization has contributed to social and political injustices, again inconsistent with Islam. It is this injustice and socioeconomic inequity in the secularizing Muslim world that today fuels the fires of Islamic revivalism.

A careful reading of the Quran and *Hadith,* two of Islam's most revered textual sources, reveals the paramount importance of justice and socioeconomic equity in Islam. According to the Quran, "the creation of justice on earth is one of the basic goals for which Allah sent his prophets and provided their guidance." (57:25) Muhammad is no exception:

> Summon them, O Muhammad. And act with justice, as you have been commanded; do not imitate their lust, but rather say: I believe in whatever Allah has set down in the Scriptures, and I am commanded to be just among you. . . ." (42:15)

God commanded Muhammad not only to set an example, but to actively preach, propagate, and instill justice in the society. Hence the powerful and wealthy Meccan elite did not see Muhammad as merely another religious preacher. They saw him as a revolutionary leader espousing an ideological message that threatened their socioeconomic and political dominance.

Quranic references to justice emphasize fairness, truth, piety, and economic equality. "If you judge between mankind . . . judge justly," (4:58) and, more specifically, "God commands you to deliver trusts back to their owners, and when you judge among men, you should judge with justice." (4:61) The principle of fairness is coupled with "performing good deeds" and is contrasted with "indecency, dishonor and insolence," which God "forbids." (15:92) In another verse: "Allah commands justice, the doing of good, and liberality to kith and kin, and He forbids all shameful deeds, and injustice and rebellion. . . ." (16:90) Elsewhere in the Quran, justice is equated with "truth," which enables one to act justly: "Of those We created are a people who guide by the truth, and by it act with justice." (8:180)

General pronouncements about justice are also linked in the Quran to more specific injunctions: justice means a roughly equal distribution of wealth, and it means piety. "All human creatures have a right to everything that Allah made available, and for this reason Allah's gifts are to be distributed equally to all. The poor and needy have the right to share in the wealth of the rich." (51:19) Also, "O you who believe! Stand out firmly for God, as witnesses to fair dealing, and let not others' hatred of you make you depart from justice and swerve towards wrong. Be just, for justice is next to piety." (5:3)

The unreligious, meanwhile, will not observe the principle of economic equality: "Signs of corruption also include the covetousness of the rich for the little that the weak and the poor possess." (38:21–24) And again the Quran states: "Hast thou observed him who believeth religion? That is he who repelleth the orphan, and urgeth not the feeding of the needy." (107:1–3)

Islam also stresses the importance of justice and moderation in conflict resolution:

> Make peace between them, but then, if one of the two [groups] goes on acting wrongfully towards the other, fight against the one that acts aggressively until it reverts to God's commandment; and if they revert, make peace between them with justice, and deal equitably [with them]; for verily, God loves those who act equitably! (49:9)

Muhammad repeatedly emphasizes the place of justice and equality in Islam. He says: "The anger of Allah against the unjust man is all the greater when the victim of injustice has no defense save in Allah."[36] Likewise, Muhammad enjoins the believer to act: "If you see evil being done, put it right with your hand. If you can't do that, use your tongue. If you can't do even that, correct it in your heart, but that last is the weakest."[37] To Muslims, the Christian ideal of turning the other cheek represents a tolerance of evil. The Quran clearly states: "We rescued those who forbade evil, but We visited the wrongdoers with a grievous punishment, because they were given to transgression." (7:165) As for punishment, the Quran states: "life for life, eye for eye, nose for nose, ear for ear, tooth for tooth, and wounds equal for equal." (5:45) However, God is also always compassionate, merciful, and just: "But if the thief repents after his crime, and amends his conduct, Allah turneth to him in forgiveness for Allah is often forgiving and most merciful." (5:39) And again: "If anyone does evil or wrongs his own soul, but afterwards seeks Allah's forgiveness, he will find Allah often forgiving and most merciful." (4:110)

On more than one occasion Muhammad said that a man enjoys no immunity when he transgresses Divine Law, whether he be a powerful king or a powerless slave, a wealthy aristocrat or a poor nomad. In a *hadith* reported by Aisha, Muhammad declares:

> The nations that lived before you declined because they punished men of humble origins for their offenses and let those of noble origin go unpunished for their crimes; I

36Quoted in Abderrahman Cherif-Chergui, "Justice and Equality in Islam," *The Month*, Vol. 13, No. 2, February 1980, p. 2.

37 Ibid., p. 6.

swear by Allah who holds my life in His hand that even if Fatimah bint-i-Muham-mad . . . committed a theft, I would have her hand amputated.[38]

Muhammad frequently states that all are equal before Allah and His divine laws on earth, whatever their race, color, or creed, and social, economic, or politi-cal status. "All people are equal, as equal as the teeth of a comb. There is no merit of an Arab over a non-Arab, or of a white over a black person, or of a male over a female. Only God-fearing people merit preference with God."[39] At the conclusion of his last pilgrimage to Mecca, Muhammad stood atop Mount Arafat to deliver his last *khutbah* (sermon) in which he said:

> In Allah's eyes, the most honored amongst you is the one who is most God-fearing. There is no superiority for an Arab over a non-Arab, nor for a non-Arab over an Arab, nor a white colored person over a black one, nor a black person over a white person, except as a result of his righteousness. All of you are descended from Adam . . . Guard yourselves from committing injustice.[40]

Living by his words, Muhammad chastises Abu Dharr Al-Ghaffari, a close com-panion of his, for mocking Bilal, an Abyssinian former slave, because the latter was black. The Prophet lambasted Abu Dharr for his prejudice and informed him that he was not superior to a man of any color, unless he surpassed him in the fear of God and good deeds.[41] This same point is made in the Quran: "The noblest among you in the sight of God is the most Godfearing and the best in conduct." (46:13)

Many non-Muslims believe that Islam is unfair to women. This misperception is based on the improper practice of Islam by some Muslims. Indeed, Islam strongly condemned and stopped the practice of female infanticide prevalent in

---

[38]Quoted in A. G. Noorani, "Human Rights in Islam," *Illustrated Weekly of India,* May 3, 1981, p. 20; Mouloud Kassim Nait-Belkacem, "The Concept of Social Justice in Islam," in Altaf Gauhar, ed., *The Challenge of Islam,* London: Islamic Council of Europe, 1978, p. 135; and in Yvonne Yazbeck Haddad, *Contemporary Islam and the Challenge of History,* Albany, New York: State University of New York Press, 1982, p. 186. The Quranic verse that prescribes amputation for theft is followed by another that says: "But whoever repents after his crime and reforms, Allah will accept his repentence" (quoted in Noorani, *Contemporary Islam,* p. 20). Thus amputation in Islam is reserved for the habitual offender who has failed to reform. Likewise, the flogging or stoning of adulterers cannot be undertaken without the testimony of four adult males who personally witnessed the offense. Since the Quran explicitly for-bids spying on individuals doing you no harm, such testimony is likely only when the offense is bla-tantly public. Hence, the aim of harsh punishments for adultery is to deter a public display of such per-missive behavior, which could lead to a decay of the social fabric (Ibid., p. 20).

[39]A *hadith* of Prophet Muhammad quoted in Darlene May, "Women in Islam: Yesterday and Today," in Cyriac K. Pullipilly, ed., *Islam in the Contemporary World,* Notre Dame, Indiana: Cross Roads Books, 1980, p. 370.

[40]This brief extract is a paraphrase of the entire sermon delivered by Prophet Muhammad at his last pilgrimage. Refer to the translation of Muhammad's sermon done by Rais-ud-Din Khan Sherani, "Muhammad: The Greatest Law-Giver and An Epitome of Justice and Compassion," *Hamdard Islam-icus,* Vol. 12, No. 4, Winter 1989, pp. 64-65; also refer to Ameer Ali, *The Spirit of Islam: A History of the Evolution of Islam with a Life of the Prophet,* London: Christophers, 1922, reprint London: Methuen & Co. Ltd., 1967, p. 114.

[41]Nait-Belkacem, "The Concept of Social Justice in Islam," p. 141.

pre-Islamic Arabia. In those days women who were lucky enough to survive till adulthood were universally treated like chattel. They were sold into marriage by their fathers, kidnapped, raped, and bought both as concubines and as members of large harems; some tribal chieftains had as many as fifty wives. Muhammad abhorred the practice of forced marriages made by a woman's guardian, and instead converted marriage into a contract between two consenting individuals. He also took the revolutionary step of limiting the number of women that men were allowed to marry to four, "provided they were treated equally." (4:4) At the time there had been several tribal wars in which many men were killed. Consequently there was an overabundance of widows and orphans. Muhammad felt that marriage would bring the warring tribes closer together and also provide care for widows and orphans. He took the lead by marrying several widows. Islam also elevated the status of women by guaranteeing them inheritance rights (although they were given half the amount assigned to corresponding males). (4:11) A woman was also given the right to own property, to manage it herself, and to earn her own living. The Quranic verse states:

> O you who believe! You are forbidden to inherit Women against their will. Nor should you treat them with harshness, that you may take away part of the dower you have given them, except where they have been guilty of open lewdness; On the contrary, live with them on a footing of kindness and equity. (4:19)

The spirit of Islamic equality and sociopolitical justice continued to be the hallmark of Islam during the period of the "rightly guided caliphs." For example, the first "pious caliph," Abu Bakr, told his audience immediately after being elected caliph:

> You have made me your leader although I am in no way superior to you. Cooperate with me when I go right; correct me when I err; obey me so long as I follow the commandments of God and His Prophet; but turn away from me when I deviate.[42]

Rhetoric alone does not suffice in Islam. On the contrary, specific measures are recommended to establish social and economic equity. These distributive measures include (1) *zakat,* in which Muslims are required to pay $2\frac{1}{2}$ percent of their wealth in alms to the poor or to charitable institutions,[43] (2) *ushr,* in which Muslim farmers are required to pay a tenth of the wealth derived from their farms to the poor or to charitable institutions; (3) *khums,* in which Shi'ah Muslims are required to pay a fifth of their savings to poor or needy Sayyids (descendants of Prophet Muhammad's family); (4) *sadaqah,* in which Muslims are encouraged to

---

[42]Quoted in A. G. Noorani, "Human Rights," p. 20.

[43]In fact, Islam stresses the principle of *haq* (legal rights or claims of an individual), especially for the poor and needy. To quote the Quran: "In the wealth of the rich is a recognized right for the needy and the deprived." (70:24–25); "And woe unto those who ascribe divinity to aught beside him; those who do not pay *zakat. . .*" (41:6–7). During the caliphate of the first caliph, Abu Bakr, for instance, those who did not pay *zakat* were regarded as sinners who should not only be criticized but also fought against, even though they claimed that they still believed in *tawhid* (oneness of God) and the finality of the Prophet Muhammad.

give money or food to the poor and needy; (5) contribution of the *zakat, ushr,* and *sadaqah* funds into the *auqaf,* which are charitable institutions operated by the government or private organizations assisting the *umma* by supporting *masjids, madrassahs,* orphanages, health clinics, and other humanitarian concerns; (6) the abolition of *riba* (usury), in which excessive interest is charged by lenders to borrowers; (7) government regulation of interest rates charged by financial institutions to lenders; (8) *mudarabah,* in which Muslim businessmen are encouraged to engage in profit-sharing with their employees; and (9) *musharaka,* in which businessmen are encouraged to engage in profit and loss sharing with investors.

Islam's heavy emphasis on justice and socioeconomic equity obliges the Islamic state—or Muslims running a modern nation state—to ensure a just distribution of the public revenues, "so that it [wealth] may not [merely] make a circuit between the wealthy among you." (41:7) Although Islam operates from within what economists would call a capitalist context, concepts like "just distribution" are espoused by twentieth-century "Islamic socialists" who quote the Quran and *Hadith* to buttress their arguments for creating a "welfare state" in the "true spirit of Islam."

Socialists notwithstanding, the importance of socioeconomic equity and justice in Islam is particularly relevant to the Islamic revivalists. It is central to their struggle to replace politically and economically unjust and, hence, "un-Islamic" regimes throughout the Muslim world with an Islamic state governed by the principles of equity and justice.

THE SIGNIFICANCE OF *JIHAD* IN ISLAM

Principal to an understanding of Islamic political action, particularly in nations that preclude the participation of Islamic revivalists in the political system, is the doctrine of *jihad.* In the West, *jihad* is a highly pejorative and much maligned term, commonly associated by the media with the most extreme Islamic revivalist factions and outrageous acts of political violence. By mistaking *jihad* for jingoism, war, kidnapping, and terrorism, the West misjudges Islam as a radical, militant, uncompromising, and intolerant faith.

For centuries, the Christian West has denigrated Islam as a faith that "never gained any Proselyte where the Sword, its most forcible, and strongest argument hath not prevailed. . . ."[44] Christians maintained that *jihad* was purely offensive war waged to spread the faith, confusing *jihad* with wars of aggression, imperialism, and forced conversion. Western scholars and mass media have contributed to these misconceptions by emphasizing the martial connotations of *jihad* and by narrowly defining it as "military 'effort' in the cause of Islam. . . "[45] usually involving the expansion of the *dar al-Islam* (the Muslim world) at the expense of the *dar*

---

[44]Cited in the preface of *The Koran Interpreted,* trans. A. J. Arberry, New York: Macmillan Publishing Co., 1955, p. 8.

[45]Gerard Endress. *An Introduction to Islam,* trans. Carole Hillenbrand, New York: Columbia University Press, 1988, p.75.

al-harb (variously defined as the non-Muslim world, the world of the "unbeliev-ers," or the world of conflict).[46] This definition, although accurate, is incomplete; it misguides the non-Muslim and fails to convey the abundant meaning embodied in *jihad* as it applies to the daily lives of 1 billion Muslims, the overwhelming ma-jority of whom will never lift a weapon in anger.

The term *jihad* is derived from the Arabic root *jhd,* which means "to strive," "to exert oneself to the utmost," "to endeavor," or "to struggle in the way of God."[47] The term does not merely mean "holy war," as it has often been defined by non-Muslims. Ideally, *jihad* has three meanings: a battle against evils within oneself (personal *jihad*), a battle against evils within Muslim community (*ummaic jihad*), and a battle in defense of the faith and the *umma* against pagan aggressors or authoritarian apostates and tyrants oppressing Muslims within a country.[48]

The personal *jihad*, or *jihad-i-akbar*, is the greatest *jihad*. It represents the perpetual struggle required of all Muslims to purge their baser instincts. Greed, racism, hedonism, jealousy, revenge, hypocrisy, lying, cheating, and calumny must each be driven from the soul by waging *jihad-i-akbar*, warring against one's lower nature and leading a virtuous life. Thus, *jihad* in the daily life of a practicing Mus-lim is the constant struggle to "avoid evil and do good." This interpretation of the greater or greatest *jihad* is very similar to the Christian injunction to "fight temp-tation." Likewise, *ummaic jihad* addresses wrongs within the community of Mus-lims, whether by the written word or by the spoken word. *Ummaic jihad* repre-sents the nonviolent struggle for freedom, justice, and truth within the *dar al-Islam*. Thus, the doctrine of *jihad* is not exclusive to Islam but is typical of monotheistic faiths that demand personal discipline, moral and ethical deeds, and community justice and responsibility.

Martial or violent *jihad* is referred to in Islam as *jihad-i-asghar* (literally, the smaller, lower, or lesser *jihad*). Martial *jihad* ideally represents a struggle against aggressors who are not practicing Muslims. In Islamic theory, martial *jihad* should be undertaken in God's name and with pure and noble intentions, never for self-aggrandizement. Martial *jihad* should be used to protect and to promote the in-tegrity of Islam and to defend the *umma* against hostile unbelievers, whether they

---

[46]It is true that Muslim Fundamentalists and Traditionalists alike perceive the world as divided into two regions: lands of those who believe in God and endeavor to do his bidding (*dar al-Islam*), and those who do not (*dar al-harb*). The *dar al-Islam* contains all lands ruled by Muslims where, ideally, Is-lamic laws are in effect. Within the *dar al-Islam*, non-Muslims are protected and live according to their own laws in matters relating to their religion and customs. Nevertheless, non-Muslims are not allowed to occupy strategic positions in the military or government. The *dar al-harb*, in contrast, contains lands ruled by non-Muslims. There, the laws, rules, and regulations are of a non-Islamic character. More-over, in the *dar al-harb*, Muslim minorities suffer discrimination, prejudice, or intolerance. Thus, a constant state of suspicion, tension, and conflict prevails between the *dar al-harb* and the *dar al-Islam*. If war does break out between the two antagonistic systems, it is for Muslims a martial *jihad* in which the *mujahideen* (freedom fighters) who die are *shaheed* (martyrs) and are rewarded with paradise.

[47]Rafiq Zakaria, *Muhammad and the Quran*, New York: Penguin Books, 1991, p. 97.

[48]Arthur Goldschmidt, Jr., *A Concise History of the Middle East*, 4th ed., Boulder, Colorado: Westview Press, 1991, p. 400.

are invading armies or un-Islamic internal despots. In the latter case, the line between *ummaic jihad* and martial *jihad* becomes blurred.

Martial *jihad*, is not the sixth pillar of Islam, as is often thought, but is strictly circumscribed by Prophet Muhammad. The use of lethal force in martial *jihad* may be authorized and conducted only by the *umma* or in the name of the *umma*. Thus, martial *jihad* is strictly a corporate responsibility directed against the *dar al-harb* by the *dar al-Islam*. The individual Muslim cannot independently wage martial *jihad* on an unbelieving individual. Likewise, Islam forbids martial *jihad* of Muslims against Muslims; only nonviolent *ummaic jihad* is permissible within the *umma* against practicing Muslims.

Muhammad said, "If you see those in authority doing something you disapprove of . . . then disapprove of the act [*ummaic jihad*], but do not resort to rebellion [martial *jihad*]."[49] When asked about fighting unjust rulers within the *umma*, the Prophet answered, "No, not so long as they pray."[50] This reply, however, leaves the door open for martial *jihad* against nonpracticing Muslim rulers and governors who oppress the people. Otherwise, martial *jihad* against Muslim leaders is discouraged in order to avoid internecine or fratricidal bloodshed. According to the books of *al-Sunnan* (a set of books which contain the Prophet's sayings), Muhammad said, "the highest [greatest] *jihad* is a word of justice addressed to an unjust ruler."[51] Thus, in *ummaic jihad* there is no mention of war.

Jihad is, in its ideal form, essentially nonviolent. To quote a famous *hadith* of Prophet Muhammad, "the scholar's ink is more precious than the martyr's blood." However, martial *jihad* is often used as a last measure because "Islam's ultimate goals might be achieved by peaceful as well as violent means."[52] But even when martial *jihad* is authorized and carried out by the *umma*, further Quranic injunctions apply. Believers engaging in martial *jihad* are cautioned to show mercy in victory just as Muhammad pardoned Abu Sufyan, his greatest persecutor. Oppressors should be given the opportunity to refrain from their actions:

> Say to the unbelievers that if they refrain, then whatever they have done before will be forgiven them, but if they turn back, then they know what happened to earlier nations. And fight against them until there is no oppression and the religion is wholly for God. But if they refrain then God is watching over their actions. But if they do not then know that God is your Ally and He is your Helper. (8:38)

This verse implies limits in the pursuit of justice. "Fight in the cause of God against those who attack you, but do not attack them first and be careful to maintain the limit since God does not love transgressors." (2:190) The force used in martial *jihad* must be restricted to the minimum sufficient to restrain attackers.

---

[49]Cited in Abdul Hamid A. Abu Sulayman, "The Quran and the Sunnah on Violence, Armed Struggle, and the Political Process," *The American Journal of Islamic Social Sciences*, Vol. 8, No. 2, 1991, p. 19.

[50]Ibid.

[51]Ibid.

[52]Majid Khadduri, *The Islamic Conception of Justice*, Baltimore: The John's Hopkins University Press, 1984, p. 164.

Theoretically, martial *jihad* must be moderate and merciful; it is not to be used to exact revenge, engage in imperialism, or conquer for personal gain.

The three carefully delimited categories of *jihad*—personal, *ummaic,* and martial—are not recommendations; they are commands. Within the *umma, ummaic jihad* is enjoined on all believers who perceive wrongdoing. *Ummaic jihad* is the means for realizing the socioeconomic equity and justice promised by Islam.

According to *Al-Tafsir al-Quran li'l Tarikh* (History of Quranic Commentary) published in Cairo in 1973, many Quranic verses place the greatest responsibility for oppression, corruption, injustice, and vice on those in positions of power and influence.[53] One such Quranic verse states:

> There is no doubt that corruption in the system of government is one of the most important factors that lead to the collapse of nations. One of the signs of this corruption is the injustice inflicted on the weak by the oppressors. (28:4)

However, according to Islam, the governing elite is not solely accountable for the deterioration of society. The ignorant, apathetic, apolitical, and cowardly people among the governed must also share the blame. When freedom of thought, conscience, and choice are denied the people by despots, devout Muslims are obliged by their faith to work to restore such freedoms, either through writing, speeches, or financial contributions, or if the oppressors and despots are unbelievers, by the sword. This point is made in the following Quranic verse:

> And how could you refuse to fight in the way of God for the sake of those utterly helpless men, women and children, who, being weak, are oppressed and are crying out: 'O our Sustainer, lead us forth [to freedom] out of this land whose people are unjust oppressors, and raise a protector for us by Thy grace and one who will bring us succor'. (4:75)

Thus, in Islam, if the oppressed do nothing to change an unjust status quo, they are partly responsible for their plight.

Moreover, the Quran teaches that "true" Muslims with *taqwa* (fear of God) must write and speak out against unjust regimes and must wage *jihad* to arouse public action: "Confound not truth with falsehood, nor knowingly conceal the truth" (2:42) and "Verily, God changes not what is in a people, until they change what is in themselves." (23:11; 8:53) Moreover,

> Those upon whom war is made by unbelievers are granted admission to fight because they are being oppressed and have been expelled from their homes in defiance of right for the sole 'crime' of saying 'Our Lord is Allah'! (22:39)

Furthermore, God will not deny the people the right to defend themselves, otherwise "corruption would surely overwhelm the earth. . . ." (2:251)

All believers are enjoined to defend God and justice, even if it seems against their own interests:

---

[53]Haddad, *Contemporary Islam*, p. 186.

> O you who believe, be firm in justice and as witnesses for God even though it be against yourselves, your parents, those close to you, and whether it concerns rich or poor. . . . So do not follow caprice, lest ye swerve truth. (4:135)

Thus, justice in Islam takes greater priority than personal well-being. The individual must strive, no matter how great the sacrifice, for the good of the community.

Martial *jihad* is required at times of crisis, and none are relieved of the duty to fight unbelieving oppressors and attackers—even fighting in the sacred months is a lesser evil than oppression:

> They ask thee about fighting in the sacred months; Say: Fighting in them is a great sin, but to prevent people from the way of God, and to reject God, and to stop people from visiting the sacred Mosque, and to expel people from their homes are a much greater sin and oppression is worse than killing. (2:217)

The Quran warns Muslims of the terrible retribution they will suffer if they ignore their duty to fight oppression and, instead, support oppressors: "And incline not to those who do wrong and oppress others, or the Fire will seize you, and you have not protectors other than God, nor shall you be supported." (11:133)

If the *umma* is oppressed by a believer, then nonviolent *ummaic jihad* is required. If the oppressor is an "unbeliever," then martial *jihad* is permitted. The Quran specifically enjoins oppressed believers to act, not to stand idly by, in the face of oppression:

> Fight against them! God will chastise them by your hands, and will bring disgrace upon them, and will succor you against them; and He will soothe the bosoms [hearts] of those who believe. (9:14)

In Islamic history, Muhammad and his first converts were cruelly persecuted in the seventh century; only by rising up against their adversaries did they enable Islam to survive. Hence, *jihad* in the face of oppression is a duty of the devout Muslim.

Although enjoined in Islam, *jihad* is not without reward to the *mujahid* (one who engages in a jihad). Muslims believe that those who engage in *jihad* will be rewarded, if not in this world, then certainly in the next: "Whatever you spend in the way of God, will be repaid to you in full and you shall not be treated unjustly." (8:60) Another Quranic verse states: "So let them fight in the way of God who sell the present life for the world to come; and whosoever fights in the way of God and is slain, or conquers, we shall bring him a mighty wage." (4:76) Yet another verse pertaining to *jihad* states:

> They ought to fight in the way of God who have sold the life of this world for the life of the hereafter and whoever fights in the way of God and is killed becomes victorious, to him shall we give a reward. Why should not you fight in the way of God for those men, women and children who have been oppressed because they are weak and call, 'Our Lord! Take us out of this place whose people are oppressors and raise for us an ally,. and send for us a helper.' Those who believe, fight in the Cause of God while those who don't believe, fight in the cause of tyranny. Then fight against the friends of Satan. Indeed, the strategy of Satan is weak. (3:74–76)

For those who give their lives in martial *jihad,* God promises the greatest reward, Paradise:

> And as for those who are slain in God's cause, never will He let their deeds go to waste. He will guide them [in the hereafter as well], and will set their hearts at rest, and will admit them to the Paradise which He has promised them. (47:4–6)

Another Quranic verse states,

> Behold, God has bought from the believers their lives and their possessions, promising them the gift of Paradise in return. (9:111)

The glory of martyrdom in *jihad* is not an exclusively Shi'ah concept but is prevalent among Sunnis as well. Islamic revivalists, whether Shi'ah or Sunni, agree that an Islamic political movement cannot succeed without dedicated and unqualified commitment both to *ummaic* and martial *jihad,* and to the readiness to die in the way of God.

Examples of martyrdom from Islam's past are numerous. Muhammad's nephew Imam Hussein is renowned among Shi'ahs and Sunnis alike for his refusal in A.D. 680 to legitimize the caliphate of the tyrannical and impious Yazid, whose credentials as a practicing Muslim were highly suspect. Imam Hussein rejected the extravagant bribes of Yazid and chose, instead, when cornered by the immoral and unjust caliph's armies on the plain of Karbala, to defend himself and die a martyr in a martial *jihad* The martyrdom of Imam Hussein and 71 male members of his extended family at Karbala, far from a defeat, made all Muslims aware of the Islamic ideals for which he stood. By upholding the revolutionary Islamic tradition of struggle and sacrifice, Imam Hussein became a role model for all Muslims. As the Quran states,

> But do not think of those who have been slain in God's cause as dead. Nay, they are alive! With their Sustainer have they their sustenance, exulting in that [martyrdom] which God bestowed upon them out of His bounty.(3:169–170)

The broad and rich meaning of *jihad* has, despite clear injunctions and proscriptions, been open more than any other Islamic doctrine to widely differing interpretations. During Muhammad's life, God enjoined martial *jihad* upon Muslims only during times of dire necessity when the nascent community of believers was in peril. Under the first four "rightly guided caliphs" who succeeded Muhammad, Islam defeated its enemies and expanded its borders; however, martial *jihad* was not unduly or frivolously waged, nor was it undertaken for the personal glory of any individual. During this period martial *jihad* was truly "just war," and those who were conquered by the Muslims were shown mercy and were not obliged to convert to Islam since the Quran clearly states that "there shall be no compulsion in religion." (2:256) Islamic tolerance is also reflected in the Quranic verse; "You have your religion and I have mine." (109:6) Meanwhile, in stark contrast, Christendom was tearing itself apart, engaging in internecine bloodbaths, and forcibly converting non-Christians.

With the establishment of the Ummayad dynasty (A.D. 661), however, martial *jihad* was increasingly declared with little or no Quranic justification. The practice of martial *jihad* following the "rightly guided caliphs" was often perverted by corrupt caliphs; "just wars" became instead naked wars of aggression and conquest. Although early Muslim scholars declared that martial *jihad* was permissible against unbelievers only after provocation from the *dar al-harb*, later scholars broadened this interpretation and declared that martial *jihad* was justified against unbelievers simply for their disbelief.[54]

Thus, the imperatives of empire overcame the letter and spirit of Islam, and the practice of martial *jihad* was perverted and abused frequently by corrupt officials. War between the *dar al-Islam* and the *dar al-harb* became inherently "just," regardless of provocation. It is this corrupted tradition of *jihad* that has drawn the condemnation of the West and has given a false impression about "true" Islam.

Varying questionable interpretations and practices of martial *jihad* today, such as hostage taking, airplane hijacking, and blowing up the World Trade Center in New York, have likewise contributed to non-Muslims' fear of revolutionary political Islam and antipathy toward devout Muslims who peacefully practice their faith. Appropriate uses of martial *jihad* have become complicated, since the *umma* has been divided and the *dar al-harb* is within the *dar al-Islam*. Accordingly, martial *jihad* has, more than ever, been directed against adversaries within the Muslim world, not on its borders. With the universal *umma* lacking a caliph, many Fundamentalists have placed themselves in the vanguard of martial *jihad*, directing a "holy war" to rid the Muslim world of unbelievers and hypocrites while reestablishing a united Islamic bloc. The Ayatollah Khomeini declared: "In this holy *jihad* and serious duty, we must lead the other people by virtue of our mission and position."[55]

The question in the Muslim world is no longer whether Islamic revivalism is necessary for change, but whether that revivalism will rely on nonviolent *ummaic jihad* or violent martial *jihad* to realize that change. Since the leaders of many Muslim nations are not perceived as practicing Muslims by their citizens, martial *jihad* is more probable. Naturally, foreigners as well as authoritarian leaders are distressed by a *jihad* that promises the blessings of Paradise in martyrdom. *Mujahideen,* mindful of such promises, have successfully waged martial *jihad* against foreign invaders and internal despots including the United States and Israel in Lebanon, the Soviets in Afghanistan, the Shah of Iran, and Pakistan's Zulfikar Ali Bhutto. Today, numerous grass roots Islamic movements struggle to overthrow what they perceive as "un-Islamic" regimes throughout the Muslim world. Revolutionaries in most Islamic movements are convinced that European imperialism succeeded because secular Muslim regimes did not establish Islamic states and did not live up to the promise and principle of pan-Islamism. By oppressing their people and depriving them of any participation in the political process, the Pragmatists governing Muslim nations today have made *ummaic jihad* impossible—and martial *jihad* inevitable.

---

[54]Khadduri, *The Islamic Conception*, pp. 165–166.

[55] Ayatollah Ruhollah Khomeini, *Islamic Government*, trans. Joint Publications Research Service, New York: Manor Books, Inc., 1979, p. 88.

SUMMARY

Islam is a vehicle for political change in the Muslim world because it is at one and the same time a "historical religion," an "organic religion," a religion that emphasizes socioeconomic equity and justice, and a faith that stresses *jihad*. Muslims who embrace it as a "historical religion" consider history to be divinely ordained, believing Islam explains the beginning and end of human history and the direction it will take. Islamic revivalists have always tried to build a political and socioeconomic order based on principles laid down not only in Islamic theology, jurisprudence, and the *Shariah*, but also in specific historical precedents set by Prophet Muhammad and his first four "rightly guided caliphs."

Islam is an "organic religion" possessing a comprehensive belief system because the divine and immutable *Shariah* incorporates the temporal within the all-encompassing spiritual realm and has something to say about every aspect of a Muslim's life. Islam posits the fusion of religion and politics. The Quran enjoins Muslims to get involved in politics because politics determines the shape of society. Moreover, Islamists believe that only politics based on Islamic foundations can be honest, just, and beneficial to the majority.

Socioeconomic equity and justice enjoy paramount importance in Islam. Quranic references to justice emphasize fairness, truth, piety, and economic equality. Prophet Muhammad repeatedly emphasized the importance of justice and frequently stated that all are equal before Allah and his divine laws on earth, whatever their race, color, sex, creed, and social, economic, or political status.

Central to an understanding of Islamic revivalism is the pivotal importance of *jihad*, which literally means "to exert oneself" or "to struggle in the way of God." There are three types of *jihad*. First, there is the personal *jihad*, involving a nonviolent "holy struggle" against evils within oneself. Second, there is the *ummaic jihad*, which is a nonviolent "holy struggle" against evils within the Muslim community (such as a struggle for freedom and justice). Third, there is the martial or violent *jihad* fought to protect, defend, and promote the integrity of Islam and the *umma* against hostile unbelievers, whether they are invading armies or "un-Islamic" internal despots. *Jihad* is popular among Muslims because of the Quranic promise that a *mujahid* martyred in a *jihad* will be rewarded with Paradise.

Chapter
3
The Muslim Fundamentalists

Muslim Fundamentalists constitute the first major category of Islamic revivalists. They are also variously referred to in both popular and scholarly literature as Scripturalists, Legalists, Literalists, Restorationists, Restitutionists, and Puritans.[56]

The term *fundamentalist,* a favorite of the mass media, is of recent coinage. Fundamentalism applied originally to a conservative Protestant movement of nineteenth-century America; the word now signifies conservative movements among most major religions—including Christianity, Judaism, Hinduism, and Islam. Certain identifying traits prevail among fundamentalists whatever their faith; namely, authoritarianism, messianic spirit, subordination of secular politics to their religious beliefs, belief in the infallibility of holy scripture, belief in the supernatural, charismatic leadership, and enforced moralism. Taken together, these distinguishing characteristics represent a political vision fundamentalists hope to achieve through aggressive political action.[57]

Muslim Fundamentalists are no strangers to aggressive political action. They occupy the vanguard of revolutionary Islam. Most are revolutionary in temperament, particularly when rapidly secularizing and modernizing political environ-

---

[56]The term *fundamentalism* has been taken from Christianity. *Webster's* defines it as "a movement in 20th-century Protestantism emphasizing the literally interpreted Bible as fundamental to Christian life and teaching." The *Encyclopaedia Britannica* defines "fundamentalism" as a "conservative movement in American Protestantism arising out of the millenarian movement in the 19th century and emphasizing as fundamental to Christianity the literal interpretation and absolute inerrancy of the Scriptures, the imminent and physical second coming of Jesus Christ, the Virgin Birth, Resurrection, and Atonement."

[57]Roy C. Macridis, *Contemporary Political Ideologies,* 5th ed., New York: HarperCollins, 1992, pp. 231–234.

ments undermine their religious convictions and perquisites. The Muslim Fundamentalists advocate rigid adherence to the fundamentals of their faith, as literally interpreted from the Quran and the *Sunnah,* and actively crusade to impose the *Shariah* on society and to purge those influences that they feel detract from or demean the fundamentals of Islam. In this regard, most Fundamentalists crusade against prostitution, pornography, the selling or use of alcohol and drugs, gambling, Western music, singing, dancing, wearing ornaments of gold and silver, palm reading, astrology, fortune-telling, fatalism, and superstition. In Iran today prohibition of these "vices" is rigorously enforced.

REVOLUTIONARIES

One of the most celebrated Muslim Fundamentalists was Muhammad ibn Abd al-Wahhab (1703–1792) (see Box 3.1). A rigid and revolutionary Arabian preacher and *qadhi* (Islamic judge), Muhammad ibn Abd al-Wahhab established a puritanical Islamic state when he forged a "holy alliance" with tribal chieftain Muhammad ibn Saud, who founded the Saudi dynasty. Together, they launched the Wahhabi movement in the second half of the eighteenth century. Eventually the Wahhabi movement, led by the Saudi dynasty, conquered much of the Arabian peninsula, giving the name of the dynasty to the peninsula.

On the Indian subcontinent, Sayyid Ahmad Barelvi (1786–1831), alias Sayyid Ahmad Shaheed, revered and emulated Muhammad ibn Abd al-Wahhab. Around 1817 Sayyid Ahmad launched his own revolutionary Islamic fundamentalist movement, the *Tariqah-i-Muhammadiyah* (The Way of Prophet Muhammad). In the 1820s Sayyid Ahmad became famous among Indian Muslims for launching a *jihad* against the Sikhs of Punjab (the followers of Guru Nanak [1469–1538] who separated from Hinduism), thereby avenging the persecution of Punjabi Muslims by Punjabi Sikhs.[58] Sayyid Ahmad also dreamed of creating an Islamic state based on scrupulous adherence to the *Shariah* in the predominantly Muslim West Punjab and in the northwest frontier of the Indian subcontinent. He eventually established an Islamic state in Peshawar; however, it was extremely short-lived (1829–1830) because it alienated the freedom-loving Pathans, who were in a majority there and did not want to live by the rigors of the *Shariah.* For instance, the Pathans resented payment of *zakat,* the severe Islamic punishments for various crimes, and the requirement for their widows to marry non-Pathan *mujahideen* from distant parts of northern India. Accordingly, the tribal Pathans declined to support the *mujahideen* in the 1831 Battle of Balakot in the Kaghan Valley, when

---

[58]Barbara Daly Metcalf, *Islamic Revival in British India: Deoband, 1860–1900,* Princeton: Princeton University Press, 1982, pp. 52–63; W. W. Hunter, *The Indian Musalmans,* The Comrade Publishers, 1945, Reprint of 1876 ed., pp. 12–13; P. Hardy, *The Muslims of British India,* London: Cambridge University Press, 1972, p. 52; Ghulam Rasul Mehr, *Sayyid Ahmad Shahid,* Lahore: Kitab Manzil, 1956, pp. 251-252; Hafeez Malik, *Moslem Nationalism in India and Pakistan,* Washington, D.C.: Public Affairs Press, 1963, pp. 142–144.

Box 3.1   MUHAMMAD IBN ABD AL-WAHHAB

THE PURITAN INTELLECTUAL AND FOUNDING FATHER OF
WAHHABISM

Muhammad ibn Abd al-Wahhab (1703–1792) was a puritanical Muslim cleric
who joined Muhammad ibn Saud, the tribal chieftain of the small town of
Dariya in central Arabia, in a "holy alliance." Al-Wahhab and ibn-Saud together started the Wahhabi movement in the Arabian peninsula during the
waning decades of the eighteenth century. The Islamic fundamentalist Wahhabi movement, allied with the fortunes of the House of Sa'ud, exists today,
institutionalized and less puritanical, as the official sect of modern Saudi Arabia.

In his youth al-Wahhab received intensive schooling in Arabic, the Quran,
and the *Hadith* from his father and grandfather, both of whom were Hanbalis
and *qadhi*s (Islamic judges) in the small Arabian town of Uyaina in Najd. The
young al-Wahhab then traveled to Mecca to perform the *haj* and to study Islamic theology and law. While traveling throughout the Arabian peninsula and
to Iraq and Iran, al-Wahhab was angered by the adulterated brand of Islam
that he witnessed. Concurrently exposed to the puritanical writings of Taqi
al-Din ibn Taymiyyah (A.D. 1263–1328), al-Wahhab returned to the town of his
fathers and assumed the respected position of a *qadhi*. As an influential Islamic judge, al-Wahhab promoted his iconoclastic brand of Islam. He ordered
the demolition of venerated shrines and tombs, and once even condemned
an adulterous woman to death. Such severe verdicts, complemented by his
puritanical sermons, alienated al-Wahhab from his townsfolk. Consequently,
in 1745 al-Wahhab journeyed to nearby Dariya, where he converted its ruler,
Muhammad ibn Saud, and many of its citizens to Wahhabism.

Wahhabism has a number of predominant features. The Wahhabis' belief
in *tawhid* (Allah's oneness) is so absolute that they denounce the practices
of venerating Prophet Muhammad and the members of his extended family
as heretical polytheism. In addition, the Wahhabis support the right of every
Muslim to interpret the Quran according to his knowledge of Islam, rather
than according to the interpretation of an *alim* (Islamic scholar). They reject all
the ceremonies, rituals, and customary traditions that were absent during the
classical period of Islam, considering them to be accretions that defile the
purity of the faith and that contribute to the decline of Islam and of Muslim
societies. Wahhabism emphasizes a return to the sources of Islam in the literal sense, demanding adherence to the actual words of the Quran and the
Sunnah while denouncing sufism, mysticism, fatalism, and numerous prevalent superstitions. Wahhabis work for a return to the simplicity, austerity, purity, and piety of Islam's classical period. This includes praying five times
daily, fasting during the holy month of Ramadan, and waging *jihad* against

infidels, which to Wahhabis include not only non-Muslims, but backsliding Muslims as well. Wahhabis support the implementation of the *Shariah* in society. In related fashion, the Wahhabis demand strict and scrupulous adherence to its severe punishments for crimes and transgressions; they prohibit the consumption of alcohol, smoking, singing, listening to music, dancing, wearing silk, wearing ornaments of gold or silver, drawing and painting animate objects, palm reading, astrology, fortune-telling, and all forms of divination.

Encouraged by their initial successes, al-Wahhab and ibn Saud launched a *jihad* to convert those beyond their immediate domain to "true" Islam. In subsequent conquests, the Wahhabis gained dominion over much of the Arabian peninsula.

Commenting on this period, historian Edward Mortimer drew some insightful parallels between the early histories of Wahhabism and Islam. Both Wahhabism and Islam propogated by Prophet Muhammad twelve-hundred years earlier began in the same region of the world. Both denounced the evils of injustice, corruption, tribalism, adultery, idolatry, and indifference to the suffering of widows and orphans. Both emphasized strict adherence to monotheism and promoted the brotherhood of all Muslims regardless of their rank and station in life. Moreover, both expanded to the detriment of unbelievers, and both created an energetic and united political unit. Mortimer, however, drew two paramount distinctions between early Islam and early Wahhabism. Unlike the early Muslims, in the classical period of Islam, the Wahhabis fought holy wars not only against admitted unbelievers, but also against "wayward" Muslims. Also, al-Wahhab, in contrast to Prophet Muhammad, was only a spiritual leader; political affairs were the principal responsibility of ibn Saud.

In 1802, only a decade after al-Wahhab's death, Wahhabi warriors led by the grandson of Muhammad ibn-Saud invaded Shi'ah Islam's holy cities of Najaf and Karbala in Iraq and demolished tombs, mausoleums, and shrines built to honor Islam's heroes. Similar scenes were repeated in Mecca and Madina.

Disdaining the Wahhabi revolution and hoping to check its expansion, the Ottoman sultan acting as the guardian of Islam's holy cities persuaded his governor in Egypt, Muhammad Ali (who would subsequently establish his own dynasty in Egypt), to send an army against the Wahhabis. After eight years of war (1811–1818), the Wahhabis were overwhelmed and driven back into central Arabia.

Nevertheless, one hundred years later, Abd al-Aziz ibn Abd al-Rahman al-Saud (popularly referred to as ibn Saud) succeeded in imposing Wahhabism throughout the Arabian peninsula by using military force, by marrying the daughters of tribal chieftains, and by settling devout Wahhabis in conquered territories.

Perhaps the greatest impact of al-Wahhab and his Wahhabi movement is that he not only reignited Islamic fundamentalism in the Arabian peninsula but spread his influence to India, North Africa, and throughout the Muslim world. As all Muslims were obliged in the *haj* to visit Arabia, all were thus exposed to the Wahhabi movement.

Sources: John Obert Voll, *Islam: Continuity and Change in the Modern World*, Boulder, CO: Westview Press, 1982; Christine Moss Helms, *The Cohesion of Saudi Arabia: The Evolution of Political Identity*, Baltimore: The Johns Hopkins University Press, 1980; Robert Lacey, *The Kingdom: Arabia & the House of Saud*, New York: Avon Books, 1981; Edward Mortimer, *Faith and Power: The Politics of Islam*, New York: Random House, 1982; Walter W. Lippman, *Understanding Islam: An Introduction to the Muslim World*, New York: New American Library, 1982; Lawrence Ziring, "Wahhabis" in *The Middle East Political Dictionary*, Oxford: Clio Press Ltd., 1984; James P. Piscatori, "Ideological Politics in Saudi Arabia," in James P. Piscatori, ed., *Islam and the Political Process*, Cambridge: Cambridge University Press, 1983.

the better armed and numerically superior Sikh army defeated and killed Sayyid Ahmad Barelvi.[59]

Mir Nisar Ali (1782–1831), popularly known as Titu Mir, was an ardent follower of Sayyid Ahmad Barelvi. From 1827 to 1831, Titu Mir preached his Islamic fundamentalist message among the Muslim peasants of predominantly Hindu West Bengal. In his sermons and lectures he encouraged the Bengali Muslims to treat each other as equals, to distinguish themselves from non-Muslims by growing beards, as Prophet Muhammad had encouraged, and by tying their sarong-like dhotis[60] in a distinctive manner, and to stand united against the Hindu landlords who generally treated their peasants like slaves.[61]

To embarrass Titu Mir's bearded Muslim followers, some Hindu landlords imposed a tax on beards. Titu Mir and his followers sought justice for this and other grievances in the local court system and even sent a representative to Calcutta to seek help. Finding no legal support, in 1831 Titu Mir led his followers to slaughter a cow, sacred to Hindus, and to defile the village temple with its blood. This unleashed a storm of Hindu fury in which Titu Mir and his followers fought off vicious attacks by Hindu landlords, Hindu peasants, and the village police. Influential landlords summoned British troops to crush the poorly armed religious dissidents. Titu Mir and all those who fought with him were killed. The corpses of slain Muslim revolutionaries were burned in intentional violation of the Islamic practice of burial; their homes were looted, and relatives and sympathizers were jailed.[62]

---

[59]Hardy, *Muslims of British India*, pp. 52–53; Ishtiaq Hussain Qureshi, *The Muslim Community of the Indo-Pakistan Subcontinent (610–1947): A Brief Historical Analysis*, 2nd ed., Karachi, Pakistan: Ma'aref, 1977, pp. 228–229; Mian Abdur Rashid, *Islam In The Indo-Pakistan Subcontinent: An Analytical Study of the Islamic Movements*, Lahore, Pakistan: National Book Foundation, 1977, pp. 38–40; K. A. Nizami, "Socio-Religious Movements in Indian Islam (1763–1898)," *Islamic Culture*, Vol. 44, No. 3, July 1970, pp. 137–139.

[60]A long, broad strip of cloth wrapped around the waist and covering the legs to the ankles.

[61]Metcalf, *Islamic Revival in British India*, p. 62.

[62]Ibid

Titu Mir's violent death in 1831 while fighting his *jihad* endeared him to the Bengali Muslim peasantry, inspiring them in their struggle against oppression by *zamindars* (wealthy landowners), indigo planters, and moneylenders.[63] Coincidentally, Titu Mir's revolt and death occurred in the same year that his mentor, Sayyid Ahmad Barelvi, died fighting in a *jihad* at the other end of India. However, the martyrdom of these two Muslim Fundamentalists did not deter their followers from continuing the Islamic crusade in India. But in the 1860s, the British, recovering from the shock of the Indian Mutiny (1857), killed or imprisoned the remaining followers of Sayyid Ahmad Barelvi and Titu Mir.[64]

Titu Mir's Islamic Fundamentalism in predominantly Hindu West Bengal stirred up the poor, weak, and formerly apathetic and apolitical Muslim peasants. Although the Muslim revolt against the exploitative and oppressive Hindu and British masters failed, Titu Mir's missionary efforts profoundly affected the Muslims of Bengal.

Another prominent revolutionary Fundamentalist was Mohsenuddin Ahmad (1819–1860), popularly known as Dadu Mian, who succeeded his father, Haji Shariatullah, to the leadership of the *Faraidhiah* movement—a movement dedicated to the promotion of Islam's five obligatory duties. Dadu Mian received his early education under the supervision of his father. At an early age he was sent for further studies to Mecca, where he was profoundly influenced by Wahhabism. After five years of intensive Islamic education in the Arabian peninsula, he returned home to support his father's missionary activities. When his father died in 1840, Dadu Mian assumed the leadership of the *Faraidhiah* movement and immediately distinguished himself.[65] While his father had devoted himself to peaceful religious, moral, and cultural reform, Dadu Mian was an aggressive political agitator and an effective organizer and administrator. He created and trained a group of fearless, obedient club-wielding volunteers to protect members of the *Faraidhiah* movement, and, when possible, to punish those *zamindars* and indigo planters known for their oppression of peasants and laborers. [66] In 1841 and 1842 Dadu Mian led successful military campaigns against two Hindu *zamindars* who had mistreated their *Faraidhi* peasants. With these successes, ranks of the *Faraidhiah* movement increased.[67]

As a devout Muslim, Dadu Mian proclaimed the equality of all men before God. He campaigned vigorously against the levying by landlords of illegal taxes

---

[63]Muinuddin Ahmad Khan, *Muslim Struggle for Freedom in Bengal: From Plassey to Pakistan 1757–1947 A.D.*, 2nd ed., Dacca, Bangladesh: Islamic Foundation Bangladesh, 1982, p. 25.

[64]Metcalf, *Islamic Revival in British India*, p. 62.

[65]S. Moinul Haq, *Islamic Thought and Movements in the Subcontinent: 711–1947*, Karachi, Pakistan: Pakistan Historical Society, 1979, p. 452; Mujib Ashraf, *Muslim Attitudes Towards British Rule and Western Culture in India in the First Half of the Nineteenth Century*, Delhi: Idarah-i-Adabiyat-i-Delli, 1982, p. 149.

[66]Haq, *Islamic Thought and Movements*, p. 452; Hardy, *The Muslims of British India*, pp. 56–57.

[67]Haq, *Islamic Thought and Movements*, pp. 453–454; Ashraf, *Muslim Attitudes*, pp. 149–150.

that were spent on polytheistic Hindu rites and shrines.[68] He also encouraged his followers to challenge the Hindu ban on cow slaughter and to eat beef against the wishes of Hindu *zamindars*.[69] As Muslim peasants exhibited a greater degree of self-confidence and assertiveness, Hindu landlords, the village *banias* (Indian Hindu moneylenders), and British indigo planters stepped-up their anti-*Faraidhiah* propaganda campaign. Moreover, the majority of powerful and powerless Muslim peasants feared harassment, unemployment, imprisonment, and misery if they joined the *Faraidhiah* movement.

The British perceived Dadu Mian as an agitator, and when the Indian Mutiny broke out in 1857, they jailed him, hoping to cripple his movement. But Dadu Mian had assiduously trained a number of *Faraidhis* in several Bengali districts to assume the leadership of the movement if something happened to him, and as a result, his two-year confinement did not adversely affect the *Faraidhiah* movement or the Islamic revival that it generated.[70]

Dadu Mian's greatest accomplishment was the creation of a well-knit hierarchical organization called the *Khilafat* system. He established *halqahs* (circles) of his followers in villages, towns, and districts. Each circle had its own leader, called a *khalifah* (caliph). The caliphs at village, township, and district levels directly reported to Dadu Mian, who was the *ustad* (teacher) and supreme leader of the *Faraidhis*. Each caliph or deputy was responsible for protecting and promoting the interests of the *Faraidhis* by teaching, preaching, and proselytizing; collecting membership fees and/or donations; settling most disputes between members instead of letting them go to British courts; and overseeing a spy network.[71] This institutionalization helped sustain the Islamic revival initiated by Dadu Mian in Bengal long after his death, despite the poor leadership qualities of his sons and successors.

Muhammad Ahmad Abdallah al-Mahdi (1843–1885), known as the Mahdi (see Box 3.2), also launched a revolutionary Islamic fundamentalist movement, known as the *Mahdiyyah*, in the Sudan, with the aim of establishing a puritanical Islamic state based on the *Shariah*. The Mahdi launched his military crusade in 1881 and, because of the religious zeal displayed by his followers, was able to win most of the early military encounters with the government's larger and better equipped forces. With each military victory the Mahdi's followers grew in number and in strength. In January 1885, with the fall of Khartoum and the overthrow of the unpopular Sudanese regime, the Mahdi could fashion the kind of Islamic state of which he dreamed. He had only just initiated the implementation of the

---

[68]A. S. Tritton, *Islam: Beliefs and Practices*, 2nd ed., London: Hutchinson & Co. Ltd., 1954, p. 160; S. M. Ikram, *Muslim Civilization in India*, New York: Columbia University Press, 1964, p. 284; Haq, *Islamic Thought and Movements*, p. 453; Ashraf, *Muslim Attitudes*, p. 149; Qureshi, *The Muslim Community*, p. 26.

[69]Haq, *Islamic Thought and Movements*, p. 453.

[70]Qureshi, *The Muslim Community*, p. 238; Haq, *Islamic Thought and Movements*, p. 454; Ashraf, *Muslim Attitudes*, pp. 150–151.

[71] Hardy, *The Muslims of British India*, p. 57; Ashraf, *Muslim Attitudes*, p. 149; Metcalf, *Islamic Revival in British India*, pp. 69–70; Murray Titus, *Islam in India and Pakistan*, Calcutta: YMCA Publishing House, 1959, pp. 187–188.

Box 3.2 MUHAMMAD AHMAD ABDALLAH AL-MAHDI

CRUSADER FOR A PURITANICAL ISLAMIC STATE IN THE SUDAN

Muhammad Ahmad Abdallah al-Mahdi (1843–1885) is famous in Islamic history for having launched the Fundamentalist *Mahdiyyah* movement in the Sudan. The Sudanese al-Mahdi founded his puritanical movement during the unpopular Turco-Egyptian regime. The *Mahdiyyah* movement, created in response to social decay, political oppression, and economic decline, culminated in the establishment of a puritanical Islamic state that would inspire Muslims throughout the world.

The Mahdi, as al-Mahdi was known, had the appropriate credentials for charismatic leadership. A descendant of Prophet Muhammad, he was a knowledgeable, pious, and ascetic sufi who had devoted a decade to community service and was perceived as a principled *mujaddid* (renewer of the faith). He openly accused the alien Turco-Egyptian regime of corruption, injustice, materialism, hedonism, and disbelief. The Mahdi conscientiously chose the end of the thirteenth century of the Islamic calendar (1881) to launch his crusade to Islamize Sudan, insofar as Islamic doctrine teaches that the restorer of the faith will appear at the end of an Islamic century in order to usher in a millennium of equity and justice.

Like many Fundamentalists, the Mahdi was extraordinarily strict and unbending in his judgments of others. He believed independent and permissive women were directly responsible for the decline of Sudanese society and, therefore, denied them their freedom. Furthermore, the Mahdi demanded scrupulous adherence to the *Shariah* and exacted the harshest punishment permissible on violators. Like any puritan, the Mahdi also banned dancing, singing, and music.

Unlike most Islamic Fundamentalists, however, the Mahdi did not advocate the exercise of *ijtihad,* although he himself exercised it. The Mahdi claimed direct inspiration from God and Muhammad in the interpretation of the Quran and the *Sunnah.*

In the initial phases of his mission, the Mahdi was fortunate to win a series of battles against better-trained and better-equipped government forces. These victories were the result of the crusading zeal of the Mahdi's followers and their willingness to be martyrs in a *jihad* and earn Paradise. The government forces, on the other hand, lacked effective leadership and good morale. With every military victory, the Mahdi's ranks swelled. Had he been killed or taken prisoner during this period, or had his poorly equipped and poorly trained followers been routed on the battlefield, the Mahdi might have been dismissed as a dangerous fanatic and terrorist. Islamic history is punctuated with many charismatic *mahdis,* messiahs, and prophets who were imprisoned and then executed by authorities when they proclaimed their mission or station. With their deaths, their movements disintegrated and disappeared. The Mahdi's initial successes gave potential supporters the time and enthusiasm to advance from skepticism to commitment.

By the end of 1883, the Mahdi began to promote pan-Islamism, with himself at the head. But before spreading Islamic Fundamentalism beyond Sudanese borders, he first had to defeat British Governor-General Charles Gordon, who was based in Khartoum. By January 1985, the Mahdi succeeded in routing the Egyptian forces of the Ottoman Empire, killing General Gordon, and becoming the undisputed ruler of Sudan. However, within a few months, the Mahdi himself was dead. His successor, Abdullahi al-Ta'ashi, ruled only a few years, until 1898, when the Anglo-Egyptian armies returned and dismantled the Mahdi's dreams.

Although Muslims in other parts of the world were generally unfamiliar with the writings of the Mahdi and the kind of Islamic state he briefly established, the fact that an Islamic movement had succeeded in expelling Anglo-Egyptian colonialists and setting up a sovereign Islamic state, however temporarily, inspired and emboldened anticolonialist Islamic revivalist movements in several parts of the world.

Sources: Leon Carl Brown, "The Sudanese Mahdiya," in Robert I. Rotberg, ed., *Rebellion in Black Africa,* London: Oxford University Press, 1971; Edward Mortimer, *Faith and Power: The Politics of Islam,* New York: Vintage Books, 1982; John Obert Voll, "The Sudanese Mahdi: Frontier Fundamentalist," *International Journal of Middle East Studies,* Vol. 10, No. 2, May 1979; F. R. Wingate, *Mahdism and the Egyptian Sudan,* 2nd ed., London: Frank Cass and Co., 1968; P. M. Holt, *The Mahdist State in the Sudan 1881–1890: A Study of Its Origins, Development and Overthrow,* 2nd ed., Oxford: Clarendon Press, 1970; Richard H. Dekmejian and Margaret J. Wyzomirski, "Charismatic Leadership in Islam: The Mahdi of the Sudan," *Comparative Studies in Society and History,* Vol. 14, 1972.

Shariah when he died in June 1885, and was succeeded by his faithful lieutenant and protégé, *Khalifah* Abdullahi al-Ta'ashi. Abdullahi ruled Sudan according to the *Shariah* for the next thirteen years, until Anglo-Egyptian armies overwhelmed his forces and dismantled the Islamic state.[72]

Egyptian revolutionary Hassan al-Banna (1906–1949), a twentieth-century Fundamentalist (see Box 3.3), created the *Ikhwan al-Muslimun,* one of the first populist and essentially urban-oriented organizations dedicated to coping with the plight of Islam in the modern world. This organization became the first transnational religiopolitical party in the Muslim world.[73] Al-Banna called for a *jihad*

---

[72]Leon Carl Brown, "The Sudanese Mahdiya," in Robert I. Rotberg, ed., *Rebellion in Black Africa,* London: Oxford University Press, 1971, pp. 9–11; Richard H. Dekmejian and Margaret J. Wyszomirski, "Charismatic Leadership in Islam: The Mahdi of the Sudan," *Comparative Studies in Society and History,* Vol. 14, 1972, pp. 205–207; P. M. Holt, *The Mahdist State in the Sudan 1881–1898: A Study of its Origins, Development and Overthrow,* 2nd ed. rev., Oxford: Clarendon Press, 1970, p. 52.

[73]"The Autobiography of Hassan al-Banna," quoted in Richard Mitchell, *The Society of the Muslim Brothers,* London: Oxford University Press, 1969, p. 235.

Box 3.3 HASSAN AL-BANNA

THE FOUNDER OF EGYPT'S IKHWAN AL-MUSLIMUN

Hassan al-Banna (1906–1949) was born in the town of Mahmudiyya, ninety miles from Cairo, to a lower middle class family. His father was a graduate of Cairo's world-renowned *Al-Azhar* University and a prayer leader in the Mahmudiyya town *masjid.* Hassan al-Banna was schooled in Islamic institutions and at sixteen attended the *Dar al-Ulum,* an Islamic teacher training college located in Cairo. There, al-Banna specialized in Islamic theology, Islamic law, and classical Arabic literature. He studied the schools of Islamic jurisprudence, sufism, and even Modernist Islamic ideology.

At twenty-one, al-Banna graduated from the *Dar al-Ulum* and taught Arabic at a public elementary school in Ismailiya on the Suez Canal. There, he and six colleagues became incensed by the inequity they witnessed between privileged foreigners and exploited Egyptian workers. In response, al-Banna founded the *Ikhwan al-Muslimun,* dedicated to political Islam. As head of this newly formed Fundamentalist party, al-Banna declared that Egyptian poverty, powerlessness, and lack of dignity resulted from Egypt's failure to adhere strictly to Islam and Egypt's adoption of Western values and culture. Islam was the answer, according to al-Banna, for all of Egypt's—indeed, all of mankind's—ills.

Al-Banna and the *Ikhwan* outlined an ambitious plan for the establishment of an Islamic state in Egypt. Al-Banna called for a constitution derived from the Quran, the *Sunnah,* and the traditions of the first four rightly guided caliphs; for the abrogation of secular laws and the imposition of the *Shariah* as the law of the land; for the collection and distribution of *zakat* among the needy; for the prohibition of usury and monopolies; for the enforcement of daily prayers and fasting during Ramadan; for the segregation of the sexes; for the banning of prostitution, gambling, alcohol, and nightclubs; and for the proscription of all customs, dress, languages, books, magazines, plays, movies, and songs not conforming to Islamic principles.

While al-Banna was interested in pan-Islamism, he was not wholly opposed to Egyptian nationalism and pan-Arabism, ideologies popular in Egypt during this period. In fact, al-Banna and the *Ikhwan* endorsed Arab unity, but only as a first step toward Muslim unity. Moreover, al-Banna was no lover of Western liberal democracy. The *Shariah,* he insisted, answered all questions with regard to law and justice.

The secular government of Egypt's King Farouk, unsettled by the political activism and growing popularity of al-Banna and his *Ikhwan,* cracked down on the organization. Although the *Ikhwan* had tried to operate as a legitimate political party working to change Egypt from within the political system, government corruption, cheating at the polls, and persecution of the *Ikhwan* convinced al-Banna that violent revolutionary struggle was necessary to transform Egypt into an Islamic state; Islamic militants took to urban guerrilla warfare. In 1948, the Farouk government banned the *Ikhwan*. The *Ikhwan* retaliated by assassinating Egypt's Prime Minister Muhammad Nuqrashi. In response, government agents assassinated al-Banna on February 12, 1949. This, however, did not put an end to the activities of the *Ikhwan*. Despite frequent government crackdowns against the organization, even after the fall of Farouk and the presidencies of Nasser, Sadat, and Mubarak, the *Ikhwan,* al-Banna's most lasting legacy, remains intact and is still a potent force for Islamic revivalist change in Egypt.

Sources: Bruce Maynard Borthwick, *Comparative Politics of the Middle East: An Introduction,* Englewood Cliffs, NJ: Prentice-Hall, Inc., 1980; M. S. Agwani, "Religion and Politics in Egypt," *International Studies,* Vol. 13, July 1974.

against ignorance, disease, and poverty. His economic program called for equal employment opportunity to all, a guaranteed minimum wage, a fixed ceiling on incomes, prohibition of usury and monopolies, a progressive system of taxation that included *zakat* and *ushr,* and a system of social security.[74]

The Fundamentalist Sayyid Abul A'la Maududi (1903–1979) lobbied for over thirty years in Pakistan (Box 3.4) with the help of his *Jamaat-i-Islami* (Islamic Association), not only for a constitution that was Islamic in letter and spirit, but also for a comprehensive Islamic state based on the *Shariah.* The *Jamaat-i-Islami's* revolutionary election manifesto of December 1969 clearly reflects Maududi's views. The party promised to "deliver a death blow to Capitalism and feudalism" by breaking up the monopoly control that a few powerful families had over industries, banks, insurance companies, and large properties in the rural areas. They promised to redistribute land and help peasants, tenant-farmers, and small landholders; to increase wages and fringe benefits, and improve the working conditions of low-income laborers; to reduce the disparity between the rich and the poor; to abolish "un-Islamic" methods of acquiring wealth (including excessive interest charges by moneylenders, illegal hoarding, and fraudulent trading); and to assist the elderly, orphans, and the children of the poor by enforcing a *zakat* tax of $2\frac{1}{2}$ percent on income. In the socioeconomic realm, laws were to be passed to cleanse society of vices and to require educational institutions to focus more intensively on Islam. Teachers' salaries were to be increased, provided that they support the Islamic ideology and were "morally capable of teaching." In the area of foreign policy, Maududi's platform opposed the Western capitalist and socialist/communist power blocs and instead supported pan-Islamism and the establishment of an international Islamic court.[75]

---

[74]Ishak Musa Husaini, *The Brethren: The Greatest of Modern Islamic Movements,* Beirut, Lebanon: Khayat College Book Cooperative, 1956, p. 165.

[75]"Election Manifesto of the Jamaat-e-Islami," *The Criterion* (Karachi), January/February 1970; reprinted in *Die Politische Role des Islam im vorderen Orient: Einfuhrung und Documentation,* Hamburg: Deutsches Orient-Institute, 1978, pp. 154–160.

Box 3.4   SAYYID ABUL A'LA MAUDUDI

FOUNDER OF SOUTH ASIA'S JAMAAT-I-ISLAMI

Sayyid Abul A'la Maududi (1903–1979) was born into a devout Hanafi Muslim middle-class family in the city of Aurangabad, India. His father was a conservative lawyer who wanted his three sons to have an education in Islamic studies uncontaminated by Western languages and ideas. Maududi attended the *Madrassah-i-Fauqaniah* and later enrolled at Hyderabad's *Dar al-Ulum* college, where he continued his Islamic studies. However, when Maududi was sixteen his father died, and Maududi left school and became a journalist for an Islamic newspaper. While writing for the paper, Maududi improved his Urdu and learned English, Arabic, and Persian. Within a few years, Maududi was working in Delhi as an editor.

Following World War I, Maududi participated in both the *Khilafat* Movement, dedicated to saving the Ottoman Empire and the *Khilafat* from Western influences, and in the *Hijrat* Movement, which urged Muslims to migrate from the *dar al-harb* of India to the *dar al-Islam* of Afghanistan, which was governed by Muslims instead of British colonialists and Hindus.

Apart from his political activities, Maududi wrote numerous scholarly books on the subject of Islam and founded a journal dedicated to breaking the intellectual hold of the West over India's Muslim intelligentsia and introducing them to Islamic ideology. Maududi not only translated Islamic precepts for Indian Muslim readers, but also interpreted those precepts in terms of contemporary applications.

Prior to 1947, Maududi expressed opposition to the Pakistan Movement's efforts to create an independent Muslim homeland in the Indian subcontinent. Indeed, he denounced the leaders of the movement as Westernized secular nationalists who were misleading the Muslims of South Asia with the un-Islamic ideology of nationalism. Maududi feared the new nation of Pakistan would be "pagan." Once Pakistan was founded, however, Maududi settled in the new Muslim nation and began a tireless effort to transform the country into an Islamic state.

Maududi envisioned the ultimate goal of Islam as a world state in which racial and national prejudices would be erased and mankind would enjoy genuine civil rights. However, Maududi, like all Muslim Fundamentalists, opposed Western democracy, in which sovereignty rests with the people. Maududi believed that sovereignty rested with God alone.

Apart from his voluminous writings, Maududi carved for himself a place in history when he founded the *Jamaat-i-Islami* (JI) in 1941. The JI has preserved Maududi's vision of an Islamic state and has worked to implement a comprehensive Islamic system in Pakistan. In 1956, Maududi and his JI played a successful role in the formulation of a Pakistani constitution that was

Islamic in both letter and spirit. Moreover, Maududi and his JI served as a successful Islamic interest group pressuring Pakistani regimes. Maududi and the JI were principally responsible for compelling Bhutto to resort to Islamic rhetoric and symbolism in domestic and foreign policy and thereby contributed to the Islamic revival that swept Pakistan in the 1970s.

In 1972, Maududi retired as the leader of the JI because of poor health. In 1977, however, he witnessed with happiness the military coup that brought the devout Muslim and Maududi admirer General Muhammad Zia-ul-Haq to power. Zia promised to establish an Islamic state. Before his death in 1979, however, Maududi expressed concern about the JI's collaboration with an increasingly unpopular military regime.

Maududi's place in Pakistani, indeed in Islamic, history is assured. His world-renowned publications and political activities provided Islamic Fundamentalism with an intellectual foundation and a clear understanding of the nature, meaning, and administration of an Islamic state. Moreover, Maududi's legacy has been perpetuated by the JI, an organization dedicated to the creation of an Islamic state after Maududi's model.

Sources: Khurshid Ahmad and Zafar Ishaq Ansari, "Mawlana Sayyid Abul A'la Maududi: An Introduction to his Vision of Islam and Islamic Revival," in Khurshid Ahmad and Zafar Ishaq Ansari, eds., *Islamic Perspectives: Studies in Honor of Mawlana Sayyid Abul A'la Maududi,* Leicester, England: The Islamic Foundation, 1979; Abul A'la Maududi, *Islamic Law and Constitution,* 6th ed., trans. and ed., Khurshid Ahmad, Lahore, Pakistan: Islamic Publications Ltd., 1977; Asaf Hussain, *Islamic Movements in Egypt, Pakistan and Iran: An Annotated Bibliography,* London: Mansell Publishing Ltd., 1983; Muhammad Arif Ghayur and Asaf Hussain, "The Religio-Political Parties (JI, JUI, JUP): Role of the Ulema in Pakistan's Politics,"; paper presented at the New England Conference, Association for Asian Studies, held at the University of Connecticut, Storrs, Connecticut, October 20–21, 1979; Khalid Bin Sayeed, "The Jama'at-i-Islami Movement in Pakistan," *Pacific Affairs,* Vol. 30, No. 1, March 1957; Sarvat Saulat, *Maulana Maududi,* Karachi, Pakistan: International Islamic Publishers, 1979; Sayyid Abul A'la Maududi, *Nationalism and India,* Pathankot, India: Maktaba-e-Jam'at-e-Islami, 1947; Aziz Ahmad, "Maududi and Orthodox Fundamentalists in Pakistan," *Middle East Journal,* Vol. 21, 1967; Syed Abul A'la Maududi, *The Process of Islamic Revolution,* Lahore, Pakistan: Islamic Publications Ltd., 1970; Kalim Bahadur, *The Jama'at-i-Islami of Pakistan: Political Thought and Political Action,* New Delhi: Chetna Publications, 1977; Charles J. Adams, "The Ideology of Mawlana Mawdudi," in Donald Eugene Smith, ed., *South Asian Politics and Religion,* Princeton: Princeton University Press, 1966.

The most prominent Fundamentalist revolutionary was Ayatollah Ruhollah Khomeini (1900–1989) of Iran (Box 3.5). The Shi'ah *alim* (Islamic scholar) became the symbolic leader of the Islamic Revolution in Iran (1978–1979) and went on to establish an Islamic state based on the *Shariah* by placing many *mullahs* (Islamic clerics) in influential governmental positions. In his book *Velayat-i-Faqih* (the guardianship of the Islamic jurist), published in 1970, Khomeini advised Muslims to shun wicked governments. He recommended that clerics, educators, journalists, lawyers, and the rest of the intelligentsia be in the vanguard of nonviolent movements enlightening, politicizing, and organizing the masses against their unjust and illegitimate governments. The passive civil disobedience that he

Box 3.5 AYATOLLAH RUHOLLAH KHOMEINI

SYMBOLIC LEADER OF THE FIRST ISLAMIC REVOLUTION IN MODERN TIMES

Sayyid Ruhollah al-Musavi al-Khomeini (1900–1989) was the youngest of six children born into a humble clerical family in the town of Khomein, 180 miles south of Tehran. His grandfather, father, and father-in-law were all *ayatollah*s (Shi'ah theologians and jurists); accordingly, the young Khomeini's education, both formal and informal, was predominantly Islamic.

At the age of twenty-seven, Khomeini taught at Isphahan and then in Qom, lecturing on Islamic philosophy, Islamic law, mysticism, and ethics. In his lectures, Khomeini alluded to contemporary problems and exhorted all Muslims to face these problems with Islamic solutions. The Traditionalist *ulama* at Qom objected to Khomeini's activist and Fundamentalist approach and had Khomeini teach classes less open to interpretation. Nevertheless, Khomeini iterated his belief that the *ulama* should not stand idly by, but become actively involved politically as Prophet Muhammad had been.

Khomeini's first years at Qom coincided with the autocratic rule of Reza Khan Pahlavi. Moved by the repression, corruption, Westernization, and secularization under Reza Kahn and his son and successor Muhammad Reza Pahlavi, Khomeini began to take an active and vocal political stand in opposition to the Shah's tyrannical and "un-Islamic" regime.

Endeavoring to cultivate his blossoming Fundamentalist ideology, Khomeini wrote a book, *Unveiling of the Secrets,* which was published in 1944. In the book Khomeini condemned the Shah's tyranny, his submission to Western powers, and his program of secularization. Moreover, Khomeini urged the *ulama* to take an activist role in social, economic, legal, and even political affairs.

Following the death of the passive and apolitical Grand Ayatollah Burujerdi in 1961, Khomeini adopted an actively confrontational role against the government. In October 1961, he led demonstrations that forced the Shah to repeal legislation permitting women and non-Muslims to contest elections to local assemblies. These demonstrations also helped the *mullahs* throughout Iran develop an easily mobilized, cohesive coalition.

In his continuing effort to effect the immediate modernization of Iran, the Shah instituted the "White Revolution" in January 1963. Khomeini objected to this program, which he believed represented an attack on the clerical establishment and an acceleration of secularization and Westernization in rural areas. Khomeini's public opposition to the program resulted in his arrest and in brief imprisonment.

Following his release, Khomeini returned to Qom more popular than ever. Continuing to publicly denounce the "White Revolution," Khomeini incited antigovernment demonstrations in 1963 and 1964 with his revolutionary rhetoric. Realizing that Khomeini could not be silenced, the Shah exiled the populist and intransigent cleric to Turkey. From Turkey, Khomeini moved to Najaf, Iraq, a major center of Shi'ah learning. For the next fourteen years he lectured at a small *madrassah,* met with Iranian pilgrims, and wrote a tract on Islamic government. In the meantime, Khomeini's absence from the Iranian political scene ended street demonstrations. Without Khomeini, the leaderless opposition could not draw significant support.

While at Najaf, Khomeini expressed his thoughts in a series of lectures that were later compiled and published as *Guardianship of the Islamic Jurists.* In this book Khomeini declared that hereditary monarchical regimes were intrinsically un-Islamic, illegitimate, and sinful; that Islam is a revolutionary political ideology enjoining Muslims violently or nonviolently to overthrow un-Islamic governments; that opposition to the government should involve noncooperation with government institutions (and the establishment of alternative Islamic institutions); that an Islamic state based on the Quran and the *Sunnah* should be established; that knowledgeable and just Islamic jurists should assume the guardianship of that Islamic state; that a single learned and just religious leader should exercise supreme leadership in that Islamic state; that all foreign influences must be extirpated from that Islamic state; and that the Islamic state's foreign policy should be one of nonalignment.

In the late 1970s, Khomeini had the opportunity to establish his "guardianship" over Iran. By 1978, the Shah had alienated most Iranians by his repression, extravagance, and tacitly encouraged nepotism. Furthermore, inflation, unemployment, underemployment, and housing shortages had increased. The Shi'ah clerical establishment was also concerned over both its diminishing pejoratives and the increase of negative Western influences.

The Shah's regime itself sparked the popular revolution in 1978 by impugning the reputation of the beloved Khomeini. A cycle of demonstrations and repressive government reactions quickened revolutionary fervor. Bootlegged audiocassette tapes of Khomeini's vitriolic anti-Shah sermons sold briskly and were played in numerous homes and mosques. His writings were disseminated nationwide. His name was the refrain of the demonstrators, and his picture was pasted on walls all over Iran.

Anxious over Khomeini's rise to preeminence in the opposition, the Shah requested the Iraqi leadership to expel the aging *Ayatollah.* The Iraqis complied, and on October 1978, Khomeini left for France and settled near Paris. In democratic France, Khomeini enjoyed far better communication with his supporters in Iran and constantly urged them to strike and demonstrate against the Pahlavi regime. Unable to stem the tide of revolution or to bring Khomeini to the negotiating table, the Shah left Iran on January 16, 1979, for an "extended vacation," a vacation from which he would never return.

In February 1979, Khomeini returned to Iran, welcomed as a conquering hero, and he vowed to create the Islamic state he had outlined in *Guardianship of the Islamic Jurists.* As "guardian" of the Islamic Republic of Iran,

Khomeini enjoyed supreme leadership of Iran for the next decade. During his "guardianship," however, Khomeini made several decisions that seriously undermined his stature and reputation on the world stage. First, Khomeini tarnished his reputation and that of the Islamic revolution by giving members of his inner circle the authority to order the executions of many officials from the Shah's regime, political dissidents, and social misfits. This led Western scholars and Khomeini's opposition to compare the Islamic regime's authoritarianism to that of the Shah. Second, Khomeini permitted and endorsed the seizure of the U.S. Embassy and its staff, an act that earned Khomeini hostile press throughout the world and branded Iran an international outlaw with whom few would deal. The diplomatic and economic isolation that Iran consequently experienced undermined the economy, adversely affected the Islamic revolution, and injured the Iranian people. Third, Khomeini angered and alienated Arab governments by denouncing all secular, monarchical, and pro-Western Arab leaders and by declaring his intention to export the Islamic Revolution. Fourth, Khomeini chose not to end the Iran-Iraq War in 1982, when the Iranians had expelled the Iraqi invaders from most of Iran. By seeking to overthrow Iraq's President Saddam Hussein, Khomeini lengthened the Iran-Iraq War by another six years, contributing to the unnecessary suffering and death of many thousands of Iranians. When Khomeini finally agreed to a cease-fire after nearly a decade of bloody stalemate with Iraq, he had little to show for his efforts.

Shortly before his death in 1989, Khomeini once again made headlines in the West by issuing a death sentence on the author Salman Rushdie for writing a "blasphemous" book, *The Satanic Verses*. Khomeini's statement underscored his radical fundamentalism and generated much global controversy (See pp. 245-249.)

In retrospect, since the death of the charismatic populist Egyptian President Gamal Abdel Nasser (1918–1970), no man has so moved the Muslim masses as the ascetic and austere Ayatollah Khomeini. Grasping the challenge of destiny, Khomeini led the first modern Islamic revolution, toppling the firmly entrenched fifty-seven-year-old Pahlavi dynasty, implementing the Islamic model of development, and making Iran genuinely nonaligned. His revolutionary brand of Islamic fundamentalism emboldened Islamic revivalists all over the world and thereby fortified the global Islamic revival.

Sources: Nicholas Gage, "Stern Symbol of Opposition to the Shah: Ruhollah Khomeini," *New York Times,* December 11, 1978; Ayatollah Ruhollah Khomeini, *Islam and Revolution: Writings and Declarations of Imam Khomeini,* translated and annotated by Hamid Algar, Berkeley: Mizan Press, 1981; Angus Deming, Scott Sullivan, and Jane Whitmore, "The Khomeini Enigma," *Newsweek,* December 31, 1979; Nicholas Gage, "The Unknown Ayatollah Khomeini: The Portrait of the Islamic Mystic at the Center of the Revolution," *Time,* July 16, 1979; Edward Mortimer, *Faith and Power: The Politics of Islam,* New York: Vintage Books, 1982; Azar Tabari, "The Role of the Clergy in Modern Iranian Politics," in Nikki R. Keddie, ed., *Religion and Politics in Iran: Shi'ism from Quietism to Revolution,* New Haven: Yale University Press, 1983;

Hamid Algar, *The Roots of the Islamic Revolution,* Markham, Ontario: The Open Press, 1983; "The Khomeini Enigma," *Newsweek,* December 31, 1979; A. T. Chaudhri, "Khomeini—the man and mission," *Dawn,* March 18, 1979; Willem M. Floor, "The Revolutionary Character of the Ulama: Wishful Thinking or Reality?" in Nikki R. Keddie, ed., *Religion and Politics in Iran: Shi'ism from Quietism to Revolution,* New Haven: Yale University Press, 1983; Shaul Bakhash, *The Reign of the Ayatollahs: Iran and the Islamic Revolution,* 2nd ed., New York: Basic Books, Inc., 1990; J. S. Ismael and T. Y. Ismael, "Social Change in Islamic Society: The Political Thought of Ayatollah Khomeini," *Social Problems,* Vol. 27, No. 5, June 1980; Ayatollah Ruhollah Khomeini, *Islamic Government,* translated by Joint Publications Research Service, New York: Manor Books, Inc., 1979; "The Enigmatic Mullah," *Time,* January 29, 1979; "Gift of God and Scourge of the Shah," *The Observer,* January 21, 1979; "Khomeini's Kingdom Qum—Rule 1: If it is Western, we don't want it," *Time,* March 12, 1979; "Portrait of an Ascetic Despot: An earthly sense of justice, an all-embracing code of behavior," *Time,* January 7, 1980; "Ayatollah Portrait: Iron-Willed Fanatic," *U.S. News & World Report,* December 3, 1979.

recommended involved noncooperation with unjust governments' institutions and laws. He suggested that this noncooperation could be achieved by establishing alternative judicial, economic, political, and cultural institutions. For instance, Khomeini wanted the masses to take their lawsuits to their own *qadhi*s (Islamic judges) rather than to the state's civil law courts, to pay their taxes to their religious establishments rather than to the government, and to respect and obey religious leaders rather than civil and political leaders.[76] Khomeini recognized the sacrifices involved in a revolutionary struggle; he repeatedly stated that fighting and dying for the Islamic cause was preferable to a life of humiliation in a state that violated Islamic principles and corrupted the *umma.* Khomeini's rhetoric carried extra weight both because of his eminent position within the Shi'ah hierarchy and because of the Islamic belief that those who die fighting a *jihad* against unjust, corrupt, and tyrannical governments are martyrs who have earned their place in Heaven.[77]

Khomeini's vision of an Islamic revolution came to pass in Iran only a decade after his book was published. Within ten years of his ascent to de facto power in 1979, Khomeini brought about an Islamic political, social, judicial, and economic revolution in Iran and completely transformed Iran's foreign policy. Khomeini not only broke Iran's dependent relationship with the West, but likewise avoided dependence on the Communist bloc for security or aid. As a result, Iran became genuinely nonaligned and truly independent, with a revolutionary Islamic foreign policy that denounces both the Western and Communist blocs. The price of such independence, however, has been high. Khomeini alienated the outside world. Iran could find no friends, no allies in the community of nations. Khomeini's Iran stood isolated in the world.

---

[76]Shaul Bakhash, *The Reign of the Ayatollahs: Iran and the Islamic Revolution,* rev. ed., New York: Basic Books, 1990, pp. 38–39.

[77]J. S. Ismael and T. Y. Ismael, "Social Change in Islamic Society: The Political Thought of Ayatollah Khomeini," *Social Problems,* Vol. 27, No. 5, June 1980, pp. 612–613.

In Khomeini's Fundamentalist Islamic state women were not only enjoined to dress "modestly," but to wear a *hijab* (veil) and not wear heavy makeup or jewelry. The *pasdaran* stopped and warned any woman caught violating this dress code. Repeat offenders were sent to prison, where they were "reeducated." Today, under the moderate Fundamentalist President Rafsanjani, the Iranian government has eased up on the rigorous enforcement of the dress code for women; however, the majority of the population still frowns on women who do not dress modestly or cover their hair.

President Muhammad Zia-ul-Haq of Pakistan (1924–1988) represented a more moderate and less confrontational brand of Islamic fundamentalism (Box 3.6). Thus, Pakistan never suffered the isolation endured by Iran. Nevertheless, Zia's Fundamentalist ardor was unqualified and the sincerity of his Fundamentalist "Islamization" campaign unquestionable. The Zia government established numerous agencies to study, plan, and implement the Islamic transformation of Pakistani society. The government arranged many conferences on Islamic topics. It ordered the mass media to cover international, regional, national, and local conferences and seminars pertaining to Islam. The government hosted national conventions of the *ulama* and *mashaikh* (spiritual leaders) and undertook a thorough revision of textbooks and course curricula to "prepare a new generation wedded to the ideology of Pakistan and Islam."[78] *Islamiyat* (Islamic studies) was made compulsory for all Muslims. A *Shariat* faculty to teach Islamic law was set up at *Quaid-i-Azam* University in 1979; a year later, the university became a separate institution, and was renamed the Islamic University.[79] Radio and television productions were ordered to conform to strict Islamic standards of morality and ethics as well as to reinforce the national identity of the citizenry. A law was introduced severely punishing those who defile the names of the Prophet Muhammad and the *Khulafah-i-Rashidin* (first four rightly guided caliphs), Abu Bakr, Umar, Uthman, and Ali.[80] In essence, Zia-ul-Haq proposed to enforce Islamic morality and piety in Pakistan.

Fundamentalist revolutions and revolutionaries are of varying types. While the ultimate goals of revolutionary Fundamentalists may be identical, the methods by which they achieve those goals may differ. For example, Iran's Ayatollah Khomeini, in his Fundamentalist zeal, rode the Islamic revolutionary wave to the zenith of absolute and unquestioned authority, imposed an authoritarian and theocratic Islamic state on his country, and crusaded against the West, and especially against America. In contrast, Pakistan's Zia-ul-Haq implemented his Fundamentalist policies and programs more moderately at home and was able to adopt a

---

[78]Ibid., pp. 150, 155.

[79]Anita M. Weiss, "The Historical Debate on Islam and the State in South Asia," in Anita M. Weiss, ed., *Islamic Reassertion in Pakistan: The Application of Islamic Laws in a Modern State*, Syracuse, New York: Syracuse University Press, 1986, p. 15; Lucy Carrol, "Nizam-i-Islam: Process and Conflicts in Pakistan's Programme of Islamisation, with Special Reference to the Position of Women," *Journal of Commonwealth and Comparative Politics*, No. 20, 1982, p. 74.

[80]William L. Richter, "Pakistan," in Mohammed Ayoob, ed., *The Politics of Islamic Reassertion*, New York: St. Martin's Press, 1981, p. 150.

Box 3.6 MUHAMMAD ZIA-UL-HAQ

PAKISTAN'S "SOLDIER OF ISLAM"

Muhammad Zia-ul-Haq (1924–1988), which literally means "Muhammad, Light of Justice," was born on August 12, 1924, in Jullunder, a city that lies today in India. His father, Akbar Ali, was a senior clerk dealing with military audits in the Indian Civil Service during the British raj. Akbar Ali was also a *moulvi* (Islamic cleric) and a strict disciplinarian who inculcated his seven children in the precepts of Islam. Every morning at dawn, Zia and his siblings were awakened to say the first of their five daily prayers. Moreover, almost since birth, Akbar Ali's children were instructed in the Quran.

Young Zia attended Saint Stephen College, New Delhi's renowned elitist Anglican missionary school. After matriculating in 1943, Zia entered the Royal Indian Military Academy at Dehra-Dun. Upon graduation in 1945, Zia was commissioned a lieutenant. He was sent to Burma, Malaya, and Indonesia.

In 1947, Zia-ul-Haq, by then a captain, migrated with his family to the newly created Muslim state of Pakistan. In Pakistan, Zia was assigned to instruct army recruits. In 1953, Zia entered the Command and Staff College at Quetta, where he took advanced courses and practical training. The new president of Pakistan, General Muhammad Ayub Khan, was impressed by Zia and in 1958 sent him to the United States for advanced military training. Zia went again to the United States to complete his training in 1963. In the meantime he taught at the Command and Staff College at Quetta.

In 1964, Zia was promoted to the rank of lieutenant colonel and appointed an instructor at the Command and Staff College. After the 1965 Indo-Pakistan War, Zia commanded a cavalry regiment for two years. He became a full colonel in 1968 and was posted with an armored division as staff colonel. In 1969, he was promoted to Brigadier and given the command of an armored brigade. But after serving only a couple of months in the latter capacity, he was sent by the new Pakistani president General Agha Muhammad Yahya Khan to serve as a military advisor to the Hashemite kingdom of Jordan. In Jordan, Zia advised the Jordanian troops who quashed the Palestine Liberation Organization (PLO) guerrilla uprising of September 1970. In July 1971, King Hussein gave Zia medals of distinction for his services.

In 1972, Pakistan's President Bhutto purged the army of senior officers whom he suspected of harboring "Bonapartic" ambitions, and promoted the apolitical Zia to the position of major general. In 1973, Zia served as the presiding judge at the Attock conspiracy case, the nationally covered court-martial proceedings of two dozen junior military officers who had conspired to overthrow the civilian regime. Zia pleased Bhutto by dispensing harsh punishments to the conspirators for their treasonous behavior against the popularly elected constitutional government.

Zia also loyally carried out Bhutto's order to crush the Baluchi separatist movement in the province of Baluchistan (1973–1977). Zia's self-effacing loyalty to Bhutto and to the constitution earned him a promotion in 1975 to lieutenant general and armored Corps Commander.

In 1976, Zia was promoted over the heads of eight senior generals and made a four-star general and army chief of staff. Bhutto felt that Zia would be the safest candidate for the top post in the potently powerful armed forces; he was a lackluster career military man who had done nothing distinguishing in the 1948, 1965, and 1971 Indo-Pakistan wars to enjoy a war-hero status that could pose a threat to Bhutto. Zia's mediocre intelligence, lack of political acumen, and lack of interest in wielding political power appealed to Bhutto. In addition, Zia came from a modest family and had no connections in Pakistan's influential elite. He was shy, humble, modest, and shunned publicity. Moreover, throughout his military career, Zia had shown the utmost obedience and loyalty to his superiors. Jordan's King Hussein had highly recommended him as a professional and loyal military officer. In addition, Zia had obediently executed the central government's policy to crush the Baluchi secessionist movement and had exhibited admirable loyalty to Bhutto when prosecuting the Attock conspiracy case in 1973.

For a year after his promotion, Zia continued to display a servile attitude toward the charismatic prime minister. Zia made ingratiating public statements and gave flattering speeches praising Bhutto. When they met, Zia would kiss Bhutto on the cheek, shake Bhutto's hand reverentially with both hands, salute Bhutto excessively, and look down with humility while talking to him. Zia-ul-Haq also attempted "to make the army safe" for the prime minister by removing ambitious senior officers who were known to dislike Bhutto. In fact, many army officers felt Zia was nothing more than a sycophant and referred to the new army chief of staff as "Bhutto's butler."

Zia, however, did attempt to exert his influence in his new position. He lectured recruits to observe the prayers and fasting obligatory in Islam, and he invited a prominent leader of the *Jamaat-i-Islami* to deliver lectures on the importance of Islam. But when Bhutto heard of Zia's activities, he ordered him to desist, and Zia, despite his strong faith and personal misgivings, submitted to the prime minister's demand.

In 1977, Bhutto faced defeat at the polls; however, he rigged the election and won a landslide victory. The Pakistan National Alliance (PNA)—a coalition of nine political parties opposed to Bhutto—rejected the outcome and demanded Bhutto's resignation. Bhutto refused, which resulted in and a series of intense and disruptive riots. After four months of virtual civil war, the top brass of the army prevailed upon General Zia to remove Bhutto and end the anarchy.

Zia assumed power in July 1977, and placed Pakistan under martial law. Although Zia promised to hold fair national elections within ninety days, he remained in power until his mysterious death in 1988 in an air-force plane crash.

Shortly after he assumed power, Zia executed Bhutto and initiated an Islamization campaign. A number of factors prompted his adoption of Islamic policies. First, the Muslim Pragmatist Bhutto had already utilized Islamic symbolism and rhetoric that, in turn, had engendered a political atmosphere of Islamic revivalism. Second, the failure of capitalism during the Ayub era (1958–1969) and socialism during the Bhutto era (1972–1977) had resulted in Pakistani demands for an Islamic alternative to address the country's chronic problems. Third, Zia faced heavy pressure from the Fundamentalists and Traditionalists to transform Pakistan into a genuinely Islamic state. Fourth, Zia realized that his military regime lacked legitimacy and, therefore, decided to use Islam to consolidate his power. Fifth, Zia felt that Pakistan could further good relations with the oil-rich Persian Gulf states by adopting the "Islamic card" in foreign policy. Finally, Zia himself had enjoyed a strict religious upbringing and thereby had strong Islamic predilections.

Zia's Islamic domestic and foreign policies were advanced by the Islamic Revolution in Iran (1978–1979) and the revivalist trend throughout the Muslim world. As a conduit for U.S. assistance to the Afghan *mujahideen* fighting the Soviets, Zia's regime fostered an Islamic resurgence in Afghanistan. Furthermore, Zia's domestic policies coupled with his enlightened foreign policy helped the country prosper and play a significant role in Southwest Asia.

Sources: Mary Anne Weaver, "Pakistan's General Zia—From Soldier to Politician," *Christian Science Monitor,* May 16, 1983; Ian Mather, "The Soldier Who Hanged Bhutto," *The Observer,* London, April 8, 1979; "General Zia-ul-Haq—Life Sketch," *Pakistan Times,* Lahore, July 9, 1977; David Dunbar, "Bhutto—Two Years On," *The World Today,* Vol. 30, No. 1, January 1974; *Washington Post,* July 6, 1977; James Haskins, *Leaders of the Middle East,* Hillside, NJ: Enslow Publishers, 1985; Anjum Matin, "Zia the Man: Piety and No Charisma," *Arabia: The Islamic World Review,* No. 10, June 1982.

pan-Islamic and pro-Western (and especially a pro-American) foreign policy. Consequently, while Khomeini isolated Iran from the rest of the world, Zia-ul-Haq, despite his Fundamentalist baggage, got a significant amount of economic and military aid from the West without surrendering his nation's sovereignty or his Fundamentalist domestic policy.

PURITANICAL MUSLIMS

Tawhid—Allah's oneness—is the central premise of Islam, a doctrine all Muslims accept. However, Muslims differ in their interpretations of *tawhid*. The Fundamentalists are often obsessed with its importance. Many Sunni Fundamentalists, for instance, have such a literal, rigid, and narrow interpretation of *tawhid* that they denounce any agent mediating between man and God as *shirk* (ascribing partners to God as sharers of His divinity) because in their eyes such an intermediary undermines and compromises the principle of *tawhid*. Therefore, these puritanical Muslims condemn such traditions as the veneration of Prophet Muhammad, Imams, saints, martyrs, and *pirs* (spiritual guides); the offering of prayers for assistance at their tombs or at shrines built in their honor; the sacrifice of animals, sanctification of water, lighting of candles, donation of money, or distribution of food in honor of those venerated with expectation of special favors; the wearing of *tawidhes* (amulets) with verses from the Quran to ward off evil or bring good luck; and excessive displays of mourning in the form of weeping, *ma'atam* (breast-beating), and *taziyah* (mourning) processions during the Islamic calendar month of Muharram to commemorate the martyrdom of Imam Hussein.[81]

One of the most prominent Fundamentalists to react to the undermining of *tawhid* in the Indian subcontinent was an East Punjabi Hanafi scholar named Shaikh Ahmad Sirhindi (1564–1624). Reverentially known as *Mujaddid Alf-i-Thani* (the renewer of the faith in the second millennium of Islamic history) and *Imam-i-Rabbani* (pious leader of a thousand years) by millions of Sunnis in the Indian subcontinent, Sirhindi served for fourteen years in the Moghul court of Emperor Jalal-ud-din Muhammad Akbar (r. A.D. 1556–1605). There Sirhindi wrote *The Epistle on the Refutation of the Shi'ah*, which was a strong indictment of the religious rituals adopted by Shi'ahs, who enjoyed influential positions in Akbar's empire.[82]

Profoundly disturbed by the un-Islamic practices that he witnessed in the emperor's court and among the Moghul elite, Sirhindi left the city of Agra in A.D. 1600 and joined the puritanical Naqshbandi *tariqah* (sufi brotherhood) headquartered in Delhi, where he spent the rest of his life writing about the plight of Islam in India. In most of his writings he courageously denounced Emperor Akbar, criticizing him for creating *Din-i-Illahi* (a liberal, eclectic, and syncretic religious ideology); for refusing to implement the *Shariah;* for prohibiting the slaughter of cows, which are sacred to Hindus, but permitting the sale of pork, which is *haram* (forbidden) in Islam; for encouraging believers in *Din-i-Illahi* to wear the emperor's likeness on their turbans and to prostrate themselves before him; for marrying non-Muslim (especially Hindu) women while prohibiting the practice of polygamy for Indian Muslims; for having many influential non-Muslim courtiers, civil servants, and officers in the armed forces; for permitting singing, dancing, gambling, charging interest, alcohol consumption, and prostitution; for posing as Allah's vice-regent on earth; for promoting Sanskritic Hindi instead of Arabic or Persian in schools; and for encouraging secular education and the study of the new syncretic faith instead of Islamic theology, jurisprudence, history, and civilization. Sirhindi's writings also condemned the Moghul elite for labeling Islamic culture the product of illiterate and uncivilized Arabs living 1300 years ago; for

---

[81]Metcalf, *Islamic Revival in British India*, pp. 57–58.

[82]Yohanan Friedmann, *Shaykh Ahmad Sirhindi: An Outline of His Thought and a Study of His Image in the Eyes of Posterity*, Montreal: McGill-Queen's University Press, 1971, pp. xiii, 4, 51–53.

doubting that the Quran was the "Word of God" and that it could have been revealed to Prophet Muhammad by Allah; for questioning life after death, the Day
of Judgment, the existence of the angels, and miracles (e.g., the ascension of the
Prophet Muhammad); for criticizing Prophet Muhammad's polygamy and holy
wars; and for slighting the importance of the five obligatory *faraidh* (duties). Finally, Sirhindi criticized a number of "worldly minded" and "unrighteous" *ulama*
who had, through their active support or passive silence, allowed Akbar and the
Moghul elite to promote the aforementioned heresies.[83]

The Islamic Fundamentalist Wahhabi movement is also fanatically dedicated
to the concept of *tawhid.* During the early years of the movement in the late eighteenth century in the Arabian peninsula, the Wahhabis strenuously objected to
the name assigned them by their detractors. The term *Wahhabi* implied that they
venerated Muhammad ibn Abd al-Wahhab, when actually they vehemently condemned the veneration of anyone but Allah. The Wahhabis preferred to be known
as *al-Muwahhidun,* or "those affirming the notion of *tawhid.*" However, since the
two English interpretations of the word *al-Muwahhidun*—Monotheists or Unitarians—were considered by the group as either too broad (encompassing all Muslims and many non-Muslims) or too loaded with Christian overtones, the term
Wahhabi stuck.[84]

In their dedication to *tawhid,* the Wahhabis demolished holy shrines and
mausoleums, pressuring all Muslims to pray directly only to Almighty Allah. In
1802, for instance, the Wahhabis invaded the Shi'ah sect's holiest cities of Najaf
and Karbala in Iraq, where they destroyed tombs, mausoleums, and shrines. They
exhibited the same kind of iconoclasm in Islam's holiest cities of Mecca and Madina in the following three years.[85]

Strongly influenced by the Wahhabi movement and equally dedicated to
tawhid, Haji Shariatullah (1781–1840)—the son of a petty *talukdar* (landowner)
in East Bengal and a product of a traditional Islamic education—spent nineteen
years in Mecca studying Islam. While remaining a Hanafi, he returned to his village of Shamail in East Bengal (now in the Faridpur district of Bangladesh) in
1818 with the puritanical ideals of the Wahhabi doctrine in mind.[86] He was so agitated to see his village folk steeped in the polytheistic influences of Hinduism that

[83]See S. Abul A'la Maududi, *A Short History of The Revivalist Movements in Islam,* 3rd ed., translated
by Al-Ashari, Lahore, Pakistan: Islamic Publications, 1976, pp. 72–77; I. A. Arshad, "Mujaddid's Revivalist Movement," in Sardar Ali Ahmad Khan, ed., *The Naqshbandis,* Sharaqpur Sahrif, Pakistan:
Darul Muballeghin Hazrat, 1982, p. 93; Muhammad Yasin, "Mujaddid Alif-i-Sani," in Khan, *The
Naqshbandis,* pp. 69–70, 75, 77–78.

[84]Robert Lacey, *The Kingdom: Arabia & The House of Saud,* New York: Avon Books, 1981, p. 56; John
Obert Voll, *Islam: Continuity and Change in the Modern World,* Boulder, CO: Westview Press, 1982,
p. 59.

[85]Edward Mortimer, *Faith and Power: The Politics of Islam,* New York: Vintage Books, 1982, p. 63;
Julius Germanus, *Modern Movements in the World of Islam,* Lahore, Pakistan: al-Biruni, reprinted
1978, p. 14.

[86]Metcalf, *Islamic Revival in British India,* p. 68; Qureshi, *The Muslim Community,* p. 237; Ikram,
Muslim Civilization in India, pp. 283–284; Hardy, *The Muslims of British India,* pp. 55–56; Haq, *Islamic Thought and Movements,* pp. 448–449.

in 1821, after performing the *haj* for a second time, he launched the *Faraidhiah* movement. Shariatullah's mission was to "save" his village folk from the evil ways they had adopted and encourage them to perform Islam's five *faraidh*.[87] In addition, he recommended that Muslims repent their sins and vow to lead lives according to the Quran and the *Sunnah*. He prohibited many of the Muslim practices that he felt had been permeated with non-Islamic influences. He forbade veneration of prophets and saints; condemned emotional displays of mourning in the form of *taziyah* (mourning) processions; disapproved of certain birth and burial ceremonies; prohibited the practice of *bai'ya*, where an aspiring *murid* (disciple) swore allegiance to his *pir* (spiritual mentor); and substituted the terms *ustad* (teacher) and *shagird* (pupil) for the terms *pir* and *murid*, to eliminate the implication of abject submission held by the latter terms.[88]

Haji Shariatullah abhorred both the oppressive and exploitative Hindu landlords and the British colonialist rulers, whose commercial monopoly seriously jeopardized Muslim interests in East Bengal. However, being a realist and a pacifist, he did not promote a martial *jihad* against them. Instead, he actively taught and preached to the downtrodden but responsive Muslim villagers. Some of his rulings were controversial and unpopular; for example, his prohibition of the customary *Jum'ah* (Friday) and *Eid* (festival) congressional prayers, because he felt India had become a *dar al-harb* (abode of conflict).[89] Nonetheless, Haji Shariatullah was revered by his Bengali coreligionists because they perceived him as a devout and learned Muslim who was genuinely concerned about their welfare and sincere about eradicating the Hindu beliefs and practices that had permeated the Islamic culture of the region. His ceaseless missionary efforts aroused the consciousness of his poor, formerly apathetic, and disenfranchised brethren.

The puritanical orientation of the Sudanese Muhammad Ahmad Abdallah al-Mahdi is evident in his proclamations and his letters, which repeatedly emphasized *tawhid*. He also strongly objected to the freedom enjoyed by Sudanese women and was appalled when approached by a prostitute. Perceiving women as the major culprits in the increasing permissiveness of the Sudanese society, he dramatically restricted their civil rights and liberties and imposed stringent penalties against men and women who violated a strict code of behavior. For example, he ordained that women must stay in their homes and be veiled in front of all but their immediate family members. Any woman caught by the Mahdi's secret informers with her head uncovered in public was to be beaten, and any man caught speaking to a female stranger was to receive one hundred lashes and be forced to

---

[87]Metcalf, *Islamic Revival in British India*, pp. 68–69; Ikram, *Muslim Civilization in India*, p. 284; Qureishi, *The Muslim Community*, pp. 237–238; also see "Faraidiya" in H. A. R. Gibb amd J. H. Kramers, *Shorter Encyclopedia of Islam*, Leiden, Netherlands: E. J. Brill, 1974, pp. 99–100; Muinuddin Ahmad Khan, *History of the Faraidi Movement in Bengal (1818–1906)*, Karachi, Pakistan, 1965.

[88] Haq, *Islamic Thought and Movements*, pp. 449–450; J. Takle, "Islam in Bengal," *The Muslim World*, Vol. 4, No. 1, January 1914, p. 15; also see Jagdish Narayan Sarkar, *Islam in Bengal: Thirteenth to Nineteenth Century*, Calcutta: Ratna Prakashan, 1972.

[89]Nizami, "Socio-Religious Movements, p. 139; Tritton, *Islam: Beliefs and Practices*, p. 160. The Friday and *Eid* prayers were revived after 1947; also see Metcalf, *Islamic Revival in British India*, p. 69.

fast for two months. Any woman caught wearing jewelry was to have her hair plucked out.[90]

Like Muhammad ibn Abd al-Wahhab, the Mahdi prohibited various forms of music, dancing, and singing.[91] He also banned the sale and consumption of alcohol and tobacco and imposed severe penalties against their use.[92]

EMULATORS OF PROPHET MUHAMMAD AND HIS PIOUS COMPANIONS

While all Muslims talk about emulating the good deeds of Prophet Muhammad and the *aslaf* (the pious companions of Prophet Muhammad), the Fundamentalists make a determined and dedicated effort to do so. As a rationale, the Fundamentalists often quote a popular *hadith* in which Prophet Muhammad declares: "The best generation is mine [i.e., of my companions]. . . . "[93] Most Fundamentalists revere those Muslims who were closest to Prophet Muhammad as paragons of Islamic austerity, purity, and piety in a context that was more religious than historical. For many Fundamentalists, the classical period of Islamic history, in which the ideal Islamic state was established and governed by Prophet Muhammad and thereafter by the first four rightly guided caliphs, became the "classic" and normative period worthy of emulation and restoration.[94]

Sayyid Ahmad Barelvi tried to emulate the life of Prophet Muhammad in the 1820s by scrupulously adhering to the *Shariah* himself and expecting his *mujahideen* to do the same. Like the Prophet Muhammad, Sayyid Ahmad Barelvi wrote letters to Muslim rulers in Central Asia. In these letters, Sayyid Ahmad used the title of *Amir al-Mu'minin* (Leader of the Faithful) and called on the Central Asian leaders to recognize his *khilafat*. In his letters he noted that while India had fallen under the rule of the Christian colonialists, he was attempting to reestablish the *dar al-Islam* (abode of Islam) in which the *Shariah* was supreme.[95]

Likewise, the Mahdi of Sudan read the life of Prophet Muhammad and tried his best to emulate him. He even imitated Prophet Muhammad's *hijra* (migration) by moving from Aba Island, where the government's forces could easily capture him, to the more inaccessible Mount Qadir in the Nuba mountains, which he renamed "Masa," after the mountain on which Prophet Muhammad had meditated. Like the Prophet, the Mahdi called on his followers to undertake the *hijra* to escape from the sinful environment controlled by the *kafirs* (infidels). Those who undertook the *hijra* were also called *muhajirun* (migrants). As the government's

---

[90]Mortimer, *Faith and Power*, p. 79; John Obert Voll, "The Sudanese Mahdi: Frontier Fundamentalist," *International Journal of Middle East Studies*, Vol. 10, No. 2, May 1979, p. 156.

[91]F. R. Wingate, *Mahdism and the Egyptian Sudan*, 2nd ed., London: Frank Cass and Co., 1968, p. 59.

[92]Voll, "The Sudanese Mahdi," p. 156; Holt, *The Mahdist State in the Sudan*, 1970, p. 131.

[93]Quoted in Fazlur Rahman, *Islam*, 2nd ed., Chicago: The University of Chicago Press, 1979, p. 236.

[94]W. C. Smith, *Islam in Modern History*, p. 43.

[95] Hardy, *The Muslims of British India*, pp. 53–54.

military campaign against the Mahdi's forces began, he made *jihad* one of the most frequent themes of his speeches and writings.[96]

Abd al-Aziz ibn Abd al-Rahman al-Saud (1880–1953) alias ibn Saud, the great-grandson of the founding father of the Saudi dynasty, also closely emulated Prophet Muhammad. He required that everyone in his movement—the *Ikhwan* (brotherhood)—treat each other as equals and call each other *akh* (brother). Each settlement was known as a *hijra*, a migration from a corrupted to a purifying existence, just as had been Prophet Muhammad's flight from Mecca to Madina.[97]

The Muslim Fundamentalists' overwhelming desire to follow the *aslaf* is also evident in their writings, speeches, statements, and interviews, and in the literature published by any Fundamentalist organization. For instance, the December 1969 election manifesto of Pakistan's *Jamaat-i-Islami,* inspired by the writings and teachings of its founder and first *amir,* Sayyid Abul A'la Maududi, promised to make "Pakistan a state where the laws of Quran and the *Sunnah* would be in full force and which would take the Rashidin Caliphate [the caliphate of the first four pious caliphs after Prophet Muhammad] as a model."[98] Moreover, when Iran's Shi'ah Fundamentalist revolutionary leader Ayatollah Khomeini was asked what he meant by an Islamic state, he replied tersely, "The only reference point, in our view, is the time of the Prophet and Imam Ali."[99]

CRUSADERS FOR THE *SHARIAH'S* IMPLEMENTATION

The Fundamentalists entirely reject the "church/state" dichotomy that non-Muslims and nonpracticing Muslims encourage, and they aggressively crusade against such separation. Fundamentalists believe that a government without the ethical foundation of Islam is unjust and easily corrupted.

Hassan al-Banna, the founder and first *amir* of the *Ikhwan al-Muslimun* in Egypt, expressed the Fundamentalist view of Islam when he said,

> We believe the rules and teachings of Islam to be comprehensive, to include the people's affairs in the world and the hereafter. . . . Islam is an ideology and a faith, a home and a nationality, a religion and a state, a spirit and work, a book and a sword.[100]

---

[96]Leon Carl Brown, "The Role of Islam in Modern North Africa," in Leon Carl Brown, ed., *State and Society in Independent North Africa,* Washington, D.C.: The Middle East Institute, 1966, pp. 9–10; Dekmejian and Wyszomirski, "Charismatic Leadership in Islam," pp. 204–205.

[97]James P. Piscatori, "Ideological Politics in Saudi Arabia," in James P. Piscatori, ed., *Islam and the Political Process,* Cambridge: Cambridge University Press, 1983, p. 58; Christine Moss Helms, "The Ikhwan: Badu Answer the Wahhabi 'Call to Unity'," in Christine Moss Helms, *The Cohesion of Saudi Arabia: Evolution of Political Identity,* Baltimore: Johns Hopkins University Press, 1981, pp. 127–150.

[98]"Election Manifesto of the Jamaat-e-Islami," p. 154.

[99]First published in *Le Monde* (Paris), May 6, 1978; later quoted in "The Start of a Gigantic Explosion: An Interview with Iranian Shi'ite Leader Ayatollah Khomenie," *Middle East Research and Information Project* (henceforth *Merip Reports*), Vol. 8, No. 6, July–August 1978, p. 20.

[100]Abd al-Moneir Said Aly and Manfred W. Wenner, "Modern Islamic Reform Movements: The Muslim Brotherhood in Contemporary Egypt," *Middle East Journal,* Vol. 36, No. 3, Summer 1982, p. 340.

Al-Banna also stated that if he came to power in Egypt, he would use the numerous government mechanisms to replace most of the prevailing secular laws with the *Shariah*. He used his party to crusade actively for the imposition of the *Shariah* in Egypt. Similarly, in Pakistan the Muslim Fundamentalist Maududi formed the *Jamaat-i-Islami* to lobby actively for the establishment of a "Kingdom of God" run in accordance with the Quran, the *Sunnah*, and the *Shariah*.[101]

Like other Muslim Fundamentalists, Ayatollah Khomeini publicly iterated the comprehensive and "organic" nature of Islam;

> Do not heed those who imagine that Islam is like present-day Christianity, that the mosque is no different than the church or that Islam is merely a relationship between the individual and his God. . . . Imperialist institutions instilled evil in the hearts of men, saying that religion does not mix with politics . . . most unfortunately some of us have given credence to those lies.[102]

On another occasion Khomeini more succinctly conveyed the holistic nature of Islam from the Fundamentalist's point of view in the phrase "This world is political!"[103] This phrase could just as easily have been said by the Mahdi of Sudan, al-Banna of Egypt, or Maududi of Pakistan.

The Fundamentalists believe that one of the most important functions of the Islamic state is to maintain and enforce the *Shariah*. In fact, the Fundamentalists consider it their Islamic duty to struggle actively and ceaselessly to implement the *Shariah* in its entirety.[104] In this regard, Khomeini stated unequivocally that "Government in Islam means obedience to the law [*Shariah*] and its arbitration."[105] On another occasion Khomeini said:

> We do not say that the government must be composed of the clergy but that the government must be directed and organized according to the divine law, and this is only possible with the supervision of the clergy.[106]

Pakistan's chief martial law administrator, General Muhammad Zia-ul-Haq, who had strong Islamic predilections of his own, felt that Pakistan had been created in 1947 to be an Islamic state. In his first speech after becoming president in 1977, Zia-ul-Haq stated that Pakistan was "created in the name of Islam" and would "survive only if it sticks to Islam."[107] Most of Zia-ul-Haq's press conferences and public speeches were in Urdu and started with a recitation from the Quran. A few days after coming to power, Zia-ul-Haq introduced a number of *Shariah*-

---

[101] Abul A'la Maududi, *Islamic Law and Constitution*, 6th ed., trans. and ed. by Khurshid Ahmad, Lahore, Pakistan: Islamic Publications Ltd., 1977, pp. 119, 132–133, 211–232.

[102] Khomeini, *Islamic Government*, p. 7; also quoted in Martin Kramer, "The Ideals of an Islamic Order," *The Washington Quarterly*, Vol. 3, No.1, Winter 1980, pp. 3–4.

[103] Quoted by Daniel Pipes, "This World Is Political: The Islamic Revival of the Seventies," *Orbis*, Vol. 24, No. 1, Spring 1980, p. 9.

[104] H. A. R. Gibb, cited in Donna Robinson Divine, "Islamic Culture and Political Practice in British Mandated Palestine, 1918–1948," *The Review of Politics*, Vol. 45, No. 1, January 1983, p. 78.

[105] Cited in Kramer, "The Ideals of an Islamic Order," p. 7.

[106] Raymond H. Anderson, "Ayatollah Ruhollah Khomeini, 89, Relentless Founder of the Islamic Republic," *New York Times*, June 5, 1989, p. B-11.

[107] *Pakistan Times*, July 7, 1977, p. 1

based Islamic punishments, including public flogging for murder, rape, theft, drinking of alcohol, fornication, prostitution, adultery, bearing false witness, and destroying government property in demonstrations and riots. These measures were taken to intimidate the opposition and to instill the fear of God in the society's criminal and disruptive elements. Several months later, Zia-ul-Haq introduced other Islamic changes: women were told to dress modestly, cover their heads, and wear little or no makeup on television, in government offices, and in other public places;[108] entertainment in all educational institutions was strictly monitored to comply with Islamic standards of morality and ethics; walls of offices and educational institutions, calendars, and billboards were adorned with quotations from the Quran and the *Hadith;*[109] and Friday was officially designated as the weekly holiday instead of Sunday.[110] A couple of years later even dancing and music were discouraged by the administration because they violated the Islamic sensibilities of the Muslim Fundamentalists.

On December 2, 1978, Zia-ul-Haq committed himself to the Islamic transformation of Pakistan. He announced his intention to establish a legal system based on *Nizam-i-Islam* (the Islamic system). He founded a permanent law commission to simplify the legal system and to bring all the existing laws into conformity with Islamic guidelines. His ultimate goal was to make the *Shariah* the basis of all law in Pakistan. In February 1979, Zia-ul-Haq announced the establishment of special *Shariat* benches (courts that would decide cases on the basis of the *Shariah*) to supplement the existing judicial system. These courts would review a limited range of laws and adjudicate cases brought under the *Shariah*. Each *Shariat* bench consisted of five judges who were advised by competent *ulama* in matters of classical Islamic law. The main function of these Islamic legal bodies was to exercise a form of Islamic judicial review, where any citizen could request the judiciary to declare a law either wholly or partially un-Islamic. The addition of a *Shariat* bench to the supreme court allowed cases to be brought challenging the validity of any law. This was a big step toward granting the supremacy of the *Shariah* over the secular Anglo-Saxon law inherited from the British.[111]

---

[108]Urdu is the national language of Pakistan. It is a hybrid of Arabic, Persian, and Sanskrit. It is written from right to left like Arabic and Persian. Spoken Urdu is similar to Hindi (the national language of India that is written from left to right in the Devnagri script). Urdu was initiated in the army barracks during the Muslim-dominated Mughul Rule that lasted from 1525 to 1857). Ironically most of Pakistan's presidents before Zia were fluent in English, but not in Urdu.

[109]Kemal A. Faruki, "Pakistan: Islamic Government and Society," in John Esposito, ed., *Islam in Asia: Religion, Politics, and Society,* New York: Oxford University Press, 1987, p. 59.

[110]Bhutto first started the practice of making Friday a holiday instead of Sunday to allow Muslims to follow the command of Prophet Muhammad to go to the mosques on Friday at noon to pray with the congregation.

[111]Craig Baxter, "Restructuring the Pakistan Political System," in Shahid Javed Burki and Craig Baxter, *Pakistan Under the Military: Eleven Years of Zia-ul-Haq,* Boulder, CO: Westview Press, 1991, p. 36; Mumtaz Ahmad, "Islamic Revival in Pakistan," in Cyriac Pullapilly, ed., *Islam in the Contemporary World,* Notre Dame, IN: Cross Roads Books, 1980, p. 266; Richter, "Pakistan," p. 146; also see Jan Mohammed, "Introducing Islamic Laws in Pakistan—I," *Dawn,* July 15, 1983, p. 15; Hakim Mohammed Said, "Enforcement of Islamic Laws in Pakistan," *Hamdard Islamicus,* Vol. 2, No. 2, Summer 1979, pp. 71–80.

On February 10, 1979, President Zia-ul-Haq utilized the happy occasion of *Eid-i-Milad-un-Nabi* (Prophet Muhammad's birthday) to introduce a more comprehensive Islamic penal code. In that announcement, the government prescribed the *hadd* (extreme) punishment of eighty lashes for adult Muslims caught drinking alcohol. If evidence was insufficient, then the *ta'azir* (lesser) punishment of three years imprisonment and/or thirty lashes would be imposed. The *ta'azir* punishment also applied to non-Muslim Pakistani citizens found drinking alcohol (except as part of a religious ritual) and to non-Muslim foreigners found drinking alcohol in a public place. Furthermore, anyone who imported, transported, manufactured, processed, sold, or allowed consumption of an intoxicant on his or her premises was liable for a maximum of five years imprisonment, thirty lashes, and a fine. For simply possesssing an intoxicant, the punishment in Zia-ul-Haq's Pakistan was two years imprisonment or thirty lashes, and a fine.[112] Under Zia-ul-Haq's strict penal code, many people were publicly flogged for a variety of crimes. There were also a couple of cases in which habitual thieves had their hands amputated under medical supervision, and one case in which a woman was stoned to death for adultery.

Though far from the comprehensive Islamic system that Zia-ul-Haq had wanted to implement, these laws nevertheless constituted one additional step in his series of sociocultural, judicial, economic, and political reforms designed to incorporate Islam more fully into the nation's daily life.[113]

ZEALOUS PROMOTERS OF THE FIVE *FARAIDH*

The Fundamentalists believe in practicing the five *faraidh* expected of all Muslims, namely, the *shahadah* (confession of the faith), *salat* (ritual prayers), *sawm* (fasting during Ramadan), *zakat* (payment of alms to the poor), and *haj* (pilgrimage to Mecca and Madina). Yet unlike other Muslims, the Fundamentalists crusade with missionary zeal for the obligatory practice of the five *faraidh*. The Fundamentalist movement launched by Haji Shariatullah in 1821 in East Bengal was called *Faraidhiah* precisely because it attempted to "save" the "wayward" Bengali Muslims by encouraging them to perform the five *faraidh*. In the same way all Islamic Fundamentalist movements could well be called *Faraidhiah* movements because of their constant exhortation to perform the five *faraidh*.

Pakistan's Zia-ul-Haq, like all Fundamentalists, encouraged and obliged his citizens to fulfill the duties of Islam. Ramadan was seriously observed; fasting was glorified and heavily promoted in the mass media; and restaurants, shops, motels, and hotels were forbidden to serve food to Muslims from dawn to dusk. Government offices were ordered to set aside appropriate times for daily prayers during

---

[112]Weiss, "The Historical Debate on Islam," p. 15; Richter, "Pakistan," p. 144; Baxter, "Restructuring the Pakistan Political System," pp. 36–37; also see Mohammad Suleman Siddiqi, "The Concept of Hudud and Its Significance," in Anwar Moazzam, ed., *Islam and Contemporary Muslim World*, New Delhi: Light and Life Publishers, 1981, pp. 160–180; Said, "Enforcement of Islamic Laws," pp. 61–90.

[113]Richter, "Pakistan," p. 144.

the work day, and tremendous governmental and peer-group pressure was applied toward prayer observation (especially the midday prayer) in offices and factories; civil and military officers were advised to lead or, at least, attend these prayers. The government publicized the annual *haj*, with high government officials photographed and televised sending off and welcoming home pilgrims at the docks and airports.[114] Zia-ul-Haq himself was shown personally seeing off planeloads and shiploads of pilgrims going to perform the *haj* or embracing *haji*s on their return.[115]

During the holy month of Ramadan in 1979, Zia-ul-Haq's regime began collecting *zakat* and *ushr* with much fanfare. A central *zakat* fund was established to help the poor and needy (such as those who were widowed, orphaned, handicapped, or aged). In the Ramadan period of 1980, Zia-ul-Haq proudly inaugurated the distribution of *zakat* on national radio and television.

On August 14, 1984, Pakistan's Independence Day, Zia-ul-Haq announced the immediate appointment of a *nazim-i-salat* (organizer of prayers) for every village and urban precinct—an action that frightened and annoyed the Shi'ahs and liberal Muslims. These prayer organizers were not only to organize the midday prayers on Fridays, but also to encourage Muslims to say all five prayers daily.[116] Zia-ul-Haq said:

> Only those persons are being appointed for this service of religion who have sound moral character and their piety is so exemplary that their words will have deep effect on the hearts of people. The procedure for this exercise for the time being is based on persuasion and motivation and not on compulsion. But we are determined to succeed in establishing the system of prayer at all cost.[117]

OPPONENTS OF *TAQLID* AND PROPONENTS OF *IJTIHAD*

Virtually all Fundamentalists reject the dogma of *taqlid*, and embrace its antithesis, the dynamic notion of *ijtihad*. *Taqlid* entails blind and unquestioning adherence to the legal rulings (of one or more schools of Islamic jurisprudence) of the learned, competent, and renowned theologian-jurists of the medieval Islamic era. *Ijtihad*, conversely, means to strive or exert oneself intellectually to the utmost in order to draw independent conclusions and judgments on legal or other issues with the assistance of the Quran and the *Sunnah*. Taha J. al-Alwani—a member of the *Fiqh* Academy of the Organization of the Islamic Conference (OIC), chairman of the *Fiqh* Council of North America, and president of the International Institute of Islamic Thought in the United States—clearly summarized the Islamic Fundamentalist point of view about *taqlid* and *ijtihad*:

---

[114]Faruki, "Pakistan: Islamic Government and Society," p. 59.

[115]Richter, "Pakistan," pp. 150–151.

[116]Faruki, "Pakistan: Islamic Government and Society," p. 61.

[117]Ibid., p. 61; *Dawn*, August 16, 1984, p. 1.

What has happened to the penetrating and enlightened mind inspired by Islam, the one which freed our ancestors from their idols and the obstacles blocking their progress? How did such a mind return to its former prison and fetters, robbed of any chance to renew and reform the *ummah* through *ijtihad?* In a word, the answer is *taqlid,* an illness which entered the Muslim mind and then fed on it until it returned to its prison.[118]

However, Fundamentalists often limit the right of *ijtihad* to those knowledgeable and competent in Islamic theology and law.

Most Sunni Fundamentalists applaud the Syrian-born Hanbali theologian-jurist Taqi al-Din ibn Taymiyyah (A.D. 1263–1328) for his courageous denunciations of *taqlid* and fearless practice of *ijtihad* at a time when such ideas were considered heretical because they were seen as sowing the seeds of division and discord in the Muslim *umma.*[119] In fact, because of his systematic and forcefully argued stand in his scholarly writings, ibn Taimiyah is regarded by most Sunni Fundamentalists as the father of Islamic fundamentalism.[120]

The archetypical Sunni Fundamentalist, Muhammad ibn Abd al-Wahhab closely emulated ibn Taymiyyah in his bitter condemnation of *taqlid* and extensive use of *ijtihad* in eighteenth-century Arabia. His beliefs spread from Arabia when Muslim pilgrims who had come to Mecca for the *haj* returned home espousing the popular ideas of the Wahhabis. For example, the East Bengali Haji Shariatullah was profoundly influenced by Wahhabism while a pilgrim and student in the Arabian peninsula in the nineteenth-century; he returned home to found the *Faraidhiah* movement. Another scholar-pilgrim heavily influenced by the Wahhabi movement was Sayyid Muhammad ibn Ali al-Sanusi (1787–1859), an Algerian of the Bani Sanus tribe (see Box 3.7). The Grand Sanusi, as he came to be known in his later years, returned from Arabia to North Africa, where he advocated *ijtihad* for men who were pious and knowledgeable about the Quran and the *Sunnah,* and categorically rejected *taqlid.*[121]

Most Fundamentalists and Modernists today wholeheartedly agree with Shah Waliullah (1702–1762), a Muslim Fundamentalist and one of the greatest Islamic revivalists of the Indian subcontinent, that the major cause for the decline of Muslim rule in the world was the discontinuance of the spirit of *ijtihad* and the dominance of the dogma of *taqlid* among the Traditionalists.[122] As Waliullah said, "The *ulama* of today are like camels with strings in their noses. They are tightened by *taqlid* and do not think over problems afresh."[123]

---

[118]Taha J. al-Alwani, "Taqlid and the Stagnation of the Muslim Mind," *The American Journal of Islamic Social Sciences,* Vol. 8, No. 3, 1991, pp. 513–514.

[119]Quoted in Maududi, *A Short History of the Revivalist Movement,* pp. 57–70.

[120]The Shi'ahs are very critical of ibn Taymiyyah because of his condemnation of accretions in Shi'ah beliefs and practices.

[121]Nicola A. Ziadeh, *Sanusiyah: A Study of a Revivalist Movement in Islam,* Leiden, Netherlands: E. J. Brill, 1958, pp. 36–40.

[122]A. D. Muztar, *Shah Waliullah: A Saint-Scholar of Muslim India,* Islamabad, Pakistan: National Commission on Historical and Cultural Research, 1979, p. 75; Freeland Abbott, "The Decline of the Moghul Empire and Shah Waliullah," *The Muslim World,* Vol. 55, No. 2, April 1965, p. 347.

[123]Quoted in Nizami, "Socio-Religious Movements in Indian Islam," p. 132.

Box 3.7   SAYYID MUHAMMAD IBN-ALI AL-SANUSI

FOUNDER OF THE SANUSIYYAH

Algerian Fundamentalist Sayyid Muhammad ibn-Ali al-Sanusi (1787–1859) was founder and first leader of the Sanusiyyah or Sanusi *tariqah* (Sufi brotherhood), which initiated an Islamic revival in North Africa. After acquiring a thorough Islamic education from learned *ulama*, the young Sayyid Muhammad left Algeria in his late teens to further his education in Fez. There he became interested in sufism and was introduced to and influenced by Shaikh Ahmad al-Tijani, the founder of the Tijaniyyah brotherhood. After spending two years with al-Tijani, Sayyid Muhammad attended the renowned Islamic university of *Al-Azhar* in Cairo and performed the *haj*. In his journey across North Africa to Cairo, he stopped at many *zawiya*s (sufi lodges). When he finally reached Cairo, Sayyid Muhammad discussed the sad state of Islam and the *umma* with the *shaikh*s (religious teachers) at *Al-Azhar*. Disappointed with their responses and with their total failure to address contemporary problems facing Muslims and the Muslim world, Sayyid Muhammad left *Al-Azhar* for the Arabian peninsula.

In Hijaz, Sayyid Muhammad studied Islam with a number of learned *shaikh*s, particularly with Sayyid Ahmad ibn-Idris al-Fasi, a Sufi who had recently become fascinated with Wahhabism. Sayyid Muhammad also met Muslim pilgrims from many countries, with whom he discussed the conditions of the *umma* and the state of Islam within their respective regions and countries. Following al-Fasi's death in 1837, Sayyid Muhammad founded the Sanusi brotherhood and established the first *zawiya* in the Hijaz. For three more years, he preached his fundamentalist vision of Islam and established additional *zawiya*s between Mecca and Madina. By 1840, Sayyid Muhammad's Sanusi brotherhood had grown popular enough to prompt the jealous enmity of Mecca's Traditionalist *shaikh*s, who pressured Sayyid Muhammad to leave the Arabian peninsula.

Sayyid Muhammad returned to North Africa, still preaching his Islamic Fundamentalist message, and began to establish a network of *zawiya*s. These Sunusi centers provided a comprehensive religious education, trained the boarders in the use of firearms, taught agricultural techniques, and instructed in the conduct of trade and commerce. More generally, the Sanusi lodges built a semblance of unity among the scattered and often conflicting local tribes of Cyrenaica and Tripolitania, bridging present-day Algeria and Libya. Sayyid Muhammad also sent committed Sanusi missionaries to Central and West Africa to propagate his fundamentalist doctrine.

Sayyid Muhammad also wrote nine books in his lifetime, the majority of which were theological. The views he espoused, usually staunchly fundamentalist in nature, revealed ibn-Taymiyyah's influence. Sayyid Muhammad denounced materialism and hedonism, exorting his followers to eschew such sins as listening to music, dancing, and smoking. Moreover, he advocated *ijtihad* and rejected *taqlid*. But unlike many fellow Fundamentalists, ibn-Taymiyyah included, Sayyid Muhammad did not denounce Sufism.

In his old age, the founder of the Sanusi movement came to be referred to as "the Grand Sanusi." His imposing personality, eloquent public speeches, effective organizing talents, depth of knowledge, and prolific scholarship won innumerable converts to his brand of Islamic Fundamentalism. Furthermore, his influence continued even after his death. His son, Sayyid al-Mahdi Sanusi, and, later, other family members continued to lead the Sanusi movement. Until 1969 when Colonel Gaddafi took over in a military coup d'état, the Sanusi movement flourished, leading the fight in North Africa against the Italians and bringing spiritual and material improvement to the lives of the people. As active missionaries, the Sanusiyyah helped tribes by digging wells, planting trees, cultivating food, promoting commerce, and establishing *zawiya*s along caravan routes. Abhorring sloth, mendicancy, and hedonism, the Sanusiyyah encouraged hard work, self-sufficiency, and asceticism.

Sources: C. C. Adams, "The Sanusis," *The Moslem World*, Vol. 36, No. 1, January 1946; Nicola A. Ziadeh, *Sanusiyah: A Study of a Revivalist Movement in Islam,* Leiden, Netherlands: E. J. Brill, 1958; John Obert Voll, *Islam: Continuity and Change in the Modern World,* Boulder, CO: Westview Press, 1982; Majid Khadduri, *Modern Libya: A Study in Political Development,* Baltimore: Johns Hopkins University Press, 1963; Edward Mortimer, *Faith and Power: The Politics of Islam,* New York: Vintage Books, 1982.

ARDENT FOES OF SECULAR NATIONALISM

While all Traditionalists and many Modernists claim to oppose secular nationalism, they display less vehemence in their opposition than do the Fundamentalists. The most extreme example of this Fundamentalist opposition is that of Maududi and his *Jamaat-i-Islami*. Maududi's stubborn and aggressive opposition to the Pakistan Movement was rooted in his belief in "Islamic universalism" as mentioned in the Quran and the *Sunnah,* and in his bitter opposition to the alien, secular, and territorial nature of nationalism, which, he was convinced, would divide and weaken the *umma* by allowing national interests to prevail over global Islamic interests. Maududi believed Islam and nationalism were totally incompatible. Writing in 1947, he stated, "'Muslim Nationalist' and 'Muslim Communist' are as contradictory terms as 'Communist Fascist,' and 'Socialist Capitalist,' and 'Chaste Prostitute!'"[124] Maududi's view was clear:

---

[124]See Sayyid Abul A'la Maududi, *Nationalism and India,* 2nd ed., Malihabad, India: n.p., pp. 9–10.

One ultimate goal of Islam is a world state in which the claims of racial and national prejudices would be dismantled and all mankind incorporated in a cultural and political system, with equal rights and equal opportunities for all.[125]

Maududi went on to elaborate how nationalism divides humanity and breeds localism, and how it inculcates the love of a particular territory, rather than the love of humanity in general. He felt nationalism was "the greatest curse in the world, . . . the greatest menace to human civilization; it makes man wolf to all other nations except his own."[126] To Maududi, Jinnah, Pakistan's founder, was a Westernized, secular nationalist who did not fulfill Islam's obligatory *faraidh* and who espoused the ideology of nationalism (which was *shirk*) instead of the religion of Islam. Maududi felt Jinnah was an inappropriate leader of the new Islamic state, and that Jinnah's Pakistan would be pagan and its leaders pharaohs, nimrods, and infidel tyrants.[127] Maududi was so bitterly opposed to the creation of a Pakistan led by the secular Muslim elite that he wrote, "When I look at the [Muslim] League's resolution [demanding Pakistan] my soul laments."[128] He went on to write:

Sad it is, that from the *Quaid-i-Azam* of the League to its lowliest followers there is not one who has an Islamic mentality and way of thinking or who looks at matters with an Islamic viewpoint.[129]

Later Maududi stated, "The result of it [Pakistan] will be a heretic government of Muslims."[130] And again:

Why should we foolishly spend our time in waiting for, or in the struggle for the creation of, this so-called Muslim government, which we know will be not only disadvantageous for our objective but a substantial hindrance to it?[131]

The election of 1946 was crucial to the creation of Pakistan, yet Maududi told his supporters to ignore it:

As a principled organization, we cannot sacrifice our principles, in which we have faith, for temporary advantage; whatever the importance of the coming elections and whatever effect they may have on our nation and our country.[132]

Muslim Fundamentalists have also spoken out virulently against secular pan-Arabism. As one Fundamentalist noted: "It [pan-Arabism] evolved into a surro-

---

[125]Ibid., pp. 10–11.

[126]Ibid., p. 18.

[127]Cited in Aziz Ahmad, "Maududi and Orthodox Fundamentalists in Pakistan," *Middle East Journal*, Vol. 21, 1967, p. 374.

[128]Abul A'la Maududi, *Musalman aur Maujuda Seyasi Kashmakash* (Muslims and the Present Political Conflict), in Urdu, Vol. 3, Pathankot, India: n.p., 1942, p. 29.

[129]Ibid., p. 29.

[130]Ibid., p. 132.

[131]Ibid., p. 138.

[132]Abul A'la Maududi, *Tarjuman al-Quran*, September–October 1945, p. 1.

gate for religious bonds under the impact of a set of ideas which had developed in Europe in a specifically Christian situation."[133] In Syria the *Ikhwan al-Muslimun* has accused President Hafiz al-Assad's regime of "apostasy" and "infidelity" for the promotion of Ba'athism, which has elements of Arab nationalism, pan-Arabism, Arab socialism, and secularism.[134]

FUNDAMENTALISTS IN THE MODERN PERIOD

Muslim Fundamentalists in the late twentieth century, unlike their predecessors, are willing to embrace what they perceive as beneficial modern values that conform to the basic tenets of Islam. For example, although they wish to follow the revered body of *Shariah* strictly, they are willing to interpret the letter of the law more broadly than in the past. Many, though certainly not all, Fundamentalists in the modern period have come to accept the Western notions of democracy, which entail periodic elections on the basis of secret balloting and one vote for every adult person, a multiparty political system, and a national assembly or parliament to pass laws for the entire nation. However, in order to ascertain that no legislation is passed or decisions made that are not in keeping with the Quran or *Sunnah,* the Fundamentalists still insist that competent Fundamentalist *ulama* advise the democratically elected representatives of the people and ratifying all legislation.

Maududi's Fundamentalist critique of the Traditionalist *ulama* articulated the Fundamentalist approach to the modern world:

> The conservatist approach, represented by the orthodox *ulama,* is unrealistic. It fails to take note of the fact that life is everchanging. . . . New situations are arising, new relationships are being formed and new problems are emerging. . . . The approach fails to grapple with the problems of the day [and] is bound to fail. It cannot but drive religion out of the flux of life and confine it to the sphere of private life. And when estrangement is effected between religion and life, then even the private life cannot remain religion's preserve. . . . Furthermore, the conservative elements had not the full understanding of the constitutional, political, economic and culture problems of the day. The result was that they could not talk the language of today and failed to impress the intelligentsia and the masses alike. . . .[135]

Maududi likewise critiqued the Muslim Modernists, charging that they were attempting to modernize Islam by emulating Western ideas, values, institutions, and processes that were alien to Islam. Although he agreed with the necessity of *ijtihad* and the use of reason to interpret God's commands, he insisted that *ijtihad* be undertaken according to, and not against, Islam's clear commands. While concurring that Islam contains nothing contrary to reason and the acquisition of the latest scientific knowledge, he disagreed with the Modernists' belief that the

---

[133]Quoted in Emmanuel Sivan, *Radical Islam: Medieval Theology and Modern Politics,* New Haven: Yale University Press, 1985, p. 49.

[134]Ibid., p. 49.

[135]Maududi, *Islamic Law and Constitution,* p. 18.

Quran and the *Sunnah* should be interpreted by the standard of reason. Instead of starting with the proposition that "true reason is Islam," the Muslim Modernists believed that "Islam was truly rational and reasonable." Like the Mutazilite *ulama* of the eighth, ninth, and tenth centuries, the Muslim Modernists had implicitly designated reason, rather than the Quran and *Sunnah,* as the final authority.[136]

SUMMARY

Muslim Fundamentalists are revolutionary and puritanical in their orientation. They are extremely critical of *taqlid* and scathing in their denunciation of Western ideas. They are obsessed with the notions of *tawhid,* the finality of Prophet Muhammad, and the five *faraidh,* and try to closely emulate Prophet Muhammad and the pious *aslaf.* Above all, Fundamentalists have the sincere and passionate desire to establish an Islamic state based on the comprehensive and rigorous application of the *Shariah.* (See the table following p. 151.)

---

[136]Mortimer, *Faith and Power,* pp. 203–204.

Chapter
4

The Muslim Traditionalists

Muslim Traditionalists constitute the second category of Islamic revivalists. The products of traditional Islamic education, Traditionalists are often drawn from the ranks of the devout and learned *ulama* and are, hence, typically Islamic scholars.

Westerners have tended to equate Fundamentalists and Traditionalists because both are religiously conservative and disapproving of the West. But there the ideological affinity ends. To depict any general ideological consensus among devout Muslims, or to portray Islam as a monolithic force is to completely misunderstand and misrepresent Islam and Islamic revivalism. Even between strictly conservative Fundamentalist and Traditionalist clerics, agreement is rarely reached on such intrinsic issues as *tawhid* and tradition, *taqlid* and *ijtihad,* and predestination and political activism. In fact, their conflicting stands on the preceding issues are what differentiate Traditionalists from Fundamentalists.

PRESERVERS OF MEDIEVAL ISLAMIC TRADITIONS WHO TOLERATE LOCAL CUSTOMS

Among the most divisive issues separating Fundamentalists from Traditionalists are their conflicting definitions of an appropriate normative period. The Fundamentalists look to Islam's classical period for inspiration and emulation and denigrate the traditions and practices of subsequent historical periods as impure and fundamentally un-Islamic "accretions" and "innovations." Often Fundamentalist opposition to such "accretions" is based on their strict interpretation of *tawhid.* Many Muslim traditions, particularly those in which saints, holy men, or *Imams* are venerated as intermediaries between man and God, violate *tawhid* by Fundamentalist standards and thus must be extirpated. Indeed, Muslim Fundamentalists are committed to eradicating all Muslim practices except those prevalent during the classical period of Islam. The Fundamentalist Wahhabis, for example, strongly denounce the practice of venerating Prophet Muhammad and members of his extended family as *shirk* (polytheism) and, therefore, heretical. This is why Wahhabi holy warriors invaded Shi'ah Islam's holiest cities in 1801 and demolished a number of tombs, mausoleums, and shrines built in the memory of Islam's heroes and saints.

In stark contrast, Muslim Traditionalists conserve and preserve not only the Islamic beliefs, customs, and traditions practiced in the classical period of Islam but also those of subsequent Islamic periods. They are tolerant of sufism, mysticism, and numerous local and regional customs and traditions commonly referred to in the aggregate as "folk Islam" or "popular Islam." Traditionalists believe that Islam is not merely a set of abstract and utopian principles, but a comprehensive and living belief system that interacts with the historical and cultural traditions of devout Muslims. To suppress these traditions, therefore, would be to weaken the popular form of devotion of the Muslim majority. The Traditionalist Farangi Mahallis (Sunni *ulama* who lived in a Farangi mahal [Farangi mansion] in late seventeenth century Lucknow, India), for instance, revered a pantheon of saints, including their own ancestors, and visited their tombs often to offer prayers and express their gratitude for prayers that had been answered.[137] In fact, the *madrassahs* (Islamic schools) in which Farangi Mahallis taught were invariably closed on the birthdays or death anniversaries of prominent saints so that both teachers and pupils could partake in celebrations to commemorate the occasions.[138]

The Barelvis (see Box 4.1) also taught that Prophet Muhammad, as well as *pirs* and *ulama,* were effective intermediaries to God and the best interpreters of His divine message.[139] The Barelvis advocated spiritualism and *tasawwuf* (mysticism), and believed that the spirits of dead saints can be invoked for help. Visits to the tombs of saints, *pirs, ulama,* and sufis are characteristic Barelvi traditions, as is *urs,* the graveside celebration of the death anniversary of a prominent saint. The Barelvis also used the widely accepted fatalism and superstition of the commoners to promote the Quranic power in healing, warding off evil, and gaining success. This was done by using relevant Quranic verses in *tawidhes* (amulets) and *imam-zamins* (arm bands).[140]

The Deobandis derived their name from a devout Hanafi and practicing sufi, Haji Muhammad Abid of Deoband, founder of the *Madrassah-i-Deoband* in his

---

[137]Francis Robinson, "The Ulama of Farangi Mahall and their Adab," in Barbara Daly Metcalf, ed., *Moral Conduct and Authority: The Place of Adab in South Asian Islam,* Berkeley, CA: University of California Press, 1984, pp. 155–156, 160–161, 164–170.

[138]Francis Robinson, "The Veneration of Teachers in Islam by Their Pupils: Its Modern Significance," *History Today,* Vol. 30, March 1980, p. 24.

[139]Metcalf, *Islamic Revival in British India,* p. 267.

[140]Mohammad Arif Ghayur and Asaf Hussain, "The Religio-Political Parties (JI, JUI, JUP): Role of the Ulema in Pakistan's Politics," paper presented at the New England Conference, Association for Asian Studies, held at the University of Connecticut, Storrs, Connecticut, October 20–21, 1979, p. 16.

Box 4.1 AHMAD RAZA KHAN BARELVI

Ahmad Raza (1856–1921) was born in the South Asian subcontinent to a family of devout and scholarly Pathans. As a child, Ahmad Raza distinguished himself with his precocious intellect and photographic memory. For example, when he was merely four years old, he recited a poem from a mosque pulpit in honor of Prophet Muhammad's birthday. When Ahmad Raza was twenty, he journeyed with his father to perform the *haj*. Ahmad Raza's amazing memory enabled the young man to memorize numerous books on Islamic jurisprudence, which helped him later to stand out as among the most outstanding scholars of the *fiqh* in his time.

A great admirer of Prophet Muhammad, Ahmad Raza wrote sixteen books and composed verses in Urdu in the Prophet's praise. He also authored a commentary on the *Hadith* and on the Prophet's family and companions. In his writing, Ahmad Raza concurred with the sufi doctrine of *Nur-i-Muhammadi,* which held that the "Light of Muhammad" was God's own light and had existed since creation, thus making the Prophet himself a point of eternal light.

In common with other Traditionalists, Ahmad Raza invoked the Prophet Muhammad as an intercessor between man and God, inasmuch as the Prophet enjoyed complete knowledge of spiritual matters, of the meaning of all metaphorical passages in the Quran, of the obscure past, and of the unknown future. Ahmad Raza regularly celebrated *milad-un-Nabi,* the anniversary of the Prophet's birthday, with a select gathering of people. Ahmad Raza would arrive at the time of *qiyam* (the period of standing, when it was believed that the Prophet was present), and when the *qiyam* ended, he would give a scholarly sermon. A *haji* himself, he treated *haji*s and sayyids with particular respect.

Ahmad Raza also believed that saints were intermediaries between man and God, and he encouraged the practice of calling upon their assistance in all situations. He annually observed *urs* (graveside celebration of a saint's death) of several saints and *pir*s. He also urged Muslims to recite specified readings and to offer food at the graves of saints to hasten the answering of prayers. As a fervent believer in folk Islam, Ahmad Raza condoned many other superstitious practices and rituals widely prevalent in India. A revered *shaikh* in the Qadiri brotherhood, Ahmad Raza handled correspondence dealing with sufism and was a master of *taksir* (the making of numerical charts to serve as amulets). He also provided recipes for formulas guaranteed to secure blessings. In addition, he approved the practice of kissing the thumbs and placing them on the eyes upon hearing the name of Prophet Muhammad in the call to prayer—a practice believed to help induce visions of the Prophet. Moreover, he condoned such superstitions as keeping a white chicken, drawing blood on Saturdays, and praising the Prophet when plucking a flower. He justified the practice of folk Islam by declaring that un-less a ritual was specifically prohibited by a *hadith*, it was legitimate.

Though a typically apolitical Traditionalist, Ahmad Raza did become politi-cally involved near the end of his life in opposition to the *Khilafat* Movement. He discouraged Muslim cooperation with Mahatma Gandhi and with the Hindu-dominated All-India Congress Party. To this end, he even convened a conference of Indian *ulama* in 1921, the year he died.

Ahmad Raza was one of the most prominent scholars, teachers, and lead-ers of the Barelvi school. His charisma and his adherence to traditional Is-lamic beliefs and practices appealed to devout Indian Muslims throughout rural northern India. His promotion of folk Islam, therefore, left a deep and lasting imprint in the history of Islamic revivalism in the South Asian subcon-tinent.

Sources: Barbara Daly Metcalf, *Islamic Revival in British India: Deoband, 1860–1900,* Princeton: Princeton University Press, 1982; A. D. Muztar, *Shah Waliullah: A Saint-Scholar of Muslim India,* Islamabad, Pakistan: National Commission on Historical and Cultural Research, 1979; Murray Titus, *Islam in India and Pakistan,* Calcutta, 1959; Muhammad Arif Ghayur and Asaf Husain, "The Religio-Political Parties (JI, JUI, JUP): Role of the Ulema in Pakistan's Politics," paper presented at the New England Confer-ence, Association for Asian Studies, held at the University of Connecticut, Storrs, Con-necticut, October 20–21, 1979; Francis Robinson, *Separatism Among Indian Muslims: The Politics of the United Provinces' Muslims 1860–1923,* Cambridge: Cambridge Uni-versity Press, 1974; Mian Abdur Rashid, *Islam in [the] Subcontinent: An Analytical Study of the Islamic Movements,* Lahore, Pakistan: National Book Foundation, 1977.

hometown in 1866.[141] The Deobandis, like the Farangi Mahalli and Barelvis, be-lieved that the bodies and souls of prophets and saints were immortal, and there-fore regularly visited their tombs to pray and ask for help from God through them.[142] However, the Deobandis, unlike the Barelvis, strongly discouraged other aspects of folk or popular Islam.

In general, the practice of folk Islam is tolerated by Traditionalists as a healthy expression of the faith since they view the "traditional" act as inherently appropriate. The Fundamentalists, in contrast, oppose folk Islam in all its mani-festations and discourage its practice, sometimes by force, as essentially un-Islamic.

---

[141]S. M. Ikram, *Modern Muslim India and The Birth of Pakistan (1858–1951),* rev. ed., Lahore, Pak-istan: Shaikh Muhammad Ashraf Publishers, 1965, pp. 124–125.

[142]Aziz Ahmad, *Islamic Modernism in India and Pakistan 1857–1964,* London: Oxford University Press, 1967, p. 107.

GENERALLY APOLITICAL PACIFISTS; OCCASIONALLY POLITICAL ACTIVISTS

The issue of folk Islam alone does not separate Fundamentalists from Traditionalists. Their comparative approaches to political action likewise differ—a difference more essential than the question of *tawhid* versus tradition. When not at the apex of power, Fundamentalists often play an aggressive political role. The Traditionalists, however, disdain political activism and are generally detached and apolitical scholars, teachers, and preachers. In fact, because of their nonviolent and apolitical orientation, Traditionalists are often easily coopted by Muslim regimes to support the status quo. There is, however, no guarantee of Traditionalist silence in times of political upheaval. Even after periods of relative dormancy, when Islam or the *umma*—whether at local, regional, or global levels—appears to be in imminent danger, Traditionalists have vigorously asserted themselves politically.

In the most recent past, this political activism on the part of Traditionalists was obvious in the case of the Islamic Revolution in Iran (1978–1979) when the Traditionalist *ulama* joined the anti-Shah opposition and toppled the Pahlavi monarchy. The most prominent Traditionalist *alim* involved in the Iranian Revolution was Ayatollah Sayyid Kazem Shariatmadari (1905–1986). Grand Ayatollah Shariatmadari was an erudite, passive, and honorable gentleman whose final years in Ayatollah Khomeini's Islamic Republic read like a Greek tragedy (see Box 4.2.)

The Farangi Mahalli school of Sunni Traditionalists, for instance, consisted of learned *ulama* and practicing sufis who, by virtue of their teaching and advisory roles, brought about a gradual Islamic revival in the Indian subcontinent during the eighteenth and nineteenth centuries. For most of those two centuries the Farangi Mahallis educated Sunnis and Shi'ahs for careers in religion, in education, and as advisors to local rulers. They also educated the sons of *pirs* and sufis, and were heavily relied upon by both Sunni and Shi'ah princes.[143]

However, between 1909 and 1926, the Farangi Mahallis under the leadership of Qayam-ud-Din Muhammad Abdul Bari (see Box 4.3) became increasingly involved in politics because they felt that the *umma* was in danger from external non-Muslim aggressors. In 1909, Abdul Bari, at the age of thirty-one, agitated for separate electorates for Indian Muslims. In 1910, he founded an organization to promote the cause of the Ottoman Empire in its war against Russia.[144] Concerned over the Balkan War, in which non-Muslim European powers were carving up the Ottoman Empire, and about possible British control over Islam's holiest shrines in Mecca and Madina, he helped initiate a major Islamic conference in Lucknow, India, in December 1913 to discuss ways to protect Islam, the holy shrines, and the *umma* from European colonialism. After the conference, he helped to estab-

---

[143]Metcalf, *Islamic Revival in British India*, pp. 29–34; Ahmad, *Islamic Modernism in India and Pakistan*, pp. 103, 107, 113.

[144]Francis Robinson, *Separatism Among Indian Muslims: The Politics of the United Provinces' Muslims 1860–1923*, Cambridge: Cambridge University Press, 1974, pp. 419–420; M. Naeem Qureishi, "The Ulama of British India and the Hijrat of 1920," *Modern Asian Studies*, Vol. 13, No. 1, 1979, p. 47.

Box 4.2   AYATOLLAH SAYYID KAZEM SHARIATMADARI

Born into the religious household of Hasan Husayni Burujerdi Tabrizi Qummi in 1905, Sayyid Kazem Shariatmadari studied Islam in the northern Iranian city of Tabriz. In his twenties he traveled to Qom, the holiest Islamic city in Iran, where he continued his studies under such erudite *alim*s as Hairi Yazdi. He then pursued his Islamic studies in the Shi'ite city of Najaf, in Iraq, under the tutelage of prominent Islamic scholars like the *ayatollah*s Naini, Iraqi, and Isfahani. After concluding his studies there, Shariatmadari returned home to Tabriz, where he taught *fiqh*. In 1949 he left again for Qom, this time as an instructor.

When the Grand Ayatollah Hussein ibn Ali Tabatabai Burujerdi died in 1961, no single clerical candidate proved learned enough to succeed him as the sole *marja-i-taqlid* (source of emulation). Consequently, Ayatollah Shariatmadari became one of the three *marja-i-taqlids* chosen to succeed the venerated Grand *Ayatollah.* Shariatmadari's personal influence was greatest among the fourteen million Turkish-speaking Azarbaijani minority living in northwestern Iran and Khorasan and the *bazaaris* in Tehran. Ayatollah Shariatmadari was senior to the Ayatollah Khomeini in the Shi'ah clerical establishment; Khomeini became *marja-i-taqlid* a year later.

Regarded by numerous Iranians as the most learned *ayatollah,* Shariatmadari founded the *Dar al-Tabligh Islami* (House of Islamic Propagation) in 1963 at Qom to encourage traditional apolitical missionary activities, worldwide distribution of Shi'ah literature, and education through modern methods. Shariatmadari also served as administrator of the *Madrassah-i-Fatimah* in Qom and gave instruction there in both the *akhlaq* (virtues) and *fiqh* to Shi'ah theological students from around the Muslim world.

The death of Grand Ayatollah Mohsen Hakim in 1970 aggravated a growing power struggle between Shariatmadari and Khomeini for leadership of Iran's Shi'ah clerical establishment. On Hakim's death, the Shah conveyed his condolences in a personal letter to Shariatmadari in an effort to secure the moderate and apolitical ayatollah's succession as the supreme *marja-i-taqlid.* The effort backfired. Already the Shah was despised between the Iranian people and by the clerics; by implying support for Shariatmadari, the Shah guaranteed that Shariatmadari would be bypassed in consideration for virtual supreme leadership in the Shi'ah clerical hierarchy. Indeed, the clerics were so incensed by the Shah's support for Shariatmadari that they turned instead to Khomeini, the Shah's most vocal and vituperative critic.

Ayatollah Khomeini had built a reputation for himself not as a great scholar but rather as an uncompromising critic of the Pahlavi monarchy. Khomeini had condemned and denounced the Shah on numerous occasions, thus earning the ire of the Shah's regime and the love of the frustrated and alienated Iranian masses. His criticism of the Shah's regime, though constructive, was couched in essentially religious terms. The gentle, humble, and passive Shariatmadari did not speak of revolution to overturn the monarchy's political economic, and social programs, but emphasized the government's need to abide more by Islamic principles. Shariatmadari refrained from making personal attacks on the shah and criticized instead his Western and secular ideas and policies. While Khomeini advocated the establishment of an Islamic government in which religion and politics were fused, the Traditionalist and apolitical Shariatmadari believed that the place of the clergy was not in government but in disseminating the message of Islam among the people. Moreover, Khomeini was willing to accept bloodshed to advance his goal of creating an Islamic state, while Shariatmadari opposed bloodshed. For example, after the Shah's paratroopers murdered a student in Shariatmadari's house in 1978, the peaceful ayatollah advised his supporters to refrain from responding with violence and revolution. He feared that such a revolution would transform Iran into a repressive and oppressive Islamic regime like those in Saudi Arabia or Libya. Although Shariatmadari demanded government compliance with Islamic precepts of the Iranian constitution, he opposed the implementation of traditional Islamic punishments for crimes, including amputations and stoning. Furthermore, while Shariatmadari preferred women in his presence to wear a *chador* (a head-to-ankle black gown) or a head scarf, he had no desire to impose this style of dress on every woman in Iran. And while he refrained from going to movies, he did not demand that movie theaters be closed as Khomeini did.

As the Iranian revolution advanced, Shariatmadari, opposing further bloodshed, accepted the shah's nomination of Shahpour Bakhtiar as prime minister; the institution of constitutional monarchy, in which the shah would be only a figurehead; and a return to the 1906–1907 constitution, which granted leading Shi'ah clerics virtual veto power over government policies. Shariatmadari, unfortunately, backed the wrong horse. When the Shah fell, the Ayatollah Khomeini became Iran's de facto leader and asked his Fundamentalist associates to devise an Islamic constitution. Ayatollah Shariatmadari expressed concern about both the Islamic constitution and Khomeini's doctrine of *Velayat-i-Faqih* (the guardianship of the Islamic jurist), which would make Khomeini the ultimate arbiter of Iran's destiny. Furthermore, Shariatmadari also disapproved of the aggressive political role of the Islamic Republican Party that comprised the radical Fundamentalist *ulama.* He predicted that with the radical Fundamentalist clerics in power opposition would be quelled and Iran would merely have exchanged the "turban for the crown." In essence, Shariatmadari maintained that the democracy people wanted during the revolution against the shah would not be attained in a theocracy. Thus, Shariatmadari criticized and boycotted election and referendum plans; he also chastised Khomeini's Fundamentalist associates on the ruling Revolutionary Council for ordering the suppression of the 1979 Kurdish uprising.

In April 1979, Shariatmadari's supporters, who were predominantly Azerbaijani merchants, middle-class politicians, and clerics, founded the Islamic People's Republican Party (IPRP) to oppose the domination of the Islamic Republican Party. Khomeini's associates, in turn, accused Shariatmadari of dividing the Islamic movement during a time of crisis, with the nascent Islamic government facing threats both foreign and domestic. In response, IPRP supporters demonstrated in the streets, particularly in Iran's Azerbaijani province. As the demonstrations intensified, a well-publicized meeting was held between Shariatmadari and Khomeini. Wishing to defuse conflict between his supporters and those of Khomeini, Shariatmadari asked millions of his supporters to end their demonstrations, which Khomeini considered a threat to the embryonic Islamic Republic. However, Khomeini, never very tolerant in nature, soon began to see Shariatmadari himself as a threat to the Islamic government.

In April 1982, a plot was uncovered to overthrow Khomeini. The ruling Fundamentalist clique used this discovery as a pretext for neutralizing Shariatmadari's influence. Because Shariatmadari was known to oppose Khomeini's regime and was on record for his belief that the *ulama* should advise rulers, not become rulers themselves, rumors were circulated that he knew about or even supported the plot against Khomeini, which was led by liberals and secularists. Accepting the rumors, Khomeini and his clerical allies, in an unprecedented move, demoted one of Shi'ah Islam's most senior and highly revered Grand Ayatollahs. After taking away the title of *marja-i-taqlid* from Shariatmadari, the ruling clerics confined the passive and apolitical Shariatmadari to his home. Notably, when Shariatmadari was formally stripped of his clerical rank, not one senior cleric dared defend him. The Shi'ah clerical establishment remained uncommonly silent as Khomeini's associates purged the Shi'ah hierarchy of Shariatmadari's allies. These actions succeeded in silencing the dissident clerics as a political force and disabled them from supporting a grass roots opposition movement against the Fundamentalist Islamic regime.

Shariatmadari, who had dreamed of a democratic Islamic Republic in Iran, was terribly disillusioned. After spending the last four years of his life in obscurity under virtual house arrest, Shariatmadari died brokenhearted in Qom in 1986. His services to Islam and the Iranian Revolution were limited to a brief obituary in the Iranian mass media.

Sources: Moojan Momen, *An Introduction to Shi'i Islam: The History and Doctrines of Twelver Shi'ism*, New Haven: Yale University Press, 1985; Lawrence M. O'Rourke, "A determined rival in Iran: The 'other' ayatollah is described as 'a kindly old man'," December 11, 1979, *Bulletin Washington Bureau;* "The Gentle Scholar of Qum, *Time,* September 18, 1978; David Menashri, "Shi'ite Leadership: In the Shadow of Conflicting Ideologies," *Iranian Studies,* Vol. 13, Nos. 1–4, 1980.

Box 4.3   QAYAM-UD-DIN MUHAMMAD ABDUL BARI

Qayam-ud-din Muhammad Abdul Bari (1878–1926) was descendant of Mullah Nizamuddin, the founder of the Farangi Mahall *madrassah* in India. Abdul Bari received a traditional Islamic education at the Farangi Mahall institution and then furthered his Islamic education in Istanbul, Turkey, and in the Hijaz, Saudi Arabia.

In 1908, at the age of thirty, Abdul Bari established the *Madrassah-i-Nizamiyyah* in Lucknow, India. A year later, he became involved in the Muslim agitation for separate electorates. The following years, he became president of the newly founded *Majlis-i-Mu'yad al-Islam* (Association to Strengthen Islam), whose immediate aim was to help the Ottoman Empire in its war against czarist Russia.

In December 1913, Abdul Bari helped organize a major Islamic conference in Lucknow to discuss ways to protect the holy shrines in Mecca and Madina and the Ottoman Empire from European colonialism. One outcome of this conference was the establishment in Delhi of the *Anjuman-i-Khuddam-i-Ka'aba* (Organization to Protect the *Ka'aba*), with Abdul Bari as president. However, as a result of the British government's harassment and imprisonment of the group's officials, the organization was dissolved in 1916.

In December 1918, Abdul Bari was instrumental in initiating the *Khilafat* Movement to protest British attempts to divide the Ottoman Empire. In this regard, he brought together the leading *ulama* of India for an All-India Muslim League conference and separately prodded Mahatama Gandhi to get involved in the *Khilafat* Movement. In September 1919, Abdul Bari was elected the leader of an influential group of *ulama* at the Lucknow All-India *Khilafat* Conference, at which he produced a plan for the Central *Khilafat* Committee. Merely two months later Abdul Bari dominated the Delhi *Khilafat* Conference and was elected president of the newly created organization of Indian *Jamiat-i-Ulama-i-Hind* (Association of Indian *Ulama*).

In 1924, Maulana Bari formed yet another pan-Islamic organization, the *Anjuman-i-Khuddam-i-Haramain* (Guardians of Islam's Holiest Shrines), and led demonstrations against the Wahhabi conquest of Mecca and Madina and the destruction of mausoleums and shrines of Muslim heroes in Islam's holiest cities. Around the same time he also resisted the growing Hindu revival that Mahatma Gandhi had ushered in with his use of Hindu rhetoric and symbolism.

Despite his political and educational commitments, Abdul Bari wrote about one hundred books and pamphlets; he founded and taught at the *Madrassah-i-Nizamiyyah;* he executed his duties as a *pir* to a large following of disciples; and he served on the boards of the shrine of Muin-ud-Din Chishti—a famous sufi saint who has a large following in the South Asian subcontinent—at Ajmere and of the *Nadwat-ul-Ulama* (Islamic scholars of Nadwa) seminary at Lucknow. He was the major catalyst responsible for the Islamic revival in the first quarter of the twentieth century and one of the most influential Muslim Traditionalists in Islamic history.

Sources: Barbara Daly Metcalf, *Islamic Revival in British India, 1860–1900,* Princeton: Princeton University Press, 1982; Francis Robinson, "The Ulama of Farangi Mahall and their Adab," in Barbara Daly Metcalf, ed., *Moral Conduct and Authority: The Place of Adab in South Asian Islam,* Berkeley, CA: University of California Press, 1984; Aziz Ahmad, *Islamic Modernism in India and Pakistan 1857–1964,* London: Oxford University Press, 1967; Francis Robinson, *Separatism Among Indian Muslims: The Politics of the United Provinces' Muslims 1860–1923,* Cambridge: Cambridge University Press, 1974; M. Naeem Qureshi, "The Ulama of British India and the Hijrat of 1920," *Modern Asian Studies,* Vol. 13, No. 1, 1979; Pran Chopra, ed., *Role of the Indian Muslims in the Struggle for Freedom,* New Delhi: Light and Life Publishers, 1979.

lish and became president of the *Anjuman-i-Khuddam-i-Ka'aba* (Organization to Protect the *Ka'aba*).[145]

Abdul Bari also played a significant role in launching the post–World War I *Khilafat* Movement. In December 1918, under the auspices of the All-India Muslim League, he convened a conference at which the leading *ulama* of India (except for the *ulama* of the Barelvi school) participated. He then cultivated a friendly relationship with Mahatama Gandhi and urged that he involve himself in the *Khilafat* movement. At the Lucknow All-India *Khilafat* Conference held in September 1919, Abdul Bari produced a plan for the Central *Khilafat* Committee and was elected the leader of the *Khilafat* Movement. In November 1919, he dominated the Delhi *Khilafat* Conference. Moreover, he was elected president of a newly created organization of Indian *ulama,* the *Jamiat-i-Ulama-i-Hind* (The Association of India *Ulama*).[146]

In 1924, when ibn-Saud and his Fundamentalist Wahhabi warriors overran Mecca and Madina, Abdul Bari perceived a new threat to the holy cities, coming for the first time not from European Christian colonialists, but from fanatical coreligionists. In response, Abdul Bari founded yet another pan-Islamic organization, the *Anjuman-i-Khuddam-i-Haramain* (Guardians of Islam's Holiest Shrines), charged to protect Islam's holy shrines. He also led peaceful demonstrations decrying the Wahhabi conquest of Mecca and Madina. At the same time, colonialist threats faded further in the background as Abdul Bari resisted the growing Hindu revival fueled by Gandhi.[147]

---

[145]Pran Chopra, ed., *Role of the Indian Muslims in the Struggle for Freedom,* New Delhi: Light and Life Publishers, 1979, p. 92.

[146]Ibid., p. 92; Robinson, *Separatism Among Indian Muslims,* p. 420; Robinson, "The Ulama of Farangi Mahall," pp. 157–158; Leonard Binder, *Religion and Politics in Pakistan,* Berkeley, CA: University of California Press, 1963, p. 53; Qureshi, "The Ulama of British India," p. 41; also see Gail Minault, *The Khilafat Movement: Religious Symbolism and Political Mobilization in India,* London: Oxford University Press, 1983.

[147]Robinson, *Separatism Among Indian Muslims,* p. 420.

When the *Khilafat* Movement was at its peak in the summer of 1920, a segment of the Traditionalist *ulama* began the *Hijrat* Movement, in which about 50,000, devout Indian Muslims were persuaded by the *ulama* to abandon their homes and immigrate to the neighboring Muslim homeland of Afghanistan because India under British rule was no longer a *dar al-Islam* (abode of Islam). Afghanistan was under the Muslim rule of Amir Amanullah and considered safe for the Muslims of the Indian subcontinent. Initially, the ruler, government, and people of Afghanistan warmly welcomed the refugees. Yet as the penniless refugees became a socioeconomic burden to Afghanistan, Amanullah's armed forces sealed the Afghan border. By autumn 1920 many of the Indian Muslim pilgrims had returned to India disillusioned, alienated and angry.[148]

The Traditionalist Deobandis also displayed political activism in their support of the *Khilafat* Movement and opposition to the Pakistan Movement. Their actions, which truly represented a political "reaction" to specific imperialist, Muslim Fundamentalist, and Hindu Fundamentalist threats, were consistent with their otherwise apolitical Traditionalist orientation.[149] In fact, during the 1980 celebrations commemorating the fourteen-hundredth anniversary of Islam, Prime Minister Indira Gandhi and other eminent Hindu politicians paid glowing tribute to the Deobandi school for its world-renowned scholarship, its exemplary patriotism, and its significant contribution to the cultural mosaic of a pluralistic society. The Indian Government also issued a thirty-paisa (three-cent) stamp in honor of the *Dar al-Ulum* of Deoband.[150] No revolutionary Fundamentalist organization crusading for a puritanical Islamic system could have been so honored by the Indian government.

The Traditionalists observed limits in their pursuit of goals and, conversely, their goals were limited. Even politicized, the Traditionalists at heart lacked the devastating and destabilizing political agenda of their crusading Fundamentalist brethren.

OPPONENTS OF *IJTIHAD* AND PROPONENTS OF *TAQLID*

Most Sunni Traditionalists reject *ijtihad* (which encourages independent thought in legal matters) and accept the dogma of *taqlid* (unquestioning conformity to prior legal rulings). For the Traditionalist, *ijtihad* represents an attack on traditional values and practices and, therefore, undermines Islam. Author Leonard Binder voices the belief of many Traditionalists:

---

[148]See Qureishi, "The Ulama of British India," p. 41; Binder, *Religion and Politics in Pakistan,* pp. 54–57; Kramer, "Political Islam," p. 33; Stanley Wolpert, *Roots of Confrontation in South Asia,* Oxford: Oxford University Press, 1982, pp. 94–95.

[149]Ziya-ul-Hasan Faruqi, *The Deoband School and the Demand for Pakistan,* Bombay, India, Asia Publishing House, 1963.

[150]Metcalf, *Islamic Revival in British India,* pp. 14–15.

To alter the decision that has been accepted for ages would be to deny the eternal immutability of God's law and to admit that earlier jurists erred would be to destroy the idea of the continuity of the divine guidance of the Muslim community.[151]

The Farangi Mahallis, the Barelvis, and the Deobandis of the Indian subcontinent all subscribed to *taqlid* and rejected *ijtihad*. In fact, it was their rigid adherence to the *fiqh* (Islamic jurisprudence) of Abu Hanifa (A.D. 699–769)—the founder of the Hanafi sect of Sunni Islam—that made famous Deobandi theologians, like Muhammad Qasim Nanautawi (d. 1879), resent and attempt to undermine the efforts of Shah Waliullah to create an interjuristic discipline of Islamic theology and law.[152]

The Fundamentalists and Shi'ah Traditionalists, in contrast, believe that Muslims schooled in the Quran and the *Hadith* should practice *ijtihad* and not blindly conform to legal judgments a millennium old. They argue that Fundamentalists are loathe to accept unquestioningly any practice, tradition, or judgment following the classical era of Islam.

FATALISTS

The Traditionalists, like all Muslims, believe that God is omnipotent, omnipresent, just, and merciful; a person is merely an *abd* (obedient servant) of God, and only God retains absolute sovereignty over His creation; God's commands are always just and right; and all determinations of right and wrong are embodied in the Quran. However, taking these beliefs to the logical extreme, many Traditionalists believe that to allow a person freedom to decide questions of right and wrong trespasses against God's omnipotence.[153] A quotation from al-Ashari (A.D. 873–935)—the Iraqi-born *alim* (Islamic scholar) who spearheaded a traditionalist movement in Islam—vividly illustrates this point:

> We believe that God created everything by bidding it 'Be' [*'kun'*] . . . that nothing on earth, whether a fortune or misfortune, comes to be, save through God's will; that things exist through God's fiat; . . . and that the deeds of the creatures are created by Him and predestined by Him;. . . that the creatures can create nothing but are rather created themselves;. . . We . . . profess faith in God's decree and fore-ordination.[154]

Thus, to al-Ashari, expressing even the concept of chance, of randomness, or of bad luck was unpardonable blasphemy since: "This was to imply that an event might occur otherwise than the will of God, or that the will of God was unjust. The correct response was an immovable clam and a reference to *kismet* [fate] or

---

[151]Binder, *Religion and Politics in Pakistan*, pp. 20, 24, 26, 42–43, 74; Freeland Abbott, *Islam and Pakistan*, Ithaca, NY: Cornell University Press, 1968, pp. 89, 225.

[152]Ahmad, *Islamic Modernism in India and Pakistan*, p. 107.

[153]Peter Hardy, "Traditional Muslim Views of The Nature of Politics," in C. H. Phillips, ed., *Politics and Society in India*, London: George Allen and Unwin, 1963, pp. 32–33, 36.

[154]Ibid.

taqdir [destiny]."[155] The Traditionalist *ulama*'s rigid viewpoint emphasizing *taqlid* and predestination was caused in part by the Asharite movement, which gained ascendency during the reign of the Abbasid caliph al-Mutawakkil (A.D. 847–861). The movement impeded the revision and reform of Islamic theological law and tradition, often branding revisionists and reformists as heretics, *kafirs* (infidels), or enemies of Islam. Furthermore, it stifled creative and critical thought and action among the public while sanctioning corruption, nepotism, and tyranny as demonstrated by its leaders. The Traditionalists, believing in predestination, reasoned, "It is God's eternal decree that these men must rule; all their actions are inevitable and destined by God. . . . A believer could not very well rebel against that."[156] These dogmatic attitudes were further reinforced after the destruction of Baghdad, the center of Islamic knowledge and learning, in A.D. 1258 by the Mongols under Hulaku. By considering man insignificant and powerless, the Traditionalists undermined the self-esteem of the Muslim people and dampened their spirit of dynamism and creativity. Belief that man could not conquer and control his environment led the Traditionalists, often considered as the spiritual guides of the Muslim community, to adopt a passive and scholarly orientation. In moments of crisis or during distressing times, they encouraged the *umma* to seek refuge and spiritual strength in the omnipotence and generosity of God. This stance was challenged by the gross corruption and hypocrisy of politics and the decline of central authority. The Traditionalists rationalized that the well-developed and appealing religion of Islam could easily survive the loss of power manifested in Muslim rulers and the depoliticization of Islam.[157] In disengaging themselves from active politics and the worldly temptations of power and wealth, the Traditionalists sincerely believed that they were protecting the integrity and cherished ideals of Islam. Thus, they tolerated the de facto separation of "church and state" where none existed in Islamic theory or history. Sometimes they were co-opted and reduced to impotent passivity by shrewd rulers.

The apolitical and fatalistic orientation of the Traditionalists was manifested in the Farangi Mahallis, with the notable exception of Abdul Bari. Most of the time the Barelvis had a similar orientation, although they became political with their involvement in the Pakistan Movement from 1940 to 1947, in the 1968–1969 anti-Ayub movement in Pakistan, and in the *Nizam-i-Mustafa* movement (movement for Prophet Muhammad's Islamic System) against President Bhutto's Pakistani regime in summer 1977. Finally, the Deobandis had a similar apolitical and fatalistic orientation, with the exception of their involvement in the *Khilafat* movement, their opposition to the Pakistan Movement, and their opposition to Ayub Khan in the spring of 1969 and to Bhutto in the summer of 1977.

---

[155]Richard H. Pfaff, "Technicism vs. Traditionalism: The Developmental Dialectic in the Middle East," in Carl Leiden, ed., *The Conflict of Traditionalism and Modernism in the Muslim Middle East,* Austin, TX: University of Texas Press, 1966, p. 104.

[156]Ignaz Goldzihar, *Introduction to Islamic Theology and Law,* trans. Andras and Ruth Hamori, Princeton: Princeton University Press, 1981, p. 76; D. S. Roberts, *Islam: A Concise Introduction,* San Francisco: Harper & Row Publishers, 1981, pp. 48–49.

[157]S. Alam Khundmiri, "A Critical Examination of Islamic Traditionalism," *Islam and The Modern Age,* Vol. 2, No. 2, May 1971, p. 7.

Fatalism by Traditionalist standards cannot be reconciled with activism. To accept God's will is to take no action opposing it but rather to submit fully. The Fundamentalists, however, reject this interpretation of predestination. They argue instead that God specifically enjoined Muslims to fight injustice, thus laying the foundation for *jihad, ijtihad,* and political and social activism. While Fundamentalists also believe in the ultimate authority of God over all things and in all matters, they insist that God invested man with free will—to choose between right and wrong, belief and disbelief. The Traditionalists, in contrast, generally reject "worldly" political activity as unseemly and un-Islamic. Nevertheless, when Islam is attacked or when Fundamentalists spark Islamic revivalism, Traditionalists will not stand idly by but will protect and defend the *umma* from aggression.

OPPONENTS OF MODERNIZATION

Traditionalists are often learned scholars of Islamic theology, law, and civilization who lead austere and pious lives. They can be spellbinding in their extemporaneous renditions of the Quran or the sayings of Prophet Muhammad, his *Sahaba* (companions), and many Islamic theologians and jurists throughout Islamic history. Traditionalists impress Muslims with their detailed knowledge of the lives and accomplishments of Prophet Muhammad and the major figures in Islamic history. They also have an authoritative grasp of *fiqh.*

Nevertheless, these respectable scholars have serious limitations when viewed in a contemporary light. They are often naive, if not ignorant, of modern natural and social sciences. If they read modern scientific theories at all, they either accept or reject these themes according to the Quran and the *Sunnah.* Traditionalists are generally oblivious to the complexities, institutions, and processes of modern governments and international relations in an interdependent world—although they do not perceive this ignorance as a shortcoming. They are convinced that the perfect religion of Islam, in which they are well versed, reveals all truths and can help to resolve all internal crises and external threats facing Muslim societies around the world.[158]

Despite gaping differences, both Fundamentalists and Traditionalists are strong opponents of modernization, secularization, and Westernization, all of which they attribute to the *dar al-harb* and the enemies of Islam. Given their narrow, almost parochial attitudes, the Traditionalists, like the Fundamentalists and even many Modernists, express serious concern about the increasing secularization of the critically important educational, legal, economic, and social realms of their Muslim societies. Secularization to them is tantamount to the elimination of the divine *Shariah;* they believe secularization will eventually erode the very foundations of the Muslim community. In the educational sphere, the Traditionalists, like the Fundamentalists, demand the generous funding of *madrassahs*; advocate syllabi that contain mainly Islamic disciplines and few, if any, modern Western sciences; and promote the segregation of the sexes and extreme modesty in dress in educational institutions. In the legal sphere, the Traditionalists demand rigid

---

[158]Ibid., p. 11.

adherence to their respective schools of *fiqh*. They want an Islamic constitution drawing heavily upon the Quran, the *Sunnah*, and the *Shariah*, and Islamic law courts presided over by *qadhi*s and based on the *Shariah*. In the economic sphere, they advocate the institution of the *zakat* and *ushr* taxes, as well as the prohibition of *riba* (usury). Unlike the Fundamentalists, however, the Traditionalists do not engage in a sustained political crusade for these beliefs.

In the social realm, the Traditionalists, like the Fundamentalists, encourage monogamy while at the same time allowing Muslims who meet certain criteria to have up to four wives. In keeping with their belief in the timelessness of morality, Traditionalists categorically reject the right of any Muslim to tamper with the practice of polygamy.[159] Like most Fundamentalists, the Traditionalists promote the segregation of the sexes. Both revivalist groups enjoin women to adopt *purdah* (veiling and segregation). Furthermore, the Traditionalists and the Fundamentalists believe that court testimony given by one man is equal to that of two women.

The Traditionalists manifest a detached attitude in their reluctance to adapt Islamic viewpoints to contemporary eras. A significant number of Muslims frown upon this detachment and reluctance to change, and feel this fatal flaw in Traditionalists' worldview has contributed to the stagnation of the Muslim world, as well as to the impotence of the *umma* on the world stage. The Traditionalists forcefully reply that Islam has not, cannot, and should never change, for it is founded on God's comprehensive and immutable words and laws. Consequently, they argue that immutability is not the cause of the Muslim world's decline, but that the problem arises from the Muslim world's inherent imperfections, and because Muslims have not steadfastly followed the letter and spirit of the religion.

SUMMARY

The emphasis given by Traditionalists to Islamic scholarship, teaching, and preaching, as well as their firm belief in *taqlid* and predestination, often gives them a passive and apolitical orientation. Thus, few Traditionalists are in the vanguard of Islamic revivals. However, Islamic revivals often spark them to abandon temporarily their passivity, and to try to leverage the revival toward their theocratic and theocentric orientation. (See the table following p. 151.)

---

[159]Modernists suggest severely restricting polygamy, while Muslim Pragmatists advocate abolishing polygamy on the grounds that there no longer exists (for all practical purposes) the two major reasons for early Islamic condoning of polygamy. First, when Islam began there was a widely prevalent practice among Arabs to be married to a number of women at the same time. Prophet Muhammad realized that he could not ban the practice completely and still make Islam attractive to the majority, so he restricted polygamy by limiting husbands to four wives, with the important qualification that all wives should be treated with complete equality, justice, and compassion. Second, during the early years of Islam there were numerous tribal and religious wars, in which many men lost their lives, leaving numerous widows and orphans without husbands and fathers to support them. All Muslim Pragmatists, and even many Modernists, conclude that because these two reasons are gone and because they believe it is humanly impossible for any man to treat four wives equally, the practice of polygamy should be abolished.

Chapter
5

The Muslim
Modernists

The third category of Islamic revivalists is the Muslim Modernists, also known as Adaptationists, Apologists, Syncretists, and Revisionists. The Modernists are devout and knowledgeable Muslims whose mission is threefold: first, "to define Islam by bringing out the fundamentals in a rational and liberal manner"; second, "to emphasize, among others, the basic ideals of Islamic brotherhood, tolerance and social justice"; and third, to interpret the teaching of Islam in such a way as to bring out its dynamic character in the context of the intellectual and scientific progress of the modern world.[160]

In contradistinction to the Traditionalists, who are concerned with maintaining the status quo, and to the puritanical Fundamentalists, the Modernists sincerely endeavor to reconcile differences between traditional religious doctrine and secular scientific rationalism, between unquestioning faith and reasoned logic, and between the continuity of Islamic tradition and modernity.

ARDENT OPPONENTS OF *TAQLID* AND VIGOROUS PROPONENTS OF *IJTIHAD*

Modernists, like Fundamentalists, vehemently disagree with the Sunni Traditionalists' belief in the dogma of *taqlid*, which requires the unquestioning and rigid adherence to one of the four schools of Sunni *fiqh* developed in the postclassical period. The Modernists feel the primary causes of the decline of Islamic culture

---

[160]Quoted in *The Muslim World*, Vol. 50, No. 2, April 1960, p. 155; also cited in Donald Eugene Smith, "Emerging Patterns of Religion and Politics," in Donald Eugene Smith, ed., *South Asian Politics and Religion*, Princeton: Princeton University Press, 1966, pp. 32–33.

and power are the inhibition of independent, creative, and critical thought, and the lack of vigorous discussion about Islamic laws and issues that resulted from what Traditionalists consider the closure of "the gates of *ijtihad*" a millennium earlier. Convinced that Islam is a progressive, dynamic, and rational religion, the Modernists denounce the inhibiting dogma of *taqlid* and advocate an unconditional reopening of "the gates of *ijtihad*" to facilitate the reinterpretation and reformulation of Islamic laws in the contemporary light of modern thought. Modernists reinforce their appeal for the restoration and exercise of *ijtihad* with Quranic quotations: "And to those who exert we show the Path (29:69)"; "God would never change His favor that He conferred on a people until they changed what was within themselves"(8:53); and "Verily, God changes not what is in a people until they change what is in themselves. "(22:10) Modernists believe these Quranic verses indicate that Islam is not a confining and inhibiting force, but an inspiration and spur to progress. Indeed, they feel dynamic change in Islam is not only possible, but desirable. Therefore, according to most Modernists, Islamic laws must be carefully revised to be flexible and adaptable enough to incorporate modern political, economic, social, cultural, and legal conditions.

Sayyid Jamal ad-Din al-Afghani (1838–1897), considered by many the father of Islamic modernism (see Box 5.1), was extremely critical of the Traditionalist *ulama* who believed in *taqlid* and who discouraged any new and creative thought. He was convinced that the medieval mentality of the Traditionalists was primarily responsible for the decline of Muslim power and influence in the world:[161]

> The strangest thing of all is that our ulema in these days have divided knowledge into two categories: one they call Muslim knowledge and the other European. . . . Because of this, they forbid others to learn some useful knowledge. They just do not understand that knowledge which is a noble thing, has no connection with any particular group. . . . How strange it is that Muslims study with great delight those sciences that are ascribed to Aristotle, as if Aristotle were a Muslim author. However, if an idea is related to Galileo, Newton, or Kepler, they consider it unbelief. . . . In fact . . . when they forbid [modern] knowledge with a view of safeguarding the Islamic religion . . . they themselves are the enemies of religion. Islam is the closest religion to knowledge and learning and there is no contradiction between [modern] knowledge and the basic principles of Islam.[162]

According to al-Afghani, "intellectual decline first penetrated" through the ranks of the influential *ulama*, who were educated in the limited and archaic Islamic studies taught in *madrassah*s and who were unexposed to the outside world. Consequently, al-Afghani believed that the traditional *ulama* contributed to the decline of the *umma*.[163]

Al-Afghani, in common with most subsequent Modernists, attributed the dynamic vitality, strength, progress, and prosperity of the West to its freer use of reason and its encouragement of scientific and technological processes that the im-

---

[161]Rashid Ahmad (Jullundhri), "Pan-Islamism and Pakistan: Afghani and Nasser," *Scrutiny,* Vol. 1, No. 2, July–December 1975, pp. 31–32.

[162]Ibid., p. 32; Mortimer, *Faith & Power,* p. 121.

[163]R. Ahmad, "Pan-Islamism and Pakistan," p. 32.

Box 5.1 SAYYID JAMAL AD-DIN AL-AFGHANI

THE FATHER OF ISLAMIC MODERNISM

Sayyid Jamal ad-Din al-Afghani (1838–1897) was born into a Shi'ah family in the village of Asadabad near the city of Hamadan in northwest Persia. However, in order to have a greater impact on reforming and uniting the predominantly Sunni Muslim world, he concealed his Persian Shi'ah origins and intimated that he was born in predominantly Sunni Afghanistan.

Al-Afghani's father was a lower middle class farmer well versed in Islam. As he instructed his son in the precepts of their faith, the father was impressed by the boy's innate intelligence and thirst for knowledge. After al-Afghani had studied at Qazvin for two years, his father sent him to Tehran to study under the renowned *alim* Agha Sayyid Sadiq. Shortly thereafter, al-Afghani traveled to Najaf in Ottoman Iraq, where he spent four years studying under a leading Shi'ah *mujtahid* (*alim* authorized to exercise *ijtihad*). There he became familiar with a variety of Islamic disciplines and was influenced by the victory of the *Usuli* school of thought in Persia, a school that favored the use of *ijtihad* to develop the Islamic theory of jurisprudence. The Traditionalist *ulama* of the *Akhbari* school, however, opposed the *Usuli* school; the *Akhbari* school believed in maintaining the status quo and felt traditional judgments were adequate. Supporting the *Usuli* school, al-Afghani came into conflict with the traditionalist *ulama,* a conflict that piqued his interest in seeing and meeting Muslims the world over.

Al-Afghani traveled from Iraq to Afghanistan, India, Egypt, Turkey, France, Britain, and Russia, which gave his political activism a cosmopolitan perspective. However, his extensive travels prevented him from writing. This changed when he spent eight years in Egypt as an instructor at *Al-Azhar* in Cairo (1871–1879). His most prominent pupil, Muhammad Abduh, later praised his mentor's dynamic and meaningful lectures. Al-Afghani's classes, which included Islamic theology, jurisprudence, mysticism, and philosophy, stressed the threat of Western imperialism, the need to unify the *umma,* and the necessity of constitutional limits on the power of kings and presidents. Moreover, al-Afghani introduced his students to Western intellectual thought and scientific achievement, encouraged them to question and analyze, helped them to write and publish articles, and assisted them to use public speaking effectively. Thus he promoted Islamic modernism specifically, and Islamic revivalism in general, among a new generation of intelligent and scholarly Muslims.

Although a critic of the *ulama* and the archaic and obsolete Islamic education it provided in *madrassahs*, al-Afghani was also critical of Muslim apologists and pro-Western Muslim Modernists who promoted Western education (like Sir Sayyid Ahmad Khan). Formal and secular Western education, al-Afghani believed, made Muslims insensitive to the injustices of pro-Western rulers.He also felt it fostered elitism and excessive individuality while promoting an expensive and materialistic lifestyle.

However, al-Afghani did not denounce nationalism as un-Islamic. Instead, he felt that pan-Arabism, pan-Islamism, and local nationalism were all necessary and appropriate ideologies, provided they promoted Muslim self-determination and solidarity. Al-Afghani returned to Persia in the late 1880s, but he was soon expelled for opposing tobacco concessions granted by the Persian monarchy to British businessmen. Al-Afghani returned to Iraq, where he convinced a revered Shi'ah *alim,* Haji Mirza Hasan Shirazi, to issue a *fatwa* (authoritative Islamic decree) opposing the tobacco concession. Consequently, in 1892, the Iranian monarchy canceled the concession. Al-Afghani's actions inspired a revolutionary fervor in Persia that eventually led to the constitution of 1907.

Al-Afghani's primary goal as a revolutionary intellectual was to establish pan-Islamic regimes free from imperialism and colonialism. He looked forward to the reconciliation between sects within Islam, the rebirth of Islamic nationalism, and the development of an Islamic confederation ruled by a devout, progressive, just, and tolerant caliph. This, al-Afghani reasoned, would more effectively counter imperialism then a plethora of divided nation-states.

Al-Afghani was a liberal and enlightened writer who sought through his writings and speeches to move fellow Muslims to action. His persuasive lectures, his magnetic personality, and his immense knowledge and eloquence attracted eager students and admirers, the most prominent of whom, Muhammad Abduh, became his greatest legacy.

Sources: Nikki R. Keddie, *An Islamic Response to Imperialism: Political and Religious Writings of Sayyid Jamal ad-Din "al-Afghani,"* Berkeley, CA: University of California Press, 1983; Nikki R. Keddie, *Sayyid Jamal ad-Din "al-Afghani": A Political Biography,* Berkeley, CA: University of California Press, 1972; M. A. Zaki Badawi, *The Reformers of Egypt,* London: Croom Helm, 1978; Edward Mortimer, *Faith and Power: The Politics of Islam,* New York: Vintage Books, 1982; Albert Hourani, *Arabic Thought in the Liberal Age 1798–1939,* 2nd ed., London: Oxford University Press, 1979; Charles C. Adams, *Islam and Modernism in Egypt: A Study of the Modern Reform Movement Inaugurated by Muhammad Abduh,* New York: Russel & Russel, 1933; Rashid Ahmad (Jullundhri), "Pan-Islamism and Pakistan: Afghani and Nasser," *Scrutiny,* Vol 1, No. 2, July–December 1975; Ali Merad, "Reformism in Modern Islam," *Cultures,* Vol. 4, No. 1, 1977; Aziz Ahmad, *Islamic Modernism in India and Pakistan 1857–1964,* London: Oxford University Press, 1967; Bruce Borthwick, *Comparative Politics of the Middle East: An Introduction,* Englewood Cliffs, NJ: Prentice-Hall, Inc., 1980; Sylvia G. Haim, *Arab Nationalism: An Anthology,* Berkeley, CA: University of California Press, 1962; S. Vahid, ed., *Thoughts and Reflections of Iqbal,* Lahore, Pakistan: Shaikh Muhammad Ashraf, 1964.

poverished and weak Muslim world refused to adopt.[164] Therefore, al-Afghani strongly recommended acquiring Western knowledge, technology, and services, as long as borrowing from the West was selective and served the basic needs and aspirations of the Muslim people. In this undertaking, which he believed would raise the standard of living of all Muslims, al-Afghani struggled to initiate an Islamic reformation similar to the successful Christian Reformation sparked by Martin Luther.[165]

The seeds of *ijtihad* planted by al-Afghani in his most prominent Egyptian student and ardent follower, Muhammad Abduh (1849–1905), bore fruit when the latter assumed positions of official religious responsibility and influence in Egypt. Like his mentor, Abduh (see Box 5.2) made a dedicated and sustained effort to liberate Islam from the dogma of *taqlid*. He insisted that Muslims could improve their lives and their society only by carefully studying the Quran in the light of reason and rationality. He taught that the Quran gives all Muslims the right to differ with even the *ulama*, if the latter were unreasonable or irrational. He justified this stance by maintaining "Islam had liberated man from the authority of the clergy; it has put him face to face with God and has taught him not to rely on any intercession."[166] He also said,

> The supposed superiority of the ancients was a mere pretext to keep intact the absurdities of the past, and such a pretext of infallibility must necessarily mean the thwarting of human intellect.[167]

Reacting to the uninspiring and stultifying Islamic education based on rote learning he had received in *madrassahs*, Abduh constantly exhorted Muslims to approach problems in the true spirit of Islam: through analysis, reason, and logic. In one instance, he declared that "when reason and [Islamic] tradition are in conflict, the right of decision rests with reason."[168] On another occasion he said,

> Of all religions, Islam is almost the only one that blames those who believe without proofs, and rebukes those who follow opinions without having any certainty. . . . Whenever Islam speaks, it speaks to reason . . . and the holy texts proclaim that happiness consists in the right use of reason.[169]

---

[164]Albert Hourani, *Arabic Thought in the Liberal Age, 1798–1939,* London: Oxford University Press, 1970, p. 109.

[165]Nikki R. Keddie, *Sayyid Jamal ad-Din al-Afghani: A Political Biography,* Berkeley, CA: University of California Press, 1972, p. 141.

[166]Quoted in Osman Amin, "Some Aspects of Religious Reform in the Muslim Middle East," in Carl Leiden, ed., *The Conflict of Traditionalism and Modernism in the Muslim Middle East,* Austin, TX: University of Texas Press, 1966, p. 91.

[167]Mahmudul Haq, *Muhammad Abduh: A Study of a Modern Thinker of Egypt,* Aligarh, India: Institute of Islamic Studies, Aligarh Muslim University, 1978, p. 181.

[168]Muhammad Abduh, *al-Islam wa'l-nasraniya ma'af-'ilm wa'l- madaniya,* Cairo, n.d., posthumously printed, p. 56; also quoted in Goldziher, *Introduction to Islamic Theology and Law,* p. 110.

[169]Amin, "Some Aspects of Religious Reform," p. 91.

Box 5.2 MUHAMMAD ABDUH

THE PREEMINENT MUSLIM MODERNIST OF EGYPT

Muhammad Abduh (1849–1905) was born in Lower Egypt into a lower middle class farming family. After learning to read and write at a village school,
Abduh was sent, at the age of ten, to the home of a *hafiz-i-Quran* (one who
has memorized the Quran) so that he, too, could memorize the Quran and
learn how to recite it eloquently. In a brief two years, Abduh had accomplished both tasks. In 1862 he started school at the Ahmadi Mosque in
Tanta. There he spent almost four years learning by rote and listening to
highly technical lectures. Consequently, the sixteen-year-old Abduh, who
loved the outdoors, left the school discouraged by its unsatisfactory method
of instruction. He returned to his village to become a farmer like his father
and relatives, and while at home got married. Soon thereafter, Abduh's father pressured the young man to return to school at the Ahmadi Mosque, but
Abduh disobeyed his father's wishes. Ostensibly on his way back to school,
Abduh decided instead to stay with some relatives. During that visit, Abduh's
great-uncle, Shaikh Darwish, instilled in Abduh an insatiable appetite for religious learning and for sufism. In 1865, Abduh returned to school in Tanta,
now motivated to acquire a religious education. Before the end of a year, Abduh left for *Al-Azhar* in Cairo, where he studied for the next four years. During this period, Abduh's interest in sufism led him to adopt a devoutly religious and ascetic lifestyle. For a brief period he even became a recluse.

In 1871, Abduh began a close association with the scholarly and politically
active al-Afghani and abandoned his absorption in the passive and mystical
realm of sufism. Instead, Abduh became involved in reforming Islam and
Muslim societies. In 1874, he began to write newspaper and journal articles;
by 1876 he had written two books. In his writings, he criticized the traditionalist *ulama* for their dogmatic and doctrinaire stand on Islamic theology and
jurisprudence. Furthermore, he emphasized the need for Muslims to study
modern science and Western progress, because, he argued, Muslims had to
adapt to the times.

After obtaining his degree and becoming an *alim,* Abduh taught at *Al-
Azhar* and at the Khedivial School of Languages, using the methods of reasoning and logical proof that he had learned from his mentor, al-Afghani.
While teaching, Abduh often discussed prospects for reforming Islamic jurisprudence and the Arabic language in an effort to improve Egyptian society.

In 1880, Abduh became one of the three editors of *Al-Wakai Al-Misriyyah*
(The Egyptian Events), a position he held for two years. But in 1882 he was
suspected of involvement in Urabi Pasha's unsuccessful nationalist revolt
against British and French influence in Egypt and banished from Egypt. Abduh
traveled to Syria and Lebanon. Then, in 1884, al-Afghani invited Abduh to join

him in Paris. There the two men published a strongly pan-Islamic, nationalist, modernist, and anti-imperialist newspaper called *Al-Urwat Al-Wuthqa* (The Indissoluble Link). The paper was soon banned and al-Afghani and Abduh were both exiled from France.

In 1889, Abduh, tired of his nomadic existence (which included travels through Europe), compromised with the Egyptian authorities, promising to work within the system to bring about gradual change and to eschew revolution if he were allowed to return home. Nevertheless, within a decade, Abduh was so popular among Egyptians for his moderate and modernist views on Islam that he was made grand mufti (supreme religious guide) of Egypt and was appointed a permanent member of the Egyptian legislative council. In these positions, Abduh introduced a number of significant reforms, especially after his appointment to the *Al-Azhar* Administrative Committee of Egypt. His reforms included a return to a thorough study of the Quran and the *Hadith;* a reinterpretation of those fundamentals in light of modern developments; a reformation of Egyptian higher education; and protection of Islam against Christian and Western influences.

Throughout his life, Abduh also sought to liberate Muslims from the inhibiting doctrine of *taqlid,* urging them to interpret the Quran and the *Hadith* themselves with reason and rationality. Abduh also encouraged Muslims to read not only the classical Arabic works of theology and jurisprudence but also the works of Western scientists and intellectuals, which, Abduh insisted, were compatible with Islam.

In 1898, Abduh launched a monthly journal called *Al-Manar* (The Lighthouse) with the help of his student Rashid Rida. The dominant theme of this periodical was the reform and revitalization of Islam and Muslim society. *Al-Manar* became a major vehicle for propagating Abduh's liberal and modernist views on Islam.

Muhammad Abduh promoted many of al-Afghani's ideas, although Abduh's manner was more moderate, systematic, sustained, effective, and productive than that of his mentor. In due course, the Islamic reformations that he helped instigate in Egypt were taken up and championed by Rashid Rida and the *Salafiyyah* movement, which had been attempting to return to the ideals of the *salaf* (the generations that lived before the establishment of the principal Islamic sects in the classical period of Islam), and the efforts of these reform-minded disciples eventually adapted Islam to a rapidly changed world. Thus, Abduh shares with al-Afghani the august status as one of the two parents of Islamic modernism.

Sources: Charles C. Adams, *Islamic and Modernism in Egypt: A Study of the Modern Reform Movement Inaugurated by Muhammad Abduh,* New York: Russel & Russel, 1933; H. A. R. Gibb, *Modern Trends in Islam,* Chicago: The University of Chicago Press, 1947; Osman Amin, "Some Aspects of Religious Reform in the Muslim Middle East," in Carl Leiden, ed., *The Conflict of Traditionalism and Modernism in the Muslim Middle East,* Austin, TX: University of Texas Press, 1966; Mahmudul Haq, *Muhammad*

Abduh: A Study of a Modern Thinker of Egypt, Aligarh, India: Institute of Islamic Studies, Aligarh Muslim University, 1978; Ignaz Goldziher, *Introduction to Islamic Theology
and Law,* trans. Andras and Ruth Hamori, Princeton: Princeton University Press, 1981;
Suhail ibn-Salim Hanna, "Biographical Scholarship and Muhammad Abduh," *The Muslim World,* Vol. 59, Nos. 3–4, July–October 1969; James A. Bill and Carl Leiden, *Politics
in the Middle East,* 2nd ed., Boston: Little, Brown and Company, 1984; M. K. Nawaz,
"Some Aspects of Modernization of Islamic Law," in Carl Leiden, ed., *The Conflict of
Traditionalism and Modernism in the Muslim Middle East,* Austin, TX: University of
Texas Press, 1966; John L. Esposito, *Islam and Politics,* Syracuse, NY: Syracuse Uni-
versity Press, 1984; P. J. Vatikiotis, "Muhammad Abduh and the Quest for a Muslim
Humanism," *The Islamic Quarterly,* Vol. 4, No. 4, January 1958.

Because of Abduh's emphasis on reason and rationality, he considered Islam and
constructive science the twin offspring of reason, which "God gave us to guide us
in the right path."[170]

Muhammad Rashid Rida (1865–1935), an Egyptian disciple of Abduh, vigorously pursued his mentor's mission for Islamic reform. He urged the *ulama* to
come together, to exercise *ijtihad,* and to produce a comprehensive revision of Islamic laws based on the Quran and *Hadith.* He wanted the *umma* and Muslim
countries to progress and acquire the positive aspects of European civilization. He
exhorted Muslims to reclaim their glorious heritage; Islamic civilization had encouraged learning that resulted in the Renaissance.[171]

The famous Indian Modernist Sir Sayyid Ahmad Khan (1817–1898) maintained that a revitalized Islam was indispensable to the intellectual, economic, social, and political progress of Muslims (see Box 5.3). Sir Sayyid, like other Modernists, dismissed the contention of Sunni Traditionalists that the "gates of *ijtihad*"
had been eternally sealed a millennium earlier, and he vehemently denounced the
inhibiting force of *taqlid:*

> If people do not shun blind adherence, if they do not seek that light which can be
> found in the Quran and the indisputable *Hadith* and do not adjust religion to the sci-
> ence of today, Islam will become extinct in India.[172]

Although a devout Sunni, Sir Sayyid's idealization of *ijtihad* led him to accept
the Shi'ah belief that every generation must have its *mujtahids* (Islamic scholars
with authority to exercise *ijtihad*), with one significant reservation: He felt *ijtihad*
was not the exclusive right of a privileged few *ulama,* but the right of all devout
and enlightened believers. He believed that the benefits derived from diverse
opinions overwhelmingly outweighed possible errors of judgment and enhanced
Muslim self-esteem.[173]

---

[170]Ibid., p. 91.

[171]Hourani, *Arabic Thought in the Liberal Age, 1978-1939,* London: Oxford University Press. 1962,
reprinted in 1970, p. 236; D. E. Smith, *Religion and Political Development,* pp. 216–217.

[172]Bashir Ahmad Dar, *Religious Thought of Sayyid Ahmad Khan,* Lahore, Pakistan: Shaikh Muhammad Ashraf, 1957, pp. 113, 247–248, 264.

[173]Ibid., pp. 113, 247–248, 264.

Box 5.3 SIR SAYYID AHMAD KHAN

THE TORCHBEARER OF ISLAMIC MODERNISM
IN THE INDIAN SUBCONTINENT

Sayyid Ahmad Khan (1817–1898) was born into an Indian Muslim family closely connected to the Moghul court. His father was a disciple of a Naqshbandi mystic and his mother a follower of the traditionalist Islamic philosophy of Shah Abd al-Aziz. Sayyid Ahmad Khan was educated, both formally and informally, in a conservative, religious environment. However, when Sayyid Ahmad turned twenty-one, his father died, and the young man was forced to seek employment in order to supplement the family's meager income of emoluments from the Moghul court.

With the assistance of a relative, Sayyid Ahmad Khan found work as a record writer in the East India Company's court of justice at Delhi. In 1841, he rose to the position of a subordinate judge. In 1846, at twenty-nine years of age, he began to seriously study the Quran, the *Sunnah,* Islamic jurisprudence, and Arabic literature written by well-known Muslim divines. During this period, he wrote several works, including a biography of Prophet Muhammad; a short tract denouncing the relationship between sufi-saints and their obedient disciples as well as various un-Islamic practices prevalent in sufi orders; and a defense of the *Sunnah* and a denunciation of *bid'a* (innovation).

The severe British suppression after the failure of the Indian Mutiny (1857–1858) marked a watershed in the life of Sayyid Ahmad Khan. He was saddened and distressed by the punitive and retaliatory measures the British had taken against disaffected Muslims in rebellious regions. Sayyid Ahmad was also devastated when his home was plundered and his uncle and cousin murdered by Sikhs during the turbulent months of the Indian Mutiny. Consequently, Sayyid Ahmad transformed himself into an outspoken and dedicated reformer of Indian Muslim conditions.

As a judicious visionary, Sir Sayyid dedicated his efforts to reducing the distrust between Indian Muslims and the British. He reasoned that were the British to leave India, the country would lose a dominant central government able to prevent communal strife and Hindu oppression of Muslims. Therefore, he felt British-Muslim rapprochement was essential in the Indian subcontinent. To encourage Muslim loyalty to the British crown, Sir Sayyid founded the British-Indian Association in 1866. Meanwhile, he authored a number of apologetic works. One of the works denounced the Muslim royalty for neglecting the needs of the common Muslims. In a second volume, he attempted to soothe tensions between Muslims and the British by expressing gratitude to the British crown on behalf of loyal Muslim civil servants. In a third major effort, Sir Sayyid wrote a commentary on the Bible and the Quran, specifically highlighting their similarities and common source.

Sir Sayyid encouraged Muslims to abandon self-pity and futile denunciations of the British and to emulate the forward-thinking Hindus by learning English; acquiring Western education; seeking government jobs; and entering the professions of journalism, law, medicine, and engineering, and teaching. In essence, he urged Muslims to adapt to the realities of modern times.

In 1864, Sir Sayyid established a library and scientific translation society in Ghazipur to translate Western works into Urdu. This center also published a newsletter in both English and Urdu to enable the British to understand and appreciate the Muslims more fully. In 1875, Sir Sayyid founded the All-India Muhammadan Anglo-Oriental College at Aligarh (later called Aligarh College and finally Aligarh University). The dynamic and enlightened graduates of Aligarh College went on to lead the Muslim League, the Pakistan movement, and the new Islamic Republic of Pakistan in 1947. In 1885, Sir Sayyid founded the All-Indian Muhammadan Anglo-Oriental Educational Conference, dedicated to the active exploration of Islamic theology, history, culture, and civilization, and to assisting needy *madrassah*s and *maktab*s (Muslim elementary schools).

In his six-volume commentary on the Quran, Sir Sayyid argued that Islam was a dynamic and flexible faith fully compatible with science, technology, justice, freedom, and other enlightened and humane Western concepts. So committed to reason was Sir Sayyid that he discounted all superstition, mythology, fatalism, prejudice, and xenophobia. But Sir Sayyid's vigorous attempt to reconcile faith with reason was countered by the traditionalist *ulama*. Ironically, even the Aligarh College that he had founded refrained from promoting his religious beliefs.

Sir Sayyid's political and sociocultural accomplishments included encouraging Indian Muslims to learn English and study Western education; reducing British-Muslim tensions; discouraging Muslim cooperation with the Hindu-controlled Indian Congress Party; advocating and supporting separate electorates; and promoting the "two-nation" separatist concept. Today, he is credited as the initiator of India's Islamic renaissance. Consequently, his legacy and impact as a Muslim Modernist and one of the founding fathers of Pakistan are secure.

Sources: Lini S. May, *The Evolution of Indo-Muslim Thought After 1857*, Lahore, Pakistan: Shaikh Muhammad Ashraf, 1970; Bashir Ahmad Dar, *Religious Thought of Sayyid Ahmad Khan,* Lahore, Pakistan: Shaikh Muhammad Ashraf, 1957; S. M. Ikram, *Modern Muslim India and the Birth of Pakistan (1858–1951),* 2nd rev. ed., Lahore, Pakistan: Shaikh Muhammad Ashraf, 1970; J. M. S. Baljon, *The Reforms and Religious Ideas of Sir Sayed Ahmad Khan,* 3rd ed., Lahore, Pakistan: Shaikh Muhammad Ashraf, 1964; Mumtaz Moin, *The Aligarh Movement—Origin and Early History,* Karachi, Pakistan: Salman Academy, 1976; Freeland K. Abbott, *Islam and Pakistan,* Ithaca, NY: Cornell University Press, 1968; Edward Mortimer, *Faith and Power: The Politics of Islam,* New York: Vintage Books, 1982; Safdar Mahmood and Javaid Zafar, *Founders of Pakistan,* Lahore, Pakistan: Publishers United Limited, 1968; Safdar Mahmood, *A Political Study of Pakistan,* Lahore, Pakistan: Shaikh Muhammad Ashraf, 1972; Aziz Ahmad, *Islamic Modernism in India and Pakistan 1857–1964,* London: Oxford University Press, 1967; Ahmad Hassan Dani, *Proceedings of History Congress,* Vol. 1, Islamabad, Pakistan: Islamabad university Press, 1975; S. Moinul Haq, *Islamic Thought and Movements in the Subcontinent (711-1947),* Karachi, Pakistan: Pakistan Historical Society, 1979.

Another well-known Modernist of South Asia, Muhammad Iqbal (see Box 5.4), admired al-Afghani's ideas and tireless efforts for betterment of the *umma*. Iqbal criticized the Traditionalists for debating issues of abstract Islamic theory that had little relevance to modern life. He also scathingly attacked their belief that scientific, technical, and technological knowledge would corrupt and weaken Muslim society and undermine the faith. Iqbal pointed out that this misrepresented Islam. Afterall, there had been numerous Muslim scientists in the heyday of Islamic power who had not left Islam but had been inspired by it; they had helped the *umma* and spread Islamic influence.[174] According to Iqbal, it was Islam's dynamism that had made it a potent force in the world. However, he attributed both the decline of Islam as a dynamic faith and the decline of the Muslim world in the most recent centuries largely to the Traditionalists' insistence on stultifying conformity and orthodoxy. At times Iqbal denounced the conservative *mullah* (Muslim teachers and preachers): "For the shortsighted [and] narrow-minded *mullah* the concept of religion is to brand others as *kafirs*."[175] He believed the *mullah*'s obscurantist worldview served no other function than "sowing corruption, perverseness and disruption in the name of God."[176]

Iqbal, like the Modernists who preceded him, did not consider the *Shariah* sacrosanct, citing that it had been formulated by fallible *ulama* three centuries after the death of Prophet Muhammad. He appealed to devout Muslims schooled in Islam and modern Western ideas to apply *ijtihad* judiciously to revise the *Shariah* in the light of the Quran and *Sunnah*, and to meet the requirements of contemporary Muslim societies.[177] He believed *ijtihad* should reflect the opinion of society and meet its interests.[178] Iqbal reasoned that if the Quran were interpreted in an enlightened, rational, and liberal way, it could awaken individuals' higher consciousness in their relationships with God and other human beings, and assist people in the changing environment.

> Islam properly understood and rationally interpreted is not only capable of moving along with the progressive and evolutionary forces of life, but also of directing them into new and healthy channels in every epoch.[179]

Ali Shariati (1933–1977), a Shi'ah Modernist (see Box 5.5), Iranian sociologist, and revolutionary Islamic ideologue, followed in the footsteps of al-Afghani and Iqbal by criticizing the traditionalist *ulama* for promoting the "old-fashioned

---

[174]Allama Muhammad Iqbal, *The Reconstruction of Religious Thought in Islam*, Lahore, Pakistan: Shaikh Muhammad Ashraf, 1977, pp. 9–14.

[175]Quoted in Masud-ul-Hassan, *Life of Iqbal*, Vol. 2, Lahore, Pakistan: Ferozsons, 1978, p. 386.

[176]Ibid., p. 386.

[177]Abbott, *Islam and Pakistan*, pp. 166–167.

[178]Riaz Hussain, *The Politics of Iqbal: A Study of his Political Thoughts and Actions*, Lahore, Pakistan: Islamic Book Services, 1977, p. 42.

[179]Donald E. Smith, ed., *Religion, Politics and Social Change in the Third World: A Sourcebook*, New York: The Free Press, 1971, p. 73.

Box 5.4 MUHAMMAD IQBAL

ISLAMIC MODERNIST POET AND PHILOSOPHER

Muhammad Iqbal (1873–1938) was born in Sialkot, India. In his youth, Iqbal was an Indian nationalist who advocated Hindu-Muslim cooperation and collaboration in a united India. However, by 1909, the thirty-six-year-old Iqbal began to consider the desirability of separating the Muslim community from the Hindu one. He feared that Indian Muslims were in danger of losing their distinct faith, culture, and identity in a predominantly Hindu nation, and he became convinced that the Muslims of the Indian subcontinent should have their own nation-state. He defined the possible boundaries of this proposed Muslim state as incorporating Punjab, the Northwest Frontier Province, Sindh, and Baluchistan. He developed this concept further by describing a distinct Muslim nation based on a common language, history, race, and religion. Muhammad Ali Jinnah, the future leader of the Muslim League and of Pakistan, adopted the separatist ideas of Iqbal and of Sir Sayyid Ahmad Khan as his own and promoted "the two-nation theory," which became the justification for the new "Islamic" state of Pakistan.

While Iqbal had traveled and studied in the West, he remained critical of Western secular education and preferred the traditional Islamic education taught in *madrassah*s. Although impressed by the achievements of Western technology and of Western intellect, he disliked the excessive competition, selfishness, materialism, hedonism, and deterioration of spiritual values found in the West. Moreover, he denounced Western secular education for its lack of humanism, which is inherent in Islam. In Iqbal's view, Western education tended to make Muslims feel Islamic culture was reactionary, backward, and inferior to Western culture and civilization. Iqbal felt that Western technological, economic, social, and political advancements were admirable, but that secularization of Muslim societies was responsible for creating a spiritual void among Muslims, and for promoting the decay and decline of the Muslim world.

Iqbal was a famous poet, a philosopher, and a founding father of Pakistan. He conceived of the Muslim state in 1930 and encouraged the Muslim League leadership to pursue the establishment of such a homeland, inspiring millions of Indian Muslims through his poetry. In this manner, Iqbal played a pivotal role in fostering an Islamic revival on the Indian subcontinent and creating Pakistan.

Sources: Refer to Iqbal's "Presidential Address Delivered at the Annual Session of the All-India Muslim League at Allahabad on 29 December 1930" in Shamloo, *Speeches and Statements of Iqbal,* Lahore, Pakistan; Al-Manar Academy, 1948; Allama Muhammad Iqbal, *The Reconstruction of Religious Thought in Islam,* Lahore, Pakistan: Shaikh Muhammad Ashraf, 1962, reprinted 1977; Masud-ul-Hassan, *Life of Iqbal,* Vol. 2,

Lahore, Pakistan: Ferozsons Ltd., 1978; Riaz Hussain, *The Politics of Iqbal: A Study of His Political Thoughts and Actions,* Lahore, Pakistan: Islamic Book Services, 1977; Shameen Akhtar, "Iqbal's Concept of a New World Order," *Pakistan Horizon,* Vol. 30, Nos. 3–4; Wilfred Cantwell Smith, *Modern Islam in India: A Sociological Analysis,* London, 1946; Jamil-ud-Din Ahmad, ed., *Historical Documents of the Muslim Freedom Movement,* Lahore, Pakistan: Publishers Ltd., 1970.

way" of "believing without thinking" and discouraging new ideas.[180] When attacked by the conservative *ulama* as an agent of "Wahhabism," "Communism," or "Christianity," he noted that moribund and stagnant organizations generally defended themselves by engaging in character assassination of the agents of change.[181] When the denunciation of Shariati by the conservative *ulama* continued, he retorted that

> Islam had abolished all forms of official mediation between God and man. . . . We have scholars of religion; they do not constitute official authorities. . . . Islam has no clergy; the word clergy [*ruhaniyun*] is recent, a borrowing from Christianity.[182]

In his lecture "Independent Reasoning and the Principle of Perpetual Revolution," Shariati implored *mujtahids* to recognize the changed realities of the contemporary world and to meet the pressing demands with enlightened Islamic solutions. He understandably angered the *ulama* by promoting the idea that devout Muslims should not unquestioningly follow *mujtahids,* but should carefully assess the rationality of their opinions. Shariati argued that by blindly following *mujtahids,* Muslims were committing the sin of *shirk* (polytheism), which greatly undermines Islam's cardinal principle of *tawhid* (oneness of God).[183]

REFORMERS OF ISLAMIC THOUGHT AND PRACTICE

In addition to being devout Muslims who are knowledgeable about Islam, Modernists are also knowledgeable about modern non-Islamic (especially Western) ideas, to which they are exposed in their formal and/or informal education, either in their homeland or abroad. Most Muslim Modernists, including al-Afghani, Abduh, Sir Sayyid, and Shariati, have been filled with new ideas and insights after exposure to the West, and have been eager to introduce them into their own soci-

---

[180]Mangol Bayat-Philipp, "Shi'ism in Contemporary Iranian Politics: The Case of Ali Shariati," in Elie Kedourie and Sylvia G. Haim, eds., *Towards A Modern Iran: Studies in Thought, Politics and Society,* London: Frank Cass & Co., 1980, p. 156.

[181]See Ali Shariati, *We and Iqbal,* Tehran: Husainiyeh Irshad, 1979, p. 207.

[182]Ali Shariati, *On the Sociology of Islam,* Berkeley, CA: Mizan Press, 1979, p. 115.

[183]Abdulaziz Sachedina, "Ali Shariati: Ideologue of the Iranian Revolution," in John Esposito, ed., *Voices of Resurgent Islam,* Oxford and New York: Oxford University Press, 1983, p. 203.

Box 5.5 ALI SHARIATI

THE INTELLECTUAL FATHER OF MODERN REVOLUTIONARY SHI'ISM

Ali Shariati (1933–1977) was born in Persia, where he received solid grounding in the fundamentals of Islam from his father, who was an Islamic scholar and teacher, and from formal primary and secondary schools. On graduating from school, he joined his father's Research Center for the Propagation of Islamic Teachings in Meshad. There he wrote, lectured, and translated works from Arabic and French into Persian. While working part-time at his father's center, he completed a two-year teacher-training course at the Meshad Teacher's College, obtained his bachelor's degree in Persian literature at the Meshad Faculty of Letters, and taught at primary schools in a village near Meshad. While attending the university, he actively supported Prime Minister Muhammad Mossadeq (1951–1953) and became involved in demonstrations staged by nationalist and Islamic socialist groups protesting the overthrow of Mossadeq and the return to power of Muhammad Reza Shah Pahlavi in 1953 with CIA assistance.

Shariati continued his political activities for the next four years, and in 1957 he was arrested and incarcerated for a short time. In 1959, he traveled to Paris to pursue a doctorate in the sociology of religion at the Sorbonne. There he studied under liberal professors and read numerous works by and about revolutionaries. He remained politically active during this period, supporting the anti-imperialist Algerian and Iranian student movements. After completing his doctorate in 1964, Shariati returned to Iran and was jailed for six months for his antimonarchical activities abroad. After his release, Shariati lectured, wrote, and briefly taught in high schools and at the University of Meshad. In 1965 he established the Husainiyeh Irshad Research Center, where he continued to lecture and write prolifically.

In 1973, the Shah's regime reacted to Shariati's antigovernment rhetoric by closing his research center and once again jailing him. However, pressured strongly by domestic and international forces, the Shah's government released Shariati two years later. But Shariati was prohibited from lecturing or publishing again. Unhappy with this prohibition, Shariati fled Iran for London, where he soon died under mysterious circumstances. Many Iranians believe that he was killed by the SAVAK, the Shah's secret police.

Shariati believed that the central message of Islam was to fight for justice and freedom. For him the official Shi'ism of the Persian Safavid rulers and the later Pahlavi monarchs was a corrupted form of Islam, since it made no effort to alter an unjust, exploitative, and oppressive status quo. For Shariati, Shi'ism represented not only a metaphysical religion or a dogmatic theology, but a progressive and revolutionary religiopolitical ideology that emphasized protest, revolution, holy war, and martyrdom—all for the sake of justice and brotherhood.

Shariati also criticized the traditionalist *ulama* for promoting *taqlid,* which, he argued, was a form of *shirk* undermining Islam's fundamental principle of *tawhid.* The traditionalist *ulama,* in response, criticized Shariati's attack on the status quo, feeling that his extensive Western education would encourage him to distort and adulterate the fundamentals of Islam.

While Shariati had proposed to integrate Islamic concepts with Western social sciences in an effort to make Islam relevant in the modern age, he nevertheless criticized Westernized and secularized Muslims in Iran and the Muslim world. Shariati argued that foreigners had politically and economically exploited Iran and the entire Muslim world.

Ali Shariati, considered by many Iranians the intellectual father of the revolutionary Islam of 1979, was a lay Muslim Modernist who was inspired by the progressive Islamic theology and political activism of such men as Abu Dhar al Ghaffari, Jamal ad-Din al-Afghani, and Muhammad Iqbal. Shariati integrated their ideas in so creative and dynamic a manner that he profoundly influenced Iranian youth; his thoughts permeated the 1979 Islamic Revolution in Iran.

Sources: Ervand Abrahamian, "Ali Shariati: Ideology of the Iranian Revolution," *MERIP Reports,* Vol. 12, No. 1, January 1982; Hamid Algar, *The Roots of the Islamic Revolution,* Markham, Ontario: The Open Press, 1983; Suroosh Irfani, *Revolutionary Islam in Iran: Popular Liberation or Religious Dictatorship?* London: Zed Books Ltd., 1983; Mansour Farhang, "Resisting the Pharaohs: Ali Shariati on Oppression," *Race and Class,* Vol. 21, No. 1, Summer 1979; Abdulaziz Sachedina, "Ali Shariati: Ideologue of the Iranian Revolution," in John Esposito, ed., *Voices of Resurgent Islam,* Oxford and New York: Oxford University Press, 1983; Shahrough Akhavi, "Shariati's Social Thought," in Nikki R. Keddie, ed., *Religion and Politics in Iran: Shi'ism from Quietism to Revolution,* New Haven: Yale University Press, 1983; Soheyl Amini, "A Critical Assessment of Ali Shariati's Theory of Revolution," in Ahmad Jabbari and Robert Olson, eds., *Iran: Essays on a Revolution in the Making,* Lexington, Kentucky: Mazda Publishers, 1981; Nikki R. Keddie, *Roots of Revolution: An Interpretive History of Modern Iran,* New Haven: Yale University Press, 1981; Mangol Bayat-Philipp, "Shi'ism in Contemporary Iranian Politics: The Case of Ali Shariati," in Elie Kedourie and Sylvia G. Haim, eds., *Towards a Modern Iran: Studies in Thought, Politics and Society,* London: Frank Cass & Co., 1980; Ali Shariati, *Iqbal: The Architect of the Reconstruction of Religious Thought in Islam,* Tehran: Husainiyeh Irshad, 1978; Ali Shariati, *Religion vs. Religion,* Tehran: Husainiyeh Irshad, 1979; Ali Shariati, *Monotheism and Polytheism,* Tehran: Husainiyeh Irshad, 1980; Ali Shariati, *On the Sociology of Islam,* trans. Hamid Algar, Berkeley, CA: Mizan Press, 1979; Ali Shariati, *The Intelligentsia's Task in the Construction of Society,* Solon, Ohio, 1979; Ali Shariati, *Selection and/or Election,* trans. Ali Asghar Ghassing, Tehran: Hamdami Foundation, 1979; Ali Shariati, *Ommat va Emamat,* Tehran; Husainiyeh Irshad, 1968.

eties. In this respect, they have lived up to Iqbal's belief that, "The West's typhoon turned a Muslim into a true Muslim . . . [in the] way waves of the ocean nourish a pearl in the oyster."[184]

---

[184]Quoted in Hafeez Malik, *Sir Sayed Ahmad Khan and Muslim Modernism in India and Pakistan,* New York: Columbia University Press, 1980, p. 99.

Consequently, unlike the Fundamentalists and Traditionalists, Modernists do not fear or dislike Western ideas and practices. On the contrary, they welcome those non-Islamic ideas and practices that they consider beneficial to the progress and prosperity of Muslim societies. The Modernists imaginatively synthesize Islamic and Western ideas to produce a reasonable and relevant reinterpretation of Islamic thought with enlightened cosmopolitan, liberal, and realistic perspectives. Modernists believe this tolerance for diversity and willingness to adjust rapidly to a changing environment contributes to the emancipation of the individual Muslim and to the progress of Muslim societies.

When al-Afghani unofficially taught at *al-Azhar* in Cairo for eight years (1871–1879), he introduced his pupils to Arabic translations of Western intellectual and scientific thought and achievement. He encouraged his students to examine, analyze, and critique whatever they read; motivated and trained them to write and publish articles on a wide variety of subjects in order to influence public opinion; and coached them in the art of public speaking.[185]

In 1892, when Muhammad Abduh joined *al-Azhar*'s administrative committee, he successfully reformed the curriculum by introducing several courses in the modern natural and social sciences.[186] In 1899, Abduh became Egypt's grand mufti, and he used his authority as Egypt's supreme official interpreter of the *Shariah* to initiate the process of progressively revising Islamic law and reforming the entire court system. Three of his *fatwas* (authoritative legal rulings) were particularly famous. In one *fatwa*, he granted Muslims permission to eat the flesh of animals slain by Jews and Christians arguing that they were also "people of the Book." In another *fatwa*, he prohibited polygamy. He noted that although the Quran permits a man to have as many as four wives, it does not endorse this practice. Furthermore, as the Quran specifically enjoins husbands to treat all wives equally, Abduh felt this was a clear, albeit indirect, prohibition of polygamy, as he felt no man could treat two or more wives equally. In the third *fatwa*, Abduh strongly disapproved of the way *talak* (repudiation of marriage) was arbitrarily and unilaterally misused by Muslim men. He forcefully argued that the Quran orders the appointment of arbitrators in the event of "discord" between husband and wife. Since *talak* implies discord between the spouses, he reasoned, repudiation of marriage should not be permitted unless authorized by the court.[187]

Modernists are generally saddened by the discrepancy between the improved status of women during Islam's classical period and their second-class status in the Muslim world of the nineteenth and twentieth centuries. They would concur with Abduh when he said, "To be sure, the Muslims have been at fault in the education

---

[185]Charles C. Adams, *Islam and Modernism in Egypt: A Study of the Modern Reform Movement Inaugurated by Muhammad Abduh,* New York: Russel & Russel, First pub. 1933, Reissued, 1968, pp. 34–35.

[186]Ibid., pp. 70–78.

[187]M. K. Nawaz, "Some Aspects of Modernization of Islamic Law," in Carl Leiden, ed., *The Conflict of Traditionalism and Modernism in the Muslim Middle East,* Austin, TX: University of Texas Press, 1966, p. 74.

and training of women, and of acquainting them with their rights in our religion. . . . "[188] Shariati, for example, while he denounced the excessive independence, materialism, and sexual permissiveness of Western women, was equally critical of Muslim societies for not giving women adequate opportunities to grow, develop, and participate in all spheres of life. He offered the Prophet Muhammad's daughter Fatimah as a role model for women because she was an ideal daughter, wife, mother, and social worker.[189]

Sir Sayyid also argued that Islam encouraged monogamy, and that polygamy should be allowed only in specific and exceptional cases. He concurred with Abduh that certain types of interest were not "usurious" and, consequently, were permissible in trade and commerce. Sir Sayyid also noted that in the classical period of Islamic history, punishment by amputation of hand or foot was seldom, if ever, imposed, and urged that the practice be discontinued in the modern age.[190]

In order to popularize modern ideas among Indian Muslims, Sir Sayyid established in 1864 a literary and scientific translation society in Ghazipur for the translation of Western books (primarily in the natural and social sciences) into simple Urdu.[191] He also established the Muhammadan Anglo-Oriental College at Aligarh in 1875 after the pattern of institutions of higher learning in England. This college provided a modern education tempered with training in Persian, Arabic, and Islamic studies. Its graduates were well-rounded individuals who, as part of the Aligarh movement of enlightened and dynamic Muslims, played a starring role in the birth of Pakistan, and subsequently assumed elite roles in government, financial, political, and educational institutions.[192]

Sir Sayyid advocated the separation of the religious and secular realms in clear violation to the "organic" and holistic nature of conventional Islamic theory and practice. He justified his argument by referring to a *hadith* in which Prophet Muhammad himself is believed to have recommended that Muslims separate the secular and religious domains. In the *hadith*, the Prophet Muhammad is reported to have encountered some farmers who were pollinating some palm trees. The Prophet recommended that they abandon this practice. Following the Prophet's

---

[188]Quoted in John L. Esposito, *Islam and Politics,* Syracuse, NY: Syracuse University Press, 1984, p. 49.

[189]Sachedina, "Ali Shariati," pp. 220–221; Ali Shariati, *Fatima is Fatima,* trans. Laleh Bakhtiar, Tehran: The Shariati Foundation and Hamadami Publishers, 1980; Adele Ferdows, "Shariati and Khomeini on Women," in Nikki R. Keddie and Eric Hoogland, eds., *The Iranian Revolution and the Islamic Republic: Proceedings of a Conference,* Washington, D.C.: Middle East Institute in Cooperation with Woodrow Wilson International Center for Scholars, 1982, pp. 75-77, 81; Shanin Tabatabai, "Women in Islam," *Islamic Revolution,* No. 1, 1979, pp. 14–17.

[190]Michael Nazir Ali, *Islam: A Christian Perspective,* Exeter, England: The Paternoster Press, 1983, p. 108; James A. Bill and Carl Leiden, *Politics in the Middle East,* 2nd ed., Boston: Little, Brown and Company, 1984, pp. 50–51.

[191]Safdar Mahmood, *A Political Study of Pakistan,* Lahore, Pakistan: Shaikh Muhammad Ashraf, 1972, p. 124; Safdar Mahmood and Javaid Zafar, *Founders of Pakistan,* Lahore, Pakistan: Publishers United, 1968, p. 31.

[192]A. Ahmad, *Islamic Modernism in India and Pakistan,* p. 37.

advice, the farmers discontinued that method of pollination and gathered far fewer ripe fruit than before. On hearing this bad news, the Prophet reportedly remarked, "I am only a human being; if I order you to do sometime regarding your religion, you must accept it. . . . You know better in matters concerning your worldly affairs."[193]

One of many examples of a Modernist presenting a Western idea in an Islamic framework is Iqbal's recommendation to expand the scope and authority of *ijma* (consensus) to encompass not only the *ulama* but also the legislative assembly—comprised of elective representatives of the people—of the nation-state:

> The transfer of the power of *ijtihad* from the individual representatives of the [medieval] school of Islamic law to a Muslim legislative assembly . . . in view of the growth of opposing sects, is the one possible form *ijma* can take in modern times.[194]

Unlike the staunch Fundamentalists and Traditionalists, who often insist that devout and learned Muslims help formulate and ratify legislation, Iqbal wished to relegate the *ulama* to an advisory role, vesting the elected representatives of the people with the final authority of the modern-day nation-state's governance. They, in turn, would be required to legislate in a manner that would not contravene the basic "spirit of Islam." Interestingly, Iqbal's novel idea has now come to be accepted by a majority of Muslims.

Muslim Modernist Rashid Rida supported the concept of a progressive, liberal, and tolerant Islamic state in which non-Muslims would be treated in an exemplary way. Rashid Rida suggested the establishment of a "caliphate of necessity" to coordinate efforts of Muslim countries against foreign threats. He even envisioned the ultimate restoration of a genuine caliphate ruled by a wise, pious, and just caliph who would consult a broad spectrum of *ulama* and who would practice *ijtihad* before making decisions.[195]

ADVOCATES OF RECONCILIATION AMONG ISLAMIC SECTS

As Modernists are concerned about the divisions and frictions between the various *madhabs* (sects), they spend considerable effort advocating Muslim reconciliation and unity. Al-Afghani spent his entire adult life preaching pan-Islamism, minimizing Shi'ah-Sunni differences, and stressing the commonalities between the two major Islamic sects. In fact, al-Afghani, who was born into a Shi'ah family in the Iranian village of Asadabad, in his ceaseless effort to unite the worldwide

---

[193]Quoted from Sahih Muslim and said to have been reported by Prophet Muhammad's wife, Aysha, Rafi bin Khadij, and Moosa bin Talhah. Quoted in Ali Abdel Wahid Wafi, "Human Rights in Islam," *The Islamic Quarterly*, Vol. 11, Nos. 1 and 2, January–June 1967, p. 66; also see Dar, "Religious Thought," pp. 245–247.

[194]Iqbal, *The Reconstruction of Religious Thought in Islam*, pp. 174–176.

[195]Hourani, *Arabic Thought*, pp. 243–244.

umma concealed his Shi'ah heritage and alluded to having been born into a Sunni family in Afghanistan.[196]

Like al-Afghani, Shariati felt that the worldview of many Traditionalists and Fundamentalists accentuated the divisions in the "House of Islam." Therefore, he did his utmost to promote the *umma*, advocating the reconciliation and acceptance of various schools of Islamic *fiqh* to promote unity.[197] At times he angered the Shi'ah *ulama* by saying that the succession of Ali after Prophet Muhammad's death was merely a difference of opinion between the Shi'ah belief in *wisaya* (designation of Ali as Prophet Muhammad's religiopolitical successor) and the Sunni belief in *shura* (a group of knowledgeable and pious Muslims who engage in discussions and reach a consensus on important issues, including the choice of a leader). Shariati concluded that Shi'ahs and Sunnis were both correct, since both had valid and persuasive arguments to support their contentions.[198]

SUMMARY

The differences between Muslim Modernists and the Traditionalists and Fundamentalists are distinct. Nevertheless, each recognizes the other as truly Muslim. The Modernists, unlike the Pragmatists, are devout and practicing Muslims whose proclivity for Westernization and modernization is tempered by their hostility against secularization. The Muslim Modernists have struggled to reappraise and reform a comprehensive religion nearly fourteen hundred years old, so that they can find constructive and feasible solutions to the new problems of a dramatically changed socioeconomic and political environment. This extensive and difficult task, intensified during Islamic revivals, often has been pursued at the cost of many cherished beliefs and traditions and in the face of unrelenting opposition from the Traditionalists and Fundamentalists. However, the Modernists continue to offer innovative insights into the Islamic scriptures, emphasizing ideas that may have long been dormant in the substantive body of Islamic scripture. They believe their work will yield dividends for the entire *umma*.[199] (See the table following p. 151.)

---

[196]Nikki R. Keddie, *An Islamic Response to Imperialism: Political and Religious Writings of Sayyid Jamal ad-Din "al- Afghani,"* Berkeley, CA: University of California Press, 1983, pp. ix, 5–8; Keddie, *Sayyid Jamal ad-Din "al-Afghani,"* pp. 10–12, 427–433; M. A. Zaki Badawi, *The Reformers of Egypt,* London: Croom Helm, 1978, p. 7.

[197]Nikki R. Keddie, *Roots of Revolution: An Interpretive History of Modern Iran,* New Haven: Yale University Press, 1981, p. 220.

[198]Sachedina, "Ali Shariati," pp. 192–196.

[199]Abbott, *Islam and Pakistan,* p. 23.

Chapter
6
The Muslim Pragmatists

The fourth and least religious of the Islamic revivalists are the Muslim Pragmatists. Although they are Muslims by name and birth, most Pragmatists have had some childhood religious socialization, may cherish Islamic ideals and values, often identify with the Muslim community and culture, and are perceived as Muslims by non-Muslims. Nevertheless, the majority of Pragmatists were originally Secularists uninterested in "political" Islam. They are latecomers to Islamic revivalism and are sometimes reluctant Islamic revivalists.

The four most prominent Muslim Pragmatists who initiated Islamic revivals are Muhammad Ali Jinnah (1875–1948), Zulfikar Ali Bhutto (1928–1979), Muhammad Anwar al-Sadat (1918–1981), and Saddam Hussein (b. 1937). While a great deal has been written about these four, they have not been considered Islamic revivalists. Nevertheless, a careful reading of their lives reveals a transition from secular nationalism to "Islamic nationalism." By manipulating Islamic symbols and rhetoric, these former Secularists willingly or unwillingly unleashed Islamic revivals at home and/or abroad and entered the pages of Islamic history as Muslim Pragmatists.

NONRELIGIOUS MUSLIMS

While faithful to their Islamic allegiance, albeit sometimes without much theological grasp of its details, and fully aware of the basic tenets of their faith, Muslim Pragmatists often do not observe the ritual obligations incumbent on all Muslims, such as offering daily prayers, fasting during Ramadan, paying the annual *zakat*, and performing the *haj* at least once in a lifetime. Despite their nonchalant attitude toward the faithful observance of their religion, they return to it in moments of personal crises or when they find it necessary to conform to social or political pressure exerted by devout Muslims. The Pragmatists are nonpracticing Muslims who subscribe to a liberal and eclectic version of Islam. Frequently their faith is reduced to a few basic ethical, moral, and spiritual principles emphasized by Islam and other religions, such as equality, justice, liberty, freedom, honesty, integrity, brotherhood, tolerance, and peace. The Pragmatists' liberal and lax approach to Islam is decried by devout Muslims, who consider them "wayward souls" at best and "unbelievers" at worst.

Except for Sadat, who was religious in his childhood and behaved like a devout believer after he became president of Egypt, the other three Pragmatists—namely, Jinnah, Bhutto, and Saddam—were nonpracticing Muslims and never attempted to hide their lack of religosity (especially their lack of commitment to saying their daily prayers and their refusal to fast during Ramadan). Jinnah and Bhutto were known to imbibe liquor—a practice forbidden in Islam. In fact, weary of the opposition's charges that he was a drunkard, Bhutto surprised his audience in one of his public speeches by lifting a glass full of water and asserting that he only drank liquor and not people's blood. The implication of this comment was that while his drinking liquor was a harmless luxury which hurt no one, the riots fomented by his political opponents were causing unnecessary bloodshed.

In addition to violating the prohibition against drinking liquor, Jinnah disregarded Islam's injunction to take a spouse from among "people of the Book" (namely, a Muslim, a Christian, or a Jew) and married an Indian Parsee (Zoroastrian) instead.[200] However, while Jinnah's marriage to a Parsee is censured in Islam, Bhutto's womanizing and adultery are harshly condemned in the religion.

SECULAR POLITICIANS

Most Pragmatists have been educated in the secular Western tradition at home or abroad, and consequently they are more knowledgeable of and sympathetic to Western intellectual thought than to Islamic concepts. Their Western educational experiences encourage them to view classical and medieval Islamic doctrines and practices as anachronistic, reactionary, and impractical for today. Instead of taking the nostalgic Fundamentalist and Traditionalist stance that the "Islamic state" of Prophet Muhammad and the *Khulafah-i-Rashidin* was the golden age of Islam, the Muslim Pragmatists wish to modernize their societies along the lines of Western societies, and they believe that secularization is not only inevitable but desirable.

Bhutto and Saddam are known to have received a predominantly secular education in their home countries and abroad. Jinnah and Sadat, on the other hand, both attended *madrassahs* early in their lives and thus received some formal Islamic education at the primary school level.

---

[200]Jinnah's Indian Parsee wife, Ruttenbai Petit, did symbolically convert to Islam, but she remained a nonpracticing Muslim.

While studying at Lincoln's Inn in London to become a barrister, Jinnah (see Box 6.1) exhibited his secularist leanings by actively supporting an Indian Parsee, Dadabhai Nawrodji, who was running for a seat in the British House of Commons. Jinnah's commitment to secularism was further demonstrated when he joined the majority Hindu—though secularist—All-India National Congress Party in 1906. It was during this period that he became an admirer of the Indian Hindu nationalist Gopal Krishna Gokhale, so much so that he wanted to be a "Muslim Gokhale." Gokhale, in turn, hailed the secular and nationalistic Jinnah as "an ambassador of Hindu-Muslim unity" in the anticolonialist struggle.[201]

As an Indian nationalist in the Congress party (which had been boycotted by the Indian Muslim majority), Jinnah was critical of the Muslim League's demands for separate but equal electorates, and even convinced a number of Muslims to join his political party. In 1913 he joined the Muslim League, but he did so without adversely affecting his Congress party membership, which he held for the next seven years. In fact, in 1917 Jinnah called on Muslims to join with their Hindu brethren:

> To the Muslims my message is: join hands with your Hindu brethren. My message to the Hindu brethren is: lift your backward brothers up. In this spirit, let the foundation of Home Rule League be consecrated and there is nothing for us to fear.[202]

Generally, Muslim leaders would not refer to Hindus (who are considered polytheistic infidels in Islam) with such affinity. In the same speech Jinnah rejected the fear in the Muslim community that Muslim identity and culture would be undermined by the domination of the Hindu majority. He said: "Fear not . . . this is a bogey which is put before you to scare you away from the cooperation and unity which are essential to self government."[203]

Jinnah's secularism and his desire to cooperate with the Congress party leadership to resolve problems facing India were evident in a public speech in which he stated, "There is no difference between the ideals of the Moslem League and of the Congress—the idea of complete freedom for India."[204] Similarly, in his correspondence with Modernist Muhammad Iqbal, Jinnah usually avoided taking the religious positions that Iqbal urged upon him. Instead, Jinnah concentrated on the economic, political, social, and cultural plight of the Indian Muslims.[205] Even as late as 1931, Jinnah referred to himself as "an Indian first and a Muslim afterwards."[206]

---

[201]Quoted in Sarojini Naidu, ed., *Mahomed Ali Jinnah: An Ambassador of Unity*, Madras: Ganesh, 1918, p. 1.

[202]Nazir Ahmad Sheikh, *Quaid-e-Azam: Father of the Nation*, Lahore, Pakistan: Qaumi Kutub Khana, 1968, p. 32.

[203]Quoted in P. Moon, *Divide and Quit*, Berkeley, CA: University of California Press, 1962, p. 270.

[204]Quoted in Khalid Bin Sayeed, *Pakistan: The Formative Phase*, Karachi, Pakistan: Pakistan Publishing House, 1960, p. 84.

[205]C. M. Naim, "Afterword," in C. M. Naim, ed., *Iqbal, Jinnah and Pakistan: The Vision and the Reality*, Syracuse, NY: Syracuse University Press, 1979, pp. 184–189.

[206]Sharif al-Mujahid, *Quaid-e-Azam Jinnah: Studies in Interpretation*, Karachi, Pakistan: Quaid-e-Azam Academy, 1981, p. 18.

Box 6.1 MUHAMMAD ALI JINNAH

Muhammad Ali Jinnah (1875–1948) was the chief architect and founding father of Pakistan. Although Western and secular in his worldview, he infused the Pakistan Movement, which had been struggling for an independent Muslim homeland, with new life and vigor when he became its leader in the late 1930s. In less than a decade Jinnah brought about an unprecedented Islamic resurgence in twentieth-century India and carved from the Indian subcontinent the new "Islamic state" of Pakistan. His remarkable achievement, which still endures, establishes his place among the great leaders not only in the annals of Islamic history but in world history as well.

Born into a *Khoja* (an Ismaili Shi'ah sect) family in Karachi, India (now in Pakistan), Jinnah was the eldest of seven children of Jinnahbhai, a prosperous hide merchant. Jinnah's father wanted his eldest son to get a better education than he himself had received. Thus, Jinnah was admitted to the predominantly secular Gokaldas Taj Primary School in Bombay, to the religiously oriented Sindh *Madrassah* School in Karachi, and to the British missionary Mission High School in Karachi at age fifteen.

After graduating from high school at the age of sixteen, the precociously intelligent teenager was sent to England in 1892 to study business and to gain some practical business experience. Instead of business, however, Jinnah decided to study law at Lincoln's Inn in London. While pursuing his legal education, Jinnah developed an interest in the British political system, and he got his first taste of British democratic politics, secularism, and liberalism when he actively supported the Indian Parsee (Zoroastrian) immigrant Dadabhai Nawrodji, who won a seat in the House of Commons.

On becoming a barrister in 1895, Jinnah returned to Karachi in British-ruled India just in time to save his father from financial ruin. Jinnah was only twenty-one years old when he successfully defended his father in court. Delighted at his first major victory in the practice of law, the ambitious and gifted Jinnah left Karachi for the bigger legal arena of Bombay. It was there that he struggled in obscurity and poverty for three years at the Bombay High Court until one of his old friends introduced him to Bombay's Advocate General Mr. McPherson. As a result of that introduction, Jinnah got to read in McPherson's legal chambers and established a successful legal practice.

Having attained prominence and financial independence in the legal profession, Jinnah went back to his second passion—politics. In 1906, Jinnah joined the All-India National Congress Party partly because Nawrodji, his former mentor, had just assumed the organization's presidency for a third time. Jinnah served as Nowrodji's secretary and got to know all the leaders of the Congress party.

In 1910, Jinnah was elected to the Imperial Legislative Council. When the Indian Home Rule League was established in 1913, Jinnah became the chief organizer and president of its Bombay branch. The Muslim League leadership was so impressed with their politically successful and influential coreligionist that in 1913 they asked Jinnah to join the Muslim League, telling him he could retain his Congress party membership if he did so. A few months later, Jinnah clearly demonstrated his continued commitment to Indian nationalism over the more narrow parochial interests of the Muslim League when he led an Indian delegation to London to put the views of the Congress party regarding the Council of India Bill before the Secretary of State for India. World War I, which began in August 1914, however, postponed the consideration of the bill. In 1916, Jinnah was the moving spirit behind the Lucknow Pact signed by the leaders of both the Congress party and the Muslim League; this agreement provided for separate Hindu and Muslim electorates when India gained its independence.

In 1919, Jinnah was appointed to represent Bombay's Indian Muslims in the Imperial legislative council, but he resigned from the council later that year in protest over legislation to prevent "revolutionary activity." In 1920, he left the Congress party and the Indian Home Rule League because he disagreed with Mahatma Gandhi's use of Hindu rhetoric and symbolism in the civil disobedience movement against the British. Jinnah was just as unhappy with the Indian Muslims who were engaging in Islamic mass politics with the *Khilafat* and *Hijrat* Movements.

By the late 1920s, Jinnah's goal of establishing Hindu-Muslim unity was going nowhere. The Hindu Congress party was completely unwilling to give Indian Muslims separate electorates or to reserve some seats for them in the Indian legislatures. The Muslim League thought Jinnah remained a committed Indian nationalist, far more committed to the Congress' goal of Indian independence and secularism than to the League's demands for greater civil and political rights and privileges. Jinnah was also increasingly frustrated with the infighting within the Muslim League. When the Punjab Muslim League, a large and influential segment within the larger Muslim League, denounced Jinnah's accomodationist views—specifically his alliance with the Congress party—Jinnah was furious and disgusted. In 1930, a disillusioned Jinnah left India for London, disgusted with politics in the Indian subcontinent. He spent his time in London practicing before the Privy Council and monitoring politics half a world away in India.

Jinnah's elevation to the presidency of the Muslim League in 1934 and the talk of elections in the Indian subcontinent under the Government of India Act of 1935 brought the political activist home at last—to the place where all the action was. At the time, Jinnah was still dreaming of close collaboration between the Muslim League and the Congress party. But this dream was shattered just after the 1937 Indian provincial elections when the Congress party won landslide victories in the provinces comprising Hindu majorities; in the wake of this victory, the Congress party decided not to include Muslim Leaguers in the formation of provincial governments. For Jinnah and the Muslim League, that action led to a parting of the ways. From that time Jinnah was the moving spirit behind the March 1940 Lahore Resolution, in which the Muslim League resolved to form the separate Muslim state of Pakistan when India gained its independence. In the same year, Jinnah coined the term the "two nation theory," and he started working single-mindedly and relentlessly to create a separate homeland for Indian Muslims. He participated in three major constitutional meetings—in 1942, in 1945, and in 1946—that culminated in the partition of the Indian subcontinent and the establishment of an independent Pakistan on August 14, 1947. Jinnah was appointed the first governor-general of Pakistan and was officially given the title of *Quaid-i-Azam* (the great leader), but in September 1948, thirteen months after Pakistan's miraculous creation, he died at age seventy of tuberculosis.

Jinnah's mark on Islamic history is great. He initiated the conversion of the 1930s incipient Islamic revival into the Islamic resurgence of the 1940s, a considerable achievement considering the fierce opposition from the Congress party and its millions of Hindu followers, from the British colonialists who wanted to leave behind a united India, and from some influential Muslim Fundamentalists and Traditionalists who were against the secular nationalists leading the Pakistan Movement. Although Jinnah was aristocratic in his deportment; Westernized, secular, and pragmatic in his worldview; fluent in refined English but poor in Urdu; and wore elegantly tailored Western suits, he effectively managed to inspire, mobilize, and galvanize the Urdu-speaking and devout Muslim masses. In the end, Jinnah's determination, hard work, and perseverance paid off, and he realized his dream of creating a tolerant, moderate, and liberal "Islamic republic" only seven years after the passage of the Lahore Resolution.

Sources: Nazir Ahmad Sheikh, *Quaid-e-Azam: Father of the Nation,* Lahore, Pakistan: *Qaumi Kutub Khana,* 1968, p. 32; *Biographical Encyclopedia of Pakistan,* Karachi, Pakistan: Biographical Research Institute of Pakistan, 1969–1970; R. J. Moore, "Jinnah and the Pakistan Demand," *Modern Asian Studies,* Vol. 17, No. 4, 1983; Sarojini Naidu, ed., *Mahomed Ali Jinnah: An Ambassador of Unity,* Madras: Ganesh, 1918; Jamil-ud-Din Ahmad, ed., *Speeches and Writings of Mr. Jinnah,* Lahore, Pakistan: Shaikh Muhammad Ashraf, 1960; C. M. Naim, ed., *Iqbal, Jinnah and Pakistan: The Vision and the Reality,* Syracuse, NY: Syracuse University Press, 1979; Stanley Wolpert, *Jinnah of Pakistan,* London: Oxford University Press, 1984; Wm. Theodore de Bary, ed., *Sources of Indian Tradition, Volume II,* New York: Columbia University Press, 1958.

Although ecstatic at the creation of Pakistan through the use of the potent emotional message of "Islamic nationalism," Jinnah agonized over the bloody communal massacres spawned by both the Islamic resurgence and its equally powerful and reactionary Hindu response. The communal bloodshed reached its worst in 1947, when millions of Muslim refugees crossed the border into Pakistan and millions of Hindus crossed the border into India. Witnessing this painful event, Jinnah was determined to use the full weight of his charismatic personality to end the communal carnage and to allay the fears of all minorities (both non-Muslim and Muslim) within Pakistan. In August 1947, Jinnah spoke to the constituent assembly of Pakistan, which was responsible for framing the country's constitution:

> If you change your past and work together in the spirit that every one of you, no matter to what community he belongs . . . is first, second and last a citizen of this state with equal rights, privileges and obligations, there will be no end to the progress you will make. . . . You may belong to any religion or caste or creed—that has nothing to do with the business of the state.[207]

Hindus and Muslims were no longer considered two incompatible nations but religious communities that could and should get along as citizens of one state where all were equal in the eyes of the government and law. In fact, the last sentence of the above quotation implies that religion has nothing to do with the state—a rather clear espousal of secularism.

Jinnah may have believed that the "two-nation theory," which he had so eloquently and aggressively advocated in prepartition India, had outlived its utility. But rather than stating this, he alluded in his speech to how Roman Catholics and Protestants, who had fought each other for generations, live harmoniously as equal citizens of Great Britain.[208] He added,

> Now, I think we should keep that in front of us as our ideal and you will find that in the course of time Hindus would cease to be Hindus and Muslims would cease to be Muslims, not in the religious sense, because that is the personal faith of each individual, but in the political sense as citizens of the state.[209]

The ideological thrust of Jinnah's speech was entirely consistent with his general worldview throughout his long political career. Having failed to establish Hindu-Muslim unity in predominantly Hindu India, Jinnah was determined to succeed in the predominantly Muslim homeland of Pakistan. Having witnessed the insecurity felt by the Muslim minority in predominantly Hindu India, he did not want the non-Muslim minorities to suffer the same fate in the predominantly Muslim state of Pakistan.

As President Muhammad Ayub Khan's foreign minister from 1963 to 1966, Bhutto improved Pakistan's relations with the atheistic and communist nation of the People's Republic of China (PRC). After resigning from Ayub Khan's cabinet in 1966 and traveling through Pakistan, Bhutto realized that the general conditions in the country demanded a new socialistically oriented political party that would address the aspirations of the majority. In November 1967, he published

---

[207]*Quaid-e-Azam Mahomed Ali Jinnah: Speeches as Governor General of Pakistan 1947–1948,* Karachi, Pakistan: Pakistan Publications, n. d., pp. 8–9.

[208]Ibid., p. 9.

[209]Ibid.

the foundation documents of his new Pakistan People's Party (PPP); formulated such appealing slogans as "Islam is our Faith," "Democracy is our Polity," "Socialism is our Economy," and "All Power to the People"; and promised *roti, kapra,* and *makan* (bread, clothing, and shelter) to all Pakistanis.

A substantial portion of PPP documents was devoted to alleviating poverty through secular scientific socialism. Bhutto's support of Fabian socialism as the panacea for Pakistan was evident in most of his speeches and statements made at the end of 1967 and during much of 1968. In one such public address he said, "We have to tackle basic anomalies and no basic anomaly can be tackled without the application of the principle of scientific socialism. . . ."[210]

On another occasion, Bhutto wrote,

Only socialism which creates equal opportunities for all, protects from exploitation, removes barriers of class distinction, is capable of establishing economic and social justice. Socialism is the highest expression of democracy and its logical fulfilment. . . . Socialism is, therefore, of direct interest to Pakistan.[211]

And again in a public address, he said,

No power on earth can stop socialism—the symbol of justice, equality, and the supremacy of man—from being introduced in Pakistan. . . . I am a socialist. . . . Some ridicule me for being a socialist. I don't care.[212]

Like Bhutto, Sadat also flirted with socialism. Sadat was an Egyptian nationalist for much of his adult life. When he joined Nasser's Free Officers Movement in the late 1940s, he became a convert to Arab socialism. As a key member of Nasser's ruling circle for nineteen years (1952–1970), Sadat was wedded to Arab socialism, pan-Arabism, and secularism.

Saddam Hussein, another modern leader, became enamored with the secular ideologies of Arab nationalism, Arab socialism, pan-Arabism, and secularism in his impressionable teenage years, largely as a result of Nasser's influence. Having come to power in Egypt in 1952, Nasser had undertaken significant reforms in Egypt aimed at reducing Western influence. The Suez Crisis in 1956 further increased the political heat in the Arab world while propelling Nasser to the zenith of popularity. Meanwhile, socialist ideologies like Ba'athism and its outgrowth, Nasserism, came into vogue. Saddam, already predisposed to revolutionary nationalism, quickly adopted these ideologies as his own and became a committed activist in the Ba'ath party.[213]

---

[210]Bhutto's address to the Muzzaffargarh Bar Association on January 17, 1968, quoted in Żulfikar Ali Bhutto, *Awakening the People: A Collection of Articles Statements and Speeches, 1966–69,* in Hamid Jalal and Khalid Hasan, eds., *Politics of the People,* Vol. 1, No. 2, Rawalpindi, Pakistan: Pakistan Publications, p. 45 (henceforth referred to as: Bhutto, *Awakening the People*).

[211]Quoted in Bhutto, *Awakening the People,* pp. 94–95.

[212]Bhutto's address to the Sind Convention in Hyderabad on September 21, 1968, quoted in Bhutto, *Awakening the People,* p. 32.

[213]"President Saddam Hussein of Iraq," *MidEast Report,* Vol. 23, No. 16, August, 5, 1990, p. 2.

BELIEVERS IN THE SEPARATION
OF RELIGION AND POLITICS

Muslim Pragmatists are pleased that Islam (especially Sunni Islam, which the overwhelming majority of Muslims belong to) does not give a privileged status to the *ulama* in the governance of Muslim societies. Pragmatists iterate the view that there is no institutionalized clergy in Islam but that all Muslims are responsible to Allah for their deeds. While Muslim Pragmatists comprise the privileged class, they point to Islam's emphasis on equality and have an aversion to the formation of any privileged class (including a priestly one) that fosters elitism and encourages inequalities. According to the Pragmatists, the *ulama* are experts in the Islamic religion only and are therefore fully entitled to provide religious guidance in the affairs of the state. However, the Pragmatists contend that in economic, political, technical, international, and non-Islamic legal matters, the *ulama* have no right to impose their viewpoint on the nation.

Jinnah, for example, opposed mixing religion and politics. On more than one occasion he declared that religion was a private affair between man and God, whereas the state and politics was a public affair between man and man. Consequently, he objected to Gandhi's use of Hindu rhetoric and symbolism to mobilize Indian Hindus for his civil-disobedience movement against British rule. In 1934, Jinnah became the president of the Muslim League. Soon thereafter he gave a speech in the Indian legislative assembly in which he stated bluntly that religion should be dissociated from politics.[214]

On one occasion, while Jinnah was passing through a small town, a crowd chanted, "*Maulana* Muhammad Ali *Zindabad!*" (Long Live Maulana Muhammad Ali!). Being called a Muslim cleric so angered Jinnah that he stopped the car, pointed the index finger of his right hand at the crowd, and said, "Stop calling me *Maulana.* I am not your religious leader. I am your political leader. Call me Mr. Jinnah or Muhammad Ali Jinnah. No more of that *Maulana.*"[215]

Likewise, Bhutto had always embraced a secular worldview, and he espoused secularism as a politican. It was this secularism that endeared him to the minorities (non-Muslims, Ahmadis, and Shi'ahs) and to the nonpracticing Muslims who voted for him and not for the Islam-oriented parties in the 1970 national elections. But his secular worldview nevertheless troubled the influential Islamic parties. They criticized Bhutto and put him on the defensive in the 1970 and 1977 elections, and again in the civil disobedience campaign, which swept across the country after the rigged 1977 national elections.

Iraq's Ba'athist regime has been secularist since it came to power in 1968, at which point Saddam became its activist vice-president, and it has remained secularist since 1979 when he became president. Secularism is enshrined in Iraq's con-

---

[214]Speech delivered by Jinnah in February 1935; reproduced in its entirety in Jamil-ud-Din Ahmad, ed., *Speeches and Writings of Mr. Jinnah,* Lahore, Pakistan: Shaikh Muhammad Ashraf, 1960, pp. 1, 5.

[215]Quoted in Hector Bolitho, *Jinnah: Creator of Pakistan,* London: John Murray Publishers, 1954, p. 213.

stitution. The educational curriculum in all public schools, colleges, and universities is secular in its orientation. *Madrassah* education, on the other hand, is frowned upon as archaic and gets little government funding. The regime's policies and programs are usually secular. Non-Muslims have not been discriminated against in Ba'athist Iraq, and since Saddam became president in 1979, the country has even had a Christian foreign minister in the person of Tariq Aziz. Iraqi girls have always gone to coeducational schools, and women work shoulder-to-shoulder with men. Bars, nightclubs, discotheques, and pornographic literature have been allowed throughout Saddam's stay in power. In fact, except for a brief period during Operations Desert Storm and Desert Shield, the government has not permitted the mixing of religion and politics. Devout Muslim activists and Islamic Fundamentalists are called "terrorists" and are hunted down by Saddam's elaborate secret police apparatus.

INFLUENTIAL MEMBERS OF THE ELITE

Though a minority in Muslim societies, the Muslim Pragmatists wield a disproportionate degree of wealth and power and hold leadership positions in the influential institutions of their countries. They are in the upper echelons of their governments' civil service and armed forces. They are heavily represented in the mass media, in educational institutions, in the business community, among landlords, and throughout a broad spectrum of professions. They keep abreast of events in their country and in the world at large, and they comprise the most assertive and vocal segment of their societies.

Bhutto was part of this wealthy, powerful, and privileged elite from the time he was born (see Box 6.2). Jinnah rose into the privileged elite from his middle-class background with the help of his barrister's training and lucrative legal practice in India. Sadat and Saddam made it into the power elite from extremely humble beginnings through dogged determination, cunning, intuition, and luck.

SHREWD PROMOTERS OF ISLAMIC POLICIES AND PROGRAMS

Ironically, despite their essentially secular worldview and their firm conviction that religion is a personal affair between man and God, Muslim Pragmatists often find it expedient to promote and implement Islamic policies and programs to capture the support of the Muslim masses. The Pragmatists' use of Islamic programs allows them to gain or enhance their legitimacy, integrate and unite their fragmented societies, and inspire and mobilize the people.

Jinnah was disillusioned with the hunger for power exhibited by the Congress party leadership during and just after the 1937 provincial elections. Not only did these Congress-run governments exclude Muslim Leaguers from power, they also

Box 6.2 ZULFIKAR ALI BHUTTO

Bhutto was born into an aristocratic, wealthy, and politically influential landowning Sindhi family. He attended the Bishops High School in Karachi and the Cathedral High School in Bombay, an institution modeled on British public schools. During this time Bhutto became friendly with the children of Bombay's elite, who came from diverse religious and ethnic backgrounds.

Bhutto, whose influential father periodically played host to prominent Muslim leaders while he was growing up, was nourished on politics from an early age. As a teenager, Bhutto admired Jinnah, who at the time was spearheading the Pakistan Movement for a separate Muslim state in the Indian subcontinent.

After completing high school in 1947, Bhutto continued his education in the United States and England. He obtained a B.A. (with honors) in political science from the University of California at Berkeley, and then he went on to get his M.A. (with honors) in jurisprudence from Oxford University and, simultaneously, a barrister-at-law degree from Lincoln's Inn in London.

Bhutto returned home to Pakistan in 1953 and became a legal assistant to a successful and prominent Hindu lawyer in Karachi. On weekends, Bhutto often returned to the family estates in Larkana, and during some of his visits, his wife's father would organize *shikar*s (hunts) at which such nationally renowned personalities as H. S. Suhruwardy, Major-General Iskander Mirza, and General Muhammad Ayub Khan were occasionally in attendance. It was on these *shikar*s that Iskander Mirza came to know and like the young Bhutto. He found Bhutto to be brilliant, well-read, widely travelled and cosmopolitan. Since Iskander Mirza was then president of Pakistan (1956–1958), he nominated the young barrister in 1958 as minister of commerce and industries. When Ayub Khan deposed Iskander Mirza that same year in a bloodless military coup d'état, Ayub Khan retained his predecessor's entire cabinet. Within four years, the bright and dynamic Bhutto became in turn minister of information and national reconstruction; minister of minority affairs; and minister of fuel, power, and natural resources; and eventually he was asked to oversee the ministry of Kashmir affairs.

In 1963, President Ayub made Bhutto Pakistan's foreign minister. In this position, Bhutto started to decrease Pakistan's dependence on the West, worked to improve his country's relations with communist China, and gradually moved Pakistan into the nonaligned movement. Bhutto became popular in Pakistan when China supported Pakistan during the 1965 Indo-Pakistan War, a war which saw the United States halt arms shipments to both subcontinental combatants. The U.S. decision hurt Pakistan far more than India because Pakistan was heavily dependent on American weapons, while India was not. After the cease-fire, the Tashkent Declaration, which glossed over the Kashmir issue, triggered antigovernment demonstrations in a number of

West Pakistan's major cities. Bhutto, perceiving the mood of the country, denounced the Tashkent peace treaty as a "virtual surrender," and a few months later he claimed to have resigned over it. A rumor that Ayub was going to dismiss Bhutto from the government at U.S. insistence further enhanced his popularity among Pakistanis.

On his travels through Pakistan, Bhutto realized that the general conditions in the country demanded a new political party that would address the aspirations of the majority. He worked to develop this new party, which he named the Pakistan People's Party (PPP). The PPP promised *roti, kapra,* and *makan* (bread, clothing, and shelter) for all Pakistanis. Bhutto's support of Fabian socialism as the panacea for Pakistan was evident in most of his speeches and statements made at the end of 1967 and during much of 1968. However, in the next two years, Bhutto made a concerted effort to move away from secular socialism to Islamic socialism, and by the end of this period, he was injecting a heavy dose of Islam into his socialist message.

Bhutto won the 1970 elections in West Pakistan, while Bengali leader Sheikh Mujib-ur-Rahman led his Awami League to a landslide victory in East Pakistan. President Agha Muhammad Yahya Khan's military junta and West Pakistan's civilian politicians found Mujib-ur-Rahman's victory unacceptable because most West Pakistanis perceived Mujib's demand for East Pakistan's autonomy as striking at the very foundations of a united Pakistan. Bhutto along with other West Pakistani politicians urged Yahya Khan to prevent Mujib from assuming the leadership of Pakistan. Mujib retaliated by calling a civil-disobedience movement in East Pakistan, which escalated into a civil war.

While the nine-month-long civil war raged in East Pakistan (March 25–December 17, 1971), Bhutto served as Pakistan's deputy prime minister and foreign minister. After the Indian armed forces militarily helped East Pakistan secede from Pakistan and become Bangladesh, Yahya Khan relinquished the presidency to Bhutto on December 20, 1971. Since Pakistanis were in a state of shock and Bhutto was their first democratically elected leader since the mid-1960s, the charismatic Bhutto had the stage of Pakistan all to himself.

In 1971, Bhutto decided to introduce the parliamentary system in Pakistan and played an active role in fashioning a new democratic constitution in the Pakistani National Assembly (Parliament). On August 14, 1971, Pakistan's Independence Day, Bhutto signed the country's third constitution into law and assumed the position of prime minister.

Bhutto was socialistically oriented and believed in the redistribution of wealth. When in power, he nationalized industries, banks, and insurance companies, and he introduced land reforms that took land away from a number of *zamindar*s (very large landlords) and gave it to landless peasants.

In March 1977, Pakistan held national and provincial elections. Eight opposition political parties, constituting the Pakistan National Alliance (PNA), joined forces to defeat Bhutto at the polls. The PPP scored a landslide victory at the polls despite the mammoth crowds that the PNA had been drawing. The disillusioned and furious PNA accused Bhutto of election fraud and launched a civil disobedience movement to remove him from office. As the PNA's civil disobedience movement gathered momentum and threatened to plunge Pakistan into civil war, the Pakistani army led by General Muhammad Zia-ul-Haq intervened. On July 6, 1977, it overthrew the PPP regime, placed Bhutto in "protective custody," and promised to hold elections in three months.

When Zia released Bhutto from "protective custody" after three weeks, the deposed leader began actively campaigning for the October 1977 elections. The mistake Bhutto made, however, was to openly flout martial law regulations, to scathingly denounce the martial law authorities, and even to suggest retribution against the military leaders if reelected. The members of the ruling military clique began to fear for their lives when they saw the charismatic Bhutto drawing huge crowds. Zia-ul-Haq ordered the arrest and jailing of Bhutto in early September 1977, after hearing rumors of Bhutto's possible involvement in a plot to murder a former protégé turned bitter political foe, a plot in which the father of Bhutto's rival was killed. On March 18, 1978, Bhutto was sentenced to death by the Lahore High Court after being convicted of charges of conspiracy to murder his political rival. A week later, Bhutto appealed the death sentence to Pakistan's Supreme Court. In a split verdict of four judges in favor and four against, the Supreme Court upheld both the Lahore High Court's conviction of Bhutto in the murder case and its sentence of death. President Zia turned a deaf ear to pressure from home and abroad to commute Bhutto's death sentence. On April 4, 1979, Bhutto was secretly hanged at the Rawalpindi jail.

As Zulfikar Ali Bhutto's body was being put to rest in his hometown of Larkana, his thirty-six-year-old daughter, Benazir Bhutto, assumed PPP's leadership. She has won two free and fair democratic elections within the space of four years: once in 1988 and the second time in 1993. Those victories are an eloquent testimony to the power of a legend.

Sources: Salman Taseer, Bhutto: A Political Biography, London: Ithica Press, 1979; Dilip Mukerjee, Zulfikar Ali Bhutto: Quest for Power, New Delhi: Vikas Publishing House, 1972; Craig Baxter, Yogendra K. Malik, Charles H. Kennedy, and Robert C, Oberst, Government and Politics in Asia, 2nd ed., Boulder, CO: Westview Press, 1991; Shahid Javed Burki, Pakistan: The Continuing Search for Nationhood, 2nd ed., rev. and updated, Boulder, CO: Westview Press, 1991.

were perceived by Muslims as promoting Hindu ideas and ideals.[216] By the end of the 1930s, Jinnah, who had spent most of his political life attempting to preserve and protect the rights, interests, and culture of the Muslim community on the Indian subcontinent through peaceful dialogue with the leadership of the Congress party, became convinced that "the Congress Party was a Hindu organization dedicated to the establishment of Hindu *raj* (rule) in India and that it had no intention of developing a nonsectarian, genuinely liberal polity that might value the diversity of religious and cultural expression in India."[217]

Moreover, by the late 1930s the slogan "Islam in Danger" had become so loud that Jinnah, as leader of the Indian Muslims, could no longer ignore it. He too adopted the rallying cry of Islam and called for an "Islamic state." With this move, Jinnah's transition from secularist to Pragmatic revivalist was complete.

By 1938, Jinnah had come to believe that the Muslim League was not merely a political party representing Indian Muslims, but the standard-bearer of Islam in the Indian subcontinent. In the same way, Jinnah identified the Congress party as the representative of India's Hindu majority.

In 1940, Jinnah—who had become a supporter of many of the ideas and ideals of Muslim Modernist Sir Sayyid Ahmad Khan, Muhammad Iqbal, and the Muslim League in general—formulated the now famous "two-nation theory," a significant innovation in Islamic political theory. In this theory he maintained that the Muslims and Hindus were not merely members of two different religions, but of two comprehensive and entirely different belief systems that diverged completely, and whose adherents pursued two strikingly different and frequently antagonistic ways of life. Hindus and Muslims neither intermarried nor dined together, and they drew inspiration from different historical episodes and heroes. In fact, often the historical or cultural hero for one was the villain for the other.

In 1947, Jinnah told an audience of lawyers at the Karachi Bar Association that "I joined Lincoln's Inn because there on the main entrance the name of the Prophet was included in the list of the great law-givers."[218]

In 1968, Bhutto was profoundly offended that his opponents were accusing him of being a socialist and an atheist who was propagating an alien and secular ideology that would make Pakistan an "un-Islamic" society. In his defense, Bhutto claimed that the socioeconomic egalitarianism of socialism was deeply embedded in the "spirit of Islam." In fact, he often used the terms "socialism," "Islamic so-

---

[216]For instance, they encouraged the use of Hindi and discouraged the use of Urdu; compelled Muslim children in municipal and government schools to sing the Congress party's national anthem—a hymn entitled *"Bande Mahtaram"* (I Hail Thee Mother India) with strong anti-Muslim undertones; hoisted the Congress party flag on public buildings; and condoned discrimination against Muslims in a broad spectrum of government and nongovernment jobs (Hafeez Malik, *Moslem Nationalism in India and Pakistan,* Washington, D.C.: Public Affairs Press, 1963, pp. 334–335).

[217]Anwar Husain Syed, "Was Pakistan to Be an Islamic State? Iqbal, Jinnah, and the Issues of Nationhood and Nationalism in Pakistan," *The Indian Review,* Vol. 1, No. 1, Autumn 1978, pp. 38–39.

[218]Safdar Mahmood and Javaid Zafar, *Founders of Pakistan,* Lahore, Pakistan: Publishers United Ltd., 1968.

cialism," "*Musawat*" (equality), "Islamic *musawat*" (Islamic equality), and *Musawat-i-Muhammadi* (Prophet Muhammad's egalitarianism) interchangeably, thereby allaying public fear of socialism. Second, Bhutto maintained that he was merely emulating Pakistan's founding fathers—Modernist Muhammad Iqbal, Pragmatist Muhammad Ali Jinnah, and Pragmatist Liaquat Ali Khan—by espousing Islamic socialism.[219] Third, Bhutto emphasized that the first guiding principle of his party was "Islam is our Faith."[220]

The Islamic emphasis in Bhutto's Islamic socialism was noticeable in 1969 but became blatantly obvious during the 1970 election year. For instance, in his address to the district bar association in Hyderabad on June 26, 1969, Bhutto said,

> Islam is our religion. . . . We will sacrifice everything for Islam. . . . If you want to serve Islam, if you want to serve Pakistan, then serve the Muslims of Pakistan. . . . Islam emphasized . . . equality [more] than . . . anything else. . . . We cannot see equality in Pakistan. We want to create equality but when we talk of equality, of socialism, we are dubbed anti-Islamic.[221]

At a public speech in Liaquat Gardens, in Rawalpindi, on January 17, 1970, Bhutto said:

> We are first Muslims and then Pakistanis . . . our foremost principle is 'Islam is our religion.' We are prepared to offer any sacrifice for the glory of Islam. . . . In Islam, socioeconomic equality or *Musawat* has been given highest priority. . . . We shall, therefore, bring about *Musawat*.[222]

In the 1970 PPP election manifesto, Bhutto declared that his party's ultimate objective was the creation of a classless society that would ensure the true equality of Pakistanis. Since this aim was deeply embedded in the socioeconomic and political philosophy of Islam, Bhutto felt that the PPP was merely striving to implement the noble ideals of the Islamic faith.[223] On one occasion, he stated, "Just as democracy is an English word for *jumhuriet*, similarly socialism means nothing but *Musawat*. Islam is the greatest champion of *Musawat*, and this equality my party wants to establish."[224] On another occasion, he said, "Islam was the first religion to give a message of equality for everyone. That is why we want Islamic equality to be established. . . ."[225]

---

[219]See Bhutto's speech at Charsada on April 29, 1970, which has been documented in Zulfikar Ali Bhutto, *Marching Towards Democracy: A Collection of Articles, Statements and Speeches 1970–71*, edited by Hamid Jalal and Khalid Hasan, Vol. 3, Rawalpindi, Pakistan: Pakistan Publications, pp. 91–92 (henceforth referred to as Bhutto, *Marching Towards Democracy*).

[220]See Bhutto's writings on the "Political Situation in Pakistan," published in April 1968 in Bhutto, *Awakening the People*, p. 95.

[221]Bhutto, *Awakening the People*, p. 240.

[222]Bhutto, *Marching Towards Democracy*, pp. 10–11.

[223]"Pakistan People's Party," *The Election Manifesto*, Lahore, Pakistan, 1970, p. 1.

[224]Bhutto's public meeting in Jhelum on January 21, 1970, quoted in Meenakshi Gopinath, *Pakistan in Transition: Political Development and Rise to Power of the Pakistan People's Party*, New Delhi: Manohar Book Service, 1975, p. 67.

[225]Bhutto's speech to a public gathering in Abbottabad on April 19, 1970, quoted in Bhutto, *Marching Towards Democracy*, p. 63.

When the mass media and the general public began to refer to the three Islamic political parties as Islam *pasand* (literally, those who like Islam), Bhutto claimed that PPP members not only *liked* Islam, but *loved* it.[226] Subsequently, when the Islam *pasand* parties tried to turn the masses against Bhutto's socialism by raising the slogan "Islam in Danger," the PPP retaliated with the slogan "Capitalism in Danger." The PPP's slogan rallied the poor majority, who had witnessed the gap between the rich and the poor widen during the Ayub era of capitalism (1958–1969).[227]

In December 1971, after the dismemberment of Pakistan and the birth of Bangladesh in what was formerly East Pakistan, West Pakistanis underwent a profound identity crisis, and a strong Islamic current emerged in the rump Pakistan (West Pakistan). Bhutto correctly assessed the growing Islamic mood in the country and took a number of steps to please his countrymen. For instance, Bhutto encouraged and approved the 1973 constitution which was far more Islamic than the two previous constitutions.

To appease and undercut the powerful Islamic interest groups in the country, Bhutto also instituted a number of Islamic measures. Between 1973 and 1976, Bhutto approved an act of parliament classifying the Ahmadis as a non-Muslim minority despite the fact that they had actively supported and voted for him in the December 1970 elections (see Box 6.3); changed the name of the Red Cross to the Red Crescent, thereby symbolically, although superficially, Islamizing the humanitarian organization in Pakistan;[228] ordered copies of the Quran to be placed in all the rooms of first-class hotels throughout Pakistan; established a Ministry of Religious Affairs;[229] encouraged the national radio and television stations to increase the number of religious programs; promoted Arabic instruction in schools and on radio and television;[230] provided increased facilities for the separate Islamic instruction of Shi'ah and Sunni children in all schools; sponsored an international conference on the life and work of Prophet Muhammad; removed quota restrictions imposed on those wanting to go to perform the *haj;* increased pilgrims' foreign exchange allowance; and saw to it that more ships and planes were made available during the *haj* season to transport pilgrims to and from Saudi Arabia.[231]

In his desire to win over the hearts of the Sindhi and Punjabi village folk, who revered their *pirs* and saints, Bhutto ordered ornate gilded doors from Iran to be placed at the entrance of two very popular shrines in Pakistan: one at Shahbaz Qalander in Sewan (Sindh) and the other at Data Ganj Bakhsh in Lahore (Punjab).

---

[226]Gopinath, *Pakistan in Transition,* p. 80.

[227]Ibid., p. 80.

[228]Zulfikar Ali Bhutto, *My Execution,* London: Musawat Weekly International, January 1980, p. 1.

[229]A. H. Syed, *Pakistan: Islam, Politics and National Solidarity,* New York: Praeger Publishers, 1982, p. 126.

[230]Within a very short space of time, numerous privately owned Arabic tutorial centers sprang up throughout the country, and Arabic began to be taught in the Open University broadcast on radio and television once a week.

[231]Syed, *Pakistan,* p. 126.

In addition, he invited to Pakistan the *imam* (prayer leader) of the Prophet's mosque in Madina and later the *imam* of the mosque at the *Ka'aba*.

In foreign policy, Bhutto embarked on what he called a "journey of renaissance," which took him to twenty predominantly Muslim countries (most of them in the Middle East). His "journey among brothers" greatly improved Pakistan's relations with the Muslim world.[232]

During the Arab-Israeli War of October 1973, Bhutto supported the Arabs diplomatically and materially.[233] He instructed Pakistan's U.N. delegation to assist other Muslim delegations in the *umma's* common cause against Israel. Bhutto's regime dispatched doctors and nurses to Egypt and Syria,[234] sent Pakistani pilots to assist the Syrian air force, and kept a few army battalions on alert in the event Damascus was attacked.[235]

As a result of Pakistan's espousal of Arab and Islamic causes since the nation's inception and, especially, under Bhutto's leadership, Pakistan was nominated as host of the Second Islamic Summit Conference in Lahore. Because of Bhutto's careful orchestration and the propitious political climate in the Muslim world, the Lahore Summit was not only the largest gathering of its kind in the post-World War II period but was also very successful.[236] The summit enhanced Pakistan's stature in the world, made Bhutto one of the most popular figures in the Muslim world, facilitated Pakistan's export of manpower to and inflow of remittances from the Middle East, and dramatically increased aid to Pakistan from the oil-rich Muslim countries.

In Bhutto's opinion, his "greatest achievement," however, was as the architect of Pakistan's nuclear energy program and the father of the yet-to-be-exploded "Islamic Bomb."[237] In a book entitled *If I Am Assassinated*, published in India, Bhutto wrote:

---

[232]See Z. A. Bhutto, *A Journey of Renaissance*, Islamabad, Pakistan: Government of Pakistan's Ministry of Information, November 1972, p. 7.

[233]See Bhutto's press statement made in Karachi on October 20, 1973, and quoted in *Prime Minister Zulfikar Ali Bhutto: Speeches and Statements, August 14, 1973–December 31, 1973*, Karachi, Pakistan: Department of Films and Publications, Government of Pakistan, 1973, pp. 126–127.

[234]*Pakistan Times*, Rawalpindi, 13 October, 1973, p. 1.

[235]M. G. Weinbaum and Gautam Sen, "Pakistan Enters the Middle East," *Orbis*, Vol. 22, No. 3, Fall 1978, p. 600.

[236]Rafiq Akhtar, ed., *Pakistan Year Book*, Karachi, Pakistan: East-West Publishing Company, 1974, pp. 122–125. Bhutto made a particular effort to ensure attendance of the distinguished guests by sending special Pakistani envoys to persuade leaders to attend the conference. Because disputes had arisen over the agenda at the First Islamic Summit Conference, Bhutto made sure that the agenda for the Lahore Summit was carefully prepared so that it won unanimous approval. The biggest reason for the success of the summit was the fact that the Muslim world was ecstatic over both a perceived victory in the 1973 Arab-Israeli War and the Muslim-dominated OPEC's oil-price increases.

[237]Rafiq Akhtar, ed., *Pakistan Year Book, 1976*, Karachi, Pakistan: East-West Publishing Company, 1976, p. 299.

Box 6.3 AHMADIS OR QADIANIS

The Ahmadis are an offshoot of Sunni Islam. The sect was founded by Mirza Ghulam Ahmad (1837–1908), who was born in a village in the Indian Punjab called Qadian (thus Ahmadis are also called Qadianis). He wrote the *Barahin-i-Ahmadiya* (Arguments of the Ahmadiya) in the 1880s. Subsequently, he claimed to have received a series of revelations from God and proclaimed himself to be the Mahdi, the second Christian Messiah, an incarnation of the Hindu god Krishna, and the *buruz* (reappearance) of Prophet Muhammad. In 1901, he founded the *Jamaat-i-Ahmadiya* (Ahmadiya Society), and had it listed as a separate Islamic sect in the official census of the Indian government. He died in 1908, leaving behind a body of theology that differs fundamentally from that of mainstream Muslims.

Mirza Ghulam Ahmad was succeeded by Khalifah Maulvi Nur-ud-Din, who died in 1914. The founder's son Mirza Bashir al-Din Mahmud Ahmad was chosen then as the second *khalifah*. This group, calling itself the "True Ahmadis" or "Qadianis," believes in Mirza Ghulam Ahmad's claim to prophethood (unlike Muslims, who regard Muhammad as the last prophet). Another group, led by Khwaja Kamal-ud-Din and Maulvi Muhammad Ali, seceded, forming the Lahori Party. This group renamed itself *Ahmadiya Anjuman-i-Isha'at-i-Islam* (Ahmadi Society for the Propagation of Islam), insisting that Mirza Ghulam Ahmad had never claimed to be the promised Messiah but that he was a great *mujaddid* (renewer of the faith) instead. All Ahmadis, on Mirza Ghulam Ahmad's instructions, have renounced military *jihad* as inhumane and sinful, but consider peaceful proselytization as a sacred duty. In 1947, with the creation of Pakistan, they officially relocated from Qadian to Rabwah (near Lahore), although they still make pilgrimages to Qadian. They number from five hundred thousand to one million and are reportedly well organized.

In Pakistan, the *Jamaat-i-Islami,* the *Majlis-i-Tahfuz-i-Khatm-i-Nabuwwat* (Council for Defending Prophet Muhammad's Finality), and the *Majlis-i-Ihmam-i-Islam* (Council of Islamic Freedom Fighters) have been in the vanguard of the anti-Ahmadi movement. In 1953, for instance, the *Jamaat-i-Islami's* Maududi wrote a pamphlet called *Qadiani Mas'ala* (The Qadiani Question), in which he attempted to prove that the Qadianis were non-Muslims and called for "excising the Qadiani cancer" (i.e., the Qadiani beliefs) from Pakistan. Besides distributing anti-Qadiani literature, Maududi actively sought the help of other *ulama* in his crusade to declare Qadianis non-Muslims and have them removed from all influential positions in government. The anti-Ahmadi campaign resulted in demonstrations and riots in the major cities of the Punjab, many deaths, and extensive destruction of Ahmadi property. It eventually was controlled in 1953 by the imposition of martial law in the Punjab; the jailing of many Muslim zealots, including Maududi; and a court inquiry presided over by secular Chief Justices Muhammad Munir and M. R. Kayani, who, in 1954, published a report on the Punjab disturbances that warned against the danger of zealots exploiting Islam.

The Ahmadi question erupted again twenty years later with the *Jamaat-i-Islami* once more in the vanguard. In May and June of 1974, anti-Ahmadi demonstrations resulted in widespread rioting, destruction of Ahmadi property, and the loss of innocent lives. Bhutto resisted using the Pakistani army to restore law and order because he feared the army might overthrow him. He also wanted to neutralize criticism that he was a nonpracticing Muslim and a secularist. In order to appease the Muslim Fundamentalists and Traditionalists, the Bhutto regime agreed to pass a constitutional amendment through the National Assembly in 1974 declaring the Ahmadis a non-Muslim minority in Pakistan.

In the late seventies and eighties, the anti-Ahmadi movement of the *Majlis-i-Tahfuz-i-Khatm-i-Nabuwwat* received help from Zia's government. Zia accelerated the purge of Ahmadis from influential positions in the army and the civil service, and decreed that for election purposes they had been allotted non-Muslim seats in the *Majlis-i-Shura* (National Assembly). In April 1984, Zia delivered an ordinance prohibiting the Ahmadis from calling their prayer houses *masjid*s (mosques), from giving *adhan* (the call to prayer), and from using Islamic terminology. The ordinance won overwhelming support from most of the nation's *ulama* and political parties.

Sources: *The Encyclopedia of Islam,* rev. ed., Leiden, Netherlands: E. J. Brill, 1960; H. A. R. Gibb and J. H. Kramers, *Shorter Encyclopaedia of Islam,* Leiden, Netherlands: E. J. Brill, 1974; *The New Encyclopedia Britannica,* 15th ed., Chicago: Encyclopaedia Britannica, Inc., 1984; Asghar Ali Engineer, *Islam—Muslims—India,* Bombay: Lok Vang Maya, 1975, pp. 70–71, 74; *Report of the Court of Inquiry Constituted Under Punjab Act 11 of 1954 to Enquire into the Punjab Disturbances of 1953,* Lahore, Pakistan: Government of Pakistan, 1953.

We know that Israel and South Africa have full nuclear capability. The Christian, Jewish and Hindu civilizations have the capability. The Communist powers also possess it. Only the Islamic civilization was without it, but that position was about to change.[238]

Circumstantial evidence suggests that Bhutto promised to share Pakistan's nuclear technology with his Arab benefactors once his country had built the "Islamic Bomb" with their money. Israel's past military successes and probable nuclear capability helped Bhutto convince the Arabs that the existence of an "Islamic Bomb" would not only deter Israel from ever using its nuclear arsenal against the Arabs but also dissuade it from invading and occupying more Arab

---

[238]Zulfikar Ali Bhutto, *If I Am Assassinated,* New Delhi: Vikas Publishing House, 1979, p. 137.

land. Moreover, Bhutto firmly believed and was able to convince his Arab friends that with the "Islamic Bomb," the Islamic bloc would no longer be weak and vulnerable; rather it could reassert itself as an influential power in international affairs.[239]

In June 1977, Bhutto alleged that foreign agents (especially the CIA) and pro-Western opposition forces were conspiring to overthrow him to prevent the completion of the "Islamic Bomb." These accusations were intended to make Bhutto a martyr should he be killed, dying in the honorable cause of Islam.[240] This readiness to die for Islam further enhanced his Islamic credentials.

Bhutto's Islamic credentials also helped shore up the Pakistani economy. Using the politics of Islam, Bhutto was able to make Pakistani manpower one of the country's major export items, bringing in nearly 48.9 percent of Pakistan's foreign exchange earnings by the fiscal year 1977–1978, compared to only 15.1 percent in the fiscal year 1974–1975.[241] By 1977, according to an International Monetary Fund (IMF) report, Pakistan topped the list of labor-exporting countries both in numbers of workers, which was estimated at over 500,000, and in volume of remittances, which was estimated at $1 billion—nearly double its 1976 figure of $590 million.[242]

Bhutto's same policies generated increased Middle Eastern grants, loans, and investments, as well as oil at concessionary prices. Statistics reveal that prior to Bhutto's assumption of power, foreign aid to Pakistan from Muslim countries was inconsequential. Starting in 1974, Pakistan became one of the prime recipients of aid from the oil-rich Muslim countries. By the end of 1976, foreign assistance to Pakistan, mainly from the Middle East, contributed about half of the approximately $1.7 billion Pakistani development budget.[243]

PPP's 1977 election manifesto contained none of the socialist rhetoric that had characterized PPP ideology when the party was founded. While socialism and even "Islamic socialism" were underplayed both in the 1977 election manifesto and in the party's official pronouncements, Islam (minus socialism) was prominently highlighted. The manifesto promised to:

---

[239]Steve Weissman and Herbert Krosney, *The Islamic Bomb: The Nuclear Threat to Israel and the Middle East*, New York: Times Books, 1981, pp. 53, 62–64

[240]On April 28, 1977, Bhutto made a dramatic and impassioned speech to Pakistan's National Assembly, in which he said that U.S. Secretary of State Henry Kissinger, on a visit to Pakistan on August 8, 1976, had personally threatened him (Bhutto) to drop Pakistan's plans to build the atomic bomb, saying if he did not, "Carter, if he comes to power, will make a horrible example of your country" (*Dawn*, April 29, 1977, p. 1; Salamat Ali, "The Options Finally Run Out," *The Far Eastern Economic Review*, July 1, 1977, p. 8).

[241]Jamil Rashid, "The Political Economy of Manpower Export," in Hassan Gardezi and Jamil Rashid, eds., *Pakistan, The Roots of Dictatorship: The Political Economy of a Praetorian State*, London: Zed Press, 1983, p. 222.

[242]*Dawn Overseas Weekly*, January 6, 1979, p. 3.

[243]Weinbaum and Sen, "Pakistan Enters the Middle East," p. 603.

hold high the banner of Islam;. . . ensure that Friday is observed as the weekly holiday instead of Sunday . . . making the teaching of the Holy Quran an integral part of eminence as a center of community life; . . . [and] establish a federal *Ulama* academy. . . .[244]

During the spring 1977 election campaign in Pakistan, Bhutto sensed the Islamic thrust of his opposition—the eight opposition political parties constituting the Pakistan National Alliance (PNA)—and instructed the PPP rank and file to drop references to "Islamic socialism." Instead, he told his PPP candidates to use the appealing term of *Musawat-i-Muhammadi* (Prophet Muhammad's Egalitarianism), to stress the regime's service to Islam in domestic as well as foreign policy during the previous six years (with particular emphasis on Bhutto's role as chairperson of the successful Islamic summit conference in Lahore), and to promise to do much more for the cause of Islam if reelected.[245]

The PPP's overwhelming election victory, despite the PNA candidates' success in drawing mammoth crowds during the election campaign, infuriated the PNA. The PNA demanded that Bhutto resign or hold new elections. When Bhutto refused to do either, the PNA launched a civil disobedience campaign. Bhutto reacted by announcing a series of Islamic measures in his press conference on April 17, 1977, including the immediate prohibition of alcohol in the country, a ban on all forms of gambling, and the closure of nightclubs. In addition, the Islamization of the Pakistani civil and criminal laws was to be completed in six months instead of the four years allowed by the 1973 constitution, and the Council of Islamic Ideology responsible for the introduction of *Shariat* law was to be reconstituted to include leaders of three Islamic political parties. These moves only heightened the Islamic revival sweeping Pakistan and emboldened Bhutto's opposition.

When Bhutto's attempt to appease the PNA with Islamic measures met with little or no success, he imposed martial law, placed tighter censorship on the media, and jailed hundreds of people who opposed his regime.[246] However, when the use of force also failed to crush the opposition movement, Bhutto once again resorted to the "Islamic card" and called on the leaders of the Muslim world to help. Saudi Arabia's ambassador to Pakistan and the foreign ministers of the United Arab Emirates (UAE), Kuwait, and Libya were asked by their governments to do all they could to resolve the differences between the Pakistani political parties in the "spirit of Islamic solidarity and brotherhood." This "Islamic Solidarity Committee" provided a face-saving way for both the PPP-led government and the

---

[244]"PPP Manifesto: Text of Third Chapter," *Dawn* (Karachi), January 26, 1977, p. 4.

[245]William L. Richter, "The Political Dynamics of Islamic Resurgence in Pakistan," *Asian Survey*, Vol. 19, No. 6, June 1979, p. 551; "A Great Manifesto," *Baluchistan Times*, January 26, 1977.

[246]William Border, "Bhutto in Crackdown on Critics Orders Martial Law for Three Cities," *New York Times*, April 22, 1977, p. 1.

PNA-led opposition to negotiate issues. Arab mediators also promised financial assistance for new elections.[247] Although compromise was almost reached, the PNA central council, sensing victory, rejected the deal that they and the PPP had tentatively approved. With the failure of PPP–PNA negotiations, violence intensified and the Pakistani army overthrew Bhutto's regime.[248]

Like Bhutto, Anwar al-Sadat (see Box 6.4) was a wily manipulator of Islamic politics. Sadat assumed the presidency of Egypt after Nasser's death in 1970. He was a compromise candidate and perceived as manipulable by the left wing and right wing members of Nasser's inner circle. To remain in power, Sadat neutralized the more powerful secular and pro-Soviet leftists. Sadat freed many *Ikhwan* activists from prison[249] and encouraged exiled leaders of the *Ikhwan* to return to Egyptian public life and publicize their cause. He even permitted the *Ikhwan* to recruit new members and to support indirectly candidates for parliament (but not to campaign under the name *Ikhwan*).[250] Furthermore, Sadat encouraged Islamic organizations, like the *Jama'at-i-Islamiyya* (Islamic Association) to form at universities, the erstwhile bastions of socialism and Nasserism. These Islamic associations multiplied in cities and villages, in factories and government offices. Moreover, Sadat permitted them to receive foreign financing, especially from Libya, Saudi Arabia, and the Persian Gulf sheikhdoms. Among the Islamic revolutionary groups established in the post-1967 period and strengthened during the early Sadat years were the *Munazzamat al-Tahrir al-Islami* (the Islamic Liberation Organization), *Al-Jamaat al-Islamiyya* (the Islamic Society), *Al-Takfir wal-Hijra* (Repentence and Flight), *Jund Allah* (Soldiers of Allah), and *Jamaat al-Jihad* (Association for the Holy War), also known as *Al-Jihad* (The Holy Struggle).[251]

Moreover, Sadat gave generous government financial grants and subsidies to *Al-Azhar*, the Traditionalist religious establishment in Cairo. As a result, the building program at *Al-Azhar*'s campus in Cairo experienced rapid growth, and educational facilities there were expanded. For the first time in Egyptian history, *Al-Azhar*'s leading spokespersons were offered jobs in government and in business ventures—areas long reserved for secular-leaning technocrats and military officers.[252]

---

[247]Surendra Nath Kaushik, "Aftermath of the March 1977 General Elections in Pakistan," *South Asian Studies,* Vol. 13, No. 1, January–July 1978, p. 75.

[248]*Dawn* (Karachi), July 6, 1977, p. 1; *New York Times,* July 6, 1977, p. 1; *Time,* July 18, 1977, p. 29.

[249]John Waterbury, "Egypt: Islam and Social Change," in Philip Stoddard, David C. Cuthell, and Margaret W. Sullivan, eds., *Change and the Muslim World,* Syracuse, NY: Syracuse University Press, 1981, p. 55; Abd al-Moneir Said Aly and Manfred W. Wenner, "Modern Islamic Reform Movements," *The Middle East Journal,* Vol. 36, No. 3, Summer 1982, p. 341; Eric Rouleau, "Who Killed Sadat?" *MERIP Reports,* No. 103, February 1982, p. 4.

[250]Robert Springborg, "The Politics of Resurgent Islam in Egypt, Syria, and Iraq," in Mohammad Ayoob, ed., *The Politics of Islamic Reassertion,* New York: St. Martin's Press, 1981, pp. 10–11.

[251]Rouleau, "Who Killed Sadat?" pp. 3–5; Saad Eddin Ibrahim, "Egypt's Islamic Militants," *MERIP Reports,* No. 103, February 1982, pp. 5–14; John L. Esposito, *The Islamic Threat: Myth or Reality,* Oxford: Oxford University Press, 1992, pp. 133–140.

[252]Springborg, "The Politics of Resurgent Islam," p. 8.

Box 6.4   MUHAMMAD ANWAR AL-SADAT

Muhammad Anwar al-Sadat (1918–1981) was born to a military hospital clerk and his Sudanese wife in the tiny village of Mit al-Kum in the Nile Delta province of Minufiyya between Cairo and Alexandria in Lower Egypt. Devout Muslims, Sadat's parents sent their son to a religious primary school, where he studied the Quran and the *Hadith*. When Sadat was seven years old, he was sent to Cairo to attend primary and secondary schools. In 1936, Sadat graduated from high school and soon thereafter entered Cairo's prestigious Royal Military Academy—later called Abbassia Military Academy—where he became Gamal Abdel Nasser's close friend.

Following his graduation in 1938, Sadat became a lieutenant in the Egyptian army. However, the nationalism that he had picked up in the military academy made him politically restless. He attended a number of Muslim Brotherhood meetings, joined the right wing *Misr al-Fatat* (Young Egypt) party, and was active in the pro-Nazi and anti-British underground. In 1942, the government learned of Captain Sadat's political activities, dismissed him from the army, and imprisoned him. After spending two years in prison, where he improved his English and learned German, Sadat escaped from the prison's hospital where he was being treated for the side effects of his hunger strike. But his freedom was short-lived, since he was arrested again in 1946 and charged with complicity in the murder of the former Egyptian finance minister, Amin Osman Pasha—an aristocrat and politician who favored British presence in Egypt. There were some who also suspected that he was involved in the plot to assassinate Egypt's ex-prime minister Mustafa al-Nahhas. In jail for over two years during the trial, he was acquitted in 1948; then while working as a journalist in a Cairo publishing house, he petitioned the Egyptian army to reinstate him. Sadat was finally reinstated to his officer's rank in 1950 with the help of his former classmates in the military academy.

Once in the army, Sadat joined Nasser's Free Officers Movement, which was dedicated to liberating Egypt from British control. After Egypt's disappointing performance in the 1948–1949 Arab-Israeli War, Sadat was the liaison between Nasser's Free Officers Movement and clandestine civilian organizations like the *Ikhwan* that were also working against the British and the Egyptian monarchy.

On the evening of July 22, 1952, the Free Officers Movement staged a bloodless and successful coup d'état against King Farouk's regime (r. 1936–1952). Nasser ruled Egypt for the next eighteen years (1952–1970) with Sadat as his quintessential yes-man and obsequious sycophant. Fearing Sadat less than any other man in Egypt, Nasser appointed him to several prominent government posts. In 1952, Major Sadat became director of army public relations and editor of the government-controlled daily newspaper, *Al-Jumhuriyyah* (The Republic). Meanwhile, he continued to serve as liaison with the popular and influential *Ikhwan* and with various right-wing groups.

In 1954, Nasser banned the *Ikhwan* and turned increasingly to the left, while aggressively espousing Egyptian nationalism and Arab socialism. Many of the *Ikhwan*'s activists were arbitrarily arrested and jailed, and a few of its leaders were even executed. When Sadat did nothing to help the Islamic group, the *Ikhwan,* which had actively supported the Free Officers Movement in the 1952 coup and had assisted the new military government in the first two critical years, felt betrayed.

After 1954, Sadat served in a variety of impressive-sounding but merely ceremonial posts. He was minister of state from 1954 to 1956, and he served from 1955 to 1956 as secretary general of the Islamic Congress, a short-lived and impotent body established by Nasser to promote Muslim unity under Egyptian auspices. In 1957, Nasser appointed Sadat secretary general of the National Union, the only political party permitted to function in Egypt and the predecessor to the Arab Socialist Union (ASU). In 1958, Sadat headed the Afro-Asian Solidarity Conference, where he scathingly denounced the West; and in 1961 Sadat became president of the National Assembly, a position he enjoyed for seven years. During the 1960s, Sadat served in the presidential council and as a representative of Egypt in ceremonial visits to the communist bloc and to the West. In the meantime, Sadat continued to denounce the West, usually from his post as editor of *Al-Jumhuriyyah,* and he even described the United States as "enemy number one" for its unwavering support of Israel. During this period, Sadat also wrote a book, *Revolt on the Nile,* which told the story of the Egyptian Revolution.

Although Nasser had abolished the post of vice-president following the disastrous 1967 war, he reestablished the post on December 20, 1969, because Nasser's health was deteriorating. Because he trusted only Sadat, Nasser appointed him vice-president. Although Sadat's prior positions had been almost entirely ceremonial, he had already acquired political experience, cultivated good relations with world leaders, and enjoyed influence at home through his relationship with Nasser.

Sadat became interim president of Egypt following Nasser's sudden heart attack in September 1970. That October, Sadat was elected president by the ruling clique to avoid a polarizing power struggle among rightist and leftist candidates for the presidency. Choosing Sadat as an easily manipulable compromise candidate, Zakariyya Muhyiud Din of the right wing and Ali Sabri of the left wing felt they would be the real powers behind the presidency. Sadat, however, was more adept than they had realized.

In order to neutralize the more powerful secular left, Sadat encouraged and assisted Islamic organizations, particularly the *Ikhwan,* which harbored deep grudges against the Nasserites and pro-Soviet leftists. After first relaxing political restrictions on Islamic organizations, Sadat in April 1971 began to purge the influential Nasserites and leftists from the Egyptian government under the pretext that they were conspiring to overthrow him. He attempted to deprive the socialists of all platforms of expression; de-emphasized the role and importance of the Arab Socialist Union (ASU), which had been one of the principal pillars of Nasser's regime; and imprisoned Ali Sabri, head of the ASU. To placate the Soviets, who had supported Ali Sabri, Sadat signed a fifteen-year treaty of friendship with the Soviet Union in May 1971.

It was Sadat who secretly convinced Syria's Hafiz al-Assad and Jordan's King Hussein to launch a surprise invasion against Israel on October 6, 1973—an invasion whose goal was to recover Arab lands. At the height of the war, it was Sadat who persuaded King Faisal of Saudi Arabia and the Organization of Arab Petroleum Exporting Countries (OAPEC) to embargo oil to the United States and the Netherlands, resulting in OPEC's quadrupling of oil prices. King Faisal also agreed to accept thousands of Egyptian workers into the Saudi work force.

Following the moderately successful 1973 Arab-Israeli War, Sadat became popular at home and abroad. Having outmaneuvered his rivals and firmly taken command, Sadat transformed Egyptian foreign and domestic policy, and he did so by distancing himself from the atheistic Soviet Union and Nasser's Arab socialism without abandoning the rhetoric of his predecessor. On the contrary, Sadat insisted that the measures he undertook were merely a "corrective revolution," restoring the true principles of the 1952 revolution.

Sadat decreased Egyptian reliance on an alliance with the Soviet Union while improving relations with the West—especially with the United States. In July 1972, he expelled 20,000 Soviet advisers stationed in Egypt. Nevertheless, later in the year relations with the Soviets improved, and the Soviet Union resumed full military aid before and during the October 1973 Arab-Israeli War. On February 28, 1974, Egypt resumed diplomatic relations with the United States after President Nixon's official visit to Cairo.

In November 1977, Sadat not only recognized the Zionist State of Israel, but he also flew to the Israeli capital of Jerusalem—which the Muslim world considers Israeli-occupied and therefore disputed territory—to discuss peace with the Israeli leaders. Sadat's historic trip to Jerusalem was followed a year later by the equally historic September 1978 Camp David agreement with Israel. In the treaty, Sadat committed his country to peace with Israel, while Begin promised to return the Sinai Peninsula to Egypt in phases. While the West rewarded Sadat and Menachem Begin with the Nobel Peace Prize, Muslims around the world condemned the Egyptian-Israeli peace agreement as a betrayal of the Palestinian cause and the Arab world. In March 1979, despite strong denunciation and isolation in the Muslim world, Sadat signed the Camp David Peace Treaty with Begin.

While Nasser had nationalized industry and embraced socialism, his successor began privatizing industries and establishing a free enterprise system. On April 18, 1974, Sadat inaugurated *infitah* (opening up), an "open door" policy that opened Egypt up to foreign investment. Attractive tax breaks and duty-free zones lured foreign multinational corporations into the country. Egypt's dynamic economic growth came with the negative side effects of inflation, socioeconomic inequity, nepotism, and corruption. Sadat's efforts to increase tourism and foreign investment resulted in the rapid growth of nightclubs, prostitution, pornography, gambling, and the sale of alcoholic beverages. These vices were strongly condemned by the Islamic organizations.

While Sadat promised an era of peace, Egypt's closer ties to the United States and a peace treaty with Israel did not end the Arab-Israeli conflict or resolve the Palestinian problem. While Sadat promised his people prosperity, unemployment, inflation, poverty, and inequality only got worse. Egyptians were also affected when most Muslim countries shunned Sadat and ostracized Egypt. Egypt was expelled from the Arab League and the Organization of the Islamic Conference (OIC). While Sadat had promised his people democracy, his September 1981 crackdown on his opponents for criticizing his domestic and foreign policies belied his pledges to them, and his action further stigmatized him in the eyes of the Egyptian people. On October 6, 1981, while reviewing a military parade in Cairo commemorating the 1973 war against Israel, the sixty-two year old Sadat was assassinated by radical fundamentalist members of *Al-Jihad* (The Holy Struggle). While few Egyptians and Muslim leaders attended Sadat's funeral, many Western leaders came to Cairo to pay their final respects to a man they revered as a great statesman.

Sources: "Sadat," in *Current Biography 1971*, p. 359; also see "Sadat" in Yaacov Shimoni, *Political Dictionary of the Arab World*, New York: Macmillan Publishing Company, 1987; Bernard Reich, ed., *Political Leaders of the Contemporary Middle East and North Africa: A Biographical Dictionary*, New York: Greenwood Press, 1991; "Egypt's Man of the Moment," *Africa Report*, Vol. 18, No. 6, November-December 1973; Thomas W. Lippman, *Egypt After Nasser: Sadat, Peace and the Mirage of Prosperity*, New York: Paragon House, 1989.

In the first years of his presidency, Sadat made "Faith and Science" the twin pillars of the new Egypt. Practicing his slogan, Sadat wrote Islam into the Egyptian constitution as the state religion; made the *Shariah* the source of legislation; introduced compulsory religious education in schools, colleges, and universities; regulated the sale of alcoholic beverages; decreed the construction of additional mosques; and ordered that small prayer rooms be designated in all offices. Sadat also encouraged the state radio and television stations to broadcast prayers, sermons, and lectures on the Quran each day.[253] Likewise, Sadat required that Egyptian airplanes carry a framed verse of the Quran.[254]

[253]Rouleau, "Who Killed Sadat," p. 4.
[254]"Cairo's Caliph," *The Economist*, July 16, 1977, p. 62.

Desirous of Libya's oil wealth, Sadat nearly accepted an offer from Colonel Muammar al-Gaddafi to integrate their two countries. Sadat also permitted al-Gaddafi to spread his brand of Islamic fundamentalism among the Egyptian masses. But when al-Gaddafi began calling for an Islamic cultural revolution in Egypt, Sadat's regime became uneasy. Saudi Arabia was also alarmed at the prospect of al-Gaddafi turning Egypt into a platform from which to denounce their regime. Consequently, the Saudis offered substantial aid to Egypt if Sadat decided against the proposed merger with Libya. Sadat agreed, and the Cairo-Riyadh axis developed—an encouraging development for Egyptian Islamic organizations.[255]

In his never-ceasing efforts to assuage Fundamentalist and Traditionalist revivalists of Egypt, Sadat introduced a law in parliament in 1977 that exacted the death penalty for apostasy. This law was targeted primarily at the Christian Copts who became nominal Muslims when marrying Muslims but who reverted back to Christianity when they were divorced or widowed. However, when the spiritual leader of the Copts, Shenouda, led the Copts in a fast to protest the law, Sadat withdrew it.[256] Nevertheless, Sadat permitted debate in parliament regarding the possible introduction of the *Shariah* as a separatist legal system to coexist with, and eventually replace, Anglo-Saxon civil law in Egypt. As another concession to the Muslim Fundamentalists and Traditionalists, Sadat put less money, personnel, and effort into Egypt's birth-control program—a program initiated by Nasser.

MANIPULATORS OF ISLAMIC SYMBOLS

Bhutto effectively used religious imagery by designating a sword as his party's election symbol, thereby alluding to the legendary *Zulfiquar-i-Ali*, the sword of the fourth *khalifah*, Ali. In so doing, Bhutto sought to identify himself with Ali ibn Abi Talib, Prophet Muhammad's wise and courageous cousin and son-in-law who had defeated many enemies of Islam with his famous sword.

Moreover, Bhutto wanted the image of the sword to inspire the masses with the ideal of a *jihad* that the PPP would wage when it came to power, fighting against the evils of capitalism and feudalism in particular, and against exploitation and injustice in general. In foreign affairs, Bhutto promised a *jihad* against the evils of imperialism, colonialism, and neocolonialism. He also stirred his audiences by saying that he was prepared to lead Pakistan into a thousand-year-long *jihad* against Hindu India and to celebrate *Shaukat-i-Islam* (Glory of Islam) day in New Delhi and Srinagar, Kashmir.[257]

During his whirlwind tours of West Pakistan, Bhutto made publicized visits to the religious shrines of a few famous *pirs* (spiritual guides). He performed public prayers at popular Islamic festivals to counteract his conservative Islamic oppo-

---

[255]Waterbury, "Egypt," p. 55.

[256]Ibid., p. 57.

[257]Gopinath, *Pakistan in Transition*, pp. 53, 57, 66, 75–76.

nents' criticism that he was a *kafir* (unbeliever). With the use of Islamic rhetoric and symbolism, Bhutto's PPP won the December 1970 election in West Pakistan.

Sadat sought to establish his legitimacy by cultivating the image of himself as a practicing Muslim when in reality he was not particularly devout. For example, he encouraged the Egyptian mass media to refer to him as the "Believer President" and the "Pious President." Sadat also encouraged the press to refer to him by his first name, "Muhammad," and made publicized visits on Fridays to the mosque, prostrating himself alongside the "common man." Likewise, he began his speeches with the ritual phrase "in the name of Allah" and ended them with verses from the Quran or with quotations of the Prophet Muhammad. The ruling elite followed Sadat's example in this regard.[258]

Sadat used Islamic symbolism in Egypt's invasion of Israel in the 1973 Arab-Israeli War. He ordered his armed forces to attack Israel during Islam's holy month of Ramadan, when Arab Muslims would be most willing to fight and die in a *jihad* against Israel.[259] Sadat instructed the Egyptian media to refer to the 1973 Arab-Israeli War as the "Ramadan War," and thus a "holy struggle." The operational code name that Sadat gave to the crossing of the Suez Canal was "Badr," the name of a victorious battle fought in 626 by Prophet Muhammad's Muslim army against the pagans, and the battle cry of the Egyptian soldiers crossing the canal was *Allahu Akbar* (God is Most Great).[260]

During Operations Desert Shield and Desert Storm (August 1990 to March 1991), Saddam Hussein, the secular warrior against revolutionary Islamic fundamentalism at home and in Iran (see Box 6.5) portrayed himself the self-styled champion of Islam engaged in a *jihad* against Christian crusaders and *munafiqun* (wayward Muslims and "hypocrites"). Fearing expulsion from Kuwait and political disaster at home, Saddam began to manipulate Islamic symbolism and to exploit Arab frustration and anger in an effort to arouse the Muslim Arab masses against the West.

Saddam, who had often denounced his enemies as "imperialists," began to denounce them as "infidel" as well. By calling for a *jihad* against the "imperialist" and "infidel" West, Saddam gained the support of many clerics in Iraq and around the Muslim world. Furthermore, he ordered the Arabic motto *Allahu Akbar* (God is Most Great) placed on the Iraqi flag and even went so far as to claim direct de-

---

[258]Hassan Hanafi, "The Relevance of the Islamic Alternative in Egypt," *Arab Studies Quarterly*, Vol. 4, Nos. 1 and 2, Spring 1982, p. 64.

[259]Ramadan is the month in the Islamic calendar when Muslims believe that the Quran was revealed to Prophet Muhammad. It is also the month of fasting, prayer, and atonement.

[260]Nazih N. M. Ayubi, "The Political Revival of Islam: The Case Study of Egypt," *International Journal of Middle East Studies*, Vol. 12, No. 4, December 1980, pp. 490–491.

scent from Muhammad. He also quoted frequently from the Quran in public speeches and official statements.

In fact, as early as August 8, 1990, Saddam's Revolutionary Command Council issued a statement, heavy with Islamic symbolism:

> because the gates of the sky open up . . . to the determination of the believers who reject oppression, tyranny and injustice. . . . After seeking God's forgiveness and help, we will demolish blasphemy with faith. . . . God is great, God is great, God is great; let the lowly be accursed, and God's peace and mercy be upon you, honorable brothers, wherever you are.[261]

Facing worldwide opposition to his invasion, Saddam visited his soldiers occupying Iraq's newly annexed "Nineteenth Province" and prayed in front of the cameras and journalists. With this symbolic gesture, Saddam attempted to portray himself as the fearless defender of Islam and the *umma,* the true *mujahid* (one who engages in a *jihad* or holy struggle) who adheres to Islam's most important dictate not to fear or submit to anyone but God. Indeed, the television images of Saddam calmly praying in the open desert while the armed forces of the West and of the pro-Western Arab regimes prepared for war against his troops and country evoked strong sentiments among many Muslims.

Saddam's justification for invading a fellow Arab nation was likewise couched in Islamic rhetoric. Pointing to the materialism, corruption, elitism, and arrogance of the Kuwaiti royal family, Saddam indicated they were hence un-Islamic. Saddam told fellow Muslims that Western colonialists had established "disfigured petroleum states" that "kept the wealth away from the masses of this nation. . . ." He implored, "Oh, Arabs! Oh, Muslims and believers everywhere, this is your day to rise and defend Mecca!"[262] At the same time, the Iraqi media questioned the right of the Saudi monarchy to govern the land containing Islam's two holiest cities and to refer to itself as the "keeper of the faith" while inviting over thousands of Christian Westerners who would fight other Muslims and desecrate Islam's holy land.

As the liberation of Kuwait by multinational forces neared, Saddam exhorted his soldiers for the final battles with intensified Islamic rhetoric: "O Iraqis, fight them with all the power you have in a people that believes in God!"[263] When on February 26, 1991, Saddam ordered Iraqi troops to evacuate Kuwait, the Iraqi dictator declared,

> Shout for victory, O brothers; . . . The soldiers of faith have triumphed over the soldiers of wrong, O stalwart men. Your God is the one who granted your victory . . . O you valiant men . . . faith, belief, hope, and determination continue to fill your chests, souls and hearts. . . . Victory is sweet with the help of God.[264]

---

[261]"Excerpts from Iraq's Statements on Kuwait," cited in *New York Times,* August 9, 1990, p. A–10.

[262]Excerpt of Saddam Hussein's speech quoted in Norman Polmar, ed., *CNN War in the Gulf,* Atlanta: Turner Publishing Inc., 1991, p. 50.

[263]Quoted in Polmar, *CNN War in the Gulf,* p. 203.

[264]Quoted in "Shout for Victory; Soldiers of Faith Have Triumphed," *USA Today,* February 27, 1991, p. A–13.

Box 6.5 SADDAM HUSSEIN

Saddam Hussein was born on April 28, 1937, to an impoverished and illiterate Sunni Muslim peasant family in Takrit, a tiny village north of Baghdad that was also the birthplace of the twelfth-century Muslim warrior Saladin. According to some reports, Saddam's father, Hussein al-Majid, died shortly before or shortly after Saddam's birth, but President Saddam Hussein's former private secretary tells a different story. He claims that Saddam's father abandoned his wife and children. Whatever the true story, Saddam's destitute mother remarried a poor, illiterate, and abusive peasant by the name of al-Haj Ibrahim al-Hassan and moved into the latter's house in the nearby village of al-Auja. Years later, Saddam recalled bitterly how his stepfather often dragged him out of bed at dawn while cursing him, forced him to steal chickens and sheep from their neighbors, and then either ate or sold the stolen livestock.

When Saddam's cousin, Adnan Khairallah, began attending school, Saddam begged his mother and stepfather to allow him to go to school as well. But Saddam's parents wanted their children to continue the family tradition of being melon farmers or sheep herders. Profoundly disappointed with his parents' response, Saddam at ten years of age slipped out of his stepfather's home in the middle of the night and travelled to Takrit to the house of Kairallah Talfah, his maternal uncle. Saddam's departure represented his first act of rebellion, acts that would become characteristic behavior throughout his adult life.

Khairallah Talfah was a frustrated and bitter man who had been dismissed from the army for his role in an ill-fated May 1941 uprising against the British-controlled Iraqi monarchy. Consequently, Saddam's disillusioned uncle and mentor instructed him in the evils of Western colonialism and the benefits of ultranationalism, teaching him the politics of hate. Saddam had already heard his mother's stories of Saddam's forebears courageously battling the Ottoman Turks and of Talfah himself struggling valiantly against the British. Such stories, coupled with his uncle's ideological influence, later propelled Saddam into revolutionary activities aimed at eliminating foreign colonialism from the Arab world. Seeking to emulate his uncle, Saddam applied to the prestigious Baghdad Military Academy to become an army officer; however, he was turned down because of his poor academic record.

Saddam attended *Al-Karkh* secondary school in Baghdad in the fall of 1955, a turbulent time throughout the Arab world. Nasser had come to power in Egypt and was undertaking significant reforms aimed at extirpating undue Western influence. A year later, the Suez crisis, further increased the political heat in the Arab world while propelling Nasser to the zenith of popularity. Meanwhile, ideologies like Ba'athism and its outgrowth, Nasserism, came into vogue. Saddam, already predisposed to revolutionary nationalism, quickly adopted these ideologies as his own.

During this period Saddam became not only politically aware, but also politically active. In late 1956, Saddam participated in a failed coup against Iraq's King Faisal II and Prime Minister Nuri as-Said. A year later, while still attending *Al-Karkh* secondary school, Saddam joined the Ba'ath party. The party fell on hard times after 1958, however, when General Abdul Karim Kassem overthrew and killed King Faisal II, ironically with Ba'ath support. Kassem and his cadre of generals, fearing Ba'ath power and popularity, turned against the Ba'athists and drove them underground.

In October 1959, Saddam was among six chosen by the besieged Ba'ath leadership to assassinate President Kassem. Considering the assignment an honor, Saddam and his cohorts ambushed Kassem's station wagon as it passed through Baghdad's main thoroughfare on the way to the ministry of defense. Saddam and his comrades killed the driver and an aide to the president, but Kassem escaped with only a minor injury. Most of the participants in the ambush were apprehended, but Saddam eluded a dragnet laid by Kassem's security forces. Sentenced to death in absentia for his role in the assassination attempt, Saddam fled from Iraq disguised as a bedouin tribesman. He reached Damascus and safety only after riding a donkey across the desert. Upon reaching Syria, Saddam received a hero's welcome from fellow Ba'athists, and his prestige and popularity soared.

In February 1960, Saddam left Damascus for Cairo, settling in the Egyptian capital with a community of fellow exiles from throughout the Arab world. In 1961, Saddam continued his education at Cairo's *Al-Qasr al-Aini* secondary school. After graduating at age twenty-three, Saddam attended a preparatory school for Cairo University's Law School. Meanwhile, during his stay in Egypt, Saddam was profoundly influenced by Nasser's anti-Western, pan-Arab revolutionary rhetoric and ideology.

In February 1963, Ba'athist military officers overthrew the Iraqi government and executed President Kassem. Saddam interrupted his studies and returned hastily to Baghdad. As the new government formed under Ba'ath party leadership, the Ba'athists asked Colonel Abdul Salam Aref to serve as president. At the time, Saddam participated in the party's fourth regional and sixth national congress. Resuming his education in the same year, Saddam studied law at Baghdad's *Al-Mustansiriyah* university. In November 1963, Saddam's education was again suspended when Colonel Aref felt strong enough to remove the fragmented, weak, and incompetent Ba'ath party leadership from the government.

Saddam, who was an important member of the Ba'ath party, was again on the most-wanted list. In 1964, Iraqi authorities caught up with Saddam, returned him to Iraq, and imprisoned him for two years, during which time he resumed his law studies. Despite his imprisonment, Saddam maintained his political contacts. He was elected to the Ba'ath party's eighth national congress in 1965 and became deputy general secretary of the Ba'ath party's regional leadership in 1966. In 1966, after mysteriously escaping from prison, Saddam went underground and dedicated himself to reorganizing the Ba'ath party into a tightly knit and effective revolutionary movement. With the help of some good writers in the Ba'ath party, Saddam wrote propaganda tracts that laid the ideological foundation for a future Ba'athist revolution and established a Ba'ath party secret police and militia.

Saddam was prominent in the 1968 overthrow of President Abd al-Rahman Aref, brother and successor of Abdul Salam Aref. However, within two months, Saddam instigated the dismissal of the ambitious non-Ba'athist army officers who had taken part in the coup, giving the Ba'ath party undisputed mastery over Iraq. General Ahmed Hassan al-Bakr became prime minister, president, and commander-in-chief of the Iraqi military. But Saddam represented the real power behind al-Bakr. As vice-president and assistant secretary general of the Iraqi Ba'ath party and deputy chairman of the Revolutionary Command Council (RCC), which oversaw Iraq's day-to-day affairs, Saddam Hussein enjoyed preeminent influence within the Ba'athist government. Nevertheless, Saddam did not yet have mass popular support or allegiance from the military's top brass.

Acting as virtual master of Iraq during the 1970s, Saddam initiated a five-year economic plan aimed at freeing Iraq from Western oil interests. In 1972, he nationalized the Iraq Petroleum Company—which had been owned by British, American, French, and Dutch firms—and thereby gained direct control of approximately 10 percent of Middle Eastern oil. According to Khalid Kistainy, who translated some of Saddam Hussein's writings and speeches during the 1970s, Saddam talked at that time like a Marxist who pointedly avoided reference to either Marx or use of related Marxist terminology.

As vice-president, Saddam approached foreign policy in a manner underscoring his political acumen and his grasp of realpolitik. He repaired relations with the West during the mid-seventies, laying the basis for good relations with the United States between 1983 and mid-1990. He also reached an agreement with Iran regarding the *Shatt al-Arab* waterway; seceded from the Rejection Front of Syria, Libya, Algeria, and Iran; and improved relations with moderate Arab states, including Egypt after the Camp David accords. Saddam's diplomacy, however, was always based on the exigencies of self-interest. For example, Saddam's 1975 agreement with Iran to share navigation rights on the bordering *Shatt al-Arab* was made in return for an end to Iranian support of the Kurdish uprising in Iraq. Maneuvering quickly and adeptly, Saddam made peace with the Iranians just as the Kurds began to undermine his control of northern Iraq.

By 1979, the aging president of Iraq, Hassan al-Bakr, had increasingly withdrawn from political life. Mourning the recent but unrelated deaths of his wife, his son, and his son-in-law, the ailing sixty-seven-year-old Bakr resigned in favor of his ambitious, 42-year-old vice-president. Thus, in mid-1979, Saddam Hussein became president, prime minister, commander-in-chief, chairman of the Revolutionary Command Council (RCC), secretary general of the Iraqi command of the ruling Ba'ath party, and deputy secretary-general of the party's pan-Arab command.

Assuming the powers of the presidency, Saddam initiated his dictatorship by executing five hundred Ba'athist leaders in Iraq whom he either did not trust or did not like. Saddam also used his absolute power to create a cult of personality rivaling those of Hitler, Stalin, and Mao. His portraits are prominently displayed everywhere in Iraq. He is pictured on large billboards, on building walls, and in every office, shop, and restaurant in various garb— as a field marshall, as a simple peasant, as a devout Muslim praying at Shi'ah shrines, and as a caring leader holding children. He purposely cultivates a fatherly image and takes credit for everything good.

Likewise, Saddam portrayed himself in the media as the modern-day successor to the glory of ancient Babylon, as the "Knight of the Arab Nation," and as the future leader of a united Arab world. While Iraqis heaped praises upon him and dedicated more paintings and sculptures of his likeness, Saddam suppressed Iraqi citizens with expulsion from jobs, with arbitrary arrests and jailings, with tortures, with executions, with bombings, and even with the use of chemical weapon attacks.

When Iraq invaded Iran, Ayatollah Khomeini immediately denounced Saddam as an "infidel" against whom he promised to fight a *jihad.* Thus, the ayatollah played right into Saddam's hands. Western governments and most regimes in the Arab world perceived that Iraq was serving their national interests and was considerably less dangerous than the Islamic fundamentalist regime in Tehran. As a result, Western governments largely ignored reports of Iraqi atrocities, use of poison gas, indiscriminate bombings of civilian targets, and deliberate destruction of nonbelligerent ships leaving Iranian harbors in the Persian Gulf. Instead of receiving condemnation, Saddam gained a reputation as a strong leader and his country was seen as a bulwark against the spread of revolutionary Islamic fundamentalism. The West and the Arab states, including Saudi Arabia and Kuwait, sided with Iraq against the Iranians.

The war went badly for Iraq. By 1982, the Iranians had removed the Iraqis from Iranian soil and Khomeini was promising to prosecute the war either until victory or until Saddam was removed from power. Meanwhile, Saddam closely identified himself with the war. The Iraqi media, under government control, each day referred to the conflict as "Saddam's *Qadessiya*" after the famous seventh-century battle the Arab Muslims fought against the Persian Zoroastrians. Already, Saddam was acting the Pragmatist revivalist. The war, however, was a blot on Saddam's record. After the war had degenerated into a bloody, decade-long stalemate, Hussein and Khomeini, to their mutual chagrin, accepted a cease-fire. Neither the Iraqis nor the Iranians had achieved much in the way of their expressed objectives.

Learning well the lessons of the war with Iran, Saddam chose next to victimize a smaller easily crushed nation: Iraq's oil-rich neighbor to the south, Kuwait. Iraq invaded Kuwait on August 2, 1990, and proceeded to loot that wealthy country. Within a week, U.S. President George Bush declared that "Iraq's occupation of Kuwait will not stand" and began using the United Nations to punish Iraq. Bush was able to get leaders of thirty nations to commit their armed forces to evicting Saddam's troops from Kuwait.

The U.N. gave Saddam until January 15, 1991, to withdraw all his troops and weapons from Kuwait. The day after the deadline, the U.S.-led multinational force started the air war against Iraq and Iraqi positions in Kuwait. The operation had been code named "Operation Desert Storm"—and that is precisely what Iraqis experienced for nearly two months. The war cost Iraq dearly: Over 100,000 Iraqis were killed; thousands were wounded; the country lay in ruins; and a proud people, who were the envy of many Third Worlders, were reduced to eking out their existence at bare subsistence levels. It was a crushing and humiliating military defeat for Saddam. A leader who was in a position to step into Nasser's shoes before he invaded Kuwait on August 2, 1990, was now friendless in the world community; a country that was fast emerging as a major power center in the Arab world had not only been declawed and defanged but was also classified as a "pariah state" or a "terrorist state"; an oil-rich country was unable to sell its oil. Things could not have been any worse for Iraq and its leader. In early March 1991, just after the war between the multinational force and Iraq had ended, the Iraqi Kurds in the north and the Shi'ahs in the south rose up to overthrow the "butcher of Baghdad." However, Saddam was not as weak and vulnerable as his opposition thought. Saddam unleashed his loyal Elite Republican Guard against the rebels and brutally crushed the insurrection.

Sources: "President Saddam Hussein of Iraq," *MidEast Report,* Vol. 23, No. 16, August 15, 1990; "Saddam Hussein," *1981 Current Biography;* Bernard Reich, ed., *Political Leaders of the Contemporary Middle East and North Africa: A Biographical Dictionary,* New York: Greenwood Press, 1991; Yaacov Shimoni, *Biographical Dictionary of the Middle East,* New York: Facts on File, 1991; Lawrence Ziring, *The Middle East: A Political Dictionary,* Santa Barbara, CA: ABC-CLIO, 1992; Elie Kedourie, "What's Baathism Anyway?" *Wall Street Journal,* October 17, 1990.

Saddam claimed repeatedly that he acted "in the name of God, the merciful, the compassionate." He proclaimed himself, in this time of crisis, a champion of Islam, like Saladin, and called all Arabs his brothers.[265]

---

[265]Polmar, *CNN War in the Gulf,* p. 52.

ISLAMIC REVIVALS AND INTENSE OPPOSITION
FROM ISLAMIC GROUPS

In addition to the Islamic advocacy of the Muslim Fundamentalists, Traditionalists, and Modernists, the Islamic rhetoric and symbolism of all four Pragmatists spawned or strengthened Islamic revivals in their respective countries, regions, and/or the entire world. Yet Islamic groups scathingly denounced all four Pragmatists as "un-Islamic" hypocrites.

After the PPP scored a landslide victory at the polls in 1977, for example, the disillusioned and infuriated PNA members, who had managed to draw mammoth crowds during the election campaign, accused Bhutto of election fraud and launched a civil disobedience movement to remove him from office. In their religiopolitical sermons and by organizing protests, numerous *masjids* throughout Pakistan encouraged their congregations to engage in a *jihad* against the hypocritical, fraudulent, and "un-Islamic" Bhutto regime. The agenda of the PNA, which was influenced by the Islamic political parties, was to replace the regime of the "Whiskey party leader," under whom "Islam was in Danger," with the pristine purity of *Nizam-i-Mustafa* (Prophet Muhammad's system) or *Nizam-i-Islam* (the Islamic system). Thus, the "politics of Islam," in which the secular and liberal Bhutto so astutely engaged in order to enhance his own power and popularity, came to haunt him in the twilight months of his tenure, and it ultimately destroyed him.

Despite Sadat's many concessions to the Islamic groups over the years, there remained four significant areas of contention between them and the Sadat government. First, Sadat had allowed the Fundamentalists to play an active role in the formulation of a new constitution, but he had failed to satisfy a number of their major demands. For instance, he had severely disappointed the *Ikhwan* when he had not established the *Shariah* as the law of the land.[266] He had annoyed Islamic groups with Article 2 of the constitution, which stated that "the State shall be responsible for maintaining the balance between women's duties toward the family and her activity in society, as well as for her equality with man in the fields of political, social, cultural and economic life, without detriment to the Islamic *Shariah*."[267] Moreover, Sadat angered the Islamic groups in 1979 when he decreed that at least thirty members of Egypt's national assembly had to be women, and he attempted to make divorce more difficult and polygamy all but impossible.

Second, Islamic groups opposed Sadat's close ties to the United States. When Sadat opened Egypt's economy to Western investment, the Islamic groups grew

---

[266]Aly and Wenner, "Modern Islamic Reform Movements," p. 349.
[267]Ibid., p. 349.

concerned about the consequent socioeconomic inequity and injustice, and the resultant nepotism and corruption. They were likewise alarmed by the rapid growth of nightclubs, prostitution, gambling, and the sale of alcoholic beverages—all of which resulted from Sadat's efforts to increase tourism and foreign investment. In essence, Sadat's goals for economic modernization were at odds with the goals of the Islamic groups for an Islamic state.

In January 1977, the Islamic groups took advantage of the demonstrations, strikes, and riots that had been precipitated by a reduction in government bread subsidies to destroy casinos, nightclubs, and bars.[268] By late 1977, Sadat's pro-Islamic policies had contributed to the landslide victory of *al-Jami'a al-Islamiyya* (the Islamic Society) in the student union elections in all Egyptian colleges and universities.

Third, Islamic groups opposed Sadat's recognition of the Zionist State of Israel, whose capital was Jerusalem. They were infuriated by his trip to Jerusalem in November 1977, with its attendant media hype. The Camp David peace treaty, which followed in 1979, alienated devout Muslims and Islamic organizations not only in Egypt but in most of the Muslim world as well.[269]

In March and April 1979, after the Camp David accords had been signed and before the official signing of the Camp David treaty, *al-Jami'a al-Islamiyya* led strikes and riots on the Asyut and Minya university campuses. Muslim students incensed by the Egyptian-Israeli "sellout of Islamic Palestinian Territory" attacked Egyptian government officials, professors known for their secular views, and Christian students.

In 1981, the Muslim-Coptic conflict that had steadily increased during the 1970s exploded into violence. In September 1981, Sadat attempted to stem the Muslim-Coptic fighting and to suppress the growing opposition to his regime. Over 1,500 people, including many Muslim Fundamentalists, were arrested on charges of fomenting sectarian strife and distorting the image of Egypt abroad. Sadat then ordered the closure of 40,000 private mosques that were located on the ground floors of apartment buildings and that had served as the focal point of both religious and social activity. He attempted to control mosque sermons by sending out prepared texts, a tactic previously used by Nasser. Moreover, Sadat banned Islamic organizations in educational institutions, at the same time introducing stringent security measures like identity cards. But Sadat's drastic actions only added fuel to the Islamic revival that he had rekindled. For several weeks that followed, Muslims were drawn every Friday in the thousands to a mosque where Shaikh Kishk, the blind prayer leader of Cairo, unabashedly criticized Sadat's regime. The mosque attendees also challenged the police outside in demonstrations at the risk of arrest or death. On October 6, 1981, while reviewing a military parade celebrating the anniversary of the October 1973 Arab-Israeli War,

---

[268]Ibid., pp. 354–356.

[269]Ibid., p. 356.

Sadat was assassinated by radical fundamentalist members of *Al-Jihad* (the Holy War).[270]

Ironically, Sadat was destroyed by the powerful currents and forces of Islamic revivalism which he himself had encouraged and cultivated. But the Fundamentalists and Traditionalists were not satisfied with Sadat's Islamic policies and programs. In Muslim Fundamentalist and Muslim Traditionalist eyes, true piety could never be reconciled with making peace with Zionists who occupied Arab lands, with allowing the production and sale of pork and alcoholic beverages, with giving asylum (in 1980) and a grand funeral (in 1981) to Iran's deposed *Shah* (king), and with declaring a separation of religion and politics. Unable to satisfy the radical Islamic revivalists, Sadat, the self-titled "Believer President," turned to and got along best with his former enemies—the Zionists of Israel, the Christians of the West, and the Western media—whom he had vociferously denounced throughout his life. The *umma* abandoned him. Few Egyptian citizens or Muslim leaders attended Sadat's funeral in Cairo, while Israeli and Western mourners were well represented. For his fellow countrymen and coreligionists around the world, Sadat was not the great international statesman lauded by the West; instead, he represented a twentieth-century pharaoh who had sold his nation short and betrayed both the Arab and Muslim worlds to the Western imperialists and Zionists.

Saddam Hussein's use of Islamic rhetoric during Operation Desert Storm—characterizing his struggle as a *jihad* against the West—belies the fact that Islamic groups like the Shi'ah-based *Da'wa* (the call) party in Iraq are considered terrorists and are brutally crushed. Immediately after Operation Desert Storm, many Shi'ah activists, who had intensified their decade-long *jihad* against Saddam's "un-Islamic" Ba'athist regime and threatened his survival, were hunted down, jailed, tortured, and even executed.

Saddam used rhetoric to arouse the passions of Muslims against the West, not to encourage Islamic revivalism within Iraq or abroad, but mainly to survive in power, and if possible, to prevail in the political war against the West. Thus, Saddam was a typical Pragmatist in that he engaged in the politics of Islam only insofar as it was useful for him to do so. However, like Muslim Pragmatists before him, Saddam spawned an Islamic revival (especially among Iraqi Shi'ahs) that threatened to overthrow him. Realizing the imminent danger to his regime and his life, Saddam abandoned all Islamic rhetoric and used his loyal Elite Republican Guard in March 1991 to ruthlessly crush the Islamic resurgence in southern Iraq.

[270]Jihad B. Khazen, *The Sadat Assassination: Background and Implications,* Monograph, Georgetown University's Center for Contemporary Arab Studies, Washington, D.C., November 1981, p. 3.

SUMMARY

Muslim Pragmatists are often only nominally Muslims; they do not even practice the obligatory duties. Influenced by their formal and informal secular education, they look to a broad spectrum of ages and philosophies for models of political and socioeconomic progress. In their search for an ideal system, they adopt concepts and ideologies from both capitalist and socialist countries, but unlike the Modernists, they do not adapt these ideas to their indigenous environments. Pragmatists concern themselves with the dynamic modernization of their societies and address practical realities in a rational manner. Though at times pressured by the Muslim Fundamentalists and Traditionalists to promote and defend the faith, Pragmatists often prefer a state whose guiding principle is secularism. They also believe that modern-day nation-states ought to be governed by lay Muslim politicians and statesmen, rather than by the *ulama,* who they feel should be limited to professional religious duties. (See the table that follows.)

A TYPOLOGY OF ISLAMIC REVIVALISTS

MAJOR CHARACTERISTICS	FUNDAMENTALISTS	TRADITIONALISTS	MODERNISTS	PRAGMATISTS
I. BELIEF IN THE FUNDAMENTALS OF ISLAM	1. All four believe in (a) *tawhid* (oneness of God); (b) omnipotence, omnipresence, justice, and infinite mercy of God; (c) Prophet Muhammad as the last in a long line of God's prophets starting with Adam and including Abraham, Moses, and Jesus; (d) The holy Quran as revealed to Prophet Muhammad as the last of God's holy books along with the Torah as given to Moses and the Bible; and (e) the Day of Judgment.			
II. DEGREE OF DEVOUTNESS	1. ——————————— Practicing Muslims ——————————— 2. Extremely devout and austere; and often puritanical.	2. Extremely devout; relatively dogmatic and orthodox, but tolerant in varying degrees of some local customs.	2. Devout to very devout; eclectic; not rigid or puritanical.	1. Nonpracticing Muslims 2. Moderately devout at best; often nonpracticing, nominal, and very liberal Muslims.
III. EDUCATION AND LEARNING	2. Minor influence of some non-Islamic (e.g., Western) ideas, ideals, and practices among Fundamentalists in the modern period.	1. Formal education acquired in Islamic educational institutions. Informal learning also primarily, but not exclusively, religious. 2. Often reject non-Islamic (e.g., Western) ideas, ideals, and practices.	1. Formal and informal education not confined to religious learning. 2. Significantly influenced by non-Islamic (especially Western) ideas, ideals, and practices.	1. Secular formal and informal education for the most part. Relatively knowledgeable about Islam and Muslims. 2. Heavily influenced by non-Islamic (e.g., Western) ideas, ideals, and practices.
IV. CLERICAL AFFILIATION	1. Not exclusively from the ranks of the *ulama* (Islamic scholars); many non clerics among them.	1. Virtually all come from the ranks of the *ulama*.	1. Though they may come from the ranks of the *ulama*, the majority have been non clerics.	1. They never come from the ranks of the *ulama*.
V. NORMATIVE PERIODS	1. Look primarily to classical period of Islam for inspiration and emulation; secondary emphasis on medieval Islamic era.	1. Look nostalgically to both classical and medieval periods of Islam for their ideas, ideals, and practices.	1. Look to classical period of Islam as well as to Western capitalist and socialist countries for their ideas, ideals, and practices.	1. Look to broad spectrum of philosophies and ages for models of political and socioeconomic development.

MAJOR CHARACTERISTICS

MAJOR CHARACTERISTICS	FUNDAMENTALISTS	TRADITIONALISTS	MODERNISTS	PRAGMATISTS
VI. RESPECT FOR TRADITION AND OPENNESS TOWARD CHANGE	1. Zealous crusaders against doctrine of *taqlid* (whereby legal rulings of one or more schools of Islamic jurisprudence are blindly and unquestioningly followed) and all accretions and innovations in Islam from postclassical period. 2. Vigorously advocate *ijtihad* (independent reasoning, especially in matters of Islamic law). 3. Extremely opposed to modern secular (especially Western or Socialist) ideas, practices, and institutions that are contrary to Islam. 4. Extremely particular about compatibility of policies and programs with the letter and spirit of Islam.	Consider true Islam's immutability and perfection to transcend time and space. Determined to prove that many popular and beneficial ideas, ideals, and practices across cultures, ideological systems, and time are Islamic in essence or have Islamic roots or influences. 1. Firmly adhere to doctrine of *taqlid* and often support or condone conservation and preservation of "Islamic" customs and traditions popular among Muslims in their particular locality or region. 2. Against *ijtihad* (except for some minority Shi'ah sects which restrict that practice to *mujtahids*—highly qualified *ulama* exercising *ijtihad*.)	2. Very particular about placing all adopted popular and beneficial non-Islamic/foreign concepts, practices, and institutions within Islamic framework. 1. Against *taqlid* and all those traditions that they consider to inhibit the progress of Muslim societies. Believe in the continuity of essential, useful, and popular traditions along with comprehensive progress (including structural change) that they deem compatible with the spirit of Islam. 2. Extremely vigorous in their advocacy of *ijtihad*. Often believe that *ijtihad* should be exercised by all devout, enlightened, and progressive Muslims who are knowledgeable about Islamic thought and practice. 3. Opposed to modern secular (especially Western or Socialist) ideas, practices and institutions which are contrary to Islam. However, in practice, often tolerate them in varying degrees. 4. Extremely particular about compatibility of policies and programs with the spirit of Islam.	2. Often adapt concepts and practices from Western capitalist and socialist countries to their indigenous environments, deriving syntheses that are often nominally Islamic, but so labeled to legitimize and popularize their use. 2. Would like to see all Muslims enjoy the right to exercise *ijtihad*. 3. Have no qualms about accepting modern secular ideas, practices, and institutions that the Fundamentalists, Traditionalists, and Modernists oppose. 4. Not concerned about compatibility of programs with Islam unless heavily pressured by the other three groups of Islamic Revivalists.

MAJOR CHARAC-TERISTICS	FUNDAMENTALISTS	TRADITIONALISTS	MODERNISTS	PRAGMATISTS
VII. TOLERANCE OF SECULARIZATION	1. Vociferously and virulently against secularization. Often launch a *jihad* (crusade) to stop and reverse secularization processes. Their active political involvement is often taken into account by regimes in power.	1. Clamorously condemn secularization of Muslim societies. The majority, however, do little to retard or reverse secularization processes. The few that do get politically involved do so because they perceive that Islam and the Muslim community of which they are a part are in danger.	1. Openly oppose secularization in principle, theory, and rhetoric, but conveniently tolerate secularization with either benign neglect or as a necessary evil that must be accommodated in contemporary times.	1. Strong advocates of secularization. Modernizers who care about progress or modernization being Islamic in coloring and outward manifestation only when challenged by Fundamentalists, Traditionalists, and Modernists.
VIII. PRINCIPAL REASONS FOR THE MUSLIM WORLD'S DECLINE	1. Ascribe decline of Muslim world (including its poverty and impotence) to two commonly shared reasons: (a) colonialism and neocolonialism (especially by Western powers) and (b) disunity within the "House of Islam."			
	2. Believe that decline is also due to (a) failure on the part of Muslims to adhere to letter and spirit of Islam; and (b) "corrupt," "incompetent," and often "dictatorial" leadership of "secular" (and thus "un-Islamic") Pragmatists.		2. Believe that decline is due to rigid, doctrinaire, and dogmatic orthodoxies promulgated by Fundamentalists and Traditionalists.	
	3. Also believe that decline is due to the lackluster leadership and inhibiting influences of the detached Traditionalists.		3. Emphasize inhibiting of *ijtihad* and banning of *bid'a* (innovation in Islamic beliefs, practices, and laws) as counterproductive practices.	3. Mention (often in passing) lack of *ijtihad* as a contributory cause.
IX. MANIFESTATIONS OF AN ISLAMIC STATE	**A. Type of Islamic State:** 1. Advocate an Islamic state, although its character differs significantly in each case.			1. Although at times call for a liberal democratic "Islamic state," often opposed in practice to the creation of a genuine Islamic state (where church and state are fused).
	2. Prefer one with puritanical manifestations.	2. Prefer one with traditional theocratic manifestations.	2. Prefer one with liberal democratic manifestations.	2. Often prefer a secular state.

MAJOR CHARACTERISTICS	FUNDAMENTALISTS	TRADITIONALISTS	MODERNISTS	PRAGMATISTS
B. Who Should Govern:	1. Convinced that enlightened, sincere, and dedicated Fundamentalists would do the best job of governing the truly Islamic state. Often very critical of nonfundamentalists.	1. Believe that Traditionalist *ulama* ought to govern the Islamic state as they are the guardians and principal interpreters of the divine *Shariah*. In practice, have become somewhat tolerant of Fundamentalists, Modernists, and Pragmatists governing Muslim societies.	1. Believe that enlightened and competent Modernists would do the best job of governing the modern-day Islamic state. In practice, are very tolerant of and even support competent Pragmatists in leadership positions.	1. Believe that competent lay Muslim politicians instead of the *ulama* govern modern-day nation-states.
C. Nature of Constitution and Laws:	1. Would like to formulate and implement a constitution that is Islamic in both letter and spirit. 2. Would like the Islamic state to be governed by the *Shariah*, which for them is sacrosanct, immutable, and capable of successful application to all given situations regardless of time and place.		1. Would like to formulate and implement a constitution consonant with the letter and especially the spirit of Islam. 2. Believe in revision of Islamic legal system in order to cope with contemporary problems. Would not remove many secular laws already implemented.	1. Would like to formulate and implement a primarily secular constitution, but are often pressured to concede a number of Islamic provisions and clauses to devoutly religious interest groups. 2. Prefer not to implement a comprehensive Islamic legal system (even if revised) at national level. Feel more comfortable relying primarily on secular laws.
D. Basis of Sovereignty:	1. Believe that sovereignty primarily rests with God. Believe all devout Muslims should reject sovereignty of man. With few exceptions, have come to accept (Western) parliamentary democracy in the modern period, implying that they do give importance to "popular sovereignty" (especially in the post–World War II period) after sovereignty of God.		1. Believe above all in God's ultimate sovereignty but next in "popular sovereignty." The latter is manifested in a form of (Western) parliamentary democracy legitimized as essentially Islamic.	1. Believe in (Western) parliamentary democracy and thereby in popular sovereignty, while not discounting ultimate sovereignty of God.
E. Integration of Society:	1. Believe in integrating a predominantly Muslim country's citizenry on the basis of Islam although the character of that Islam differs markedly in each case.			

MAJOR CHARACTERISTICS	FUNDAMENTALISTS	TRADITIONALISTS	MODERNISTS	PRAGMATISTS
	Based on Islamic fundamentalism.	Based primarily on Islamic orthodoxy with a minimum of custom and occasionally on custom-laden "popular Islam" or "folk Islam."	Based on progressive Islam and/or Islamic nationalism.	Based on Islamic nationalism, although Islamic component is largely rhetorical and symbolic.
X. DEGREE OF FATALISM AND ACTIVISM	1. Vary in their fatalism, believing in such notions as *kismet, taqdir* (fate), predestination, and preordination.			
	2. Very fatalistic, but extremely active religiopolitical crusaders for Islamic fundamentalism/puritanism.	2. Very fatalistic; often passive, apolitical, contemplative, and mystical scholars, teachers, and preachers of traditional Islamic doctrine and practice. However, do get involved in politics if and when they perceive that Islam is threatened by non-Muslims or by "wayward" Muslims.	2. Moderately to very fatalistic, though extremely dynamic reformers of Islam and Muslim societies. Imbued with and desirous of promoting the spirit of Islam.	2. Minimally fatalistic; extremely dynamic reformers and modernizers of Muslim societies. Perceptive and astute politicians imbued with the vestiges of the spirit of Islam.
XI. MAJOR FOREIGN POLICY ORIENTATION	1. Often extremely insular and parochial.		1. Often relatively cosmopolitan, broad-minded and highly principled pragmatists.	1. Often cosmopolitan, broad-minded, liberal, and pragmatic.
		2. Ardent exponents of a united Muslim world/Islamic bloc		
	3. Believe in *dar al-Islam* (Abode of Islam) and *dar al-Harb* (Abode of the Infidel) dichotomy of the world. Thus end up with a We-They, Us-Them, Good-Evil dichotomous orientation toward outside world.		3. Hardly preoccupied with *dar-al-Islam* and *dar al-Harb* dichotomy.	3. Not at all concerned about *dar al-Islam* and *dar al-Harb* dichotomy. Considered by the devout as well as by non-Muslim observers as having made controversial alliances with non-Muslim (even atheistic/communist) states in their preoccupation with promoting their country's national inter-
COMMON STEREOTYPES	**A. Critics:** Puritans; Iconoclasts; Religious Zealots.	Obscurantists; Reactionaries.	Apologists; Revisionists; Syncretists.	Secularists; Westernizers; Opportunists; Manipulators.

MAJOR CHARAC- TERISTICS	FUNDAMENTALISTS	TRADITIONALISTS	MODERNISTS	PRAGMATISTS
	B. Defenders: Purists; Literalists; Scripturalists; Religious Ideologues/ Revolutionaries; Restorationists; Restitutionists.	Islamic Scholars; Learned Theologians; Conservatives.	Progressives; Reformers; Modernizers; Adaptationists; Realists; Liberals.	Pragmatic, populist politicians.
PROMINENT ISLAMIC REVIVALISTS	Shaikh Ahmad Sirhindi (1564–1624)	*The Farangi Mahallis* The most prominent of whom was: Qayam-rund-Din Muhammad Abdul Bari (1878–1926)	Pragmatically oriented Islamicists.	
	Shah Waliullah (1702–1762)		Jamal Ad-Din al-Afghani (1838–1897)	Muhammad Ali Jinnah (1875–1948)
	Muhammad ibn-Abd al-Wahhab (1703–1792)	*The Barelvis* The most prominent of whom was: Ahmad Raza Khan Barelvi (1856–1921)	Sir Sayyid Ahmad Khan (1817–1898)	Zulfikar Ali Bhutto (1928–1979)
	Sayyid Ahmad Barelvi (1786–1831)		Muhammad Abduh (1849–1905)	Muhammad Anwar al-Sadat (1918–1981)
	Mir Nisar Ali /Titu Mir (1782–1831)	*The Deobandis* The most prominent of whom were: Haji Imdadullah (1815–1899)	Muhammad Iqbal (1873–1938)	Saddam Hussein (b. 1937)
	Haji Shariatullah (1781–1840)		Ali Shariati (1933–1977)	
	Mohsenuddin Ahmad/Dadu Mian (1819–1860)	Muhammad Qasim Nanautwi (1833–1877)	Mehdi Bazargan (1905–)	
	Sayyid Muhammad ibn-Ali al-Sanusi (1787–1859)	Rashid Ahmad Gangohi (1829–1950)	Abolhassan Banisadr (b. 1933)	
	Hassan al-Banna (1906–1949)	Mahmud al-Hassan (1850–1921)		
	Muhammad Ahmad Abdullah al-Mahdi (1844–1885)	Ayatollah Sayyid Kazem Shariatmadari (1905–1986)		
	Sayyid Abul A'la Maududi (1903–1979)			
	Ayatollah Ruhollah Khomeini (1902–1989)			
	Muhammad Zia-ul-Haq (1924–1988)			
	Ali Akbar Hashemi Rafsanjani (b. 1934)			

Chapter
7

Failure of Secular Ideologies and Developmental Crises

By the ninth century, the Islamic empire stretched over the face of the earth from the Indus River in the east to the Atlas Mountains in the west. Europe, the stronghold of Christendom, saw the Crescent rising over its stone walls. Islam held Spain, Southern France, part of Italy, and the islands of Crete, Corsica, Sicily, Sardinia. Islam led the world in science and art, in mathematics and military might. Islam was first intellectually and politically—its supremacy was unequaled.

One thousand years later, Islam's conspicuous glory was faded, and the Crescent eclipsed by an inexorably modernizing Europe that had surpassed the Islamic empire in military and industrial technology. One Muslim land after another fell into Western hands as Europeans gradually dismembered the debilitated empire of the Ottoman Turks and imposed colonial rule throughout the Muslim world. The Europeans not only exploited these colonies, rich in cheap raw materials and labor, but used them as export markets for their surplus producer goods (like machines) and consumer goods. Moreover, the Europeans introduced modernization[271] and Western secular education. In the process, they penetrated

---

[271]The terms "modernization" and "development" are often used interchangeably in scholarly literature and the popular media to refer to the movement of a society or country from the traditional, through the transitional, and into the modern stage of economic, social, and political development. Some scholars (like Samuel Huntington), however, see a major difference between the two terms. In Huntington's words, "[Development is] an evolutionary process in which indigenous institutions adapt

all levels of society and regulated the political, economic, social, and cultural lives of their Muslim subjects. The indigenous elite, simultaneously impressed and antagonized by European power, both emulated and cooperated with their colonial masters. They embraced Westernization and secularization: They served the Western powers that governed their people while they sent their own children to European universities. The elite, armed with thoroughly Western attitudes, lifestyles, and ideologies, were poised to take power following independence.

The First World War marked the decline of colonial rule. The European promised the Muslims independence in exchange for their cooperation against the Axis nations in general, and the Ottoman Turks in particular, igniting nationalist passions throughout the Muslim world. Following Allied victory, however, the promised independence was not forthcoming. Instead, the West enlarged its colonial possessions at the expense of the defeated countries. For example, in the 1916 Sykes-Picot Agreement, Britain and France divided the former Ottoman territories between themselves and justified the action under the League of Nations' mandate system.

Following the final dismemberment of the Ottoman Empire and the termination of the *Khilafat,* disappointed Muslims traded one inscrutable tyrant for another. Even the Western-favoring elite grew restless with the colonial rulers and despaired of their own stagnation. Thus, anticolonial sentiment gathered momentum throughout the Muslim world. Finally, following the Second World War, the West, exhausted spiritually and economically by the war, initiated the process of decolonization, hoping to extricate itself from its increasingly troublesome and strife-filled colonial possessions.

Despite formal independence, the newly emerging Muslim nation-states of Asia and Africa were not yet independent of Western ideologies and Western notions of secular, territorial nationalism. These independent Muslim nations emphasized the "national interest," and abandoned the traditional Islamic *umma.* Instead, ultimate authority rested in the state—and the state demanded total political obedience. This concept was understood by the governing Westernized elite, but lost on the governed, who identified themselves not according to Western-delineated national boundaries but on the basis of the *umma.*

Moreover, these newly independent and predominantly Muslim states were economically poor and politically fragile. To survive and to consolidate power, they turned to the competing superpowers. The West needed allies and military bases throughout the world to contain and combat communism. In turn, those

---

and control change and are not simply caught up in imitating and reacting to outside forces. Modernization is often contemporary, imported, and creates a dependency on the technologically advanced urban-industrial centers without helping local political and social institutions to grow and adapt. Development means that a system has some ability to be selective in the type and pace of changes, often imported, that occur in a country." (Herbert Winter and Thomas Bellows, *People and Politics,* New York: Wiley, 1977, pp. 352–353; Samuel P. Huntington, "Political Development and Political Decay," *World Politics,* Vol. 17, 1965, p. 389).

Muslim states in need of aid and hostile to the characteristic atheism of communism joined the Western-sponsored antisocialist and anticommunist alliance scheme. A much smaller number tilted, instead, toward the socialist camp, while the rest chose nonalignment. Thus, although the colonial era was over, the impoverished states of the Muslim world grew dependent on foreign aid, were drawn into geopolitical conflicts, and were divided among themselves both on a national and an ideological basis.

FAILURE OF SECULAR IDEOLOGIES ESPOUSED BY PRAGMATISTS

In the immediate aftermath of independence, the Muslim Pragmatists, who were influenced by Western ideologies, often Western-educated, and impressed by the Western nations' order and progress, comfortably filled the political void left by the departing colonial administrators. The euphoria of independence from the West initially endeared these Muslim Pragmatists to the masses and they were enthusiastically swept into power. However, the Pragmatists no longer saw through the eyes of the masses; they saw their nations as backward and sought to emulate the model of progress of the West. The Pragmatists worked to transform the predominantly rural and traditional Muslim world into modern urban nation-states by pursuing programs of modernization, Westernization, and secularization.

Despite the Pragmatists' early popular support, within a few decades the credibility and legitimacy of their government had dangerously eroded. Their poorly implemented modernization programs have proved incompatible with traditional Islam. The Pragmatists carelessly and thoughtlessly imposed secular socialism, secular capitalism, or a mixture of both, but have failed to deliver on their promises of economic, social, and political development.[272] Even the rapid economic growth registered in some Muslim countries has not significantly benefitted the impoverished majority. Instead, any economic gains have been enjoyed almost exclusively by the wealthy elite. The Muslim Pragmatists have interpreted modernization as the adoption, not the adaptation, of Western ideology and industry. This modernization has not occasioned development that involves finding the best use of a nation's potential for mitigating the poverty of and raising the

---

[272]The example of secular socialism implemented in the communist world has disappointed the Muslim masses because they have learned more about the lack of political, economic, and social freedoms prevalent in the communist bloc. Moreover, the Muslim elite has also stopped looking at socialism and communism as model ideologies because the Soviet-dominated communist bloc itself has renounced and repudiated communism. The Muslim masses, however, have been equally disappointed by the example of secular capitalism practiced in the West. Many Muslims feel that capitalism breeds excessive greed, individuality, materialism, and hedonism, while lacking compassion for the poor and needy.

standard of living for the majority.[273] In fact, in the Muslim world, rapid modernization has precluded appropriate development.

The Pragmatists, hoping to become partners with the Western industrial world, have espoused the Western idea of nationalism to integrate and to unify their fragmented societies and to consolidate political power. However, nationalism instead has further divided the Muslim world as a whole, and the leadership has pursued national interests at the expense of the *umma*. In the interests of realpolitik, Muslim nations have ignored fellow Muslims in distress, whether starving in Ethiopia and Somalia, or bearing Israeli assaults in southern Lebanon.

The ideology of pan-Arabism, which was pursued by Pragmatists to rectify the failure of nationalism, enjoyed popularity in the 1950s and 1960s. However, the ideology lost favor when Arab Muslims realized that pan-Arabism was a thinly disguised extension of secular nationalism promoted primarily by those leaders who sought to dominate the world. Pan-Arabism neither unified the Arabs against Israel nor settled the Palestinian problem. Pan-Arabism was discredited first with the Arab defeat in the 1967 Arab-Israeli War, second by its failure to increase trade and commerce among Arab nations, and third by the failure of Arab governments to break the bonds of dependency with the West or, in a few cases, with the communist bloc.

The Pragmatists have also failed to fulfill their postindependence promise of implementing liberal parliamentary democracy. Of all Western values and ideologies, democracy was the first dissociated by the Muslim Pragmatists from their modernization policies. Most regimes in the Muslim world are authoritarian and dictatorial; some are as callous, oppressive, and tyrannical as prior colonial regimes.

Nor have the Muslim Pragmatists delivered on their promised postindependence utopia of genuine independence and sovereignty. Their desire to modernize has retarded the process of breaking dependency relationships with the West. Instead, modernization programs have reinforced dependency.

The secularization process promoted by the Pragmatists throughout the Muslim world in modernization's name has not brought the development they promised their citizens. Instead, secularization has resulted in the transplantation of alien Western institutions, laws, and procedures that have eroded the traditional and holistic system of Islam and have thus created an acute identity crisis. Not surprisingly, in those states where Pragmatists have most aggressively pushed

---

[273]E. Bradford Burns, *Latin America: A Concise Interpretive History*, 5th ed., Englewood Cliffs, NJ: Prentice-Hall, 1990, p. 357. Although a Latin Americanist, Burns's views on and definitions of key concepts like "modernization" and "development" are applicable throughout the Third World; too many other studies are based heavily on the experience of the developed West. See also E. Bradford Burns, *The Poverty of Progress: Latin America in the Nineteenth-Century*, Berkeley and Los Angeles: University of California Press, 1983, which details the Positivist-inspired, elite-mandated modernization process in Latin America, and its disastrous consequences; and E. Bradford Burns, "The Modernization of Underdevelopment: El Salvador, 1858–1931," *The Journal of Developing Areas*, Vol. 18, April 1984, which chronicles the above-mentioned struggle in El Salvador.

secularization, Islam has become the primary idiom of protest. For example, in Syria, Iraq, Algeria, Tunisia, and Egypt, the Islamic backlash endures despite and, ironically, because of the efforts of those secular regimes to crush it by force.

The failure of the Muslim Pragmatists and their imported policies and programs is the most significant cause of Islamic revivalism. The Pragmatists have not reconciled their policies with tradition; instead, they have attacked it. They have secularized education and have driven traditional belief underground. This war waged against tradition has been sustained on exaggerated and unreasonable promises that have not come through. Thus, those beleaguered traditions enjoy enhanced credibility. Westernization and secularization, as panaceas for people's spiritual and material ills, have proven deficient. While Western industry and ideology increasingly disappoint the Muslim masses, Islam is renascent, and erstwhile traditions have been invigorated. Thus, Islamic revivalism has become the focus of opposition to the policies and regimes of the Pragmatists.

The Muslim Pragmatists have failed to deliver on the promises they made at the time of independence. They have failed to achieve the high level of development they anticipated through secular capitalism, socialism, nationalism, pan-Arabism, and secularization. Thus, Islam—which is a comprehensive system—has become an attractive alternative among the masses, who indentify themselves with the *umma,* not with the secular, Westernizing nation-state. Seeing the resurgence of Islam, the astute Pragmatists have exploited Islamic rhetoric and symbolism in domestic and foreign policy to shore up wavering support. Yet, instead of appeasing the more sincere Islamic revivalists, the Pragmatists' political use of Islam has legitimized Islamic revivalism and, thus, undermined government secularization programs—the linchpin of the Pragmatists' modernization policies. Moreover, rather than being perceived as devout "born-again Muslims," the Pragmatists are seen as hypocrites and opportunists not to be trusted.[274]

MANIFESTATIONS OF SIX DEVELOPMENTAL CRISES IN MUSLIM NATIONS

While Muslim nations are undergoing rapid modernization, their development is neither holistic nor healthy. What may seem, at first, a paradox is merely a difference in context. In the West, where modernization and development have proceeded gradually and simultaneously, many equate the two and bundle them together under the value-laden term "progress." In contrast, modernization has occurred rapidly in the Muslim world, while appropriate development has not happened.

In essence, modernization is a complex, multidimensional, prolonged, and unsettling process of technological, economic, political, social, and cultural innovation. Since modernization has been successful in the West, it has become identi-

---

[274]Fouad Ajami, *The Arab Predicament: Arab Political Thought and Practice Since 1967,* Cambridge: Cambridge University Press, 1981, p. 171.

fied with Westernization, secularization, and the sweeping adoption of Western industry, ideology, and institutions.

Western technology, introduced into the Muslim world by the Pragmatists, instantaneously supplanted the indigenous technology. Industrialization and urbanization followed. Transportation and communications were revolutionized. Differentiated and specialized roles and structures have emerged, and the people have increasingly adopted rational and secular attitudes. Old centers of power have disintegrated, giving way to new and emerging power centers. Modernization involves a comprehensive transformation in all sectors and at all levels of society. Nevertheless, old ideas, ideals, traditions, institutions, and processes, often sanctified by Islam, have resisted the encroachment of modernization. There is still continuity within change.[275]

Development, in contrast to modernization, denotes the relative welfare of a nation's population. In the West, modernization accompanied the growth of a large middle class. In this respect, development occurred because a large number of Westerners enjoyed the fruits of modernization. However, in the Muslim world, modernization has not coincided with the growth of a substantial middle class. Although small "middle sectors" have emerged, they lack class consciousness and tend to ally themselves with the elite, whom they emulate, against the "rabble," whom they disdain. Modernization throughout the Muslim world has led to politicoeconomic polarization and social fragmentation. Resources have not been freely or fairly distributed. Instead, the elite has been the primary beneficiary while the impoverished masses have borne the burden of subsequent underdevelopment. In effect, the Muslim Pragmatists, convinced or deluded about the benefits of modernization, have unwisely neglected appropriate development. As a result, they have sacrificed the welfare of the many for the prosperity of a few.

Political development, a more specific and precise distillation of general development, involves the formation of political institutions to improve popular participation in government and to incorporate new power contenders. Political development signifies the capacity of government not only to sustain and adapt to the stresses of modernization, but to direct the course and rate of economic, social, and political change.[276] As authors James Bill and Robert Springborg wrote, "the rewards and priorities of the [modernizing] society need to be allocated and reallocated in a way that permits all to expect equal opportunity and to receive just treatment."[277] The problem of achieving political development is particularly relevant in the Muslim world as the modernization process has undermined and over-

---

[275]James A. Bill and Robert Springborg, *Politics in the Middle East,* 3rd ed., Glenview, IL: Little, Brown and Co., 1984, pp. 1–10.

[276]Since political development is defined here as relative to the process of modernization, it becomes impossible to discuss political development prior to the Industrial Revolution. Although the empires of the Romans, the Byzantines, and the Incas, for example, may have had, at their height, ample capacity to meet the demands made upon them, they did not suffer the numerous stresses and crises of accelerated modernization and, therefore, the concept of political development, circumscribed in time, is inapplicable (Huntington, "Political Development and Political Decay," p. 389).

[277]Bill and Springborg, *Politics in the Middle East,* p. 7.

whelmed existing political institutions. Political development is usually associated with the secularization of government, which in turn often involves the differentiation of governmental institutions and processes from religious organization, influence, and control.[278] The same process of secularization in the Muslim world is often perceived as the chief perpetrator of underdevelopment. Moreover, since such political development in conjunction with modernization has been achieved only in the West, it is generally associated with the formation of Western democratic institutions. The capacity of a government to absorb change and solve problems, however, may have nothing to do with Western-style democracy. For example, political participation can be realized through referendums or plebiscites, which bypass democratic institutions.

Theoretically, the problem of achieving political development is linked to the imperatives of differentiation, equality, and capacity.[279] Differentiation suggests political development to the extent that the more highly developed a political system becomes, the greater the specialization of roles and functions within its administrative and political structures.[280] Equality, the second imperative of political development, involves national citizenship (equality as a participating member of society), a universalistic legal order (equality under the law), and achievement norms (equal opportunity).[281] The third imperative, capacity, signifies a polity's ability to adapt to the pressures inherent in pursuing equality and differentiation. More than mere adaptation, capacity indicates proficiency in planning, organizing, implementing, and manipulating new changes while striving to achieve new goals. The main attributes of "creative capacity" are scope and effectiveness, which are aspects of a developing polity's performance and rationality.[282] In this manner, capacity is not only adaptive, but a creative force.

Unless the imperatives of differentiation, equality, and capacity are satisfied as a polity modernizes, specific developmental crises will arise. The crises of identity, legitimacy, penetration, distribution, and participation are interrelated; one can give rise to another and any number can occur simultaneously.

The Identity Crisis

The ancient command, "know thyself," is an enduring feature of human history and a recurring theme of philosophy. The search for personal identity begins with an assessment of one's past ("What are my roots?"), one's present ("Who am I?"), and one's future ("What is the purpose of my life?"). Only when these questions are answered does the quest for self-knowledge end.

---

[278]James S. Coleman, "The Developmental Syndrome: Differentiation-Equality-Capacity," in Leonard Binder, James S. Coleman, Joseph LaPalombara, Lucien W. Pye, Sidney Verba, and Myron Weiner, eds., *Crises and Sequences in Political Development*, Princeton: Princeton University Press, 1971, p. 77.

[279]Ibid., pp. 74–75.

[280]Ibid., p. 75.

[281]Ibid., p. 76–78.

[282]Ibid., p. 78–79.

During periods of rapid modernization (especially industrialization and urbanization), when the familiarity of traditional society is broken, a widespread identity crisis can ensue. People are uprooted from their tightly knit rural communities and migrate to the cities, where many become victims of unemployment or underemployment, inflation, and unhygienic living conditions. Often these individuals arrive in the cities with high expectations; instead they find a world of excessive materialism, selfishness, and crime. The depersonalization, alienation, and frustration of the "urban jungle" disillusion them and threaten their security and identity. For Muslims, this identity crisis often draws them closer to the religion into which they were socialized as children. Their religion acts as an anchor, alleviates their fears, and gives them a sense of stability, direction, and faith in the future. Therefore, Islam, as both a "historical" and an "organic" religion, is especially significant in the modernizing Muslim world.

Just as the identity crisis must be resolved by individual Muslims if they are to develop into mature and stable adults, similarly, the first and most crucial hurdle facing a new nation-state is to achieve a common or "national" identity. This means that citizens of a new nation-state must come to recognize their national territory as their homeland and must feel that their personal identities are in part defined by their identification with their country.[283] In essence, only when a nation's citizens identify themselves with the nation can a stable yet adaptable and mature political system be realized.[284] This entails government effort to integrate its citizenry and to form a single patriotic political community owing its primary loyalty to the national entity rather than to its primordial groups, which include the extended family and tribal, racial linguistic, religious, sectarian, class, or regional communities. Most members of a traditional developing society are closely tied to their primordial groups and find it difficult to shift allegiance to the "nation-state." In the process of political development, individuals and groups within a multiethnic nation-state must transcend traditional kincentric loyalties and become patriotic citizens. Thus it is imperative that the government translate the loose and uncoordinated sentiments of nationalism into a cohesive spirit of patriotism, citizenship, and solidarity. In this respect, political development entails nation-building.[285]

Traditional community loyalties are not so easy to overcome, however. In fact, they often become intensified under the pressures of modernization. Identity crisis in the traditional community involves profoundly ambivalent feelings about the modern world and one's own historical, religious, and cultural traditions.[286] An appropriate resolution of the identity crisis must then involve reconciliation of one's sociocultural traditions and modern practices. Until and unless there is a satisfactory reconciliation of tradition and modernity, people remain ambivalent,

---

[283]Lucien W. Pye, *Aspects of Political Development,* Boston: Little, Brown and Co., 1966, p. 53.

[284]Lucien W. Pye and Sidney Verba, *Political Cultural and Political Development,* Princeton: Princeton University Press, 1965, p. 529; and Lucien W. Pye, *Politics, Personality and Nation Building: Burma's Search For Identity,* New Haven: Yale University Press, 1962, pp. 52–53.

[285]Pye, *Aspects of Political Development,* p. 38.

[286]Gopinath, *Pakistan In Transition,* p. 7.

conflicted, and rootless. This rootlessness, in turn, hinders the development of identity, which is necessary for building a stable and modern nation-state.[287]

The people in a modernizing state must recognize and accept a national identity over rival primordial claims to their loyalty. Political development requires, during sociopolitical integration, that the people perceive themselves as forming a single political community and feel their personal identities partly defined by their attachment to that community and the country's national interests. Third World countries, including the Muslim world, have yet to resolve their identity crisis. Thus, they are plagued by periodic sociopolitical explosions.

A major factor that has contributed to an identity crisis among Muslims all over the world—and still does for many devout Fundamentalist and Traditionalist Muslims today—is the preeminence of the *umma* in Islamic theory. Derived from the Arabic word *um,* meaning "mother," the term *umma,* in Islam, refers to "the nation or brotherhood of Muslims." In the *umma,* Muslims all over the world are brothers and sisters despite their history, region, culture, color, language, or socioeconomic and political status. Both *umma* and nationalism involve a peoples' sense of group identity and loyalty due to shared heritage. Both demand the prime loyalty of their followers. However, the Western secular ideology of nationalism attempts to engender solidarity among the diverse people living within the territorial boundaries of a particular nation-state, rather than grouping persons by their beliefs.[288] People in countries all over the world are indoctrinated to love their country from an early age. They are thus influenced, manipulated, and even coerced into being or becoming patriotic, owing their allegiance to their government, and fighting for their country's national interests.[289] The Islamic *umma,* on the other hand, is concerned with improving the welfare of and forging a sense of solidarity among all Muslims. While this pan-Islamic vision seems utopian and difficult to achieve today, it is nevertheless the dream that figures prominently in the Islamicist's worldview.

The Legitimacy Crisis

Closely related to the identity crisis is the legitimacy crisis: problem of reaching a consensus on the legitimacy of a nation's political institutions.[290] Legitimacy can be defined as "the basis on which and the degree to which the decisions of

---

[287]Pye, *Aspects of Political Development,* p. 63.

[288]Many developing countries cannot be considered "nations" as the term was initially used by Western scholars and media. Instead, developing countries are more or less artificial aggregates of various ascriptively defined communities (tribal, ethnic, racial, linguistic, and religious). However, the national integration of these multiethnic and multinational societies still remains the principal goal of all Third World governments.

[289]National interests involve the critically important and enduring considerations that lie at the very core of a nation's value system. These include such matters as national security against external and internal threats; protection of the country's political, economic, and sociocultural system; enhancement of the country's economic well-being or the development of a higher standard of living; and protection and promotion of a country's honor and ideology.

[290]Pye, *Aspects of Political Development,* p. 63.

government are accepted by the populace of a society because of normative beliefs as to the rightness of the ways in which decisions were made."[291] The population must acknowledge, without coercion, their regime's authority to govern. People may disagree with specific governmental decisions or actions without necessarily denying the right of the regime to remain in power. Yet the population will support existing political institutions only as their values correspond. Thus, the greater the public's conviction that a regime is honest, fair, and interested in the general welfare, the more popular that regime will be, the more power it can exercise, and the more effective it can be. The moment a regime loses the confidence of the people, its political institutions will be incapable of governing and the regime will either fall or become increasingly repressive.

Legitimacy is a moral bond between the government and the governed. The greater that bond, the more likely that people will see the government's existing political institutions, as appropriate for their society and will obey those institutions, even when obeying may be unpleasant or harmful to the individual. A political system that enjoys no legitimacy is forced to resort to increasing degrees of coercion to maintain itself.

Establishing legitimacy is the first best step to political development. A government that is legitimate will be more able to adapt to and to overcome developmental crises. Conversely, developmental crises can erode legitimacy.[292]

A legitimacy crisis exists in the Muslim world, the result of immense differences in values between the rulers and the ruled. The governing Pragmatists are in varying degrees Westernized and secularized. They speak Western languages and have acquired Western education either at home or abroad. In contrast, the culture of the people is permeated with the religious tradition of Islam, which is in direct conflict with secularism and the secular society of the Pragamatists. Most Muslims are uneducated and therefore do not understand the language (figuratively, and, at times, even literally) of their elitist leaders. Hence the Pragmatists are unable to legitimize their rule, mobilize their populations behind their policies and programs, or integrate their multiethnic citizenry. Lacking mass support, the Pragmatists are ever vulnerable to overthrow. Thus, to stay in power they have resorted to a mixture of secular indoctrination, cooptation, and coercion. However, this oppression has further divided the power elite from the governed, and, in turn, further destabilized the existing political institutions.

The Penetration Crisis

The penetration crisis refers to the problem faced by central governments of all modernizing nations to reach down to the level of their citizenry.[293] Governments that are unable to enforce their decisions at the local level are ignored, and are

---

[291]Monte Palmer and William R. Thompson, *The Comparative Analysis of Politics,* Itasca, IL: F. E. Peacock Publishers, Inc., 1978, p. 74.

[292]Raymond Grew, "The Crises and Their Sequences," in Raymond Grew, ed., *Crises of Political Development in Europe and the United States,* Princeton: Princeton University Press, 1978, p. 25.

[293]Pye, *Aspects of Political Development,* op. cit., p. 64.

thus inherently unstable. Effective penetration involves controlling previously insulated institutions and segments of society. This is often accomplished with the help of political institutions such as governmental agencies, political parties, and local village councils, which link the governing elite with the governed to implement the country's laws and the regime's policies and programs. This process of state building results in a centralized bureaucracy with increased coercive capacity to effectively enforce national authority, secure public compliance, and govern the society.

All political systems are created and controlled by the governing elite. Yet the long-term survival of these systems depends on popular support. The penetration crisis can be resolved only by bridging the conspicuously wide gulf between the governing and the governed so that the developmental needs of the country can be met. This task in the developing Muslim world is particularly formidable as the ambitious modernization programs of the governing elite far exceed the comprehension of people accustomed to old parochial ways. The wide "cultural gap" or "cultural cleavage," which blocks any resolution of the legitimacy crisis, is also impeding leaders from developing a rapport with the people they govern and from reaching down to the grass roots level to change old values and behaviors. Hence, the Pragmatists are unable to motivate and mobilize the masses to support their modernization programs.

Paradoxically, when governments successfully resolve the closely related crises of penetration, legitimacy, and identity, widespread pressures for greater participation in government decision making are unleashed.

The Distribution Crisis

The most visible and extended crisis in political development involves the division of the nation's economic wealth. In essence, the distribution crisis involves the vitally important question about how government powers are to be used to allocate, distribute, and redistribute values, material goods, services, and other benefits in society.[294] The processes and policies of distribution are what government is all about. The distribution crisis is the most difficult of the developmental crises to resolve because the wealthy and powerful elite are seldom willing to surrender their privileges. Their resistance to redistribution can manifest itself by lower economic activity and even monetary support to demonstrators who oppose reform-minded regimes and who, on occasion, bring them down. Thus, the ultimate gauge of a government's political performance is its management of the distribution crisis in terms of national security, general welfare, and individual liberties.

The distribution crisis is compounded in the Muslim world by the population explosion characteristic of developing countries.[295] The population explosion has

---

[294]Pye, *Aspects of Political Development*, p. 66.

[295]Dorothy Nortman, *U.N. Reports on Population/Family Planning*, No. 2, September 1976, p. 4; Lester Brown, *World Without Borders*, New York: Vintage Books, 1972, p. 134; J. Faaland and J. R. Parkinson, *The Political Economy of Development*, New York: St. Martin's Press, 1986, p. 168; Gerald O. Barney, *Global 200*, Arlington, VA: Seven Locks Press, 1991, pp. 1, 8–9; Michael P. Todaro, *Economic Development in the Third World*, New York: Longman, 1989, p. 187.

meant that the working population carries a larger "dependency load." In Muslim countries, nearly half the population is under fifteen years of age. As a result, a high percentage of the countries' capital is expended on feeding, housing, clothing, educating, and training these young individuals. Moreover, the demographic preeminence of youth in Muslim countries indicates that fertility rates will not soon decline.

Since the population of the major cities in the Muslim world is doubling every fifteen years, rapid urban growth is putting heavy pressure on food and water supplies, housing, sanitation, health care, education, and employment. Given the current inadequate distribution of goods and services and its relation to sociopolitical instability and violence, it is likely that cities throughout the Muslim world will be the focal points of future revolutions.

The population explosion contributes to a chronic shortage of resources (such as food, drinking water, clothing, housing, education, health care, consumer goods, and electricity); leads to the chronic overcrowding of cities and towns; contributes to inflation and the sharp rise in the cost of living; greatly reduces the opportunities that job seekers will have obtaining relevant job training programs and jobs; and accelerates ecological degradation. Shortages of food, consumer goods, and services drive up the prices of these goods and services, making them less accessible to the needy majority, more of whom are slipping into the category of the "absolute poor." This, in turn, results in a chronic distribution crisis that most Muslim governments are finding difficult to resolve. Robert McNamara, former president of the World Bank, summarized the consequences of the population explosion best when he said:

> Rapid population growth in sum, translates into rising numbers of labor force entrants, faster-expanding urban populations, pressure on food supplies, ecological degradation, and increasing numbers of 'absolute poor.' All are rightly viewed by governments as threats to social stability and orderly change. Even under vigorous economic growth, managing the demographic expansion is difficult; with a faltering economy it is all but impossible.[296]

Muslim governments have been unwilling to crusade against the explosive population growth for various reasons. Some Secularists and Pragmatists have placed their faith in the "demographic transition" theory, positing that economic and social modernization will inevitably lower population growth rates as it has done in the West. Also, Muslim leaders are afraid of the power conservative and fundamentalist clerics who oppose aggressive population control measures. Muslim leaders are also wary of the costs involved in instituting a successful family planning program. Other leaders, usually nationalist and socialist-oriented, are suspicious of the West's emphasis and propaganda on the population issue and are opposed to the encroachment of secular Western governments or groups in their internal affairs.

The distribution crisis is accentuated by the problem of "relative deprivation," or reduced expectations, which causes sociopolitical instability. Prominent intellectuals of the last twenty-three centuries have said that people act aggressively,

---

[296]Robert S. McNamara, "The Population Problem," *Foreign Affairs,* Summer 1984, pp. 1, 119.

and even violently, not only because they are poor and deprived in an absolute sense, but because they feel deprived relative to others, or relative to their own expectations. Thus, feelings of relative deprivation result when people realize that others have done better than they in the past, are doing better than they in the present, and/or are expected to do better than they in the future.[297] Aristotle, for instance, contends that the principal cause of revolution is the desire of the entrenched oligarchy for more power and wealth conflicting with the desire of the poor for greater equity and justice.[298]

Relative deprivation is today defined as "the discrepancy between those conditions of life to which people in society think they are justifiably entitled (value expectations) and those desirable social circumstances which they feel they are capable of achieving and maintaining (value capabilities). This discrepancy induces social discontent, which may lead to widespread anger, which, in turn, may be triggered into collective political violence."[299]

Political instability can be attributed to the significant discrepancy between expectations of the population and the degree to which the people have realized those expectations.[300] Similarly, the gap between what people want and what they get results in increasing frustration among the masses, which in turn leads to revolution.[301]

Rebellions and revolutions may also occur when a society, having enjoyed a prolonged period of rising expectations and gratification, suddenly experiences a sharp reversal. A period of rapid growth often heightens people's expectations of continuing improvement in their lives. Thus, when a sudden reversal occurs, the gap between the accelerating expectations and the realities of plummeting gratifications is far more distressing and intolerable than if the reversal had followed a period of relative stagnation. These accumulated and intolerable frustrations eventually seek violent outlets. If frustration and bitterness have been festering for a long time and are sufficiently widespread, intense, and focused on the established regime in power, violence may explode into revolution that may displace the ruling regime, undermine the old and discredited power structure, and radically transform the entire society through coercion and attendant bloodshed. If the outbreak of violence is not focused, intense, or widespread enough, the result may merely be a coup at the apex of power, or against government oppression. In the latter case, potential rebels may prefer to live with their frustrations than endure job loss, long prison terms, torture, or execution. Just as often, the govern-

---

[297]Bruce Russet and Harvey Starr, *World Politics: The Menu For Choice*, 4th ed., New York: W. H. Freeman and Company, 1992, p. 89.

[298]J. E. C. Weldon, *The Politics of Aristotle*, trans., New York: Macmillan, 1905, p. 338.

[299]Ted R. Gurr, *Why Men Rebel*, Princeton: Princeton University Press, 1970, p. 37.

[300]Harold Lasswell and Abraham Kaplan, *Power and Society*, New Haven: Yale University Press, 1950, p. 264.

[301]Daniel Lerner, "Toward A Communication Theory of Modernization," in Lucien W. Pye, ed., *Communications and Political Development*, Princeton: Princeton University Press, 1964, pp. 330–350.

ment partially or completely addresses the grievances of the discontented masses.[302]

In Muslim societies today, the distribution crisis is particularly acute because the gap separating the rich and powerful few from the poor and powerless majority has grown wider. Since Islam emphasizes socioeconomic equity and justice, and enjoins devout Muslims to play an active role in politics, religion has become a powerful revolutionary ideology used by the poor, disenfranchised, exploited, frustrated, and alienated masses (socialized in Islam) to challenge the governing elite. Some of the poor adopt violent measures to pressure the government to improve the distribution of goods and services in the society. This is vividly evident in Lebanon, where a segment of the Shi'ah majority has given up on the peaceful and legal parliamentary means of pressuring the Christian-dominated government to improve their economic, social, and political welfare. The same distribution crisis manifests itself in most other Muslim countries. However, major sociopolitical upheavals are prevented and contained by the authoritarian methods of the civil, monarchical, and military regimes ruling the Muslim world.

The Participation Crisis

Although relative deprivation usually signifies perceived economic inequity, people can also suffer from relative political deprivation. The population in a modernizing, secularizing, and Westernizing society inevitably asks for greater political participation, particularly when such participation is routine in Western nations. Relative political deprivation, or the participation crisis, occurs when the governing elite does not accommodate the aspirations and expectations of citizens to participate in the political system's decision-making process.

In essence, the participation crisis results when the governing elite ignores or rejects the public's demand to participate in the political system.[303] In reaction to pressures for increased participation, a government may become more authoritarian as it struggles to stay in power, or may organize a rigged election or referendum. Sometimes the participation crisis will cause a military coup d'état or, more rarely, a broad-based revolution.

Rapid modernization intensifies relative political deprivation "when there is uncertainty over the appropriate rate of expansion and when the influx of new participants creates serious strains on the existing institutions." The pressures accompanying increased participation upset the status quo and the "continuity of the old polity is broken and there is the need to reestablish the entire structure of

---

[302]James C. Davies, "Satisfaction and Revolution," in David H. Everson and Joann Popard Paine, eds., *An Introduction to Systematic Political Science,* Homewood, IL: The Dorsey Press, 1973, pp. 158–160. For a much more detailed discussion of the hypothesis forwarded by James Davies and others on the subject of relative deprivation, see James Chowning Davies, ed., *When Men Revolt and Why: A Reader in Political Violence and Revolution,* New York: The Free Press, 1971.

[303]Myron Weiner, "Political Participation: Crisis of the Political Process," in Leonard Binder et al., eds., *Crises and Sequences in Political Development,* p. 187.

political relations."[304] The consequent political chaos and dislocation could easily overwhelm the fragile nation-states of the Muslim world.

The participation crisis is often related to the legitimacy and penetration crises. Legitimacy can become untenable either under conditions of severely limited participation, which is common in the Muslim world, or under conditions of widespread participation outside existing political institutions. Excepting controlled forms of pluralism and democracy in Pakistan, Malaysia, Turkey, Jordan, and Turkey, there are no other functioning democracies among the remaining forty-four predominantly Muslim countries. Most authoritarian leaders, whether civilian or military, are Muslim Pragmatists who manipulate Islamic rhetoric and symbols to stay in power. The Pragmatists often mask modernization with indigenous concepts (like Islamic democracy or Islamic socialism) to encourage mass participation, rather than by holding general elections based on Western-oriented liberal parliamentary democracy. Moreover, the Pragmatist's efforts usually are intended to mobilize support for government programs, seldom to give the masses any real say in the governance of society.[305]

In most Muslim societies there are few democratic institutions through which the masses can vent their grievances or from which they can expect justice. This institutional void has been filled by the *masjid,* which has served throughout the Muslim world as an oasis of freedom in a desert of despotism. Most Muslims— whether rulers or the ruled—respect the sanctity of the *masjid* and are loathe to shed blood therein. The most cruel and dictatorial tyrant will hesitate in his repression under the shadow of the minaret. To do otherwise, to murder in a house of worship, invites political suicide.

*Masjid*s in the Muslim world often require no government license to operate, and authoritarian Muslim governments generally refrain from closing even politically objectionable *masjid*s. Since Prophet Muhammad strongly urged congregational prayer, especially on Friday afternoons (the Muslim Sabbath), disallowing such prayer or barring the doors of the mosque would cause a furor among worshipers. Because *masjid*s are, to a certain degree, immune from blatant government repression, the *masjid* has become the focal point of antigovernment, antisecularist, and anti-Western opinion in the Muslim world. Many Muslim clerics, following the example of Prophet Muhammad, utilize the sacred premises of the *masjid* not only to worship God, but as a political platform from which to enlighten the faithful and to mobilize political action. Some clerics deliver sermons sharply critical of government policies, programs, and leadership. Thus, the clerics in the Muslim world have risen to positions of leadership in opposition to unpopular and tyrannical secularist and Pragmatist regimes and their corrupt and unrepresentative political institutions. This clerical class largely has no knowledge of Western intellectual thought, has not traveled abroad, and can speak no Western languages. Therefore, when the clerics communicate with the people through Is-

---

[304]Pye, *Aspects of Political Development,* p. 65.

[305]Norman D. Palmer, "Changing Patterns of Politics in Pakistan: An Overview," in Manzooruddin Ahmad, ed., *Contemporary Pakistan: Politics, Economy, and Society,* Durham, NC: Carolina Academic Press, 1980, pp. 48–49.

lamic symbols, they are seen as sincere, unlike the Pragmatists. These Islamic revivalists have risen repeatedly throughout Islamic history, leading mass movements against foreign and domestic despots. The last decade represents a cyclical renewal of this Islamic revivalism. The Fundamentalists and the Traditionalists, often insulated from direct government control in the mosques, have effectively used the potent Islamic concepts of *khurooj* (the right to revolt against an unjust, tyrannical ruler), of *jihad* (the right to engage in holy struggle against nonbelievers and the unrighteous), and of *shahadat* (martyrdom attained in a *jihad*) to agitate and mobilize Muslims against repressive regimes throughout Islamic history.

Aware of this history, the Pragmatists have not stood idly by in the face of *masjid*-instigated antigovernment activity. Government troops have been placed within sight of *masjid* entrances to deter possible spontaneous demonstrations following congregational prayer. The Egyptian government has taken this strategy a step further and exercises direct control over urban *masjids*. The Egyptian government pays the salaries and screens the Friday sermons of as many as one-third of Egypt's mosque *imans* (preachers). Thousands of other *imans* serving in mosques throughout Egypt, especially in rural areas, regularly denounce the government for being "un-Islamic."[306] Egypt's control of the *masjid,* perhaps the most extensive of any secularist regime, is truly inadequate. The dynamism of Islamic revivalism in Egypt is undampened, the clerics are undeterred, and the mosque remains the focal point of opposition to the secularists and Pragmatists, and their Modernist supporters. Thus, in Egypt and throughout the Muslim world, the *masjid* represents a safe haven for antigovernment opposition.

The nations of the developed Western world are fortunate to have become modernized gradually over the centuries, giving the West sufficient time to resolve each developmental crisis in turn. In the Muslim world, modernization is occurring at such an accelerated pace that centuries of transformation are condensed into a single generation. Hence, the crises that occurred serially in the West are coming simultaneously in the Muslim world and are imposing intolerable demands on political systems that have neither the time nor the opportunity to adapt. Sociopolitical explosions are frequent, usually leading to authoritarian civil or military regimes, and sometimes even to civil wars and revolutions.

Iran experienced all five crises simultaneously and with such elevated intensity that the compound mixture reached "critical mass" and exploded in an Islamic revolution in 1978. Iran's Muhammad Reza Pahlavi had initiated a process of rapid modernization, but he had been unwilling to resolve the consequent developmental crises. The youth of Iran questioned the legitimacy of the Shah's authoritarian regime, the lack of popular participation, and even their own identity. Meanwhile, the distribution crisis worsened meanwhile as the material needs and wants of an expectant population went consistently unfulfilled. The crises of development become cumulatively acute in the final years of the Shah's regime, despite U.S. President Jimmy Carter's encouraging the Iranian monarch to liberalize his political system. Overwhelmed by the developmental crises, the Shah fled and

---

[306]Caryle Murphy, "Islam's Crescent of Change," *The Washington Post National Weekly Edition*, May 25–31, 1992, p. 7.

his regime collapsed. The Ayatollah Khomeini, representing the "Islamic" alternative, assumed power and promised to reverse the pro-Western policies of the Shah and to establish a "true" Islamic state.

Sudan, like Iran, is experiencing all five developmental crises at once. However, the identity crisis is particularly acute. Southern Sudan, which is primarily Christian and animist, does not identify itself with the predominantly Muslim north that governs Sudan. The overwhelming majority of those living in Southern Sudan resent the authoritarian control exercised by the army in the north and have waged guerrilla warfare for autonomy for nearly two decades. The situation worsened in the late 1970s when Sudan's Muslim Pragmatist President Jafar al-Numeiri imposed the *Shariah* and started an aggressive Islamization program. Though Numeiri was overthrown in a military coup in 1985, subsequent Sudanese regimes have continued his Islamization program. The current military regime has appointed several prominent Islamic fundamentalists in the National Islamic Front (dominated by the *Ikhwan al-Muslimun*) to high-level government positions, and is seriously committed to instituting Islamic policies and programs and making Sudan an Islamic state. Unhappy with the current Sudanese regime's worldview and its refusal to participate in Operation Desert Storm, the West and the conservative oil-rich Arab kingdoms of the Persian Gulf have stopped most of their aid to Sudan. The abrupt discontinuation of all aid has further aggravated and compounded all five developmental crises in Sudan.

The seventeen-year-long civil war in Lebanon can be attributed to the convergence of the five developmental crises. First, this predominantly Muslim country has been controlled by the Christian minority since it gained independence on November 22, 1943. Over time, the Muslim population grew at a rate faster than that of the Christians, while individual Muslims became more conscious of their Islamic identity and their state of relative deprivation vis-à-vis the governing Christian elite. Next, the Palestine Liberation Organization (PLO), which had been targeted by King Hussein's army in Jordan, escaped into Lebanon in September 1970. The PLO and their families were first treated as refugees by the Lebanese Shi'ahs of South Lebanon; however, by the late 1970s the PLO had assumed control of the Shi'ah heartland of South Lebanon and were perceived by the Lebanese to be a state within the state of Lebanon. The Lebanese identity crisis worsened after the Israeli invasion of Lebanon in 1982. Initially, the Shi'ah majority welcomed the Israeli invaders as liberators. Yet when the Israelis, like the PLO, overstayed their welcome and victimized the Lebanese Shi'ahs, the Shi'ah majority of Lebanon emboldened by the successful Islamic revolution in Iran, rose and challenged an unjust status quo. The fact that Lebanon is a poor country and a complex mosaic of different ethnic groups have complicated its tragic fate. The divided Christian elite, the fragmented Palestinians, the polarized Shi'ah (with moderates and pro-Iranian Islamic Fundamentalists), the Sunnis, and the Druze are all proud of their identity, are highly politicized, and are heavily armed. As though these divisions and rivalries were not bad enough, the Lebanese system is also deeply penetrated by Syria, Israel, Iran, the United States, France, and the PLO. Each external power manipulates its surrogates in the Lebanese system, often to Lebanon's detriment. The penetration of the Lebanese system by outside powers has greatly destablized the fragile ethnic balance of a once peaceful and prosperous country and has contributed to the prolongation and exacerbation of its seventeen-year civil war. Today, Lebanon is plagued by all five developmental crises; they will be difficult to alleviate.

The civil war that has consumed Ethiopia since 1962 involves the simultaneous combustion of all five crises. Again, the identity crisis manifested itself first. Over half the population of forty-four million is in rebellion (four million Eritreans, five million Tigreans, and fifteen million Oromoans). Eritrea, increasingly populated by Arabic-speaking Muslims, became a province of Ethiopia with Western help following World War II. When the Ethiopian government formally and permanently annexed Eritrea in 1962, the Eritreans rose in rebellion against the Marxist-Leninist regime of Ethiopia. At first the Muslims were in the vanguard of the struggle against Ethiopian Addis Ababa regime; however, in the 1970s, a Christian Eritrean rebel movement usurped the leadership role. Besides the Eritreans, the Ethiopian government has had to suppress the movement for self-determination among the Tigrean people (one-third of whom are Muslim). Government mismanagement and callousness cost over a hundred thousand Tigreans their lives to hunger and disease in the Ethiopian famine of 1972 to 1973. The Tigreans vowed never to die quietly again and have since engaged in guerrilla warfare against the government. In turn, Ethiopia's military government has spent over seventeen years trying to crush the Eritrean and Tigrean movements. In this effort it has received enormous help from the Russians and Cubans. When these two benefactors stopped supporting the Mengistu Haile Miriam's regime in Addis Ababa, the Ethiopian regime fell. The Eritreans took over of all of Eritrea, the Tigreans took over the Tigre province, and the country slid into anarchy.[307]

Algeria has been rocked recently by the legitimacy and participation crises. Beginning with the massive uprisings in October 1988 in which more than six hundred people were killed and over ten thousand were injured, the military regime of Chadli Benjedid relented and in February 1989 announced its decision to adopt a multiparty system. This was the first time since Algeria's independence from France in 1962 that Islamic groups had been allowed to organize themselves into political parties. The Islamic Salvation Front (FIS), which stressed a plan to establish an Islamic state with the Quran as the constitution, won 55 percent of the vote in the June 1989 regional elections and 49 percent of the vote in the first round of the general election on December 26, 1991. In fact, the FIS won 188 out of 430 seats in the national legislature and needed only an additional 28 out of 199 seats in the second round of runoff voting to be held on January 16, 1992. The secular socialist National Liberation Front, on the other hand, won only 15 seats in parliament. Although the party has governed Algeria since independence, the National Liberation Front was perceived by the Algerian people as guilty of authoritarianism, corruption, nepotism, close ties with France (Algeria's unpopular former colonial master), and above all, gross mismanagement of an economy suffering from 100 percent inflation and 25 percent unemployment.

---

[307]James F. Dunnigan and Austin Bay, *A Quick & Dirty Guide to War: Briefings on Present and Potential Wars,* rev. ed., New York: William Morrow and Co./Quill, 1991, pp. 308–310.

Western leaders and Pragmatists in the Muslim world were shocked that the Islamicists walked away with almost half the national vote despite competition from forty other political parties. The secularized elite of the Algerian army, fearing the victory of the Islamic fundamentalists and the loss of their positions, privileges, and comfortable lives at the very minimum, pressured Benjedid to resign and cracked down on the FIS. On the day Algerians were to celebrate the occasion of the Arab world's first genuine multiparty democracy, the army called on Muhammad Boudiaf—a hero from Algeria's war of independence against France who had just returned to Algiers after three decades of exile in Morocco—to head an army-backed five-member "collegial presidency" and run the country in place of the elected leaders until new elections were held. Boudiaf was assassinated by Islamic fundamentalists in early July 1992. The country is sitting today on a time bomb because of the legitimacy, participation, and distribution crises.[308]

SUMMARY

The unhappy predicament of the nation-building, modernizing, and secularizing Muslim world invites certain conclusions. The five developmental crises, in no discernible or definitive sequence, have afflicted the fragile nation-states of the developing world. However, the identity crisis is often the precipitating crisis in the Muslim world; it triggers political chaos and national catastrophe. Nevertheless, the identity crisis is not a priori; it is both symptomatic of and a contributor to the other crises. In essence, it serves as catalyst.

The apparent primacy of the identity crisis suggests the government's failure of achieving political development, of establishing valid political institutions, and of instilling national consciousness; it is a failure of nation-building. Regimes throughout the Muslim world have been incapable of understanding or undertaking successful political development. Unlike Europe and the United States, the Muslim world was initially conceived as a single political and religious unit. The creation of nation-states from the dismemberment of this unit was an artificial and arbitrary contrivance of the colonial powers; it was not wholly consensual. Consequently, the resulting false borders were rejected as truly legitimate among Muslims. This rejection has been exacerbated by the oppressive, but otherwise ineffectual, leadership of Muslim secularists who are loyal to the secular nation-state and want their countrymen to be as well.

In reaction, Muslims have sought more legitimate, more comforting, and more effective definitions of identity and community—definitions excluding "nation-state," but including everything from tribe and race to language and religion.

---

[308]Alfred Hermida, "Algeria: Fundamentalists Sweep to Near Victory," *Middle East International,* January 10, 1992, pp. 7–9; "Algeria: An Alarming No Vote," *Time,* January 13, 1992, p. 28; "Fundamentalist Leaders Reported Arrested in Algeria," *New York Times,* January 20, 1992, p. A-3; Stephen Budiansky, "Democracy's Detours: Holding Elections Does Not Guarantee that Freedom will Follow," *U.S. News & World Report,* January 27, 1992, p. 49; Howard La Franchi, "Algeria's Leadership Chooses Head of Ruling Council," *The Christian Science Monitor,* January 16, 1992, p. 3; "Algerian Islamic Parties," *The Minaret,* Summer 1989, Vol. 10, No. 3, p. 36.

The question becomes. On what basis and at what level should "community" be delineated? Sincere revivalists, particularly the Fundamentalists and Traditionalists, wish to unify Muslims under the banner of the universal *umma,* under the universal law of the *Shariah;* they advocate pan-Islamism. At the other extreme, community units smaller than the nation-state are arising—units based on family, a religious sect, a tribe, or a village. But whether the pull is toward utopian universalism or narrow parochialism, the pull is decidedly away from the nation-state. As an appropriate and acknowledged unit of community, the nation-state, like the Muslim secularist leadership advocating it, is discredited.

The developmental crises are cumulatively hastening the dissolution of the Muslim nation-state. The Muslim secularists and Pragmatists have been unable to establish national institutions to forestall or resolve the developmental crises or to satisfy the imperatives of differentiation, equality, and capacity. Hence, these nations are politically underdeveloped, and are today held together by raw force alone. The Muslim secularists and Pragmatists have failed to build working political institutions or cohesive nations. Their regimes are illegitimate and their ideologies inappropriate, and they have chosen to oppress the masses rather than to submit to the inevitable—that is, the dissolution of the nation-state.

Chapter
8

Islamic Revivalism in the Arab-Israeli Context

The Arab-Israeli conflict has contributed to the global revival of political Islam in two ways. The Palestinian people's inability since 1948 to wrest any substantive concessions from the Israeli government through peaceful negotiations, and the failure of the secular PLO leadership after decades of struggle to deliver on their promise of Palestinian autonomy, have disenchanted Palestinian Muslims specifically and all Muslims generally. Furthermore, the military ineffectiveness of secular Arab regimes in wars with Israel has frustrated and alienated many Muslims. Consequently, the people of the Muslim world are turning increasingly to Islam as the answer to this muddled, bewildering, and long-festering conflict.

No question, the truest victims of this dispute are the Palestinians—a people homeless, stateless, and friendless. They have been ill-served by incompetent and unscrupulous leaders and have been exploited and persecuted by colonial and neocolonial powers. The leaders of Muslim countries have paid mere lip-service to their dream of a Palestinian homeland. Moreover, their most basic human needs for food, clothing, shelter, and jobs have gone largely unmet.[309]

In 1948, as the state of Israel took its first breath, thousands of Palestinians were terrorized and driven from their homes by overzealous Zionists. Others maintain that these Palestinians fled on the urging of neighboring Arab governments, who initially rejected Israel's right to exist and considered the Jewish state a foreign neocolonial cancer in the heart of the Arab world.

---

[309]David M. Rosenbaum, "The Possibility of Middle East Peace," paper presented for the International Relations of the Middle East course at the University of South Alabama, May 23, 1992, p. 3.

Despite these conflicting accounts of the initial Palestinian diaspora, it is indisputable that many thousands of Jewish refugees were emigrating to Israel from around the world while 700,000 Palestinians were becoming refugees, living in squalor in Egypt's Gaza Strip, Jordan's West Bank, Syria, and Lebanon. As the Jews returned to Zion, the Palestinians lost their state and home.[310] The Arab-Israeli wars of 1967 and 1973 contributed to the Palestinian exodus, and to swelling refugee camps. Likewise, many Palestinians were victimized in the Jordanian Civil War of 1970 and in two Israeli invasions of Lebanon in 1978 and 1982. Although these conflicts targeted the Palestine Liberation Organization (PLO), many innocent Palestinians suffered. For example, following the PLO evacuation of Beirut in 1982, two thousand Palestinians, most old men, women, and children, were slaughtered in the Sabra and Shatila refugee camps in Lebanon. The attackers, who acted with Israeli army complicity, were members of the paramilitary wing of the Christian Phalangists—a tightly organized rightist political party committed to preserving the Maronite Catholic control of Lebanon.

The 1.2 million Palestinians who remained in what had been Palestine and was now under Israeli jurisdiction were hardly any better off. Through a systematic policy of discrimination and persecution, the powerless Palestinians in Israel were relegated to second-class Israeli citizenship or became little more than refugees in the occupied West Bank and Gaza Strip. A dramatic increase in numbers in the Israeli government's settlement policy in those territories uprooted thousands of Palestinians to make way for newly arriving Zionists.

The predicament of the Palestinians in the last fifty years has been psychologically devastating. They have been stripped not only of the land of their fathers, but of their very identity. While they have focused primarily on the Israelis in their struggle to establish a Palestinian state, whether adjacent to or in the place of Israel, their enemies are not always Zionists.

Serious and sometimes explosive tension underlies the relationship between Palestinians and other Arabs. While Egypt, Syria, and Jordan have warred with Israel ostensibly in the name of the Palestinian plight, Palestinians recognize that Egypt fights only for Egypt, Syria fights only for Syria, and Jordan fights only for Jordan. National interests motivate the actions of the Arab states neighboring Israel. Their promotion of the Palestinian cause is often symbolic. Meanwhile, the Palestinians are "reviled by self-proclaimed sympathizers. . . ."[311] One Palestinian explained that

> the real enemy of the Palestinians is the other Arabs. That is because we know the Zionists are against us, but the Arabs say they are friends and brothers, but the truth is that they just use us for what they need.[312]

Thus, the alienation of the Palestinians is complete; their identity, uncertain. They cannot identify themselves according to a homeland. They have none.

---

[310]Geoffrey Regan, *Israel and the Arabs,* Cambridge: Cambridge University Press, 1984, pp. 20–23.

[311]Nels Johnson, *Islam and the Politics of Meaning in Palestinian Nationalism,* London: Kegan Paul International Ltd., 1982, p. 61.

[312]Ibid.

Yet they consider themselves once and future Palestinians. Their current situation is best characterized as being in limbo with their identity in flux. In fact, many Palestinians refer to their struggle as not merely an independence movement, but an unfolding revolution.[313] Given this chronic and unresolved crisis of identity, the Palestinians are susceptible to Islamic revivalism, and Islam as a source of identity and security.

However, the homeless Palestinians have traditionally embraced secular nationalism and have fought ceaselessly since 1948 to establish a homeland in any part of the former Palestine. They have trusted politically adept leaders like Yasir Arafat and have avoided Islamic revivalism as an idiom of their struggle. Nevertheless, the Palestinians are predominantly Muslim, and their forty-six-year failed struggle against Israel has led to the empowerment of Fundamentalist factions within the Unified Leadership of the Uprising (UNLU), which the traditionally secular PLO has long controlled. In response, PLO chairman Yasir Arafat has turned recently to Islam. Facing presumably in the direction of Mecca while in his jet, he portrays himself as the devout Muslim, caressing his prayer beads. In this respect, Arafat has become a Pragmatist. He has sensed the growing revivalism among Palestinians and is effecting revivalist tendencies, contributing to the movement. The conflict, therefore, between the pan-Islamism of revivalism and Palestinian nationalism is unresolved. Arafat considers the PLO's raison d'être the establishment of Palestine, a sovereign nation-state. This is conceptually irreconcilable with true revivalist pan-Islamism.

As a Muslim Pragmatist, Arafat embraces Islam today because secular nationalism has become increasingly discredited among Palestinians as a motivating force in the struggle against Israel. A chief advisor to Arafat, Hani Hassan, told Alan Hart in 1988 that, "[W]e discovered that not less than *sixty percent* of our young people in the occupied territories were thinking that Islamic fundamentalism had more to offer than the PLO."[314] Although Arafat remains much adored by most Palestinians, the failure of the PLO to achieve appreciable success in its struggle against Israel, even as it moderates its policy toward the Jewish state, has disheartened Palestinians. Defeat after defeat, in combat and in negotiation, has gradually soured Palestinians toward the secular and pragmatic direction of the PLO. The Pragmatists, like Arafat, have been demonstrably ineffectual, even as they change tactics against the Israelis. Therefore, the desperate and alienated Palestinians are turning to religion—and to Islamic revivalism as their new idiom of protest.

Muslims all over the world are understandably exasperated with their leaders for having failed to defeat the Israelis, either militarily or diplomatically, in the last five decades. Politically active Fundamentalist and Traditionalist groups are today successfully attacking the status quo and mobilizing the masses by promising to defeat and destroy Israel. The Muslim people tired of their dictatorial regimes—mainly governed by Muslim Pragmatists and Modernists—are heeding the call of

---

[313]Ibid.

[314]Quoted in Alan Hart, *Arafat: A Political Biography,* Bloomington and Indianapolis, IN: Indiana University Press, 1989, p. 519.

the Fundamentalists and Traditionalists. Thus, the Arab-Palestinian-Israeli conflict, unresolved after fifty years, is not only contributing to the Islamic revival, but is radicalizing it.

THE FIRST ARAB-ISRAELI WAR: 1948–1949

In November of 1947, the United Nations General Assembly adopted Resolution 181, which called for the partition of Palestine into two sovereign states, one Jewish and one Arab. The Palestinian Arabs and the Arab League rejected the resolution, and conflict between Palestinian and Jewish settlers in the region grew more pronounced. The British, who for decades had administered Palestine, evacuated their forces on May 15, 1948, unable to further referee the conflict. Immediately, Jewish settlers proclaimed the establishment of the state of Israel. Concurrently, five Arab armies, in the name of the Arab League, invaded Palestine to eradicate the new Jewish state. However, the Arab advantage in numbers and strategic positioning were squandered by their gross ineptitude and consistent failure to mount a joint offensive. Thus, the Israelis won the war by December of 1948.

The results of the first Arab-Israeli war were profound. First, the land allocated to the Palestinians by U.N. Resolution 181 had been either conquered by the Israelis or divided between Egypt and Transjordan. No Palestinian state, with three foreign powers occupying it, could come into being. Arab-Palestinian tension was rooted in this development. Arab defense of Palestinian rights had degenerated into a land grab—Transjordan took the West Bank, Egypt the Gaza Strip. The Palestinians grew increasingly aware that they could count only on themselves. Second, the Palestinian refugee problem became acute. Banished from their homes in Israel, the Palestinians were now truly homeless and stateless. And third, the victory of tiny Israel against numerically superior Arab forces was both surprising and embarrassing to the Muslim world.[315] The people accused their civilian governments of incompetence and corruption. Consequently, incapable of defending either the Palestinians or themselves, these corrupt governments were toppled by military coups and populist leaders.

The failure of Arab regimes to defeat Israel and the consequent internal upheaval was particularly significant in Egypt. Different groups coalesced in common opposition to the discredited government of King Farouk. In this atmosphere of despair, Egypt's Gamal Abdel Nasser, leader of the Free Officers Movement, overthrew Farouk's regime in 1952. Nasser rose to power concomitantly with an ideology of Arab socialism, pan-Arabism (pan-Arab nationalism), and anti-Zionism, becoming president himself in 1954. (See Box 8.1.)

Ironically the Fundamentalist *Ikhwan al-Muslimun* originally supported Nasser and the Free Officers Movement in 1952. The *Ikhwan* had been consistently outspoken in its displeasure at the Farouk government, which it blamed for the Israeli victory in the 1948 Arab-Israeli war. Moreover, the Fundamentalist

---

[315]Itamar Rabinovich, "Seven Wars and One Peace Treaty," in Alvin Z. Rubinstein, ed., *The Arab-Israeli Conflict: Perspectives,* New York: Praeger Publishers, 1988, p. 46.

Box 8.1 AYATOLLAH KHOMEINI AND GAMAL ABDEL NASSER COMPARED

The fact that Iran's Ayatollah Khomeini and Egypt's Gamal Abdel Nasser differed in so many respects, particularly with respect to their ideological proclivities, makes the shocking commonalities in their lives that much more worthy of examination. Nasser and Khomeini were of humble birth, neither was a prince, neither had the world handed to him. Both men lived simple and austere lives. The material trappings of power had no hold over them. Both were unpretentious in speech. Nasser spoke the language of the people, inspiring millions of Arabs in colloquial and not classical Arabic. Likewise, Khomeini eschewed the classical Persian in which he was proficient in favor of colloquial Persian. Identifying themselves with the poor and underprivileged masses, both overthrew unpopular, pro-Western monarchies. Neither explicitly assumed political power in the initial phase of their revolutions, but both were king-makers and wasted no time assuming power themselves. Khomeini and Nasser alike craved power both within and beyond the borders of their nations.

As a revolutionary, Nasser utilized a growing Arab nationalism to take power in Egypt. Similarly, Khomeini, as the senior Muslim divine in Iran, stood in the vanguard of revolutionary upheaval in Iran. Khomeini and Nasser were transformational revolutionaries who overturned the status quo and inaugurated massive social changes in their respective countries. But they

---

Ikhwan at that time accepted the secular vision of pan-Arabism, in contrast to "ideal" revivalism, but only as a first step toward pan-Islamism. Nevertheless, relations soon became strained when the *Ikhwan* demanded to select representatives to the revolutionary government. The Revolutionary Command Council (RCC), governing Egypt at the time, rejected these demands. In 1953, the government outlawed all political parties except its own. Then, in early 1954, the *Ikhwan* and the RCC came to blows again. As Nasser struggled to assume control of Egypt, the *Ikhwan* rose in protest.

Politically threatened by the extremist *Ikhwan*, Nasser began systematically to suppress the organization in the first year of his presidency. Using as his pretext an assassination attempt by a member of the *Ikhwan*, Nasser condemned the entire organization and arrested its activists. With most of its leaders behind bars and Nasser making a meteoric rise to popularity throughout the Muslim world, the Fundamentalist *Ikhwan*, and like-minded revivalists, saw a decade-long decline in fortunes. Within two years, Nasser emerged as a charismatic Arab statesman—an emergence effected by his defiance of the West and of Israel in the Suez War of 1956.

shook not only their own countries but the world around them as well. Both were supremely self-confident—and it was this self-confidence which was Nasser's undoing in the 1967 War with Israel and Khomeini's despair in the fruitless war with Iraq. Nevertheless, Khomeini and Nasser both stood up to the great powers. Nasser faced down Britain, France, and Israeli in the Suez Crisis (with a little help from Eisenhower), while Khomeini defied the United States. Their repudiation of Western assistance endeared both men to the masses, and their attempts to export revolution throughout the Muslim world frightened their pro-Western neighbors. Moreover, Khomeini and Nasser piqued Western anger with blatantly anti-Western policies and in-flammtory rhetoric, promising and delivering on promises to break their countries' dependency on the West and to take positions of leadership in the Muslim world. Both repudiated imported Western political, economic, and social systems and values. They opted instead to pursue their own models and ideologies.

Khomeini and Nasser will both be remembered as uncompromising authoritarians, as ideologues and as revolutionaries. Yet both were poor administrators who mismanaged their economies. But they remain figures who appealed to the masses with their populist styles and with their fearlessness in the face of incredible odds. Destiny, they believed, was theirs, and no matter what one thinks of them, history will remember their names and deeds.

Source: Rafael Calis, "Letter from the Editor," *The Middle East*, Issue No. 62, December 1979, p. 7.

THE 1956 SUEZ WAR

On July 26, 1956, Nasser nationalized the strategically vital Suez Canal, a decision that prompted British, French, and Israeli forces to stage a military strike against Egypt. Although the Israelis performed well, the Anglo-French operation floundered. Immediately, the United States forced the British and the French to abandon their efforts, and likewise persuaded the Israelis to evacuate the Sinai Peninsula and the Gaza Strip.

The results of the brief Suez War were threefold. First, Israel proved, yet again, it was militarily powerful. Second, the Egyptians agreed to the demilitarization of the Sinai and the stationing of U.N. forces in the Gaza Strip. Third, the war was a major political victory for Nasser.[316] By standing up to the West and to Israel, Nasser now enjoyed unequaled stature throughout the Muslim world. He became the idol of the masses. The popularity of his ideologies of pan-Arabism and Arab socialism became enshrined in "Nasserism."

---

[316]Leon Carl Brown, "The June 1967 War: A Turning Point?" in Yehuda Lukas and Abdalla M. Battah, eds., *The Arab-Israeli Conflict: Two Decades of Change*, Boulder, CO: Westview Press, 1988, p. 133.

Nevertheless, the voices of Islamic revivalist discontent could still be heard within Egypt. As Nasser undertook the socialist transformation of his country and improved relations with the Soviet Union, the Egyptian religious establishment feared their country was drifting toward atheistic communism. To defend his policies from the attacks of the Traditionalist *ulama*, Nasser co-opted clerics (with such offers as money or jobs for relatives). When this failed, he intimidated them. Thus, Nasser persuaded a number of the *ulama* either to endorse his foreign and domestic policies, or to abstain from criticizing them.

The *Ikhwan*, meanwhile, was unsatisfied. In August 1965, fearing a resurgence of the Fundamentalist organization, Nasser spread a story of a second *Ikhwan*-sponsored plot to assassinate him. Again, Nasser's security forces hunted down, arrested, and imprisoned *Ikhwan* leaders and activists. This, however, was hardly the end of the Fundamentalist revivalism in general, or the *Ikhwan* in particular. Events in 1967 would favor the reemergence of Islamic revivalism, and would discredit Nasser's ideologies of pan-Arabism and Arab socialism. In fact, Nasser himself made the transition from secularist to Pragmatist.

THE 1967 ARAB-ISRAELI WAR

For ten years following his spectacular performance in the 1956 Suez Crisis, Nasser decided to avoid direct military confrontation with Israel while he strengthened the Egyptian military and gloried in his position of preeminence among Arab leaders. Nevertheless, by 1967 events overtook the charismatic Egyptian president, resulting in a war that humiliated his military and tarnished his glory.

Unable to resist either challenges to his reputation or Soviet reports of a fictitious Israeli attack plan against Syria, Nasser took steps that would test the legitimacy of his regime and of his ideology and that would provoke the Israeli leadership.[317] Nasser sent U.N. forces packing, remilitarized the Sinai Peninsula, and proclaimed a blockade, which he never enforced, of the strategically important Strait of Tiran. Initially, these steps restored Nasser's standing as the leader of Arab nationalism.[318] However, Nasser's decisions would soon embarrass and humble him.

Considering Nasser's actions as equivalent to a declaration of war, Israel launched a preemptive air attack against Egypt and Syria that destroyed the Arab air forces on the ground. Israel then took the Sinai Peninsula from Egypt, the West Bank and East Jerusalem from Jordan, and the Golan Heights from Syria. The Arab response, where it occurred, was inconsequential. Within six days, Israel had crippled the military capability of Egypt, Syria, and Jordan; had conquered large segments of Arab land, which could be used as a bargaining chip in future peace negotiations; and had seized the holy city of Jerusalem. Having achieved its objectives fully, Israel accepted a U.N.–brokered cease-fire.

---

[317]Rabinovich, "Seven Wars and One Peace Treaty," p. 49.

[318]Ibid., p. 50.

In Egypt and throughout the Muslim world, the psychological injury inflicted by the Israelis was enormous. A period of intense self-examination descended upon Muslims. Nasser, his secular socialist ideologies discredited by the overwhelming defeat, turned to Islamic themes and ritual observances to heal the wounds and relieve the trauma plaguing the Egyptian people. Nasser, famed for his erstwhile secular orientation, turned Pragmatist. He stopped using socialist rhetoric and resorted to an Islamic idiom to rationalize the astounding Arab defeat on the battlefield.[319] Nasser maintained that defeat had been God's will and, therefore, not preventable by any precaution or preparation. He stressed Islamic virtues, like patience and perseverance in the face of adversity.[320] The government even encouraged Islamic activities to help the nation cope with its failure and shame.[321] For instance, on June 19, 1967, Nasser personally participated in the festivities marking the Prophet Muhammad's birthday. This event was heavily covered by the Egyptian media, which prior to the 1967 war had been discouraged from covering such religious events. Moreover, as Nasser continued to emphasize Islam, he fired his secular socialist advisors or encouraged them to resign; he introduced economic liberalization; and he made fraternal overtures to the wealthy, traditional, pro-Western, monarchical regimes of the Persian Gulf whom he had scathingly denounced and even subverted in the previous decade (1957-1967).[322] Meanwhile, numerous Islamic institutions, *masjids*, and the *ulama*, which had been tightly controlled by the government, were allowed to function with relative freedom in the prevailing environment of shock, humiliation, and sadness. Even restrictions on the Fundamentalist *Ikhwan* were relaxed, and many of its members were released from jails.[323]

Muslim Fundamentalists quickly took advantage of their newfound freedom and of the emotional religious atmosphere to offer a simple explanation for the Arab world's shattering defeat: Egypt and other countries had strayed from the "straight path" of Islam that had brought progress and glory in the past. By importing and embracing alien Western ideologies like nationalism and socialism, the Muslim world suffered chronic divisiveness, greater poverty, lack of freedom, and a weaker belief in Islam.[324]

The *Ikhwan al-Muslimun* went further and declared that Arab defeat in the 1967 war was an effective condemnation of the secular policies characteristic of present regimes that ignored or violated the principles of the *Shariah;* a sign of God's revenge for the oppression Muslims had endured under Nasser's dictatorial

---

[319]Waterbury, "Egypt," p. 54; Dessouki, "The Resurgence of Islamic Organization in Egypt," p. 114.

[320]Hanafi, "The Relevance of the Islamic Alternative in Egypt," p. 61.

[321]Waterbury, "Egypt," p. 54.

[322]Dessouki, "The Resurgence of Islamic Organization in Egypt," p. 114; Ayubi, "The Political Revival of Islam," p. 490.

[323]Raphael Israeli, "Islam in Egypt Under Nasir and Sadat: Some Comparative Notes," in Metin Heper and Raphael Israel, eds., *Islam and Politics in the Modern Middle East,* New York: St. Martin's Press, 1984, p. 70.

[324]Ali E. Hillal Dessouki, "Arab Intellectuals and *Al-Nakba:* The Search for Fundamentalism," *Middle Eastern Studies,* Vol. 9, No. 2, May 1973, p. 189.

regime; and God's punishment for Nasser's alliance with the atheistic Soviet state.[325] The *Ikhwan,* in essence, attributed defeat to a lack of faith and stated, "Israel is a religious state, based upon the tenets of Judaism. The Egyptians, who had depended upon a secular ideology, could not hope to withstand the power of religious faith."[326] The *Ikhwan* believed firmly that the imported Western ideologies of socialism, nationalism, and secularism—enshrined in Nasserism—had been defeated, and the only cure for the Muslim world's ills lay in Islamic fundamentalism. Only the staunch practice of Islam would renew Egyptian dignity and courage, or would inspire Egyptians to give their lives as martyrs in a martial *jihad* against Israel.[327] Thus, revivalism gained favor, as had Nasserism before it, on the promise to vanquish Israel.

ARSON AT *AL-AQSA* MOSQUE AND NASSER'S DEATH

After the 1967 Israeli occupation of Jerusalem's eastern section, frustration and anger steadily built throughout the Muslim world. This frustration was aggravated by the Israeli government's attempts to Judaize the city after 1967 by expropriating Arab lands, demolishing Arab homes, expelling eminent political and intellectual leaders of the Arab community, and requiring Arab schools to teach a history that destorted Arab claims to Palestine.

On August 21, 1969, a deranged Australian Zionist set fire to the *Al-Aqsa* mosque in East Jerusalem, and the Muslim world rose up in protest. The arsonist's sacrilege seemed to many Muslims all too symptomatic of Israeli abuses upon East Jerusalem.

Two days following the fire, Nasser penned a letter rife with Islamic imagery and symbolism to his defense minister.

> We shall return to Jerusalem and Jerusalem will be returned to us . . . we shall not lay down our arms until God grants His soldiers the victory and until His right is dominant, His house respected and true peace is restored to the city of peace.[328]

Meanwhile, there was a vigorous discussion in the media and a proliferation of literature examining the centrality of Jerusalem for Islam. Later, in 1970, the fifth conference of *Al-Azhar*'s Academy of Islamic Research devoted a substantial part of its proceedings to a discussion of the Islamic nature of Jerusalem and Palestine.[329] In essence, in Egypt and throughout much of the Muslim world, the arson and desecration of the *Al-Aqsa* mosque reinforced the revivalist trend already pronounced since the 1967 war. Likewise, it reminded revivalists that Israel

---

[325]Aly and Wenner, "Modern Islamic Reform Movements," p. 345; Dessouki, "The Resurgence of Islamic Organization in Egypt," p. 114.

[326]Aly and Wenner, "Modern Islamic Reform Movements," p. 345.

[327]Dessouki, "The Resurgence of Islamic Organization in Egypt," p. 114.

[328]Quoted in Haddad, *Contemporary Islam,* pp. 35–36.

[329]Ibid., p. 36.

stood between the *umma* and sacred Jerusalem. Israel, therefore, remained a significant enemy.

The death of Nasser in 1970 increased the Egyptian regime's reliance on the politics of Islam and thus directly contributed to Islamic revivalism. Nasser's successor, Anwar Sadat, heightened political Islam by fully lifting the ban of the political activities of the *Ikhwan al-Muslimun*. Sadat's motives were simple. Unleashing the *Ikhwan* effectively neutralized the influence of the socialists who sought to topple the Sadat government. Sadat, like Nasser following the 1967 War, was an adept Pragmatist, engaging in revivalist politics in domestic and foreign policies. Many of Sadat's speeches, statements, and actions were intentionally given Islamic overtones. Sadat's emphasis on the Islamic idiom was epitomized within three years by the 1973 war with Israel.

THE 1973 ARAB-ISRAELI WAR

While the defeat inflicted on the Arabs by Israel in 1967 led to a period of intense self-evaluation and laid the groundwork for the Islamic revival in several Arab nations, the Arab-Israeli War of October 1973 added great impetus to the incipient revival. Although the 1973 war was fought to a military stalemate, and the Arabs regained none of the lands lost to them in 1967, the conflict began with a successful Arab invasion of Israel's fortified military positions. There were three consequences of this initial success. First, throughout the Muslim world the Arab effort was perceived as a limited victory. Second, the widely held myths of Arab disunity and military inferiority were dashed. And third, the myth of Israeli invincibility was similarly discredited.

An important feature of the 1973 war was the Arab emphasis on religious symbolism, an emphasis indicative of the influential role played by religion in Egyptian society following the 1967 war. For example, the 1973 war was launched by Sadat during Islam's holy month of Ramadan. The operational code name for the crossing of the Suez Canal by Egyptian forces was "Badr," a reminder of the first Islamic victory under Prophet Muhammad over the *kafirs* in A.D. 623. Moreover, the battle cry in the 1973 Ramadan War was *"Allahu Akbar"* (God is most Great). The battle cry of the Arabs in the Six Day War of June 1967 had been the less-than-inspiring "Land, Sea and Sky," which implied protecting the territory of the Arab world—a secular nationalist idea, rather than a religious one. The 1967 battle cry also implied faith in military equipment and the tactics of military engagement, rather than in God. Many Muslims throughout the world attribute the 1973 Arab victory to God and His modern-day, holy warriors.[330] Thus, Islamic revivalists could later point out that trust in Islam is the surest way to defeat the Israelis.

---

[330]Yvonne Haddad, "The Arab-Israeli Wars, Nasserism, and the Affirmation of Islamic Identity," in John L. Esposito, ed., *Islam and Development: Religion and Sociopolitical Change*, Syracuse, NY: Syracuse University Press, 1980, p. 120.

ISRAEL'S 1982 INVASION OF LEBANON

Following the 1979 Camp David peace agreements, in which Egypt made peace with Israel, the Arabs no longer posed a viable military threat to Israel. Having secured its border with Egypt, Israel could prosecute a limited war on its northern border without risking a substantial regional escalation of hostilities. In this context, Israel invaded Lebanon in 1982 with the following objectives: first, to prevent the PLO from further shelling northern Israel by expelling it from its last "autonomous territorial base"; and second, to establish a Lebanese government favorably disposed to Israel.[331]

The war in Lebanon lasted three months, beginning in June of 1982 under the code name "Operation Peace for Galilee." By early September, Israeli forces laying siege to West Beirut forced the PLO to evacuate from Lebanon. The PLO's departure, however, did not signal an end to the Lebanese war. Instead, the war entered a new phase, marked by Israeli conflict with the majority Lebanese Shi'ah population.

When the Israelis first invaded Lebanon in 1982, Lebanese Christians and Shi'ahs alike rejoiced. Living by the motto, "the enemy of my enemy is my friend," the Shi'ahs welcomed the Israeli soldiers as liberators who would finally rid Lebanon of the overbearing Palestinians. However, while the Lebanese Shi'ahs had begun to dislike and resent the Palestinians for destabilizing their lives, they distrusted and feared the Israelis more.[332]

Although a "tacit understanding" did exist between the Israelis and Shi'ah guerrilla groups, this understanding ended abruptly when, after the Israelis had expelled the common enemy, the Palestinians, the conquerors overstayed their welcome and oppressed the local population. Although welcoming the elimination of the PLO as a political and military presence in Lebanon, the Shi'ahs soon realized they had merely witnessed the substitution of one occupation force by another.[333] In effect, the Shi'ahs had invited the cats inside to frighten away the mice. Now they could not get rid of the cats.

Various Shi'ah guerrilla organizations began a long, aggressive, and even violent campaign against the Israelis. The Shi'ah group *Amal* represented, at least initially, the most popular and most secular Shi'ah guerrilla group. Other, more radical organizations had significant support among the Shi'ahs, however, and soon eclipsed the *Amal*. These radical groups included the Fundamentalist Islamic *Amal* and the Fundamentalist *Hezbollah* (Party of God).[334] These two organizations represented radical revivalism in the struggle against the Israeli in-

---

[331]Rabinovich, "Seven Wars and One Peace Treaty," p. 52; Daniel C. Diller, ed., *The Middle East,* 7th ed., Washington, D.C.: Congressional Quarterly, Inc., 1990, p. 33.

[332]Augustus Richard Norton, *Amal and the Shi'a: Struggle for the Soul of Lebanon,* Austin, TX: University of Texas Press, 1987, p. 85.

[333]Ibid., p. 86.

[334]Clinton Bailey, "Lebanon's Shi'is After the 1982 War," in Martin Kramer, ed., *Shi'ism, Resistance, and Revolution,* Boulder, CO: Westview Press, 1987, p. 220.

vaders, and enjoyed friendly relations with Iran's newly founded Islamic Republic. While the goal of the *Amal* was to stabilize Lebanon and transform it into a secular state ruled by the Shi'ah majority and sovereign from undue outside influence, the goal of the radical Fundamentalist Islamic *Amal* and *Hezbollah* was an Islamic revolution in Lebanon and the establishment of an Islamic republic.[335]

The campaign of the Shi'ahs against the Israelis inflicted heavy Israeli casualties, which made the Lebanese war increasingly unpopular in Israel. By 1985, Israel evacuated most of Lebanon, having achieved only the expulsion of the PLO. Even this success, however, was tarnished. The PLO fighters in southern Lebanon were replaced by *Amal,* Islamic *Amal,* and *Hezbollah* fighters whose skill in harassing the Israelis has impressed even the exiled PLO.

Revivalist success on the battlefield in Lebanon proved to many Muslims that Israel could be checked not by secular leaders and secular forces, but only by true, Fundamentalist *mujahids.* The Shi'ahs had achieved success against the Israelis that the PLO had not. The lesson was not lost on the PLO or on Palestinians living in the Occupied Territories. Taught by example and distraught by the consistent failures of the past, the Palestinians turned ever more fully to Islam and to fundamentalism.

THE *INTIFADAH*

According to the 1947 U.N. Partition Plan, the territories of the West Bank and the Gaza Strip were to be integral components of the Arab Palestinian state. However, following the 1948 invasion of Palestine by Arab armies ostensibly in support of the Palestinian cause, the Egyptians assumed control of the Gaza Strip and King Abdullah of Transjordan officially annexed the West Bank.

The 1967 war replaced the Arab occupiers of Palestinian land with Israeli occupiers, and Israel has administered both the West Bank and the Gaza Strip ever since. Originally, Israel considered the occupied territories as bargaining chips to exchange with the Arabs for peace. The stunning victory of 1967, however, emboldened the Israeli government to reject Arab peace overtures immediately after the war. Israeli intransigence hardened, while the Palestinians living in the West Bank and the Gaza Strip continued to endure occupation.

Although West Bank Palestinians enjoyed material economic gains in the late 1960s and early 1970s, benefitting from a boom in the Israeli economy, the Palestinians still recognized their occupiers as foreigners. In fact, the Palestinians in the occupied territories paid in taxes the cost of the Israeli occupation. Add to that a litany of human rights abuses perpetrated on the Palestinians, and a portrait of resentment, frustration, and alienation emerges, a portrait that no material gain could ever erase or obscure.[336]

---

[335]Ibid.

[336]Charles D. Smith, *Palestine and the Arab-Israeli Conflict,* 2nd ed., New York: St. Martin's Press, 1992, pp. 241–243.

The first anti-Israeli uprising occurred immediately following the Israeli victory and occupation in June 1967. As civil-disobedience campaigns in the Occupied Territories devolved into rebellion in Gaza, the Israeli army stepped in, forcefully suppressed the demonstrators, and restored order. The West Bank experienced popular upheaval after the 1973 Arab-Israeli War. The Israelis responded with arrests and deportations. In the early 1980s protests and demonstrations again took place in the Occupied Territories. The Israeli expulsion of the PLO from Lebanon, however, quieted the desperate and demoralized populace. In addition, Israeli treatment of demonstrators toughened under Defense Minister Yitzhak Rabin's "Iron Fist" policy, inaugurated in 1985.[337]

Fearing eradication as a political and social unit, the Palestinians, provoked by a relatively minor incident, rose against their Israeli occupiers. The *intifadah* (translated variously as "shaking" or "uprising") of Palestinians, which began in December 1987, for the first time in the Arab-Israeli conflict drew world attention to the plight of the long-forgotten Palestinians living in the Israeli-occupied territories. Israel's tempestuous relations with her Arab neighbors were suddenly eclipsed. Now the focus shifted to "Israel's relations with the Arabs who lived under its occupation."[338]

On December 8, 1987, four innocent Palestinian workers driving into the Gaza Strip were rammed by an Israeli military tank transport and killed. This traffic accident ignited the *intifadah*—the massive, popular, and sustained Palestinian uprising against Israeli occupation. Soon after the *intifadah* began, Palestinian activists from various groups and factions formed the Unified National Leadership of the Uprising (UNLU) to coordinate their strategy and tactics. While local grass roots committees were the backbone of the UNLU, the PLO was its dominant member. Acting as an umbrella organization, the PLO/UNLU invited the participation in the uprising of Islamic revivalists, who represented the most serious opponent to the PLO's secular nationalism and to its overtures of peace and compromise with Israel embodied in the Palestinian National Council's Palestinian Declaration of Independence of November 1988. The PLO/UNLU realized that "the major organizational and political challenge to the UNLU came . . . from the avowedly Moslem political organizations. . . ."[339]

While most Palestinians remained loyal to the PLO, Islamic revivalists increasingly gained adherents in the Occupied Territories, particularly in the Gaza Strip. At first the revivalist activities centered around local *masjids*, schools, colleges, and universities, where Muslim clerics and teachers inculcated Palestinian youth with a politically activist Islamic message. Ironically, the Islamic revivalists

---

[337]Ann Mosely Lesch, "Anatomy of an Uprising: The Palestinian Intifada," in Peter F. Krogh and Mary C. McDavid, eds., *Palestinians Under Occupation: Prospects for the Future,* Washington, D.C.: Georgetown University Press, 1989, pp. 90–91.

[338]Diller, *The Middle East,* p. 37.

[339]Helena Cobban, "The PLO and the Intifada," in Robert O. Freedman, ed., *The Intifada: Its Impact on Israel, the Arab World, and the Superpowers,* Miami: Florida International University Press, 1991, p. 76.

established effective institutions in Gaza with Israeli complicity. Fundamentalist and Traditionalist leaders were seldom harassed by the Israelis to the extent that PLO members were. Apparently the Israelis hoped to undercut PLO support and essentially divide and weaken the Palestinian movement by pitting the Islamicists against the secular-leaning PLO. However, this strategy backfired when the Islamic fundamentalists entered the forefront of the opposition to the occupation.[340] Even the PLO itself supported the more radical fundamentalist Islamic *Jihad* in 1979 to undermine the relatively moderate Islamic fundamentalist *Ikhwan's* growing popularity in Gaza Strip.[341]

The growth of Islamic revivalism in the West Bank and Gaza increased after the Iranian Islamicists succeeded in defeating and overthrowing the Shah's powerful security apparatus, establishing an Islamic republic, and remaining in power despite formidable odds. The success of the Lebanese Shi'ah fundamentalists, inspired by the example of the Iranian Revolution, in expelling the Western multinational forces and Israelis from southern Lebanon in the fall of 1983 further accelerated the growth of the Islamic movement in the Occupied Territories. Thousands of young, energetic, and zealous Palestinian students joined Islamic student organizations and youth groups in the Gaza Strip and West Bank during the 1980s.[342]

Despite the phenomenal growth of Islamic revivalism in the Israeli-occupied territories, the Islamic revivalists played an inconsequential role in the first days of the *intifadah.* Initially, the *Ikhwan* termed the uprising inappropriate "Muslim social behavior," and took a nonactivist approach to the *intifadah.* Apparently, the formerly-fundamentalist *Ikhwan* had mellowed with age. Although accepting compromise with the Israeli state and openly hostile to the secular nationalist PLO, the *Ikhwan* backed up its rhetoric not with militarism, but by espousing "an essentially educational and social role for its adherents."[343] The *Ikhwan* controlled three universities in the Occupied Territories with a strictly Traditionalist Islamic curriculum.[344] Consequently, the *Ikhwan,* having become moderate in its orientation, was left behind in the *intifadah.*

Shaikh Ahmed Yassin, the *Ikhwan's* influential spiritual leader and the head of the Islamic Center in Gaza, was unhappy with the *Ikhwan's* emphasis on merely cultivating more religious, moral, and ethical Palestinian Muslims. More important, he was inspired by the example of Ayatollah Khomeini standing up to the Western powers and came to believe that Palestinian Muslims ought to actively struggle to achieve an Islamic state in Palestine and should fight courageously in the front lines of the *intifadah.* Therefore, in August 1988, he founded

---

[340]Don Peretz, *Intifada: The Palestinian Uprising,* Boulder, CO: Westview Press, 1990, p. 43.

[341]Cobban, "The PLO and the Intifada," p. 78.

[342]Lisa Taraki, "The Islamic Resistance Movement in the Palestinian Uprising," *Middle East Report,* Vol. 19, No. 1, January–February 1989, p. 30.

[343]Cobban, "The PLO and the Intifada," p. 77.

[344]Charles D. Smith, *Palestine and the Arab-Israeli Conflict,* op. cit., p. 295.

the Islamic fundamentalist *Harakatal-Muqawama al-Islamiyya* (Islamic Resistance Movement), known better by its Arabic acronym, *Hamas*.[345] Shaikh Yassin's *Hamas* dubbed itself the newest in a historical chain of militant fundamentalist organizations,

> beginning with the revolt of Shaikh 'Izz al-Din al-Qassam and his Muslim Brotherhood comrades in the 1930s through the *jihad* of the Palestinians in 1948 and the operations of the Muslim Bretherin since 1968.[346]

Hamas portrayed itself as the Muslim answer to Jewish Zionism. In its Communiqué Number 30, *Hamas* refers to Palestine as a *waqf*, an "Islamic trust" to be governed by Muslims until the Day of Judgment. Yassin said Palestinian Muslims were therefore obliged to undertake a *jihad* against the Israeli occupiers who had usurped Muslim land. Yassin's view is remarkably similar, perhaps intentionally, to the Zionist ideology, which views the same land as a divine trust granted to God's chosen people, the Jews, for all time.[347] In contrast to the *Ikhwan*, *Hamas* assumed a more aggressive political role in opposing the Israeli occupation of the West Bank and Gaza Strip. *Hamas* became a powerful organization mobilizing and agitating the Palestinians in the *intifadah*.[348]

The PLO/UNLU attempted to coopt the "increasingly popular Palestinian Islamic groups. . . ."[349] However, while the Islamic *Jihad* accepted UNLU membership and by extrapolation PLO leadership, *Hamas* rejected active membership in the UNLU. Both *Hamas* and Islamic *Jihad* differ with the PLO, first by virtue of their Fundamentalist revivalism and second in their ultimate goals. The revivalists favor the liberation of all of Israel and replacement of the Jewish state with a fundamentalist Islamic one.

In the short run, however, the PLO and the revivalists share the cause of liberating the Occupied Territories from the common Israeli foe. Yet despite official and unofficial coordination of efforts with the PLO, the revivalists emphatically reject all compromise or peaceful coexistence with the Israeli state. Instead, they demand the end of the Zionist state.

Sensitive to fundamentalist belligerency, the Israelis have ceased to give preferential treatment to *Hamas* and Islamic *Jihad*. The Israelis have labeled *Hamas* a "terrorist organization," have arrested Yassin, and have sought to destroy the fundamentalist movement they themselves cultivated.[350] Such efforts, however, have been largely ineffectual against growing Islamic revivalism in the territories, and have entirely failed to quell the Palestinian uprising; instead, they have "unified it,

---

[345]Ibid., p. 299.

[346]Taraki, "The Islamic Resistance Movement in the Palestinian Uprising." p. 30.

[347]Ibid., p. 31.

[348]Cobban, "The PLO and the Intifada," p. 79.

[349]Ibid., p. 81.

[350]Ibid.

solidifying ties that had been tenuous."[351] Israeli repression brought the revivalists and the secular nationalists together, spread the *intifadah* from the Gaza Strip to the West Bank, and attracted all classes of Palestinians to the ranks of the uprising. In contrast to Israel's violent and brutal methods, the Palestinians have reacted rarely with lethal force but with stones, strikes, economic boycotts, and resistance to taxes.[352]

THE GULF WAR AND THE PALESTINIANS

By mid-1990, the Palestinian *intifadah,* in its third year, had begun to founder, and the Palestinians had grown increasingly desperate. Through the *intifadah* they had attracted international attention, but the world community had shed an occasional tear and done nothing else. This explains the ebullient Palestinian response to Iraqi President Saddam Hussein's invasion and occupation of neighboring Kuwait beginning August 2, 1990. After all, "any shakeup in the Arab world could only help the Palestinian cause; things couldn't get worse."[353]

Enthusiasm for Saddam Hussein's actions cut across ideological lines within the Palestinian community and united, if briefly, nationalists and revivalists. For example, the Traditionalists and Fundamentalists in occupied Palestine raised their voices during Friday congregational prayers in support of the secularist-turned-Pragmatist Saddam Hussein. Revivalist support for Hussein, however, represented no love for the Iraqi dictator's pan-Arabism or Arab nationalism; it represented a more intrinsic rejection of Western imperialism against the *umma* and an attack on "the presence of foreign troops in Saudi Arabia," which defiled "the holiest land for Islam."[354]

The Islamic revivalists were joined in their condemnation of Western interventionism by Yasir Arafat. The ubiquitous PLO chairman, taking an enormous political risk in relations with most Arab countries, threw his support behind Saddam Hussein. Yet Arafat's stance was widely misinterpreted in the West and in Arab capitals. Thus, Arafat hastily announced,

> the Palestinians' principled position against taking land by force, but at the same time opposing a foreign military presence in Arab countries and the demand that the Gulf crisis should be solved within an Arab context.[355]

Palestinian support for Hussein, bolstered by the Iraqi president's attempt to link Iraqi withdrawal from Kuwait to simultaneous Israeli withdrawal from the

---

[351]Charles D. Smith, *Palestine and the Arab-Israeli Conflict,* p. 298.

[352]Ibid., pp. 298–299.

[353]Daoud Kuttab, "Emotions Take Over," *Middle East International,* No. 382, August 31, 1990, p. 13.

[354]Ibid.

[355]Daoud Kuttab, "Forgotten Intifada," *Middle East International,* No. 383, September 14, 1990, p. 16.

West Bank and Gaza, was rooted not in dislike of Kuwait, but in "their deep desire for national liberation, their feeling of having been victimized, betrayed, or ignored by the West, and their deep sense of despair at the failure of their leadership, its moderation, and rational political processes to produce tangible change in their living conditions under a brutal occupation."[356]

The "principled position" of the Palestinians during the Gulf crisis brought immediate and substantial cost to the PLO, *Hamas,* and other Palestinian institutions. Significant aid from Kuwaiti and Saudi benefactors ended abruptly after the Palestinians gave their support to Saddam Hussein. In addition, thousands of Palestinian workers and students, expelled from angry Arabic-speaking Persian Gulf kingdoms, returned to the Occupied Territories, requiring jobs and places to live and placing further burdens on an already struggling economy.[357] Since earlier survey information in the Occupied Territories indicated that "the revivalist trend was most evident among the youth and the college-educated,"[358] the revivalists received a political boost with the Palestinian "ingathering" of young workers and students.

The state of the *intifadah,* meanwhile, increasingly stagnated. One journalist observed that "the Gulf crisis has so absorbed everyone's attention that the *intifadah* has been almost completely forgotten."[359] Before the crisis, the uprising was receding. During the crisis it was eclipsed. After the crisis, it became "a kind of permanent state," which began, "to harden and to lose the bright colors of its early days."[360]

Conflict within the Palestinian community since the end of the Persian Gulf War has also heightened as the *intifadah* falters and unity between revivalists and secular nationalists disintegrates. On June 2, 1991, for example, *Hamas* and PLO supporters battled in the streets and suburbs of Nablus. While the conflict was patched up with promises to work together against the common Israeli foe, the days of "national unity" were past.[361]

The keen attraction of revivalist politics in the Occupied Territories can be dulled only if Israel satisfies a few Palestinian demands. Otherwise, political Islam will continue to grow and will replace a discredited PLO. After all, Islamic revivalism offers Palestinians, "ethnic identity, attachment to the land, and cultural purity as Palestinians."[362] Arafat, the lifelong secularist, is moving reluctantly to be-

---

[356]James J. Zogby, "The Strategic Peace Initiative Package: A New Approach to Israeli-Palestinian Peace," *American Arab Affairs,* No. 35, Winter 1990–1991, pp. 181–182.

[357]Kuttab, "Emotions Take Over," p. 14; Kuttab, "Forgotten Intifada," p. 15; Daoud Kuttab, "The Palestinian Economy and the Gulf Crisis," *Middle East International,* No. 383, September 14, 1990, p. 16.

[358]Cobban, "The PLO and the Intifada," p. 77.

[359]Kuttab, "Forgotten Intifada," p. 15.

[360]Azmy Bishara, "Palestine in the New Order," *Middle East Report,* Vol. 22, No. 2, March/April 1992, p. 6.

[361]Daoud Kuttab, "Worries About the Intifada," *Middle East International,* No. 402, June 14, 1991, pp. 12–13.

[362]Emile Sahliyeh, *In Search of Leadership: West Bank Politics Since 1967,* Washington, D.C.: The Brookings Institution, 1988, p. 137.

coming a half-hearted Pragmatist. If the occupation of the West Bank and the Gaza Strip continues much longer, the Fundamentalists will sweep the chairman and his organization away in an ecstasy of fanaticism.

ISRAEL'S 1992 INTERVENTION IN LEBANON

The 1982 Israeli intervention in Lebanon, while signaling the end of Palestinian hegemony in southern Lebanon, bolstered radical and militant revivalist groups within the Shi'ah population of the country. Since 1982, these groups, foremost among them Islamic *Amal* and *Hezbollah,* have staged repeated attacks against Israeli forces in the self-proclaimed "security zone" in south Lebanon. Choosing to answer violence with violence, on February 16, 1992, Israeli helicopter gunships attacked a convoy carrying *Hezbollah* leader Sheikh Abbas Musawi, killing him, his wife, and his six-year-old son. The Lebanese Shi'ahs, avenging the death of their leader, elected a more radical Fundamentalist to succeed Musawi and launched rocket attacks against Jewish settlements in northern Israel.

Unable to break the cycle of violence it had initiated, Israel and its surrogate Lebanese Christian forces invaded *Hezbollah* villages in south Lebanon, brushing aside poorly armed U.N. peacekeeping forces stationed on the border. Within twenty-four hours, the Israelis withdrew and "jubilant Muslim militiamen swarmed back into the region."[363]

Syria's Hafiz al-Assad, just beginning to enjoy hegemony over Lebanon, feared another deeper invasion of Lebanon by the Israelis. He therefore asked Iran to rein in the zealous *Hezbollah* fighters. Consequently, *Hezbollah* evacuated the border region with Israel, but not before scoring a significant political victory within the Muslim community.

ISRAEL'S 1993 HEAVY BOMBARDMENT OF SOUTHERN LEBANON

In the summer of 1993, trouble flared again in southern Lebanon. *Hezbollah* expressed its vehement opposition to ongoing Middle East peace talks by attacking Israel's self-declared "security zone" in Lebanon. Over a period of months, *Hezbollah* launched a number of rocket attacks against northern Israel and, in July, killed seven Israeli soldiers in Israeli-occupied southern Lebanon.[364]

Using these deaths as a pretext, Prime Minister Yitzhak Rabin's government launched "Operation Accountability" on July 25. 1993.[365] Israeli ships bombarded

---

[363]Gerald Butt, "Iran and Syria Curb Hizbullah Attacks, But Group Gains," *The Christian Science Monitor,* February 25, 1992, p. 5.

[364]"Operation Exodus," *The Economist,* Vol. 328, No. 7822, July 31, 1993, p. 35; Tom Masland, "Fire on the Border," *Newsweek,* Vol. 121, No. 6, August 9, 1993, p. 17; Bruce W. Nelan, "What's Peace Got to Do With It?" *Time,* Vol. 142, No. 6, August 9, 1993, p. 32.

[365]"Operation Exodus," p. 30.

the Lebanese coastal cities of Sidon and Tyre, and Israeli fighter-bombers and helicopter gunships razed villages and leveled houses throughout southern and eastern Lebanon. *Hezbollah* answered by firing 131 Soviet-made Katyusha rockets at northern Israel. Two Israelis were killed.[366]

When after a week of constant bombardment, the Israeli offesive in southern Lebanon ended, 130 Lebanese civilians were dead, 450 to 500 were wounded, and 250,000 were homeless refugees. Ten thousand houses were leveled and 30,000 damaged in seventy villages. Less than ten *Hezbollah* guerrillas were reported killed.[367]

Israel's objective, however, was not simply to kill *Hezbollah* fighters. Instead, Israel sought to intimidate the civilian populace in the south and to create a refugee problem for the government in Beirut. The Rabin government hoped that Syria and its puppet government in Lebanon would rein in *Hezbollah* to prevent further Israeli incursions into the country. Although *Hezbollah* received its ideological prompting from Iran, Syria controlled the organization's supply lines and could thus be greatly influential. However, Syria publicly refused. *Hezbollah*, Syria maintained, had legitimate cause to oppose the Israeli occupation of southern Lebanon.[368]

Nevertheless, Syria did not wish to jeopardize the Middle East peace talks. Assad wanted to regain the Golan Heights. Continued negotiations with Israel were vital. Thus, Syria stayed aloof from the confrontation and was praised by President Bill Clinton for its "considerable restraint," even after Syrian soldiers were killed in the Bekaa Valley, victims of Operation Accountability.[369] Assad then defused the situation by wresting a promise from *Hezbollah* to refrain from further rocket attacks on northern Israel. Nevertheless, *Hezbollah* "maintained their right to take action against Israel's 'security zone.'"[370]

The Israelis accepted *Hezbollah's* promise and ended Operation Accountability. However, Israel also exacted a promise from the Lebanese government to deploy the Lebanese army in the south to offset the power of *Hezbollah*. To further strengthen the Lebanese military, Arab ministers meeting in Damascus promised $500 million to the government in Beirut.[371]

The ultimate success of Operation Accountability is in question. The heavy bombing of southern Lebanon's villages has only embittered the civilian Shi'ah population in Lebanon. If the Lebanese government does not engage in a major

[366]Ibid., p. 35; Brian Duffy, "Israel Takes on the Party of God," *U.S. News & World Report,* Vol. 115, No. 6, August 9, 1993, p. 16.

[367]Masland, "Fire on the Border," p. 30; Nelan, "What's Peace Got to Do With It?" p. 33; "Assault Course," *The Economist,* Vol. 328, No. 7823, August 7, 1993 p. 42; Jim Muir, "Rabin's Revenge Exacts an Appalling Toll," *Middle East International,* No. 456, August 6, 1993, p. 3.

[368]Masland, "Fire on the Border," p. 30; Nelan, "What's Peace Got to Do With It?" p. 33; "Operation Exodus," p. 35.

[369]"Operation Exodus," p. 35.

[370]"Assault Course," p. 42.

[371]Ibid.

effort to improve the quality of life of the Lebanese villagers, *Hezbollah* could end up with many more recruits in the future.

THE *IBRAHIM* MOSQUE MASSACRE OF PALESTINIAN WORSHIPPERS

At dawn on February 25, 1994, a zionist settler from the orthodox Jewish settlement of Qiryat Arba entered the crowded *Ibrahim* (Abraham's) Mosque,[372] which is located in the ancient biblical town of Hebron on the Israeli-occupied West Bank. Dressed in an Israeli Army uniform, he opened fire with his automatic assault rifle on as many as 800 worshippers, who had just started their Ramadan fast and were kneeling in prayer with their foreheads touching the ground. One profile cast him not as a "lunatic" or "psychopath" who had callously slaughtered as many as 29 Palestinian Muslims and wounded as many as 150; some pictured him instead as a man who passionately despised Arabs, believing them to be the avowed enemy that was trying to destroy Israel—in other words, he was a man who "believed" that Arabs had to be expelled or destroyed before they expelled or destroyed Israelis. This is the same anti-Arab ideology that permeates the worldview of a significantly large segment of the gun-toting zionist settlers in the Gaza Strip and West Bank. Little wonder that most settlers from Qiryat Arba and other settlements gave the mass murderer a funeral of a martyr who had been killed in a noble crusade against a deadly enemy.

The mass murderer was a 42-year old American-born orthodox Jewish physician named Dr. Baruch Goldstein who in 1983 immigrated to Israel from the New York City borough of Brooklyn. He had long been a committed follower of the radical Jewish fundamentalist Rabbi Meir Kahane.[373] In Israel, Goldstein became part of Kahane's inner circle and even ran Kahane's political campaign for the Is-

---

[372]The *Ibrahim* Mosque or *al-Haram al-Ibrahimi* (The Tomb of Ibrahim) is named after Prophet Abraham who is venerated in Judaism, Christianity, and Islam. Muslims reverentially refer to Prophet Abraham as *Khalil Allah* (God's friend). Adherents of all three faiths believe that Abraham is buried there. The Bible states that Abraham purchased the site as a burial ground for his wife, Sarah. The Jews call the hallowed site the Tomb of the Patriarchs or the Cave of Machpela because they believe that the sacred tombs of the patriarchs Isaac and Jacob and matriarchs Rebecca and Leah are also to be found there. Both Jews and Muslims worship in separate sections of the same Tomb of the Patriarchs and therefore the hallowed site has been a flashpoint since 1929 when sixty-nine Jews were massacred there by Arabs (Joel Greenberg, "Biblical Tomb Long a Site of Arab-Jewish Conflict," *New York Times,* February 26, 1994, p. 6).

[373]Rabbi Meir Kahane, a Brooklyn-born native, had founded the Jewish Defense League (JDL) in 1968; as its founder and leader, he had been largely responsible for defining its mission. According to Kahane, the organization was dedicated to fighting anti-Semitism and protecting Jews in America. In 1971, the radical and demagogic rabbi immigrated to Israel and founded the right-wing *Kach* party. The goal of this Jewish fundamentalist party was to expel all Arabs from the biblical land of Israel and from Israeli-occupied lands and to make Israel a truly Jewish state based on the Torah (See "Meir Kahane," in Susan Hattis Rolef, ed., *The Political Dictionary of the State of Israel*, New York: Macmillan Publishing Company, 1987, p. 176).

raeli Knesset (legislative body). Because the two zionist soulmates had grown so close, Kahane's assassination in New York City in 1990 left Goldstein seriously disturbed. He must have been further angered by the trial of Kahane's accused assassin. At trial's end, the Arab-born American Al-Sayyid al-Nosair, who was the principal suspect, walked away a free man due to insufficient evidence. Goldstein is said to have repeatedly told his friends thereafter that Kahane's murder must be avenged.[374]

As the leader of the local emergency medical team for his Jewish settlement, Goldstein had seen several of his close friends and neighbors die under his care. He therefore considered "Arabs to be Nazis" and refused to treat them when they came in for emergency treatment.[375]

Furthermore, the Israeli government's peace accord with the PLO and the Arafat-Rabin handshake on September 13, 1993, must have enraged and incensed him. He believed that Arafat was a "terrorist" and that the PLO was a "terrorist organization" that had killed many Israelis. For the Israeli government to be legitimizing the PLO and elevating Arafat to the august status of a statesman was a betrayal of the Jewish people and the Jewish state. Goldstein was determined to sabotage the Israeli-PLO peace talks with a dramatic and explosive event.

He chose Friday, February 25, 1994, because it was the second Muslim sabbath during Islam's holy month of Ramadan, a time when fasting Muslims make every effort to get involved in the congregational prayer sessions enjoined by Prophet Muhammad. It was also the Jewish festival of Purim, when Jews celebrate the deliverance of Persian Jews from a plot to destroy them in the fifth century B.C. In the Purim story, a courageous Jew called Mordechai plays a central role in the awesome revenge that the Jews mete out to their enemies.[376]

The cry that went up in the *Ibrahim* Mosque just after the mass murderer had emptied three 35-shot magazines into the congregation of worshippers was: "Where are you Arafat? Where is the peace?" This cry mingled with the Islamic rallying cry of *Allahu Akbar* which was immediately taken up by furious Palestinians venting their disillusionment and anger at the deaths of their brethren and at the disappointing results from the peace talks that Arafat had said would soon give his people a Palestinian state. It was a cry heard by Israeli Prime Minister Yitzhak Rabin, who immediately went on Israeli television to condemn the massacre and apologize on behalf of the Israeli people for it. It was a cry heard by U.S. President Bill Clinton, who invited both Israeli and Palestinian negotiators to Washington so that they could tie up all the loose ends of their peace accord on limited Palestinian autonomy. It was a cry likewise heard by Yassir Arafat at his PLO headquarters in Tunis, Tunisia. Immediately suspending the Israeli-PLO peace

---

[374]Russel Watson, Caroline Hawley, Jeffrey Bartholet, Chritopher Dickey, Karen Breslau, and Eleanor Clift, *Newsweek*, Vol. 123, No. 10, pp. 34–37; Tom Masland, Carrol Bogert, Robin Sparkman, and Caroline Hawley, "Benjie Was Always an Extremist," *Newsweek*, Vol. 123, No. 10, p. 36.

[375]Richard Lacayo, "The Making of a Murderous Fanatic," *Time,* Vol. 143, No. 10, March 7, 1994, p. 52.

[376]Chris Hedges and Joel Greenberg, "A Seething Hate, a Gun, and 40 Muslims Died," *New York Times,* February 28, 1994, p. 1–A.

negotiations, the PLO Chairman now made the Israeli settler issue the principal problem requiring urgent attention; no longer, he insisted, could it be a secondary matter to be addressed in 1995 as agreed to in the Israeli-PLO Declaration of Principles signed on the White House lawn on September 13, 1993 and sealed with an Arafat-Rabin handshake.[377]

While significantly undermining Arafat's secular and moderate leadership of the Palestinian movement, the Hebron massacre has further strengthened the Islamic fundamentalist organizations like *Hamas* and Islamic *Jihad,* and it has likewise intensified the Palestinian *intifadah* not only in the Israeli-occupied West Bank and in Gaza but also among Israeli Palestinians in Israel as well. With the Islamic organizations now dominant, the Palestinian *intifadah* is now looking more and more like an Islamic resurgence, and if the process is not aborted by the overwhelmingly powerful Israeli authorities, one could witness an Islamic revolution leading to an Islamic state of Palestine consisting of the Gaza Strip and Jericho— and of whatever else the Israeli government decides to give up in the West Bank to the far more accommodating PLO.

SUMMARY

It is, indeed, ironic that both explosive conflicting events and dramatic peace agreements between the Arabs and Israelis have contributed to the Islamic revival. This was especially true after the Six-Day War of June 1967 when the Islamic revival in Egypt began. After growing and spreading throughout the Middle East for the next six years, the Islamic revival got much media attention during the 1973 Yom Kippur/Ramadan War. Then, the Israeli invasion of Lebanon in the summer of 1982 inflamed the revival of political Islam, particularly in Lebanon but more generally in the entire Muslim world, as television pictures of that invasion were broadcast all over the world. Israel's periodic bombing of Lebanese villages and towns by air, sea, and land for much of the 1980s and even the early 1990s has kept the Islamic revival in Lebanon simmering.

In the last quarter century, two terrorist incidents in the West Bank have infuriated the Muslim world and intensified the revival of political Islam: One was the Australian Zionist's arson at the *Al-Aqsa* Mosque in Jerusalem in 1969, and the other was an American-born Zionist settler's massacre of worshippers at the *Ibrahim* Mosque in Hebron in February 1994.

One would think that Arab-Israeli peace agreements would dampen the rise of political Islam, but they seem to have had the opposite affect. Sadat's trip to Jerusalem and the Camp David Peace Agreements between Sadat and Begin were widely condemned by the *umma* as a "sell-out" and a betrayal of the Arab and Muslim cause. Thus, Sadat's efforts at peace with Israel may have actually reinforced the reassertion of political Islam, not only in Egypt but in the Middle

---

[377]Peter Ford, "The Peace Process After Hebron: Attack Prompts Calls For End to Talks, but Some See New Impetus," *The Christian Science Monitor,* February 28, 1994, p. 3.

East at large. Just as Sadat lost his leadership of the Arab world and then his life to Islamic fundamentalists, Arafat is in danger of losing his leadership of the Palestinian movement and his life to Islamic fundamentalists as a result of the Declaration of Principles for limited Palestinian self-rule in Gaza and Jericho. Many Palestinians in the Israeli-occupied territories and in the diaspora see the Arafat-Rabin handshake over the Declaration of Principles as a "raw deal" for the Palestinians. Thus, the Arafat-Rabin agreement has greatly swollen the ranks of radical Palestinian Islamic organizations such as *Hamas* and Islamic *Jihad*. With the Hebron massacre of Palestinian worshippers in the *Ibrahim* Mosque, the Islamic revival in the West Bank and Gaza Strip seems to look more and more like an Islamic resurgence. The major question is: Can the Israeli army and Zionist settlers crush the Islamic resurgence sweeping the Israeli-occupied West Bank or will a Jewish-Muslim crusade make the West Bank ungovernable and therefore an unbearable liability for Israel? If the latter scenario results, then the Israeli government will have to eventually give back the entire West Bank to the Palestinians and allow them to establish a Palestinian state in much of the West Bank and Gaza Strip, with Jerusalem eventually becoming an international city under U.N. supervision.

Chapter
9

OPEC, OIC, and Islamic Politics

The Organization of Petroleum Exporting Countries (OPEC), established in 1960 by Saudi Arabia, Iran, Iraq, Kuwait, and Venezuela, has since its inception been misunderstood. Westerners erroneously believe that OPEC (1) completely monopolizes and manipulates the world's oil market, (2) is comprised solely of wealthy harem-keeping kings, *amirs*, and *shaikhs*, (3) is united in purpose, identity, and ideology, and (4) is bent on undermining Western economic and political stability. Despite these and a myriad of other popular misconceptions, OPEC has had a significant impact on the West as an organization comprising important oil producers and consumers of Western products.

Within the Muslim world, OPEC has effected the enrichment of a few Arab Muslim nations, like Saudi Arabia, Kuwait, UAE and Libya, while the vast majority of Muslims throughout the Muslim world remain destitute and impoverished. This, in turn, has fueled the fire of Islamic revivalism on several levels. First, devout Muslims have perceived the relative success of OPEC during the 1970s, despite Western interference, as God's blessing for pursuing the "straight path" following the disastrous 1967 Arab-Israeli War. The success of OPEC, in their eyes, has vindicated them and testified to the will of God. Second, the money that OPEC has brought to the oil producers of the Muslim world has in limited amounts found its way through the agency of OPEC member nations to various and often competing Islamic revivalist organizations—whether to build *masjids* or to buy mortars. And third, the failure of OPEC member nations to substantially redistribute their oil wealth throughout the Muslim world, regardless of national delineation, has engendered great envy and frustration among impoverished Muslims. Accordingly, Islamic revivalists have sometimes turned against the oil-rich OPEC nations, labeling them personally corrupt and un-Islamic.

The creation of OPEC has contributed to global Islamic politics in often contradictory and ironic ways, and yet the connection of OPEC to the global Islamic revival is seldom made in either the popular or the scholarly literature. To understand the true and substantive effects of OPEC on the development and growth of the global Islamic revival requires a thorough examination of OPEC, its origins, and its actions.

PRELUDE TO OPEC'S ASCENDENCY

The oil-producing nations of the Muslim world, after many years of struggle, achieved full political independence following World War II and immediately sought economic independence from the West as well. At the time the Seven Sister[378] dominated and monopolized the oil industry, acting arrogantly and disrespectfully to their host nations and denying them fair and appropriate compensation. This situation aggravated tensions between the foreign oil companies and the governments of the nations in which they operated and in which "oil as a commodity represented the primary, and often only, resource . . . and an important, and often prime, energy input for the countries in which it was consumed. Private enterprise was sandwiched between strong governmental interests."[379] Savoring their newfound political independence, these governments began to give precedence to their economic interests at the expense of the Western oil companies. By the 1950s, host governments fought the foreign oil companies for "basic modifications in the concessions terms, which originally granted the companies, in addition to the right of exploiting the oil, extraordinary privileges."[380] The era of the virtual sovereignty of the Western oil companies in the region was coming to a close.

The establishment of OPEC was the result of increasing anger among oil-producing nations over foreign governments' reduction of the posted price for oil, a reduction that threatened to cut into desperately needed oil revenue. The stated resolutions of OPEC were (1) that the governments of oil-producing nations needed to assume a more direct and active role in the determination of oil prices and not leave the decisions to the private companies; (2) that sudden price fluctuations were intolerable and that oil prices must be stabilized; and (3) that oil policies among OPEC member nations needed to be reconciled and unified to achieve desired benefits for the organization generally and for each member indi-

---

[378]A nickname for seven of the biggest oil corporations in the world: Exxon, Royal Dutch-Shell, Texaco, Standard Oil Company of California (Socol; marketed as Chevron), Mobil, Gulf, and British Petroleum.

[379]Ian Skeet, *OPEC: Twenty-Five Years of Prices and Politics,* New York: Cambridge University Press, 1991, p. 2.

[380]Shimoni, *Political Dictionary of the Arab World,* p. 358.

vidually. In brief, OPEC was founded with the expressed purpose of coordinating the petroleum policies of member states and thereby safeguarding their individual and collective interests.[381]

Since stabilization of oil prices and maintenance of steady oil revenues were the immediate short-term goals of OPEC, the organization was successful in the 1960s despite a continuing worldwide recession and a declining demand for oil. In fact, as realized prices fell, revenues for OPEC members rose. However, since demand for oil remained weak for the first decade of OPEC's existence, OPEC was yet incapable of showing economic or political muscle.

Egypt's devastating and demoralizing defeat in the Six Day War with Israel in 1967 cost Nasser and his ideologies of pan-Arabism and Arab socialism much of their attraction among the masses. In turn, Islam strengthened as a source of identity and solace strengthened. Egypt's defeat, coupled with long-standing economic problems, compelled the once-proud Nasser to turn to his erstwhile ideological foes, the oil-rich members of OPEC, who were conservative antirevolutionary cheerleaders for Islamic, not Arab, solidarity. In exchange for desperately needed financial assistance, Nasser embraced the oil producers and compromised his own ideological zeal.[382] To further appease the Saudis and their allies and also to enhance his own letitimacy at home, Nasser began to utilize Islamic symbols and rhetoric. Thus, conservative oil-producing OPEC member nations like Kuwait and Saudi Arabia emerged as new centers of regional power, handing out money and aid to gain friends and partisans throughout the Muslim world.

Accompanying the successes was a notable failure. During the 1967 war OPEC attempted to turn "the oil weapon" against those nations supporting Israel. This first short-lived oil embargo collapsed as the economic consequences for the oil producers became too burdensome. Therefore, in 1968, Saudi Arabia, Kuwait, and Libya established the Organization of Arab Petroleum Exporting Countries (OAPEC)—an organization similar to OPEC but which excluded non-Arab oil producers—to achieve Arab political unity within the cartel and to employ that unity and Arab control of substantial oil resources as a weapon.[383] Thus, the stage was set for the vastly more successful oil embargo of 1973.

A confluence of factors, many rooted in the events of the 1960s, brought OPEC to the apogee of power and influence during the 1970s. First, the 1970s were years of remarkable and unprecedented economic expansion both in the industrialized West and in the Third World. As industry grew, after a long decade of worldwide recession, demand for oil grew as well and OPEC members prospered. Second, this prosperity underscored OPEC's predominant position in the oil in-

---

[381]See Resolutions I 1.2 and I 3.4 adopted at the first OPEC conference in Baghdad, Iraq, on September 1966, and quoted in Abdul Kubbah, *OPEC: Past and Present*, Vienna, Austria: Retro Economic Research Center, 1974, p. 21.

[382]Shireen T. Hunter, *OPEC and the Third World*, Bloomington, IN: Indiana University Press, 1984, pp. 58–60.

[383]Shimoni, *Political Dictionary of the Arab World*, p. 361.

dustries. Prior to the establishment of OPEC, not even one oil-exporting nation accounted for more than one-third of total world exports and no single oil-producing nation accounted for more than one-fifth of world petroleum production. Yet by 1974, more than half the world's oil production and more than three-quarters of the world's exports were concentrated in the hands of the cartel.[384] Third, the world had begun a transformation from bipolarity, in which the two superpowers—the United States and the USSR—completely dominated their spheres of influence, to global multipolarization, in which numerous powerful countries acted with relative independence from the superpowers. Hence, oil producers like Saudi Arabia and Kuwait, feeling no particular affinity for Moscow or for Washington, were given new encouragement to stand up for their rights. Fourth, smaller independent oil companies had started to deal with the OPEC cartel. These companies offered larger royalties and taxes to the governments of the oil-producing countries, giving the cartel greater clout in negotiations with the Seven Sisters. Fifth, in the late 1960s, the Trans-Arabian Pipeline (TAPline) bringing Saudi Arabian crude oil to the Eastern Mediterranean over land was temporarily closed, and long-haul Gulf crude oil was shipped in to satisfy excessive demand. A tanker shortage ensued and freight rates skyrocketed. This situation, coupled with the closure of the Suez Canal after numerous ships were sunk there in the 1967 Arab-Israeli War, also pushed up the value of low-sulphur Libyan crude oil that the independent oil companies were taking to the European markets.[385] While these new conditions resulted in the tightening of the oil supply, which increased the profits of the oil corporations, the revenues enjoyed by the governments of the oil-producing countries did not much increase. OPEC members discovered that only when they took matters in their own hands was their prosperity fully realized.[386]

In 1969, Libya's Colonel Muammar al-Gaddafi rose to power through a military coup and began his long tenure as leader of Libya, replacing the conservative regime of King Idris with his own peculiar brand of Islamic fundamentalism. The increasingly favorable winds of OPEC prosperity were at al-Gaddafi's back; he had ascended to leadership at an especially propitious time for oil producers. Al-Gaddafi was in a unique position to improve OPEC leverage vis-à-vis the oil companies. As leader of OPEC's Mediterranean Group, Libya initiated policies to cut petroleum production and thereby to increase revenue taken in by OPEC member nations. Libya's position of prominence and leadership in OPEC was bolstered by the fortuitous bulldozer accident that temporarily closed Saudi Arabia's TAPline, which increased the value of Libyan oil. Al-Gaddafi took this opportu-

---

[384]Jeffey Hart, "Three Approaches to the Measurement of Power in International Relations," *International Organization,* Vol. 30, No. 2, Spring 1976, p. 303.

[385]Philip Connelly and Robert Perlman, *The Politics of Scarcity: Resource Conflicts in International Relations,* London: Oxford University Press, 1975, p. 72.

[386]Abbas Alnasrawi, "Arab Oil and the Industrial Economies: The Paradox of Oil Dependency," *Arab Studies Quarterly,* Vol. 1, No. 1, Winter 1979, p. 5.

nity to demand larger revenues and higher taxes from foreign oil corporations operating in Libya.

Libya's unprecedented success exacting concessions from the oil companies changed the pattern of compliancy that had prevailed for the previous six decades, injected new life and vigor into OPEC, and spurred other OPEC members into action. The twenty-first meeting of OPEC in Caracas, Venezuela, in December 1970, resulted in an across-the-board increase in posted prices of thirty-three cents per barrel and a tax rate increase to a minimum of 55 percent.[387]

Although the balance of power between the oligopolistic multinational oil corporations and the oil-producing nations had shifted decidedly in favor of the latter in the 1970s, this shift did not grip international attention until OPEC flexed its economic muscle during and after the Arab-Israeli War of October 1973. Within two weeks of Egypt's surprise attack on Israeli positions in the Sinai Peninsula, OAPEC instituted an oil embargo against the United States and the Netherlands. OAPEC members, indignant at the United States for its substantial economic, political, military, and moral support for Israel, imposed the embargo after President Nixon requested from the United States Congress $2.5 billion in immediate arms deliveries to the beseiged Zionist state. Meanwhile, a Dutch offer to provide a relay center for emigrating Soviet Jews and charter flights to Israel on the official Dutch airline, KLM, triggered Arab antipathy toward the Netherlands.[388]

The oil embargo, coupled with a simultaneous cut in oil production, occurred at a time when demand for oil in the industrialized world was already stretching OPEC production, refining, and transportation beyond capacity. Taking advantage of this development, OPEC exercised its formidable market power by raising the posted price of oil to $5.11 in October 1973. Sensing no reaction among the powerful industrialized oil-consuming nations that might threaten OPEC members' collective or individual interests, OPEC again raised the posted price per barrel of crude oil to an unprecedented $11.65 in January 1974, thus quadrupling the price since the outbreak of the Ramadan War in October 1973. All of this occurred without the consent of the oil companies.[389]

Immediate U.S. reaction was to "bite the bullet." Even after the imposition of the embargo, the Nixon administration increased its arms shipments to Israel. Nonetheless, the sudden and devastating oil-price increases undermined economies around the world. The disruption resulting from OPEC and OAPEC actions induced a worldwide recession between 1974 and 1975. Meanwhile,

---

[387]Kubbah, *OPEC: Past and Present*, p. 54; Connelly and Perlman, *The Politics of Scarcity*, p. 72.

[388]George Lenczowski, "The Oil-Producing Countries," in Raymond Vernon, ed., *The Oil Crisis*, New York: W. W. Norton & Co., 1976, p. 68. The embargo against the United States was lifted in March 1974 (Bill and Leiden, *Politics in the Middle East*, p. 426).

[389]Bill and Leiden, *Politics in the Middle East*, p. 426; Ramon Knauerhase, "The Oil Producing Middle East States," *Current History*, Vol. 76, No. 443, January 1979, p. 9.

OPEC member nations were enjoying oil revenues that before they could never have imagined.[390]

Although the relative success (or at least the lack of outright failure) of the Arab combatants in the 1973 war boosted morale throughout the Muslim world, the unmistakable success of OPEC positively electrified Muslims. OPEC's ability to quadruple oil prices and OAPEC's embargo of oil to a superpower gave Muslims the world over a sense of pride, a taste of power, and a vision of the future that had looked for the past century only bleak. For devout Muslims, OPEC's economic and apparent political empowerment was a token of divine providence—vindication for their belief that God was at last granting His believers their just rewards after so much struggle and hardship. OPEC, again, directly contributed to Islamic politics.

While OPEC's economic success in the 1970s was extraordinary, its political success was dubious at best. OPEC achieved none of its political objectives. While Muslim regimes within OPEC were able to influence subtly the domestic and foreign policies of needy Muslim and non-Muslim Third World countries and even to influence Europe and Japan to tilt, at least symbolically and rhetorically, toward Arab anti-Israeli and pro-Palestinian causes, little headway was made in wringing substantive concessions from the West on any issue. Moreover, the major political objectives of the oil embargo—the withdrawal of Israel from all territories captured in the 1967 war, the "affirmation of the Arabism of Jerusalem," and the restoration of the "legitimate rights" of the Palestinians—were not achieved.[391] The United States, meanwhile, encouraged OPEC members to invest their wealth of petrodollars in U.S. producer goods, consumer goods, military hardware, and agricultural produce. Consequently, OPEC economic health became tied to the well-being of the U.S. economy. From this point on, OPEC discouraged and dismissed any attempts to destabilize the U.S. economy with excessive price hikes or an oil embargo. Saudi Arabia, the most influential OPEC member, for example, had become the largest importer of American military hardware with purchases totaling $5.1 billion in 1980.[392]

Since the end of the oil embargo in 1974, OPEC has failed repeatedly to take action in the face of bold Israeli aggression and unqualified U.S. support for Israel. While OPEC has done nothing, Israel has built more settlements on the West Bank; made Jerusalem the unified capital of Israel; attacked OPEC-member Iraq's nuclear reactor at Osirik; annexed the Golan Heights; repeatedly invaded Lebanon; mauled Syria's antiaircraft batteries and air force after Syria attempted to check Israel's 1982 advance into Lebanon; dismantled the PLO infrastructure, driving the PLO fighters out of Lebanon; permitted the barbaric massacre of Palestinian men, women, and children in the Sabra and Shatila refugee camps; and continued to terrorize the Lebanese Shi'ahs without any condemnation, let

---

[390]Lawrence Ziring, *The Middle East: A Political Dictionary,* Santa Barbara, CA: ABC-CLIO, Inc., 1992, pp. 292–293.

[391]Joseph A. Szliowicz, "The Embargo and U.S. Foreign Policy," in Bard E. O'Neil, ed., *The Energy Crisis and U.S. Foreign Policy,* New York: Praeger Publishers, 1975, pp. 185, 204.

[392]George Thomas Kurian, *Encyclopedia of the Third World,* 3rd ed., Facts on File Inc., 1987, p. 1698.

alone united action, from the regimes in the Muslim world. This in turn has disillusioned many Islamic revivalists, even those receiving financial assistance from OPEC member nations.

Of the prominent Muslim nations of OPEC only Iraq is secular in its ideological orientation. The rest are religious conservatives promoting distinct brands of Islamic revivalism through the disbursement of petrodollar aid.[393] Despite an apparent unity of interest in Islamic politics, no uniform policy of aid disbursement has ever emerged from an OPEC meeting. OPEC member nations have preferred overwhelmingly to channel their petrodollar aid to recipients on a bilateral rather than a multilateral basis. Joint development projects are, by comparison, rare and underfunded. Furthermore, the promotion of Islam by individual OPEC nations is sometimes no more than the promotion of selfish national interest through the agency of a particular brand of Islam. However, in the process, OPEC has strengthened the Islamic revival to such an extent that it too can no longer overlook Islam's demands.[394]

Libya's al-Gaddafi has taken keen interest in exporting his version of Islamic revivalism and, consequently, his personal influence into non-Arab African nations with substantial Muslim populations. In addition, a Libyan payroll tax has long supported the *Jihad* fund, which distributes money to militant, anti-Israeli Muslim groups and to Muslim guerrillas in the Philippines and in Ethiopia.[395] Ideologically speaking, al-Gaddafi believes that "Islam is the best answer to the Third World's problems, and for the Islamic countries a return to Islamic principles is the best solution to their difficulties."[396]

Iran, like Libya, has supported militant and clandestine Islamic revivalist organizations that are anti-Western and anti-Zionist in ideology. As a nation calling itself an Islamic republic and governed by Shi'ah religious clerics, Iran considers itself the greatest benefactor to Islamic revivalism and has expended substantial oil revenues to prove it.[397] Radical Lebanese Shi'ah organizations, for example, look to Iran not only for petrodollar aid, but for leadership as well. Iran has also involved itself in the Central Asian Muslim republics newly independent from Moscow. Iran has vied, with Turkey and Saudi Arabia, for influence there by promoting commercial ties. More important, Iran has sent clerics and religious teachers to the former Soviet Muslim republics to heighten and politicize the Islamic revival taking place there.

Of all OPEC members, Saudi Arabia provides the best documented case for the use of petrodollar aid to promote national interests and to disseminate Islamic revivalism, two essentially compatible goals. Saudi Arabia's King Faisal (1906–1975) promoted a moderate brand of Islamic fundamentalism and pan-

---

[393]Roy R. Anderson, Robert F. Seibert, and Jon G. Wagner, *Politics and Change in the Middle East: Sources of Conflict and Accomodation*, 3rd ed., Englewood Cliffs, NJ: Prentice-Hall, 1990, p. 239.

[394]Hunter, *OPEC and the Third World*, p. 68.

[395]Kurian, *Encyclopedia of the Third World*, p. 1206.

[396]Hunter, *OPEC and the Third World*, p. 68.

[397]Anderson, *Politics and Change in the Middle East*, p. 239.

Islamism in the 1960s to counter Nasser's attempts to destabilize pro-Western regimes by exporting radical Arab socialism. Faisal greatly increased and expanded monetary loans and grants to needy Muslim countries and to Muslim minorities in non-Muslim countries during the 1970s. Through aid, the Saudi government subsidized (a) the building of *masjids* and *madrassahs*, (b) the publication of Islamic books, journals, magazines, and newspapers, and (c) clandestine Muslim Fundamentalist groups like the *Ikhwan*, who were outlawed in Egypt, Sudan, and Syria. Saudi loans and grants were partly responsible for influencing Egypt's Sadat, Sudan's Numeiri, and Somalia's Said Bari to remove their countries from the Soviet sphere of influence and to embark on a more pro-Western foreign policy. Partly to counter and neutralize entrenched socialist elements in Egypt, and partly to please Saudi patrons, Sadat allowed Islamic groups to operate freely in Egypt again. He also introduced a policy entitled *infitah* or "open door policy" in which Western multinational corporations were encouraged to invest in Egypt. Similarly, Pakistan's Bhutto was no doubt courting Saudi aid when he adopted an uncharacteristically strong Islamic emphasis in Pakistan's foreign and domestic policy.

Saudi aid often influenced political decisions. With the promise of millions of dollars in aid, the Saudis convinced the leadership of the newborn and needy nation of Bangladesh to abandon its desire for revenge against Pakistani army officers—some marked for execution—languishing in Bangladeshi jails, to forego demanding war reparations from Pakistan, and to try to improve relations with Pakistan. The Saudis also offered the regime of Ferdinand Marcos aid in return for his promise to soften the Filipino government's militaristic policy against the Muslim rebels in Mindanao.

In essence, OPEC members have used their vast petrodollar wealth and petroleum resources to support and to encourage their particular views of Islam and the prerequisites of their national interests. Unified OPEC disbursement of petrodollar aid has failed to occur since views of Islam and national interests vary from country to country. Consequently, OPEC has evoked envy and resentment by giving petrodollar aid selectively to the governments of a few Muslim countries while most Muslim countries suffer privation from high oil prices, global inflation, rising unemployment, and a heavier debt burden. Some members of OPEC have further incurred the anger of many Muslims by squandering the petrodollar wealth on the purchase of huge quantities of Western arms; on industrialization and urbanization on the materialistic Western model; on investment in Western banks, real estate, and companies; on the purchase of gold; and on the importation of numerous luxuries. Moreover, throughout the Muslim world, Muslims have come to regard OPEC as a paper tiger, unwilling or unable to force substantive concessions from Israel or the West. Instead, OPEC has aggravated and perpetuated poverty and inequality by failing to share its enormous wealth with less fortunate Muslim brethren, as enjoined by Islam. Thus, while the oil embargo of 1973 to 1974 and the oil-price increases of 1973 through 1981 contributed positively to Islamic revivalism, the disillusionment inspired by OPEC's failure to improve the lives of most Muslims, in turn, further fueled the global Islamic revival.

THE OIC AND PAN-ISLAMISM

Religion in society has always inspired two apparently contradictory tendencies: the first toward union, the second toward distinctness. In Islam, for example, believers are united in the *dar al-Islam* (abode of Islam), as distinguished from the *dar al-harb* (abode of war or conflict.) Pan-Islamism represents the most modern ideological expression of these tendencies and is enshrined in the idea of the *umma*—an idea as ancient and as compelling as the Quran. An integral component to Islamic revolution, pan-Islamism reflects the ultimate aspirations of today's devout Muslim. It is an ideology that calls upon believers to cast aside the veils of secular nationalism and racial, linguistic, and tribal loyalties to reunite the long-divided *umma*. In this sense, Islam asks for more than personal devotion and submission to the will of God; Islam demands the devotion and submission of the community of believers to the precepts revealed in the Quran and set forth in the *Shariah*.[398] It is upon this fourteen-hundred-year-old concept of community, of the universal *umma* so alien to the West, that the modern Organization of the Islamic Conference (OIC) is based.

The *umma* is more than some distant or utopian goal rooted deeper in faith than in immediate fact. It represents more than divine promise, like the Kingdom of God foretold in Judaism, Christianity, and Islam alike. After Prophet Muhammad's death in A.D. 632, the Muslim world, which spanned the Arabian peninsula, retained its unity as the *umma*. The basis of this unity was brotherhood and equality among believers as well as the primacy of Islamic law and *ummaic* loyalty over tribal claims to individual fealty that for millennia had prevailed among the pagan Arabs. Muhammad's death did briefly inspire a challenge to *ummaic* authority, rested in the institution of the *khilafat*, by rebellious Arab tribes. Abu Bakr, Islam's first caliph and Muhammad's immediate successor, quickly suppressed this defiance. Thus, Abu Bakr established the superiority of *ummaic* over tribal identity and reminded Muslims that their first loyalty lay in submission to God and to his earthly *umma*.[399]

Over the centuries as Islam spread, the *umma* remained intact. Nevertheless rivalries for power within the *khilafat* eroded its effectiveness, and the *umma* as a designation of the political unity of the Muslim world gradually dissolved. As the *khilafat* crumbled, its political authority disintegrating in the hands of those who had paid every price to wield it, the vacuum was filled increasingly by Westerners. Finally, in 1924, the Turks terminated the *khilafat* as a political entity. This dissolution of the *khilafat* and the continued role of non-Muslim Western colonial powers in the Muslim world engendered the "romance" of the *umma*, the popularization of the Muslim world's political unity. Consequently, many took advantage of the *umma*'s renewed popularity as a number of prominent Muslim rulers

---

[398]Shimoni, *Political Dictionary of the Arab World*, p. 397.

[399]Abdullah al-Ahsan, *OIC: The Organization of the Islamic Conference,* Islamization of Knowledge Series, Herndon, VA: International Institute of Islamic Thought, 1988, pp. 8–9.

aspired to assume the role of Caliph of the Muslim world.[400] Among the most notable were Mecca's Sharif Husayn at a conference in 1924; Egypt's King Fu'ad in 1926; Arabia's King Abd al-Aziz Ibn Saud, also in 1926; and the Mufti Amin al-Husayni in 1931.[401] Yet these efforts came to naught. Instead, the secular ideal of the nation-state was adapted without modification from the West, dashing hopes for a reborn *khilafat*. Yet Muslims could not so blithely cast their history and their culture aside, nor so easily reconcile their new political identity with their identity as members of the community of Islam—the *umma*.

If pan-Islamism had no longer a political reality, it retained a psychological one. As the boundaries of nation-states in the Muslim world divided the *umma*, learned Islamic revivalists advanced the notion that the secular nation-state, as a Western imposition, had rendered impotent the formidable power that the *umma*, in the vesture of the *khilafat*, had once been. Only pan-Islamism, they argued, could reverse the damage inflicted by secular nationalism and could loosen the bonds of Western domination. In effect, Islamic revivalists recognized the great inherent potential of an Islamic bloc and, indeed, derided secular nationalism, the foundation on which the Muslim world was now being rebuilt, as un-Islamic. After all, they pointed out, the glory of Islam was historically the glory of the *umma*, the fragmentation of which had undermined the strength of Islam and opened the doors to the Western colonialists.

Moreover, Muslims throughout the world continued to feel a special bond with their coreligionists without regard to race, tribe, language, or even nation. Islam, after all, turned all Muslims to the *qiblah* (the direction of Mecca, toward which Muslims must pray), called all Muslims from the minaret, and brought all Muslims to the *Ka'aba*, irrespective of homeland. Spiritually, Islam was their home. The psychological and spiritual unity of Muslims continued despite the dissolution of their political unity.

The psychological *umma*, however, could not give life to its political manifestation. After the Muslim nations achieved independence from the West, secular nationalism enjoyed greater popularity than did the ideology of pan-Islam. Abu Bakr could not lead armies against Nasser, and Nasserism for a time waxed triumphant. Arabism, not Islam, Nasser insisted, was an appropriate framework on which to construct unity.

Nasser's political rivals, particularly the Saudis, who resented Nasser's interference in Yemen and his threats to their legitimacy, also became his ideological rivals. The obvious alternative to Nasser's pan-Arabism, Arab socialism, and personal cult of secular leadership was pan-Islamism. The attempts of King Faisal to promote and to popularize pan-Islamism were welcomed by many Muslim

---

[400]Shimoni, *Political Dictionary of the Arab World*, p. 398.

[401]Trevor Mostyn, ed., *The Cambridge Encyclopedia of the Middle East and North Africa*. Cambridge: Cambridge University Press, 1988, p. 477.

nations, at least in principle, but were condemned vigorously by the regimes of Egypt, Syria, and Iraq. Nasser, meanwhile, had reached the height of his popularity among the masses. The Saudis, using their credentials as the guardians of Islam's two holiest cities—Mecca and Madina—countered Nasser's vast appeal and kept the Egyptian president at bay.

The Saudi royal family's sponsorship of pan-Islamism before 1967 resulted in the creation in 1962 of the Muslim World League, a pan-Islamic organization. However, this organization served as little more than "a propaganda forum for the Saudis," against Nasser.[402] Despite Saudi Arabia's continued efforts, pan-Islamism made little progress during the height of pan-Arab nationalism and did nothing to diminish Nasser's soaring popularity.

Ironically, what the Saudis could not in a decade accomplish with pan-Islam and the creation of pan-Islamic organizations, the Israelis accomplished in six days. The 1967 war with Israel humiliated Egypt, humbled Nasser, and undermined the credibility of nationalism, Arab socialism, and pan-Arabism. Nasser's popularity plummeted; no more could he impede the development of an institutionalized subsystemic organization devoted to the promotion of Islamic unity.[403] The political ascendancy of Saudi Arabia at Nasser's expense coupled with the devastating psychological trauma inflicted upon the Muslim world by the swift defeat of 1967 granted pan-Islamism and the concept of the *umma* a renewed ideological life; secularism had utterly failed to defeat Israel. A profound sense of despair pervaded the Muslim world, a despair assuaged by renewed faith in Islam, by Islamic revivalism, and by the promise and potential of pan-Islamism.

Over two years passed between the 1967 war and the establishment of the OIC. Although pan-Islamism was growing in popularity—even in Nasser's Egypt—the creation of the OIC occurred only after a second shock to the Muslim world; the August 21, 1969, arson at the *Al-Aqsa* mosque in Jerusalem. Although the fire and its consequent damage were the work of Denis Michael Rohan, a lone and fanatical Australian Zionist, Muslims all over the world were outraged and, in one way or another, held the Israeli government responsible.[404] A conference of twenty-five Muslim nations was convened in Rabat (Morocco) on September 22, 1969. Then a March 1970 meeting of the foreign ministers of Muslim countries directed the creation of the OIC, a pan-Islamic organization based upon the philosophy of the *umma* and charged first to protect Islamic holy sites (like the *Al-Aqsa* mosque), second to encourage Islamic solidarity among Muslim states, third to end all manifestations of colonialism and imperialism, and fourth to assist Palestinians in the liberation of their land.[405] These, in abbreviated form, represent both the immediate reasons and the ultimate objectives for which the OIC was formed.

---

[402]Mostyn, *The Cambridge Encyclopeida of the Middle East and North Africa*, p. 479.

[403]Ibid., p. 480.

[404]Ibid.

[405]al-Ahsan, *OIC*, pp. 23–24.

THE OIC'S ROLE IN INSTITUTIONALIZING THE ISLAMIC REVIVAL

Today the OIC consists of fifty-four member states, and at least twenty subsidiary bodies and affiliated specialized associations. By organizing conferences that periodically bring Muslim leaders, government officials, and nongovernmental groups of the fifty member nations together, the OIC plays a vitally important organizational role not only by fostering a greater sense of solidarity in the fragmented Islamic bloc but also by institutionalizing the Islamic revival. Muslims the world over no doubt feel pleased and hopeful when they learn through the media that leaders of the Muslim countries—with sometimes diametrically opposite ideological orientations and national interests—are sitting down to discuss their common problems, coming up with unanimous resolutions, and formulating solutions for the Muslim world in the true spirit of Islamic brotherhood. The OIC has also published a considerable amount of literature on Islam in its twenty-three-year existence. This Islamic literature has been disseminated not only in predominantly Muslim countries but also in non-Muslim countries with significant Muslim minorities.

Because the OIC was established as a consequence of the Israeli occupation of Jerusalem, the Arab-Israel conflict is central to OIC members. Indeed, the fifth stated objective in Article 2 of the OIC charter is "to coordinate efforts for the safeguard of the Holy Places and support of the people of Palestine, and help them regain their rights and liberate their land."[406] The OIC has remained true to this founding principle; for example, in 1981 then announced a *jihad* and an economic boycott against Israel.[407] Nevertheless, despite the great emphasis placed on the Arab-Israeli conflict by the OIC, the organization since its establishment has cultivated the more ancient and agreeable traditions of the *umma*. Consequently, the first and second objectives of the OIC defined in Article 2 of the charter are "to promote Islamic solidarity among member states"; and, "to consolidate co-operation among member states in economic, social, cultural, scientific and other fields of activities, and facilitate consultation among member states in international organizations."[408] Thus, the OIC was founded primarily on principles of Islamic unity and is rooted, at least theoretically, in the tradition of the *umma*. In practice, however, the OIC's roots in the ideal politically united *umma* are weak. The organization, fragmented and poorly anchored, is often powerless and ineffective in the face of political storms.

While the OIC is hardly a vision of pan-Islamism or of a sturdy Islamic solidarity, the organization has made serious and concerted strides toward greater unity culturally, intellectually, economically, and politically over the last two decades, often through various subsidiary or affiliated institutions. The Islamic

---

[406]Ibid., p. 128.

[407]*The Middle East and North Africa 1984–85,* London: Europa Publications, 1984, p. 205.

[408]al-Ahsan, *OIC,* p. 128.

Development Bank (IDB), for example, was established in 1975 by the finance ministers of OIC member nations in an effort, "to encourage economic and social progress of member countries and Muslim communities in accordance with the principles of the Islamic *Shariah*. . . ."[409] The IDB, abiding by Islamic law, forbids usury and provides interest-free loans while charging only a service fee. These loans are granted to the poorest member states so that they can attend to their most urgent socioeconomic problems. The IDB also encourages investments within and joint ventures among member states.[410] Moreover, the IDB's special assistance account renders emergency financial aid and promotes Islamic education for Muslims not in the OIC member countries.[411]

Other subsidiary and affiliated OIC institutions include the *Al-Quds* fund, founded to resist Israeli-sponsored Judaization policies in Arab Jerusalem and to support the Palestinians generally; the Islamic Commission of the International Crescent, which is the OIC's answer to the Red Cross; the Islamic Solidarity Fund, founded to build *masjids, madrassahs,* and hospitals; the International Islamic Law Commission, charged with the promotion of the *Shariah;* the Islamic Center for the Development of Trade, founded to encourage mutually beneficial commercial ties among member nations; the Islamic Center for Technical and Vocational Training and Research, which trains individuals, conducts research in relevant technologies, and encourages exchanges of technologies between member-nations; the Islamic Civil Aviation Council, which promotes member-nation cooperation in air transport; the Islamic Jurisprudence Academy, established to study the problems besetting the modern Muslim world, to devise solutions in accordance with the *Shariah* and, more generally, to promote the unity of the Muslim world; the Islamic Foundation for Science, Technology and Development, which promotes research in science and technology within an Islamic framework; the Research Center for Islamic History, Art and Culture, founded to research the common past of the Muslim world; and the Statistical, Economic and Social Research and Training Center for the Islamic Countries, which collects and evaluates socioeconomic data on member nations.[412] Among additional OIC-related institutions are the International Islamic News Agency; the Islamic States Broadcasting Organization; the Islamic Capitals Organization; the Islamic Chamber of Commerce, Industry and Commodity Exchange; the Islamic Educational, Scientific and Cultural Organization; and the Islamic Shipbuilders Association.[413]

Although many OIC organizations specifically encourage the cooperation of OIC member nations in cultural, economic, and political realms, their success has been hindered by questions of national interest in even less ambitious projects. The IDB, for example, is not funded or equipped to rectify the poles separating the rich Muslim states from the poor. But because rich OAPEC nations prefer to

---

[409]*The Middle East and North Africa,* p. 196.

[410]al-Ahsan, *OIC,* pp.95–96.

[411]*The Middle East and North Africa,* p. 196.

[412]al-Ahsan, *OIC,* pp. 30–37; *The Middle East and North Africa,* p. 204.

[413]*The Middle East and North Africa,* p. 204.

promise and disburse aid money to poorer states on terms conducive to their national interests, the IDB, which sets no such preconditions, cannot take their money. Meanwhile, the success of organizations promoting sociocultural unity in the Muslim world is, when possible to gauge, undermined by dictatorial regimes that can endure only by drawing distinctions between "us" and "them" within their own nations and between their nations and others within the Muslim world. Iraq, for example, won support from the oil-rich Gulf states in its war with Iran only by portraying itself as an impediment to Persian-dominated Iran's revolutionary Shi'ah brand of Islamic fundamentalism. Underlining the essential sociocultural similarities between Iran and Iraq would, in contrast, have been an unproductive strategy.

In essence, the national interests of OIC member states far outweigh any commitment to Islamic solidarity. The OIC's attempt to study and coordinate Muslim affairs, particularly in political matters, may prove unproductive since the OIC itself is handicapped by significant internal contradictions. The OIC purports to represent its members, but its members prefer to represent themselves; the OIC wishes to unify the *umma*, but the *umma* and the modern nation-state system have a difficult time coexisting. Consequently, constant internal squabbling, turmoil, and dissension have rendered OIC a pale shadow of its own ideals.

The OIC's chronic inability to enforce the collective will over the objections of specific member nations represents the subordination of international Islamic law to Western international law in the Muslim world. In the days of the *khilafat*, the *umma*, was ruled entirely on the basis of the *Shariah*. In contrast, however, member states of the OIC "are stronger authorities than the OIC itself."[414] The law of individual states—whether secular or religious—takes precedence over *Shariah* law at the subsystemic and systemic levels. Submission of member nations to OIC rulings based on the *Shariah*, no matter if there is overwhelming support of most members, is wholly voluntary. Therefore the OIC, unlike the *umma* during the *khilafat*, is not a sovereign entity but, like other equally impotent international organizations, is obeyed, manipulated, or ignored by member nations according to their perceived best interests. Thus, while the OIC brilliantly and lucidly transcribes the ideal of the universal *umma* into its finely worded charter, it is unable to translate that ideal into action.

The OIC succeeds and fails according to the dictates of sovereign nation-states, which are able on the surface to make common cause, but which all too often pursue national interests that are essentially irreconcilable with the interests of their neighbors and with the OIC. Even on the issue of Israel, the issue that directly inspired the creation of the OIC, member states have fallen into argument and disunity. When Egypt signed the Camp David agreement with Israel in 1978, the OIC suspended Egyptian membership for its "flagrant violation of the U.N. and OIC Charters."[415] Egypt, to regain the Sinai Peninsula, to secure its border

---

[414]al-Ahsan, *OIC*, p. 48.

[415]"Islam Spreads Political Mantle," *The Middle East,* No. 57, July 1979, p. 5.

with Israel, and to end the devastating cycle of war in the region, jettisoned, in the view of many Muslims, the very principles on which the OIC was founded. Thus, Egypt was deprived of its OIC membership for having sacrificed collective objectives for national benefit. Yet no other penalties were exacted, and within five years Egypt was reinstated. In fact, the reinstatement required no compromise of the Camp David peace by Egypt and was based on no conditions. The OIC had no power to enforce its most basic decisions.[416]

The Soviet invasion of Afghanistan in 1979 further complicated the Israeli issue within the OIC and damaged the organization's credibility as a consistently just and principled organization. Many OIC members likened the Soviet invasion and occupation of Afghanistan to Israeli occupation of Palestine and therefore condemned the Soviet action on terms no less explicit. Other OIC members, however, refused to offend their Soviet patron and remained silent, despite the cries of their Afghan coreligionists. The OIC, in turn, demanded Soviet troop withdrawal "without condemning the Soviet Union for the invasion."[417] Consensus building in the highly diverse and fragmented OIC has compromised the organization's ideological integrity. Deep divisions within the Muslim world have greatly undercut the OIC's power on the world stage. Furthermore, the authoritarian leaders of several Muslim nations in the OIC have merely paid lip service to the organization's noble principles and goals.

Today, after Operation Desert Storm, the OIC is predominantly in the hands of Saudi Arabia and Kuwait. The sixth OIC conference, held on December 9, 1991, in Senegal, was nothing but a formal get-together in which all the delegates dutifully repeated the old rhetoric of fraternity and solidarity, but did little to help the poor and needy or redress the inequality and tyranny widely prevalent in the Muslim world. Many members departed the conference before its scheduled end. The OIC, meanwhile, harshly denounced and maintained sanctions against Iraq. Pakistan inserted a resolution condemning the Indian government over its harsh treatment of the Kashmiri Muslims. OIC members promised to resist the repeal of the UN resolution equating Zionism with racism—a promise few kept. The OIC demanded Israeli withdrawal from the Occupied Territories but, despite a five-hour speech by Yasir Arafat, omitted the word *jihad* from that demand. Terrorism was denounced and United States–backed peace talks were encouraged. Even the prospect of future applications to enter the OIC from the Central Asian republics of the former Soviet Union, brightened by acceptance of Azerbaijan into the organization, failed to kindle excitement at the summit.[418] In short, divisions in the OIC appear greater than ever and the Islamic revivalist dream of pan-Islam remains unfulfilled.

---

[416]"Egypt to Rejoin Islam Group," *Philadelphia Inquirer,* January 31, 1984, p. A-3.

[417]al-Ahsan, *OIC*, pp. 71–72.

[418]"OIC: Can It Meet the Challenge?" *The Economist,* December 14, 1991, pp. 35–36.

SUMMARY

The predominantly Muslim OPEC established in 1960 did not flex its muscles until the early 1970s. It was Gaddafi's success in demanding larger revenues and higher taxes from foreign oil companies operating in Libya that was soon repeated by other members of OPEC. Then came the 1973 Yom Kippur/Ramadan War, which was soon coupled with the OAPEC oil embargo against Israel's allies in the West. The resulting oil shortage put an upward pressure on oil prices. The oil-price explosion that the world witnessed from 1974 to 1982 helped in the rapid modernization of the oil-rich countries. The Muslim members of OPEC (especially, Saudi Arabia, Libya, Kuwait, UAE, and Iran) donated much aid to poverty-stricken Muslim countries, gave a number of financially strapped Muslim countries a discount on oil, purchased food and had it distributed among starving Muslims, financed a number of Islamic organizations, built mosques, and purchased and distributed Quran to *madrassahs*. The *umma* interpreted OPEC's success during the "oil boom" years as Allah coming to the assistance of His "chosen people."

But the euphoria was short-lived. The governments of many Muslim countries complained that they were promised far more by their oil-rich brethren than they received. Moreover, OPEC's dramatic oil price increases contributed to goal inflation, followed by higher interest rates, and recession. All three of the aforementioned economic problems plagued the oil-poor Muslim countries many times more than the developed Western world and resulted in the Third World being far worse off than before the oil price explosion. Furthermore, the glut of oil and decline of oil-prices in 1982, the effort by OPEC member-states to sell more oil than their OPEC-allotted quota, the Iran-Iraq War, Operations Desert Shield and Desert Storm, and division in OPEC ranks between pro- and anti-Western member states virtually emasculated the once powerful oil cartel.

There is a widespread perception in the Muslim world that both OPEC and the OIC have failed to protect and defend the rights of the *umma*. Among other things, they have failed to achieve their principal objective of getting Israel to withdraw from all territories captured in the 1967 war and restoring the legitimate rights of the Palestinian people; they have done nothing to stop the periodic Israeli aggression in Lebanon or the rapid growth of Israeli settlements in the West Bank and Gaza Strip; they have failed to prevent two disastrous Persian Gulf wars; they have been impotent to prevent the starvation of Muslims in Somalia or the massacres in Bosnia-Herzegovina, Israel, India, Burma, and other parts of the Muslim world; and, they have failed to unite the Muslim world and improve the lot of the *umma*.

Chapter
10

The Islamic Revolution in Iran

In 1978 the people of Iran, led by Iran's Shi'ah clerical establishment and their theological students, rose in demonstrations throughout the country to challenge the forty-year tyranny of the Shah. A little more than a year later the Shah, overwhelmed by the revolutionary tide, fled Iran on an "extended vacation"; his secular, pro-Western monarchical regime, long considered by Western analysts an anchor of stability in the stormy Middle East, collapsed unconditionally, catching the West by surprise. Suddenly, a political void opened in Iran, and the Shi'ah *ulama* stepped in, assuming total power, setting up an Islamic model of development, breaking Iran's ties of dependency with the West, and forging a sovereign and nonaligned Islamic republic on the anvil of past Iranian grievances against despot and imperialist alike. The Islamic Revolution signified a watershed in world history, its repercussions shaking both East and West. Seizing the attention of all Muslims, the Iranian Revolution became the "source of emulation" for Islamic revivalists throughout the world. Inspired by its success and stirred by its utopian appeal to pan-Islam, Muslim Fundamentalists were emboldened by the Revolution to remake their countries in the "Iranian model." Muslim Pragmatists and secularists trembled at the triumph of the Islamic Revolution. Western analysts, in turn, perceived a new threat to Western hegemony; the specter not of communism, but of Islamic fundamentalism.

Although the West, and particularly the United States, was jarred by the Iranian Revolution, its roots were deep in Iranian soil. Political, social, and cultural inequities and their synergistic impact undid the Iranian monarchy, overturned the status quo, and enabled the Shi'ah religious hierarchy to supplant the government of the Shah. An exploration of this synergism reveals the genesis of the Iranian Revolution and exposes the anatomy of Islamic revivalism.

THE GENESIS OF A REVOLUTION

In 1953, the U.S. CIA engineered the ouster of Iran's popular Prime Minister Muhammad Mossadeq. Although Mossadeq was respected by Iranians for his uncompromising nationalism, the United States worried that Mossadeq's regime was opening Iran to communist influence. Thus, the staunchly pro-Western Shah, who had escaped to Paris, returned triumphant to the Peacock Throne. The unmistakable U.S. role in deposing Mossadeq poisoned relations between the United States and the Islamic Republic of Iran after the fall of the Shah and contributed to decades of anti-U.S. sentiment among the Iranian people. Iranians believed, following the overthrow of the popular Mossadeq, that the meddlesome Americans were but "leasing" the Peacock Throne to the Shah who, with the support of a powerful and oppressive U.S.-trained security apparatus (SAVAK), maintained his tyrannical and absolute dominion over Iran. Indeed, the Pahlavi Shah permitted no form of political dissent.

U.S. motives in supporting the Shah were simple. The Shah had been a steadfast ally of the West and owed his political survival to it. The strategic value of Iran amplified the Shah's importance to Washington. During the Cold War, the United States was determined to contain the USSR and to deny it influence in the oil-rich Persian Gulf region. Possessing large oil and gas reserves, sharing a 1,600-mile border with the Soviet Union, and hugging the critical Persian Gulf and the narrow mouth of the Strait of Hormuz, Iran represented an irreplaceable strategic asset. The Shah became the United States' ally in Tehran, his personal faults notwithstanding.

By 1976, the Shah began to realize the necessity of modest and gradual political liberalization after decades of harsh autocratic rule. Increasingly frequent attacks against government targets by urban guerrillas disturbed the Shah, and his closest security advisors, among them General Hussein Fardust, counseled him to moderate his repressive policies. Furthermore, the Shah was ailing and wished to ensure the succession to the Peacock Throne of his eldest son, the sixteen-year-old Crown Prince Muhammad Reza. By gradually building legitimate democratic institutions, the Shah hoped that his son could govern Iran in a less authoritarian manner than he had and that the longevity of the Iranian monarchy would be ensured. The persistence of despotism was simply counterproductive.

The Shah was also moved to adopt a more moderate government by events in the West. The Western media, long friendly to the Shah, began to decry his shameful human-rights record. The emphasis of then-president Jimmy Carter also forced the Shah to rethink his policies of repression. Thus, from 1976 onward, the Shah replaced a number of his old advisors with younger, more progressive, and more able technocrats. Concomitantly, the Shah liberalized Iran's long-restrained political system enough to allow his oppressed and resentful subjects an opportunity to vent their frustration. The Shah, however, had waited too long to liberalize. Forty years of rage and alienation could not so easily be assuaged by the Shah's momentary indulgence. The Iranian people began openly to criticize their government's domestic and foreign policies. Iranians protested their nation's trade with Israel and South Africa, and criticized Iran's dependence on the United

States. They denounced the presence of U.S. military advisors and technicians, and the expenditure of billions of dollars on the purchase of U.S. weapons. The feeling was widespread that the Shah was nothing more than a puppet of a meddlesome imperial power. Enraged by such criticism and fearing a loss of control, the Shah changed his mind and ordered SAVAK to tighten up and to crush dissent. It was too late.

Two ill-conceived public statements both made within one week inspired Iranians to rise against the Pahlavi monarchy. On December 31, 1977, President Carter misread the depth of the anti-Shah sentiment in Iran and praised the Shah's "great leadership" for bringing stability to Iran. "This is a great tribute to you Your Majesty," Carter said, "and to your leadership, and to the respect, admiration and love that your people give to you."[419] Distrusting of the United States, the Iranian people saw Carter's statement as American government support and encouragement for the Pahlavi regime's repressive methods. Despite his talk of human rights, Carter's praise for the Shah earned the United States only the ire of Iranians.

Within a week of Carter's shortsighted statement, the Shah's ministry of information planted a rash personal attack against the prominent Shi'ah cleric and uncompromising opponent of the Shah, Ayatollah Khomeini. The Iranian newspaper *Ittila'at* ran an article on January 7, 1978, entitled "Iran and Red and Black Colonialism," which read in part,

> In order to acquire name and fame, Ruhollah Khomeini became a tool for the red and black colonialists who have sought to discredit the revolution of the Shah and the people. . . . Actually, Khomeini is known as the Indian Sayyid (Sayyid Hindi).. . . He lived in India for a time where he was in touch with British colonial circles and it is said that when young he composed love poems under the pen name of Hindi.[420]

The article reflected the Shah's suspicions that Khomeini was the agent of both red leftist intellectuals and black religious reactionaries. Although the article was planted in a transparent effort to slander Khomeini and thereby to deprive him of popular support, its publication had precisely the opposite effect. Indeed, after the article's publication, crowds of Iranians demonstrated in defense of the *Ayatollah's* reputation.

From January 1978 to February 1979, anti-Shah demonstrations rocked Iran, shaking the foundations of the Pahlavi monarchy. During this fourteen-month period, the Shah's security forces confronted and killed as many as twelve thousand unarmed men, women, and children and wounded fifty thousand Iranians. The "extended family phenomenon" increased casualty figures and broadened the opposition to the Pahlavi regime. For instance, when an Iranian died during the demonstrations, his relatives engaged in public mourning processions every forty days as is the Shi'ah custom. These traditional processions for the dead became

---

[419]Quoted in James Bill, "The Shah, The Ayatollah, And The U.S." *Headline Series,* No. 285, New York: Foreign Policy Association, June 1988, p. 21.

[420]Ibid.

overtly political and occasioned the violent and frequently lethal response of government security forces. The revolution was thus cumulative in character and spread rapidly in major Iranian cities.[421]

Ayatollah Khomeini, safe from the Shah while in exile in the Iraqi city of Najaf, encouraged the revolutionary fervor without ever personally leading the revolution. He gave angry sermons denouncing the Pahlavi regime and calling for revolution. Tapes of these sermons were then disseminated throughout Iran, where they inflamed the Iranian people.[422]

The Shah turned to the United States for advice. When the Iranian people learned this, their anger further escalated and they turned to the streets in rage. National Security Advisor Zbigniew Brzezinski counseled the Shah to crack down harder. Following the torching of a public theater in the city of Abadan, presumably by SAVAK agents, hundreds of thousands of Iranians protested in the streets. The Shah, taking the advice of Brzezinski, declared martial law. However, it was already over for the Shah. Demonstrators continued to take to the streets.[423]

With the Shah's government and the Iranian economy paralyzed by mass strikes and student demonstrations, the Shah became increasingly conciliatory. Desperate to save the monarchy, the Shah made an unprecedented public plea:

> I commit myself to make up for past mistakes, to fight corruption and injustices and to form a national government to carry out free elections. . . . Your revolutionary message has been heard. I am aware of everything you have given your lives for.[424]

After a year of terrible bloodshed, the Iranian people were not prepared to forgive the Shah. The aging monarch realized by mid-January 1979 that his position in Iran was untenable. His subjects universally despised him; his continued suppression of them had only strengthened their resolve. There was nothing left for the Shah to do. On January 16, 1979, the last Pahlavi monarch left Iran, again "on vacation."[425] The Iranians were left only with bitter memories of the Shah's terrible reign and of the United States' part in perpetuating it.

Western analysts failed to predict the revolution. That failure was often justified by the Westerners' conviction that the Islamic Revolution was nothing more than barbaric madness against a leader too ahead of his time. In reality, however, Western analysts were surprised by the revolution because they had neglected to study the crisis adequately. Indeed, the media emphasized immediate political history while slighting the economic, sociocultural, and religious factors contribut-

---

[421]George Lenczowski, *Americal Presidents and the Middle East,* Durham, NC: Duke University Press, 1990, pp. 188–189.

[422]Ibid., p. 189.

[423]Robert D. Schulzinger, *American Diplomacy in the Twentieth Century,* Oxford: Oxford University Press, 1984, p. 333.

[424]An extract of Muhammad Reza Shah Pahlavi's speech quoted in *Newsweek,* 20 November, 1978, p. 38.

[425]Philip Lee Ralph, Robert E. Lerner, Standish Meacham, and Edward McNall Burns, *World Civilizations: Their History and Their Culture,* Vol. 2, 8th Ed., New York: W. W. Norton & Co., 1991, p. 691.

ing to the revolution. If only the political features of Iran are examined, the revolution is mysterious and unpredictable. However, the introduction of Iran's economic woes and sociocultural disharmony makes sense of the Iranian Revolution and dispels many of the misconceptions and much of the mystery.

As a major oil-producing country, Iran benefitted greatly from the 1973 oil-price explosion that triggered a fivefold jump in the nation's oil revenues. Flushed with a $20 billion inflow of petrodollars in 1974, the Shah inaugurated a development plan that over a period of five years would cost $70 billion. The plan dangerously inflated expectations. The government promised expensive new weapons for the armed forces, the latest technology and foreign expertise for industrialists, and employment and expanded social services to the Iranian people. The Shah bragged that he would fashion Iran into the world's fifth greatest industrial power by the turn of the century.[426] The Shah and his subjects, however, were in for terrible disappointment.

To transform Iran into a modern nation-state by the turn of the century, the Shah accelerated the pace of modernization and dismissed the good advice of technocrats who counseled a more gradual and holistic approach to socioeconomic development. Consequently, the Shah's unrealistic, hasty, and haphazard modernization targets induced shortages in manpower and material. A lack of skilled and professional manpower prompted the Pahlavi monarchy to recruit thousands of foreigners by offering handsome salaries to work in Iran. Simultaneously, soaring petroleum prices escalated costs for all imports, while excessive government spending coupled with ballooning manpower costs fueled an inflationary spiral that devastated the majority of Iranians.[427]

Preoccupied with the Shah's modernization policies, the Iranian government gave inadequate attention to agrarian development in the countryside where the majority of Iranians resided. Economic stagnation resulted in villages throughout rural Iran. Meanwhile, members of the royal family, royal courtiers, and highly placed bureaucrats accepted payments from Western agribusiness corporations to open large tracts of valuable food-growing tillage for the cultivation of cash crops. Consequently, large numbers of unemployed farmers and peasants fled rural poverty and flooded into towns and cities in search of work. By the mid-1970s, rural to urban migration numbered 250,000 people annually. As a result, the bad situation in housing, health, and education in the cities worsened; unemployment and inflation soared; and the gap between rich and poor widened and was alarmingly evident in the growth of slums.[428]

The Shah, meanwhile, set an example of garish extravagance that contrasted obscenely with the poverty of migrants to the cities who lived on the edge of existence in filthy shanty towns. The Shah reasoned that his personal dearth of charisma could be remedied by building a cult of worship around the institution of the monarchy itself. Such a cult could be built, the Shah imagined, by continually

---

[426]Akbar Husain, *The Revolution in Iran*, East Sussex, England: Wayland Publishers Ltd., 1986, p. 41.

[427]Ibid.

[428]Ibid., pp. 42, 45, 47; Ralph et al., *World Civilizations*, p. 680.

and flamboyantly displaying the riches of the royal family. The Shah's ostentation, however, did nothing to increase his popularity. For instance, the bacchanal celebration at Persepolis to mark the twenty-five-hundredth anniversary of the Persian monarchy was a memorable insult to Muslim sensibilities throughout Iran. The history of Zoroastrian Persia was honored in the feasts and festivities while Islamic precepts were flouted. Western-dressed men and women drank alcoholic beverages; dancing was encouraged; and pork was served during the banquets.[429] The expenditures on the festival were enormous—in the range of millions of dollars. Meanwhile, the Shah maintained five palaces for his family, bought shares in powerful Western corporations, and stashed away millions of dollars abroad in Western banks.[430] The ostentation of the Shah inspired not love of the monarchy among Iranians; it inspired resentment. Acting on this resentment, the Shi'ah *ulama* easily turned the Shah's penchant for big spending against him. But as long as the petrodollars continued to pour into the Iranian economy, the Shah could afford to throw Iran's money away and pursue shortsighted modernization policies.

The United States nurtured and nourished the Shah's ambition to modernize Iran. U.S. leaders saw the conservative, anticommunist, pro-Western government of the Shah as a reliable ally against the spread of Soviet communism. In fact, Iran served the United States as a well-situated listening post from which Soviet missile activity could be scrutinized. Moreover, during a time when the United States was haunted by the "Vietnam syndrome" and feared direct military intervention in the developing world, the Shah cultivated an image as America's policeman in the oil-rich Persian Gulf region. Accordingly, Iran's armed forces grew to half-a-million men while the Shah's regime eagerly purchased an incredible $20 billion worth of U.S. armaments between 1973 and 1978.[431] The Shah also spent considerable amounts of money to beef up his internal security forces. Local and national police agencies received a financial boost from the Shah. Likewise, Iran's intelligence service, SAVAK, benefitted from a generous and paranoid monarchy.[432]

Massive and widespread corruption accompanied the unprecedented exploitation and export of petroleum, the heavy inflow of petrodollars, the excessive military spending, the rapid industrialization and urbanization, and the Shah's ambitious but unrealistic modernization programs. When hard times returned to Iran in 1976, the disillusioned Iranian people were convinced that the nation's oil wealth had been squandered by the unscrupulous royal family, the Iranian elite, and Westerners. Indeed, increasingly indignant Iranians viewed the 100,000 Westerners living and working in their country as neocolonialist interlopers exploiting Iran in the grand imperialist tradition.[433] Educated and ambitious Iranians resented that a growing population of foreigners enjoyed responsible, influen-

---

[429]Karl W. Deutsch Jorge I. Dominguez, and Hugo Heclo, *Comparative Government: Politics of Industrialized and Developing Nations,* Boston: Houghton Mifflin, 1982, pp. 419–422.

[430]Ibid.

[431]Glenn E. Perry, *The Middle East: Fourteen Islamic Centuries,* Englewood Cliffs, NJ: Prentice-Hall, 1983, p. 297.

[432]Deutsch et al., *Comparative Government,* pp. 419–422.

[433]Akbar Husain, *The Revolution in Iran,* pp. 42–43.

tial, and high-paying positions in the Iranian government and in the private business sector. Iranian's resentment was heightened when they learned that foreigners were earning far more than Iranian citizens in comparable positions. The effect of this realization was profound for the future of Iran and of Iranian-Western relations. Ayatollah Khomeini capitalized on antiforeign sentiment; he consistently condemned foreign domination of Iran and became, in Iranian eyes, an authentic Iranian patriot.[434]

Widespread was the belief that the Shah had mismanaged Iran's economy, and every class that bore the burdens of the 1976 recession blamed the Pahlavi monarchy and the West for its economic ills. In fact, the Shah had made enemies even of the well-to-do *bazaaris,* who were largely conservative and religious entrepreneurs. They never forgave the Shah for undercutting them by establishing state-purchasing corporations selling wheat, meat, and sugar; for establishing government-subsidized supermarkets that decreased the bazaar's clientele; for engaging in town-planning and road-construction programs that destroyed sections of the bazaar; and, above all, for dispatching aggressive young government inspectors to the bazaars in 1977, who arbitrarily fined and jailed those *bazaaris* suspected of price gouging.[435]

Despite the incredible petrodollar windfall beginning in 1974, the Shah earned the anger of nearly every economic class excepting the Iranian elite. The impoverished peasants who had hopefully migrated to the cities remained jobless. The *bazaaris* felt their economic status slipping. The Iranian people in general saw none of the expected social services promised by the Shah. Indeed, the Shah's modernization policies had turned the petrodollar blessing into Iran's curse.

While the Shah's modernization policies during the 1970s damaged the economic standing of the middle and lower classes, they also had a social and cultural impact on Iran. Indeed, the Shah's transformational approach to Iranian life precipitated an identity crisis among Iranians, the vast majority of whom did not enjoy a standard of living comparable to the West and who, therefore, could not emulate Western lifestyles. Consequently, many Iranians sought for redefinition. Just what was it to be Iranian when Iran was turning upside down?

The poor who thronged to the slums of Iran's cities, and who grew daily more cognizant of the widening gap between their standard of living and that of the foreigners and the wealthy Iranian elite, were lost and alienated in their new environment. Their traditional ways of life were disrupted by the move from village to city, and they hungered for a renewed sense of belonging and of self. Consequently, they represented an enormous pool of anti-Shah sentiment from which the opposition could and did draw support.[436]

As petrodollars inundated Iran during the 1970s, Western goods and cultural influences transformed Iranian cities. Materialistic and hedonistic elements of Western culture infiltrated Iran and undermined the country's traditional Islamic

---

[434]Ibid., pp. 37–41.

[435]Ibid., p. 38

[436]Deutsch et al., *Comparative Government,* pp. 419–422; Lenczowski, *American Presidents and the Middle East,* p. 185.

sociocultural values. The royal family led the way. Queen Farah Deeba herself became a patron of the Annual Arts Festival that showed Western avant-garde and X-rated films. Nightclubs, dance halls, cinemas, bars, and brothels proliferated in major Iranian cities to serve foreigners and wealthy Iranians looking for a good time, and pornographic literature was widely available in city streets. Bikini-clad Iranian women displayed themselves on beaches around the nation; Iranian cities were teeming with prostitutes; and upper middle class Iranian women aped prurient and unseemly Western dress and behavior.[437] In reaction to widespread immorality and depravity, many Iranian women, even in universities, were veiling themselves by 1978. Asked why she had donned the traditional veil, one young Iranian woman at Isfahan University in 1977 responded, "I am making a statement."[438]

The backlash to the Westernization, secularization, materialism, hedonism, and widespread permissiveness prevalent in Iranian society was especially strong within the Shi'ah clerical establishment. After all, the Shi'ah *ulama* nursed a grudge against the Shah for usurping a significant portion of their rural land holdings during the "White Revolution" in the early 1960s. Furthermore, the fire of their anger was stoked again during the oil bust of the late 1970s when the Shah terminated all subsidies to the clerics as part of a severe austerity program.[439]

Although the Shah's policies had effectively reduced the Shi'ah clerics' central role as educators, judges, and advisors, the clerical establishment still maintained a vast network of *masjids* through which they now politicized and mobilized their discontented congregations against a corrupt and increasingly illegitimate monarchy.[440] The appeal of the clerics to Islamic socioeconomic equity and justice swayed many unhappy Iranians—and in no part of Iran did this appeal go unheard. Wherever stood a *masjid* stood a bastion of opposition against the policies of the Shah. Furthermore, the Shi'ah clerical establishment had contributed to the political, spiritual, and intellectual development of the Iranian people. Politically conscious and armed with their faith, the Iranian masses went on to make an Islamic revolution in their country.[441] Indeed, the Shi'ah *ulama* in Iran were particularly suited to assuming the reins of government after the fall of the Shah. After all, for many years prior to the revolution, the *ulama* "emerged as a class providing not only religious leadership in the narrow and technical sense but also leadership of a national and political nature, given increasingly to contesting the monarchical institution."[442] In fact, the Shi'ah *ulama* had a long history of political involvement in protests between 1891 and 1892 and during the constitutional revolution of 1905 to 1911. The Pahlavi monarchy, which began in 1925, harassed and persecuted the *ulama*, but to little avail. The Shi'ah clerical establishment rose again to

---

[437]Akbar Husain, *The Revolution in Iran*, p. 45.

[438]Bill, "The Shah, The Ayatollah, and The U.S," p. 12.

[439]Ibid. p. 11.

[440]Ibid., p. 41.

[441]Quoted in Kalim Siddiqui, Iqbal Asaria, Abd Al-Rahim Ali, and Ali Afrouz, *The Islamic Revolution: Achievements, Obstacles and Goals,* Toronto: Crescent Internationl, 1980, p. 40.

[442]Ibid.

challenge the government in 1963, when it was suppressed, and in 1978 when it emerged victorious.[443]

Aware of the *ulama*'s political interests and its opposition to his policies of land redistribution, women's rights, secular education, and modernization, the Shah attempted to check clerical influence among the Iranian people.[444] Stripping the clerics of their special perquisites, closing down Islamic presses, breaking up religious assemblages, and imprisoning, exiling and even executing clerics, the Shah hoped to undermine clerical power. Instead, his suppressive policies strengthened it.[445] The Shah could not easily enforce his edicts within the sacred *masjid*. Thus, while the *masjid*'s became safe forums for political dissent, the Shi'ah clerical establishment become an alternative government.

The role of the *masjid* in the genesis of the Iranian Revolution is central to an understanding of the *ulama*'s political functions in Iran. Despite the Shah's cultural campaign to modernize and secularize his country, most Iranians remained resolute in their religious faith and traditions. Shi'ah Islam was heavily reinforced by the central role played by the *masjid* in Iranian communities. In the *masjid*, daily prayers were recited, sermons delivered, weekly religious assemblies held, and community activities planned. These organized religious gatherings often had political overtones, especially during the 1970s.[446]

The Shi'ah clerical establishment had the only truly nationwide organization in Iran, penetrating deeper than even the Shah's regime. *Masjids* stood in every community in Iran and remained independent of the government and relatively free to operate in the Shah's repressive police state. By 1978, 180,000 clerics (1 Iranian cleric for every 200 Iranians) communicated their displeasure with the Shah's policies directly to the Iranian people in every community in Iran.[447]

The *ulama*'s function as an alternative government was girded during the revolutionary period of 1978 to 1979 with the generous financial assistance of the *bazaaris*. The clerics, in turn, distributed the money honestly and efficiently to the unemployed, poor, and needy, and to the families of murdered antiregime demonstrators. Increasingly, district and neighborhood *masjids* gained control over the daily affairs of their communities. Prior to the overthrow of the Shah, *masjids* operated as local power centers that brought together all opposition to the Shah under their banner, including the dispossessed, the *bazaaris*, the intelligentsia, the nationalists, and even the leftists. During this time, in the twilight of the Pahlavi monarchy, Islam permeated the Iranian consciousness. No secular ideology emerged as a rival to the *ulama* against the Shah. Leftists and national-

---

[443]Nikki Keddie, "The Revolt of Islam and Its Roots," in Dankwart A. Rustow and Kenneth Paul Erickson, eds., *Comparative Political Dynamics*, New York: HarperCollins Publishers, 1991, pp. 292–293.

[444]Robert W. Strayer, Edwin Hirschmann, Robert B. Marks, and Robert J. Smith, *The Making of the Modern World: Connected Histories, Divergent Paths (1500 to the Present)*, New York: St. Martin's Press, 1989, pp. 321, 323.

[445]Deutsch et al., *Comparative Government*, pp. 421–422.

[446]Ramy Nima, *The Wrath of Allah: Islamic Revolution and Reaction in Iran*, London: Pluto Press, 1983, p. 77.

[447]Ibid.

ists, for example, could not match the widespread influence of the *masjid* on Iran. Thus, following the collapse of the Shah's regime, Muslim Fundamentalist clerics who had stood in the vanguard of the revolution were well positioned to step into the political vacuum. Indeed, it was only natural.[448]

The collective grievances of the Iranian people, compounded by decades of oppression under the Shah, erupted in 1978 like a match dropped in a sea of gasoline. During his reign the Shah had angered and alienated nearly all sectors and classes of Iranian society. The educated, politically conscious, and ambitious middle class felt economically excluded and politically stifled in the police state of the Pahlavi monarchy. The middle class also resented the presence of 100,000 Westerners who enjoyed positions of power and influence in the Iranian government and who earned higher wages than native Iranians. The *bazaaris* were angry with the Shah for his policies to undercut them economically. The clerics were aroused by the Shah's secularization policies and his sometimes blatantly anticlerical programs. Workers in the cities were infuriated by the Shah's crackdown on competent organized-labor movements. Even the upper middle class was unsatisfied with the Shah's inept, unprofessional, and often corrupt government.[449] The poorest 40 percent of the population was incensed by the Shah's government not only for ignoring their plight, but for contributing to it. The Shah's failure to earn the support of any class or to root his regime in anything more substantial than promising handouts cost him the Peacock Throne. Unified against his tyranny, the Iranian people cast the Shah aside. The *bazaaris* rendered financial assistance, the clerics provided the leadership, and the frustrated and disaffected urban poor became the foot soldiers of the Islamic Revolution in Iran.[450]

Ironically, the Shah precipitated the final revolutionary crisis himself. Relative deprivation, fueled by the Shah's extravagant promises to remake Iran into a modern, Western-style nation-state, exploded into popular discontent following the oil bust. The Shah had lifted Iranian expectations and reality had dashed them. Therefore, the Shah became the target of popular anger. When the recession hit Iran in 1976, the Shah's policies of Westernization were considered failures. Indeed, millions of devout Iranian Muslims considered the Shah's secular ideologies unsuitable for Iran and felt vindicated by the widespread dissatisfaction they precipitated. The perceived failure of "imported" development plans strengthened the appeal of Islam as the only alternative to the Shah and his U.S. masters.

Moreover, the Shah's modernization policies aggravated and amplified the five common crises of development. The Shah never had much legitimacy while the clergy did. The Shah's government did not penetrate far into Iran; *masjids* were everywhere. The government failed to secure the fair and appropriate distribution of goods and services; the Shi'ah clerics did. The Shah's government permitted no popular participation; all Muslims were welcomed in the *masjid*. And the Shah's policies precipitated a crisis of identity that the Shah could not resolve;

---

[448]Ibid., p. 142.

[449]Deutsch et al., *Comparative Government*, pp. 419–422.

[450]Ibid.; Rod Hague, Martin Harrop, and Shaun Breslin, *Political Science: A Comparative Introduction*, New York: St. Martin's Press, 1992, pp. 80–81.

the clergy could. Therefore, the fall of the Shah was inescapable, and the rise of the Shi'ah clerical establishment in his place, inevitable.

Although political, economic, and sociocultural factors contributed significantly to the Islamic Revolution in Iran, the catalytic role played by two devout Iranian Muslim personalities—Ali Shariati and Ayatollah Khomeini (see Box 10.1)—is critical to understanding the timing, direction, and temperament of the Islamic revival and revolution that overswept Iran in the late 1970s.

EXPORTING REVOLUTIONARY ISLAM

With the Shah permanently exiled, Khomeini returned triumphantly from exile in Paris to preside over a new phase of the Iranian Revolution: the establishment of an Islamic government. To this end, Khomeini appointed the respected and devout Mehdi Bazargan (see Box 10.2) as Iran's prime minister. Bazargan's government was short-lived, however. Meant only to be an interim prime minister, Bazargan was directed to lay the foundations for the Islamic form of government that Khomeini envisioned. The new Islamic Republic would be ruled not by the people, but by the precepts of Islam as interpreted by the Fundamentalist Shi'ah *ulama*. Khomeini, assuming the title *Velayat-i-Faqih*, appointed himself and was accepted by most Iranians as the last word in scriptural interpretation. In essence, the new government of Iran would be a theocracy. The Fundamentalist *ulama*, and Khomeini especially, advocated direct clerical rule of Iran. Given Khomeini's incomparable popularity in the flush of victory against the Shah, few Iranians were willing to question the eighty-year-old Ayatollah's judgment. The Traditionalist *ulama*'s view that the Shi'ah clerical establishment should not rule but should only advise temporal rulers was abandoned. Traditionalists like the Ayatollah Shariatmadari and Modernists like interim prime minister Bazargan, who felt the *ulama* should maintain only an advisory role in Iranian government, lacked the stature and popularity enjoyed by the Fundamentalist Ayatollah Khomeini among the Iranian people and were left by the wayside.

In Khomeini's mind and in the minds of most Iranians, the Iranian Revolution was more than a popular revolt against the tyranny of the Shah. The Iranian Revolution was synonymous with an Islamic Revolution. The monarchy was discarded, certainly, but only to be replaced by an Islamic theocracy. The Fundamentalist *ulama* sought to transform Iranian society from top down. Iran would be "Islamized." The clerics would reorganize and reform Iran's legal system, its cultural institutions, its system of education, and even its economic system according to the letter and spirit of Islam.[451]

Consolidating the gains of the Iranian Revolution meant securing the Ayatollah Khomeini's personal power over the nation while simultaneously pursuing policies of Islamization in all sectors of society. Almost immediately following Khomeini's assumption of power in February 1979, Fundamentalists began systematically and thoroughly to purge any individuals suspected of loyalty to the

---

[451]Strayer et al., *The Making of the Modern World*, pp. 326–327.

Box 10.1

THE ROLE OF SHARIATI AND KHOMEINI IN THE IRANIAN REVOLUTION

Although numerous clerical and lay Iranian citizens made the Iranian Revolution possible, the preeminent roles played by Ali Shariati and Ayatollah Khomeini need special mention and comparison.

Although political, economic, and sociocultural factors contributed significantly to the Islamic Revolution in Iran, one cannot discount the preeminent part played by two devout Iranian Muslim personalities. The catalytic role of Ali Shariati and Ayatollah Khomeini is principal to understanding the timing, direction, and temperament of the Islamic revival and revolution that overswept Iran in the late 1970s.

An Iranian sociologist with a degree from the Sorbonne in Paris, Shariati was never the leader of an Islamic movement or party, although a party was built around his revolutionary Islamic ideology. Shariati formulated a popular and attractive synthesis of the ideals of Islamic theology and Marxist ideology adapted to the contemporary Iranian environment. He also authored nearly two dozen books, pamphlets, and monographs in his life and published more than fifty articles that elucidated his musing on Islam in Iran. Shariati's revolutionary and populist Islamic ideology appealed to restless and confused university students, offering an exciting alternative to the sometimes tiring and obtuse sermons of the *ulama*. Consequently, Shariati's revolutionary ideals provided the ideological foundation for the People's *Mujahideen* Organization of Iran (PMOI), popularly known as the *Mujahideen-i-Khalq*. Under the PMOI banner, students and unemployed youths gathered to spread Shariati's gospel and to distribute transcripts and recordings of his lectures.

Widely disseminated, Shariati's ideals were influential during and immediately after the Iranian Revolution, when nearly 80 percent of books on display on Iranian cities streets were authored by Shariati. Before that, in the late 1960s and throughout the 1970s, the PMOI had commenced a guerrilla campaign to overthrow the Pahlavi monarchy. Likewise, during the 1978–1979 revolution the PMOI mobilized Iranian youth to demonstrate in the streets against the Shah. Yet although Shariati's ideas were ubiquitous during the revolution, Shariati did not live to see the end of the Pahlavi monarchy. In 1977 Shariati, who had no known health problems, died suddenly and mysteriously in London. Many attributed his death to SAVAK, the Shah's intelligence service. Lamenting the loss of a principled opponent of the Shah and recognizing his service to the cause of political Islam, the Shi'ah *ulama* eulogized the murdered Shariati in their sermons—no doubt increasing his popularity among the Iranian people. In contrast to Shariati, Ayatollah Khomeini was revered by the Iranian people as a senior-most Shi'ah religious leader and brother were rumored to have been murdered by the monarchy's security apparatus and Khomeini himself endured sixteen years in exile for his vitriolic public denunciations of the monarchy. The Shah exiled Khomeini from Iran following the cleric's vociferous opposition to the Pahlavi regime's surrender to demands that all the U.S. military and civilian personnel in Iran be governed by U.S. and not Iranian law. Khomeini was enraged by this insult to Iranian national sovereignty and said so, loudly and often. But exile, for Khomeini, was a hidden blessing. While in Iraq and later in France, Khomeini was out of the Shah's reach and could speak against the Pahlavi regime with impunity.

Khomeini's influence was likewise strengthened by his connections with friends inside Iran. While a religious leader in Qom, Khomeini earned the respect of innumerable theological students over the years. These students, many of whom became Islamic clerics themselves, became eager disciples of the Ayatollah and transmitted Khomeini's ideas and teachings to Iranians while he languished in exile. When the revolutionary fuse was lit in the first week of 1978, Khomeini's many Fundamentalist clerical supporters agitated and mobilized the people in *masjid*s throughout Iran. Admirers broadcast Khomeini's proclamations from his exile in Najaf that condemned the Shah's corruption, injustice, and oppression; denounced the United States for supporting the unpopular Pahlavi monarchy; and honored Iranians demonstrating in the streets. The Shi'ah clerical establishment revered Khomeini and portrayed him as a heroic figure. Khomeini's personality entered the public consciousness through easily accessible reproductions of his speeches and sermons on audiocassette tapes. Demonstrators against the Shah carried huge posters of Ayatollah Khomeini through the streets. His portraits bedecked the walls of city slums, and many booksellers and street vendors sold Khomeini's writings. The Ayatollah, in the public eye, symbolized the revolution against the Shah. Indeed, many among the impoverished and downtrodden people of Iran were convinced by the hero-worship lavished upon Khomeini in *masjid* and marketplace alike that he was the representive of the Twelfth *Imam* or *Mahdi;* the vicar of Ali coming to free Iran from the tyranny and corruption of the Pahlavi monarchy and its Western supporters.

While the middle-aged Shariati died a few months before the start of the Iranian Revolution, the elderly Khomeini not only lived to witness a political earthquake, which completely shattered and destroyed the Shah's monarchical system, but he also got the opportunity to start building the Islamic Republic that he had spent so many years envisioning and praying for.

Both Islamic revivalists brought to the Iranian theater their own unique Islamic worldviews. The Muslim Modernist Shariati's Islamic worldview was very different from that of the Muslim Fundamentalist Khomeini's. Shariati's profound understanding of the Western social sciences and the Western world was in sharp contrast to that of Khomeini's *madrassah* education that discounted the importance of an understanding of the Western social sciences and the Western world itself. Had Shariati lived through the Iranian Revolution, he may have disagreed with many of the policies and programs pursued by Khomeini's Islamic Republic. Probably, Shariati may even have suffered the same fate as Bazargan and Banisadr, two other Iranian Muslim Modernists who enjoyed Khomeini's confidence and who even got Khomeini's blessing when they became president of Iran for a few months—but who were eventually discredited and swept aside by Khomeini when they clashed with the powerful Shi'ah clerical establishment.

Sources: Ervand Abrahamian, "Ali Shariati: Ideology of the Iranian Revolution," *MERIP Reports,* Vol. 12, No. 1, January 1982; Hamid Algar, *The Roots of the Islamic Revolution,* Markham, Ontario: The Open Press, 1983; Abdulaziz Sachedina, "Ali Shariati: Ideologue of the Iranian Revolution," in John Esposito, ed., *Voices of Resurgent Islam,* Oxford and New York: Oxford University Press, 1983; Shahrough Akhavi, "Shariati's Social Thought," in Nikki R. Keddie, ed., *Religion and Politics in Iran: Shi'ism from Quietism to Revolution,* New Haven: Yale University Press, 1983; Nikki R. Keddie, *Roots of Revolution: An Interpretive History of Modern Iran,* New Haven: Yale University Press, 1981; Mangol Bayat-Philipp, "Shi'ism in Contemporary Iranian Politics: The Case of Ali Shariati," in Elie Kedourie and Sylvia G. Haim, eds., *Towards a Modern Iran: Studies in Thought, Politics and Society,* London: Frank Cass & Co., 1980; Nicholas Gage, "Stern Symbol of Opposition to the Shah: Ruhollah Khomeini," *New York Times,* December 11, 1978; Angus Deming, Scott Sullivan, and Jane Whitmore, "The Khomeini Enigma," *Newsweek,* December 31, 1979; Nicholas Gage, "The Unknown Ayatullah Khomeini: The Portrait of the Islamic Mystic at the Center of the Revolution," *Time,* July 16, 1979; Edward Mortimer, *Faith and Power: The Politics of Islam,* New York: Vintage Books, 1982; Robert Stephens, "Gift of God and Scourge of the Shah," *The Observer,* January 21, 1979; Ayatollah Ruhollah Khomeini, *Islam and Revolution: Writings and Declarations of Imam Khomeini,* trans. and annotated by Hamid Algar, Berkeley: Mizan Press, 1981; Shaul Bakhash, *The Reign of the Ayatollahs: Iran and the Islamic Revolution,* 2nd ed., New York: Basic Books, Inc., 1990; J. S. Ismael and T. Y. Ismael, "Social Change in Islamic Society: The Political Thought of Ayatollah Khomeini," *Social Problems,* Vol. 27, No. 5, June 1980; Ayatollah Ruhollah Khomeini, *Islamic Government,* translated by Joint Publications Research Service, New York: Manor Books, Inc., 1979; Marvin J. Folkertsma, Jr., *Ideology and Leadership,* Englewood Cliffs, NJ: Prentice-Hall, Inc., 1988.

Shah from the military and government. Paranoid of a military coup against the nascent Islamic Republic and determined never to trust the Shah's U.S.-trained armed forces, the ruling clerics purged the officer corps repeatedly. Furthermore, tens of thousands of young and unemployed supporters of the revolutionary government were recruited to serve in a paramilitary group known variously as the *Pasdaran,* the Revolutionary Guards, or Guardians of the Islamic Revolution. These young soldiers comprised the Praetorian guard of clerical government, loyal only to the *ulama.*

During the Islamic Revolution, committees were established in workplaces to organize strikes to protest the Pahlavi monarchy. With the victory of the revolution, these committees undertook to run those workplaces whose owners and management had fled the country, or share control with owners and managers

Box 10.2 MEHDI BAZARGAN

Mehdi Badar Bazargan was born in 1905. His father was of Turkish descent and plied a successful trade selling rugs and fruit in Tabriz. His family was among the wealthy and influential class of *bazaaris* that later played a prominent role in financing Khomeini's revolution. The young Bazargan showed promise early, receiving a scholarship from the government of Reza Kahn Pahlavi to study engineering at the École Centrale in Paris. Receiving his engineering degree in thermodynamics, Bazargan went home in 1942 to teach at Tehran University. Winning an immediate reputation as one of Iran's best mathematicians, Bazargan was awarded the chair at the technical college of Tehran University. While a young professor there, Bazargan established the Islamic Students Society and the Society of Engineers.

While in France, Bazargan developed a lasting admiration for liberal parliamentary democracy. Therefore, following the Second World War, Bazargan became increasingly involved politically in the National Front's opposition to the Shah and became allied with Muhammad Mossadeq. During Mossadeq's nationalist government, from 1951 to 1953, the Shah was forced into exile and the British-owned Anglo-Iranian Oil Company was nationalized. Mossadeq appointed Bazargan to oversee its operations. In 1953, however, Mossadeq was ousted and the Shah returned to power. Interested in being the bridge between Islamists (including the clerics) and secular intellectuals, Bazargan drifted away from Mossadeq's secular National Front party and founded the more religiously oriented Iran Freedom Movement in 1961 along with Ayatollah Sayyid Mahmood Taleqani and Yadollah Sahabi. In his new leadership role, Bazargan organized Islamic discussion groups and lecture series, and became a tireless speaker and a prolific writer of articles, pamphlets, and books in which he addressed and advocated Islam's compatibility with modern science and technology. Moreover, Bazargan believed that no distinction existed whatsoever between the spiritual and temporal realms. Religion, Bazargan insisted, should function as the guiding star of politics. Furthermore, in his writings Bazargan viewed the West with a mixture of admiration and revulsion. Although he felt its scientific and technological advances were wondrous and worthy of respect and emulation, he believed its secularization had undermined its spirit. Without a prominent role for religion, he posited, the West was incomplete and soulless.

Although Bazargan was an advocate of religious faith in society, he wanted to break the monopoly of the Traditionalist and Fundamentalist Shi'ah clergy over religion. Bazargan preferred a strictly Modernist path, in which the best elements of Western civilization would be adapted to function within an Islamic context. But Bazargan was no advocate of theocracy. He encouraged the clerics to awaken their students politically and to involve themselves in political affairs. The clerical establishment, he believed, should serve as the political conscience of the nation. However, he was totally opposed to the clerical establishment becoming the government.

A vocal advocate of substantive change in Iran, Bazargan quickly ran afoul of the Shah and was deprived of his position as chairman of Tehran University's engineering college and imprisoned for five years. Upon his release, Bazargan was banned from the classroom and was forced to open a heating and air-conditioning company to feed his family. But while working, the engineering professor headed the Iranian Human Rights Committee, thereby forging closer ties with a wide array of anti-Shah opposition movements.

After spending sixteen years in exile, Mehdi Bazargan returned to Tehran during the Islamic Revolution. The Ayatollah Khomeini capitalized on Bazargan's reputation as a pious, popular and "untouchable" man by appointing him prime minister of Iran's "provisional" government. Khomeini praised his new prime minister as "a devoted Muslim, a righteous man, a nationalist without any inclinations that go against Islamic law." Indeed, even Shahpour Bakhtiar looked favorably on the decision Khomeini had made. Bazargan, Bakhtiar stated, "is an old friend, I trust and respect him." Suddenly, this meek and soft-spoken seventy-two-year-old engineer, with a reputation as a devout Muslim and as a tireless human rights advocate during the reign of the Shah, was in a position to realize his Modernist vision of Islam. He explained to a *Newsweek* correspondent that his role was "between the political nationalists and the Islamic clergy. . . . I am a liaison man between modern culture and tradition. My task now is to prove that modernism is not alien to Islam." Called "Mr. Clean" in reference to his unstained character during the Shah's corrupt regime, Bazargan has written numerous books and articles that explore Islam's inherent compatibility with democracy, reason, and science.

Having weathered the Iranian Revolution and having been handpicked by Khomeini to become prime minister of the provisional revolutionary government, Bazargan had effectively spanned the turbulent period between the old monarchical regime of the Shah and the new Islamic order about to be born. As prime minister, Bazargan selected the ministers and other high-ranking officials in his government on the following criteria: Nominees must be devout and reputable Muslims, must be competent in their fields, and must have actively opposed the Shah's regime. Consequently, Bazargan's cabinet consisted of clean-shaven, middle-class professionals in suits and neckties. The Shi'ah clerics were insulted by their lack of representation in the Bazargan government and swore to replace it with an Islamic government in which they would predominate.

Bazargan's authority was increasingly undermined by radical political parties, by ethnic uprisings throughout Iran, and by the Revolutionary Council, which frequently organized large-scale street demonstrations and which served together with local revolutionary committees, Islamic courts, and the Islamic Republic's paramilitary force of the *Pasdaran-i-Enqelab-i-*

Eslami (Guardians of the Islamic Revolution) as an alternative government challenging Bazargan. These organizations, coupled with the newly created Islamic Republican Party (IRP), finally brought down the Bazargan government. The prime minister had been photographed and filmed during an official visit to Algeria shaking hands and speaking amiably to U.S. National Security Advisor Zbigniew Brzezinski—notorious in Iran as a staunch supporter of the Shah and an early advocate of U.S. intervention in Iran to support the Shah in crushing the Islamic Revolution. The outcry against Bazargan for cozying up to the Americans caused him to resign the premiership and to return to his position of leadership in the Iran Freedom Movement. His criticism was aimed no longer at the deposed Shah. He targeted the zealous Fundamentalists in the Revolutionary Council whom he accused of misgoverning Iran. Bazargan would survive to be one of the few voices of dissent permitted in Iran.

Sources: David Butler with Elaine Sciolino, *Newsweek,* February 19, 1979; "In Iran, He's Mr. Clean," *Philadelphia Inquirer,* February 7, 1979; Shaul Bakhash, *The Reign of the Ayatollahs: Iran and the Islamic Revolution,* rev. ed., New York: Basic Books, 1990; Nikki R. Keddie, *Roots of Revolution: An Interpretive History of Modern Iran,* New Haven: Yale University Press, 1981.

who remained in Iran.[452] Meanwhile, the clerical establishment also inaugurated committees, known as *komitehs*, in numerous *masjids*. In larger Iranian cities, two forms of *komitehs* were established; the first based in the *masjid* to control and organize the neighborhood, and the second, called a central *komiteh*, with far greater powers to coordinate and direct the policies of Islamic revolution throughout the city. Central *komitehs* rapidly became the primary governing bodies in large urban centers. They controlled the prices and distribution of goods; policed city streets; enforced law and order; and meted out justice based on the basis of the *Shariah.* The central *komitehs* combined the administrative and judicial functions of government while higher authorities, like the Islamic Revolutionary Council and Khomeini himself, executed legislative powers.[453]

In institutionalizing the Islamic Revolution, Iran's Shi'ah clerical establishment hurriedly formulated an Islamic constitution and an Islamic legal system in which clerics would officiate as judges over criminal cases and would punish offenders according to *Shariah* law. The ruling clerics also established a new political organization called the Islamic Republican Party (IRP) under the astute leadership of the Ayatollah Beheshti. Clerics and Muslim Fundamentalists elected under the IRP banner became a new breed of politician in Iran.

True to his Fundamentalist credentials, Khomeini undertook a "cultural revolution" in 1980 to Islamize Iran domestically. Khomeini's militant Fundamentalist

---

[452]Nima, *The Wrath of Allah,* p. 79.

[453]Ibid., pp. 77–79.

partisans attacked leftists in Iranian colleges and universities. In June 1980, Khomeini closed all Iranian institutions of higher education to expedite a purge of Westernized and secular elements. Public education from kindergarten up was also revamped. Secular teachers and administrators were fired to make room for devout Muslim teachers who were more amenable to the new Islamic curriculum. Khomeini also purged the Iranian bureaucracy and staffed ministries with "good" Muslims.[454]

Both domestically and internationally, Khomeini pursued a policy of unwavering opposition to Western influences of any sort. Indeed, for Khomeini, everything beyond Islam was truly *dar al-harb;* the Muslim world was beset by various un-Islamic evils that included secular and Pragmatist governments ruling Muslims, and meddlesome imperialist powers like the United States and the USSR. Indeed, Khomeini perceived the U.S. government as the "Great Satan," the leader of the immensely powerful Western world that was a controlling force in Iran and the Muslim world. He called on Muslims all over the world to engage in a ceaseless *jihad* against their pro-Western and pro-Russian rulers and against dependency on the powerful but morally "degenerate" powers of the West and the Communist world.[455]

Despite Khomeini's death in 1989, his anti-Western and anticommunist rhetoric continues to attract and inspire Islamic revivalists throughout the world. His call to eradicate Western and communist influence from the Muslim world remains powerful and popular, even though many Fundamentalist revivalists, particularly of the Sunni sect of Islam, resist emulating the "Iranian model" because of its Shi'ah overtones and adverse publicity in the world. For Islamists throughout the Muslim world, the victory of the Islamic Revolution in Iran signified a new type of revolution in which secularization, modernization, and Westernization did not prevail but were, in fact, overthrown in the name of non-Western Islamic values and cultures. The appeal of such a victory even in the most general sense generated widespread outbursts of Fundamentalist militancy throughout the Muslim world, including Egypt, Saudi Arabia, Kuwait, the Sudan, and Algeria, even though Khomeini's leadership itself was rejected. Consequently, Iran's Islamic Revolution has had unprecedented international impact. Its reverberations are still being felt throughout the Muslim world. Furthermore, Muslims worldwide were affected by Khomeini's Islamic message of justice, equality, and Islamic purification. His frequent admonitions to Muslims to overthrow the secular and Pragmatist regimes that oppress them greatly emboldened both legitimate and revolutionary Islamic political movements in nearly all Muslim countries.

Khomeini's proclamations that he would export the Islamic Revolution to all Muslim countries alarmed the regimes of those countries and angered the governments of the West and of the communist world. Fear that Khomeini or his successors might make good on threats to undermine and overthrow secular, Pragmatist,

---

[454]John L. Esposito and James P. Piscatori, "Introduction," in John L. Esposito, ed., *The Iranian Revolution: Its Global Impact,* Miami: Florida International University Press, 1990, p. 3.

[455]Ralph et al., *World Civilizations,* pp. 691–692.

or conservative neighboring governments by spreading Fundamentalism, has motivated and directed U.S. policy toward the Muslim world for over a decade now. Khomeini's hatred of the United States itself was always obvious.

THE U.S. EMBASSY HOSTAGE CRISIS

Although he despised the West and the communist bloc with equal vigor, Khomeini focused his xenophobic rage against the United States, the longtime ally of the hated Shah. Generally, Khomeini decided that Iran must rely neither on West nor East. Foreign influence was to be eschewed. However, Iran emerged from its partly self-imposed isolation from the international community in 1988 when Iranian President Ali Akbar Hashemi Rafsanjani (see Box 10.3) repaired Iran's ties with several European nations. Rafsanjani's efforts to improve U.S.-Iranian relations have failed because they have been contaminated by mutual mistakes and misconceptions. Years of Khomeini's rhetoric deriding the "Great Satan" were answered by equally irrational anti-Iranian outbursts in the United States. For Iran, the trouble with the United States began in 1953. In U.S. eyes, however, Iran started trouble in 1979 by taking U.S. diplomats as hostage.

The fall of the Shah and the "loss" of Iran was traumatizing for the West. The U.S. government was thoroughly unprepared to deal with the new government in Tehran, especially one consisting of Muslim clerics.[456] Worse than that, however, the United States totally undermined the chances of a U.S.-Iranian reconciliation after the revolution by permitting the Shah to enter the United States for medical treatment. The United States justified the action on "humanitarian grounds." Furthermore, the Shah still commanded the friendship of men like Henry Kissinger and David Rockefeller. Nevertheless, the Shah had no friends in Iran. By admitting the Shah into the United States, President Carter stoked the paranoia of the Iranian people who remembered the U.S. role in the 1953 ouster of Mossadeq. Playing on this paranoia, Khomeini declared that "America expects to take the Shah there, engage in plots, and our young people are expected to simply remain idle." Khomeini therefore called for mass demonstrations, which he got. Three million Iranians marched on the U.S. Embassy in Tehran on November 1, 1979. Three days later, hundreds of young militants stormed the embassy, with Iranian government complicity, and took U.S. diplomats hostage. So powerful was the image of Iranians attacking the U.S. embassy that similar attacks were made against U.S. diplomatic offices in Libya and Pakistan.[457]

The radical Iranian youths in control of the U.S. Embassy in Tehran accused the United States of spying in Iran and of supporting the Shah while he massacred protestors, tortured political prisoners, squandered and plundered the nation's wealth, and introduced Western values at the expense of Islamic values. Although

---

[456]Ralph et al., *World Civilizations,* p. 691.

[457]Schulzinger, *American Diplomacy,* pp. 333–334.

Box 10.3 ALI AKBAR HASHEMI RAFSANJANI

Iran's Ali Akbar Hashemi Rafsanjani was born in 1934 into the middle-class family of a pistachio-nut farmer and dealer in the southwestern desert village of Rafsanjan near the city of Kerman. At age fourteen he went to Iran's world-renowned holy city of Qom to receive an Islamic education. There he studied at *Madrassah-i-Faiziyeh* (Faiziyeh Seminary) under Ruhollah Khomeini and other clerics. The impressionable teenager was greatly influenced by Khomeini's revolutionary Islamic worldview that contrasted sharply with Shi'ah Islam's apolitical and quietist tradition. Under Khomeini's tutelage, Rafsanjani came to believe that the salvation of Islam and the Muslim world lay in the assumption of temporal power by the *ulama.* Thus, Rafsanjani turned against the Shah and Iran's monarchical, secular, and Westernizing system. Also while at Qom, Rafsanjani first met and cultivated close ties with several Fundamentalist clerics later to play major roles in the 1978–1979 Islamic Revolution.

In the early 1950s, Rafsanjani joined Muhammad Mossadeq's struggle against the Shah. In 1962, he was conscripted from his seminary in Qom along with other Islamists to serve in the Iranian army, but was soon re-trenched for preaching Khomeini's Islamic worldview to his fellow army conscripts. When Khomeini opposed the Shah's "White Revolution," his students were in the vanguard of the Islamic resistance movement. At that time, Rafsanjani developed even closer ties with the future leaders of Iran's Islamic Revolution. When the Shah exiled Khomeini, Rafsanjani was among those clerics who kept his former mentor informed about developments within Iran for the next sixteen years. On a number of occasions, Rafsanjani was arrested and detained by the Shah's notorious SAVAK. On at least one occasion, Rafsanjani was even tortured in jail.

Rafsanjani has often been described as a very bright, clever, and knowledgeable cleric. He has written three books in Persian: *Champion of the Struggle Against Colonialism,* about Amir Kabir, a prime minister of Nazreddin Shah in the late nineteenth century and a prominent reformer *The Story of Palestine,* on the Palestinian dilemma; and *Revolution or a New Resurrection,* about Iran's Islamic Revolution. He was also promoted in the Shi'ah clerical establishment to *Hojatolislam* (literally, "authority on Islam").

As one of the founders of the Tehran Association of Militant Clergy, Rafsanjani was in the vanguard of Iran's Islamic Revolution. After Ayatollah Khomeini's return to Tehran from exile on February 1, 1979, *Hojatolislam* Rafsanjani was on the Revolutionary Council, in the ayatollah's inner circle of confidants, one of the founders and central committee members of the Islamic Republican Party (IRP) until the influential organization was dissolved in 1987, and a major patron of the *Pasdaran* (Revolutionary Guards)—a powerful organization that gave him considerable clout in the government.

Soon after the formation of the Islamic regime, Rafsanjani was elevated to the position of minister of the interior. In this position, he organized the referendum on the new constitution in December 1979, and the first presidential elections in January 1980. He subsequently resigned from his ministerial post to stand for Iran's *Majlis* (National Assembly) in March 1980. Elected to the *Majlis* as a representative from Tehran, Rafsanjani became speaker of the *Majlis* later in the same year, a position of considerable influence. He was reelected as speaker of the *Majlis* in 1984 and 1988, no mean accomplishment for a middle-level cleric during the turbulent and uncertain times when many around him were losing their jobs and even their lives.

In 1988, Ayatollah Khomeini appointed Rafsanjani commander-in-chief of the armed forces, a promotion that made Rafsanjani the second most powerful man in Iran after his aging mentor and patron. In this capacity, Rafsanjani established the full coordination of the armed forces, the Revolutionary Guards, SAVAMA (the security forces), and the *Basij* (volunteer mobilization forces). As Khomeini's representative in the Supreme Defense Council, Rafsanjani persuaded the inflexible and uncompromising Khomeini to agree to the cease-fire in the devastating Iran-Iraq war in August 1988 to preserve the Islamic Revolution.

After Ayatollah Khomeini's death in 1989, Rafsanjani was elected president of Iran, a position strengthened by the revised constitution of 1988. As president, he initially endeavored to preserve unity and maintain the balance between rival factions. However, Rafsanjani dismissed most of the radical Fundamentalist ministers and surrounded himself with progressive technocrats. As a leading member of the Council of the Cultural Revolution, he was one of the founders of an Open Islamic University on Iranian television and radio. He established priorities to reconstruct Iran's war-ravaged economy and end his country's international isolation. While reaffirming his commitment to a foreign policy of "neither East nor West" and while fully capable of denouncing the "Great Satan" (the United States), he adds that this "does not mean cutting ties with the East and the West, but rather maintaining healthy relations with outside powers." Instead of exporting Iran's brand of revolutionary Islamic Fundamentalism, Rafsanjani has expanded oil exports, improved economic relations with the West and with the former communist bloc, signed economic cooperation agreements with the former Soviet Union, and even expressed a willingness to improve relations with the United States—willingness he illustrated when he persuaded the Lebanese Shi'ite leaders of *Hezbollah* and Islamic *Amal* to release their Western hostages. Moreover, when a devastating earthquake struck northwestern Iran in June 1990, President Rafsanjani welcomed American relief organizations over the strong objections of the radical Fundamentalists in his government. In early April 1991, when Iraqi Kurds began fleeing Iraq for Iran, Rafsanjani again turned to the West to provide international relief.

During operations Desert Shield and Desert Storm, Rafsanjani maintained a position of strict neutrality, while many Fundamentalists, Traditionalists, and nationalists were calling for Iran to join Iraq in a *jihad* against the "Great Satan" and its coalition partners. Rafsanjani declared that sending Iranians to die for Iraq was "suicide," and that Iraq remained a greater threat to Iran than did the United States Rafsanjani's strategy paid off handsomely. In August 1990, Iran and Iraq concluded a peace treaty to their just-ended war that satisfied all Iranian demands. Saddam Hussein then sent one hundred Iraqi airforce jets over to Iran to avoid their destruction by Western air attacks. The consequent destruction of Iraq's nuclear, chemical, biological, and conventional military industries and the isolation of Iraq in the world community has removed the greatest threat posed to Iran's security. Thus, Rafsanjani's "practicable" policies have enabled the Iranian government to rebuild at home, and reassert itself abroad.

Notwithstanding these successes, Rafsanjani has faced harsh opposition within Iran. Radical Islamic Fundamentalists have tried to undermine Rafsanjani's power by denouncing his realism in foreign policy. For instance, they leaked information about his role in the Iranian government's secret arms deals with the United States and Israel. Nevertheless, Rafsanjani has kept the radical Fundamentalists at bay and has continued to run domestic and foreign policy his way. President Rafsanjani's brother controls the influential Iranian television and radio stations, which gives Rafsanjani positive coverage in the media. Rafsanjani's eloquent oratory helps him deliver moving sermons when he officiates as the provisional leader of Friday's congregational prayers in Tehran, one of the most influential platforms in the country.

Although the late Ayatollah Khomeini was Rafsanjani's teacher, leader, and patron, the mentor and student could not have differed more in temperament and outlook. While Khomeini was born into a family of clerics, Rafsanjani was born into a middle-class business family. Khomeini lived the ascetic life of a "puritan intellectual" and had a serious, stern, introverted, and reflective personality. Rafsanjani, meanwhile, is an extrovert with a friendly and charming disposition, a man not averse to leading a comfortable life. Rafsanjani once declared that there is nothing in Islam against living in comfort and enjoying one's life. Khomeini was an ideologue, a charismatic and transformational religiopolitical leader given to controversial decisions and momentous gambles. Rafsanjani, in contrast, is a moderate, pragmatic, and competent administrator, a dynamic politician with a keen political sense, skilled at negotiation, compromise, and consensus building. Khomeini's worldview was idealistic, radical, dogmatic, doctrinaire, and even xenophobic. Rafsanjani, on the other hand, is a realist with a remarkably progressive, open-minded, and cosmopolitan Islamic worldview. In essence, both men are Fundamentalists. Rafsanjani, however, avoids Khomeini's brand of messianic Islamic Fundamentalism. Rafsanjani has addressed the existential needs of his people, adopted a nonconfrontational policy with the world community, and been a consummate politician.

Sources: Yaacov Shimoni, *Biographical Dictionary of the Middle East,* New York: Facts on File, 1991; see Rafsanjani in *1989 Current Biography Yearbook,* New York: H. W. Wilson Co.; Richard Johns, "Rafsanjani: Pragmatic Power Behind the Revolution," *Financial Times,* June 29, 1988; David Hirst, "In the Shadow of Khomeini," *Guardian Weekly,* July 15, 1990; David Hirst, "The Shark of Iran Fights his Corner," *Guardian Weekly,* April 21, 1991; Kamran Fazel and Andrew Gowers, "Practical Man in the Shadow of Khomeini," *Financial Times,* July 28, 1989; *The Christian Science Monitor,* September 10, 1985; *International Who's Who, 1989–1990.*

they originally detained ninety persons in the Embassy, the hostage takers released all non-U.S. hostages, all African-Americans, and all women excepting one. The remaining fifty-two were branded as spies and held prisoner for 444 days. The "hostage crisis" enraged and humiliated the United States and became a lesson in the limits of U.S. power. The inability of the United States, the world's foremost military and industrial power, to expeditiously resolve the crisis or to pressure a Third World Muslim country to submit to U.S. demands sobered Americans. The world watched, captivated and bewildered, as the drama of the hostage crisis dragged on and on. Never before had the United States appeared so absolutely helpless, particularly when, in April of 1980, the Carter administration bungled a military rescue attempt to free the hostages. America itself was held hostage by militants in Tehran. The sight of U.S. powerlessness, in turn, encouraged Muslim Fundamentalists around the world and terrified Muslim Pragmatist leaders, who, seeing that Fundamentalism could paralyze the United States, feared what it could do to "un-Islamic" regimes in the Muslim world itself.

The hostage crisis poisoned Iranian relations with the outside world. The United States and its Western allies successfully used the United Nations and the Western media to portray Iran as a "pariah state" and isolated it in the world community for its breach of international law. Nevertheless, the spectacle of the hostage crisis amazed Muslims throughout the world who saw the Khomeini regime courageously (some say "imprudently") defiant in the face of a preeminent superpower equipped with the most advanced military technology in the world and with a truly frightening nuclear arsenal. Khomeini's gamble of supporting the hostage-taking was a big one. However, when the U.S. attempt to free the hostages failed in an Iranian desert sandstorm, Muslim Fundamentalists were convinced that the tide was turning against the West at last and that God was fighting in Iran's corner.[458]

The hostage crisis represented the inauguration of a new phase of the Iranian Revolution; its export. Although Iran was in no condition to spread its fundamen-

---

[458]Richard H. Foster and Robert V. Edington, *Viewing International Relations and World Politics,* Englewood Cliffs, NJ: Prentice-Hall, 1985, p. 18.

talist revolution militarily, it commanded significant influence in the world among Muslim Fundamentalists.

The hostage crisis ended peacefully, and all American hostages were released on January 20, 1981, after 444 days of incarceration. While America's superpower status was called into question, the major losers were President Carter, Khomeini, and Iran. The hostage crisis, coupled with the serious economic problems facing the United States, made Carter look weak and incompetent, and it cost him the 1980 presidential election. However, Ayatollah Khomeini, Iran, Islam, and the Shi'ah sect were hurt far more.

Iran's violation of international law was universally condemned. Many Iranians—including Muslim Modernist Mehdi Bazargan, who was Khomeini's choice to be the first interim president of Iran (February 1, 1979, to November 6, 1979), and Muslim Modernist Abolhassan Banisadr (see Box 10.4), who was the first popularly elected president of the Islamic Republic (January 25, 1980, to June 22, 1981)—disagreed with their supreme spiritual leader on the hostage crisis. While the hostage crisis may have had much to do with Bazargan's and Banisadr's short stays in office, it damaged Ayatollah Khomeini's reputation and greatly undermined Iran's Islamic Revolution even more. Khomeini was demonized in the non-Muslim world, and even many Muslims felt that his confrontation with the West was hurting Islam, and more particularly, Khomeini's Shi'ah sect, to which the majority of Iranians belong. Iran was isolated in the world community and was blacklisted as a "terrorist state." This, in turn, emboldened Iraq's Saddam Hussein to invade Iran on September 22, 1980. The Iran-Iraq war, which dragged on for eight long years, resulted in over 500,000 Iranian casualties, bankrupted the Islamic Republic's treasury, and kept the Khomeini regime from focusing on the vitally important task of economic and social development.

A number of prominent leaders in Iran—including Ali Akbar Hashemi Rafsanjani, Speaker of Iran's *Majlis* (Parliament)—convinced Khomeini to end the Iran-Iraq war and save the Islamic Republic. On July 18, 1988, Khomeini reluctantly agreed to accept the United Nations Security Council Resolution 598 calling for an immediate cease-fire in the Iran-Iraq war. A formal cease-fire went into effect on August 20, 1988.

With the end of the Iran-Iraq war, Iran's foreign ministry went into high gear and started a major diplomatic "peace offensive" in order to end their country's isolation in the world. Iran's relations with the rest of the world were just beginning to improve when Ayatollah Khomeini infuriated the West again by issuing a *fatwa* (edict) on February 14, 1989, calling on Muslims to execute Salman Rushdie and his publishers for insulting Islam in his novel, *The Satanic Verses*. (See Box 10.5, pages 245–249, following the summary.)

Ayatollah Khomeini died on June 3, 1989, and with his burial Iranians put to rest a turbulent decade in their country's history. Khomeini's former theological student and former Speaker of Iran's *Majlis*, Hashemi Rafsanjani, was elected president of Iran on July 28, 1989. Rafsanjani, a moderate Muslim Fundamentalist, has been making a concerted effort to improve Iran's diplomatic relations with the rest of the world. While the process of rehabilitating Iran in the world community is slow and tedious, progress has been made.

Box 10.4 ABOLHASSAN BANISADR

Abolhassan Banisadr was born in northwestern Iran in 1933. His father and grandfather were well-to-do landowners, who occupied positions of respect and prominence in the Shi'ite clerical establishment. Consequently, Banisadr received an Islamic education in an atmosphere that profoundly impressed upon him the faults of the Pahlavi dynasty.

Banisadr attended Tehran University and completed his undergraduate education in theology, economics, and sociology. As a student activist he joined the movement to oust the Shah and to replace him with the secular nationalist Muhammad Mossadeq. By 1953, however, a CIA-backed coup overthrew Mossadeq's government and restored the Shah to power. Banisadr then aligned himself with the Islamic groups in underground opposition to the Shah.

Engaging in anti-Shah activities, Banisadr was arrested twice by the Shah's secret police, the SAVAK. He spent two years in prison after his arrest in 1959, and he was arrested again in 1963 for his part in the uprising at Qom, which was led by Ayatollah Khomeini against the Shah's "White Revolution." After four months in jail, Banisadr joined a doctoral program in economics at Sorbonne University, where he then taught economics and sociology.

While in France, Banisadr wrote extensively on such topics as Islam, Iran, economics, and opposition to the Shah. Heavily influenced both by Iranian populist, Islamic socialist, and Muslim Modernist Ali Shariati and by Iranologist and Marxist economist Paul Vielle, Banisadr co-authored (with Vielle) the book *Oil and Violence: White Terror and Resistance in Iran* (1974). Banisadr postulated that Iran was a "tributary" which was dependent on foreign patrons, since Iran exported oil to buy consumer goods while neglecting agriculture. Banisadr argued that Iran's dependency on the West both as a market and as a producer put Iran in increasing debt. He outlined his solution in his book *Economics of Divine Unity*. Banisadr proposed to build an independent and egalitarian Iran by founding Iranian national development on principles of Islam and socialism as described in the Quran.

During this time Banisadr also continued his opposition to the Shah and involved himself in the Iranian emigré community. He became general secretary of the Confederation of Iranian Students in 1965 and also headed the religiously oriented wing of the emigré dissident movement against the Shah. In 1972, Banisadr first met Ayatollah Khomeini at his father's funeral in the Shi'ite holy city of Najaf in Iraq. Thereafter, Banisadr kept the Ayatollah abreast of conditions within Iran.

Saddam Hussein, as a favor to the Shah, expelled Ayatollah Khomeini from Iraq in 1978. Khomeini traveled to Paris at Banisadr's invitation. Banisadr therefore joined the Ayatollah's inner circle and helped bring together both the secular nationalists, socialists, and communists on the one hand, and the Muslim Fundamentalists, Traditionalists, and Modernists on the other. Recognized for his contribution to the Iranian Revolution, Banisadr joined Khomeini on the Ayatollah's triumphant return to Iran by plane in February 1979.

In Iran, Banisadr founded the *Inqilab-i-Islami* ("Islamic Revolution"), a daily newspaper that proposed radical development economics coupled with egalitarian Islamic principles. His views were similar to Mossadeq's but with a greater emphasis on Islam. The lessons were the same: Iran should cautiously export oil but simultaneously promote its own productive resources. Superpower influence should be stemmed not only in Iran but throughout the Third World. The United States, Banisadr believed, was responsible for undermining Iranian economic, political, and socio-cultural life, especially since the overthrow of Mossadeq. The USSR, however, was no more worthy of trust. Banisadr despised both U.S. and Soviet brands of imperialism and suggested instead a total nonalignment. Indeed, following the Soviet invasion of Afghanistan, Banisadr suggested the Iranian boycott of the Moscow Olympic Games in 1980.

In November 1979, Banisadr found himself in a position to realize his policies for Iran both domestically as minister of economics and finance and internationally as minister of foreign affairs. Among his first projects as a cabinet minister, Banisadr established an elaborate microfilm filing system that correlated his own economic ideas with Quranic verses to ensure that Iranian economic policy was in accordance with Islam. This system, Banisadr insisted, would guide and develop Iran's economy along the lines of Islam, thereby creating an egalitarian *tawhid* society.

Banisadr has been labeled an Islamic socialist because he favored nationalization and proposed an expansion of the public sector at the expense of the private sector. He sought to end foreign domination and dependency, to expel Western multinational corporations, to regulate monopolies, and to sponsor agricultural development and small industries. True to his writings, Banisadr strove to create a classless society in which wealth was fairly distributed and in which jobs were guaranteed for all. And as finance minister, Banisadr realized the nationalization of banks and insurance companies in the summer of 1979.

As foreign minister, meanwhile, Banisadr worked indefatigably to free the American hostages held in Tehran. He proposed a meeting of the U.N. Security Council, in which criticism of the U.S. role in Iran could be aired. Iran would then release the American hostages, abandoning the demand that the Shah be returned for trial. The Fundamentalist clerics in Iran, however, criticized Banisadr as soft on the United States; they also denounced him for his "excessive criticism" of the Iranian militants who had detained the American diplomats after initially storming the U.S. embassy. By garnering 76 percent of the popular vote in January 1980, Banisadr became the country's first popularly elected president after two thousand five hundred years of monarchical rule. Ayatollah Khomeini swore in the forty-six-year old Banisadr on February 4, 1980, and extolled all Iranians to support the new president. Later in February, the Ayatollah appointed Banisadr head of the ruling Revolutionary Council, chairman of the supreme defense council, and commander-in-chief of the Iranian armed forces. Banisadr now promised to remake Iran in the image he had envisioned as a graduate student at the Sorbonne. However, Banisadr faced incredible obstacles. He had neglected to develop a base of support in the *Majlis* (parliament), he had angered the Fundamentalist clerics who dominated the government, and he personally accused an aide of the formidable Fundamentalist Ayatollah Sayyid Muhammad Beheshti of complicity in a failed military coup in June 1980. The Fundamentalists struck back by purging the armed forces and the civil service of Banisadr's backers. Moreover, the waning of Banisadr's powers was demonstrated in August 1980 when his compromise choice for prime minister was rejected by the *Majlis*. Instead, the Fundamentalists chose a man for the post that Banisadr had earlier characterized as unfit. The Fundamentalist Islamic Republican Party (IRP) was now in a position to rival the president and isolate him politically.

Banisadr benefitted politically by the September 1980 Iraqi invasion of Iran because he enjoyed greater popularity with the armed forces than did the clerics of the IRP. But as commander-in-chief he spent his time touring the battlefield and directing Iranian military operations while his Fundamentalist foes in Tehran defeated his domestic programs. Personally annoyed by Banisadr's accusations against the Fundamentalists and surrounded by equally annoyed Fundamentalist advisors, the Ayatollah turned against Banisadr. Banisadr responded by accusing the Fundamentalists of trying to establish a dictatorship, and he asked the people to show their support for their beleaguered president. The Fundamentalists perceived this statement as a call for a counterrevolution, and within two weeks, Banisadr was dismissed as commander-in-chief.

Afraid for his personal safety, Banisadr escaped by jet to Paris. Consequently, the *Majlis* impeached the exiled president in June 1981, giving his former posts to his Fundamentalist rivals. Meanwhile, Banisadr continued to oppose the direction of the Islamic Revolution in Iran, but unlike other exiled opposition leaders, he would not side with Iraq in its war against Iran. Instead, in his magazine "Islamic Revolution," he condemned Iraqi atrocities and denounced Iranian exiles who failed to condemn Iraq.

Banisadr like Abduh, Iqbal, and Shariati was a Muslim Modernist par excellence. Devout and enlightened, a tolerant Muslim intellectual, knowledgeable of Western intellectual thought and its social science methodology, Banisadr was both willing and able to adapt Western ideas and ideals to his vision of a modern Islamic nation.

Sources: Yaacov Shimoni, *Biographical Dictionary of the Middle East,* New York: Facts on File, 1991; Tony Schwartz, "Apparent Victor in Iran's Voting: Abolhassan Bani-Sadr," *The New York Times,* January 28, 1980; Ronald Koven, "He sees answers to Iran's plight in the Koran," *The Philadelphia Inquirer,* November 15, 1979; Jonathan C. Randal, "Bani-Sadr: Advocate of Iranian Independence," *The Washington Post,* November 26, 1979; Fred Halliday, "Iran Chooses," *The Nation,* February 9, 1980; "For Bani-Sadr the Enemy was always Close By," *The Philadelphia Inquirer,* June 22, 1981; Claude von England, "Iran's divided exiles struggle to be heard," *The Christian Science Monitor,* April 27, 1984.

SUMMARY

The significance of the Islamic Revolution in Iran for the Islamic revival throughout the Muslim world is simple: the Iranian Revolution was the Islamic movement to topple a secular, Western-looking government purely "in the name of Islamic purification." For Muslims around the world, and especially those enduring suppression of secular and Pragmatic governments that predominate in Muslim nations, the Islamic Revolution in Iran was truly "an inspiring feat for devout men who have seen their aspirations for political and religious reforms crushed repeatedly in the 20th century."[459] Indeed, Islamic revivals, particularly those with radical fringe elements, are especially active in countries that have suffered the ills of "rapid economic growth and subsequent dislocation; . . . massive inequalities in urban areas; and a . . . period of pro-Western and relatively secular rule."[460] These conditions, which contributed to the Islamic Revolution in Iran, exist throughout the Muslim world, although the Shah's ouster gave a much-needed boost to the Islamic revival. In fact, the Islamic Revolution in Iran directly and indirectly inspired and motivated many Muslims and Muslim groups around the world. It accelerated and fortified the forces of Islamic revivalism, and even initiated a revitalization of Islam among Muslims in both Muslim and non-Muslim countries. In essence, the Islamic Revolution in Iran provided a banner around which the oppressed and impoverished people of the Muslim world have rallied to protest the continued influence of the West in their societies and the continued rule of usually Western-supported governments that have persecuted the people they were created to serve.[461]

---

[459]William Beeman, "Khomeini's Call to the Faithful Strikes Fear in the Arab World," *Philadelphia Inquirer,* May 29, 1992, p. 12-A.

[460]Nikki Keddie, "The Revolt of Islam and its Roots," p. 304.

[461]Hague et al., *Political Science,* pp. 80–81.

Box 10.5 THE RUSHDIE CONTROVERSY

"The author of *The Satanic Verses* book that is against Islam, the Prophet and the Koran, and all those involved in its publication who were aware of its content, are sentenced to death." With this declaration, Iran's late Ayatollah Khomeini enraged the West, gave the Fundamentalists and Traditionalists a new issue with which to attack the Western animosity toward Islam, polarized the Muslim world, and made Salman Rushdie's novel an international best-seller in nations where it was not banned.

Rushdie, born a Muslim but no longer practicing his faith when he wrote *The Satanic Verses,* was educated in Britain, where he resided until driven into hiding by Khomeini's death sentence. His 1988 novel *The Satanic Verses* was roundly condemned throughout the Muslim world as an affront to Islam. But it was Ayatollah Khomeini who, more than anyone, thrust the Rushdie controversy onto the world stage, contributing to a confrontation of rhetoric between Islam and the West.

The Muslim world was justifiably galled by Rushdie's inflammatory book. The very title, *The Satanic Verses,* inherently questions the validity of the Quran as holy scripture. Rushdie consciously impugns the Quran and imputes upon it satanic overtones—that it is the work of the Devil. Likewise, the second part of *The Satanic Verses* is entitled "Mahound," the insulting name given to Muhammad—Islam's last and most revered Prophet—by medieval Christians to discredit Islam. "Mahound" is an intentional caricature of Muhammad insofar as Rushdie parallels the life of semifictional "Mahound" with the life of Muhammad. Moreover, Rushdie insinuates that Muhammad manufactured the Quran for his own benefit under "Satanic" influence and, thus, that the holiest book of Islam is not the revealed word of God. Hence, the "businessman-turned-prophet" is portrayed as a fake, and Islam a work of clever forgery. Along the way, Rushdie gratuitously names twelve prostitutes after Muhammad's wives, thereby even further infuriating Muslims. In essence, as worded by Mahmood Monshipouri, "to devout Muslims, this book challenged and even violated the centrality of their beliefs, the very words of God, the integrity of their religious doctrine, and the image and dignity of the person of prophet Muhammad." Harvard professor William Graham explains that "it's as if you took the Bible, and in the middle of the Sermon on the Mount, you showed Jesus fantasizing copulation with whores."

It is a testament to the Western media's ethnocentricity and culturally myopic worldview that, upon publication of *The Satanic Verses,* the vehemently negative reaction of one billion Muslims was unanticipated and totally misperceived. Immediately, calls came from Muslim communities to ban Rushdie's novel, and many developing nations obliged.

To Westerners and Muslims alike, the Rushdie controversy warranted outrage, but for different reasons. Westerners, particularly those in the liberal media, viewed Muslim attempts at censorship as at least unseemly, and at most an affront to principles of freedom of speech and expression. Muslim Fundamentalists, Traditionalists, and even the majority of Muslim Modernists viewed Western attempts to glorify Rushdie and promote his novel as the continuation of a 1,400-year-old cultural crusade against Islam. Above all, the Rushdie controversy became a rallying cry of militant Fundamentalists to reject all things Western. The West, meanwhile, watched in horror as Muslims in Britain staged book burnings, and as protestors marched on the American Cultural Center in Islamabad, Pakistan, throwing stones, roughing up a few Americans, and demanding Rushdie's death. For the West, the coup de grace came on February 14, 1989, with Khomeini's death sentence.

Sadly, the West responded to these unreasonable emotional outbursts with a few of its own. Western commentators and politicians heralded Rushdie's "inalienable" right to offend Muslims, while the Western news media, with an eye to the sensational, portrayed all Muslims as primitive religious fanatics burning books, donning shrouds, and proposing to hunt Rushdie down and "send him to Hell."

Death threats aside, Muslim calls for censorship of *The Satanic Verses* are understandable. Since Muslims identify themselves not with the nation-state, as Westerners do, but with the *umma*, it is reasonable for them to charge Rushdie with religious treason and to demand suppression of his book, which represents an obscene attack on their community of believers. If, after all, the United States can plot to kill Fidel Castro of Cuba, Ngo Dinh Diem of South Vietnam, Rafael Leonidas Trujillo of the Dominican Republic, and Muammar al-Gaddafi of Libya; if it can overthrow Jacobo Arbenz Guzman, Salvador Allende of Chile, and Muhammad Mossadeq of Iran; and if it can invade Panama, Granada, and Iraq in the name of "democracy" and "human rights," why cannot the Muslim world in the name of the Quran, which is "the ultimate constitution of the community of believers," prohibit publication of Rushdie's libelous book, given that permitting publication is analogous to inciting a riot? Indeed, for the sake of the public order, banning Rushdie's book is not a repressive act; it is a responsible act. Professor Ali A. Mazrui, the director of the Institute of Global Cultural Studies at the State University of New York at Binghamton, put it best when he wrote that "[If] American political morality expects its citizens to be ready to 'uphold, protect and defend the Constitution of the United States'," against enemies foreign and domestic, how can the West deny the right of Muslims to uphold, protect, and defend the integrity of the Quran? These questions were never addressed by the Western media. Instead, the news media turned to simple stereotypes in which, once again, according to Edward W. Said, professor of literature at Columbia University in New York, "Islam is reduced to terrorism and fundamentalism and now, alas, [was] seen to be acting accordingly, in the ghastly violence prescribed by the Ayatollah Khomeini."

Both Britain and the United States, whose staunch defense of individual freedoms is admirable, consistently censor information for reasons of national security (i.e., Britain's ban of the book *Spycatcher*) or to avoid unduly offending minority groups. Although the latter form of censorship is practiced less by their governments than by private corporations and interest groups, it is still censorship. Moreover, thoughtful censorship in a free society is not necessarily bad so long as reasonable limits are observed. The "political correctness" fad currently sweeping the United States campuses is based on gagging individuals who might otherwise offend. This form of censorship is characteristic of the struggle between individual and corporate rights.

Muslims naturally wonder why censorship of culturally treasonous material is commonplace in the West (see if you can find a legally displayed swastika in Germany), while the reasonable concerns and requests of Muslims are either ignored or deemed unreasonable. Meanwhile, Rushdie wins literary accolades, and the Muslim world perceives Western hostility toward Islam. The West bestows upon Rushdie the right to blaspheme Islam and slander its one billion believers—in fact, congratulates him for it—while the right of those one billion believers to apply their community standards against Rushdie's heretical, hate-inspiring book is denied.

In contrast, when Irish singer Sinead O'Connor tore up a photograph of Pope John Paul II on an airing of "Saturday Night Live" in 1992, press sympathy was clearly for millions of rightly offended American Catholics. No mention was ever made of O'Connor's right to free speech while a mob cheered on a steamroller as it crushed hundreds of O'Connor's CDs—a picture sadly analogous to the burning of Rushdie's book by a handful of Muslims in different parts of the world.

There was no question in the Muslim world, or even in the West, that Rushdie maligned Islam. However, there was a question among Muslims regarding what constituted an appropriate response to Rushdie's blasphemy. While the Western media characterized riots, book burning, and death sentences as the universal reaction of Muslims to *The Satanic Verses,* this was not the case. While all Muslims justly condemned Rushdie's book, not all demanded Rushdie's death.

However, many Muslims openly supported Khomeini's death edict and made comments that truly shocked Western sensibilities and which therefore enjoyed great exposure in the mass media. One zealot said, "I think we should kill Salman Rushdie's whole family. . . . His body should be chopped into little pieces and sent to all Islamic countries as a warning to those who would insult our religion." But many more Muslims, finding no such publicity in the Western media, regretted and repudiated the Ayatollah's actions: "[Rushdie] should never have said those things against the prophet. . . . But it is also not right to call for his death." In India, where the Rushdie book has been banned, prominent Muslims denounced Khomeini's death sentence and felt that the anti-Rushdie movement had been co-opted by the Iranian

Ayatollah. Furthermore, they conceded that "this ban has made the book more popular. Just ignoring it would have been better for Muslims." Another Muslim expressed similar misgivings about the Rushdie uproar: "It has set back Islam. It conveys to non-Muslims a picture of Islam that is barbaric, rabid, and extreme."

Few Muslims felt any warmth or sympathy for Rushdie's self-imposed plight, and many Westerners were similarly inclined to denounce Rushdie's manifest insensitivity. Former President Jimmy Carter, for example, insisted that "while Rushdie's First Amendment freedoms are important, we have tended to promote him and his book with little acknowledgment that it is a direct insult to those millions of Muslims whose sacred beliefs have been violated. . . ." Rushdie had insulted the most sacred beliefs of Islam. Nevertheless, the news media refused to swallow the contention that blasphemy and apostasy were at the heart of Muslim anger. Instead, a story was widely disseminated that Khomeini's death sentence was no better than a cynical effort to prop up the floundering Iranian Revolution and not to defend the integrity of Islam. Western journalists perceived hidden motives behind Khomeini's death threats, particularly in statements the Ayatollah made indicating that "the dispute over *The Satanic Verses* proved that it was pointless [for Muslims] to pursue moderate policies. . . ."

There is little doubt that Khomeini's behavior can be partly attributed to his falling stature in the Muslim world by 1989. His nation was in economic shambles and social decline; he had been forced by a prolonged and bloody stalemate to accept a cease-fire with sworn enemy Iraq; and his own future successors had begun to decry the failures and shortcomings of the Islamic Revolution. By seizing the anti-Rushdie banner from those who first unfurled it and making it his own, the aging Ayatollah sought to stoke the smoldering embers of the Islamic Revolution in Iran and reassert himself and his brand of Islamic fundamentalism on the Muslim world.

Unfortunately, many analysts seized upon this interpretation of the Ayatollah's actions as though Rushdie's blasphemy was irrelevant to the story or as though one billion offended Muslims were the brainwashed minions of the Shi'ah *Imam.* The Rushdie controversy was symptomatic of the ever-widening chasm between East and West. When, on February 12, 1989, enraged Muslims marched on the American Cultural Center in Pakistan, they "carried placards attacking Zionism as well as Rushdie's book and its publisher." Evidently, the Rushdie book represented only the latest in a series of perceived Western-instigated affronts to Muslims and their Islamic faith. Just as the West had used the Rushdie controversy to vilify Islam and to ridicule its alleged "medievalism," so did Fundamentalists on the same basis justify their rejection of Westernization and secularization as evils inherently incompatible with the "straight path" of Islam. The Rushdie controversy did not occur in a vacuum but must be considered in the context of the fusion of religion and politics in Islam and in the growing Islamic revivalism in the Muslim world.

In fact, the Rushdie controversy represents the spark which ignited an explosive mixture already present in the world of Islam. Thus, Muslim Fundamentalists, like Khomeini, have utilized the Rushdie book to galvanize mass support against Western influence generally, and against the Muslim Pragmatists and Muslim Modernists specifically. By extrapolation then, the Rushdie controversy is not merely a manifestation of radical Islamic revivalism, but has positively contributed to its strength and popularity.

Sources: Russell Watson, "A Satanic Fury," *Newsweek,* Vol. 113, No. 9, February 27, 1989; Mahmood Monshipouri, "The Islamic World's Reaction to the Satanic Verses: Cultural Relativism Revisited," *Journal of Third World Studies,* Vol. 3, No. 1, Spring 1991; Donna Foote, "At Stake: The Freedom to Imagine," *Newsweek,* Vol. 113, No. 9, February 27, 1989; Sheila Tefft, "Muslim Debate Rushdie Uproar," *The Christian Science Monitor,* February 27, 1989; John Hughes, "Authors, Death Threats, and Islam," *The Christian Science Monitor,* February 22, 1989; Youssef M. Ibrahim, "Khomeini Assails Western Response to Rushdie Affair," *New York Times,* February 22, 1989; Alex Efty, "Khomeini Aimed his 'Verses' Attack to Stop Liberal Trends," *Birmingham News,* February 26, 1989; Barbara Crossette, "Muslims Storm U.S. Mission in Pakistan," *New York Times,* February 13, 1989.

Chapter
11

Islamic Revival in Central Asia

Alarms are sounding in the West and in the Russian Federation that Islamic fundamentalism threatens the five Central Asian republics of the former Soviet Union.[462] However, any statements regarding the Islamic revival occurring in Muslim Central Asia must consider first that it is not exclusively Fundamentalist, second that it is not yet predominantly political, and third that it is not remotely anti-American or anti-Western in character. The region's Muslims, after seven decades of Soviet rule and repression, are only now permitted to discard the failed ideology of communism, to free their spirits from the shackles of ideological purity, and to embark on a journey of open cultural and spiritual rediscovery. Such an Islamic revival is hardly antithetical to Western interests. The example and encouragement of the United States was a source of solace for Central Asians enduring Soviet occupation and Russification. Consequently, Central Asian Muslims just emerging from behind the Iron Curtain are venting their frustrations on Russia, not the United States. After all, communist modernization and Russification policies were an importation of Moscow, not Washington. Thus, the Western experience enjoys a more favorable audience in Central Asia than in Iran. In fact, the Muslim peoples of Central Asia "have a certain fascination with America. . . ."[463] Therefore, the United States has an opportunity, greater than perhaps at any other time or place, to coexist peacefully in a good relationship with Central Asian Islamic revivalism. The West could successfully cultivate

---

[462]John Kohan, "Five New Nations Ask Who Are We?" *Time*, Vol. 139, No. 17, April 27, 1992, p. 45.

[463]David Kaye, "Struggling with Independence: Central Asian Politics in the Post-Soviet World," *Middle East Insight*, Vol. 8, No. 6, July–October 1992, p. 32.

Islamic revivalists and prevent popular expressions of Islam from degenerating into anti-Western hatred. However, the United States and its allies must learn to accept Islam as a legitimate sociopolitical force and not work to defame or discredit it.[464] Otherwise, Western hostility toward the Islamic revival in Central Asia may make dire predictions of Central Asian fundamentalism sadly self-fulfilling.

For more than seventy years of Soviet rule in Central Asia, Moscow bureaucrats strived to eradicate Central Asian culture and religion. In fact, the erstwhile Soviet Central Asian Republics, among them Uzbekistan, Turkmenistan, Tajikistan, Kirgizistan, and Kazakhistan, were calm and passive props for hardline communist rule. Following the failed Soviet coup of August 1991, Soviet control evaporated, despite the support of Central Asia's communist leadership. The region was forced from the Russian nest to forage alone as newly independent states, the poorest and most destitute to emerge from the now defunct USSR. However, the composition of regional leadership remains largely intact and unchallenged. Only Tajikistan has assailed its communist regime at the price of chaos and civil war. Otherwise, those enjoying positions of authority and influence remain the same. Any systematic and substantive structural reform would entail many communist party members to lose power and their jobs. As a result, economic and political change proceed incrementally.[465] This does not bode well for an economically troubled Central Asia in which underdevelopment predominates.

The republics of Central Asian are neophytes to the processes of nation building and can therefore expect to suffer, as deeply as any impoverished newly independent state, from developmental crises. Democratic pluralism and Western-style capitalism are concepts with which these republics are unfamiliar. The population is overwhelmingly rural and undereducated. Overnight these republics have been thrust into independence, yet they remain uncertain of their own identity.

The West is interested in the outcome of the Central Asian identity crisis because of the strategic importance of these republics long thought secure in the smothering embrace of the Russian bear. Top-level Western diplomats visited Central Asia within months of the failed coup and immediately established diplomatic ties with the republics. Unfortunately, Western financial assistance has been paltry to a region so rich in raw materials. Central Asia's potential for riches, however, is outweighed in the minds of both Western policymakers and businessmen by a greater potential for political chaos. Nevertheless, Western interest in the region is keen because of its natural resources and its proximity to Iran, which shares with the republics a common religion. The West has worked to undercut Iranian influence in the region with its own diplomatic initiatives and by supporting the diplomatic initiatives of secular Muslim Turkey. The Central Asian republics, however, have rejected geopolitical commitments to any one nation or ideology.

---

[464]Ibid.

[465]Ibid., p. 27.

The West has entered the diplomatic fray to promote liberal Western democratic values and modernization policies. Otherwise, the West fears, the Central Asian republics will become thrall to Islamic fundamentalist revivalism. Soviet control of the region prior to August 1991 had been iron-clad and impossible to undermine. With the USSR defunct, the peoples of the Central Asian republics have sought to fill the political vacuum with traditional values and practices, which are often defined by Islam, the region's dominant religion. Although the Soviets had kept a lid on Islamic revivalism, first by co-opting and controlling the Islamic religious establishment and second by crushing groups that employed Islam as an idiom of dissent, this lid is off and the people are returning to their Islamic roots. The question in the West is whether Central Asian Muslims will fashion countries like Turkey, a predominantly Muslim but secular and West-leaning country, or like Pakistan, or worse, Sudan or Iran.

THE ORIGINS OF THE ISLAMIC REVIVAL

The isolation and obscurity of Central Asia, compounded by seven decades of subjugation to the totalitarian Soviet empire, enabled the region to develop a unique Islamic culture and tradition dissociated from the mainstream of the Muslim world. Because Central Asia's contact with the outside world has been tenuous at best, the flowering in the region of the Islamic revival merits particular attention; indeed, Central Asia's place as wholly unique Muslim region makes it a natural laboratory of the Islamic revival. No one, after all, has exported the revival to the Muslim republics; it has not been transplanted from Iran or from Afghanistan, but has sustained itself—in fact, has thrived—in the rich soil of Central Asia's singular Islamic tradition.

Thinking that the practice of Islam had been effectively depressed in the Muslim republics, the Soviets were surprised by its resurgence, particularly in the final years of the USSR. Foreign influence was often cited, by Western and Soviet scholars alike, as the true inspiration behind the unanticipated renewal and revitalization of Islam in Central Asia, despite seventy years of intensive and presumed successful anti-Islamic propaganda and administrative steps. The Soviets and the West singled out Iran as the culprit. Revolutionary Iran's enthusiasm for Islam had suddenly and without warning contaminated Muslim Central Asia, analysts maintained. Articles proliferated in the media promising to assess the development and implications of the Muslim "threat" to Soviet authority and stability. Yet, in spite of the world-shaking Islamic revolution in Iran, few repercussions were felt in Central Asia. Although Central Asia shares a border with Iran, the 1979 revolution was a distant event for the average Central Asian, particularly under the watchful eye of the restrictive Soviet administration.[466] Revivalist influences from Iran were, therefore, minimal at best. Events in Afghanistan, however,

---

[466]Martha Brill Olcott, "Soviet Central Asia: Does Moscow Fear Iranian Influence?" in John L. Esposito, ed., *The Iranian Revolution: Its Global Impact,* Miami: Florida International University Press, 1990, p. 205.

weighed more heavily in the thoughts of Central Asians. Three Muslim republics share borders and all share ethnic ties with Afghanistan. Thus, the revival of Islam in Afghanistan, partly influenced by the Iranian example, in turn affected Central Asia. However, the implications of the 1979 Soviet invasion of Afghanistan and Central Asians' involvement in it, conscripted on the Soviet side, are even today uncertain and contradictory.[467] The defeat of the Soviets at the hands of the Afghan holy warriors after years of terrible bloodshed was unquestionably an example for Central Asians, though not one most would choose to emulate. Reportedly, in Uzbekistan radical revivalists were inspired by the success of the Afghan *mujahideen*.[468] Nevertheless, there is no way to gauge the influence of the Afghan revival over Soviet Muslims. Little evidence of such influence is documented. Also, the roots of the Central Asian revival antedated the invasion of Afghanistan. Thus, if Afghanistan at best only "influenced" the Islamic revival in Soviet Central Asia, from where did the revival orignally come? What were its sources?

Charges that the Islamic revival in Central Asia drew its strength from external sources are not strongly supported by evidence. Central Asians have always seen Islam as integral with their identity and their cultural heritage.[469] The revival of Islam in Central Asian owes its vigor to domestic sources.[470] The roots of the Islamic revival were in Central Asia all along, always under the surface, sometimes dormant, but somehow defiant and resilient in the face of a prolonged and vigorous Soviet campaign to eradicate them.

After conquering Central Asia after the Bolshevik revolution, Soviet policymakers proposed "to reduce Islam to a 'private affair,'"[471] Social, economic, and political manifestations of Islam were to be extirpated from Central Asian life through programs of secularization, modernization, industrialization, reduction and co-optation of Central Asia's religious establishment, and displacement of the traditional regional elite in favor of a new peasant elite.[472]

The success of the Soviet policy was mixed. While most blatant political expressions of Islam disappeared or were, at least, sublimated, Islamic traditions and culture thrived.[473] Central Asian Muslims accepted Soviet control but, in many ways, subverted it as well. In fact, Central Asia's traditional elites succeeded in reestablishing themselves in positions of power and influence after the Bolshevik revolution had run its course.[474] They emulated only the veneer of Soviet culture.

---

[467]Ibid., p. 206; Vitaly Naumkin, "Islam in the States of the Former USSR," *The Annals of the American Academy of Political and Social Science,* No. 524, November 1992, p. 134.

[468]Dilip Hiro, "Islamist Strengths and Weaknesses in Central Asia," *Middle East International,* No. 443, February 5, 1993, p. 20.

[469]Olcott, "Soviet Central Asia," p. 220

[470]Alexandre K. Bennigsen, "Islam in the Soviet Union," in Philip H. Stoddard et al., eds., *Change and the Muslim World,* Syracuse, NY: Syracuse University Press, 1981, p. 123.

[471]Bennigsen, "Islam in the Soviet Union," pp. 120–121

[472]Ibid., p. 121.

[473]Ibid., p. 132.

[474]Martha Brill Olcott, "Introduction," in Sergei P. Poliakov, ed., *Everyday Islam: Religion and Tradition in Rural Central Asia,* Armonk, NY: M. E. Sharpe, 1992, p. xvi.

And although Soviet Muslims adopted such Russian traits as drinking vodka, Central Asian Muslims held on to their faith and remained the most unassimilable people in modern Soviet society.[475] Despite the efforts of the Soviets to transform life in the Muslim republics of Central Asia, the village communities of the region were left largely undisturbed. Such communities became the principal advocates of a "popular Islam" that was both tolerant and flexible.[476] Traditional culture survived, indeed flourished in Central Asia and, thus, Islam flourished with it. Even despite the lack of *masjids* throughout Central Asia, believers prayed regularly in private as well as public facilities.[477] Most important, Soviet control of the official religious leadership led to the establishment of unofficial institutional Islam in the countryside. These underground *mullahs* handed down Islamic learning and tradition and thereby did the ground-work for the Islamic revival that we are witnessing today. . . ."[478] Although the Soviet government had suppressed the teaching and propagation of Islamic doctrine, much of the traditional Islamic culture that prevailed in Central Asia prior to the Bolshevik Revolution has been preserved. This Islamic culture has, throughout Soviet rule, expressed itself economically, socially, and politically.[479] Instead of asking how the Islamic revival began in Central Asia, one might wonder if it ever ended.

Although Islam always operated just below the surface of Central Asian life under the Soviets, internal changes within the Soviet system and society itself, more than any other single factor, sped the pace at which overt political Islam gained acceptance.[480] Beginning in the last stagnant years of the Brezhnev administration, the Kremlin paid little attention to the Muslim republics. As a result, Central Asian communist leaders ignored the growth of the Islamic revival and failed to compete for the ideological affections of the people.[481] The morally and ideologically bankrupt Brezhnev years discredited communism in the eyes of many Central Asians, while policies of openness inaugurated and pursued during the Gorbachev administration assured that both Islam and ethnonationalism would emerge as idioms of protest against Soviet rule. Islam increasingly became a panacea for the spiritual and material ills experienced by Soviet Muslims.[482]

In the early 1990s, Islam, at last, regained the political voice of Central Asia. Islamic slogans and symbols were increasingly employed by political activists who recognized that Islam was a powerful and reliable means of mobilizing people.[483] In fact, even the rise of secular nationalism boosted political Islam, since Central

---

[475]Michael Rywkin, *Moscow's Muslim Challenge: Soviet Central Asia*, rev. ed., Armonk, NY: M. E. Sharpe, 1990, p. 105; Bennigsen, "Islam in the Soviet Union," p. 120.

[476]Naumkin, "Islam in the States of the Former USSR," p. 133.

[477]Ibid.

[478]Ibid.

[479]Olcott, "Soviet Central Asia," p. 207.

[480]Ibid., p. 206; Naumkin, "Islam in the States of the Former USSR," p. 134.

[481]Olcott, "Soviet Central Asia," p. 206

[482]Ibid., p. 220.

[483]Naumkin, "Islam in the States of the Former USSR," p. 134.

Asians had blurred the distinctions between religious, ethnic, and national identities.[484] Suddenly, under Soviet rule, Islam became "a symbol of national identity"
and a response to Soviet imperialism.[485] Most reform and opposition groups utilized Islamic themes and symbols to identify with the people and to distinguish
themselves from Central Asia's Soviet overlords. Thus, Central Asia's quietness
during the coup against Gorbachev belied the growth of opposition groups
throughout the region, and the growth of the Islamic revival in particular.[486]

ISLAM IN OPPOSITION

The failure of the hardline coup of August 1991 did little to change the Central
Asian status quo. Yet with the collapse of the Soviet central control, democratic,
nationalist, and Islamic opposition surged forward to challenge the entrenched regional communist leadership for the mantle of government. However, as political
parties opposing former communist leaders have proliferated, political Islam has
had to cooperate with a plethora of opposition groups not founded on Islamic
principles but on principles of nationalism. Nevertheless, the opposition is
strongly sympathetic to Islam at least insofar as both nationalists and Islamic revivalists can make common cause against the status quo.

Uzbekistan established two opposition parties to communist rule: the *Birlik*
(Unity) party (also called the Uzbekh Popular Front) and the *Erk* (Nation) party.
In the last year, Uzbek expressions of nationalism have led to violence against fellow Muslims of other ethnic groups. Muslim Kirgiz and Meshkhetian Turk minority groups in Uzbekistan, for example, have been victims of Uzbek nationalism;
the brotherhood of Islam has been conspicuously absent. In the northernmost republic of Kazakhistan, meanwhile, two prominent nationalist parties emerged; the
Alash and the *Jeloqsan*. Like the Uzbek parties, Islam has been a focal point of
their antigovernment opposition. In Kirgizistan, a wide variety of political parties
have banded together under the organization of the Kirgiz Democratic Movement (KDM). One branch of the KDM, called the Kirgiz Democratic Wing, has
expressed plans to build *masjids* and *madrassahs* throughout the republic. In
Turkmenistan, opposition to the government has been insubstantial, with the nationalist Agsybirlik Party in the vanguard. In Tajikistan, the nationalists have been
comparatively weaker under the opposition leadership of the Democratic Party of
Tajikistan. Nevertheless, Tajikistan has been beset by a powerful anticommunist
Islamic revivalist insurrection, proving that Islam can provide an influential idiom
of protest in Central Asia. Indeed, both Russia and the West have viewed cautiously and with great trepidation events in Tajikistan.[487]

---

[484]Olcott, "Soviet Central Asia," p. 206; Bennigsen, "Islam in the Soviet Union," p. 125.

[485]Naumkin, "Islam in the States of the Former USSR," p. 141.

[486]Olcott, "Soviet Central Asia," p. 207.

[487]Hoseyin Abiva, "The Islamic Revival in the Soviet Union and Its Implications," *The Message International*, Vol. 15, No. 5, October 1991, pp. 15–16.

The notable absence of well-defined exclusively revivalist opposition parties in Central Asia is partly the consequence of continued government policies to co-opt and suppress political Islam throughout the region. Again, although the Soviet Union is no more, Muslims throughout Central Asia are still subjects of regimes headed by ex-communists who have shed their outward affiliations but not their communist methods or beliefs. Many of these regimes have banned Islamic political parties and operate on the assumption that no opposition is legitimate.

The Islamic Renaissance Party (IRP) represents the one truly Islamic party with an exclusively revivalist agenda in the Central Asian republics. Established in 1990, the IRP has branches in most of the fifteen republics of the former Soviet Union and is Central Asia's most prominent representative of political Islam. Unfortunately, given the depth of divisive tribal loyalty throughout the region, the IRP has encountered, when permitted to operate, little political success despite its pan-Islamic agenda.

The IRP does not enjoy widespread popular support throughout Central Asia for its brand of Islamic politics. However, the IRP has been just popular enough to frighten the ex-communist governments of the Central Asian republics, despite the fact that the IRP is not an organization dominated by radical Muslim Fundamentalists. The IRP is a revivalist party that, at least in its Moscow offices, is moderate and Modernist in temperament.[488] Although the IRP has been perceived as a significant threat to the status quo both by the West and by the regimes in power in Central Asia, ethnonationalism is actually the predominant political expression of the region. Such nationalism has divided ethnic groups within the republics and divided the republics from one another. While a personal rediscovery of Islam is taking place in the region, pan-Islamism and Islamic fundamentalism are secondary ingredients in the Central Asian stew. While Muslims are turning ever more openly to the practice of Islam, they are not yet overwhelmingly advocating the politicization of Islam.[489] Nevertheless, the Western media points to Iranian overtures to the Central Asian republics, to harsh government crackdowns against revivalists in Uzbekistan, and to political turmoil in Tajikistan as prima facie evidence of a Fundamentalist conspiracy.

TAJIKISTAN AFLAME

The revival of Islam in Central Asia has proved most spirited and resolute in Tajikistan, where *masjids* and *madrassahs* are being built with wondrous alacrity and where year after year more Tajiks than ever before are undertaking the *haj* to the *Ka'aba* at Mecca. The revival is more intense in both Tajikistan and Uzbekistan, where Islam arrived during the Middle Ages and where Islamic traditions are strongly ingrained, than elsewhere in Central Asia. In Kirgizistan, for example, Is-

---

[488]"The Next Islamic Revolution," *The Economist,* Vol. 320, No. 7,725, p. 58.

[489]Abul Kalaam, "Muslim Remain Communist Serfs," *The Message International,* Vol. 15, No. 5, October 1991, p. 21.

lam won converts only by the close of the seventeenth century.[490] As a result, the West has portrayed Islam as the power motivating Tajikistan politics. In truth, however, the greatest danger to stability in Tajikistan stems from a worsening economic picture.[491]

Coincidentally, just as Tajikistan is the most "Islamized" society in Central Asia, so is it the most impoverished. A destitute nation, the poorest of the Central Asian republics according to per capita income, Tajikistan suffers a lack of consumer goods, a chronic fuel shortage, and widespread unemployment.[492] Furthermore, independence brought the old leadership new economic adversity; The disappearance of Soviet authority meant also the end of vitally important Soviet food subsidies. Just as the political survival of Tajikistan's President Rakhman Nabiev became most dependent on economic improvement, such improvement appeared least likely. Thus, as Tajikistan's frail economy unraveled, so did the Nabiev regime.

Complicating economic troubles in Tajikistan are divisive ethnic, regional, and clan rivalries—each representing a chasm difficult even for Islamic brotherhood to bridge. Although Tajikistan is a predominantly Sunni Muslim, Persian-speaking republic, its population of 5.1 million is 70 percent Tajik, 23 percent Uzbek, and 7 percent Russian.[493] Moreover, regional friction has played a preeminent part in escalating the conflict in Tajikistan and contributing to the ongoing civil war. Regional rivalries surfaced in the political arena because positions in the Nabiev government were monopolized by members of Nabiev's northern *Khodjent* clan. Envying and frustrated by northern domination of a government that ruled all Tajikistan, and many southerners believe, mismanaged Tajikistan's economy, southerners increasingly rose in regional opposition.[494] In spring 1992, demonstrations sparked by the dismissal of a southern-born government minister brought down the Nabiev government. The day after the miniter's dismissal crowds of southerners demonstrated against the government in the streets of Dushanbe. Opposition political parties quickly arose, but most expressed opposition in terms that were not merely, or even primarily, regional.[495] The Tajikistan Democratic Party (TDP), for example, has promoted liberal parliamentary democracy, while the Islamic Renaissance Party (IRP), has favored the eventual establishment of an Islamic state—both as panaceas for ills that are largely economic and regional.[496] Nevertheless, support for the communists and the allied

---

[490]Robert M. Danin, "Tajikistan's Turbulent Spring," *Middle East Insight,* Vol. 8, No. 6, July–October 1992, p. 36; Simon Crisp, "Kirgiz," in Edward Allworth, ed., *Central Asia: 120 Years of Russian Rule,* Durham, NC: Duke University Press, 1989, pp. iv, 246–247.

[491]David Kaye, "Struggling with Independence," p. 27.

[492]"The Next Islamic Revolution," p. 58; Kaye, "Struggling with Independence," p. 27.

[493]Kaye, "Struggling with Independence," p. 27; "The Next Islamic Revolution," p. 58.

[494]Kaye, "Struggling with Independence," p. 28.

[495]Ibid.

[496]"In Trouble," *The Economist,* Vol. 324, No. 7,770, August 1, 1992, p. 31; Kaye, "Struggling with Independence," p. 28.

opposition divided on ethnic and regional lines. During the May 11, 1992 demonstrations, however, the communists and the opposition hammered out a compromise to establish a National Reconciliation Government headed by Nabiev. In return, Nabiev appointed eight leaders of the opposition to posts in his cabinet and established a *majlis* (parliament) with its seats divided between the Communists and the opposition. The compromise solved nothing, however. Nabiev's interim government proved unequal to the task of holding together a state plunging into civil war and national catastrophe.[497]

Although Tajikistan's branch of the IRP was a latecomer to the regionally inspired spring demonstrations, nevertheless Islamic revivalism enjoyed a prominent role as the protests continued. Every day throngs of protestors listened to Muslim religious leaders deliver sermons on Islamic issues. In fact, so popular were the daily congregational prayer sessions, that they increased from one to five over the rally's two month life.[498] Southerners gradually but inexorably embraced political Islam as an expression of their differences with the northern-dominated atheistic Nabiev regime.

Answering communist accusations that the IRP was a radical Fundamentalist organization devoted to the establishment of an Iranian-style theocratic state, moderate IRP leaders defended their party's democratic credentials by declaring unwavering support for representative democracy, like the TDP, but only as a first step toward eventually achieving an Islamic state founded on principles of socioeconomic equity and justice. IRP radicals, meanwhile, insisted on the immediate establishment of an Islamic state governed by the *Shariah*. Prior to the onset of civil war, at least, the moderate vision of an eventual, gradual approach to Islamic government predominated within IRP ranks under the spiritual leadership of Hajji Akbar Turadzhon Zoda (known as the *Qadhicolon*—the Supreme Islamic Judge—or the *Qadhi* for short), whose position in the official Islamic establishment neither tarnished his image nor eroded his considerable popular support. Although the *Qadhi* was never officially a leader of the IRP, his position of influence among devout Muslims was and probably remains, considerable. During the spring demonstrations, the *Qadhi* insisted that "politics and religion should be kept separate."[499] Nevertheless, the *Qadhi* joined the IRP and the TDP in opposition to the Nabiev regime and adopted an activist role in forging the May 11, 1992, compromise agreement with Nabiev.[500] The Islamic and democratic opposition opted to keep Nabiev less as a gesture of friendly conciliation and more in an attempt to defuse northern anger and to avert civil war. Ironically, Nabiev's clan supporters revolted anyway. Nabiev's northerner-manned National Guard, disheartened by the idea of a National Reconciliation Government, left Dushanbe on

---

[497]"In Trouble," p. 31; Kaye, "Struggling with Independence," p. 27; Danin, "Tajikistan's Turbulent Spring," p. 36.

[498]Danin, "Tajikistan's Turbulent Spring," p. 36.

[499]Ibid., p. 36.

[500]Kaye, "Struggling with Independence," p. 28.

May 11, 1992, with a significant arsenal and a regional grudge to settle. Forming northern paramilitary "self-defense" groups, Nabiev's well-armed fellow clan members raided areas supporting the anticommunist opposition. Consequent warfare in arid southern regions ignited by the intense and bitter north-south rivalry claimed the lives of hundreds.[501] IRP and TDP opposition leaders in the coalition government demanded an end to the attacks, but Nabiev was either unwilling or unable to stop the activities of his fellow clan members. The National Reconciliation Government left the opposition reconciled only to an inevitable civil war.

In mid-September 1992, IRP and TDP coalition members forced Nabiev to resign at gunpoint. However, this did not halt the fighting, which had intensified in the south. Northern procommunist militias with Russian army help soon recaptured Dushanbe and completely ousted the opposition from power, and fifty thousand opposition supporters fled for their lives to Afghanistan's refugee camps. Installing a northern-controlled procommunist government, the northern militias continued to prosecute their war, primarily in the south, to eradicate southern anticommunist IRP and TDP resistance.[502]

By January of 1993, the communist forces of Tajikistan had gained the upper hand in the civil war. From Dushanbe, communist militias cleaned out nearby villages sympathetic to the opposition. Tajiks suspected of anticommunist inclinations disappeared from and around Dushanbe and are reported to be in communist-run concentration camps. Mass graves were unearthed in the south and in the outskirts of Dushanbe. Dedicated to crushing southern opposition, the north conducted systematic executions of southern clansmen, journalists, and businesspeople.[503]

Hope for the beleaguered opposition is small. Pointing to Fundamentalist Afghan support for the Tajik opposition, Tajikistan's communist leaders have won the support of the Commonwealth of Independent States (CIS), including Uzbekistan, Kazakhistan, and Turkmenistan, to send thousands of soldiers to secure the border with Afghanistan. By drumming up fear of Islamic revivalism in all its forms, the Tajik communists may have assured themselves power in Tajikistan for a few years. Yet the brutal victory of the communists will also ensure a popularization and radicalization of the Islamic revival in Tajikistan. By crushing the moderate Muslim secularists and Modernists in the IRP and the TDP, the communists may have guaranteed the ascendancy of the radical Fundamentalist opposition in their place, radical Fundamentalists who will forsake the democratic methods that moderate Islamic revivalists, like the *Qadhi,* dared to uphold.

---

[501]Ibid., p. 35.

[502]Justin Burke, "Tajik Refugees Tell Tales of Rights Abuses," *The Christian Science Monitor,* January 26, 1993, p. 8; Jan Cienski and Jeff Trimble, "See No Evil: Unnoticed, A Civil War Rages in Tajikistan," *U.S. News & World Report,* Vol. 114, No. 4, February 1, 1993, p. 62.

[503]Burke, "Tajik Refugees Tell Tales of Rights Abuses," p. 8.

UZBEKISTAN OPPRESSED

The repercussions of the Tajik civil war are felt far beyond its borders. The regimes of neighboring Central Asian states and the government of the Russian republic eye with suspicion events in Tajikistan. Immediate concern is that Uzbekistan, which shares both a common border and similar endemic social, political, and economic hardship, is vulnerable to a spillover of violent unrest.[504]

Burdened with a rapidly growing population of almost twenty million, Uzbekistan is the most populous of the Central Asian Muslim republics. Ethnic Tajiks comprise one million of this population and are concentrated most heavily along the border with Tajikistan in the Samarkand-Bukhara area and the Ferghana valley, where ethnic strife has been exacerbated by jingoistic rhetoric from Dushanbe. Tajik nationalists, whether living in Tajikistan or Uzbekistan, claim Samarkand and Bukhara, which are historically Tajik cities, as their own, and denounce the Uzbek overcrowding of the cities. This has prompted the Uzbek government to worry over the loyalty of Tajik subjects on the border.[505]

Moreover, in Samarkand, Bukhara, and the Ferghana valley, the Islamic revival is gaining ground—particularly in the countryside, where Uzbek central authority is weakest. Also, weapons from Tajikistan via Afghanistan have slipped into Uzbekistan, contributing to regional tension and distrust.[506] As a consequence, Uzbek authorities are particularly keen to keep things calm in Samarkand.[507]

Further complicating matters in Uzbekistan is the large urban population of ethnic Uzbeks inhabiting Tajikistan and making up nearly 20 percent of the Tajik population. According to reports, Tajikistan's Uzbeks have largely sided with pro-communist forces.[508] Fear of a Islamic revivalist or nationalist backlash among Tajiks in Uzbekistan to cover ethnic Uzbek support for Communists in northern Tajikistan has contributed to paranoia in the Uzbek government of any Tajik-style unrest.

Uzbekistan President Islam Karimov has reason to fear antigovernment unrest in his country. Like Tajikistan prior to the civil war, Uzbekistan remains tightly under communist control. The former Uzbek Communist party has renamed itself the People's Democratic Party (PDP) and has retained Karimov as its leader. Uzbekistan's government ministries, bureaucracy, and secret police still operate under old Communist party officials, although now under the PDP ban-

---

[504]Theresa F. Weber, "Tajikistan's Troubles Could Embroil Others," *The Christian Monitor*, October 9, 1992, p. 19.

[505]Kaye, "Struggling with Independence," p. 27; Weber, "Tajikistan's Troubles Could Embroil Others," p. 19.

[506]Daniel Sneider, "Uzbek Opposition Asserts Government Increases Repression," *The Christian Science Monitor*, October 2, 1992, p. 7; Justin Burke, "Uzbek Leaders Pick Stability Over Reform," *The Christian Science Monitor*, December 11, 1992, p. 10.

[507]Justin Burke, "Uzbek Leaders Clamp Down to Keep Peace," *The Christian Science Monitor*, January 5, 1993, p. 8.

[508]Ibid.; Weber, "Tajikistan's Troubles Could Emberoil Others," p. 19.

ner.[509] Although Karimov and the PDP have promised to initiate political and economic reform, the Tajik civil war has provided a convenient pretext to delay such reform indefinitely.

To cull support from its neighbors, especially Russia, the Karimov government has claimed that if upheaval comes to Uzbekistan, another domino might fall beneath the onslaught of revolutionary Islamic fundamentalism. Uzbek leaders insist that "fundamentalism," which they define as any Islamic opposition to the communist government, no matter how moderate and mainstream that opposition, must be contained and that Uzbekistan's role should be as a buffer state, without which even Russia would fall victim to Islamic Fundamentalism in the south.[510]

Perhaps greater than the threat posed by the Tajik civil war to Uzbek stability is that posed by the actions of the communist Uzbek government. More threatening to Uzbekistan than the Islamic revival is President Islam Karimov. By enlisting Russian support, Karimov has offended Uzbek nationalists. By abandoning reform, Karimov has lost any hope of support from capitalists and democrats. And by labeling the Islamic opposition as purely fundamentalist, he has radicalized the revival of Islam in Uzbekistan. But Karimov's hardline tactics are the most counterproductive of all his actions. His vicious crackdowns on the democratic and Islamic opposition have invited comparison to the hardline attitude of Tajikistan's President Nabiev just prior to the outbreak of civil war.[511] Thus, Uzbekistan's democratic opposition predicted that in due course, the Uzbek republic would be embroiled in the same kind of civil war as Tajikistan.[512]

Popular opposition to the Karimov regime has been generally democratic and nationalist in temperament. The *Birlik* (Unity) party, by far the largest of Uzbek opposition groups (although it goes unrecognized by the Karimov government), proposes that Uzbekistan adopt secular democracy. Yet like the prodemocratic TDP in Tajikistan, *Birlik* is allied with the growing Islamic Renaissance Party, although its Uzbek wing operates illegally. Alliances notwithstanding, as government repression of the opposition continues, *Birlik* is losing members to the banned IRP, first because many are losing faith in the effectiveness of Birlik to change the status quo or to oust peacefully to oust the intransigent communists, and second because in some regions *masjids* have become the dominant focal points for antigovernment opposition.[513] Even within *Birlik*, Islamic revivalism is gaining recognition and influence in direct proportion to increasing government suppression. One regional branch of *Birlik*, for example, advocates Islamic educa-

---

[509]Sneider, "Uzbek Opposition Asserts Government Increases Repression," p. 7; Kaye, "Struggling with Independence," p. 29.

[510]Ibid., p. 10; Burke, "Uzbek Leaders Clamp Down to Keep Peace," p. 8; Sneider, "Uzbek Opposition Asserts Government Increases Repression," p. 7.

[511]Justin Burke, "Uzbek Leaders Pick Stability Over Reform," *The Christian Science Monitor,* December 11, 1992, p. 10.

[512]Sneider, "Uzbek Opposition Asserts Government Increases Repression," p. 7.

[513]Ibid.

tion and the adoption of Arabic script in Uzbekistan.[514] Thus, as the pressure on *Birlik* has increased, *Birlik,* and other opposition groups have shifted from a predominantly secular to an Islamic orientation.

The prodemocracy *Birlik* movement has agreed with the government of Islam Karimov that civil unrest should be prevented and Uzbek stability preserved—but not through "Stalinist methods."[515] *Birlik* denounces Karimov's policy of repression against the democratic and Islamic opposition. Two prominent *Birlik* leaders tasted government anger when they were accosted in public and beaten with iron pipes by several men presumably on the government payroll.[516] Furthermore, in January 1992, the president used similarly tough tactics at Tashkent State University, where students were protesting economic chaos. Acting swiftly, Karimov cracked down and sent the students home, some in caskets.[517] Meanwhile, "illegal arrests, searches of homes, firings from jobs, and physical attacks on activists," have persisted in Uzbekistan.[518] Following the spring demonstrations in Tajikistan that toppled the Nabiev government, Karimov increased his suppression and intensified the crackdown. In essence, the civil war in Tajikistan provoked Uzbek leaders into using repression to maintain law and order.[519] And, indeed, Uzbekistan's voices of opposition have been temporarily silenced, but at what future cost for Uzbekistan?

Uzbek foreign minister Ubaidullah Abdurasakov explained the motivation behind government oppression in frank but familial terms: "If you are the head of a family and someone begins to act up, you must assert your authority to keep everyone in line."[520] But *Birlik* leaders counter that excessive policies of repression and oppression will not reduce the likelihood of internal upheaval, but rather increase it; "When a man feels he cannot be protected by the law, it pushes him to defend himself in another way—with arms."[521] Conflict in Uzbekistan is not being averted, it is being aggravated. "Suppression of emocratic rights" breeds "further resistance." and strengthens "the more extreme Islamic fundamentalist wing of the antigovernment movement."[522]

Oppression of internal democratic and Islamic antigovernment dissent has not been the Uzbek communist government's only response to the civil war in Tajikistan. To prevent a feared spillover of upheaval from Tajikistan, President Karimov has closed his border with the unstable Tajik republic.[523] Moreover,

---

[514]Kaye, "Struggling with Independence," p. 30

[515]Burke, "Uzbek Leaders Pick Stability Over Reform," p. 10.

[516]Sneider, "Uzbek Opposition Asserts Government Increases Repression," p. 7.

[517]Kaye, "Struggling with Independence," p. 29.

[518]Sneider, "Uzbek Opposition Asserts Government Increases Repression," p. 7.

[519]Burke, "Uzbek Leaders Pick Stability Over Reform," p. 10.

[520]Quoted in ibid.

[521]Quoted in ibid.

[522]Sneider, "Uzbek Opposition Asserts Government Increases Repression," p. 7; Burke, "Uzbek Leaders Clamp Down to Keep Peace," p. 8.

[523]Burke, "Uzbek Leaders Clamp Down to Keep Peace," p. 8.

Uzbekistan has joined Kazakhistan, Kirgizistan, and Russia in dispatching troops to Tajikistan to prevent both arms smuggling and possible spring 1993 offensives from Tajik refugee camps inside Afghanistan. Such actions are meant to undermine allied prodemocracy and Islamic groups from ousting Tajikistan's hardline communist government.[524] In addition, Karimov has urged CIS forces—dominated by a Russian officer corps—to remain in Uzbekistan presumably "in hopes that Moscow's military presence would help prop up his conservative government, if upheaval threatened."[525] But these moves, like the Karimov regime's violent tactics in crushing the opposition, may produce exactly the opposite of the desired effect, which is to preserve Uzbek stability. Karimov has taken sides in the Tajik civil war, and leaders of the underground democratic and Islamic opposition have denounced Karimov's cozy ties with the Russians as suggestive of a sellout, a cynical ploy to exchange Uzbekistan's independence and sovereignty in return for Russian assistance in keeping his regime in power.[526]

Perhaps more than any other factor, increasing economic hardship has produced a climate advantageous to the politicization of the Islamic revival in Uzbekistan. Economic trouble and disparity fan the flames of politically oriented Islamic revivalism, given Islam's emphasis on socioeconomic equity and justice. Indeed, the Karimov regime has been so preoccupied with maintaining political order that economic development has been entirely neglected. However, by ignoring economic reform, Karimov exacerbates tensions and contributes to political unrest.[527]

Fearing Islamic Fundamentalism, Karimov has cracked down on the opposition, thus strengthening radical Islamic revivalism as the people's last recourse for fundamental change. By neglecting to address the social, political, and economic ills fueling that opposition, Karimov is again strengthening radical revivalism. Islam Karimov has not only accelerated the pace of the Islamic revival in Uzbekistan, but has radicalized the revival's political manifestations.

Nevertheless, the Communists in Uzbekistan are not blind to the potency of the Islamic revival and have attempted to portray themselves as good Muslims to maintain a semblance of legitimacy for their regimes.[528] Karimov, for example, judiciously made a pilgrimage to Mecca in April 1992.[529] However, like Sadat's pragmatic self-made image as the "believer" president, Karimov's Islamic overtures may convince few. In any case, with or without Karimov's stamp of approval, the Islamic revival moves forward. Islam and Islamic revivalism have survived governments far more hostile than Karimov's, and Islam will assuredly survive him. As new *masjids* rise, and as the voice of the muezzin is heard over the face of Tashkent, Islam Karimov can only commiserate with his fellow communist comrades.

---

[524]Sneider, "Uzbek Opposition Asserts Government Increases Repression, p. 7.

[525]Burke, op. cit., p. 8.

[526]Ibid., p. 10.

[527]Ibid., p. 8.

[528]Daniel Sneider, "Soviets Face Muslim Activists," *The Christian Science Monitor,* February 5, 1991, p. 5.

[529]Kaye, "Struggling with Independence," p. 30.

ALL QUIET ON THE RUSSIAN FRONT?

The prospects of the Islamic revival in Central Asia cannot be discussed without addressing Russia's active role in the region, a role that far eclipses the importance there of the West or even the Muslim world. The presence of Russia in Central Asia is ubiquitous and overwhelming. The Russian Federation represents the mightiest military and economic power present in the region and is, more important, Central Asia's most important link to the outside world.[530] Russia, in turn, has historically interested itself in conquering and administering Central Asia. Thus, the people of the Muslim republics view with great suspicion continued Russian interest and intervention in the region as symptomatic of Russia's long imperialist history.[531]

The civil war that is raging in Tajikistan and the ethnic, regional, and ideological conflicts destabilizing the Muslim republics that border Russia on the south, have encouraged the growth of political Islam as an idiom of dissent within Central Asia. At the same time, in Moscow Russian nationalists have increasingly pushed for the colonization and pacification of their ostensibly independent neighbors, despite the denial of Russian diplomats and policymakers. Although Russia, in the name of the Commonwealth of Independent States (CIS), of which the Muslim republics are members, maintains border troops and an army division in Tajikistan, Russia claimed neutrality in the civil war there.[532] Moreover, Russia asserts the actions of the CIS forces throughout Central Asia are intended to avert a spillover of civil unrest from Tajikistan into neighboring states.[533] Russia, by its own admission, is making policy designed to keep order in Central Asia. Russia and three of the Muslim republics released a declaration in September 1992 that "the southern borders of the commonwealth must not be violated and that the escalation of the civil war in [Tajikistan], which is threatening the security of our nations and upsetting political stability in the region, must not be permitted."[534] Already Moscow is dictating what is and what is not permissible in ostensibly sovereign Central Asia. Furthermore, Moscow's claims of neutrality in the region are contested in Tajikistan; the Russian army has sided with the communists, although Russian officials adamantly deny such assertions. Trepidation remains that Russia's "peacekeeping" in the name of the CIS is but a facade masking Russia's wishes to reassume its influential role in neighboring regions.[535] Russian-con-

---

[530]Martha Brill Olcott, "Central Asia's Catapult to Independence," *Foreign Affairs,* Vol. 17, No. 3, Summer 1992, p. 120.

[531]Ibid., p. 130; Jim Hoagland, "Choosing Camps," *The Washington Post Weekly Edition,* March 30–April 5, 1992, p. 29.

[532]Cienski and Trimble, "See No Evil," p. 62.

[533]Burke, "Uzbek Leaders Clamp Down to Keep Peace," p. 8.

[534]Daniel Sneider, "Russia's 'Peacekeeping' Raises Issue of Neutrality," *The Christian Science Monitor,* September 14, 1992, p. 8.

[535]Ibid., p. 4; Daniel Sneider, "Critics Wary of Russian Army's Role in Republics," *The Christian Science Monitor,* October 2, 1992, p. 6.

trolled CIS forces stationed in Central Asia are well positioned to fulfill that desire.

With the collapse of the USSR, Russia retains the only effective, modern, and disciplined military in the region. Inevitably, Russia plays a significant role as "big brother."[536] For although one of every two enlisted men in CIS forces stationed in Central Asia is Central Asian, the officers are predominantly ethnic Russian and therefore reflect Russian interests in the region.[537] Thus, accusations against the impartiality of the Russian forces are rooted to some extent in regional nationalism. One leader of a nationalist opposition party in Uzbekistan is convinced that the Russian army is sowing trouble in the region to divide and reconquer Central Asia. To support these contentions, opposition parties throughout Central Asia have pointed to Russian involvement in the Tajik civil war. Russia's 201st Motorized Rifle Division, which was deployed only to guard strategic sites, aided the northern Tajik communists against the Islamic and democratic opposition with tanks and armored vehicles.[538] Russian soldiers claiming to be mercenaries are battling southern Tajiks along the border with Afghanistan.[539] Protestations of neutrality coming from Moscow are discounted by the Central Asian nationalist, democratic, and Islamic opposition parties, who maintain that while Russian officers and CIS troops act on orders from Moscow, they are at heart strongly influenced by Russian nationalists.[540]

Russia has involved itself, and taken sides, in Central Asia for four reasons. First, the frightened leadership of the Central Asian republics has requested Moscow to intervene and to dispatch "peacekeepers" to Tajikistan to restore order. Uzbekistan, Kazakhistan, and Kirgizistan have specifically requested Russian military assistance to contain civil unrest in Tajikistan.[541] Second, the Russians have acted to ensure the safety and well-being of the ten million ethnic Russians living in the Muslim republics.[542] Already, half-a-million or more Russians have fled Central Asia for fear of the indigenization of the region and the increasingly strong anti-Russian backlash. Maintaining order—that is, perpetuating the power of pro-Russian regimes—is a priority in Moscow. Consequently, in the battle between communist militias and IRP and TDP forces in Dushanbe, the Russian military helped drive the democrats and revivalists out ostensibly as the best way to restore and preserve order. With as many as 300,000 ethnic Russians residing in the Tajik capitol, the Russian army's decision to assist the communists and to neutralize the democratic and Muslim opposition may indeed have been inspired by a

---

[536]Quoted in Sneider, "Russia's 'Peacekeeping' Raises Issue of Neutrality," p. 4.

[537]Olcott, "Central Asia's Catapult to Independence," p. 119.

[538]Ibid.; Burke, "Uzbek Leaders Clamp Down to Keep Peace," p. 8.

[539]Sneider, "Russia's 'Peacekeeping' Raises Issue of Neutrality," p. 1

[540]Ibid., p. 5.

[541]Ibid., p. 7.

[542]Olcott, "Central Asia's Catapult to Independence," p. 123.

desire to restore order.[543] Third, Russian interventionism is motivated by the rising tide of Russian nationalism in Moscow. The "Eurasianists," for example, are strong proponents of a future Russia much in the spirit of its imperial past; for them, the borders of the former Soviet Union are the borders appropriate to Russia. Thus, the independence of areas like Central Asia from direct Russian rule is simply illogical.[544] In response, Russian President Yeltsin has begun to emphasize the strengthening of the CIS, the protection of ethnic Russians living in former Soviet republics, and, most ominously, the maintainance of pro-Russian regimes in Central Asia.[545] Fourth, Russia's fear of the Islamic revival borders on paranoia. The commander-in-chief of the CIS forces has iterated Russia's unofficial position: "We are now faced with a desire to build a new union on the basis of the Islamic factor in [Central Asia]. As a result of this, a line of new global confrontation may appear on the north-south axis."[546] Such blatant antirevivalist sentiments typify the grip of "Islamaphobia" over the Russian brass, and help explain why Russia has engaged itself in a region that, after the Afghanistan debacle, should frighten Russia away. Indeed, talk of the "domino theory" is current among Russian leaders. In their eyes, Tajikistan is potentially the first domino to fall. If the democrats and revivalists emerge as victors in Tajikistan, the Russians fear that Islamic Fundamentalism will take hold in the republic and from there spread throughout Central Asia, or even into Tartarstan in Russia.[547] Although now no credible Islamic Fundamentalist movement threatens the region, and although there is little to support the contention that all the Muslim republics would fall like dominoes to Fundamentalist revivalism, the paranoia is real enough to prod Russian planners into action and into supporting friendly but oppressive regimes at the expense of both revivalists and democrats. In short, Russia is compelled for many reasons to become the "imperial arbiter" of Central Asia's fate. In the end, Russia will make all Central Asia's decisions, but may not make the right ones.[548]

The exercise of Russia's manifest hegemony in Central Asia is simply counterproductive. Although Russian military presence has turned the tide against the opposition in Tajikistan and has ensured at least temporary order in the region, the opposition has only been driven underground and radicalized. The obsequiousness of the communist regimes in Central Asia toward Russian forces has opened those regimes up to charges of giving away regional sovereignty to the Russians. Moreover, by crushing and delegitimizing all dissent in Central Asia, Russia has guaranteed that future dissent will be far more radical and anti-Russian in temperament. The radicalization of the Islamic revival caused by Russian inter-

---

[543]"The New Domino Game," *The Economist*, Vol. 325, No. 7,790, December 19, 1992, p. 31.

[544]Daniel Sneider, "A Russian Movement Rejects Western Tilt," *The Christian Science Monitor*, February 5, 1993, p. 4.

[545]Ibid., p. 4.

[546]Sneider, "Critics Wary of Russian Army's Role in Republics," p. 6.

[547]"The New Domino Game," p. 31.

[548]"Russia to Decide," *The Economist*, January 30, 1993, p. 48.

vention in the region will encourage further Russian intervention that will, in turn, accelerate the radicalization of the Islamic revival. Thus, an action-reaction syndrome has begun in Central Asia, in which opposition is polarized by Russian intervention and suppression. If the Russians want to find the real culprit exacerbating the Islamic revival and assuring that its manifestations will be violently anti-Russian, they need not look to Iran, they need only look in the mirror.

SUMMARY

Central Asia's procommunist regimes are as responsible as is the Russian Federation for the oppression and consequent radicalization of the Islamic revival there. Ironically, by crushing all antigovernment protest and by permitting the operation of no political party, however moderate, the Central Asian communist regimes are ensuring that the democrats and moderate revivalists will lose support to militant Islamic Fundamentalism. Alienated, frustrated, and no longer allowed to work within the system, political Islam will take its case to the battlefield, as it has been compelled to do in Tajikistan and may yet do in Uzbekistan. These reborn Central Asian *mujahideen* will borrow extensively from the examples of their militant Islamic revivalist brethren in Iran and Afghanistan. If Russia and procommunist regional regimes want Islamic Fundamentalism to gain a foothold in the former Soviet Muslim republics, they should continue to pursue the policies of oppression. Islamic Fundamentalism will intensify in direct proportion to the harshness of measures meant to eradicate it.

No matter the outcome of the civil war in Tajikistan or the success of communist regimes throughout Central Asia in quelling the Islamic opposition, Islam will maintain its prominent role in all spheres of Central Asian life because it is intertwined with the area's culture, tradition, and ethnonationalism. Although the expression of political Islam may be driven underground by oppressive regimes, Islam will endure and will long outlast those regimes dedicated to eradicating it. Political Islam will again surface in a region that is experiencing an almost perpetual Islamic revival.

Suppression can only succeed for so long in Central Asia. When the Soviets first persecuted Islam, closed *masjids*, and banned Islamic literature, there was still food on the table. Central Asia today, however, cannot feed itself, and those communist governments still entrenched in power are increasingly feeling the brunt of popular anger. To control this anger, the hardline regimes of the Muslim republics will turn increasingly to internal suppression, thus forcing democrats and revivalists alike to forgo ballots for bullets. These regimes will then look more frequently to Moscow to exercise its hegemony. However, while the Russians can provide soldiers and armaments, they can hardly satisfy Central Asia's economic needs. Indeed, the future of the Central Asian governments depends on their ability to reverse the rapid decline in endemic socioeconomic conditions and to allow greater political participation. This is unlikely to occur in the near future as these governments enjoy such limited legitimacy. Distribution of economic goods has ceased, the political opposition has been denied a legitimate voice, regional identity is confused, and regional governments have little authority in the country-side. All of this fuels the fires of Islamic revivalism. In fact, despite Central Asia's place as a unique Muslim region, the oppression, the economic ills, the lack of po-litical participation, the failure of secular ideologies, and the meddling of a foreign power there make Central Asia sound not so very different from modern Egypt or Algeria. Central Asia is a fascinating laboratory for the study of Islamic revivalism. Given the area's present circumstances, Central Asia is ripe for political Islam.

Chapter
12

Conclusion

The modern Islamic revival is best defined as the reawakening and the recrudescence of Islam as a political idiom in which Islamic symbols, ideas, and ideals are cultivated by practitioners (Islamic revivalists) both sincere and insincere, violent and pacifist. Islam, in the Islamic revival, is the wellspring of political legitimization. Islam serves as the source of community unification, whether in opposition to or commensurate with nationalism. Manifestations of the Islamic revival will invariably include growing interest in political Islam as a key to governing society, grass roots support for an Islamic system, and an organization or organizations dedicated to the implementation of an Islamic system. Sometimes such organizations are national governments, as in Pakistan, Iran, or Afghanistan. More often, however, these organizations operate outside the government, opposing the government, as in Egypt and Iraq, and become increasingly revolutionary.

Prominent features of today's Islamic revival include the widespread and grass roots dissemination of political Islam from homes and places of worship, observance of Islamic precepts, efforts to establish Islamic governments based on the application of the *Shariah,* and the popular discussion and debate of Islamic issues in the media. The Islamic revival emphasizes the centrality in Islam of socioeconomic equity and justice while reasserting Islam's relevance to solve contemporary problems in contrast to Westernization and secularization. Most important, the Islamic revival has proved a powerful response to years of real and perceived Western and communist political influence.

Islamic revivalists may differ to a significantly large degree as to which direction the Islamic revival should take or, indeed, the very meaning of the revival itself. Thus, an Islamic revivalist is defined as any individual who has contributed to the renewal and revitalization of political Islam. Within this almost infinitely broad framework are four categories of Islamic revivalists: Fundamentalists, Traditionalists, Modernists, and Pragmatists. Sadly, however, the Fundamentalists are often perceived by the West as the only type of revivalist. Therefore Islamic revivalism and Islamic fundamentalism are mistakenly taken to be synonymous.

The current Islamic revival sweeping the world has had profound implications for nations both Muslim and non-Muslim. The long arm of radical Islamic fundamentalism, one brand of the Islamic revival, has reached across the seas and has struck even at the heart of New York City, at the World Trade Center, where a car bomb killed six and rocked the financial epicenter of the Western world. Such manifestations of the Islamic revival, however rare and unrepresentative of the revival at large, demand the world's attention. This attention must be tempered, however, with the realization that Fundamentalist revivalism is but one aspect of the Islamic revival, one that most Muslims shun yet which has enjoyed inordinate media exposure due to Fundamentalism's usually sensational appeal. Most Islamic revivalists and devout Muslims disparage and repudiate such acts as car bombings and hostage taking as inherently irreconcilable with Islam.

There are over fifty predominantly Muslim nations in the Muslim world pursuing sometimes contradictory agendas. Furthermore, Muslims differ by race, history, and culture, and therefore represent a pluralistic and heterogeneous people. Even the Muslim Fundamentalists themselves are distinguished from one another according to divisions within Islam, differing interpretations of Quranic teaching, and invariably national differences unrelated to Islam. Thus, Islamic fundamentalism specifically and, more generally, the revival of political Islam are something less than monolithic.

So different are the people of the Muslim world from one another that often their only connection is through a common faith, although that faith is usually differently interpreted. Nevertheless, in every community of Muslims there exists, always has existed, and will always exist a tendency, inherent in the faith, for politicization of Islam, for making Islam an idiom of dissent against shared injustice and inequity. Thus, Islam is the key to understanding the Islamic revival, its roots in Muslim communities around the world, and its implications for Muslims and non-Muslims alike. Political Islam need not be violent or revolutionary. It has operated sufficiently well within a democratic context, and many Islamic revivalists have attempted to work within that context with mixed results. It is the war waged against Islamic revivalism that has radicalized political Islam and that has made at least some manifestations of Islamic revivalism violent ones.

Islam is itself the core of political Islam, and the separation of the two is a misleading one. The first Islamic state was founded by Muhammad himself when, after the *hijra* in A.D. 622, he governed the people of Madina in God's name. So successful was this first Islamic state under Muhammad's rule that by the time of his death, Muslims were in control of the whole of the Arabian Peninsula. Thus, Muslims today wish to emulate the example of this "once and future" Islamic state by establishing their own, one governed by Islamic law encoded in the *Shariah,* the comprehensive legal guide to both individual and community life in Islam.

The faith of Islam has forever emphasized free will and stresses the significance of making "the right decision" in all aspects of life. Thus, Islamic education occupies a central place in the revival of political Islam. Extraordinary importance is given to the Islamic scholars who interpret Islam and the Islamic institutions of education that bring such interpretations to the population, for they both strengthen and perpetuate the current Islamic revival. For students of Islamic institutions, Islam is presented as a way of life governing every aspect and nuance of existence—and of thus having significant political implications. Consequently, in Egypt, for example, the most devout, most radical, and most revolutionary Fundamentalists are young students attending these institutions.

Political Islam's attraction for Muslim students, teachers, and laypersons alike is nothing new. Yet the modern Islamic revival of the last two decades differs from the many revivals of Islam preceding it. The Islamic revival today differs insofar as it lacks geographic boundaries and because its expression has been varied to an unprecedented extent.

The universality of the Islamic revival has been a significant development in international relations. This universality is explained by the links that bind the world together in ways often unknown in the past. The communications, transportation, and computerization revolutions have shrunk the world drastically. Significant occurrences in Iran, Saudi Arabia, Kuwait, or Iraq, for example, are communicated to the world through CNN almost instantaneously. Furthermore, the establishment of nongovernmental and transnational Islamic organizations, like the OIC or the *Ikhwan al-Muslimun,* has spread the message that "Islam is the answer" in all human endeavors. Moreover, global economic and political interdependence have shattered formerly secure borders. No nation's population is long unaffected by events around the world. Today, the Islamic revival is well known; Islam has reentered the people's consciousness.

Ironically, the shrinking of the global village has united the people of the Muslim world in common cause but has also made the modern Islamic revival polycentric and heterogeneous, with as many aspects as there are Islamic revivalists. In this sense, the Islamic revival is not yet conducive to the creation of an Islamic bloc or a unified Muslim *umma.* Nevertheless, the Islamic revival progresses each day with greater vigor than the last. The many faces of the Islamic revival have prevented the revival from being discredited as a whole. Thus, the Islamic revival has remained a popular idiom of political activity among the majority of Muslims. Any action the world takes to suppress the revival will only serve to continually "relegitimize" it in the eyes of frustrated and angry Muslims the world over.

Islam is a vehicle for political action primarily because it is both a "historic" and an "organic" faith. As a historic religion, Islam offers a definite direction to human history; every human action becomes another element in the divine scheme. Human history and its direction are important to Islam, and therefore Muslims work to understand history, to emulate it where it has been divinely guided, and to avoid its repetition where it has angered God. Thus, Muslim Fundamentalists, for example, insist that Muslims return to the "fundamentals" of Islam as exemplified by the rule of Muhammad and the first four rightly guided caliphs over the earliest Muslim community. Less dogmatic Muslims likewise see the importance of history to Islam and interpret success and failure in the recent, even immediate, past as indicative of divine grace or anger respectively.

Islam is also an organic or holistic religion in which, by definition, no distinctions exist between the world of individual worship and community government. Islam sets forth universal principles of human behavior, and these principles are binding on Muslims and provide for them an answer in all areas of human endeavor. When secular ideologies and systems cannot answer the gigantic political, economic, social, and cultural grievances of Muslims, there is always recourse in Islamic revivalism.

Centrally important to Islam as a political idiom is the Islamic emphasis on socioeconomic equity and justice. This emphasis is in marked contrast to secular political ideologies that in the Muslim world have led to the increasing misery of the population and the funneling of wealth into fewer and fewer hands. The consequent injustice and inequity in Muslim societies have made Islamic revivalism that much more popular. Islam stresses justice and moderation in all human endeavors, political and otherwise. In Islam, no one is above the law of God; all people are equal in the eyes of God and no individual goes unpunished for a crime. Furthermore, Islam provides for specific measures in which socioeconomic equity and justice are to be ensured and safeguarded. This emphasis on equity and justice has greatly enhanced the attraction of Islamic revivalism in a Muslim world where equity and justice are notably absent.

The achievement of Islamic justice is possible in Islam through the application of *jihad*, a term much maligned and misunderstood. Three categories of *jihad* exist in Islamic theology: personal, *ummaic,* and martial. Personal *jihad* is the struggle waged by Muslims to purge themselves of their base desires and evil impulses. *Ummaic jihad* is the peaceful correction of wrongs within the *dar al-Islam* (the community of Muslims in which devout Muslims rule). Martial *jihad,* the least favored in the eyes of God and the last resort of Muslims according to the Quran, is the prosecution of war against un-Islamic oppressors who have precipitated confrontation. Nonpracticing Muslims and other unbelievers are combated in martial *jihad,* at least ideally. However, the misapplication of martial *jihad* has given it a bad name. What *jihad* represents to most Muslims, particularly *ummaic jihad,* is the peaceful means for realizing socioeconomic justice and equity in the Muslim world. Nevertheless, martial *jihad* gains proponents in proportion to the oppression of political Islam in the Muslim world and to the increasing impossibility of nonviolent *ummaic jihad* in the face of such oppression. The question becomes: In which direction will the Islamic revival go? The nonviolent struggle—or martial *jihad?*

Central to a prediction of the future of Islamic revivalism is an examination of the four different categories of Islamic revivalists, namely, the Muslim Fundamentalists, Traditionalists, Modernists, and Pragmatists. Fundamentalist revivalists are often the more puritanical and revolutionary advocates of political Islam. However, they are never inherently opposed to the West, only to undue Western influence in the Muslim world. Nor are they innately revolutionary, but government or imperialist oppression of their activities will often inspire them to revolutionary activity. Traditionalist revivalists, usually drawn from the ranks of Islamic scholars, prefer to avoid political activity unless the integrity of Islam is violated by internal un-Islamic despots or external unbelievers. Modernist revivalists, although politically active like the Fundamentalists and devoutly concerned about the integrity of Islam like the Traditionalists, possess none of their inordinate fear of the West and advocate the incorporation of many Western ideas into the current scene in the Muslim world, provided the ideas are not essentially un-Islamic. Muslim Pragmatists, often not considered revivalists at all by many scholars, nevertheless have contributed as much as the other three groups to the strengthening and the perpetuation of the Islamic revival in the Muslim world. The Pragmatists utilize Islamic symbols to rebuild mass support for themselves, although they are usually considered by other Muslims as unbelievers. Nevertheless, the contributions of the Muslim Pragmatists to the revival have been remarkable. In brief, Islam represents a political idiom accepted, however grudgingly by some, throughout the Muslim world. All categories of Islamic revivalists are using Islamic symbols and ideals to attract support and to build mass movements; in this respect, the Islamic revival is purely a political one.

While much of the recent literature on the Islamic revival emphasizes the importance of militant fundamentalism to the revival, it is the dynamic interaction of the four types of revivalists that fuels the revival. Thus, the Islamic revival today is open to much interpretation; the meaning, the methods, and the ultimate aim of the revival differ according to changes in the Muslim world. In this respect, the revival represents a constructive Islamic dialogue in which varied Islamic systems are debated and in which Islamic practice is applied to realities in the Muslim world. Thus, this interaction represents the beginning of an "Islamic reformation."

Following the independence of the Muslim world from colonial rule, the Muslim Pragmatists were the first to fill the power vacuum. Their emphasis on imported Western ideologies and their policies of Westernization were related to the evident disparity between the strength of the West and the weakness of the Muslim world. However, the policies and programs of Westernization, modernization, and secularization that the Pragmatists initially pursued with such relish have fallen far short of expectations. While the Muslim world has experienced unprecedentedly rapid modernization, appropriate economic, political, and sociocultural development has been lacking.

The Muslim Pragmatists' applications of Western and pseudo-Western ideologies have utterly failed to achieve comprehensive and equitable development in much of the Muslim world. In fact, the imported and "un-Islamic" ideologies of capitalism, socialism, communism, nationalism, Ba'athism, Nasserism, pan-Arabism, secularism, and secularization are no longer seriously discussed as solutions to endemic socioeconomic dysfunction in the Muslim world. Instead, such ideologies are now equated with the causes of such dysfunction. Political Islam stands ready to fill the developmental void wholly unaffected by the failed ideologies of the past. Therefore, by default Muslims look to political Islam as the answer to their socioeconomic and political ills, and Muslim Pragmatists turn to Islam when they need to shore up wavering internal support. This effort has backfired, however. Far from undermining or co-opting political Islam, the Muslim Pragmatists have legitimized political Islam as an idiom of antigovernment dissent. Few Muslims are fooled by the Islamic rhetoric of the Pragmatists; for instance, when kneeling and praying for media consumption, Saddam Hussein, a murderer of devout Muslims, is nothing but a blatant fraud.

The failure and discrediting of secular ideologies have been precipitated and accompanied by the developmental crises that have beset the Muslim world. By adopting rather than adapting Western technology and innovation, the Muslim Pragmatists have ignored the the uniqueness of the Muslim world, whose potential and pitfalls differ from those of the West. The crises of identity, legitimacy, penetration, distribution, and participation are severe in the Muslim world and have paralyzed the governments of the region. Rapid urbanization, immigration, and a frightening population explosion have each contributed to the dire political, economic, social, and religious conditions of most Muslim nations. In contrast to the Western world, where modernization and secularization occurred gradually, the Muslim world is beset by all five developmental crises simultaneously. Consequent civil unrest has therefore brought civil war and revolution, demagogues and firebrands to the forefront of politics in the Muslim world.

The identity crisis has impeded the resolution of the other four crises and may serve as the key to political, economic, and social stability in the region. Yet the processes of modernization pursued by the Muslim Pragmatists and secularists have worsened the identity crisis and need to be suspended. A more effective and attractive idiom of identity is required for Muslims; Islam is their natural alternative. Islamic unity, through the agency of the *umma,* and narrow community loyalty at the other end of the spectrum are working together as a centrifugal force tearing apart the nation-states of the Muslim world. Only by force can the Muslim Pragmatists hold these states together; and force has accelerated the delegitimization of the nation-state as a source of identity for Muslims.

The Arab-Israeli conflict has also contributed significantly to Islamic revivalism's attraction for Muslims. The failure of either Arab regimes or secular Palestinians to defeat Israel has reinforced a Muslim inferiority complex, has discredited secular and Pragmatist regimes devoted to the defeat of Israel, and has contributed to an Islamic backlash to perceived Western neocolonialism through the Israeli "surrogate." Thus, the conflict, still unresolved after fifty years, is fueling the revival by playing upon anti-Western sentiment among Muslims and by underscoring the incompetence of any but purely Islamic regimes in the region.

The astounding defeat of Arab forces at Israeli hands in the 1967 Six Day War was a watershed for the global revival of political Islam. After so much boasting and bravado, Egyptian President Nasser in the space of a week discredited himself and his secular and pseudo-Western ideology of Nasserism. Islamic groups throughout the world were quick to ascribe the defeat of the Arabs to the emphasis on the fashionable secular ideologies of the Muslim world's political and economic elites. Political Islam, it was increasingly claimed, could defeat the Israelis—a conclusion bolstered by the improved showing of the Arabs against the Israelis in the 1973 war.

The Arab-Israeli conflict also empowered two pan-Islamic international organizations that have played significant roles in the financial enrichment and institutionalization of the Islamic revival: the Organization of Petroleum Exporting Countries (OPEC) and the Organization of the Islamic Conference (OIC). OPEC, which first flexed its economic muscle in the aftermath of the 1973 Arab-Israeli War, fueled the fire of Islamic revivalism on several levels: first by breaking the Arab world's bonds of dependency on the West; second by providing finances to revivalist organizations around the world; and third by failing to contribute significant monies to financially strapped Muslim nations, thus underscoring the disparity between the few oil-rich Muslim countries and the many non-oil producing and exporting countries (NOPEC) of the Muslim world. The initial satisfaction, indeed euphoria, in the Muslim world for the apparent successes of OPEC were short-lived, tempered by the realization that OPEC, excepting Iran and Libya, represented status quo powers uninterested in revolutionary Islam. Nevertheless, Saudi distribution of oil money has benefitted innumerable revivalist groups and has contributed positively to the resurgence of Islam both on the grass roots level and in the corridors of power in the Muslim world.

The 1969 burning of the *Al-Aqsa* mosque in Israeli-occupied Jerusalem infuriated Muslims around the world and led to the establishment of the Organization of the Islamic Conference (OIC) in the same year. Dedicated to principles of Islamic solidarity, the OIC has contributed to the revival by institutionalizing the lost but never-forgotten Islamic dream of the universal *umma*. Like OPEC, however, the promise of the OIC has not yet been realized; but the very existence of the OIC is both the result of and a contribution to the strength of the Islamic revival. Its affiliated institutions, like the Islamic Development Bank, have shown Muslims around the world the potential power of an Islamic bloc dedicated to Islamic politics. Islamic revivalists are encouraged to fulfill the potential inherent in pan-Islamism and institutionalized by the OIC.

Iran's Islamic Revolution has, more than any other single event, accelerated and radicalized the Islamic revival. Its implications are felt throughout the world even today, nearly fifteen years after the fall of the Shah. The Iranian Revolution traumatized the West and invigorated the Islamic revival in such diverse countries as Egypt, Algeria, Iraq, Syria, and Saudi Arabia. The events leading to the Islamic Revolution, for all its mystery, are commonplace in the Muslim world. The Shah of Iran pursued modernization policies incompatible with his people's traditional ways of life. In turn, the Shah aggravated the five crises of development. He permitted no political participation in the system and thus delegitimized himself and his government. He failed to ensure the just and equitable distribution of resources and goods to all Iranians; the Shah's policies and programs benefitted the upper middle class far more than it did the masses. The rapidity of the Shah's modernization programs also caused incredible dislocation in the countryside. The cities were suddenly filled with a growing population of job-seeking ex-farmers. This dislocation and the consequent frustration and alienation felt by most Iranians engendered a crisis of identity that left Iranians unsatisfied with the government of the Shah and more interested in returning to traditions in the countryside, traditions centered around Islam. Moreover, the Shah's reign was further undermined by the singular place in Iranian society of the Shi'ah clerical establishment. The clerics' ability to solve, at least to a greater degree than had the Pahlavi monarchy, the developmental crises besetting the nation and the popular leadership of the charismatic Ayatollah Khomeini made the transition of power from the secular government of the Shah to the Islamic Republic both possible and, in Iranian eyes, desirable.

The implications of the Iranian Revolution extend far beyond Iran's borders. As a classic case study illuminating the causes of the Islamic revival, the Iranian

Revolution also provides a model to other revivalists around the world. The anti-Western and anticommunist temperament of the new Islamic regime under the leadership of the Ayatollah Khomeini inspired and excited Islamic revivalists everywhere. The victory of the Iranian Revolution, in the face of palpable Western hostility, encouraged radical revivalists to struggle for victory. Widespread outbreaks of Fundamentalist militancy have resulted.

The Iranian Revolution also radicalized the Islamic revival both directly and indirectly. Declarations from Tehran that the new government would work actively to export the Fundamentalist revolution throughout the Muslim world infuriated the West and terrified the Muslim Pragmatist leaders of nations in the region. Their response? Repression of revivalism, regardless of whether it was radical or moderate, without distinction. The result? A self-perpetuating positive feedback of Islamic revivalism. This is perhaps the truest significance of the Islamic Revolution in Iran.

Events in the former Soviet republics of Central Asia have confirmed the validity of Islam as a vehicle for political action. In a region isolated for decades from the rest of the Muslim world, an Islamic revival is in evidence, demonstrating that Islam needs no external influence to become politicized. Today, in Central Asia, the action-reaction syndrome of oppression and radicalization of the Islamic revival, common in the Muslim world, has begun in earnest. Already, the Central Asian republic of Tajikistan has undergone a terrible and costly civil war in which Islamic revivalist groups and democrats in the south of the nation have been crushed by communist northern Tajik militias with the assistance of the Russian military. This, however, does not signify the end of the revival in Tajikistan; it signifies its radicalization. No longer permitted to operate legitimately in Tajik politics, Islamic revivalists will become increasingly Fundamentalist in orientation to get their message of Islamic justice and socioeconomic equity across to the people and to transform Tajikistan into a nation more in line with Islamic principles. Fundamentalism will increase in popularity in Tajikistan in proportion to the attempts of Russia and its Pragmatist surrogates in Central Asia to oppress Islamic revivalists.

The causes of the politicization of Islam in Central Asia are everywhere. The crises of development are pronounced in the region. Distribution of goods and services has broken down. Governments are illegitimate communist holdovers and have barely penetrated down to the grass roots of Central Asian communities, providing little popular participation or identity for the people. Consequently, an Islamic identity has reemerged, having survived the cultural pogroms of the atheistic Soviet communists. Islamic politics are gradually emerging as the greatest power for change in the region, slowly eclipsing even the efforts of secular democrats. As a result, many former communists who still command power in the region are playing the Islamic card to shore up popular support for themselves. Yet these neophyte Pragmatists are fooling themselves, especially in Uzbekistan and Tajikistan. By fueling the fires of the Islamic revival they will eventually themselves be consumed.

Again and again, the Islamic revival has been radicalized and co-opted by the most militant and dangerous demagogues, not because Islam is "barbarous" or "medieval," but because the West is funding oppressive secular regimes in the Muslim world that detain, torture, and often execute all political opponents, among them the Islamic revivalists. By refusing to allow a voice to the people, the Muslim Pragmatists ruling the Muslim world have been delegitimized and the appeal of an Islamic system promising nirvana has been strenthened.

The West has misperceived the "Islamic explosion" and the much-heralded "Islamic threat" to Western interests. Even the most radical and revolutionary Islamic revivalists pose little inherent danger to the powerful West. Western analysts and policymakers often overlook the curious history of decent United States-Fundamentalist relations. Sadly, when Westerners think of Islamic fundamentalism, they inevitably focus on Iran in the first years of its revolutionary rage or on Lebanon in the thick of its civil war. The West forgets its alliance with Zia-ul-Haq's Fundamentalist regime in Pakistan. Fundamentalist Pakistan was the beneficiary of the third-largest U.S. aid disbursement in the 1980s. Furthermore, the United States allied itself with several Fundamentalist Afghan *mujahideen* factions fighting Soviet colonialism in Afghanistan. The *mujahideen* received substantial military and economic aid from a generous Washington. Moreover, Sadiq al-Mahdi's moderate Fundamentalist Sudanese regime enjoyed good relations with the United States and received U.S. assistance. The moderate Wahhabi Fundamentalists of Saudi Arabia have also gotten along well with the United States. Even Iran has expressed an interest in reconciliation with the United States. Moderate Fundamentalist Shi'ah cleric Hashemi Rafsanjani has made positive steps to improve relations with the West and even with the United States. Rafsanjani pressured Lebanese hostage takers to release all Western hostages, maintained Iran's neutrality during Operation Desert Shield and Operation Desert Storm, and is opening Iran to Western multinational corporations.

In any event, militant and radical fundamentalism, in the name of any religion, is historically short-lived after its empowerment. Sustaining revolutionary fervor when the revolution has succeeded is all but impossible. Cultural revolutions, whether on the Chinese or Iranian models, become tiresome to the average citizen and are a drain on popular support. However, when external or internal forces threaten the regime, as Iraq threatened Iran during the 1980s, the revolutionary spirit is prolonged. Furthermore, when external forces crush fundamentalist movements as a matter of policy, such movements are proportionately popularized and radicalized. Religious and nationalist passions are easily inflamed when foreign powers intervene in the Muslim world. The Iranian Revolution burned hotter and brighter directly as the result of U.S. meddling and Iraq's war of aggression, which was supported by the West and the moderate Arab states and perpetrated against Iran by Iraq. There was no better way to guarantee that the revolution would be radicalized, uncompromising, and militantly anti-Western.

The United States has long-term interests in the Muslim world. Therefore, the United States should forge a long-term policy in the region. Supporting secular and Pragmatist dictatorships that ruthlessly suppress their subjects is shortsighted policy, as evidenced in Iran. The United States can win the lasting friendship of the people of the Muslim world simply by staying true to its own democratic ideals and by emphasizing human rights.

By committing itself to the promotion of human rights, the United States would be making the surest long-term investment. The United States would again become a beacon of hope in an increasingly appreciative world. As a military and economic superpower, it is the United States' obligation to stand as the world's moral superpower. After all, the best way to guarantee freedom and human rights at home is to guarantee their victory abroad.

The United States can take realistic and definitive steps to prevent the indefinite perpetuation of prior policies supporting tyrants. The first best step the U.S. government can take is to promote greater understanding of the Muslim world among American citizens. U.S. policies toward the Muslim world can never improve if the country's perceptions continue to be plagued by prejudice and misunderstanding. The U.S. perception of Islam, of Muslims, and of the Muslim world, built on ancient and deep-seated stereotypes, is a definite impediment to understanding the feelings, the wants, and the needs of Muslims throughout the world. Although there probably is little malice in U.S. misperceptions of the Muslim world, there is much that can be done to remedy those misperceptions and to remedy a history of unnecessarily strained relations between Muslims and Americans.

High schools and universities throughout the United States often give short shrift to the Muslim world in educating young Americans. Both U.S. public schools and the Western media need to dispel stereotypes of Muslims, not perpetuate them. Americans are barely knowledgeable about Islam, a religion whose adherents account for one of five human beings on the planet. On this basis alone, a closer and more equitable treatment of Islam is warranted. It is in school and through television that Americans form negative opinions of Islam. Thus, these opinions can be tempered by the portrayal of Muslims as human beings, not as terrorists, oil *shaikhs,* and religious fanatics.

To create a better understanding between the United States and the people of the Muslim world, the U.S. Department of State, the National Security Council, and the CIA should employ experts on Islam and the Muslim world. Hiring American Muslims might also improve relations with the world of Islam. Recognizing the central place of Islam in the cultures of Muslim countries and in the Islamic revival will avert unnecessary misperception and misinterpretation of a region strategically so important to the United States.

The United States must also pursue a strategy of reduced dependency on the Muslim world—in particular, dependency on Middle East oil. Only then will U.S. policy be truly objective; only then will the United States be able to address the wants and needs of the people of the Muslim world, not merely its own wants and needs. More generally, the United States must revitalize itself economically if it is to compete for markets and for products in a world increasingly linked by trade. If the United States succeeds economically, it can abandon its fear of Islamic fundamentalism; after all, Islam and capitalism are almost wholly compatible.

It has long been the intention of the United States to encourage its surrogates throughout the world to pursue a measure of political liberalization. However, with some pro-U.S. regimes it has gone too far for that. The people of Egypt, for example, would be unimpressed with U.S. pressure on the Mubarak regime to reform. Mubarak, like the Shah, will turn conciliatory only when the revolutionary surge threatens immediately to overwhelm him. The United States should do its best to avoid being perceived as a supporter of oppressive regimes in the Muslim world. The United States could abjure its ties with tyrannies of any sort, without regard to their friendship or the benefits they promise to bestow; indeed, where are the casinos in Havana which Cuban dictator Fulgencio Batista once frequented? The United States must cut its losses—and cut off its erstwhile allies before it is implicated in the oppression and terror they have wreaked upon their subjects. Only then will U.S. rhetoric in support of human rights have the force of truth.

The United States must stand for human rights not only by turning its back on tyrannical regimes that oppress their own people but also by applying its standards evenly and without regard to its short-term interests. By condemning all who violate human rights and perpetuate abuse on their neighbors and citizens, the United States better serves its long-term interests—that is, the United States earns the trust and the friendship of the people of the world.

The foreign policy agenda of the United States must come into line with post-Cold War reality. The United States can abandon the search for an enemy with whom to grapple for world dominance and consider new objectives. At home, the United States needs to focus on infrastructure development, crime, health care, education, the national debt, and the budget deficit. Abroad, the United States needs to orchestrate a global effort to fight global poverty, hunger, disease, illiteracy, the population explosion, environmental hazards, and drug smuggling and addiction.

The United States should also refocus national security in an interdependent world. The United States must consider the security of the world, and it can safeguard that security by checking the proliferation of weapons of mass destruction. Yet today the United States applies its standards unevenly, sometimes illogically. For instance, if Iraq fails to comply with U.N. demands for inspection of sites where nuclear material is allegedly hidden, the United States bombs Iraq. Yet the United States has averted its eyes while India, Israel, and South Africa built nuclear weapons. While Iraqis dig themselves out from the rubble of U.S. anger during Operation Desert Storm, the United States threatens a stubbornly noncompliant, indeed defiant, North Korea with a possible economic embargo—and nothing more. The Muslim world is particularly attentive to this double standard, and the outcry against U.S. belligerence toward Iraq might be quieted if only the United States applied such force consistently in the name of world security, as a protector of the common good. Hostility for, as well as mistrust and mistreatment of, U.S. citizens in the Muslim world would be alleviated.

Setting the stage for an eventual rapprochement with the Islamic Republic of Iran deserves serious consideration. Although a loving and forgiving embrace of Iran is currently very unpopular in the United States, relations with the Iranians could be gradually eased. Iran offers a large and hungry market for goods and services. Japan and Europe are already moving in while the moderate Fundamentalist Rafsanjani rules the nation with his government of technocrats. President Rafsanjani is no radical and prefers to pursue good relations with the United States if only to lift Iran from a decade of isolation and economic stagnation. If the United States misses the opportunity, if it continues its openly hostile policy toward Iran, Rafsanjani may be replaced by militant anti-American Fundamentalists much like the late Ayatollah Khomeini.

U.S. policymakers must continue mediating the Arab-Israeli dispute until a just and comprehensive peace settlement in the Middle East is realized. The Arab-Israeli conflict has gone on too long and cost the adversaries too much in blood and treasure. It has also contributed to the radicalization of the Islamic revival, which is undermining the pro-American regimes of Egypt, Jordan, and Lebanon. The Israeli-PLO mutual recognition agreement of September 1993 and the Israeli pledge to give Palestinians limited self-rule in the Gaza Strip and the West Bank town of Jerico is a political breakthrough. However, there is a long and difficult road ahead. The United States has the power to ensure Israel's security, and Israelis should enjoy such security. But the Palestinian people are also entitled to a homeland; the Syrians are entitled to the Golan Heights, which they lost to the Israelis in the June 1967 Six Day War; and the Lebanese would like an end to the Israeli Security Zone in southern Lebanon.

If the Middle East peace process should falter and grind to a halt again, the high expectations raised would soon be translated into frustration and anger, and the Middle East could once again become the hotbed of terrorism that it was during the 1970s and 1980s. If the Palestinians are denied their national rights indefinitely, radical Fundamentalist organizations like *Hamas* will swell with new members. A continuation of the Arab-Israeli conflict translates into a continuation of radical Islamic revivalism. It is this radicalization the United States should avoid. Otherwise, the United States will continue to have troubled relations with the Muslim world.

The United Nations has a role to play in the Muslim world, and the United States should make certain that the United Nations can play that role untroubled by a lack of financial, political, or moral support. While the United States can accomplish a great deal internationally on its own, its efforts are bolstered through multilateral and international cooperation. The United States should encourage the United Nations economically and politically to expand its peacekeeping missions and to care for the world's millions of refugees. However, the United States must avoid the appearance of controlling the United Nations. If the people of the Muslim world see the United Nation as no more than an extension of the U.S. State Department or the Pentagon, then the United Nations' reputation will be undermined and little will be accomplished. The United Nations must act fairly and consistently. If the United Nations were, for example, to hold war-crimes trials of Serbian political and military leaders who had engaged in genocide against Bosnian Muslims, the Muslim world would cheer.

Can the United States undertake these measures? Does the political will exist? There are few signs of any substantial change in U.S. foreign policy. What the Clinton administration apparently offers, however, is a shift away from the activist international role pursued by Bush. With domestic concerns so great, it is a wonder that the "Islamic threat" ever comes up at all.

Temptation has grown in the United States to view Fundamentalist militancy specifically and all revivalist activism generally as antithetical to the national interest. Accusations of terrorism are every day leveled at Muslim Fundamentalists, particularly after the arrest of Muhammad A. Salameh in March 1993 for the bombing of the World Trade Center. Immediately, the media seized on Salameh's attendance at a *masjid* in New Jersey where the blind Fundamentalist cleric Shaikh Omar Abdel Rahman preached his vituperative, anti-Western sermons. Although Rahman denied any involvement in the act and condemned it as inappropriate, the media nevertheless considered Salameh's ties to the Fundamentalist cleric de facto evidence of an Islamic conspiracy against Western interests.

Abdel Rahman's connections to El-Sayyid Nosair, an Egyptian serving time in the United States for involvement in the murder of Jewish fundamentalist Rabbi Meir Kahane, also guaranteed that the press, and thus the people, would view the World Trade Center bombing as an act of Fundamentalist terrorism. Moreover, Abdel Rahman himself stood trial in Egypt for alleged involvement in the assassination of Anwar Sadat. Although Abdel Rahman had issued the *fatwa* (formal Islamic decree) sanctioning Sadat's death, he was acquitted of the crime. However, the Egyptian government and the United States still considered Abdel Rahman a considerable threat and labeled him a terrorist. Nevertheless, Abdel Rahman entered the United States on a tourist visa in 1990. He is the recognized leader of radical Fundamentalist groups in Egypt who are working to overthrow the authoritarian rule of Mubarak. What more did the media need to know? The American people became suddenly convinced that Salameh's role in the bombing was irrelevant, his motives unworthy of closer examination. His guilt was unquestioned. His ties to Islamic fundamentalism proved his guilt—and the guilt of Rahman and even of the jailed Nosair.

Muslims in the United States were torn between denouncing the conspirators who bombed the World Trade Center as "terrorists"—and thus, "un-Islamic"—and denying they had anything to do with the bombing. Yet, although the conspirators' fellow worshipers at Rahman's Jersey City *masjid* distanced themselves from the attack on the World Trade Center and were quick to condemn the bombing, some Americans felt that all Muslims bore collective guilt for the crime. Consequent vandalism against the Jersey City *masjid* confirmed the fears of Muslims in America. Is this the beginning of a new Cold War, a new East-West conflict in which the East represents not communism and the communist world but Islam and the Muslim world?

The bombing prompted an immediate, though cursory, examination of fundamentalism in Egypt, given the connection between the prominent Egyptian cleric Abdel Rahman and the Palestinian Salameh. Suddenly, U.S. reporters stumbled upon a virtual civil war being waged in the land of the pharoahs, a civil war that had already cost the lives of tourists and of many Egyptians. The World Trade Center bombing quickly focused international attention on the Egyptian situation. Egypt's President Mubarak used the bombing as a convenient pretext to abort any political reform or dialogue between the Egyptian government and Egyptian Fundamentalists, who enjoy the support of the people to a far greater extent. The World Trade Center bombing has thus become in Egypt another spark pushing the cycle of action and reaction to greater and more bloody extremes. Egypt's government has cracked down on Fundamentalists, thus stimulating a more violent popular Fundamentalist outburst. Egypt may soon descend into chaos, a chaos from which the United States must extricate itself by denying support for those who abuse or deny human rights. Thus, the United States can distance itself simultaneously from the most radical Fundamentalists as well as a government that indulges in the arbitrary arrest and torture of its own citizens. Fears that the fall of the Egyptian government will usher in an Islamic Fundamentalist government opposed to the West and interested in exporting revolution are unwarranted. The people of Egypt do not want to war against their neighbors, nor do they wish to incur the wrath of the United States; what they wish for is a government free of corruption and nepotism and which can provide jobs, goods, and services to an impoverished and long-suffering population. The Mubarak government can provide nothing more than oppression and poverty and bloodshed. How could this possibly be satisfactory for U.S. national security?

The bombing at the World Trade Center, however, has brought distant events home to Americans. The United States has no personal experience with the authoritarian, corrupt, and unjust regimes ruling Egypt and other Muslim countries. These regimes are what Muslims the world over despise. These regimes are what Islamic revivalists, and not just Fundamentalists, have sacrificed their livelihoods and even their lives to destroy. Why then are some Muslim zealots attacking the United States? It is mainly because these Muslim zealots believe that the United States has supported the very governments that deny them their basic human rights and because the United States is singling out Muslim countries such as Iran, Iraq, Libya, and Sudan for punishment. The bombing at the World Trade Center should alert the United States not to the dangers of Islamic fundamentalism but to the tragedy of poverty, inequality, corruption, and oppression wracking the Muslim world. Although four Arabs were found guilty in the World Trade Center bombing and sentenced to life imprisonment without parole, Muslims who engage in rhetoric or revolution against the tyrants of the Muslim world deserve fair judgment and clear understanding. The United States need not embrace Islamic revivalists working to overthrow their oppressive governments in their homelands; but the United States should not embrace oppressive Secularist and Muslim Pragmatist rulers from fear of Islamic revivalism. Branding sincere revivalists as "terrorists" and "fanatics" while describing their oppressive governors as "moderates" only alienates many Muslims, and it enhances the appeal of the fringe anti-Western Muslim Fundamentalist zealots.

Political Islam and radical Muslims threaten the United States in no way. No country can turn its back on the United States or wage war against the United States and keep its people happy at the same time. In the end even the radical fringe of Islamic fundamentalism will recognize the utility of amicable relations with the United States.

Glossary

Abbreviations:

(A) = Arabic word; (P) = Persian word; (U) = Urdu word; sing. = singular; pl. = plural; d = died; r = reign.

ABBASIDS: The Arab Abbasid dynasty came to power after the collapse of the Ummayyad dynasty (A.D. 661–750) and reigned over the Islamic Empire from A.D. 750 to 1258. They were the descendants of Prophet Muhammad's uncle, Al-Abbas ibn-Abd al-Mutalib.

ABRAHAM: In Islam, Abraham is revered as one of the most important Prophets sent by God.

ABU (A): Literally, "the father of"; commonly used in proper names such as Abu Abbas which means "the father of Abbas."

ABU BAKR: One of the first converts to Islam, Prophet Muhammad's close companion, and the first caliph of Islam (r. 632–639).

ABU HANIFA: The Iraqi-born Imam Abu Hanifa (A.D. 699–769) was the founder of the Hanafi *madhab* (sect) of Sunni Islam. The Hanafi sect was actively promoted by a number of Abbasid and Ottoman rulers. A majority of Sunni Muslims in Turkey, Afghanistan, Egypt, Central Asia, China, and South Asia belong to the Hanafi sect.

ADHAN (A): "The call" to prayer made by a prayer-caller.

ADL (A): The act of justice, an attempt to give everyone his due, and the hallmark of a devout Muslim.

AHKAM (A): In Islam, it often applies to the numerous directives embodied in the *Shariah* that Muslims should observe.

AHL AL-BAYT (A): Literally, "People of the House." A term for Prophet Muhammad's extended family. Shi'ahs restrict the term to Prophet Muhammad's daughter, Fatimah, Prophet Muhammad's son-in-law and Fatimah's husband, Ali ibn Abi Talib, and the couple's recognized descendants.

AHL AL-KITAB (A): Literally, "People of the Book," referring to Jews, Christians, and Muslims.

AHL-I-HADITH (U): From the Arabic term *Ahl al-Hadith* (partisans of the *Hadith*); those belonging to this group are Sunni Muslims who, besides the Quran, prefer the authority of the *Hadith* over that of a conflicting legal ruling accepted by one of the four Sunni schools of jurisprudence.

AHL-I-SUNNAH (U): Followers of the *Sunnah*. Often refers to Sunnis.

AHMADIS: An offshoot of Sunni Islam that was founded by Mirza Ghulam Ahmad (1837–1908), who was born in a village in the Indian Punjab called Qadian (thus Ahmadis are also called Qadianis).

AJAMI (A): Those Arabs, who exhibited strong linguistic nationalism, chauvinistically considering non-Arabic speaking foreigners (especially Persians) as "dumb."

AL (A): Literally, "the" (in an article form) or "the clan."

AL-AQSA MOSQUE: Also called *Masjid al-Aqsa, Bait al-Muqaddas* (The Holy House), or The Dome of the Rock; it is located in Jerusalem and is one of the holiest mosques in the world of Islam.

ALAWITE: Offshoot of the Twelver Shi'ah sect who glorify Ali ibn Abi Talib to such an extent that they consider him an incarnation of divinity. Also called Nusayri because the sect was founded by Ibn-Nusair (d. 873), who was the follower and emissary of the eleventh apostolic Shi'ah *Imam*, Hasan al-Askari.

AL-AZHAR: First built as a mosque in Cairo, Egypt, on the orders of the Fatimid caliph al-Muizz in A.D. 970, it is one of the oldest and most pretigious Islamic centers of learning in the world. It was formally organized as an Islamic university by A.D. 988.

AL-BAYT AL-HARAM (A): Literally, "the holy house"; refers to the cube-shaped shrine that is situated at the center of the Grand Mosque in Mecca. *See* Grand Mosque, *Haram al-Sharif*, and *Khana-i-Kaaba*.

ALIDS: A term used for the recognized descendants of Ali ibn Abi Talib. Those claiming descent from Ali are numerous and spread all over the world. They are distinguished from other Muslims by the title of Sayyid, Sharif, or Mir.

ALI IBN ABI TALIB was the son of Abu Talib, the cousin and son-in-law of Prophet Muhammad, one of the first converts to Islam, and the fourth caliph of Islam (r. 656–661).

ALIM, pl. ulama (A): Literally, "one possessing knowledge or *ilm*," hence a learned person. In Islam, it refers to a Muslim who is learned in Islamic theology and jurisprudence. The term is also generally used for muftis, *imams, moulvis, mullahs,* and *maulanas*.

ALLAH: The Islamic term referring to the one and only omnipotent, omnipresent, just, and merciful God. Belief in Allah is the first and most essential tenet of Islam.

ALLAHU AKBAR (A): Literally, "God is Most Great" or "God is Greatest."

AMIN (A): Literally, "trustworthy"; Arabs referred to Prophet Muhammad as *al-Amin* even before he began to propagate Islam.

AMIR AL-MU'MININ (A): The honorific title of "Supreme Commander of the Faithful," given to the first four rightly guided caliphs.

AMIR/EMIR (A): It is the title given to military commanders, governors, and princes. The title is used by a number of present-day Muslim rulers and leaders of some Islamic political parties.

ANJUMAN (P): "Assembly," "association," or political organization.

ANSAR (A): Plural of nasir or *naseer*, which means "helper" or "supporter." In Islamic history it refers to the residents of Madina who gave asylum to Prophet Muhammad and actively supported him when he emigrated from Mecca in A.D. 622.

AQAID, sing. aqidah (A): Islamic beliefs and doctrines.

AQL (A): Reason, intellect.

ARAB: A Semite who most often speaks Arabic and identifies with Arab culture. A majority of the 200 million Arabs are Muslims and live in twenty-one Arabic-speaking countries in the Middle East. Thousands of Arabs also live in non-Arabic-speaking countries worldwide.

ARABIC: A Semitic language originating in the Arabian peninsula. Written from right to left, it is spoken by 200 million people living in at least twenty-one countries of the Middle East, but also by millions of Arabic-speaking Palestinians, Arab minorities, and non-Arabs located all over the world.

ARYAMEHR (P): The title of "Sun of the Aryans" assumed by Muhammad Reza Shah Pahlavi in the mid-1960s.

ASHAB (A): Companions of Prophet Muhammad.

ASHARITE: The followers of the Iraqi-born *alim* Abul Hassan al-Ashari (A.D. 873–935), who spearheaded a traditionalist Islamic movement. Abbasid rulers (A.D. 833–942) used al-Ashari's theological arguments to silence the liberal rationalism of the Mutazilites and thereby played a role in retarding Islam's dynamism.

ASHRAF (A): Literally, "well-born." In Islam, people who trace their lineage to Prophet Muhammad or his close companions are considered "well-born" and thus are highly respected.

ASHURA (A): The tenth day in the first Islamic month of Muharram when Muslims commemorate the anniversary of the martyrdom of Prophet Muhammad's grandson, Hussein ibn Ali.

ASLAF (A): Refers to the pious companions of Prophet Muhammad who are considered to have had special insight into the requirements of the faith because of their close association with Prophet Muhammad.

AULIYA, sing. Wali (A): Literally, "favorites of Allah"; often applied to prophets, *imams,* and *mujaddids.*

AUQAF, sing. waqf (A): Charitable organizations operated by the government and/or private organizations that help mosques, *madrassahs*, orphanages, and the poor and needy.

AYAT (A): "Sign," "mark," "token," or "miracle." The term is often used to refer to any of the approximately 6,200 verses in the Quran.

AYATOLLAH (P): Literally, the "sign" or "token" of Allah on earth. A revered Shi'ah theologian and jurist who studies and interprets God's directives embodied in the Quran.

BA'ATH (A): Literally, "rebirth" or "renaissance." The Ba'ath ideology or Ba'athism initially emphasized nationalism, pan-Arabism, Arab socialism, anti-Western imperialism, secularism, and democracy. Authoritarian Ba'ath parties govern Iraq and Syria.

BAI'YA (A): An "oath of allegiance" that is taken pledging one's total loyalty and obedience to a religiopolitical leader.

BANIAS: A Hindi term for Indian Hindu moneylenders.

BARAKAH (A): The "gift of God's blessing," or spiritual influence emanating from a holy man, a charismatic leader, a place, or a thing, making the person, place, or thing worthy of veneration.

BARELVIS: Muslims who follow the Indian Muslim Traditionalist Ahmad Raza Khan Barelvi of Bareilly, India.

BASIJ (A): Literally, "mobilization"; *basij* is the auxiliary force of the Islamic Revolutionary Guards (the *Pasdaran*). The *basij-i-mustazafin* (mobilization of the oppressed) was established in Iran in early 1980 by *Ayatollah* Khomeini's Islamic government.

BAZAAR (P): Market.

BAZAARI (P): Merchants; the *bazaaris* played an important role in financing the Iranian Revolution.

BEDOUIN: Nomad in the Arab world.

BID'A (A): Literally, "innovation"; some Sunni Fundamentalists consider any "innovation" in the purity of Islamic beliefs and practices of the *aslaf* as *bid'a,* and thus reprehensible.

BISMILLAH (A): Literally, "In the name of Allah," a statement with which Muslims ought to begin any undertaking.

CALIPH: The Anglicized term for *khalifah.*

CALIPHATE: The Anglicized term for *Khilafat.*

CHADOR (P): The long garment worn by conservative Iranian women to cover their head and entire body. See *Hijab.*

DAR AL-HARB (A): Literally, "abode of war"; refers to a land ruled by non-Muslims where non-Islamic laws prevail. There was a widespread feeling among the *umma* that in these lands Muslims were not allowed to freely practice their religion, felt insecure, and suffered discrimination. Thus, a state of conflict prevails between the non-Muslim rulers and their Muslim subjects and between the *dar al-harb* and the *dar al-Islam* (abode of Islam or the Muslim world).

DAR AL-ISLAM (A): Literally, "abode of Islam"; often refers to all those lands where Muslim regimes govern and where, ideally, Islamic laws are practiced and Islamic institutions exist.

DAR AL-ULUM (A): An institution where Islamic instruction is imparted. In Egypt it often refers to *al-Azhar* in Cairo.

DARS-I-NIZAMIYYA: The Islamic curriculum developed by *Mullah* Nizamuddin (d. 1748) of Oudh, India, and popularized by the Traditionalist *ulama* of Farangi Mahall in Lucknow, India, during the eighteenth and nineteenth centuries. It still exerts influence over *madrassah* education in the South Asian subcontinent.

DA'WA (A): The "call," "invitation," or "summons" to acknowledge religious truth and join a religious community, missionary movement, or religiopolitical organization.

DEOBAND: A town in Saharanpur district in the state of Uttar Pradesh, India, which is famous for its traditionalist *madrassah* education.

DEOBANDIS: Those Muslims who got a traditionalist *madrassah* education in Deoband, India, or are the followers of Muslim clerics who studied there. *See Deoband.*

DHIMMIS (A): Derives from the Arabic term *dhimma* (an agreement of protection); often applied to free non-Muslims (especially "people of the Book," namely, Christians and Jews) who lived in Muslim countries and were guaranteed freedom of worship and security by the state. *Dhimmis* paid no *zakat* or *ushr* taxes, but paid a capitation tax called *jizya* for the state protection guaranteed them and for not bearing the responsibility of defending the *dar al-Islam* in times of war.

DHOTI: A Hindi word for a long, broad strip of cloth wrapped around the waist and covering the legs to the ankles. Worn in parts of India and Bangladesh.

DIN (A): The sum total of a Muslim's faith.

DIN-I-ILLAHI (U): The eclectic "Religion of the Supreme Being" initiated by India's Moghul Emperor Jalal-ud-din Muhammad Akbar (r. 1556–1605) and combining the best features of the major religions in India. The new religion, however, was accepted by only a few Moghul courtiers and faded away soon after Akbar's death.

EID (A): Literally, "festival"; Muslims celebrate two *Eids* annually: *Eid al-Fitr,* literally "the festival breaking the fast," which is held one day after the month of Ramadan, and *Eid al-Adha,* the "festival of sacrifice," which is held at the close of the *haj* season and commemorates Abraham's willingness to sacrifice his son Ishmael when commanded by God in a dream to test his faith.

EID-I-MILAD-UN-NABI (U): Called Maulud in Arabic, it is a festival commemorating Prophet Muhammad's birthday.

FAQIH (A): An expert in Islamic jurisprudence.

FARAIDH, sing. Fardh (A): Literally, "compulsory duties" or "obligations." In Islam, omission of these duties will be punished and the commission of them will be rewarded. The five obligatory *faraidh* enjoined on all Muslims are: (a) the *shahadah* (proclamation of one's faith in Islam); (b) *salat* (prayers); (c) *sawm* (fasting during Ramadan); (d) *zakat* (alms to the poor); and (e) *haj* (pilgrimage to Mecca).

FARANGI MAHALL: The name of a mansion in Lucknow, India, that was built by a French indigo merchant. It came to be the home of an extended family of Traditionalist Sunni *ulama*—popularly known as the Farangi Mahallis because they lived in Farangi Mahall—in the late seventeenth century.

FARSI (P): The Persian language spoken by Persians/Iranians.

FATAH (A): Literally, "conquest" or "victory."

FATIMAH BINT MUHAMMAD: Daughter of Prophet Muhammad, wife of Ali, mother of Hassan and Hussein, and regarded by all Muslims as a paragon of virtue, piety, and compassion. Many Muslims add the honorific title *Al-Zahra* (The Shining One) to her name.

FATWA (A): A formal and authoritative Islamic decree on a civil or religious issue that is often formulated and promulgated by a mufti or a qualified and respected Islamic theologian-jurist.

FEDAYEEN (A): Those willing to sacrifice themselves in a *jihad*.

FIQH (A): Islamic jurisprudence, which covers all aspects of religious, political, economic, and social life. While a *fiqh* is not as comprehensive, divine, eternal, and immutable as the *Shariah*, each *madhab* within the "House of Islam" has its own *fiqh*.

FIQH-I-JAFARIYYAH (A): The Shi'ah school of jurisprudence that was codified by the sixth Shi'ah *Imam*, Ja'far al-Sadiq (d. A.D. 765).

GHAIR-MUQALLID (P): A Muslim who does not want to be restricted to only one school of Islamic jurisprudence (such as *Ahl-i-Hadith*).

GHAYBA (A): The condition of anyone who has been physically withdrawn by God from the sight of human beings and whose life during that period of disappearance may have been miraculously prolonged. Shi'ah doctrine says the twelfth *Imam* disappeared and will reappear at a foreordained time to lead people back to "true" Islam. In the meantime, supreme *mujtahids* have the authority to interpret the twelfth *Imam*'s will in his absence.

GHAZI (A): A Muslim who fights in a *jihad* to defend his faith, his community, and/or his Islamic state/Muslim homeland. The Ottoman sultans conferred this title upon generals and warriors of renown.

GRAND MOSQUE: *See Haram al-Sharif.*

HADITH (A): Sayings of Prophet Muhammad.

HAJ (A): Literally, "pilgrimage." Adult Muslims of sound mind and body have been enjoined by their faith to undertake the *haj*, the spiritual journey to Mecca, once in their lifetime, if they can afford it. *Haj* is the fifth pillar of Islam and it is formally undertaken between the seventh and tenth of *Dhul-Hijj*, the last month in the Islamic calender. *See Faraidh.*

HAJI (A): A pilgrim to Mecca who has performed the *haj* during the annual *haj* season. Also a title assumed by someone who has successfully completed the pilgrimage.

HAJR AL-ASWAD (A): Literally, "black stone"; on the wall and near the door at the northeast corner of the *Haram al-Sharif* is embedded the holy "Black Stone," which was given to Abraham by God.

HANAFIS: The Hanafis are Sunni Muslims who follow the teachings of the Iraqi-born *Imam* Abu Hanifa al-Nu'man ibn-Thabit (A.D. 699–569). The Hanafi sect was actively promoted by a number of Abbasid and Ottoman rulers and is widely prevalent in Turkey, Afghanistan, Egypt, Central Asia, China, and South Asia.

HANBALIS: Those Sunnis who follow the teachings of the Iraqi-born theologian and jurist Ahmad ibn-Hanbal (A.D. 780–855). The puritanism of the Hanbalis combined with the promotion of the Hanafi *madhab* by the Ottoman rulers who crushed the Wahhabis (adherents of the Hanbali *madhab*) resulted in the Hanbalis being the smallest of the four Sunni *madhabs*. Hanbalis are concentrated in Saudi Arabia and Qatar.

HAQ: That which is true, for example, the Quran and Islam itself. In Islamic law it is the legal rights or claims of an individual. For sufis the term refers to the "Divine Essence," or Allah.

HARAMAIN (A): Refers to two of the holiest cities in the Muslim world, namely, Mecca and Madina. It also refers to the holy mosques, mausoleums, and shrines in those cities.

HARAM AL-SHARIF: In Islam it refers to "the sacred ground" of the Grand Mosque in Mecca, which houses the *Al-Bayt al-Haram, Bayt-Allah* or the *Khana-i-Ka'aba* (U). The *Ka'aba* was first built by Prophet Abraham and his son Ishmael for worship of one God. It was later rebuilt by Prophet Muhammad in A.D. 605 for the worship of Allah. Muslims turn to the *Ka'aba* when they pray and have been enjoined by their faith to come to the *Ka'aba* once in their lifetime to perform the *haj.*

HAZRAT (A): A title of respect that is the equivalent of "your reverence" or "his reverence" when applied to eminent spiritual leaders. It is also indiscriminately used for any intellectual.

HEZBOLLAH (P)/Hizb Allah (A): Literally, "Party of Allah." The name was adopted by radical Shi'ah organizations in Iran and Lebanon.

HIJAB: The "veil" or covering worn by conservative Muslim women when they are in public. The basic reason for the *hijab* is to wear simple and nonprovocative dress.

HIJAZ: A mountainous region of the Arabian Peninsula adjacent to the Red Sea coast, which includes the holy cities of Mecca and Madina, where Islam originated.

HIJRA (A): Refers to the "migration" of Prophet Muhammad and his close companions from Mecca to Madina in A.D. 622. The Islamic calendar begins with this migration and the establishment of the first Islamic state in Madina.

HIJRAT (A): Literally, "migration" or "emigration"; In Islam, some devout Muslims have from time to time emigrated from areas ruled by *kafirs* or "wayward Muslims" to areas where "true" Islam was practiced or would be practiced.

HILAL: Refers to the "new moon" or "crescent." The new moon is important in Islam because of the Islamic lunar calendar. The crescent, analogous to the Christian "cross," the Jewish "star of David," and other religious symbols, is found on the flags of a number of Muslim countries.

HINDUSTAN: Hindi term meaning "Land of the Hindus," also known as India.

HOSAYNIYYEH (P): Religious center for the commemoration of the martyrdom of *Imam* Hussein and the performance of related ceremonies.

HUSSEIN IBN ALI: The son of Ali ibn Abi Talib and Fatimah bint Muhammad, the grandson of Prophet Muhammad, and the third Shi'ah *Imam,* who was martyred at Karbala in A.D. 680 *See* Ali ibn Abi Talib, Fatimah bint Muhammad, Shi'ah, Karbala.

IBADAT (A): Performance of ritual religious practices, including prayer, fasting, and making the pilgrimage to Mecca.

IBN (A): Literally, "son of"; corresponds to "ben" in Hebrew.

IBN TAYMIYYAH, TAQI AL-DIN (1263–1328): A Syrian-born theologian-jurist who spent his life elaborating upon Hanbali teachings in his puritanical writings and sermons. He rejected *taqlid* and *ijma,* insisted on the literal interpretation of the Quran and *Sunnah,* condemned *bid'a,* crusaded against the influences of Greek philosophy, denounced sufism, and censured the cult of Prophet Muhammad and the practice of saint worship.

IJMA (A): "Agreement," "unanimity," or "consensus"; considered to be the third *usul* or source of Islamic law. The consensus can be that of the first generation of Muslims, the great theologian-jurists of the medieval era of Islam, the *umma* scattered all over the world, or even an entire nation.

IJTIHAD (A): The word *ijtihad* derives from the same Arabic root as *jihad* and literally means "to exert oneself." Technically, *ijtihad* implies a Muslim jurist exercising his personal, independent reasoning, knowledge, and judgment to give his opinion on a legal issue where there is no specific order in the Quran. The term now commonly implies the independent interpretation or reinterpretation of Islamic laws.

IKHWAN (A): Literally, "brotherhood" or "brethren."

IKHWAN AL-MUSLIMUN (A): Muslim Brotherhood or Muslim Brethren. Hassan al-Banna founded an Islamic political party by this name in Egypt in 1928. In due course, it spread to other Arab countries.

ILM (A): Literally, "to know," "knowledge," and "learning." It is often used by Muslims for the knowledge of Islam that is regarded as all-encompassing. One possessing *ilm* is called an *alim.*

IMAM (A): A prayer leader or officiating cleric in a mosque; a very learned and competent *alim;* a term used interchangeably with caliph. In the Shi'ah sect, the title of *Imam* is also used for the divinely guided, rightful, and infallible religiopolitical successors of Prophet Muhammad starting with *Imam* Ali.

IMAMAT (A): The divine right of Ali ibn Abi Talib and his male descendants to lead the *umma.*

IMAN (A): Refers to the five articles of the Islamic creed, which are (a) belief in Allah; (b) belief in angels; (c) belief in the prophets of Allah with Adam as the first prophet and Muhammad as the last; (d) belief in the holy books revealed by Allah, i.e., the Torah, the Bible, and the Quran; and (e) belief in the Day of Judgment.

INFITAH (A): Literally, "opening up"; Egypt's President Muhammad Anwar al-Sadat inaugurated an "open door" policy that opened Egypt up to foreign investment. Attractive tax breaks and duty-free zones lured foreign multinational corporations to Egypt.

INJIL (A): The Quranic term for God's revelations to Jesus Christ embodied in the Bible, which is the holy book of the Christians. Muslims believe in the Old Testament, but not in the New Testament. This is because in the latter, Jesus Christ is mentioned as the son of God, which in Islam is *shirk* (polytheistic, and therefore sinful). *See Shirk.*

INSAF (A): Literally, "impartiality," "objectivity," "integrity," and "equity"; refers to a code of ethics and morality becoming of a devout Muslim.

INSHALLAH (A): Literally, "God willing."

ISLAH (A): In Islam, the term for reform, purification, and revitalization of the Muslim community based on Islamic principles.

ISLAM (A): Derived from the Arabic root *salama,* which means "peace." Muslims believe that Islam is the final and perfect religion of God. They also believe that only by surrendering to the will of Allah and by obeying His laws can one achieve true peace and happiness in this world and in the hereafter.

ISLAMIC CALENDAR: The Islamic lunar calendar begins with Prophet Muhammad's migration from Mecca to Madina and the establishment of the first Islamic state. The twelve months of the Islamic calendar in proper sequence are (1) *Muharram,*

(2) *Safar*, (3) *Rabi al-Awwal*, (4) *Rabi al-Thani*, (5) *Jumadi al-Awwal*, (6) *Jumadi al-Thani*, (7) *Rajab*, (8) *Shaban*, (9) *Ramadan*, (10) *Shawwal*, (11) *Dhul-Qadah*, and (12) *Dhul-Hijj*.

ISLAMIC REVIVAL: The renewal of heightened interest in Islamic symbols, ideas, and ideals subsequent to a period of relative dormancy of interest.

ISLAMIC REVIVALISM: The generic term for the phenomenon of Islamic revivals occurring around the world. It incorporates the dynamic action, reaction, and interaction of four types of Islamic revivalists, namely, the Muslim Fundamentalists, Traditionalists, Modernists, and Pragmatists. It can also be viewed as the ideologization of Islam, whereby Islam becomes a comprehensive political ideology.

ISLAMIC REVIVALIST: A term used generically in the literature of Islamic revivalism to refer to any participant in an Islamic revival. However, it is more specifically used for prominent Islamic revivalists who make a significant contribution to bringing about an Islamic revival at crucial moments in history. In propagating their perception of the "true" Islam, all Islamic revivalists frequently, but not necessarily, promote the creation of an Islamic state by teaching, preaching, and/or writing, and on rare occasions even by the force of arms. There are four types of Islamic revivalists: the Muslim Fundamentalists, Traditionalists, Modernists, and Pragmatists.

ISLAMIYAT: Islamic studies.

ISMA'ILIS: A branch of Shi'ism which follows the religiopolitical leadership of Isma'il, a son of Ja'far al-Sadiq and his descendants.

ISNAD, sing. sanad (A): Literally, "a chain of authorities." In Islam, it refers to the chain of people responsible for transmitting the *hadith*. The validity of the *hadith* depends on the transmitters being perceived as men of honesty and integrity in Islamic history.

ISTHNA ASHARI (A): The Twelver Shi'ah sect, which believes that Ali ibn Abi Talib should have been Islam's first caliph because Prophet Muhammad had nominated him. They follow twelve infallible *Imams* beginning with Ali and ending with Muhammad Mahdi, who disappeared in A.D. 873 and is promised to reappear as "true" Islam's savior.

JAHANNAM (A): "Hell"; where sinners will go after death.

JAHILIYYAH (A): Derived from the Arabic word *jahila*, "to be ignorant." Muslims claim that the pre-Islamic period in Arabia was a "time of ignorance" and "primitive savagery."

JAMAAT (A): A group, an association, an assembly, a congregation, an organization, or a political party.

JIHAD (A): Literally, "to struggle"; in Islam it means "to struggle in the way of God." A *jihad* is a "holy struggle" sanctioned by the *ulama* and fought against aggressors, tyrants, and "wayward Muslims." Also refers to the spiritual struggle waged against one's own baser instincts.

JIHAD-I-AKBAR (A): The greatest "holy struggle"; to purge one's baser instincts and impulses.

JIHAD-I-ASGHAR (A): The smaller "holy struggle"; the military campaign waged against aggressors, tyrants, and "wayward Muslims."

JIZYA (A): The poll tax or capitation tax levied on *dhimmis* or non-Muslims for protection, exemption from military duty, and full rights of citizenship given to them in an Islamic state.

JUM'AH (A): In Islam, it refers to the "meeting" or "assembly" of the *umma* on Fridays when Muslims have been enjoined by their faith to undertake their midday prayers along with their brethren. These congregational prayer services often include a sermon by a respected Islamic cleric called *Imam-i-Jum'ah wa Jama'at* (Friday congregational prayer leader).

KA'ABA: *See Al-Bayt al-Haram, Haram al-Sharif.*

KAFIR (A): The term was first applied to "unbelieving" Meccans who rejected Prophet Muhammad's message and denounced him. The term has also been used for Islam's enemies and nonpracticing Muslims. *See Mushrikun.*

KALAM (A): Literally, "speech," or "dialectic"; in Islam, it is applied to Islamic theology, which is the study of God's Words, the subject that attempts to give rational proofs for religious beliefs, deals with the problems of God's oneness, His attributes, and human free will and self-determination, among other philosophical issues.

KARBALA: A town in southeastern Iraq where in A.D. 680 a historic battle took place between the armies of Yazid ibn Mu'awiyah, who had become the ruler of the Islamic empire, and Hussein ibn Ali, the grandson of Prophet Muhammad, who refused to endorse Yazid as the new caliph. In the ensuing battle, Hussein and his male relatives and followers were killed on the tenth of Muharram. Annually, Muslims all over the world commemorate Hussein's martyrdom, over 1,300 years ago, and vow to struggle against corruption, injustice, and tyranny even if it means giving up their lives. Shi'ahs make every effort to visit the tombs and shrines of the martyrs in Karbala once in their lifetime.

KHADIJAH BINT KHUWAYLID (A.D. 554–619): The daughter of a respected chieftain of the Meccan Qureish tribe. After her father's death, she managed his thriving business. One of her business agents was Muhammad, who had a reputation for being honest and trustworthy. She subsequently married Muhammad. Khadijah was the first to accept Islam and was her husband's staunchest supporter.

KHALIFAH (A): Caliph; Prophet Muhammad's religiopolitical successors and leaders of the worldwide *umma.* Most Muslims only revere the first four rightly guided caliphs and consider all caliphs thereafter as political rulers, lacking the mantle of spiritual leadership.

KHAN: Mongol and Tartar chieftains were referred to as khans, as were the Ottoman sultans and provincial governors in Safavid Persia. In India under the Turkish kings of Delhi, khan was the title of the principal nobles, especially those of Persian or Afghan heritage. Today it is a common surname of Muslims.

KHANA-I-KA'ABA: *See Haram al-Sharif, Hajr al-Aswad.*

KHARIJITES, sing. khariji (A): Derived from the Arabic term *Khuruj,* which means "to rebel" and "secede." Another possible derivation is the Arabic word *kharij,* which means "to go out." In Islamic history, Kharijites or the Khawarij were one of the earliest revolutionary Muslim Fundamentalists.

KHATIMUN-NABIYIN (A): The title reserved by Muslims for Prophet Muhammad, who was the last of God's prophets and brought His last message. *See* Prophet Muhammad, Quran.

KHILAFAT: Literally, "Caliphate"; refers to the religiopolitical rule by a *khalifah.* Most Muslims look up to the Caliphate of the first four rightly guided caliphs, namely Abu Bakr, Umar, Uthman, and Ali. However, many scholars have broadened the term to include the regimes of many Muslim rulers in Islamic history. Mustafa Kemal Ataturk abolished the institution of the *Khilafat* in 1924.

KHILAFAT-I-RASHIDAH (U): The Caliphate of the first four righteous caliphs of Islam, namely Abu Bakr, Uthman, Umar, and Ali. *Also see Khilafat, Khulafah-i-Rashidin.*

KHULAFAH-I-RASHIDIN: Literally, "rightly guided *khalifahs.*" The religiopolitical rule of the first four righteous *khalifahs* of Islam, namely Abu Bakr, Umar, Uthman, and Ali.

KHUMS (A): Besides the voluntary donation of *zakat,* Shi'ahs have been enjoined by their faith to give *khums,* which is a donation of one-fifth of their savings to provide maintenance for and support for the work of needy Sayyids, who are Prophet Muhammad's descendants.

KHUTBAH (A): In Islam, it is a sermon delivered by a cleric to a congregation, usually at the Friday congregational prayers.

KISMET: The idea that evolved in the *umma* that their fate has been preordained and predestined. It is more a tradition than a principle of faith.

KUFR (A): In Islam it means blasphemy, hypocrisy, lies, and disbelief. A person guilty of *kufr* is a *kafir*.

MADHAB (A): Literally, "a direction"; in Islam, it applies to the four recognized Sunni schools or rites of jurisprudence, namely the Hanafi, Hanbali, Maliki, and Shafi'i sects. There is also one major school of Shi'ah jurisprudence called *Figh-i-Jafariyyah*.

MADINA: A city in Saudi Arabia. In Islamic history, Prophet Muhammad and a few of his close companions migrated to Madina in A.D. 622 and set up the first Islamic state. It was in Madina that Prophet Muhammad died (A.D. 632) and where his tomb can be found.

MADRASSAH (A): A school, college, seminary, or academy where the primary emphasis is on a broad spectrum of classical Islamic disciplines, which are taught by the *ulama*. Students also learn such subjects as Arabic, astronomy, logic, mathematics, medicine, literature, philosophy, and metaphysics.

MAHDI (A): Literally, "the divinely guided one," "the expected deliverer," "the redeemer," or "the savior." The doctrine of the Mahdi in Islamic history first originated in the Shi'ah sect with its belief in the hidden twelfth *Imam* who will be sent by God to establish "true Islam." In due course, the appealing Mahdist hope also came to be held by many Sunnis and non-Muslims.

MAJLIS (A): Literally, "session," "meeting," "assembly," or "council." In Shi'ah Islam a *majlis* is a religious session in which a knowledgeable Muslim discusses the life and works of the *Ahl al-Bayt*. It is also the term used for the national legislature or parliament in some Muslim countries.

MAJLIS-I-SHURA (A): Literally, a "consultative body" or an "elected council" to make recommendations to the ruler of an Islamic state or a Muslim homeland. It is also a term used for the national legislature or parliament in some Muslim countries.

MAKTAB (A): An elementary school for teaching children recitation of the Quran, the *Hadith,* and Arabic.

MAKTABI (P): A student or graduate of a *maktab* or Quranic school. In Iran, it refers to the doctrinaire, dogmatic, and orthodox Muslim Fundamentalist or Traditionalist.

MALIKIS: Sunnis who follow the Islamic jurisprudence of jurist Abu Abd Allah Malik ibn Anas (A.D. 716–795). The Maliki sect spread in Muslim Spain and Africa.

MARJA-I-TAQLID (P): Literally, "source of emulation." In the Ithna Ashari Shi'ah sect any *mujtahid* who has reached the position of ayatollah can be *marja-i-taqlid*.

MASHAIKH: Spiritual leaders.

MASJID (A): Derived from the word *sajdah,* meaning "to prostrate oneself." It is the Muslim house of worship, also called a mosque.

MASJID AL-AQSA (A): Also called the *Al-Aqsa* mosque, *Bayt al-Muqaddas* (The Holy House), or "The Dome of the Rock." It is located in Jerusalem and is the site from which Prophet Muhammad is said to have gone on his miraculous nocturnal journey to the seventh heaven and returned. It was also the direction in which Muslims prayed before Prophet Muhammad directed Muslims to pray in the direction of the *Ka'aba*.

MA'SUM (A): A sinless and infallible person.

MAULANA (A): Derived from the Arabic root *maula,* which means "lord," "patron," "master," and "tutor." The title is applied to scholars of Islamic theology, jurisprudence, and history.

MAULUD (A): An anniversary celebrating the birth of Prophet Muhammad. It is celebrated on the twelfth day of the third Islamic calendar month of *Rabi al-Awwal* with speeches, writings, and *gawwalis* (poems and hymns praising God, Prophet Muhammad, or a Muslim saint).

MECCA: A major city in Saudi Arabia. The holiest city in the world of Islam because it is the birthplace of Prophet Muhammad (A.D. 570), the site of the *Ka'aba*, to which Muslims from all over the world come to perform the *haj,* and the direction in which all Muslims say their daily prayers.

MESSIAH (A): Literally, "the anointed one," the religiopolitical leader who is sent by God to lead people back to the straight path. Jews, Christians, and Muslims believe that it is he who will establish the Kingdom of God on earth.

MIDDLE EAST: The term Middle East is said to have been coined around 1900 by Captain Alfred T. Mahan, the noted American naval historian/strategist. Most Middle East scholars include all the Arabic-speaking countries, Turkey, Iran, and Israel in the region.

MUDARABAH (A): Profit and loss sharing in economic transactions.

MUFTI: A learned, and respected expert on Islamic theology and jurisprudence. The mufti has the authority not only to interpret Islamic law but also to issue *fatwas.*

MUHADDITH (A): A scholar of the *Hadith.*

MUHAJIRUN, sing. Muhajir (A): Literally, "the emigrants"; it is the name given to the earliest converts to Islam from the Meccan tribe of Qureish who went with Prophet Muhammad to Madina. Also called *muhajirs* in Urdu.

MUHAMMADANISM (A): A term that is incorrectly given by non-Muslims to Islam. Prophet Muhammad did not create or start the religion nor is he worshiped by Muslims. The creator of Islam as well as of everything else according to Muslims is Allah.

MUHARRAM is the name of the first month in the Islamic calendar. It was the month in which Hussein ibn Ali and his male followers were martyred on the battlefield of Karbala in A.D. 680.

MUJADDID (A): Literally, "renewer," "restorer," or "regenerater" of Islam; Sunni Muslims believe that *mujaddids* are sent by God in times of spiritual crisis to set the world on the right path again.

MUJADDID ALF-I-THANI (U): The renewer of Islam in the second millennium of Islamic history.

MUJAHID (A): A Muslim who fights in a *jihad.*

MUJAHIDEEN (A): Those Muslims who fight in a *jihad.*

MUJTAHID (A): An erudite Muslim (usually an *alim*) who practices *ijtihad* and has the right to give *fatwas.*

MULHID (A): In the Islamic context, it is a Muslim who has deviated from Islam, hence becoming a heretic, infidel, or *kafir.*

MULLAH: Formerly another term for *alim,* and thereby someone to be revered. However, now it is commonly used for any Muslim religious teacher and preacher. *Also see Maulana* and *Alim.*

MU'MIN: Literally, "a true believer"; a practicing Muslim who has tried to get as close to the ideal human being as possible.

MUNAFIQUN (A): Literally, "doubters," "waverers," and "hypocrites." In Islamic history it was a term first used by Prophet Muhammad for those residents of Madina who, during his first stay in that city, ostensibly joined Islam but were secretly doubting the Word of Allah and were critical of His messenger.

MUQALLID (A): A Muslim who considers himself bound by the principle of *taqlid.* Also called "imitators."

MURID (A): Literally, "one who is desirous of knowledge"; a student. In the Islamic context, it applies to the disciple of a *pir* or sufi teacher.

MURTADD (A): One who renounces Islam; an "apostate."

MUSA: The Arabic term used for Prophet Moses in the Quran.

MUSAWAAT-I-MUHAMMADI (U): Literally, "Prophet Muhammad's Egalitarianism." It refers to the socioeconomic equality and justice of the ideal Islamic system.

MUSHARAKA (A): Profit and loss sharing in economic transactions.

MUSHRIKEEN (A): "Unbelievers," "infidels," or "heretics" who believe in and worship many gods and are perceived as the enemies of Islam and Muslims. *See Kafir.*

MUSLIHUN (A): Those who work for *islah* (reform).

MUSLIM, pl. Muslimun (A): Literally, "one who submits or surrenders to the will of Allah." It was a term that came to apply to those who followed the religion of Islam that Prophet Muhammad preached.

MUSLIM FUNDAMENTALISTS: A group often revolutionary and puritanical in its religiopolitical orientation. Fundamentalists usually believe in *ijtihad* and are extremely critical of *taqlid* and Western ideas. They often have a passionate desire to establish an Islamic state based on the comprehensive and rigorous application of the *Shariah.*

MUSLIM MODERNISTS: Knowledgeable and religiously devout Muslims who vehemently criticize *taqlid,* pursuasively advocate *ijtihad,* and make a dedicated effort to reconcile the differences between traditional religious doctrine and secular scientific rationalism. Modernists advocate the incorporation of numerous "modern-day" ideas and emphasize major revisions in Islamic laws.

MUSLIM PRAGMATISTS: Muslims by name and birth who cherish Islamic ideals, identify with the Muslim community and culture, and are perceived as Muslims by non-Muslims. However, frequently the Pragmatists do not practice the obligatory duties expected of all Muslims. Due to their formal and informal Western educational experiences in their homeland and/or in the West, they often know more about Western intellectual thought than about Islamic intellectual thought. They view the classical and medieval Islamic doctrines and practices as anachronistic, reactionary, and impractical in the modern age, and they look to a broad spectrum of ages and philosophies for their models of political and socioeconomic progress. Despite their secular worldview and desire to promote secularization and secularism, some Pragmatists engage in the politics of Islam to enhance their legitimacy; to integrate and unite their fragmented citizenry; and to inspire, mobilize, and galvanize Muslims.

MUSLIM TRADITIONALISTS: Muslims (often Islamic scholars) who tend to conserve and preserve not only the Islamic laws, customs, and traditions practiced in the classical period of Islam but in the medieval period as well. The major hallmark of Traditionalists is their rejection of *ijtihad* and belief in the dogma of *taqlid.* Though often apolitical, passive, and status-quo oriented, these scholarly minded custodians of Islam do get involved in politics when they perceive Islam and/or the *umma* to be in imminent danger.

MUSTAKBIRIN (A): Literally, "the rich and exploitative elite."

MUT'AH (A): A temporary marriage for a stipulated period of time. Mut'ah is still practiced by some Shi'ah sects. *Caliph* Ali allowed the practice, which was common in Arabia, and it was even condoned by Prophet Muhammad, according to the *Ithna Ashari* Shi'ah sect. The practice is denounced by Sunnis because *Caliph* Umar prohibited it.

MUTAZILITES: A school of Islamic theologians and jurists advocating rationalism and free will. It was founded by Wasil ibn Ata, who separated from the conservative and literalist school of Hasan al-Basri around A.D. 732. The school's reasoned arguments were a criticism of those Muslims who read the Quran literally. The Mutazilites influenced the intellectual environment in the eighth and ninth centuries.

MUTTAQI (A): A devout and "God-fearing" Muslim. *See Taqwa.*

MUWAHHIDDUN, sing. muwahid (A): Literally, "monotheists" or "unitarians" who are staunch believers in "the unity and oneness of God"; Wahhabis preferred to be known as *Al-Muwahhidun.*

MUZTAZAFIN (A): A Quranic term for the poor, oppressed, and exploited people. A term popularized during the Iranian Revolution.

NABI (A): Literally, "prophet." Muslims believe that Adam was the first prophet, Muhammad the last, and that there were 124,000 prophets in between.

NABUWAT (A): The office or work of a *Nabi* who has been directly inspired by Allah and to whom a special mission has been entrusted.

NAMAZ (P): *See Salat.*

NAZR (A): Literally, an "offering," "gift," or "present."

NIZAM (P): Literally, "system" or "order."

NIZAM-I-MUSTAFA (U): Literally, "the Islamic Order of Prophet Muhammad." It was the rallying cry of the nine opposition parties in the three-month-long Islamic mass movement in Pakistan just after the "rigged" election of 1977.

OTTOMAN: The name given to a member of the Turkish ruling dynasty descended from Uthman (d. 1324), which ruled over a multinational empire from the fourteenth century until 1923 when Mustafa Kemal Ataturk assumed power. It also refers to any member of the ruling class in the Ottoman Empire or a subject of the Ottoman Empire.

PAHLAVI: The language of ancient Persia. It was also the name that Reza Khan—a commander of the Cossack Brigade who assumed power in Persia in 1921—gave his dynasty. Reza Khan was deposed and exiled by the British in 1941 for his pro-Nazi sympathies and replaced by his nineteen-year-old son, Muhammad Reza Pahlavi (r. 1941–1979).

PALESTINIANS: Called Filistini in Arabic because they belong to *Filistin* (Palestine), which in 1948 became the Zionist State of Israel. While most of the 5.5 million Arabic-speaking Palestinians scattered all over the world (including Israel and the Israeli-occupied West Bank and Gaza) are Muslims, there is a significant Christian minority among them.

PARSEE/PARSI: Those who belong to the Zoroastrian faith in South Asia. *See Zoroastrian.*

PASDARAN-I-INQELAB-I-ISLAMI (P): Literally, "Guardians of the Islamic Revolution." Called *Pasdaran* (security guards) for short, this paramilitary force was created by Khomeini's Islamic regime immediately after assuming power in Iran in February 1979.

PERSIA: The name given to Iran by the ancient Greeks. Iran was called Persia until 1935, when the name was changed by Reza Khan (r. 1921–1941, called Reza Shah Pahlavi I in 1925).

PERSIAN: The name given to the national language of Persia written in a modified Arabic script from right to left. The Persian language is also called *Farsi* by native Persians or Iranians. A Persian is also an inhabitant of Persia (called Iran since 1935) and a member of the majority ethnic group of Iran.

PERSIAN GULF: The body of water separating Iran from the Arabian peninsula and connecting the *Shatt al-Arab* waterway to the Arabian Sea. Also called the Arabian Gulf or just "the Gulf."

PHALANGIST: A well-organized, right-wing Lebanese political party formed by Pierre Gemayel in 1936 along fascist lines. It also has a paramilitary wing dedicated to preserving the Maronite Catholic political and socioeconomic control of Lebanon.

PIR (P): A spiritual leader, guide, and teacher. In South Asia, it refers to a sufi or a religiopolitical leader of a tribe.

PURDAH (A): The term applies to the veiling and segregation of women in the Muslim world.

QADHI (A): A judge who administers Islamic law and justice.

QAWWALI: Devotional poems or hymns praising God, Prophet Muhammad, or a Muslim saint.

QIBLAH (A): In Islam, it is the direction (facing the *Ka'aba* in Mecca) in which a Muslim must pray.

QIYAS (A): Literally, "analogical reasoning." Technically, the fourth *usul* or founding principle of the *Shariah* after the Quran, the *Sunnah,* and *ijma.* An Islamic theologian-jurist may use analogical reasoning with situations that are covered in the Quran and the *Sunnah* to arrive at an Islamic solution.

QOM (A): A world-renowned center of Shi'ah learning in Iran.

QUAID-I-AZAM (U): Literally, "The Great Leader," it is the reverential title used by Pakistanis for Muhammad Ali Jinnah, the founding father of Pakistan.

QURAN (A): Literally, "recitation." According to Muslims the Quran is the collection of revelations sent by Allah to Prophet Muhammad through the agency of Archangel Gabriel (who recited them to Prophet Muhammad in Arabic). Prophet Muhammad in turn recited these revelations to his companions, who wrote them down aand recited them to others. The name Quran was later given to the holy book containing these revelations. According to Muslims, the Quran is the last of all holy books sent by God.

RAB (A): Literally, "Allah," "God," or "Lord."

RA'I (A): Literally, "opinion" or "personal judgment" of the *faqih* in interpreting the Quran, the *Hadith,* and the *Shariah.*

RAMADAN (A): The ninth month of the Islamic calendar. The name "Ramadan" is derived from *ramz,* which means "to burn." Therefore, fasting from dawn to dusk during the month of Ramadan is said to burn away one's sins. It was in the month of Ramadan that God revealed the Quran to Prophet Muhammad through the agency of Archangel Gabriel. *See Sawm.*

RASUL (A): A term used for God's Messenger, Apostle, *Nabi,* Prophet, or Messiah.

RIBA (A): The term used for "usury" or charging "excessive" interest on loans; it has been prohibited in Islam.

RUKN, pl. Arkan (A): Literally, "pillar," "principle," or "tenet" of faith. In Islam there are five pillars or tenets of faith called the *faraidh. See Faraidh.*

SADAQAH (A): The voluntary charitable contribution of money or food for the sake of acquiring merit with Allah and the saints. It is often criticized by Sunni Fundamentalists.

SAHABA (A): Literally, "companions"; in Islamic history, it specifically refers to the companions of Prophet Muhammad.

SALAF (A): A pious companion of Prophet Muhammad. *See Aslaf.*

SALAT (A): The term often used for ritual of prayers in Islam. Each session of prayers comprises a fixed pattern of recitation of verses from the Quran and prostrations.

SAVAK: Persian acronym for *Sazeman-i-Ettelaat-va-Amniyat-i-Kashvar* (State Organization for Intelligence and Security). SAVAK was the feared secret police of the Shah of Iran. Established in 1955 to combat antigovernment activities and cited by Amnesty International in the mid-1970s for the torture and murder of political prisoners, it was disbanded by the Islamic revolutionary government of Iran in 1979.

SAWM (A): The term for fasting from dawn till dusk during the month of Ramadan. One of the *faraidh* required of all adult Muslims. *See Faraidh, Ramadan.*

SAYYID (A): A title reserved for the descendants of Prophet Muhammad. It has come to mean "sir" or "your honor."

SECULAR: The civil, nonreligious, or temporal realm in contradistinction to the ecclesiastical, religious, sacred, or spiritual realm.

SECULARISM: Exclusion of religious conditions. A government that promotes secularism clearly separates the church/mosque from the state, refuses to act as the promoter and defender of a particular faith, and rejects religious ideas as the basis of its political legitimacy.

SECULARISTS: Those who believe that religion should not enter into the conduct of governmental affairs and promote secularization.

SECULARIZATION: The separation of religion from politics; the government's promotion of secularism; the gradual transformation of people's values from the strict adherence of religious beliefs and practices to an increasingly rational and pragmatic orientation; the gradual decline in the influence of religious leaders and groups in the society.

SHAFI'IS: Those who follow the teachings of Muhammad ibn Idris ash-Shafi'i (A.D. 767–820), who tried to reconcile the Maliki and Hanafi schools of Islamic jurisprudence.

SHAGIRD (P): A term that refers to a student, apprentice, or novice.

SHAH (P): A title that has often been used for Iranian monarchs.

SHAHADAH (A): A declaration of faith in God and in the prophethood of Muhammad which reads, "There is no God but Allah and Muhammad is His Prophet." It is the first pillar of the Islamic faith.

SHAHEED (A): A Muslim who dies fighting in a *jihad* and who becomes a martyr. Such a person is destined to go to Heaven because he died in "the path of Allah."

SHAIKH (A): Literally, an "elderly," and, therefore, a "wise man." It is often used for tribal chieftains, members of the *ulama*, sufi teachers in religious brotherhoods, and generally for men enjoying positions of authority in a Muslim society. Also written as *sheikh*.

SHAIKH AL-ISLAM (A): The highest religious office in Sunni Islam.

SHAIKHDOM: A land or country ruled by a *shaikh*. *See Shaikh.*

SHARIAH (A): The comprehensive, eternal, and immutable body of law that governs the individual and community life of Muslims.

SHARIF, pl. Ashraf (A): Literally, "noble," "high-born," or "exalted." Initially the term applied to a descendant of Prophet Muhammad's family, but now it includes a member of a prominent family or a descendant of illustrious ancestors.

SHAYTAN (A): Satan; God's principal enemy and mankind's biggest tempter to commit evil deeds.

SHERWANI (U): The long coat made of cotton or wool worn by Muslims of the Indian subcontinent.

SHI'AH (A): Members of this minority sect of Islam are "partisans" or "followers" of Ali ibn Abi Talib and believe that God and Prophet Muhammad wanted Ali to be Islam's first caliph.

SHIRK (A): Polytheism or idolatry. From the Arabic verb *shirika* (to associate). *Shirk* occurs when more than one God is worshiped (polytheism) and/or when anyone or anything other than Allah is assigned divine attributes and powers (idolatry). Ascribing partners to God as sharers in His divinity. Those guilty of *shirk* are called *mushrikun*.

SHURA (A): A group or assembly of knowledgeable and pious Muslims who engage in discussions and reach a consensus on important issues, such as the choice of a leader. The

Quran has recommended "consultation" with erudite and pious Muslims in matters where there is no specific guidance in the Quran and the *Sunnah.*

SIKH: The followers of Guru Nanak (1469–1538) who separated from Hinduism.

SIRAT AL-MUSTAQIM (A): Literally, "the right path" and "the path pursued by righteous Muslims."

SUFIS: The term *sufi* was derived from early Muslim ascetics and pious mystics who wore simple clothes made out of *suf* (coarse wool). Sufis are Muslims who became lax in their observance of the *Shariah* and devoted their lives to meditation and proselytization. They emphasize the spirit rather than the literal interpretation of the Quran and the *Sunnah,* and a search for eternal truth and goodness.

SUFISM: That body of Islamic beliefs and practices which promotes a mystical communion between Muslims and God. *See Sufis.*

SULTAN: The title of some Muslim monarchs.

SULTANATE: The office of and territory ruled by a sultan.

SUNNAH (A): Literally, "trodden path," "way," "custom" or "tradition." In Islam, the *Sunnah* comprises both the words and deeds of Prophet Muhammad. It complements the Quran as the major source of Islamic faith and practice.

SUNNI (A): The majority sect of Islam (approximately 80 percent of the Muslim world), as well as a member of that sect. Sunnis follow the *Sunnah* or "the way, the path, or the road shown by Prophet Muhammad." *See Sunnah, Madhabs, Fiqh.*

SURA (A): In Islam the term is used exclusively for each of the 114 chapters of the Quran, comprising a "series" of revelations.

TABARRUK (A): Literally, "that which brings a blessing." In Islam, it refers to food, flowers, and other offerings made at a saint's shrine.

TABLIGH (A): Islamic missionary activity and proselytization directed at Muslims and non-Muslims.

TAFSIR: The interpretation, explanation, or commentary of the Quran.

TAGHUT (P): Literally, "false god." A pre-Islamic idol at Mecca.

TAGHUTI (P): Figuratively, it refers to an individual and/or a regime that has been corrupted by power. Ayatollah Khomeini often referred to the shah of Iran as a *taghuti.*

TAJDID (A): Literally, "revival" or "renewal."

TALUKDAR: A Hindi term for "landowner" in India.

TAQDIR (A): Literally, "destiny," "predestination," or "fate."

TAQIYYAH (A): From the Arabic word *waga* which means "to safeguard" or "to protect oneself." The concealment of one's religious beliefs in order to avoid imminent harm. Though permitted in Islam, Shi'ahs have had to resort to dissimulation far more often because Sunnis have dominated the Muslim world for most of Islamic history.

TAQLID (A): Literally, "following without inquiry." In Islam, it means "legal conformity." Traditionalist Sunnis require rigid and unquestioning adherence to the legal rulings of one or more of the Sunni schools of jurisprudence compiled during Islam's medieval period.

TAQVEEAT-UL-IMAN (U): From an Arabic term, *taqveeat-al-Imam,* literally meaning "strengthening of the faith."

TAQWA (A): "Fear of God" and "piety." Since Islam believes God is omnipresent and is aware of a person's innermost thoughts, it not only refers to doing good deeds, but also to avoiding evil thoughts.

TARIQAH (A): The path or method of mysticism and spiritualism promoted by sufi teachers; also, the social groups (like sufi brotherhoods) formed by followers of such sufi teachers.

TATBIQ (A): Accommodation, harmonization, and integration.

TAWAAF (A): The ritual of going around a shrine. Often used for going around the *Ka'aba* seven times during the *haj* and *umrah*. *See Al-Bayt al-Haram, Haj, Haram al-Sharif.*

TAWBA (A): Repentence for one's sins and transgressions and a commitment to follow the "true" path.

TAWHID (A): In Islam, the term signifies the unity and oneness of God and His sovereignty. This is the most important tenet of Islam.

TAWIDHES, sing. Tawidhe (A): Amulets with Quranic verses worn to ward off evil and bring luck.

TAZIYAH (A): In Islam, Shi'ahs commemorate the martyrdom of *Imam* Hussein on the tenth of Muharram by participating in *taziyah* mourning processions with replicas of tombs (made of paper, wood, or metal) of the martyrs of Karbala. Some Sunnis also participate in *taziyah* processions.

ULAMA (A): Learned scholars of Islamic theology and jurisprudence.

UMMA (A): In Islam it refers to the Muslim "nation" or the "Brotherhood of Believers" (Muslims).

UMMAYYADS: Descendants of Ummayya within the Qureish tribe. They were one of the most influential families at the time of Muhammad and established the first hereditary caliphate in A.D. 661.

UMRAH: The pilgrimage to Mecca and Madina undertaken by a Muslim at any time other than during the *haj* period. *See Haj.*

UNITED ARAB EMIRATES (UAE): A political confederation formed in 1971 of seven Persian Gulf states formerly under British control. The UAE comprises Abu Dhabi, Dubai, Sharjah, Ajman, Umm al-Qaywayn, Al-Fujayrah, and Ras al-Khaimah.

UNITED ARAB REPUBLIC (UAR): The name given to the union of Syria and Egypt in 1958. Syria seceded in 1961, but Egypt continued to call itself by this name until Muhammad Anwar al-Sadat changed the name back to the Arab Republic of Egypt in 1971.

URS (A): The graveside celebration of the death anniversary of a saint. The popular belief is that the saint goes and meets God upon his death.

USHR (A): In Islam, a ten-percent voluntary tax that is expected from farmers owning irrigated farmland. The levy is payable in money or kind by each landholder to the poor or to charitable institutions.

USTAD (U): Literally, "teacher" or "instructor."

USUL (A): In the Islamic context, it is the term for the fundamentals of Islam. The four *usul* of Islam are the Quran, the *Sunnah, ijma,* and *qiyas.* Some *ulama* include *ijtihad* as a fifth *usul.*

USUL AL-FIQH (A): Literally, "principles," "roots," or "foundations" of Islamic jurisprudence.

USULI (A): From the root *usul*, or principles (of jurisprudence). The movement that advocates *ijtihad* and is for greater rationalism in Islamic jurisprudence; it is the movement that became influential in Shi'ah Islam after the 1770s.

UTHMAN IBN AFFAN: A wealthy Meccan merchant in the Qureish tribe, among the first converts to Islam, Prophet Muhammad's son-in-law, and the third caliph of Islam (r. A.D. 644–656).

VELAYAT-I-FAQIH (P): Literally, "Guardianship or Government of the Islamic Jurist." Ayatollah Ruhollah Khomeini's idea that a devout, learned, and just Islamic jurist ought to be the supreme guardian of the Islamic state during the absence of the awaited twelfth *Imam*. In Iran, Khomeini was the *velayat-i-faqih* for much of the 1980s.

WAHHABIS: Followers of Muhammad ibn Abd al-Wahhab (A.D. 1703–1792). They belong to the Hanbali school of Islamic jurisprudence and are concentrated in contemporary Saudi Arabia.

WAJIB (A): Literally, that which is "obligatory," "mandatory," "incumbent," or "binding."

WALI (A): In Islam, it denotes a learned *pir*, sufi, cleric, or saint who enjoys God's favor and consequently possesses significant powers. In Islamic law, the *wali* is the guardian or legal representative of an individual.

WAQF (A): *See Auqaf.*

WASI (A): Literally, "legatee," an "appointed guardian," or "executor of a will."

WATAN (A): Literally, "homeland" or "nation"; a concept borrowed from Western nationalism.

WISAYA (A): Literally, "the appointment or designation of someone to assume specified responsibilities." Among Shi'ahs the term refers to Prophet Muhammad's designation of Ali ibn Abi Talib as the religiopolitical leader of the entire Muslim world.

YAZID IBN MU'AWIYAH: The son of Mu'awiyah and the second Ummayyad ruler (r. A.D. 680–683). He is notorious in Islamic history because he was responsible for the deaths of *Imam* Hussein ibn Ali and seventy-one of his male relatives and followers on the battlefield of Karbala.

ZAKAT (A): The fourth pillar of Islam in which Muslims are enjoined by their faith to donate $2\frac{1}{2}$ percent of their wealth annually to the poor or to a charitable institution.

ZAWIYA (A): In North Africa it is a small room in a mosque or in a saint's shrine where members of a tribe or a sufi order gather. It may also comprise a building complex that includes a mosque, a *madrassah*, and living quarters.

ZIONISM: The Jewish nationalist movement advocating the migration of Jews from all over the world to Palestine. Theodor Herzl, an Austrian Jewish journalist, was primarily responsible for launching the Zionist movement with the publication of his book *Der Jüdenstaat* (The Jewish State) in 1896, and with his establishment of the World Zionist Organization (WZO) in Basel (Switzerland) in 1897. The WZO was instrumental in establishing the sovereign Jewish state of Israel in Palestine on May 14, 1948.

ZIONIST: One who believes in Zionism.

ZIYARAT (A): The visit or pilgrimage that Muslims make to the grave, tomb, mausoleum, or shrine of a venerated Muslim.

ZOROASTRIAN: A follower of Zoroaster/Zarathustra (B.C. 630–541), who established a religion in pre-Islamic Persia. There are still some Zoroastrians in Iran and Indo-Pakistan, where they are called Parsees/Parsis.

ZULM (A): Oppression

Selected Bibliography

ARTICLES

Abbott, Freeland K. "The Jama'at-i-Islami of Pakistan," *Middle East Journal*, Vol. 11. 1957.

———. "Maulana Maududi on Quranic Interpretation," *The Muslim World*, Vol. 48, No. 1. January 1958.

———. "Pakistan's New Marriage Law: A Reflection of Quranic Interpretation," *Asian Survey*, Vol. 1. 1962.

———. "The Decline of the Moghul Empire and Shah Waliullah," *The Muslim World*, Vol. 55, No. 2. April 1965.

Abdulla, Ahmed. "Causes of Muslim Decline—XII," *Dawn* (Karachi). December 12, 1975.

Abdullah, Aslam. "When Is Muslim Might Right?" *Arabia*, No. 26. October 1983.

Abiva, Hoseyin. "The Islamic Revival in the Soviet Union and Its Implications," *The Message International*, Vol. 15, No. 5. October 1991.

Abrahamian, Ervand. "Ali Shariati: Ideology of the Iranian Revolution," *MERIP Reports*, Vol. 12, No. 1. January 1982.

AbuSulayman, Abdul Hamid A. "The Quran and the Sunnah on Violence, Armed Struggle, and the Political Process," *The American Journal of Islamic Social Sciences*, Vol. 8, No. 2. 1991.

Adams, C. C. "The Sanusis," *The Muslim World*, Vol. 36, No. 1. January 1946.

Adams, Charles J. "The Ideology of Mawlana Mawdudi," in Donald Eugene Smith, ed., *South Asian Politics and Religion*. Princeton, NJ: Princeton University Press. 1966.

Ahmad, Aziz. "Cultural and Intellectual Trends in Pakistan," *Middle East Journal*, Vol. 19. 1965.

———. "Maududi and Orthodox Fundamentalists in Pakistan," *Middle East Journal*, Vol. 21. 1967.

———. "Sayyid Ahmad Khan, Jamal al-Din Al-Afghani, and Muslim India," *Studia Islamica*, Vol. 13. 1960.

Ahmad, Eqbal. "Pakistan—Signposts to a Police State," *Journal of Contemporary Asia,* No. 4. 1974.

Ahmad, Khwaja Harris. "The Concept and Principals of Quaranic Justice," *The Law Journal* (Pakistan), Vol. 40, No. 1. 1978.

Ahmad, Manzooruddin. "The Classical Muslim State," *Islamic Studies* (Karachi), Vol. 1, No. 3. September 1962.

———. "The Political Role of the Ulema," *Journal of Islamic Studies* (Islamabad). 1962.

Ahmad, Mumtaz. "Facing Up to Change: The Muslim Alternatives," *Arabia,* No. 25. September 1983.

———. "Islamic Fundamentalism in South Asia," in Martin E. Marty and R. Scott Appleby, eds., *Fundamentalisms Observed.* Chicago: University of Chicago Press. 1991.

———. "Islamic Revival in Pakistan," in Cyriac Pullapilly, ed., *Islam in the Contemporary World.* Notre Dame, IN: Cross Roads Books. 1980.

Ahmad, Rashid (Jullundhri). "Pan-Islamism and Pakistan: Afghani and Nasser," *Scrutiny,* Vol. 1, No. 2. July–December 1975.

Ahmed, Bashiruddin. "Pakistan: A Dream Gone Sour," *The Times of India.* September 5, 1982.

Ahmed, Ziauddin. "Socio-Economic Values of Islam and their Significance and Resurgence to the Present Day World," *Islamic Studies,* Vol. 10. 1971.

Ahsan, Manazir. "Mawlana Mawdudi's Defense of Sunnah," *Arabia,* No. 26. October 1983.

Akhavi, Shahrough. "Shariati's Social Thought," in Nikki R. Keddie, *Roots of Revolution: An Interpretive History of Modern Iran.* New Haven, CT: Yale University Press, 1981.

al-Alwani, Taha J. "Taqlid and the Stagnation of the Muslim Mind," *The American Journal of Islamic Social Sciences,* Vol. 8, No. 3. 1991.

al-Djani, Ahmad Sidqi. "The Relationship Between Arab Nationalism and Islam," *Current World Leaders—Biography and News/Speeches and Reports,* Vol. 26, No. 8/9. September 1983.

Ali, Salamat. "The Options Finally Run Out," *The Far Eastern Economic Review.* July 1, 1977.

Alnasrawi, A. "Collective Bargaining Power in OPEC," *Journal of World Trade Law.* 1973.

Alnasrawi, Abbas. "Arab Oil and the Industrial Economies: The Paradox of Oil Dependency," *Arab Studies Quarterly,* Vol. 1, No. 1. Winter 1979.

Altman, I. "Islamic Movements in Egypt," *Jerusalem Quarterly,* Vol. 10. 1979.

Aly, Abd al-Moneir Said, and Manfred W. Wenner. "Modern Islamic Reform Movements: The Muslim Brotherhood in Contemporary Egypt," *Middle East Journal,* Vol. 36, No. 3. Summer 1982.

Amin, Osman. "Some Aspects of Religious Reform in the Muslim Middle East," in Carl Leiden, ed., *The Conflict of Traditionalism and Modernism in the Muslim Middle East.* Austin, TX: University of Texas Press. 1966.

Anderson, Raymond H. "Ayatollah Ruhollah Khomeini, 89, Relentless Founder of the Islamic Republic," *New York Times.* June 5, 1989.

Ansari, Javed. "Themes in Islamic Revivalism," *Arabia,* No. 24. August 1983.

Aruri, N. "Nationalism and Religion in the Arab World: Allies or Enemies," *The Muslim World,* Vol. 67. 1977.

Ashraf, Ali. "The Challenge of Modernization and the Response in Turkey and India," *Islam and the Modern Age,* Vol. 12, No. 3. August 1981.

Ayoob, Mohammed. "Two Faces of Political Islam: Iran and Pakistan Compared," *Asian Survey,* Vol. 19, No. 6. June 1979.

Ayubi, Nazih N. M. "The Political Revival of Islam: The Case of Egypt," *International Journal of Middle East Studies*, Vol. 12, No. 4. December 1980.

————. "The Politics of Militant Islamic Movements in the Middle East," *Journal of International Affairs*, Vol. 36, No. 2. Fall/Winter 1982/1983.

Badeau, John S. "Islam and the Modern Middle East," *Foreign Affairs*, No. 38. 1958.

Bahadur, Kalim. "The Jamaat-i-Islami of Pakistan: Ideology and Political Action," *International Studies* (India), Vol. 14. January 1975.

Bailey, Clinton. "Lebanon's Shi'is After the 1982 War," in Martin Kramer, ed., *Shi'ism, Resistance, and Revolution*. Boulder, CO: Westview Press. 1987.

Balta, Paul. "The Boiling Islamic World: A False Religosity Fuels Fundamentalist Violence," *World Press Review*. February 1980.

Bari, Muhammad Abdul. "The Politics of Sayyid Ahmad Barelwi," *Islamic Culture*, Vol. 31, No. 2. April 1957.

Barraclough, Colin. "Central Asia's Muslims Shy Away from Adopting Iranian Model," *The Christian Science Monitor*. August 6, 1992.

————. "Muslim Republics Welcome Israeli Irrigation Expertise," *The Christian Science Monitor*. September 23, 1992.

Batatu, Hanna. "Iraq's Underground Shi'ah Movements: Characteristics, Causes and Prospects," *Middle East Journal*, Vol. 35, No. 4. Autumn 1981.

Baxter, Craig. "Pakistan Votes—1970," *Asian Survey*, Vol. 11, No. 3. March 1971.

————. "Restructuring the Pakistan Political System," in Shahid Javed Burki and Craig Baxter, *Pakistan Under the Military: Eleven Years of Zia-ul-Haq*. Boulder, CO: Westview Press. 1991.

Bayat-Philipp, Mangol. "Shi'ism in Contemporary Iranian Politics: The Case of Ali Shariati," in Elie Kedourie and Sylvia G. Haim, eds., *Towards a Modern Iran: Studies in Thought, Politics, and Society*. London: Frank Cass & Co. 1980.

Beeman, William. "Khomeini's Call to the Faithful Strikes Fear in the Arab World," *Philadelphia Inquirer*. May 29, 1992.

Bill, James A. "Power and Religion in Revolutionary Iran," *Middle East Journal*, Vol. 36, No. 1. Winter 1982.

————. "Resurgent Islam in the Persian Gulf," *Foreign Affairs*, Vol. 63, No. 1. Fall 1984.

————. "The Shah, The Ayatollah, And The U.S.," *Headline Series*, No. 285. New York: Foreign Policy Association. June 1988.

Binder, Leonard. "National Integration and Political Development," *American Political Science Review*, Vol. 63. 1964.

————. "Pakistan and Modern Islamic Nationalist Theory," *Middle East Journal*, Vol. 12. 1958.

————. "Problems of Islamic Political Thought in the Light of Recent Developments in Pakistan," *Journal of Politics*, Vol. 20, No. 4. November 1958.

————. "The Proofs of Islam: Religion and Politics in Iran," in George Makdisi, ed., *Arabic and Islamic Studies*, Leiden, The Netherlands: E. J. Brill. 1965.

Bishara, Azmy. "Palestine in the New Order," *Middle East Report*, Vol. 22, No. 2. March/April 1992.

Blum, Patrick. "Islamic Revival Fuels Maghreb Discontent," *Middle East Economic Digest*, Vol. 24, No. 9. February, 29, 1980.

Booth, Newell S. "The Historical and Non-Historical in Islam," *The Muslim World*, Vol. 60, No. 2. April 1970.

Border, William. "Bhutto in Crackdown on Critics Orders Martial Law for Three Cities," *New York Times*. April 22, 1977.

Borthwick, B. "Religion and Politics in Israel and Egypt," *Middle East Journal*, Vol. 33. 1979.

Brett, Michael. "Islam in the Maghreb: The Problem of Modernization," *Magreb*, Review 3. 1978.

Brohi, A. K. "Islam and Other Secular and Religious Ideologies," *The Muslim* (Pakistan). January 12, 13, and 14, 1981.

Brown, Leon Carl. "The June 1967 War: A Turning Point?" in Yehuda Lukas and Abdalla M. Battah, eds., *The Arab-Israeli Conflict: Two Decades of Change.* Boulder, CO: Westview Press 1988.

———. "The Role of Islam in Modern North Africa," in Leon Carl Brown, ed., *State and Society in Independent North Africa*. Washington, D. C.: The Middle East Institute. 1966.

Budiansky, Stephen. "Democracy's Detours: Holding Elections Does Not Guarantee That Freedom Will Follow," *U. S. News & World Report*. January 27, 1992.

Burke, Justin. "Afghan Arms And Mujahideen Slip Past Border Guards and into Tajik Civil War," *The Christian Science Monitor*. September 24, 1992.

———. "Afghan Refugees Are Seen as Threat In Tajikistan," *The Christian Science Monitor*. September 30, 1992.

———. "Russians Flee War, Rising Intolerance," *The Christian Science Monitor*. September 30, 1992.

———. "Tajik Refugees Tell Tales of Rights Abuses," *The Christian Science Monitor*. January 26, 1993.

———. "Uzbek Leaders Clamp Down to Keep Peace," *The Christian Science Monitor*. January 5, 1993.

———. "Uzbek Leaders Pick Stability Over Reform," *The Christian Science Monitor*. December 11, 1992.

Burns, E. Bradford. "The Modernization of Underdevelopment: El Salvador, 1858–1931," *The Journal of Developing Areas*, Vol. 18. April 1984.

Butt, Gerald. "Iran and Syria Curb Hizbullah Attacks, But Group Gains," *The Christian Science Monitor*. February 25, 1992.

Calder, G. J. "Constitutional Debates in Pakistan," *The Muslim World*, Vol. 46. January, April, and July 1956.

Carrol, Lucy. "Nizam-i-Islam: Process and Conflicts in Pakistan's Programme of Islamisation, with Special Reference to the Position of Women," *Journal of Commonwealth and Comparative Politics*, No. 20. 1982.

Cherif-Chergui, Abderrahman. "Justice and Equality in Islam," *The Month*, Vol. 13, No. 2. February 1980.

Chowdhury, Anwar. "State and Politics in Islam," *The Muslim*. September 28, 1983.

Cienski, Jan, and Jeff Trimble. "See No Evil: Unnoticed, A Civil War Rages in Tajikistan," *U. S. News and World Report*, Vol. 114, No. 4. February 1, 1993.

Cobban, Helena. "The PLO and the Intifada," in Robert O. Freedman, ed., *The Intifada: Its Impact on Israel, the Arab World, and the Superpowers*. Miami: Florida International University Press. 1991.

———. "When Arabs Face an Identity Crisis," *The Christian Science Monitor*. May 20, 1980.

Coleman, James S. "The Developmental Syndrome: Differentiation-Equality-Capacity," in Leonard Binder, James S. Coleman, Joseph LaPalombara, Lucien W. Pye, Sidney Verba, and Myron Weiner, eds., *Crises and Sequences in Political Development*. Princeton: Princeton University Press. 1971.

Crossette, Barbara. "Muslims Storm U.S. Mission in Pakistan," *New York Times,* February 13, 1989.

Danin, Robert M. "Tajikistan's Turbulent Spring," *Middle East Insight,* Vol. 8, No. 6. July-October 1992.

Dar, B. A. "Wali Allah: His Life and Times," *Iqbal Review,* Vol. 6, No. 3. October 1965.

Davies, James C. "Satisfaction and Revolution," in David H. Everson and Joann Popard Paine, eds., *An Introduction to Systematic Political Science.* Homewood, IL: The Dorsey Press. 1973.

Dawn, C. Ernest. "Islam in the Modern Age," *Middle East Journal.* 1965.

Dekmejian, Richard H. "The Anatomy of Islamic Revival: Legitimacy Crisis, Ethnic Conflict and the Search for Islamic Alternatives," *Middle East Journal,* Vol. 34, No. 1. Winter 1980.

———. "Islamic Revival and the Arab-Israel Conflict," *New Outlook,* Vol. 23. 1980.

———. "Islamic Revival in the Middle East and North Africa," *Current History,* No. 456. April 1980.

——— , and Margaret J. Wyszomirski. "Charismatic Leadership in Islam: The Mahdi of the Sudan," *Comparative Studies in Society and History,* Vol. 14. 1972.

Deming, Angus, Scott Sullivan, and Jane Whitmore. "The Khomeini Enigma," *Newsweek.* December 31, 1979.

Dessouki, Ali E. Hillal. "Arab Intellectuals and Al-Nakba: The Search for Fundamentalism," *Middle Eastern Studies,* Vol. 9, No. 2. May 1973.

———. "The Resurgence of Islamic Organization in Egypt: An Interpretation," in Alexander S. Cudsi and Ali E. Hillal Dessouki, eds., *Islam and Power in the Contemporary Muslim World.* Baltimore: Johns Hopkins University Press. 1981.

Deutsch, Karl. "Social Mobilization and Political Development," *American Political Science Review,* Vol. 55. September 1961.

Dil, Shaheen F. "The Myth of Islamic Resurgence in South Asia," *Current History,* No. 456. April 1980.

Dunbar, David. "Bhutto—Two Years On," *The World Today,* Vol. 30, No. 1, January 1974.

Dupree, Louis. "Islam: Design for Political Stability," *The Christian Science Monitor.* February 15, 1980.

Efty, Alex. "Khomeini Aimed his 'Verses' Attack to Stop Liberal Trends," *Birmingham News.* February 26, 1989.

el-Affendi, Abdel Wahab. "Martyrdom, Godhead and Heresy," *Arabia,* Vol. 4, No. 43. March 1985.

el-Guindi, Fadwa. "Veiling Infitah with Muslim Ethic: Egypt's Contemporary Islamic Movements," *Social Problems,* Vol. 28, No. 4. April 1981.

Enayat, Hamid. "The Resurgence of Islam: The Background," *History Today,* Vol. 30. 1980.

Entelis, J. "Ideological Change and an Emerging Counter-Culture in Tunisia," *Journal of Modern Asian Studies,* Vol. 12. 1974.

Fakhry, Majid. "The Search for Cultural Identity in Islam: Fundamentalism and Occidentalism," *Cultures,* Vol. 4. 1977.

Farhang, Mansour. "Resisting the Pharaohs: Ali Shariati on Oppression," *Race and Class,* Vol. 21, No. 1. Summer 1979.

Faruki, Kemal A. "Pakistan: Islamic Government and Society," in John Esposito, ed., *Islam in Asia: Religion, Politics, and Society.* New York: Oxford University Press. 1987.

Faruqi, Zia-ul-. "Orthodoxy and Heterodoxy in Muslim India," *Islam and the Modern Age,* Vol. 9, No. 4 and Vol. 10, No. 1. November 1978 and February 1979.

Fekrat, M. Ali. "Stress in the Islamic World," *Journal of South Asian and Middle Eastern Studies*, Vol. 4, No. 3. Spring 1981.

Ferdows, Adele. "Shariati and Khomeini on Women," in Nikki R. Keddie and Eric Hoogland, eds., *The Iranian Revolution and the Islamic Republic: Proceedings of a Conference*. Washington, D. C.: Middle East Institute in cooperation with Woodrow Wilson International Center for Scholars. 1982.

Fischer, Michael M. J. "Islam and the Revolt of the Petite Bourgeoisie," *Daedalus*, Vol. 111. Winter 1982.

Foote, Donna. "At Stake: The Freedom to Imagine," *Newsweek*, Vol. 113, No. 9. February 27, 1989.

Ford, Peter. "Israel and Hizbullah Trade Artillery Fire in Retaliatory Attacks," *The Christian Science Monitor*. February 18, 1992.

Friedman, Thomas. "Islamic Militants: Religion Is a Focus for Opposition to Mideast Regimes," *New York Times*. October 8, 1981.

Gage, Nicholas, "Stern Symbol of Opposition to the Shah: Ruhollah Khomeini," *New York Times*. December 11, 1978.

―――. "The Unknown Ayatullah Khomeini: The Portrait of the Islamic Mystic at the Center of the Revolution," *Time*, July 16, 1979.

Ghayur, Mohammad Arif, and Asaf, Hussain. "The Religio-Political Parties (JI, JUI, JUP): Role of the Ulema in Pakistan's Politics," paper presented at the New England Conference, Association for Asian Studies, held at the University of Connecticut, Storrs, Connecticut, October 20–21, 1979.

Gibb, H. A. R. "An Interpretation on Islamic History," *Journal of World History*, Vol. 1. 1953.

―――. "Structure of Religious Thought in Islam," *The Muslim World*, Vol. 38. 1948; article reprinted in S. J. Shaw and W. R. Polk, eds., *Studies on the Civilization of Islam*. Boston: Beacon Press, 1962.

―――. Cited in Donna Robinson Divine, "Islamic Culture and Political Practice in British Mandated Palestine, 1918–1948," *The Review of Politics*, Vol. 45, No. 1. January 1983.

Godsell, Geoffrey. "From Libya to Indonesia, the Muslim Belt's Crisis Points Are on Display—An Analysis," *The Christian Science Monitor*. December 2, 1979.

Grew, Raymond. "The Crises and Their Sequences," in Raymond Grew, ed., *Crises of Political Development in Europe and the United States*. Princeton: Princeton University Press. 1978.

Griffith, William E. "The Revival of Islamic Fundamentalism: The Case of Iran," *International Security*, Vol. 4. 1979.

Guiney, Errell. "The Power and the Peril: Growing Solidarity Centered on Anti-Americanism," *World Press Review*. February 1980.

Gwertzman, Bernard. "An Anxious Washington Studies the Fever in Islam," *New York Times*. December 9, 1979.

Haddad, Yvonne. "The Arab-Israeli Wars, Nasserism, and the Affirmation of Islamic Identity," in John L. Esposito, ed., *Islam and Development: Religion and Sociopolitical Change*. Syracuse, NY: Syracuse University Press. 1980.

Halliday, Fred. "Iran Chooses," *The Nation*. February 9, 1980.

Hanafi, Hassan. "The Relevance of the Islamic Alternative in Egypt," *Arab Studies Quarterly*, Vol. 4, Nos. 1 and 2. Spring 1982.

Hardy, Peter. "Traditional Muslim Views of the Nature of Politics," in C. H. Phillips, ed., *Politics and Society in India*. London: George Allen and Unwin. 1963.

Harley, Richard M. "Islam Is Not Reactionary, Experts Say," *The Christian Science Monitor*. March 27, 1979.

Hart, Jeffrey. "Three Approaches to the Measurement of Power in International Relations," *International Organization*, Vol. 30, No. 2. Spring 1976.

Hasanal-Masumi, M. S. "An Appreciation of Shah Waliyullah Al-Muhaddith Ad-Dihlawi," *Islamic Culture*, Vol. 22, No. 4. October 1947.

Helms, Christine Moss. "The Ikhwan: Badu Answer The Wahhabi 'Call to Unity,'" in Christine Moss Helms, *The Cohesion of Saudi Arabia: Evolution of Political Identity.* Baltimore: Johns Hopkins University Press. 1981.

Hermida, Alfred. "Algeria: Fundamentalists Sweep to Near Victory," *Middle East International.* January 10, 1992.

Hiro, Dilip. "Islamist Strengths and Weaknesses in Central Asia," *Middle East International*, No. 443. February 5, 1993.

Hoagland, Jim. "Choosing Camps," *The Washington Post Weekly Edition.* March 30–April 5, 1992.

Hodgkin, Thomas. "The Revolutionary Tradition in Islam," *Race and Class*, Vol. 21, No. 3. Winter 1980.

Hodgson, Marshall G. S. "The Role of Islam in World History," *International Journal of Middle Eastern Studies*, Vol. 1, No. 2. April 1970.

Hodson, H. V. "The New Third Force: A Global Rival of Communism and Democracy," *World Press Review.* June 1979.

Hopwood, Derek. "A Pattern of Revival Movements in Islam?" *The Islamic Quarterly*, Vol. 15, No. 4. October–December 1971.

Hughes, John. "Authors, Death Threats, and Islam," *The Christian Science Monitor.* February 22, 1989.

Humphreys, Steven. "The Contemporary Resurgence in the Context of Modern Islam," in A. E. H. Dessouki, ed., *Islamic Resurgence in the Arab World.* New York: Praeger Publishers. 1982.

———. "Islam and Political Values in Saudi Arabia, Egypt and Syria," in Michael Curtis, ed., *Religion and Politics in the Middle East.* Boulder, CO: Westview Press. 1981.

Huntington, Samuel P. "The Change to Change: Modernization, Development and Politics," *Comparative Politics*, No. 3. April 1971.

———. "Political Development and Political Decay," *World Politics*, Vol. 17. 1965.

——— , and Jorge I. Dominguez. "Political Development," in Fred Greenstein and Nelson Polsby, eds., *Handbook of Political Science: Macropolitical Theory*, Vol. 3. Reading, MA: Addison-Wesley Publishing Co. 1975.

Hurewitz, J. C. "The Persian Gulf: After Iran's Revolution," *Headline Series*, Monograph No. 244. April 1979.

Husain, Ahred. "A Myth of Legislative Supremacy in Pakistan, 1947–51," *Journal of History and Political Science*, Vol. 1, Lahore, Pakistan: Government College. 1971–1972.

Husain, Asaf. "Ethnicity, National Identity and Praetorianism: The Case of Pakistan," *Asian Survey*, Vol. 16. No. 10. October 1976.

Husain, Mir Zohair, "Ayatollah Ruhollah al-Musavi al-Khomeini," *The Search: Journal for Arab and Islamic Studies*, Vol. 7. Winter 1986.

———. "Hassan al-Banna: Founder of the Ikhwan al-Muslimin," *Islam and the Modern Age*, Vol. 17, No. 4. November 1986.

———. "Iqbal on the Islamic Agenda," *Journal of the Institute of Muslim Minority Affairs*, Vol. 7, No. 2. July 1986.

———. "Islam in Pakistan Under Bhutto and Zia-ul-Haq," in Hussin Mutalib and Taj ul-Islam Hashmi, eds., *Islam, Muslims and the Modern State: Case-Studies of Muslims in Thirteen Countries,* London: Macmillan Publishing Company and New York: St. Martin's Press, Inc., 1994.

————. "Maulana Abd al-Bari Farangi Mahalli: Scholar and Political Activist," *Pakistan Journal of History and Culture,* Vol. 7. No. 1. January–June 1986.

————. "Maulana Sayyid Abul A'la Maududi: Founder of the Fundamentalist Jammat-e-Islami," *South Asia: Journal of South Asian Studies,* Vol. 9, No. 1. June 1986.

————. "Muḥammad Abduh: The Pre-Eminent Muslim Modernist of Egypt," *Hamdard Islamicus,* Vol. 9, No. 3. Autumn 1986.

————. "Muslim Modernists: The Torch-Bearers of Progressive Islam," *The Islamic Quarterly,* Vol. 31, No. 3. 1987.

————. "The Prototypical Muslim Pragmatist and Unconventional Islamic Revivalist: Muhammad Ali Jinnah (1875–1949)," *Journal of the Pakistan Historical Society,* Vol. 36, Part 4. October 1988.

————. "Shah Waliullah Al-Dihlawi: The Indian Subcontinent's Most Revered Scholar," *The Journal of Religious Studies,* Vol. 14, No. 2. Autumn 1986.

————. "A Typology of Islamic Revivalists," in Sheikh R. Ali, ed., *The Third World at the Crossroads.* New York: Praeger Publishers. 1989.

Ibrahim, Saad Eddin. "Anatomy of Egypt's Militant Islamic Groups: Methodological Note and Preliminary Findings," *International Journal of Middle East Studies,* Vol. 12, No. 4. 1980.

————. "Egypt's Islamic Militants," *MERIP Reports,* No. 103. February 1982.

Ibrahim, Youssef M. "Khomeini Assails Western Response to Rushdie Affair," *New York Times.* February 22, 1989.

Ismael, J. S., and T. Y. Ismael. "Social Change in Islamic Society: The Political Thought of Ayatollah Khomeini," *Social Problems,* Vol. 27, No. 5. June 1980.

Israeli, Raphael. "Islam in Egypt Under Nasir and Sadat: Some Comparative Notes," in Metin Heper and Raphael Israel, eds., *Islam and Politics in the Modern Middle East.* New York: St. Martin's Press. 1984.

————. "The New Wave of Islam," *International Journal,* Vol. 34, No. 3. 1979.

Jansen, Godfrey. "Moslems and the Modern World," *The Economist.* January 3, 1981.

Kalaam, Abul. "Muslim Remain Communist Serfs," *The Message International,* Vol. 15, No. 5. October 1991.

Kaslow, Amy, and George D. Moffet III. "Pakistan Seeks Influential Role in Central Asia," *The Christian Science Monitor.* November 25, 1992.

Kaushik, Surendra Nath. "Aftermath of the March 1977 General Elections in Pakistan," *South Asian Studies,* Vol. 13, No. 1. January–July 1978.

Kaye, David. "Struggling with Independence: Central Asian Politics in the Post-Soviet World," *Middle East Insight,* Vol. 8, No. 6. July–October 1992.

Keddie, Nikki R. "Iran: Change in Islam; Islam and Change," *International Journal of Middle East Studies,* Vol. 11. 1980.

————. "The Revolt of Islam and Its Roots," in Dankwart A. Rustow and Kenneth Paul Erickson, eds., *Comparative Political Dynamics.* New York: HarperCollins Publishers. 1991.

Kédourie, Elie. "What's Baathism Anyway?" *Wall Street Journal.* October 17, 1990.

Khundmiri, S. Alam. "A Critical Examination of Islamic Traditionalism," *Islam and The Modern Age,* Vol. 2, No. 2. May 1971.

Knauerhase, Ramon. "The Oil Producing Middle East States," *Current History,* Vol. 76, No. 443. January 1979.

Kohan, John. "Five New Nations Ask Who Are We?" *Time,* Vol. 139, No. 17. April 27, 1992.

Koven, Ronald. "He Sees Answers to Iran's Plight in the Koran," *The Philadelphia Inquirer.* November 15, 1979.

Kramer, Martin. "The Ideals of an Islamic Order," *The Washington Quarterly*, Vol. 3, No. 1. Winter 1980.

———. "Political Islam," *The Washington Papers*, Vol. 8, No. 73. Beverly Hills: Sage Publications. 1980.

Kuttab, Daoud. "Emotions Take Over," *Middle East International*, No. 382. August 31, 1990.

———. "Forgotten Intifada," *Middle East International*, No. 383. September 14, 1990.

———. "The Palestinian Economy and the Gulf Crisis," *Middle East International*, No. 383. September 14, 1990.

———. "Worries About the Intifada," *Middle East International*, No. 402. June 14, 1991.

La Franchi, Howard. "Algeria's Leadership Chooses Head of Ruling Council," *The Christian Science Monitor*. January 16, 1992.

Lamb, David. "Islamic Fundamentalism: A Growing Force in the Mideast," *Current World Leaders: Biography and New/Speeches and Reports*, Vol. 26, No. 8/9. September 1983.

———. "Islamic Revival Grows, But Stays Largely Benign," *Philadelphia Inquirer*. February 19, 1984.

———. "Muslim Faithful Worldwide Preparing for Annual Pilgrimmage to Mecca," *Los Angeles Times*. August 19, 1984.

Lapidus, Ira M. "The Separation of State and Religion in the Development of Early Islamic Society," *International Journal of Middle East Studies*, Vol. 6, No. 4.

Lekhi, M. V. "Islamic State Controversy in Pakistan," *Political Science Review*, Vol. 6. 1967.

Lenczowski, George. "The Oil-Producing Countries," in Raymond Vernon, ed., *The Oil Crisis*. New York: W. W. Norton & Co. 1976.

Lerner, Daniel. "Toward a Communication Theory of Modernization," in Lucien W. Pye, ed., *Communications and Political Development*. Princeton: Princeton University Press. 1964.

Lerner, Eran. "Mawdudi's Concept of Islam," *Middle Eastern Studies*, Vol. 17, No. 4. October 1981.

Lesch, Ann Mosely. "Anatomy of an Uprising: The Palestinian Intifada," in Peter F. Krogh and Mary C. McDavid, eds., *Palestinians Under Occupation: Prospects for the Future*. Washington, D. C.: Georgetown University Press. 1989.

Lewis, Bernard. "Islamic Concepts of Revolution," in P. J. Vatikiotis, ed., *Revolution in the Middle East*. London: Oxford University Press. 1972.

———. "The Return of Islam," *Commentary*. January 1976.

———. "The Roots of Muslim Rage," *The Atlantic*, Vol. 266, No. 3. September 1990.

Low, Helen, and Howe Low. "Focus on the Fourth World," *The U. S. and World Development: Agenda for Action 1975*. New York: Praeger Publishers. 1975.

Lughod, Ibrahim Abu. "Retreat from the Secular Path? Islamic Dilemmas of Arab Politics," *The Review of Politics*, Vol. 28. October 1966.

Malik, Hafeez. "Islamic Political Parties and Mass Politicization," *Islam and the Modern Age*, Vol. 3, No. 2. May 1972.

———. "Islamic Theory of International Relations," *Journal of South Asia and Middle Eastern Studies*, Vol. 2, No. 3. Spring 1979.

Marshall, Susan E. "Islamic Revival in the Maghreb: The Utility of Tradition for Modernizing Elites," *Studies in Comparative International Development*, Vol. 14, No. 2. Summer 1979.

May, L. S. "Dr. Muhammad Iqbal: Islam and Muslim Nationhood," paper presented at conference on Pakistan at the Asia Society, New York, New York. June 2, 1979.

McNamara, Robert S. "The Population Problem," *Foreign Affairs*. Summer 1984.

Millward, William G. "Aspects of Modernism in Shi'ah Islam," *Studia Islamica*, Vol. 37. 1973.

Mohammed, Jan. "Introducing Islamic Laws in Pakistan—I," *Dawn*. July 15, 1983.

Monshipouri, Mahmood. "The Islamic World's Reaction to the Satanic Verses: Cultural Relativism Revisited," *Journal of Third World Studies*, Vol. 3, No. 1. Spring 1991.

Moore, R. J. "Jinnah and the Pakistan Demand," *Modern Asian Studies*, Vol. 17, No. 4. 1983.

Moorsteen, Richard. "Action Proposal: OPEC Can Wait—We Can't," *Foreign Policy*, Vol. 18. Spring 1975.

Morris, Joe Alex. "Across the Muslim World, a New Militancy Spreads," *Philadelphia Inquirer*. December 3, 1978.

Murphy, Caryle. "Islam's Crescent of Change," *The Washington Post National Weekly Edition*. May 25–31, 1992.

Muthalib, Hussin. "Confusion on Islam's Role in Malaysia," *Arabia*, No. 21. May 1983.

Muzaffar, Chandra. "Islamic Resurgence: A Global View," in Taufik Abdullah and Sharon Siddique, eds., *Islam and Society in Southeast Asia*. Singapore: Institute of Southeast Asian Studies. 1987.

Nait-Belkacem, Mouloud Kassim. "The Concept of Social Justice in Islam," in Altaf Gauhar, ed., *The Challenge of Islam*. London: Islamic Council of Europe. 1978.

Naqvi, M. B. "An Impossible Dream," *Newsline*, Vol. 3, No. 7. January 1992.

Naumkin, Vitaly. "Islam in the States of the Former USSR," *The Annals of the American Academy of Political and Social Science*, No. 524. November 1992.

Nawaz, M. K. "Some Aspects of Modernization of Islamic Law," in Carl Leiden, ed., *The Conflict of Traditionalism and Modernism in the Muslim Middle East*. Austin, TX: University of Texas Press. 1966.

Nizami, K. A. "Socio-Religious Movements in Indian Islam (1763–1898)," *Islamic Culture*, Vol. 44, No. 3. July 1970.

Nizami, Khaliq Ahmad. "Naqshbandi Influence on Mughal Rulers and Politics," *Islamic Culture*, Vol. 39, No. 1. January 1965.

——. "Shah Wali-Ullah Dehlavi and Indian Politics in the 18th Century," *Islamic Culture*, Vol. 25. January, April, July, and October 1951.

Noorani, A. G. "Human Rights in Islam," *Illustrated Weekly of India*. May 3, 1981.

Nye, Joseph S., and Robert O. Keohane. "Transnational Relations and World Politics: An Introduction," *International Organization*, Vol. 25. 1971.

Olcott, Martha Brill. "Central Asia's Catapult to Independence," *Foreign Affairs*, Vol. 17, No. 3. Summer 1992.

——. "Soviet Central Asia: Does Moscow Fear Iranian Influence?" in John L. Esposito, ed., *The Iranian Revolution: Its Global Impact*. Miami: Florida International University Press. 1990.

Onaran, Yalman. "Transition Proves Hard for Ex-Soviet Republics," *The Christian Science Monitor*. November 18, 1992.

Osman, Fathi. "Ayatullah Khomeini: A Genuine 'Alim-Leader' in the Contemporary World," *The Minaret*, Vol. 10, No. 3. Summer 1989.

——. "The Life and Works of Abu al-A'la al-Mawdudi," *Arabia*, Vol. 4, No. 40. December 1984.

Palmer, Norman D. "Changing Patterns of Politics in Pakistan: An Overview," in Manzooruddin Ahmad, ed., *Contemporary Pakistan: Politics, Economy, and Society*. Durham, NC: Carolina Academic Press. 1980.

Pasha, Mustapha Kamal. "Muslim Militancy and Self-Reliance—1, 2, 3," *The Muslim* (Karachi). April 18–20, 1982.

Paul, Jim. "Insurrection at Mecca," *MERIP Reports,* No. 91. October 1980.

Pipes, Daniel. "This World Is Political: The Islamic Revival of the Seventies," *Orbis,* Vol. 24, No. 1. Spring 1980.

Piscatori, James P. "Ideological Politics in Saudi Arabia," in James P. Piscatori, ed., *Islam and the Political Process.* Cambridge: Cambridge University Press. 1983.

Qureishi, M. Naeem. "The Ulama of British India and the Hijrat of 1920," *Modern Asian Studies,* Vol. 13, No. 1. 1979.

Rahbar, Muhammad Daud. "Shah Wali Ullah and Ijtihad," *The Muslim World,* Vol. 45, No. 4. October 1955.

Rahman, Fazlur. "Currents of Religious Thought in Pakistan," *Islamic Studies,* Vol. 7, No. 1. March 1968.

———. "Islam and the New Constitution of Pakistan," *Journal of African and Asian Studies,* Vol. 8. 1973.

———. "Islam: Legacy and Contemporary Challenge," *Islamic Studies,* Vol. 19. Winter 1980.

———. "Islamic Modernism: Its Scope, Method and Alternative," *The Journal of Middle East Studies,* Vol. 1. 1970.

———. "The Thinker of Crisis: Shah Waliy-Ullah," *Pakistan Quarterly,* Vol. 6, No. 2. Summer 1956.

Rana, Mohammed. "The Concept of State in Islam," *The Law Journal* (Pakistan), Vol. 40, No. 1. 1978.

Randal, Jonathan C. "Bani-Sadr: Advocate of Iranian Independence," *The Washington Post.* November 26, 1979.

Rashid, Jamil. "The Political Economy of Manpower Export," in Hassan Gardezi and Jamil Rashid, eds., *Pakistan, the Roots of Dictatorship: The Political Economy of a Praetorian State.* London: Zed Press. 1983.

Rehman, Hamood-ur. "The Concept of Justice in Islam," *Pakistan Administration,* Vol. 16, No. 2. July–December 1979.

Richter, William L. "Pakistan," in Mohammed Ayoob, *The Politics of Islamic Reassertion.* New York: St. Martin's Press. 1981.

———. "Pakistan: Impasse, Islamic Revolution, and Impending Crisis," *Asian Thought and Society,* Vol. 4, No. 10. April 1979.

———. "Pakistan Under Zia," *Current History,* Vol. 76. April 1979.

———. "Persistent Praetorianism: Pakistan's Third Martial Law Regime," *Pacific Affairs,* Vol. 51, No. 3. Fall 1978.

———. "The Political Dynamics of Islamic Resurgence in Pakistan," *Asian Survey,* Vol. 19, No. 6. June 1979.

Robinson, Francis. "Studies of Islam," *Modern Asian Studies,* Vol. 12, No. 1. 1979.

———. "The Ulama of Farangi Mahall and Their Adab," in Barbara Daly Metcalf, ed., *Moral Conduct and Authority: The Place of Adab in South Asian Islam.* Berkeley, CA: University of California Press. 1984.

———. "The Veneration of Teachers in Islam by Their Pupils: Its Modern Significance," *History Today,* Vol. 30. March 1980.

Rouleau, Eric. "Who Killed Sadat?" *MERIP Reports,* No. 103. February 1982.

Sachedina, Abdulaziz. "Ali Shariati: Ideologue of the Iranian Revolution," in John Esposito, ed., *Voices of Resurgent Islam.* Oxford and New York: Oxford University Press. 1983.

Said, Edward W. "Islam Rising," *Columbia Journalism Review.* March/April 1980.

———. "Islam Through Western Eyes," *The Nation.* April 26, 1980.

Said, Hakim Mohammed. "Enforcement of Islamic Laws in Pakistan," *Hamdard Islamicus,* Vol. 2, No. 2. Summer 1979.

Saleem, Elie. "Nationalism and Islam," *The Muslim World,* Vol. 52. 1962.

Sardar, Ziauddin. "The Greatest Gathering of Mankind," *Inquiry,* Vol. 1, No. 4. September 1984.

Sareen, Rajendra. "Political Scene in Pakistan," *The Institute for Defense Studies Analysis Journal,* Vol. 13, No. 2. October–December 1980.

Sayeed, Khalid Bin. "How Radical Is the Pakistan People's Party?" *Pacific Affairs,* Vol. 48. Spring 1975.

———. "The Jama'at-i-Islami Movement in Pakistan," *Pacific Affairs,* Vol. 30. No. 1. March 1957.

———. "Religion and Nation-Building in Pakistan," *Middle East Journal,* Vol. 17. 1963.

Schwartz, Tony. "Apparent Victor in Iran's Voting: Abolhassan Bani-Sadr," *The New York Times.* January 28, 1980.

Sciolino, Elaine. "Iran's Durable Revolution," *Foreign Affairs,* Vol. 61, No. 4. 1983.

Shah, Mowahid H. "Modernity Is Not What Muslims Resent," *The Christian Science Monitor.* January 22, 1980.

Shahi, Agha. "Roots of Islamic Reassertion," *The Muslim* (Karachi). July 1984.

Sharabi, Hisham. "Islam and Modernization in the Arab World," *Journal of International Affairs,* Vol. 19, No. 1. 1965.

Sherani, Rais-ud-Din Khan. "Muhammad: The Greatest Law-Giver and An Epitome of Justice and Compassion," *Hamdard Islamicus,* Vol. 12, No. 4. Winter 1989.

Siddiqi, Mohammad Suleman. "The Concept of Hudud and Its Significance," in Anwar Moazzam, ed., *Islam and Contemporary Muslim World.* New Delhi: Light and Life Publishers. 1981.

Siegman, Henry. "The State and the Individual in Sunni Islam," *The Muslim World,* Vol. 54, No. 1. January 1964.

Sivan, Emmanuel. "How Fares Islam?" *The Jerusalem Quarterly,* Vol. 13. Fall 1979.

———. "The Two Faces of Islamic Fundamentalism," *The Jerusalem Quarterly,* Vol. 27. Spring 1983.

Smith, Donald Eugene. "Emerging Patterns of Religion and Politics," in Donald Eugene Smith, ed., *South Asian Politics and Religion.* Princeton, NJ: Princeton University Press. 1966.

———. "The Politics of Islamic Resurgence," *Almanac* [University of Pennsylvania, Philadelphia, Pennsylvania], Vol. 27, No. 6. September 30, 1980.

———. "Secularization in Bangladesh," *World View.* April 1973.

Sneider, Daniel. "Critics Wary of Russian Army's Role in Republics," *The Christian Science Monitor.* October 2, 1992.

———. "A Russian Movement Rejects Western Tilt," *The Christian Science Monitor.* February 5, 1993.

———. "Russia's 'Peacekeeping' Raises Issue of Neutrality," *The Christian Science Monitor.* September 14, 1992.

———. "Uzbek Opposition Asserts Government Increases Repression," *The Christian Science Monitor.* October 2, 1992.

Springborg, Robert. "Islamic Revivalism in the Middle East," *Current Affairs Bulletin,* Vol. 56, No. 1. June 1979.

———. "On the Rise and Fall of Arab Isms," *Australian Outlook,* Vol. 31, No. 1. April 1977.

———. "The Politics of Resurgent Islam in Egypt, Syria, and Iraq," in Mohammed Ayoob, ed., *The Politics of Islamic Reassertion.* New York: St. Martin's Press. 1981.

Stephens, Robert. "Gift of God and Scourge of the Shah," *The Observer,* January 21, 1979.

Syed, Anwar Husain. "Was Pakistan to Be an Islamic State? Iqbal, Jinnah, and the Issues of Nationhood and Nationalism in Pakistan," *The Indian Review*, Vol. 1, No. 1. Autumn 1978.

Szliowicz, Joseph A. "The Embargo and U. S. Foreign Policy," in Joseph A. Szliowicz and Bard E. O'Neil, eds., *The Energy Crisis and U. S. Foreign Policy.* New York: Praeger Publishers. 1975.

Tabatabai, Shanin. "Women in Islam," *Islamic Revolution,* No. 1. 1979.

Taraki, Lisa. "The Islamic Resistance Movement in the Palestinian Uprising," *Middle East Report,* Vol. 19, No. 1. January–February 1989.

Tefft, Sheila. "Muslims Debate Rushdie Uproar," *The Christian Science Monitor.* February 27, 1989.

Tehranian, Majid. "Iran: Communication Alienation and Revolution," *Monthly Public Opinion Survey,* Vol. 24, No. 67. March–April 1979.

Temko, Ned. "Behind Islamic Ferment Is Anger Over Lowly Status," *The Christian Science Monitor.* December 18, 1979.

Tinnin, David B. "The Saudis Awaken to Their Vulnerability," *Fortune.* March 10, 1980.

Voll, John O. "The Islamic Past and the Present Resurgence," *Current History,* Vol. 456. April 1980.

———. "The Sudanese Mahdi: Frontier Fundamentalist," *International Journal of Middle East Studies,* Vol. 10, No. 2. May 1979.

von England, Claude. "Iran's Divided Exiles Struggle to Be Heard," *The Christian Science Monitor.* April 27, 1984.

Wafi, Ali Abdel Wahid. "Human Rights in Islam," *The Islamic Quarterly,* Vol. 11, Nos. 1 and 2. January–June 1967.

Waterbury, John. "Egypt: Islam and Social Change," in Philip H. Stoddard, David C. Cuthell, and Margaret W. Sullivan, eds., *Change and the Muslim World.* Syracuse, NY: Syracuse University Press. 1981.

Watson, Russel. "Across the Line, Israel Hits Hizbullah," *Newsweek,* Vol. 119, No. 9. March 2, 1992.

———. "A Satanic Fury," *Newsweek,* Vol. 113, No. 9. February 27, 1989.

Weber, Theresa F. "Tajikistan's Troubles Could Embroil Others," *The Christian Science Monitor.* October 9, 1992.

Weinbaum, M. G., and Gautam Sen. "Pakistan Enters the Middle East," *Orbis,* Vol. 22, No. 3. Fall 1978.

Weiner, Myron. "Political Participation: Crisis of the Political Process," in Leonard Binder et al., eds., *Crises and Sequences in Political Development.* Princeton: Princeton University Press. 1971.

Weiss, Anita M. "The Historical Debate on Islam and the State in South Asia," in Anita M. Weiss, *Islamic Reassertion in Pakistan: The Application of Islamic Laws in a Modern State.* Syracuse, NY: Syracuse University Press. 1986.

Westwood, Andrew F. "The Problems of Westernization in Modern Iran," *Middle East Journal,* Vol. 2. January 1948.

Woollacott, Martin. "Coming to Power: Theocracy Envelopes New Urban Masses," *World Press Review.* February 1980.

Young, Oran. "Interdependence in World Politics," *International Journal,* Vol. 24. Autumn 1969.

Ziring, Lawrence. "Pakistan and Bangladesh: Quest for Identity," in C. I. Eugene Kim and Lawrence Ziring, eds., *An Introduction to Asian Politics.* Englewood Cliffs, NJ: Prentice-Hall. 1977.

Zogby, James J. "The Strategic Peace Initiative Package: A New Approach to Israeli-Palestinian Peace," *American Arab Affairs*, No. 35. Winter 1990–1991.

BOOKS

Abbott, Freeland K. *Islam and Pakistan*. Ithaca, NY: Cornell University Press. 1968.

Adams, Charles C. *Islam and Modernism in Egypt: A Study of the Modern Reform Movement Inaugurated by Muhammad Abduh*. New York: Russel & Russel. 1933, reissued 1968.

Ahmad, Aziz. *Islamic Modernism in India and Pakistan 1857–1964*. London: Oxford University Press. 1967.

Ahmad, Jamil-ud-Din, ed. *Speeches and Writings of Mr. Jinnah*. Lahore, Pakistan: Shaikh Muhammad Ashraf. 1960.

Ajami, Fouad. *The Arab Predicament: Arab Political Thought and Practice Since 1967*. Cambridge: Cambridge University Press. 1981.

Akhtar, Rafiq, ed., *Pakistan Year Book*. Karachi, Pakistan: East-West Publishing Company. 1974.

al-Ahsan, Abdullah. *OIC: The Organization of the Islamic Conference*. Islamization of Knowledge Series. Herndon, VA: International Institute of Islamic Thought. 1988.

al-Mujahid, Sharif. *Quaid-e-Azam Jinnah: Studies in Interpretation*. Karachi, Pakistan: Quaid-i-Azam Academy. 1981.

Algar, Hamid. *The Roots of the Islamic Revolution*. Markham, Ontario: The Open Press. 1983.

Ali, Ameer. *The Spirit of Islam: A History of the Evolution of Islam with a Life of the Prophet*. London: Christophers, 1922. Reprint. London: Methuen & Co. Ltd. 1967.

Ali, Michael Nazir. *Islam: A Christian Perspective*. Exeter, England: The Paternoster Press. 1983.

Anderson, Roy R., Robert F. Seibert, and Jon G. Wagner. *Politics and Change in the Middle East: Sources of Conflict and Accommodation*, 3rd ed. Englewood Cliffs, NJ: Prentice-Hall. 1990.

Arberry, A. J. trans. *The Koran Interpreted*. New York: Macmillan Publishing Co. 1955.

Azam, Ikram. *Pakistan and the Nationalities Notion*. Lahore, Pakistan: Amir Publications. 1980.

Badawi, M. A. Zaki. *The Reformers of Egypt*. London: Croom Helm. 1978.

Baig, M. R. *The Muslim Dilemma in India*. New Delhi: Vikas Publishing House. 1974.

Bakhash, Shaul. *The Reign of the Ayatollahs: Iran and the Islamic Revolution*, 2nd ed. New York: Basic Books. 1990.

Barnds, William. *India, Pakistan and the Great Powers*. New York: Praeger Publishers. 1972.

Beg, Aziz. *The Quiet Revolution: A Factual Story of Political Betrayal in Pakistan*. Karachi, Pakistan: Pakistan Patriotic Publications. 1959.

Bhutto, Zulfikar Ali. *Awakening the People: A Collection of Articles Statements and Speeches, 1966–69*, in Hamid Jalal and Khalid Hasan, eds., *Politics of the People*, Vol. 1, No. 2. Rawalpindi, Pakistan: Pakistan Publications. 1972.

———. *If I Am Assassinated*. New Delhi: Vikas Publishing House. 1979.

———. *A Journey of Renaissance*. Islamabad, Pakistan: Ministry of Information, Government of Pakistan. November 1972.

———. *Marching Towards Democracy: A Collection of Articles, Statements and Speeches 1970–71,* Vol. 3, edited by Hamid Jalal and Khalid Hasan. Rawalpindi, Pakistan: Pakistan Publications. 1972.

———. *My Execution.* London: Musawat Weekly International. January 1980.

Bill, James A., and Carl Leiden. *Politics in the Middle East,* 2nd ed. Boston: Little, Brown and Company. 1984.

Bill, James A., and Robert Springborg. *Politics in the Middle East,* 3rd ed. Glenview, IL: Scott, Foresman and Company. 1990.

Binder, Leonard. *Religion and Politics in Pakistan.* Berkeley, CA: University of California Press. 1963.

Bolitho, Hector. *Jinnah: Creator of Pakistan.* London: John Murray Publishers. 1954.

Burke, S. M. *Pakistan's Foreign Policy: An Historical Analysis.* London: Oxford University Press. 1973.

Burns, E. Bradford. *Latin America: A Concise Interpretive History,* 5th ed. Englewood Cliffs, NJ: Prentice-Hall. 1990.

———. *The Poverty of Progress: Latin America in the Nineteenth-Century.* Berkeley and Los Angeles: University of California Press. 1983.

Chopra, Pran, ed. *Role of the Indian Muslims in the Struggle for Freedom.* New Delhi: Light and Life Publishers. 1979.

Dar, Bashir Ahmad. *Religious Thought of Sayyid Ahmad Khan.* Lahore, Pakistan: Shaikh Muhammad Ashraf. 1957.

Davies, James Chowning, ed. *When Men Revolt and Why: A Reader in Political Violence and Revolution.* New York: Free Press. 1971.

Dawood, N. J. *The Koran,* 4th ed., trans. with notes. Baltimore: Penguin Books. 1974.

Dessouki, Ali E. H., ed. *Islamic Resurgence in the Arab World.* New York: Praeger Publishers. 1982.

Deutsch, Karl W., Jorge I. Dominguez, and Hugo Heclo. *Comparative Government: Politics of Industrialized and Developing Nations.* Boston: Houghton Mifflin. 1982.

Dorman, William A., and Mansour Farhang. *The U. S. Press and Iran: Foreign Policy and the Journalism of Deference.* Berkeley, CA: University of California Press. 1987.

Dunnigan, James F., and Austin Bay. *A Quick & Dirty Guide to War: Briefings on Present and Potential Wars,* rev. ed. New York: William Morrow and Co./Quill. 1991.

Endress, Gerard. *An Introduction to Islam,* trans. Carole Hillenbrand. New York: Columbia University Press. 1988.

Esposito, John L., ed. *The Iranian Revolution: Its Global Impact.* Miami: Florida International University Press. 1990.

———. *Islam and Politics.* Syracuse, NY: Syracuse University Press. 1984.

———. *The Islamic Threat: Myth or Reality.* Oxford: Oxford University Press. 1992.

Farhang, Mansour. *U. S. Imperialism: The Spanish-American War to the Iranian Revolution.* Boston: South End Press. 1981.

Faruqi, Ziya-ul-Hasan. *The Deoband School and the Demand for Pakistan.* Bombay: Asia Publishing House. 1963.

Folkertsma, Marvin J., Jr. *Ideology and Leadership.* Englewood Cliffs, NJ: Prentice-Hall. 1988.

Foster, Richard H., and Robert V. Edington. *Viewing International Relations and World Politics.* Englewood Cliffs, NJ: Prentice-Hall. 1985.

Frankel, Joseph. *Contemporary International Theory and the Behavior of States.* London: Oxford University Press. 1973.

Germanus, Julius. *Modern Movements in the World of Islam.* Lahore, Pakistan: al-Biruni. Reprinted 1978.

Gibb, H. A. R., and J. H. Kramers. *Shorter Encyclopedia of Islam*. Leiden, Netherlands: E. J. Brill. 1974.

Goldschmidt, Arthur, Jr. *A Concise History of the Middle East*, 4th ed. Boulder, CO: Westview Press. 1991.

Goldzihar, Ignaz. *Introduction to Islamic Theology and Law*, trans. Andras and Ruth Hamori. Princeton: Princeton University Press. 1981.

Gopinath, Meenakshi. *Pakistan in Transition: Political Development and Rise to Power of the Pakistan People's Party*. New Delhi: Manohar Book Service. 1975.

Gurr, Ted R. *Why Men Rebel*. Princeton: Princeton University Press. 1970.

Haddad, Yvonne Yazbeck. *Contemporary Islam and the Challenge of History*. Albany, NY: State University of New York Press. 1982.

Hague, Rod, Martin Harrop, and Shaun Breslin. *Political Science: A Comparative Introduction*. New York: St. Martin's Press. 1992.

Haq, Mahmudul. *Muhammad Abduh: A Study of a Modern Thinker of Egypt*. Aligarh, India: Institute of Islamic Studies, Aligarh Muslim University. 1978.

Hart, Alan. *Arafat: A Political Biography*. Bloomington and Indianapolis, IN: Indiana University Press. 1989.

Hassan, Masud-ul-. *Life of Iqbal*, Vol. 2. Lahore, Pakistan: Ferozsons Ltd. 1978.

Holt, P. M. *The Mahdist State in the Sudan 1881–1898: A Study of its Origins, Development and Overthrow*, 2nd ed. rev. Oxford: Clarendon Press. 1970.

Hourani, Albert. *Arabic Thought in the Liberal Age, 1798–1939*. London: Oxford University Press. 1962, reprinted 1970.

Hughes, William, ed. *Western Civilization: Pre-History Through the Reformation*, Vol. 1, 4th ed. Guilford, CT: The Dushkin Publishing Group Inc. 1987.

Husain, Akbar. *The Revolution in Iran*. East Sussex, England: Wayland Publishers Ltd. 1986.

Husaini, Ishak Musa. *The Brethren: The Greatest Modern Islamic Movements*. Beirut, Lebanon: Khayat College Book Cooperative. 1956.

Hussain, Riaz. *The Politics of Iqbal: A Study of his Political Thoughts and Actions*. Lahore, Pakistan: Islamic Book Services. 1977.

Ikram, S. M. *Modern Muslim India and the Birth of Pakistan (1858–1951)*, 2nd rev. ed. Lahore, Pakistan: Shaikh Muhammad Ashraf. 1970.

Iqbal, Allama Muhammad. *The Reconstruction of Religious Thought in Islam*. London. 1934. Reprinted Lahore, Pakistan: Shaikh Muhammad Ashraf. 1962 and 1977.

Jansen, G. H. *Militant Islam*. New York: Harper & Row Publishers. 1979.

Johnson, Nels. *Islam and the Politics of Meaning in Palestinian Nationalism*. London: Kegan Paul International Ltd. 1982.

Jones, Walter S. *The Logic of International Relations*, 7th ed. New York: HarperCollins Publishers Inc. 1991.

Keddie, Nikki R. *An Islamic Response to Imperialism: Political and Religious Writings of Sayyid Jamal ad-Din "al-Afghani."* Berkeley, CA: University of California Press. 1983.

———. *Roots of Revolution: An Interpretive History of Modern Iran*. New Haven: Yale University Press. 1981.

———. *Sayyid Jamal ad-Din al-Afghani: A Political Biography*. Berkeley, CA: University of California Press. 1972.

Khadduri, Majid. *The Islamic Conception of Justice*. Baltimore: Johns Hopkins University Press. 1984.

Khan, Muin-ud-Din Ahmad. *Muslim Struggle for Freedom in Bengal: From Plassey to Pakistan, 1757–1947*, 2nd ed. Dacca, Bangladesh: Islamic Foundation Bangladesh. 1982.

Khazen, Jihad B. *The Sadat Assassination: Background and Implications*. Monograph, Georgetown University's Center for Contemporary Arab Studies, Washington, DC. November 1981.

Khomeini, Ayatollah Ruhollah. *Islamic Government.* Trans. Joint Publications Research Service. New York: Manor Books, Inc. 1979.

———. *Islam and Revolution: Writings and Declarations of Imam Khomeini.* Trans. and annotated by Hamid Algar. Berkeley, CA: Mizan Press. 1981.

Kubbah, Abdul. *OPEC: Past and Present.* Vienna, Austria: Retro Economic Research Center. 1974.

Kurian, George Thomas. *Encyclopedia of the Third World,* 3rd ed. Facts on File Inc. 1987.

Lacey, Robert. *The Kingdom: Arabia & The House of Saud.* New York: Avon Books. 1981.

Lasswell, Harold, and Abraham Kaplan. *Power and Society.* New Haven: Yale University Press. 1950.

Lenczowski, George. *American Presidents and the Middle East.* Durham, NC: Duke University Press. 1990.

Lippman, Thomas W. *Egypt After Nasser: Sadat, Peace and the Mirage of Prosperity.* New York: Paragon House. 1989.

Macridis, Roy C. *Contemporary Political Ideologies,* 5th ed. New York: HarperCollins Publishers. 1992.

Mahmood, Safdar. *A Political Study of Pakistan.* Lahore, Pakistan: Shaikh Muhammad Ashraf. 1972.

Mahmood, Safdar and Javaid Zafar. *Founders of Pakistan.* Lahore, Pakistan: Publishers United Ltd. 1968.

Mahmud, Y. Zahid. *The Meaning of the Quran,* 5th ed. Beirut: Dar al-Choura. 1980.

Malik, Hafeez. *Moslem Nationalism in India and Pakistan.* Washington, DC: Public Affairs Press. 1963.

———. *Sir Sayed Ahmad Khan and Muslim Modernism in India and Pakistan.* New York: Columbia University Press. 1980.

Maududi, Abul A'la. *Islamic Law and Constitution,* 6th ed., trans. and ed., Khurshid Ahmad. Lahore, Pakistan: Islamic Publications Ltd. 1977.

———. *A Short History of the Revivalist Movement in Islam,* 3rd ed., trans. Al-Ashari. Lahore: Islamic Publications. 1976.

———. *Nationalism and India,* 2nd ed. Pathankot, India: Maktaba-e-Jamaat-e-Islami. 1948.

Mazrui, Ali. *The Satanic Verses or a Satanic Novel? The Moral Dilemmas of the Rushdie Affair.* Greenpoint, NY: The Committee of Muslim Scholars and Leaders of North America. 1989.

Metcalf, Barbara Daly. *Islamic Revival in British India: Deoband, 1860–1900.* Princeton: Princeton University Press. 1982.

Minault, Gail. *The Khilafat Movement: Religious Symbolism and Political Mobilization in India.* London: Oxford University Press. 1983.

Mitchell, Richard. *The Society of the Muslim Brothers.* London: Oxford University Press. 1969.

Moon, P. *Divide and Quit.* Berkeley, CA: University of California Press. 1962.

Morgan, Patrick M. *Theories and Approaches to International Politics: What Are We to Think?* 3rd ed. New Brunswick, NJ: Transaction Books, Inc. 1981.

Mortimer, Edward. *Faith and Power: The Politics of Islam.* New York: Vintage Books. 1982.

Mostyn, Trevor, ed. *The Cambridge Encyclopedia of the Middle East and North Africa.* New York: Cambridge University Press. 1988.

Mukerjee, Dilip. *Zulfikar Ali Bhutto: Quest for Power.* New Delhi: Vikas Publishing House. 1972.

Muztar, A. D. *Shah Waliullah: A Saint-Scholar of Muslim India.* Islamabad, Pakistan: National Commission on Historical and Cultural Research. 1979.

Naidu, Sarojini, ed. *Mahomed Ali Jinnah: An Ambassador of Unity.* Madras: Ganesh. 1918.

Naim, C. M., ed. *Iqbal, Jinnah and Pakistan: The Vision and the Reality.* Syracuse, NY: Syracuse University Press. 1979.

Nardo, Don. *The Persian Gulf War.* San Diego: Lucent Books. 1991.

Nima, Ramy. *The Wrath of Allah: Islamic Revolution and Reaction in Iran.* London: Pluto Press. 1983.

Norton, Augustus Richard. *Amal and the Shi'a: Struggle for the Soul of Lebanon.* Austin, TX: University of Texas Press. 1987.

Palmer, Monte, and William R. Thompson. *The Comparative Analysis of Politics.* Itasca, IL: F. E. Peacock Publishers, Inc. 1978.

Perry, Glenn E. *The Middle East: Fourteen Islamic Centuries.* Englewood Cliffs, NJ: Prentice-Hall. 1983.

Pickthall, Mohammed Marmaduke. *The Meaning of the Glorious Koran.* New York: Mentor Books. 1953.

Pirzada, Syed Sharifuddin, ed. *Foundations of Pakistan All-India Muslim League Documents,* Vol. 2 (1924–1947). Karachi, Pakistan: National Publishing House. 1969.

Poliakov, Sergei P., ed. *Everyday Islam.* Armonk, NY: M. E. Sharpe. 1992.

Polmar, Norman, ed. *CNN War in the Gulf.* Atlanta: Turner Publishing, Inc. 1991.

Pullapilly, Cyriac K., ed. *Islam in the Contemporary World.* Notre Dame, IN: Cross Roads Books. 1980.

Pye, Lucien W. *Aspects of Political Development.* Boston: Little, Brown and Co. 1966.

——— and Sidney Verba. *Political Cultural and Political Development.* Princeton: Princeton University Press. 1965.

Rahman, Fazlur. *Islam,* 2nd ed. Chicago: University of Chicago Press. 1979.

Ralph, Philip Lee, Robert E. Lerner, Standish Meacham, and Edward McNall Burns. *World Civilizations: Their History and Their Culture,* Vol. 2, 8th ed. New York: W. W. Norton & Co. 1991.

Regan, Geoffrey. *Israel and the Arabs.* Cambridge: Cambridge University Press. 1984.

Reich, Bernard, ed. *Political Leaders of the Contemporary Middle East and North Africa: A Biographical Dictionary.* New York: Greenwood Press. 1991.

Roberts, D. S. *Islam: A Concise Introduction.* San Francisco: Harper & Row Publishers. 1981.

Robinson, Francis. *Separatism Among Indian Muslims: The Politics of the United Provinces' Muslims 1860–1923.* Cambridge: Cambridge University Press. 1974.

Rosenau, James N., ed. *Linkage Politics.* New York: Free Press. 1969.

Russet, Bruce and Harvey Starr. *World Politics: The Menu for Choice,* 4th ed. New York: W. H. Freeman and Company. 1992.

Rywkin, Michael. *Moscow's Muslim Challenge: Soviet Central Asia,* rev. ed. Armonk, NY: M. E. Sharpe. 1990.

Sahliyeh, Emile. *In Search of Leadership: West Bank Politics Since 1967.* Washington, DC: The Brookings Institution. 1988.

Sayeed, Khalid Bin. *Pakistan: The Formative Phase.* Karachi, Pakistan: Pakistan Publishing House. 1960.

Schulzinger, Robert D. *American Diplomacy in the Twentieth Century.* Oxford: Oxford University Press. 1984.

Shariati, Ali. *Fatima Is Fatima,* trans. Laleh Bakhtiar. Tehran: The Shariati Foundation and Hamadami Publishers. 1980.

———. *On the Sociology of Islam,* trans. Hamid Algar. Berkeley, CA: Mizan Press. 1979.

———. *We and Iqbal.* Tehran: Husainiyeh Irshad. 1979.

Sheikh, Nazir Ahmad. *Quaid-e-Azam: Father of the Nation.* Lahore, Pakistan: Qaumi Kutub Khana. 1968.

Shimoni, Yaacov. *Biographical Dictionary of the Middle East.* New York: Facts on File. 1991.

Siddiqui, Kalim, Iqbal Asaria, Abd Al-Rahim Ali, and Ali Afrouz. *The Islamic Revolution: Achievements, Obstacles and Goals.* Toronto: Crescent International. 1980.

Smith, Donald Eugene. *Religion and Political Development.* Boston: Little, Brown and Co. 1970.

———, ed. *Religion, Politics and Social Change in the Third World: A Sourcebook.* New York: The Free Press. 1971.

———, ed. *Religion and Political Modernization.* New Haven: Yale University Press. 1974.

Smith, Wilfred Cantwell. *Islam in Modern History.* New York: Mentor Books. 1957.

Stoddard, Philip H., David C. Cuthell, and Margaret W. Syllivan, eds. *Change and the Muslim World.* Syracuse, NY: Syracuse University Press. 1981.

Strayer, Robert W., Edwin Hirschman, Robert B. Marks, and Robert J. Smith. *The Making of the Modern World: Connected Histories, Divergent Paths (1500 to the Present).* New York: St. Martin's Press. 1989.

Syed, A. H. *Pakistan: Islam, Politics and National Solidarity.* New York: Praeger Publishers. 1982.

Tahir-Kheli, Shirin. *The United States and Pakistan: The Evolution of an Influence Relationship.* New York: Praeger Publishers. 1982.

Taseer, Salman. *Bhutto: A Political Biography.* London: Ithica Press. 1979.

Toprak, Binnaz. *Islam and Political Development in Turkey.* Leiden, The Netherlands: E. J. Brill. 1981.

Voll, John Obert. *Islam: Continuity and Change in the Modern World.* Boulder, CO: Westview Press. 1982.

Waltz, Kenneth. *Theory of International Politics.* Reading, MA: Addison-Wesley Publishing Co. 1979.

Watt, W. Montgomery. *Muhammad in Medina.* Oxford: Clarendon Press. 1968.

Weiss, Anita M. *Islamic Reassertion in Pakistan: The Application of Islamic Laws in a Modern State.* Syracuse, NY: Syracuse University Press. 1986.

Weissman, Steve, and Herbert Krosney. *The Islamic Bomb: The Nuclear Threat to Israel and the Middle East.* New York: Times Books. 1981.

Wingate, F. R. *Mahdism and the Egyptian Sudan,* 2nd ed. London: Frank Cass and Co. 1968.

Winter, Herbert, and Thomas Bellows. *People and Politics.* New York: Wiley. 1977.

Wolpert, Stanley. *Jinnah of Pakistan.* London: Oxford University Press. 1984.

———. *Roots of Confrontation in South Asia.* Oxford: Oxford University Press. 1982.

Zakaria, Rafiq. *Muhammad and the Quran.* New York: Penguin Books. 1991.

Ziadeh, Nicola A. *Sanusiyah: A Study of a Revivalist Movement in Islam.* Leiden, The Netherlands: E. J. Brill. 1958.

Ziring, Lawrence, *The Middle East: A Political Dictionary.* Santa Barbara, CA: ABC-CLIO. 1992.

Ziring, Lawrence, Ralph Braibanti, and W. Howard Wriggins, eds. *Pakistan: The Long View.* Durham, NC: Duke University Press. 1977.

Index

Abduh, Muhammad, 97, 98, 99–102, 107,
110–111, 157, 238
Abdul Bari, Qayam-ud-Din Muhammad,
84, 88–90, 92, 157
Abdurasakov, Ubaidullah, 262
Abid, Haji Muhammad, 81–83
Abu Bakr, 7, 61, 209
Abu Dhar al-Ghaffari, 34, 109
Abu Hanifa, 91
Adaptationists. *See* Modernist revivalists
al-Afghani, Sayyid Jamal ad-Din, 96–101,
105, 107, 109, 110, 112–113, 157
Afghanistan, 3, 23, 30, 252–253, 259, 266
in former Soviet republics, 24
Indian Muslims in, 90
Soviet invasion of, 17–18, 215
Afro-Asian Solidarity Conference, 137
Ahmad, Mirza Bashir al-Din Mahmud, 131
Ahmad, Mirza Ghulam, 131
Ahmad, Mohsenuddin (Dadu Mian),
49–50, 157
Ahmadis, 131–132
Akbar, Jalal-ud-din Muhammad, Moghul
emperor, 65
Algeria, 3
developmental crises in, 175
Islamic Fundamentalism in, 75–76
Islamic Salvation Front (FIS), 1, 23, 175
Ali, Maulvi Muhammad, 131
Ali, Mir Nisar (Titu Mir), 48–49, 157
Ali, Muhammad, 47
Aligarh University (All-India Muhammadan
Anglo-Oriental College at Aligarh),
104
Ali ibn Abi Tahib (Caliph/*Imam* Ali), 5, 7,
8, 9, 61, 69, 113, 140

Ali ibn Abi Talib, 5, 140
Ali Kabar, 62
Allah, 5
All-India National Congress Party (Con-
gress Party), 116, 117
All-Indian Muhammadan Anglo-Oriental
Educational Conference, 104
Alwani, Taha J. al-, 73–74
Amal, 188, 195, 242
Amanullah, Amir, 90
Amin Osman Pasha, 136
Anjuman-i-Khuddam-i-Haramain
(Guardians of Islam's Holiest Shrines),
89
Anjuman-i-Khuddam-i-Ka'aba (Organiza-
tion to Protect the *Ka'aba*), 88, 89
Apologists. *See* Modernist revivalists
al-Aqsa Mosque (Jerusalem), arson at,
186–187, 275
Arab-Israeli conflict, 178–200, 274–275
al-Aqsa Mosque arson attack (1969),
186–187, 275
Gulf War (1990–1991), 141–142, 147,
174, 193–195, 215, 242–243, 277
Ibraham mosque massacre (1994),
197–199
intifadah, 190–193, 194, 199
Israeli interventions in Lebanon,
188–189, 195–197
and Organization of the Islamic Conference (OIC), 212–216
Palestinian diaspora, 178–180, 181
Suez war (1956), 183–184
war of 1948–1949, 181–182
war of 1967, 15, 21, 30, 161, 179,
184–186, 189, 203, 211, 274, 280